The Archaeology of the Eastern Nevada Paleoarchaic, Part 1

Number 126 2009

The Archaeology of the Eastern Nevada Paleoarchaic, Part 1

The Sunshine Locality

by Charlotte Beck and George T. Jones

with contributions by
Jack M. Broughton, Michael D. Cannon, Amy Dansie,
Amy M. Holmes, Gary A. Huckleberry, Phillip W. Hutchinson,
Stephanie D. Livingston, Gary Noyes, and Donald R. Tuohy

The University of Utah Anthropological Papers
The University of Utah Press
Salt Lake City

The Defiance House Man colophon is a registered trademark of the University of Utah Press. It is based on a four-foot-tall, Ancient Puebloan pictograph (late PIII) near Glen Canyon, Utah.

12 11 10 09 08   1 2 3 4 5

LIBRARY OF CONGRESS CATALOGING-IN-PUBLICATION DATA

The archaeology of the eastern Nevada paleoarchaic. Part I, The Sunshine Locality / [edited] by Charlotte Beck and George T. Jones ; with contributions by Jack M. Broughton...[et al.].
p. cm. — (The University of Utah anthropological papers)
Includes bibliographical references.
ISBN 978-0-87480-939-8 (pbk. : alk. paper) 1. Sunshine Locality Site (Nev.) 2. Paleo-Indians—Nevada—White Pine County. 3. Tools, Prehistoric—Nevada—White Pine County. 4. Projectile points—Nevada—White Pine County. 5. Animal remains (Archaeology)—Nevada—White Pine County. 6. Excavations (Archaeology)—Nevada—White Pine County. 7. White Pine County (Nev.)—Antiquities. I. Beck, Charlotte, 1948– II. Jones, George Thomas. III. University of Utah. IV. Title: Sunshine Locality.
E78.N4A75 2008
979.3'15—dc22   2008037411

Printed and bound by Sheridan Books, Inc., Ann Arbor, Michigan

We dedicate this volume to Phillip Hutchinson and Gary Noyes, two avocational archaeologists who were the first to work at the Sunshine Locality. Phil's love for the site and his belief in its scientific promise ultimately led to the work done by the Nevada State Museum, Desert Research Institute, and finally, Hamilton College.

Contents

Figures

Tables

Acknowledgments

In our work at the Sunshine Locality we received help from a number of people and organizations supporting our field work, collection research at the Nevada State Museum, and manuscript production. The BLM Ely Field Office provided logistical support throughout the project. BLM archaeologists Brian Amme, Carolyn Sherve, and Mark Henderson arranged field camps and coordinated loans of camp trailers and heavy equipment with operators. Fred Nials generously worked with us in the 1992 coring exercise and shared his geological field notes from the NSM/DRI projects in 1989 and 1990. Ariane Pinson volunteered during the 1995 season, while Don Grayson, Stephanie Livingston, and Mike Cannon offered expertise and muscle to our 1996 field work. Don Tuohy, Amy Dansie, Sueann Monteleone, Maggie Brown, Gene Hattori, Alanah Woody, and Rachel Malloy were congenial hosts during our several visits to the Nevada State Museum. Joel Janetski and Dave Rhode provided detailed comments on the manuscript. Lastly, of course, we thank three seasons of field-school students and teaching assistants without whom we could not have completed this work. Support for various phases of this project was provided by grants from Hamilton College, the National Science Foundation (Grant SBR-9600999), the Orr Foundation of the Nevada State Museum, and the American Philosophical Society.

1

Introduction

George T. Jones and Charlotte Beck

This volume presents the results of archaeological and geologic investigations at the Sunshine Locality, White Pine County, Nevada. The Sunshine Locality, located in southern Long Valley, about 60 km northwest of Ely, has been the focus of scientific research since the mid-1960s when Tadlock (1966) reported on a collection of crescents from the area. The Nevada State Museum (NSM) conducted studies there between 1973 and 1978, returning with the Desert Research Institute (DRI) between 1987 and 1992. We began studies at the Sunshine Locality in 1992 and carried out excavations there between 1993 and 1997 with the assistance of the Hamilton College field school. In addition, the extensive terminal Pleistocene/early Holocene (TP/EH) surface artifact record at the Sunshine Locality drew the attention of avocational archaeologists in 1971, one of whom, Phil Hutchinson, continued to collect there through the early 1990s.

Although several published articles, three short reports, and two master's theses have resulted from these various activities at the Sunshine Locality, no synthetic treatment of these investigations has appeared in print. Consequently, one of the goals of this volume is to present the history and results of research by various researchers at the Sunshine Locality, especially studies of the site geology by NSM and DRI personnel. The second goal is to describe the rich and varied artifacts recovered from surface contexts that are housed in the collections of the NSM. These collections, primarily made by Phil Hutchinson and Gary Noyes, contain a wide array of diagnostic lithic tools, including fluted and unfluted lanceolate projectile points, hundreds of Great Basin Stemmed Series projectile points and crescents, and a variety of other tools, such as gravers, scrapers, and notches, common in Paleoindian tool kits across North America. Although significant in their own right, these collections also provide a basis of comparison for the artifacts recovered from our own excavations at Sunshine as well as with TP/EH assemblages from elsewhere in the Great Basin.

The third goal of this volume is to present the results of our studies and those by cooperating scientists who first began work at the Sunshine Locality in 1992. Those studies fall into two main areas. The first concerns analysis and interpretations of the stratigraphic sequence in Sunshine Wash. Analyses of sedimentary textures and structure, depositional processes, and chronology are combined with the study of faunal remains to evaluate local and regional environmental changes. Our second focus is the artifacts recovered from excavations. Among the issues we address are the nature of the processes that created the record, the age of this record, and whether artifacts and remains of extinct mammals also recovered at the site are associated.

The present volume is the first of two that report on our studies into the prehistory of the central Great Basin. This work began in 1986 and, until 1993, focused on the surface archaeology in adjacent Butte Valley coupled with less extensive studies in Jakes and Long valleys. The goal of our surface surveys was to develop a representative sample of TP/EH assemblages to assess questions about land use and mobility during this period. These topics are addressed in the second monograph.

The present volume presents our studies at the Sunshine Locality. Although this work was undertaken with a narrow research focus and employed different field procedures than our work in Butte and Jakes valleys, there is a great deal of overlap in these projects. Thus, we frequently refer to our work in Butte and Jakes valleys, especially in chapters 5 and 6 where comparisons are made between the assemblages collected in these valleys and that from the Sunshine Locality.

Background: Butte Valley Archaeological Project

Despite what most of us learn from introductory texts in archaeology, field programs originate for a variety of reasons, not solely to address specific research questions. That was certainly the case when we first envisioned a field project in eastern Nevada in 1985. As much as anything we simply wanted to establish a geographic base from which we could begin a long-term research and teaching program. No single research question was foremost in our minds, although we had several candidates to test out in our first field season. Mainly, we wanted to study an area where little was known and where we could expect to build knowledge about the archaeological record from the ground up, so to speak.

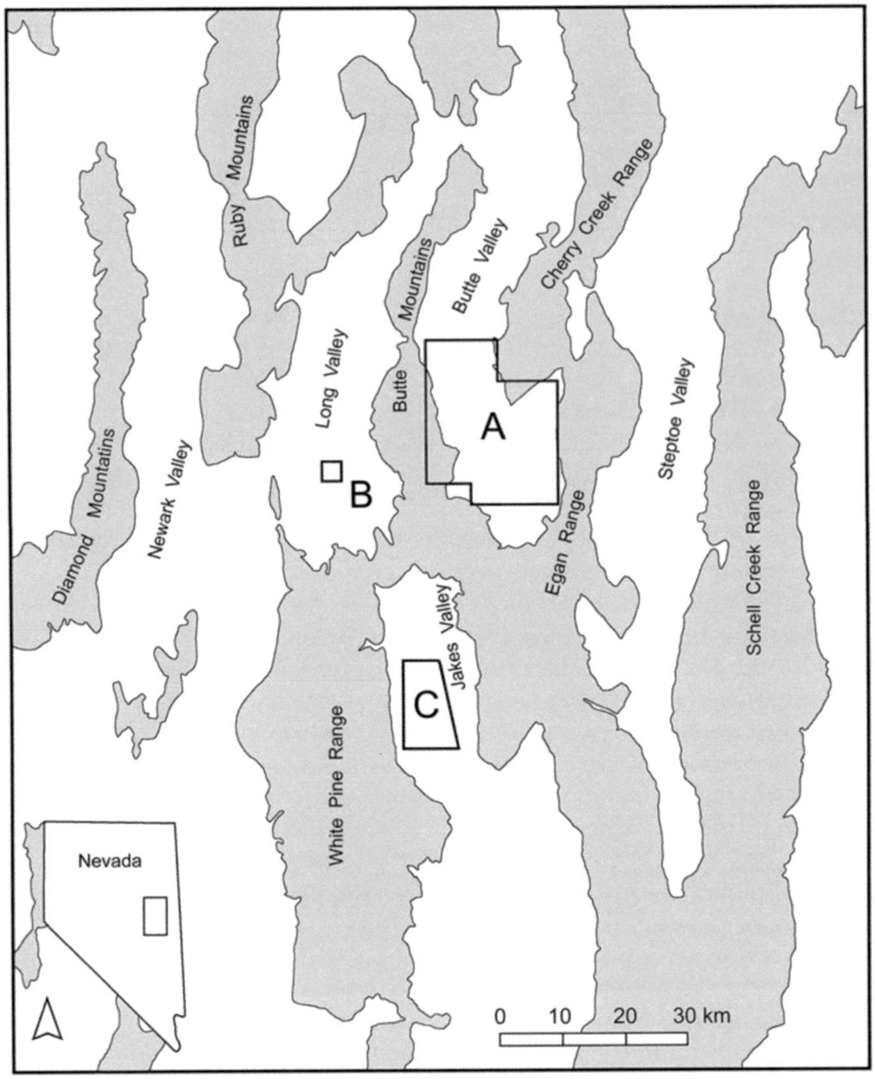

FIGURE 1.1. Locations of (A) our Butte Valley research area, (B) the Sunshine Locality, and (C) our Jakes Valley research area.

Following a suggestion made by Richard Hanes, then the Nevada state archaeologist for the Bureau of Land Management (BLM), we selected Butte Valley as the focus of our fieldwork (Figure 1.1). We thought Butte Valley might hold promise to address several problems, but our first few weeks of field study proved disappointing to say the least. We began working first in the Egan Range on the eastern side of the valley, but our surveys revealed virtually no surface record. When we shifted attention to the valley bottom, however, we began to locate sites of substantial age almost from the start. Thus, the Butte Valley Archaeological Project—BVAP as we came to call it—turned its focus toward a single general issue: the nature of cultural adaptive changes among human populations during the terminal Pleistocene and early Holocene, an adaptation we have come to call the Paleoarchaic (Beck and Jones 1997).[1]

Given the nature of the record—a surface lithic record—we decided that our research interests could best be answered through studies of mobility, especially using lithic source provenance analyses to assess movement patterns. But a host of companion issues, not the least of which was chronology, needed study.

During our first field season, in the summer of 1986, we visited the Sunshine Locality in adjacent Long Valley with BLM archaeologist Sarah Johnston. Johnston told us that the site had been placed on the National Historic Register in 1978, based on its truly extensive surface assemblage, which covered over 3 mi^2. We asked about the possibility of extending our work to include this site but were discouraged from conducting field studies there *because* of its status. Therefore, we continued our work in Butte Valley and then, in 1991, moved into Jakes Valley.

Through our 1991 field season we focused mainly on surface survey to obtain regional samples of artifacts and learn about settlement patterns and assemblage variation. All of our attempts to discover subsurface records at the sites we studied proved fruitless, however, and thus it seemed unlikely that we would ever recover classes of data like subsistence remains or datable materials to help support or refute our conjectures developed from the surface lithic record. So when the opportunity to work at the Sunshine Locality presented itself, we eagerly pursued it.

In 1989, a team from the Nevada State Museum and the Desert Research Institute began studies at the Sunshine Locality (Figure 1.2). The BLM archaeologist at this time, Brian Amme, was anxious to see research conducted at this site. The focus of the NSM–DRI work was not the extensive lithic scatters that rested on the terraces along the alluvial channel, for which the site had been accepted into the National Historic Register and which had been studied in the 1970s, but the sediments within the channel itself. NSM–DRI personnel hoped not only to show how the alluvium articulated with the terraces but to determine if buried archaeological deposits were preserved in the channel deposits. Long trenches excavated by backhoe revealed a deep stratigraphic record, reaching as much as 3 m below the modern surface of the channel. Out of the alluvium at the base of their trenches the NSM–DRI team extracted bones of extinct camel and other mammals, bird and fish remains, and a few artifacts, all dating to nearly 11,000 radiocarbon years (rcy) ago.

The deaths of two key participants, Jonathan Davis and Cynthia Irwin-Williams, caused a significant setback for the NSM–DRI investigations. Fred Nials continued geologic reconnaissance at Sunshine, but archaeological investigations were not pursued until, at the end of our 1991 field season, we were asked by the BLM to join in the study of the site. We made a brief visit with Nials to Sunshine in 1992 to conduct auger coring and began full-scale archaeological testing in 1993 with a field school group from Hamilton College. We returned to continue testing in 1995 and undertook additional work in 1996 and 1997. Gary Huckleberry joined us in 1995 as the project geologist and continued to work with us through the last field season in 1997.

Through the course of this work, we opened 19 stratigraphic exposures along an approximately 2,200-m stretch of Sunshine Wash (Figure 1.3), including six units that were systematically excavated by hand. The main artifact-bearing strata appear to date to before 9800 rcy BP. Artifacts and extinct fauna co-occur in alluvial gravels near the base of the stratigraphic section in the channel, but all evidence suggests that these associations are geologic rather than cultural. A sizable number of radiocarbon dates permits high resolution of the stratigraphic sequence at Sunshine and enables reconstruction of environments there during the period of human occupation.

The Sunshine Project

Our initial studies at the Sunshine Locality were purely exploratory, meant to assess the stratigraphic sequence and the ages of deposits and any cultural materials they might contain and to determine if in situ archaeological remains were preserved. Although we improved our interpretations of the stratigraphy and better constrained the ages of deposits with the completion of each field season, our basic exploratory goals did not change in the course of study. Even as late as 1997 we were still trying to locate buried primary cultural deposits to reveal surfaces that retained spatial patterning among artifacts and features and contained artifacts that would be preserved only in buried contexts.

We recovered quite a sizable collection of artifacts, which, because of the sedimentary contexts, made investigation of depositional processes an important focus of our studies. As part of this concern we also attempted, as fully as possible, to determine the ages of the sedimentary units and the artifacts they contained. Hence chronology, revealed by both radiocarbon analysis and analysis of time-sensitive projectile points, was one of our primary research goals. An important component of this goal was to extend chronological insights to better control the age of surface artifacts at Sunshine and, indeed, to provide age control of surface assemblages from throughout the region.

Whereas taphonomic and chronological questions dominate concerns over the archaeological record, the second principal objective of testing at the Sunshine Locality was to use the stratigraphic sequence to reveal information about past climate and environment in eastern Nevada during the glacial–interglacial transition. The backhoe excavations done by the NSM and DRI in 1989 and 1990 produced a consistent stratigraphic sequence (Nials 1990) as well as a small assemblage of mammal, bird, and fish bones (Dansie 1990) and several obsidian flakes (Hicks 1990; Nials 1990). Included in the mammal bones were elements identified as *Camelops* sp. (Dansie 1990). Together the components of this record promised great potential, if not archaeological, certainly paleoenvironmental, of a particularly important period in prehistory—the TP/EH transition.

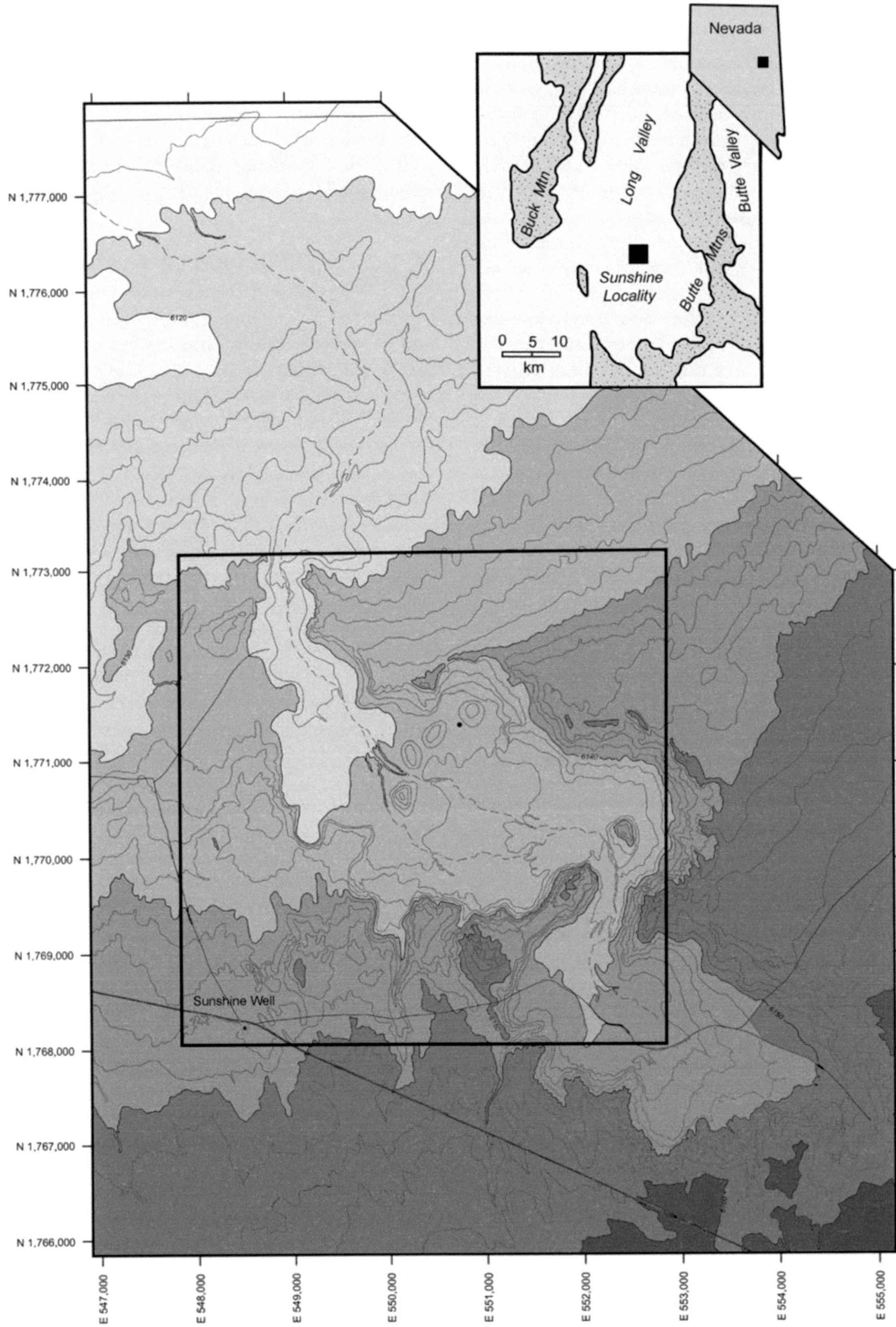

FIGURE 1.2. The Sunshine Locality. The box outlines the area within which the fieldwork discussed in this volume took place (see Figures 2.2, 2.11, and 3.1). The grid is the 1,000-ft state grid.

FIGURE 1.3. The Sunshine Locality in southern Long Valley. Sunshine Wash is contained within the bordered area, and the solid circle marks the location of Sunshine Well. Note the playa to the north and the paleobeaches to the south.

Setting

The Sunshine Locality is a National Historic Register District of 60 km^2 located in southern Long Valley, White Pine County, Nevada (Figure 1.2). Named after nearby Sunshine Well (Figure 1.4), the district contains a broad stream channel at its center that is incised into the lower beach terraces and alluvial fans of Long Valley for several kilometers. On both sides of the channel are extensive lithic scatters. Exposed by wind deflation, these artifact clusters contain numerous Paleoarchaic diagnostics, including fluted points and crescents. In an effort to preserve these surface scatters, the area was accepted to the National Register of Historic Places in 1978 (Federal Register 1978:5249).

Sunshine Wash is the name we apply to an incised channel that develops east of Sunshine Well and runs generally northwest for several kilometers before ending in multiple distributary channels on the valley floor. Sunshine Wash formed after the recession of pluvial Lake Hubbs, which probably stood over the site until ca. 13,000 rcy BP. This part of southern Long Valley is unremarkable today. Outside the wash proper, eolian processes presently dominate, producing dune hillocks within broad sheets of blow sand and deflation basins. The wash itself carries water periodically and contains a stream channel incised to a depth of less than a meter and 2 m in width. Irregular flooding events continue to deposit fine sandy alluvium in the wash and have done so, perhaps, for several thousand years.

In most other parts of Long Valley single drainages make their way across alluvial fans to the valley floor. In contrast, Sunshine Wash lies at the terminus of several

FIGURE 1.4. The Sunshine Well from which the Sunshine Locality gets its name. The site is to the right (north; photograph by Tom Jones).

channels that collectively drain a sizable upland watershed. Although these drainages today do not contribute much surface water to the wash, Sunshine once held a significantly more energetic stream system as evidenced by the depth and width of the paleochannel. In places the wash is 500 m wide, with its surface several meters below adjacent terraces. Even where constricted, the wash is over 100 m wide.

Long Valley, a "high desert" valley at a base elevation of 1873 m, lies near the geographic center of the Great Basin. At the center of a drainage basin of slightly more than 1692 km^2 (Mifflin and Wheat 1979), Long Valley is bound on its eastern and southern sides by the Butte Mountains. The southern extension of the Ruby Mountains forms the western border of the valley. Long Valley is one of several hydrographically independent basins confined by the major drainage systems of the Great Basin, the Bonneville system to the east, the Lahontan system to the north and west, and the White River drainage to the south.

Long Valley lies within the Calcareous Province, so named for the dominance of Paleozoic limestones and shales in the geologic section of this region. The Paleozoic section is overlain in many areas, particularly the Butte Mountains in the southern part of Long Valley, by a thick section of early to middle Tertiary volcanic rocks dating to 40–34 million years ago (Gans et al. 1989). There has been no volcanic activity in the area since this time (Grunder 1992:220). The Quaternary rocks of the region are sedimentary and largely unconsolidated (Hose and Blake 1976:3). Pleistocene and Holocene sediments in Long Valley are the result of alluvial and eolian processes.

Long Valley contains a typical high desert plant association, dominated by xerophytes and salt-tolerant shrubs, herbs, and grasses. The dominant shrubs are shadscale (*Atriplex confertifolia*), sagebrush (*Artemisia tridentata* and *A. nova*), and rabbitbrush (*Chrysothamnus puberulus*); several species of grasses, such as Indian ricegrass (*Achnatherum hymenoides*), are interspersed. Shadscale is dominant in and adjacent to Sunshine Wash. Relatively continuous patches of winterfat (*Kvaschenin-nikovia lanata*), several hectares in size, cover the silty fan piedmont/skirt surfaces.

The mountain slopes support sparse stands of Rocky Mountain juniper (*Juniperus scopulorum*) with an undercover of sage and Indian ricegrass. Piñon (*Pinus monophylla*) is found at higher elevations.

A number of small mammals inhabit the area today, including lagomorphs, such as black-tailed jackrabbit (*Lepus californicus*) and cottontails (*Sylvilagus* sp.), and rodents, such as ground squirrels (*Spermophilus* sp.), pocket gophers (*Thomomys* sp.), and kangaroo rats (*Dipodomys* sp.). An occasional pronghorn (*Antilocapra americana*) is visible, but these animals are rare today. Wild horses abound, growing in numbers every year (Figure 1.5). During the last field season in 1997, a herd of nearly 100 horses ran across the valley quite near to our excavation.

Why Sunshine?

Great Basin environments, like those in the rest of North America, were quite different during the terminal Pleistocene from those of the present. Climatic changes during this period were dramatic and were accompanied by equally dramatic changes in the diversity and range of plant and animal species (Grayson 1993). Because the best evidence to date suggests that the first major human migrations into the continent occurred during this volatile period, the TP/EH climate has been of great interest to archaeologists for nearly 100 years.

The Great Basin today experiences a continental climate with large differences between summer and winter temperatures, but during the terminal Pleistocene

FIGURE 1.5. Wild mustangs at the Sunshine Locality (photograph by Robert York).

this difference was much less. Climate simulations (e.g., Barry 1983; COHMAP Members 1988; Hostetler and Benson 1990; Hostetler et al. 1994) indicate that the presence of the Laurentide ice sheet had a profound influence on the Great Basin during the late glacial. The jet stream is believed to have split into two tracks around the continental ice sheet at the Last Glacial Maximum (ca. 18,000 rcy BP). Strong anticyclonic circulation over the ice sheet brought higher precipitation to the southwestern United States and higher-than-modern lake levels to the Great Basin. The Bonneville and Lahontan lake systems reached their maximum volume and surface area between 18,000 and 14,000 rcy BP (Benson et al. 1990; Currey 1990) and subsequently began to regress to levels as low as or lower than anytime during the Holocene (Madsen 1999).

With the retraction of the ice sheets, anticyclonic flow weakened, and the southern branch of the jet stream migrated northward. With this migration, effective precipitation began to decrease, with a concomitant decrease in overall lake levels across the Great Basin. This trend was reversed for a short period during the Younger Dryas, with a return to "near-glacial conditions" (Madsen 1999: 76), but winter atmospheric circulation is believed to have reached modern conditions about 9000 BP (Kutzbach and Guetter 1986).

Traditional descriptions of Great Basin TP/EH environments have been based on studies of Antevs (1948), who suggested that environmental change was gradual over long periods of time and who "illustrated his interpretation with figures employing broad sweeping curves to connect climate episodes spanning thousands of years" (Madsen 1999:75). But as Madsen argues, such gradual change was not the case, and "simple north-to-south or east-to-west analyses of evolving basin environments during the TP/EH period of human occupation can misrepresent the often complex changes that were taking place" (1999:75). It is exactly for this reason that the Sunshine Locality has captured the interest of archaeologists and amateurs alike over the past 40 years and particularly since 1989, when the NSM–DRI backhoe excavations exposed an 11,000-rcy-old stratigraphic record at the site at least 3 m below the surface.

Since the 1930s, when the Campbells discovered artifacts lying on the beaches of Pleistocene Lake Mojave, Great Basin archaeologists have known about the region's early occupants' affinity for lakes and marshes. Although this discovery was overshadowed by the search for associations between extinct fauna and "early man" in order to demonstrate the latter as "big game hunters," the association between early assemblages and pluvial lake features once again assumed importance with Bedwell's (1973) work in the Fort Rock Valley. Bedwell proposed the "Western Pluvial Lakes Tradition," which describes early human adaptation focused on pluvial lakes. This proposal quickly gained popularity (e.g., Hester 1973) as more and more discoveries of early tools were found in these contexts. We now know the situation is somewhat more complex than Bedwell presents it, but it does appear to be a fact that Paleoarchaic populations had an affinity for shallow-water resources (Grayson 1993).

Like most valleys in the Great Basin, Long Valley held a lake during the late Pleistocene. Named for Carl L. Hubbs, who contributed pioneering studies of the biogeography of native Great Basin fish (e.g., Hubbs and Miller 1948), Lake Hubbs attained a maximum size of ca. 507 km^2 and reached a depth of ca. 78 m (Mifflin and Wheat 1979). The chronology of Lake Hubbs's transgressive and regressive phases is unknown, but Mifflin and Wheat (1979) suggest that it is correlative with Lake Lahontan; radiocarbon-dated mollusks from shorelines indicate a high stand at ca. 17,520 ± 570 rcy BP (Young and McCoy 1984). A number of well-developed shorelines encircle the southern end of the valley. The uppermost of these is regarded by Mifflin and Wheat to be pre-Lahontan in age. The lower shorelines, which are not breached as extensively by stream channels, presumably mark the late Pleistocene regression of Lake Hubbs.

The northern end of the valley contains another extensive, complex pluvial landform, and pluvial landforms are also evident in aerial photographs near the Sunshine Well to the south, though they contribute far less relief. These geologic landforms indicate that Long Valley was a much more attractive location to human populations in the TP/EH than it is today. As York (1974:5) noted in 1974, Long Valley today is a desolate place, considered by locals as second only to Death Valley, a place to be crossed as quickly as possible on your way elsewhere. Looking specifically at the Sunshine Locality, the primary geologic processes in this area have been stream erosion and deposition, eolian deposition, and probably sheet wash deposition. North of the Sunshine Locality is the Long Valley playa, where sand/silt dunes rise 10–20 m above the playa on the northern (leeward) edge. Sediments scoured from the playa have also produced longitudinal dunes, which rise 5–10 m, near the center of Long Valley. At the Sunshine Locality proper, however, eolian processes contribute a thin sand veneer usually on the order of .5 m in thickness, although localized dune hummocks and ridges occur just to the northeast of Sunshine Well.

The thousands and thousands of Paleoarchaic artifacts of TP/EH age that lie on the Sunshine Locality dunes, however, attest to the fact that this was not an area "to be crossed as quickly as possible" during the TP/EH but, rather, a primary destination that populations continued to visit repeatedly for at least several hundred years. The small number of later Archaic points and the almost complete lack of ground stone, though, suggest that the attractive nature of this locality ended rather quickly, ca. 8500 rcy BP. Sites such as the Sunshine Locality are rare in the Great Basin. Aside from the thousands of stemmed points that have been collected from this site, at least 20 fluted points have also been collected. In addition, hundreds of other tools, typical of those found in Paleoindian tool kits across North America, have been found, including gravers, end and slug scrapers, and notches; further, several hundred crescents have been collected. None of the sites we have located in our work in adjacent Butte and Jakes valleys has revealed anything comparable to the Sunshine Locality assemblage, either in sheer numbers of artifacts or in the diversity of tools. The few other localities like Sunshine in the Great Basin include the Alkali Lake Basin of north-central Oregon (Fagan 1988; Pinson 1999; Willig 1988, 1989, 1991), China Lake in southeastern California (Davis 1978a, 1978b), and the vicinity of Pleistocene Lake Tonopah in southern Nevada (Campbell and Campbell 1940; Pendleton 1979; Tuohy 1988). These localities represent important archaeological and paleoenvironmental resources of TP/EH age that have the potential for answering a number of our burning questions about that period: What was the TP/EH environment like in this area? Is the Younger Dryas represented, and was it as volatile as Madsen (1999) and others suggest? What is the relation between humans and extinct fauna in the Great Basin? What is the age of fluted points in the Great Basin? What is the temporal and functional relationship between Great Basin fluted and stemmed points? What was (were) the function(s) of stemmed points? And finally, what was the adaptation of Paleoarchaic peoples of the TP/EH? Given this potential, it is no wonder that so many avocational and professional archaeologists and geologists have spent so much time and effort at this remarkable site.

Organization of the Monograph

As stated at the beginning of this chapter, the purpose of this monograph is not just to describe the Hamilton College excavations from 1993 through 1997 but to pull together the work that has been conducted at the Sunshine Locality over the last 40 years. To set the stage in chapter 2, Amy Dansie, Don Tuohy, Phil Hutchinson, and Gary Noyes, who were involved in the work at Sunshine since the early 1970s, present a history of the work done prior to Hamilton College's involvement. In chapter 3, we present a detailed description of our fieldwork, beginning in 1992. The specific goals of our project are discussed in this chapter. In chapter 4, Amy Holmes and Gary Huckleberry discuss the stratigraphy and the geologic processes contributing to sediment deposition. A discussion of the radiocarbon dates is also presented in chapter 4. The next two chapters present the artifact analyses: the general and special analyses of all artifact categories but projectile points are presented in chapter 5, while the latter are the focus of chapter 6. Mike Cannon, Stephanie Livingston, and Jack Broughton describe the faunal assemblage in chapter 7. In the final chapter, we present an overview and discussion of the data, addressing a number of questions concerning the Paleoarchaic occupation at the Sunshine Locality. We also address the Sunshine Locality in the context of several larger issues regarding the Paleoarchaic in this region of the Great Basin.

Note

1. The term *Paleoarchaic* was first used by Judy Willig (1989). We adopted the term because the more commonly used *Paleoindian* is associated with certain technologies, such as Clovis; subsistence strategies, such as "big game hunting"; and specific time periods, for example, the dates for Clovis on the Plains and in the Southwest. Fluted points in the Great Basin, however, are not well dated and thus have never been demonstrated to be part of the Clovis technology. Further, the early economy in the Great Basin, believed to have been focused on shallow-water resources, changed gradually and not abruptly from the terminal Pleistocene through the early Holocene, at least until ca. 8000 rcy BP. Steve Simms (1988) pointed out years ago that a Paleoindian/Archaic distinction in the Great Basin is misleading, and we agree. Although Gary Haynes recently argued that translated, *Paleoarchaic* means "Old old" and is not particularly useful, we have adopted this term as an alternative to *Paleoindian* because it does not carry with it the same assumptions as the latter.

2

History of Fieldwork at Sunshine Well, Long Valley, Nevada, 1962–1990

Amy Dansie, with Donald R. Tuohy, Phillip W. Hutchinson, and Gary Noyes

It doesn't get any better than this.

—JONATHAN O. DAVIS AT SUNSHINE WELL

The "Tadlock Period"

The earliest formal research in the vicinity of the Sunshine Locality was undertaken in the early 1960s by Emma Lou Davis and Lewis Tadlock, which Tuohy refers to as the "Tadlock Period" (Tuohy, Hutchinson, and Tadlock 1990). Two surface surveys were done on the Long Valley playa, the first in 1962 and the second in 1963. This work resulted in the publication of Tadlock's well-known article in *American Antiquity*, "Certain Crescentic Stone Objects as a Time Marker in the Western United States" (1966). Although this work was not done at the Sunshine Locality itself, it is important because Tadlock's article was the catalyst for the eventual involvement of two avocational archaeologists, Gary Noyes and Phil Hutchinson, who "put Sunshine on the map."[1]

According to Tadlock (Tuohy, Hutchinson, and Tadlock 1990), a geologist named Ferris Borden living in Long Beach, California, came into contact with a private collector who had made collections on the Long Valley playa. His collection included a number of projectile points as well as approximately 75 crescents. When Tadlock became involved in the 1960s, this collection could not be located, but its existence intrigued him and Emma Lou Davis, both of whom were in graduate school at the University of California–Los Angeles (UCLA). Tadlock states that "due to the threat of removal of all surface evidence from Long Valley by private collectors" (in Tuohy, Hutchinson, and Tadlock 1990:2), the suggestion for a survey of the area gained the support of Clement Meighan, Davis's dissertation adviser. Davis contacted the UCLA Archaeological Survey Facility, the Nevada State Museum (NSM), and the Bureau of Land Management (BLM) to gain permission to work in Long Valley; the NSM subsequently issued a site number (26-WP-83) to be assigned to the material collected. After the work was completed, Davis submitted a report to the NSM.

In 1963 Tadlock wrote a term paper on crescents for Meighan; this paper was based on, and pictured, 29 crescents from Long Valley Lake, 11 of which had been collected during the 1962 and 1963 surveys, but 18 of which were from a private collection owned by Victor L. Slawson of Santa Ana, California (Tadlock 1966:664; Tuohy, Hutchinson, and Tadlock 1990:3). Meighan encouraged him to send the paper to *American Antiquity*, which he did, and it was published in 1966. In this article Tadlock discusses three fluted points found in association with the crescents, one identified by Marie Wormington as Folsom and two, as Clovis. Tadlock was convinced that even though the crescents were found with stemmed as well as fluted points, they were most likely associated with the latter.

Tadlock wrote no more about Long Valley until 1990, when he contributed a section to a paper given at the Great Basin Conference in Reno; in this paper Tadlock states,

> An important observation of the archaeological evidence from Long Valley not discussed in the 1966 crescent report is the presence of artifacts resembling Eden or Yuma type blades. Evidence consists of narrow, long, bilaterally balanced blades with a waxy appearance, made of black fine-grained basalt. Further evidence includes intricate parallel oblique flaking running from right to left (proximal to distal) and continuing over the entire face of the blade. From my experience I find that this highly sophisticated flaking technique is on rare occasion observed in Colorado, Wyoming, Montana, Nevada, and the Owens Valley in California. It appears to be restricted to a period of time following fluted points and is associated with the Plano complex (Scottsbluff and Angostura points), which

FIGURE 2.1. Gary Noyes examining a scatter of bones at the Sunshine Locality, June 1973 (photograph by Phil Hutchinson).

> is older than the later, more pronounced and diversified types of stemmed points. The sophistication and flaking technique is so unique that it can be recognized from blade fragments. Due to the delicate nature of the blade and its susceptibility to breakage, whole specimens are very rarely found. Several center sections and one basal with center section were recorded [in Tuohy, Dansie, and Tadlock 1990].

Tadlock's and Davis's work in Long Valley ended with the two surveys and the publication of Tadlock's paper; this paper, however, and the artifacts found on the Long Valley playa piqued the interest of two avocational archaeologists who began working at the Sunshine Locality in 1971 and paved the way for all of the subsequent work done there by the NSM, BLM, Desert Research Institute (DRI), and eventually, Hamilton College.

Hutchinson and Noyes

Gary Noyes (Figure 2.1) first visited Long Valley in June 1971, after reading Tadlock's (1966) article on crescents in *American Antiquity*. Noyes had been locating and collecting artifacts in the vicinity of Pleistocene Lakes Tonopah and Mud since 1967. According to Noyes,

> The Campbells' report, *The Archeology of Pleistocene Lake Mohave* [Campbell et al. 1937], was of great interest to me as it described beach ridges similar to those at Pleistocene Mud Lake. After reading articles criticizing their lack of site mapping and location of artifacts within sites at Lake Mohave, I set up my procedures to include establishing a site marker stake and then take a compass reading and distance from the marker to each artifact. Later, these data would be entered on sheets in my Site Record book and an accession number assigned. Artifacts were then labeled [personal communication 2007].

Noyes used this procedure for all of his future collections, including at the Sunshine Locality.

Phil Hutchinson (Figure 2.2) joined Noyes for a three-day expedition in June 1972, when he did the field photography of the first systematic observations of the Sunshine Locality (known to them as Sunshine Well). Following Noyes's procedure, they placed aluminum datum poles at each artifact concentration, starting with Sunshine Well, Site 1 (SW1) and eventually ending at SW7. In assigning field specimen numbers to the artifacts, they kept track of who collected each one by following the number with

FIGURE 2.2. Phil Hutchinson at North Spring, the nearest natural water to the Sunshine Well (photograph by Phil Hutchinson associate).

TABLE 2.1. Locations of the Hutchinson and Noyes Surface Sites

Site Designation	Distance to Sunshine Well (m)	Distance to Sunshine Well (ft)	Azimuth from Sunshine Well (° from North)
SW1	346	1,135	24
SW2	454	1,490	50
SW2A	485	1,590	65
SW2B	555	1,820	12
SW3	1,143	3,750	25
SW3A	1,387	4,550	6
SW3B	1,394	4,575	0
SW3C	1,303	4,275	355
SW4	1,341	4,400	50
SW5	1,439	4,720	90
SW6	884	2,900	80
SW7	~1,827[a]	—	13

[a] The distance to SW7 is not given by Hutchinson (1988), but this site was located on the map in his Figure 2. The distance given here is estimated via its location on that map relative to the other sites.
Source: From Hutchinson 1988:304.

an "N" for Noyes, an "M" for Hutchinson's son Matt, and no letter for Hutchinson. In all, over 4,000 artifacts were collected from 12 mapped localities as shown in Figure 2.3 and Table 2.1 (Hutchinson 1988).

Hutchinson and Noyes established the location of each datum pole relative to a permanent datum at the Sunshine Well windmill (see Figure 1.4) using a surveyor's wheel to measure distance and a pocket transit to establish the bearing. Once this was done the provenience of each artifact relative to its closest site datum (using the same approach) could be recorded. After documentation the artifacts were collected and placed in labeled envelopes. Hutchinson and Noyes collected Great Basin Fluted, unfluted lanceolate, and Great Basin Stemmed points as well as Pinto and later Archaic points; they also collected over 200 crescents. An impressive array of flake tools was also collected, "including domed discoidal scrapers, end and side scrapers, single and multiple gravers, numerous beak-nosed gravers, choppers, leaf and oval shaped knives and one partial metate" (Hutchinson 1993:7).

The original surface density was remarkable, and Hutchinson says of this first year's fieldwork: "Great quantities of broken stems were found at site SW3. One could literally walk on them" (1993:7). This locality (SW3) eventually became the focus of more intensive subsurface work by the NSM, DRI, and Hamilton College.

On August 25, 1972, Hutchinson and Noyes returned for their second trip to Long Valley. They mapped the seven Sunshine Well sites and visited Don Tuohy "nearby" in Ruby Valley, where he was working in a small cave, in conjunction with Laurel Casjens's (1974) fieldwork. Hutchinson showed Tuohy his artifact photographs from Sunshine, which were mounted and displayed in a binder with all of the field documentation for each artifact. Tuohy then visited the locality for the first time with Hutchinson and Noyes, encouraging them to continue their documentation. Tuohy at that time decided to conduct a professional project sponsored by the NSM the following year.

Hutchinson and Noyes's third trip was in September 1972, when they were joined by some friends who agreed to conform to their field procedures. On this trip they found what they believed to be a Folsom point (Hutchinson 1988:Figure 8). Also on this trip they encountered a severe and sudden thunderstorm. During their return to camp they observed small rivulets of water transporting archaeological debitage down the sides of the silty dunes, documenting firsthand one of the means by which a surface assemblage is exposed and redistributed by rainfall.

Hutchinson and Noyes returned to the site once more in October 1972 and again in April 1973. They were convinced, as Tadlock (1966) had been, that the crescents

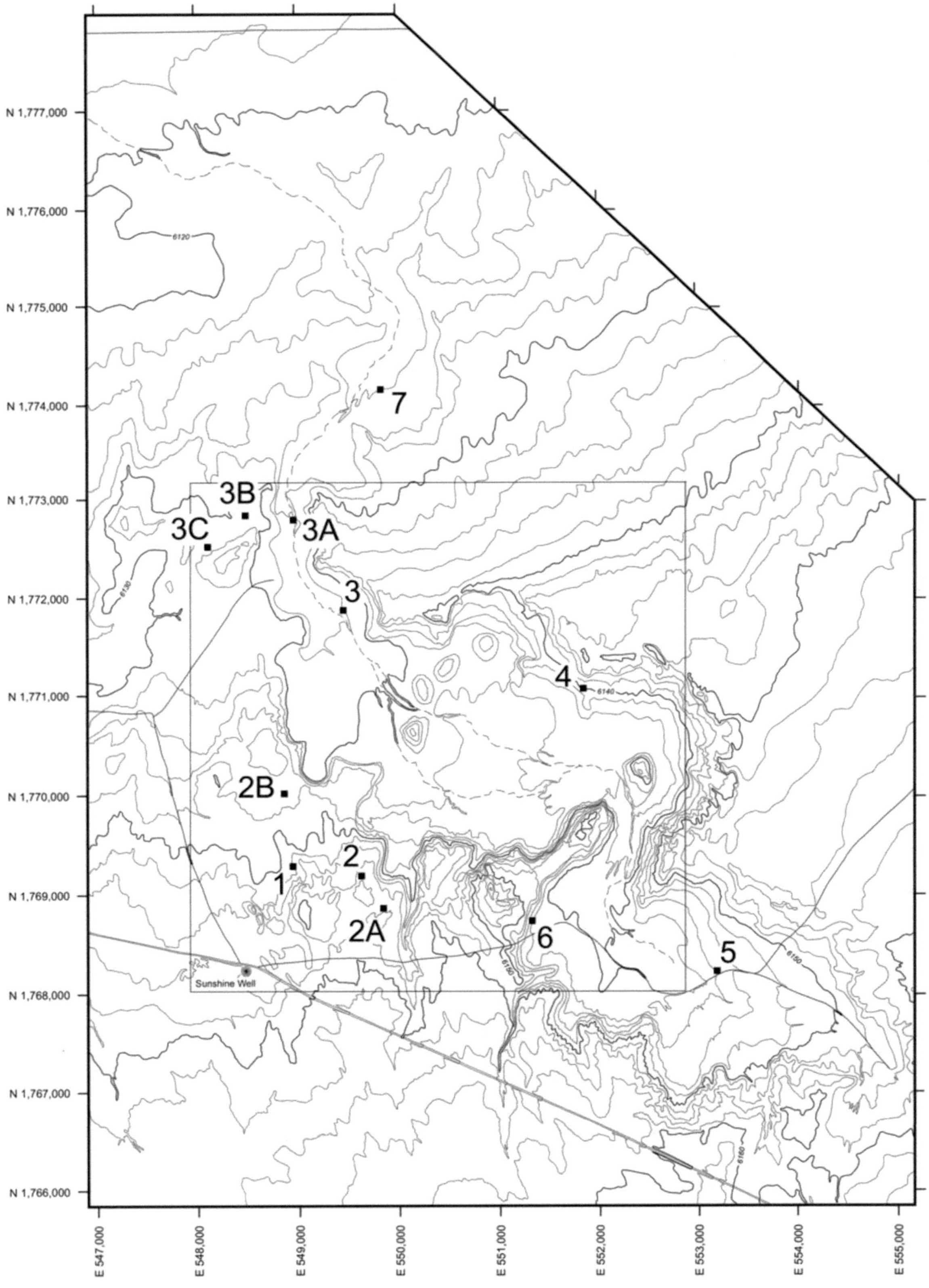

FIGURE 2.3. Location of the Hutchinson and Noyes surface sites at the Sunshine Locality (enclosed area). Table 2.1 shows the distance and direction of each site from the Sunshine Well.

FIGURE 2.4. Phil Hutchinson setting up his transit near Reno, September 1998 (photograph by Alanah Woody).

were more often associated with the fluted points, but they also knew that the exposed surface artifacts could not be dated without buried components associated with charcoal or other datable material and that only professional archaeologists could hope to resolve the timing of these vast assemblages of early stone tools.

During their April 1973 trip Hutchinson spent his first days designing and making his first homemade transit:

> It consisted of a circular aluminum disk ¼ inch thick and 5 inches in diameter with a compass attached; a plastic rosette, with the center band fastened to the top of the disk. Copper bus bars formed the sides which supported a four-power rifle scope. The whole assembly was mounted on ¼ inch threaded brass bolts and secured with brass nuts. No ferrous material was used. Several army surplus levels were fastened to the disk and the scope. This device was made with a speed drill, taps, dies and hard work [1993:22–23].

Hutchinson and Noyes worked at SW1 and again noted the co-occurrence of crescents and fluted points: "Invariably when we found several crescents, we found a concave base, sometimes fluted" (Hutchinson 1993:25). They also noted the characteristic "chisel tip" and "reverse bevel" on most of the Lake Mohave points, traits that had been recently described in a publication by Tuohy (1969).

In June 1973, Hutchinson and his family visited Long Valley for two days, meeting Robert York, who was conducting the first systematic fieldwork by the NSM at the Sunshine Locality (see below). Hutchinson shared his maps and knowledge of the locality and straightened his site datum poles, which had been bent by cattle. Interestingly, these datum poles can still be seen at the Sunshine sites, whereas the wooden datum stakes put in by York have, for the most part, disappeared.

York's work failed to produce much in the way of subsurface cultural materials, and thus, after he completed his work, Hutchinson and Noyes, with Don Tuohy's permission, conducted more than 50 hand–core drilling operations. Most of the cores were 8 ft deep and also failed to locate artifacts below the surface.

In August 1974, Hutchinson, his son Matt, and Noyes returned to the site with Hutchinson's second homemade transit (Figure 2.4), a much better device, and they reshot the datum pole locations, making corrections for several of them. They confirmed that new artifacts were continuing to be exposed on the previously collected sites, suggesting the presence of at least shallow buried deposits. They also observed something noted by York, that the weathering on the Sunshine artifacts was minor to absent, in contrast to many early sand-blasted assemblages around Tonopah with which they were familiar. This suggested to them that the artifacts had only recently been exposed and that they continued to erode out every year.

During this same visit Hutchinson and Noyes explored other "promising" areas of Long Valley and found nothing but later artifacts; no other "early man" sites were found. They reported the sites to Tuohy and returned their attention to the Sunshine vicinity.

Hutchinson and Noyes continued to work at Sunshine, returning in July and September 1975, July 1976, June and September 1977, and September 1978. They had hoped to find another Folsom point, but they never did. They believed that, except for Tadlock's small collection, they were the first to collect from the Sunshine Locality, and they took this responsibility very seriously. Most of the formed and complete tools, including points, gravers, drills, beaks, scrapers, and knives were plotted individually relative to the site datum, but the debitage and broken stems were not. Hutchinson states that "most importantly, our camera was used to take numerous *in situ* photographs. This was one of the items Gary [Noyes] emphasized," quoting Noyes as saying, "We need a better way to show how and where artifacts are found and how they weather out" (1993:49; see Figure 2.5). The close-up

FIGURE 2.5. Fluted point preform in situ, June 1993 (photograph by Phil Hutchinson).

photographs, using 2.25-in film for maximum resolution, and detailed location data were their effort to meet this perceived need.[2]

Hutchinson and Noyes donated their collection to the NSM in May 1989; it was cataloged under NSM accession CM-3705. A collection of about 1,700 artifacts was stored by Hutchinson and Noyes in 102 large plastic battery trays, lined with cotton, and labeled with Sunshine site numbers. The photographs and location documentation that they recorded of finished artifacts were prepared and kept in large binders, completely cross-referenced for detailed study. Samples of flakes and flake tools were collected, and most were documented by site. Hutchinson published a paper describing his and Noyes's work (Hutchinson 1988), and together they made a significant contribution to Great Basin archaeology (e.g., Hutchinson 1979, 1990, 1993; Noyes and Hutchinson 1972). Hutchinson continued to collect through 1993, donating these artifacts to the NSM as well.

It is hard to imagine digging 50 8-ft cores just for the love of the quest, but these two dedicated avocationals worked harder than most professional archaeologists. In light of later work, it is not surprising that they found no archaeological materials at depth, because they would have had to core to 11 ft in just the right place to find what the NSM, DRI, BLM, and later, Beck and Jones discovered far below the surface of the modern stream channel, the first deeply buried late Pleistocene archaeological site in the Great Basin. Hutchinson and Noyes were sure it was there, and they were right.

The Nevada State Museum Fieldwork Under Robert York

From June 7 to August 17, 1973, Robert York conducted archaeological fieldwork for the NSM, under the general supervision of Don Tuohy.[3] Six anthropology students from various universities across the West worked hard for food and experience.[4]

York's (1974) report to the U.S. Department of the Interior consulting archaeologists and the BLM describes the work in detail. He hoped to find buried cultural and paleoenvironmental data that would help determine the timing and nature of early human occupation in the Great Basin and to explore the function and temporal position of crescents in early cultures. The pristine nature of the archaeological complex around Sunshine was a primary factor in this research, the visits by Hutchinson and Noyes being the only known impact on the surface archaeology. York's crew located and recorded 55 sites, several of which corresponded to those first recognized by Hutchinson and Noyes (Table 2.2).

York summarized the bleak modern environment of Long Valley and pointed out that the extremely sparse late Archaic and Protohistoric archaeology confirm

FIGURE 2.6. Jean Ostrander recording stratigraphy at 26-WP-304, 1973 (photograph by Robert York).

FIGURE 2.7. The 26-WP-317 trench, 1993 (photograph by Robert York).

TABLE 2.2 Sites Located by York that Correspond to Sites Defined by Hutchinson and Noyes

HUTCHINSON–NOYES SITE DESIGNATION	YORK/SMITHSONIAN DESIGNATION
SW1	26-WP-306, 26-WP-307, and possibly part of 26-WP-308
SW2	26-WP-308, 26-WP-412, and 26-WP-413
SW2A	26-WP-413
SW2B	26-WP-306 and 26-WP-414
SW3	26-WP-311 and 26-WP-406
SW3A	26-WP-410
SW3B	26-WP-312 and/or 26-WP-408
SW3C	26-WP-408
SW4	26-WP-403, 26-WP-404, and 26-WP-405
SW5	26-WP-396, 26-WP-399, 26-WP-400, and 26-WP-401
SW6	26-WP-317 and 26-WP-393
SW7	26-WP-411

Source: From York 1995:195, Table 12.

Steward's (1938) data suggesting that the Shoshone found the situation in Long Valley to be as unattractive as it was to all but the earliest inhabitants. Only one out of 55 sites located by York (1974:6) yielded Shoshone ceramics or late points. As York states, the locals compared Long Valley to Death Valley, "something to be traversed as quickly as is possible on their way north to the lush marsh-lands of neighboring Ruby Valley" (1974:5).

Three locations were located for subsurface testing; one of these corresponded to Hutchinson and Noyes's Site 6 (26-WP-317), whereas the two others were newly recorded in 1973 (26-WP-304 and 26-WP-318). Locations were selected based on several factors, including differences in observed surface lithic distributions and perceived differences in geomorphology, in an attempt to find buried cultural deposits (R. York, personal communication 2004). Test units ranged from a single 1-×-1-m pit (Figure 2.6) to two 12-×-1-m, hand-dug trenches (Figure 2.7). The trenches were dug to a depth of ca. 80 cm on average, up to 1.7 m in some units, but they were all on the deflated sediments perched on the old lake bed, away from the channel. Most of the fill was screened through ⅛-in screens, but only a few flakes were found, all in the upper eolian sands and slope wash within 40 cm of the surface.

Surface surveys of the higher beach terraces produced only scattered isolated finds, including one complete Hell Gap point and a Pinto point. As had Hutchinson and Noyes before him, York observed that little or no weathering was apparent on the artifacts. He also noted that cobbles of chert and basalt suitable for knapping were available in the higher beach gravels.[5] He concluded that the small sites and isolates were contemporaneous with the main sites near the Sunshine Locality and may have been used primarily as toolstone procurement loci. He briefly mentions some "weathered lithics of a 'crude' nature" from the higher terraces, which might be much older, possibly contemporaneous with the higher lake stands of Lake Hubbs.

York believed that he and his student crew had satisfactorily compiled a "complete surface inventory" of the 6100-ft terrace (the Sunshine Locality) and that the NSM collection represented a "statistically valid" sample of all raw material and artifact types originally present (1974:9). He (1974:10) emphasizes an important correlation between a Pinto point and a Type III "Butterfly" crescent (Tadlock 1966) that may have been made from the same heat-treated chert core (specimens 26-WP-398:4 and 26-WP-398:46). This pair of artifacts was inconsistent with Tadlock's association of crescents with fluted points. This statement was later refuted by York in his 1978 report, after he had the artifacts examined at the U.S. Bureau of Mines in Reno (R. York, personal communication 2004). York noted that there are many Pinto points and a few ground-stone artifacts in the Long Valley assemblage, in contrast to Tadlock's report, which reports none. But as pointed out in note 1, it is unclear exactly where Tadlock collected. Further, if Tadlock actually collected from the Sunshine Locality, he was not there for long, and the site covers over 3 km^2.

A secondary purpose of York's work was to evaluate the nearby hills for toolstone sources and any other findings. He identified the probable quarries for a distinctive green chert and wonder stone from which several artifacts were made. His observation concerning the rarity of obsidian was questioned by Hutchinson and Noyes, who found many obsidian artifacts.[6] While surveying the uplands, York's crew found several rockshelters that were of sufficient size and location that they may have seen some aboriginal use, but only one seemed to have any potential; nothing older than Elko or Gatecliff Contracting Stem points was found on the slopes near this shelter. None of these shelters was tested by York. He concluded that the people who left the abundant stemmed and related artifacts on the valley floor did not use the uplands much, if at all, except for toolstone procurement.

In his conclusions York suggests that the people were camped along a stream flowing into a shallow lake and that fishing may have been important. He emphasizes the Pinto component of the sites and, citing Tuohy's (1974) postulation of a "Lake Mohave–Pinto Tradition" that may be represented here, suggests a date between 11,000 and 7000 rcy BP for the primary occupation.

York's summary of the paleoenvironmental reconstruction reveals the thinking of that time, that early Holocene, or "Anathermal" (Antevs 1948), environments gradually warmed and dried, with the shallow lakes drying into stagnant ponds before disappearing entirely around 7000 rcy BP. York includes an observation that Ruby Valley began to see increased human occupation at about the same time Long Valley was being abandoned, based on Laurel Casjens's (1974) work. He recommends backhoe trenches and detailed paleoenvironmental studies for the area. York bemoans how archaeological fieldwork often gets no further than the exploration stage and states that "in order for Long Valley to contribute effectively to our understanding of Great Basin ecology, and on a wider scale, to our understanding of how human beings have coped or have failed to cope with their environments, this project will have to be pursued through at least another field season" (1974:17). Now, 28 years later, considering the additional fieldwork spent on this marvelous archaeological locality, this is an incredible understatement.

York (e.g., 1974, 1978, 1979) reported his findings in several short reports as well as a paper presented at the Society for American Archaeology meeting in Vancouver in 1979. Although he did plan another field season in Long Valley, he was diverted by the new director of the museum, Thomas Layton, to work at Last Supper Cave. He eventually took a job with the BLM, but he never forgot the Sunshine Locality. In 1976 he prepared a nomination for the BLM to list the Sunshine Locality on the National Register of Historic Places, which finally happened in 1978.[7]

The nearly 8,000 artifacts collected by York remained unanalyzed until Gigi York (1995) analyzed the collection for her master's thesis. Approximately 71 percent (5,588) of the artifacts are formal tools, cores, or utilized flakes; the remaining 29.1 percent (2,970) of the assemblage is composed of debitage (see Table 5.1). Table 2.3 provides a summary of the artifacts minus the debitage by elevational zone, as presented by G. York (1995:89).

The Nevada State Museum–Desert Research Institute Consortium, 1988–1990

No further work was done by the NSM at the Sunshine Locality until the late 1980s, when the museum developed a research consortium with the DRI Quaternary Science Center under Cynthia Irwin-Williams and Jonathan O. Davis. We shared a compelling interest in the

FIGURE 2.8. Brian Amme (Bureau of Land Management), Cynthia Irwin-Williams (Desert Research Institute), and Amy Dansie (Nevada State Museum) at the Sunshine Locality, October 11, 1989; this was Cynthia's last field trip (photograph by Phil Hutchinson).

TABLE 2.3. Summary by Elevational Zone of the Tools Collected by York

	Elevational Zone				
Tool Type	Valley Floor	Wash	Fan	Mountain	Total
Projectile Point	321	4	2	32	359
Crescent	28			1	29
Multipurpose Tool	1,103		2	375	1,480
Utilized Flake	1,651	9	49	488	2,197
Knife	243		8	65	316
Biface	124			52	176
Graver	148			52	200
Scraper	553	1	1	133	688
Chopper/Cleaver	21		1	27	49
Ground Stone	19			2	21
Hammer Stone	6			4	10
Core	47	1		14	62
Total *N*	4,264	15	63	1,245	5,587
%	76.3	.3	1.1	22.3	100.0

Source: From York 1995:89.

early human occupation of the Far West and worked together in the Black Rock Desert, the Carson Desert, and the Sunshine Locality until the untimely deaths of both Irwin-Williams and Davis in 1991. The BLM, under archaeologist Brian Amme of the Ely District, was a full partner in this phase of work at Sunshine, providing the backhoe and operator and a field trailer. Generous private support from the Truman-Orr Foundation, later renamed the Calhoun Foundation, provided for the needed field and laboratory expenses.

The goal of this work was to establish whether there was buried evidence of early human occupation and an intact paleoenvironmental record to serve as a foundation for more systematic excavations under full funding. Planning began in 1988 for our first serious fieldwork in 1989.

The 1989 Field Season

On October 10, 1989, a team of archaeologists and geologists from the NSM and DRI met with the BLM archaeologist, Brian Amme (Figure 2.8), at the Sunshine Locality to conduct subsurface testing. Cynthia Irwin-Williams (Figure 2.8) and Fred Nials of DRI and I (representing the NSM), with Phil Hutchinson, worked for four days in the field.

A total of 15 backhoe trenches were excavated across the paleochannel (Sunshine Wash; Figure 2.9). The trenches were located in order to maximize the exposure of stratigraphy in the paleochannel as well as that representing eolian activity and slope deposition (Nials 1990). Because of time limitations in the field, no detailed sediment descriptions were done; efforts were concentrated on describing the stratigraphic sequence, searching for datable materials, and evaluating depositional processes. Nials (1990) presents a detailed description of the stratigraphy, including stratigraphic sections and textural correlations across the site, from which the following summary is taken.

Eight of the 15 trenches (Trenches 1–4, 8–11) were excavated in or adjacent to the bottom of Sunshine Wash (Figure 2.9). Almost identical stratigraphic profiles were visible in all of the trenches, one of which is shown in Figure 2.10. The base of the profile reveals cross-bedded coarse sand to small pebble alluvium, believed to have been deposited by an abraded stream. The sediments become finer toward the top of the deposit. A clear contact separates the alluvium from the overlying dark, organic-rich paludal deposit (Nials 1990). Above the marsh are silt, sand, and silty loam deposits accumulating from slopewash and eolian activity. Extensive local bioturbation was evident in these upper deposits.

In Trench 10 the alluvium contained charcoal, fauna, and several lithic flakes (Figure 2.10). Charcoal samples

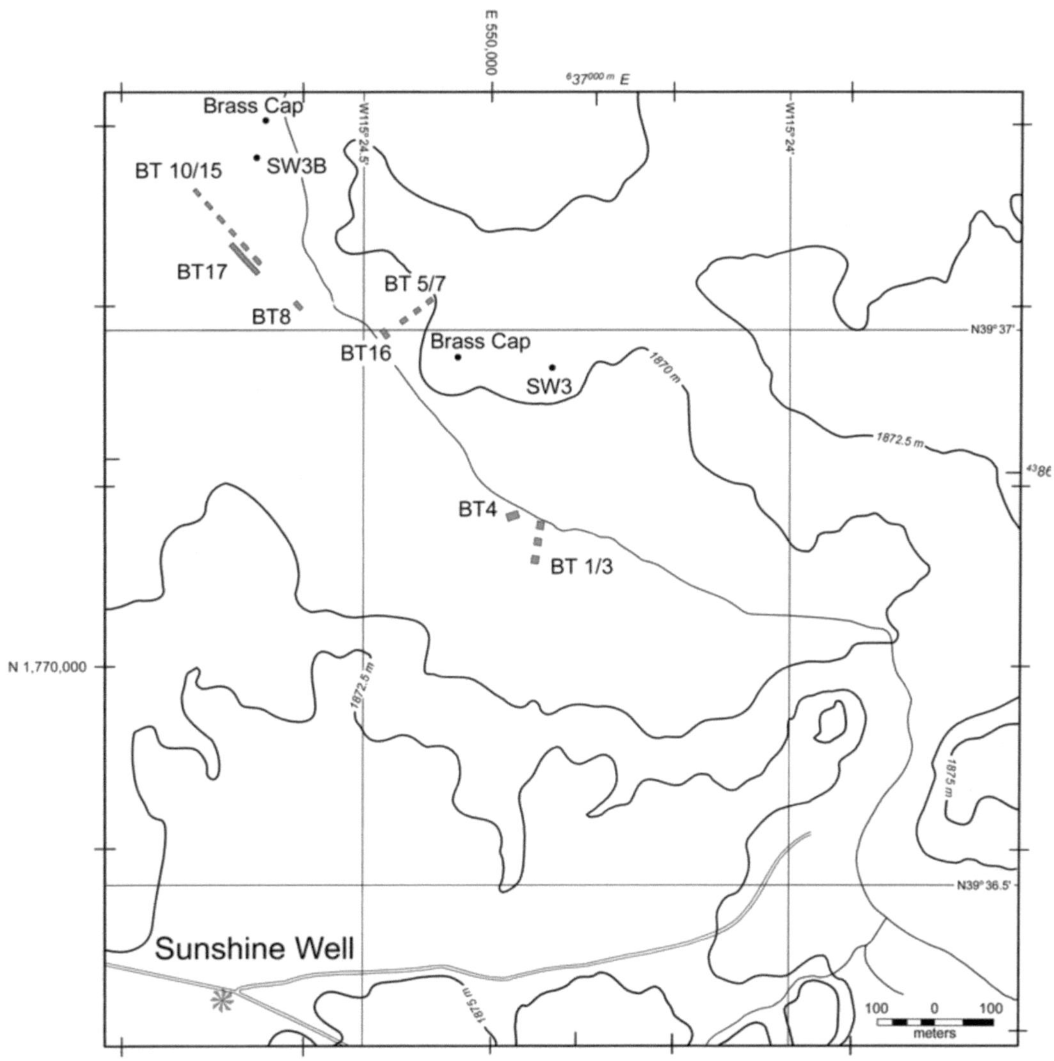

FIGURE 2.9. Location of the 1989 (1–8, 10–15) and 1990 (16–17) Nevada State Museum–Desert Research Institute backhoe trenches (BTs).

were taken approximately 2.6–3.0 m below the present surface. This charcoal was sent to Beta Analytic for radiocarbon dating and yielded a date of 10,690 ± 430 rcy BP. A variety of faunal remains were recovered from the alluvium, about 3 m below the present surface; these include a large mammal long bone, several vole jaws, fish cranial bones, a single jackrabbit element, and a single element of a medium-sized bird. Finally, several lithic flakes were also recovered from the alluvium.

The remaining seven trenches (5–7, 12–15) were excavated in the valley margin along the eastern and western sides of the wash (Figure 2.9). Five of these trenches show eolian sands underlain by lacustrine sediments; the marsh is not represented. The remaining two trenches were excavated on valley-margin escarpments and show a slopewash component overlying eroded lacustrine sediments.

At the end of our four days we made plans for fieldwork during the following summer, July 1990. Excavation was planned for four additional trenches in the hopes of exposing more cultural and paleontological material; we hoped to find an in situ archaeological deposit. Further, we hoped to gather enough data to develop a grant proposal for more intensive archaeological and geologic fieldwork. All work up to this point had been voluntary (i.e., unfunded). We planned to also ask the Truman-Orr Foundation for minimal support for Irwin-Williams and Nials during the 1990 field season and for time investment to provide a finished report of the fieldwork, analysis and interpretation of materials gathered to date, and a

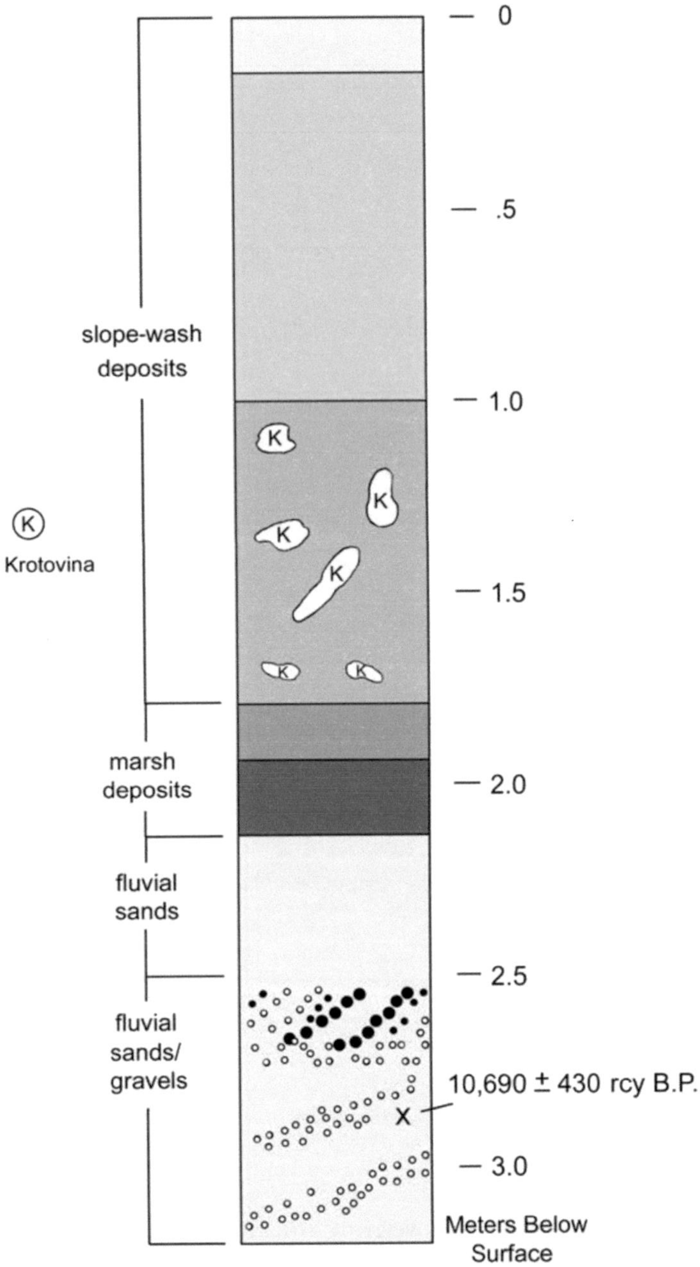

FIGURE 2.10. Profile of Trench 10 excavated in 1989 by the Nevada State Museum–Desert Research Institute field crew. A single radiocarbon date, marked by an X, was obtained from charcoal retrieved from the alluvial gravels (modified from Nials 1990:Figure 7). Small solid circles indicate lithic flakes; large solid circles indicate charcoal; open circles indicate gravels.

major portion of grant proposal text for future funding. The NSM committed to provide the time of its professional staff as well as a per diem.

In February 1990, Nials, Irwin-Williams, Hutchinson, Tuohy, and I met to plan the upcoming field season. The locations of the four trenches were planned, and priorities were mapped out. Everyone was assigned a task: Nials had responsibility for describing stratigraphy and depositional environments; I, the paleontology and paleoenvironments; Irwin-Williams, the archaeological evidence; Hutchinson, the history of work in Long Valley; Tuohy, the Sunshine Locality in late Pleistocene/early Holocene perspective; and Amme, the BLM management concerns.

We were very excited about this next field season because we knew there were bone, charcoal, and artifacts 3 m below the surface. Unfortunately, a few months later, having suffered from a debilitating illness for many years, Cynthia Irwin-Williams died before the 1990 field season began.

The Last Great Field Trip and the Great Basin Conference, 1990

Despite our deeply felt loss, we decided to proceed with the work at the Sunshine Locality. We had received a grant from the Truman-Orr Foundation to continue geologic probing at the site. On October 1, about a week and a half before the Great Basin Anthropological Conference was to be held in Reno, we returned to Long Valley. Jonathan Davis rejoined the team in the field. We began by opening two additional backhoe trenches (Figure 2.9) but focused most of our attention on Trench 17 (see Figure 2.11).

These few days in the field produced exciting results: bones and teeth of an extinct camel in the same stratum with an artifact! From Trench 17 we recovered two teeth and a mandible with incisors that we definitely believed to be from a camel (Figures 2.12–2.13). A relatively large, flat bone was also recovered, which we thought could also be from a camel. In addition to the camel bones, an obsidian flake was recovered in the same alluvial gravels, about 36 cm below the second camel tooth. Finally, several rodent and possibly amphibian or reptile bones were found in this trench.

The stratigraphy of Trench 17, as described by Nials, was consistent with that in the 1989 trenches excavated into, and adjacent to, the channel (see Figure 2.9). At the base was the alluvium and interspersed coarse sand and pebbles, overlain by fine sand. The alluvial deposits were overlain by the marsh and then "loessy" alluvium, or slopewash. A datum was established at the top of the marsh at the eastern end of the trench. Table 2.4 shows

FIGURE 2.11. Amy Dansie (Nevada State Museum) and Fred Nials (Desert Research Institute) in Trench 17 at the Sunshine Locality, October 5, 1990 (photograph by Phil Hutchinson).

FIGURE 2.12. *Camelops hesternus* mandible in Trench 17, exposed in situ by Amy Dansie, October 5, 1990 (photograph by Phil Hutchinson).

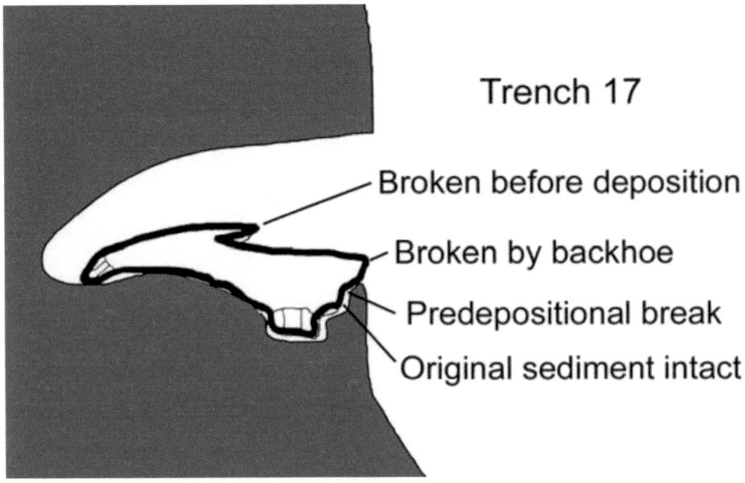

FIGURE 2.13. Schematic of *Camelops* mandible in situ. The base of the incisors was decayed and sand filled. The teeth were removed as the mandible was stabilized on extraction.

TABLE 2.4. Locations of Bones and the Single Flake Recovered from Trench 17

Field Specimen Number[a]	Distance West of East Datum (m)	Depth Below Datum (m)[b]	Element
2 (N)	18.65	1.21	Tooth
3 (S)	24.5	1.1	Tooth
4 (N)	47.9	.15	Mandible
5 (N)	12.6	1	Flat bone
6 (S)	14.1	1.15	Phalanx
7 (N)	14.2	1.24	Flat bone
9 (S)	24.6	1.47	Obsidian flake
11a (E)	1.25	1.01	Skull fragment?
11b (E)	1.42	1.19	Rib
11c (E)	1.99	.99	Unidentified

[a] Taken from the north/south wall.
[b] Datum established at the top of the marsh.

the location of bones and the obsidian flake relative to the datum.

Field specimen number 4, the mandible, which has since been identified as *Camelops hesternus* (see chapter 7), was probably the most exciting find of the trip (Figures 2.12–2.13). It was carefully cleaned in the field with polyvinyl acetate, a weak acetone solution, after removal from the trench wall; also, the four ventral incisors were removed from the mandible and cleaned. Many coats of polyvinyl acetate were applied to both the mandible and the tooth roots. After drying, each individual piece was packed in ziplock bags and Styrofoam peanuts for transport back to the NSM.

We presented the results of the 1989 and 1990 excavations at the 1990 Great Basin Anthropological Conference in Reno, Nevada. Table 2.5 summarizes the artifacts collected during these investigations.

The End of an Era

The October 1990 field trip was our last as the NSM–DRI consortium. I will never forget that last field trip to Sunshine, a remote spot so much a part of my life over the last 30 years. The evening of the day we found the Camelops jaw and the flake, we stopped to relax only when it was too dark to see, after a day we all agreed had been successful beyond our wildest dreams. The fact that the backhoe exposed the camel jaw by less than a centimeter, breaking only a tiny piece of the broken end, was the miracle of the day. Marveling at our luck, and the cold October sunset, my dear friend Jonathan said, "It doesn't get any better than this."

A few weeks later Jonathan Davis was killed by a drunk driver. Figure 2.14 shows Jonathan on his last field trip, October 5, 1990, operating the total station. Fred Nials went on to work with Charlotte Beck and Tom Jones (e.g., Jones et al. 1996), but the museum involvement died with Jonathan.

Afterthoughts and Conclusions

It was not until 2001 that we learned the age of the camel jaw and tooth from our 1990 trench work. The two University of California–Riverside AMS dates, corrected for δ13 values, are 11,340 ± 50 rcy BP and 11,910 ± 50 rcy BP. No matter how you look at it, it seems the megafauna bones are older than the sediments bearing cultural evidence, and although these are relatively late dates for Camelops,

TABLE 2.5. Artifacts Collected from the 1989 and 1990 Backhoe Trenches

TRENCH	DEPTH	ARTIFACT	RECOVERY	MATRIX
12	52 cm below surface	1 obsidian flake	in situ	slope wash
No information	no information	1 obsidian flake	in screen	slope wash
16	147 cm below datum	1 chert flake	in situ	upper marsh deposits
17	no information	1 obsidian flake	in screen	alluvial sand/gravel
10 and 17	no information	1 welded tuff flake, 1 basalt flake, 1 chert flake	in screen	wall scrapings
No information	no information	3 chert flakes, 2 basalt flakes, 1 welded tuff flake, 1 obsidian flake	in screen	backdirt

Source: Data compiled from Hicks 1990.

they do not change the estimated dates of camel extinctions in the New World. If the big bones are older and were redeposited, then maybe the fish bones are also. So after all that hard work, we still do not even know when the fish became locally extinct or if they survived through the Bolling/Allerod desiccation of Lake Hubbs through the early Younger Dryas. The longer time estimates since the drying of Lake Hubbs make it difficult to imagine fish surviving in this closed basin. However, all of us working on these earlier phases of the Sunshine prehistory agreed it was possible that the vast alluvial fans to the south may have "oozed" water into springs feeding Sunshine Wash, well after the pluvial lake dried. If the water flowed throughout the post-pluvial times, as indicated by the stream gravels and sands, the fish, and some of the megafauna, may have been available to the people who left the thousands of artifacts along the banks of the wash, but the evidence remains equivocal.

FIGURE 2.14. Jonathan Davis (Desert Research Institute) at the Sunshine Locality, October 5, 1990; this was Jonathan's last field trip (photograph by Donald Tuohy).

Notes

1. Robert York, in offering comments on this chapter, stated that he could not believe these collections came from the Long Valley playa, which lies about 8 km north of the Sunshine Locality. During his work in 1973 and 1978, York surveyed the playa and found no artifacts at all. In 1997 Tom Jones and his crew did the same and also found nothing. York suggested that perhaps Tadlock was using a more literal translation of *playa* from Spanish to mean "beach" or "shoreline," and if this is the case, the artifacts most likely came from within the area eventually designated the Sunshine Locality.
2. Hutchinson's photographs are excellent black-and-white renditions that are exactly to scale. As Alanah Woody of the NSM recently pointed out to Beck and Jones, you can take an artifact and place it on the photo and it fits perfectly.
3. We are grateful to Robert and Gigi York for their extensive comments on this chapter. They provided important clarification and additional information concerning the NSM work in the 1970s as well as a number of photographs of that work.
4. The students who worked on York's project were Dana Stone, Susan Clymer, Alan Ferg, Elizabeth Young, Steven Stearns, and Jean Ostrander. I worked as the cataloger and cook.
5. Although most archaeologists refer to the fine-grained volcanic material used to manufacture many of the Paleoarchaic tools as basalt, work by Jones et al. (1997) has demonstrated that the material used, at least in eastern Nevada, is most often dacite, which has a higher silica content and is thus of better flaking quality.
6. We now know that York was correct with regard to the rarity of obsidian outcrops in the vicinity of the Sunshine

Locality. Extensive surveys of most of eastern Nevada as well as parts of western Utah by Beck and Jones (1994; Jones et al. 2003) have failed to reveal any obsidian sources closer than about 100 km, with the exception of an outcrop of small pebbles in the Butte Mountains. Although only a few have been analyzed as to their chemical composition, the obsidian artifacts collected by Hutchinson and Noyes are undoubtedly manufactured from exotic toolstone.

7. The following is summarized from Robert York's description, provided to Beck in a personal communication in 2004:

> This was a unique nomination for that time, as there was no precedence for listing such a large archaeological district (34,560 acres), that contained no "ruins," on the NRHP [National Register of Historic Places]. Another "ahead of its time" aspect of this nomination was its landscape preservation goal. An explicit recognition that it was not only important to preserve the Sunshine Locality's archaeological materials but also the context or "integrity of location, feeling, and setting." Also, the nomination expressly endorsed that archaeological research should continue and be fostered by the BLM.

There were objections from several areas (e.g., the keeper of the National Register, the National Park Service, and BLM management personnel) relating to the need for such a large district to be listed. Other objections came from both professional and avocational archaeologists who worried that listing the site would open the area to illegal collecting. But the proposal was strongly supported by the State Historic Preservation Office and eventually the BLM, and thus the site, now officially named the Sunshine Locality, was listed on January 30, 1978. As a result, York returned to the site in 1978, conducting a survey to assess the archaeological potential of Long Valley outside of the Sunshine Locality. This work resulted in a 1978 report that was filed with the BLM, NSM, and Nevada State Historic Preservation Office.

3

The Hamilton College Excavations, 1992–1997

George T. Jones and Charlotte Beck

After consulting with Bureau of Land Management (BLM) and Desert Research Institute (DRI) personnel in 1991, we assumed responsibility for archaeological testing at the Sunshine Locality, continuing work that had been undertaken by DRI and the Nevada State Museum (NSM) in 1989 and 1990. Up to this point, our field efforts in Butte, Long, and Jakes valleys had been concerned nearly exclusively with surface archaeology (see, e.g., Beck and Jones 1990a, 1990b). Our subsurface tests were unsuccessful in identifying buried archaeological deposits at sites in those valleys, and thus the prospect of test excavation at the Sunshine Locality offered new opportunities for answering questions about which we were most interested.

In 1990 stratigraphic explorations by the NSM–DRI team exposed the mandible of an extinct camel *(Camelops hesternus)* and artifacts in alluvial gravels at a depth of about 2.75 m below the surface of Sunshine Wash. Alluvial charcoal from that deposit returned a radiocarbon age of 10,690 ± 430 rcy BP, confirming that terminal Pleistocene deposits occurred within Sunshine Wash. The preservation of bone and other organic materials suggested that this record might inform on climate and environment during that and subsequent periods.

Based on these few pieces of information several questions about the Sunshine record were easily envisioned. First, under what circumstances were the bones of extinct mammals deposited? Did they lie in an in situ context, and was that context cultural? Second, did artifacts lie in even deeper strata? Again, we wondered if primary cultural deposits were preserved. Finally, what were the ages of the deposits, and what processes contributed to their deposition? How might this information inform on the paleoenvironment of the area? These basic questions framed our research in the coming years.

Research Goals

We had a number of goals for our excavations at Sunshine, concerning geology, paleoclimate, and human activity at this site. The first was to refine the field descriptions of stratigraphy made in 1990 by Fred Nials and Jonathan Davis from the NSM–DRI backhoe trenches and to obtain datable organic material in order to better interpret the geologic history of the site. Because the alluvial gravels at the base of one of the trenches contained the remains of an extinct camel and had returned a terminal Pleistocene radiocarbon age, Nials suspected that the period during which these gravels were deposited might represent a local record of the Younger Dryas climatic interval, during which there was a return in the Great Basin, as elsewhere, to near full glacial conditions (Madsen 1999). Deciphering the geochronology of these lower strata, we believed, was extremely important.

The second goal of the Sunshine excavations was to evaluate the deposits, especially those in the lower strata, for the presence of an in situ cultural record. We already knew that it was quite possible we would find additional remains of extinct mammals; we also hoped to determine if these deposits held an associated cultural record. The relation between the extinct megafauna and humans in the Great Basin remains a mystery, for all previously reported "associations" are regarded generally as questionable (Beck and Jones 1997; Grayson 1993; see also Grayson and Meltzer 2002). Thus, if such an association could be found in unequivocal context, we might begin to answer some of the questions regarding human adaptation during the terminal Pleistocene, questions that had been of concern to us for the previous seven years in our eastern Nevada research.

Third, we hoped to gain some insight into the age of fluted points in the Great Basin. Fluted points are poorly dated in the Great Basin; in only five instances have they been reported from stratigraphic contexts, and in only one of these are radiocarbon dates and fluted points unequivocally associated (Beck and Jones 1997). That evidence comes from the Henwood site in the Mojave Desert (Douglas et al. 1988; Warren 1990; Warren and Phagan 1988), where a fluted point is associated with radiocarbon dates of 8470 ± 370 rcy BP and 4360 ± 280 rcy BP. The latter date is discounted by the excavators as too young, but the other date is still quite recent when compared with dates from outside the Great Basin and thus is viewed with skepticism by most archaeologists. But it could certainly be the case that fluted points in the Great Basin date somewhat later than Clovis on the Plains and in the Southwest (Beck and Jones 2008), and as the Sunshine

Locality fluted points are a significant component of the surface record, we hoped to find examples in undisturbed and datable stratigraphic contexts.

Finally, we hoped to improve our understanding of the temporal relation between fluted and stemmed points. Most researchers maintain that fluted points represent an earlier and different technology (and possibly adaptation) than do stemmed points (e.g., Basgall and Hall 1991; Grayson 1993; Pinson 1999), although most would agree that there is at least some degree of temporal overlap. In fact, existing data suggest that stemmed points could be as old as fluted points in the Great Basin, especially if fluted point use persisted into post-Clovis times and was coeval with Folsom (Beck and Jones 1997; Beck and Jones 2008). If fluted and stemmed points are contemporaneous, what is the technological/functional relation between the two? Thus, the finding of these two point forms and associated tools in undisputed stratigraphic context, also with datable material, remains an important goal for terminal Pleistocene/early Holocene archaeology in the Great Basin and was a primary goal of our excavations at the Sunshine Locality.

The 1992 and 1993 Field Seasons

The 1992 Field Season

In addition to excavating 17 backhoe trenches (see chapter 2), the NSM–DRI team completed a soil resistivity survey in the vicinity of the DRI long trench (Trench 17; see Figure 3.1). They detected an anomaly that projected from the edge of the wash into the main axis of the channel. Jonathan Davis believed the anomaly might represent a subsurface feature, perhaps a terrace that was capped by more recently deposited sheet-wash alluvium.

In an effort to evaluate Davis's hypothesis, Fred Nials and George T. Jones tested the area in 1992 using a hand-operated auger core, reasoning that such a feature, if present, might have been an ideal occupational surface. Because of its elevated position, a terrace would have been relatively isolated from high-energy fluvial processes operating in the stream channel. With subsequent burial such a surface might retain spatial patterns among artifacts as well as preserve faunal remains normally not found in surface contexts.

After establishing a grid over the target area, Nials and Jones proceeded systematically using a 4-in-diameter barrel hand auger. Sediments were recovered to a depth of between 2.0 and 2.5 m. Coring penetrated sandy and fine gravelly alluvium below this depth, which proved difficult to recover. Despite this, it was clear that the anomaly that had registered in the resistivity survey was not the signature of a buried terrace, at least within 2 m of the surface, and that the sampled area was itself part of the main axis of the channel or a major tributary channel.

The stratigraphic sequence developed by augering was identical to that evident from the NSM–DRI trenching (see Figure 2.10). The dark organic lens that was such a clear stratigraphic marker within the channel deposits across the length of the long trench was encountered in each of the auger holes. Importantly also, this unit contained artifacts; sediments brought up were passed through ⅛-in mesh screens from which numerous small flake artifacts were recovered. Although the dark lens clearly postdated 10,700 rcy BP, we were not sure of its actual age. In part to assess the age of this sedimentary unit and to determine if it was a cultural deposit, we planned to conduct our first test excavation in this same area.

The 1993 Field Season

During the summer of 1993 we held our first Hamilton College field school at the Sunshine Locality. The crew consisted of 12 students; Philip LeTourneau, then a Ph.D. student at the University of New Mexico, served as our field assistant. On June 10, before most of the students arrived, we began several test pits in order to make our decision as to where the primary excavation should take place, eventually selecting an area about 40 m southwest of NSM–DRI Backhoe Trench 17 (Figure 3.1). Based on results of the 1992 coring exercise, it appeared quite clear that artifacts occurred at least as deep as 2 m below the surface in this area. We did not know if they continued to even greater depth because we had been unable to penetrate the sandy sediments much below 2 m. We began by laying out a 20-×-20-m area (Figure 3.2), which we first surface collected before siting our excavation unit. A datum was established west of the excavation area and given an arbitrary elevation of 10 m; all depth measurements were referenced to this elevation. (In subsequent years we used actual elevation referenced to average sea level.)

With completion of the surface collection two 1-×-2-m test units, separated by 2 m, were laid out on a roughly east–west baseline (east–west axis of 307° and north–south axis 37°; Figure 3.2). Test Pits (TPs) 1 and 2 were excavated in 10-cm levels within the natural strata; sediments were screened through ⅛-in mesh screen. A number of small flakes (<1 cm in diameter) were found in the upper two levels; greater numbers were found in TP 2, which was slightly upslope (west).

TP 1 and TP 2 were excavated to depths of 70 cm, at which point the number of artifacts recovered dropped. The sediments, however, were riddled with krotovina, adding to our suspicions that artifacts in these upper sediments were not in situ but had been derived through deflation, slope wash, and bioturbation of sediments. A third 1-×-2-m test pit (TP 3), the center of which was along the same east–west line, was opened 14 m west of and further upslope from TP 2 (Figure 3.2). In addition, the

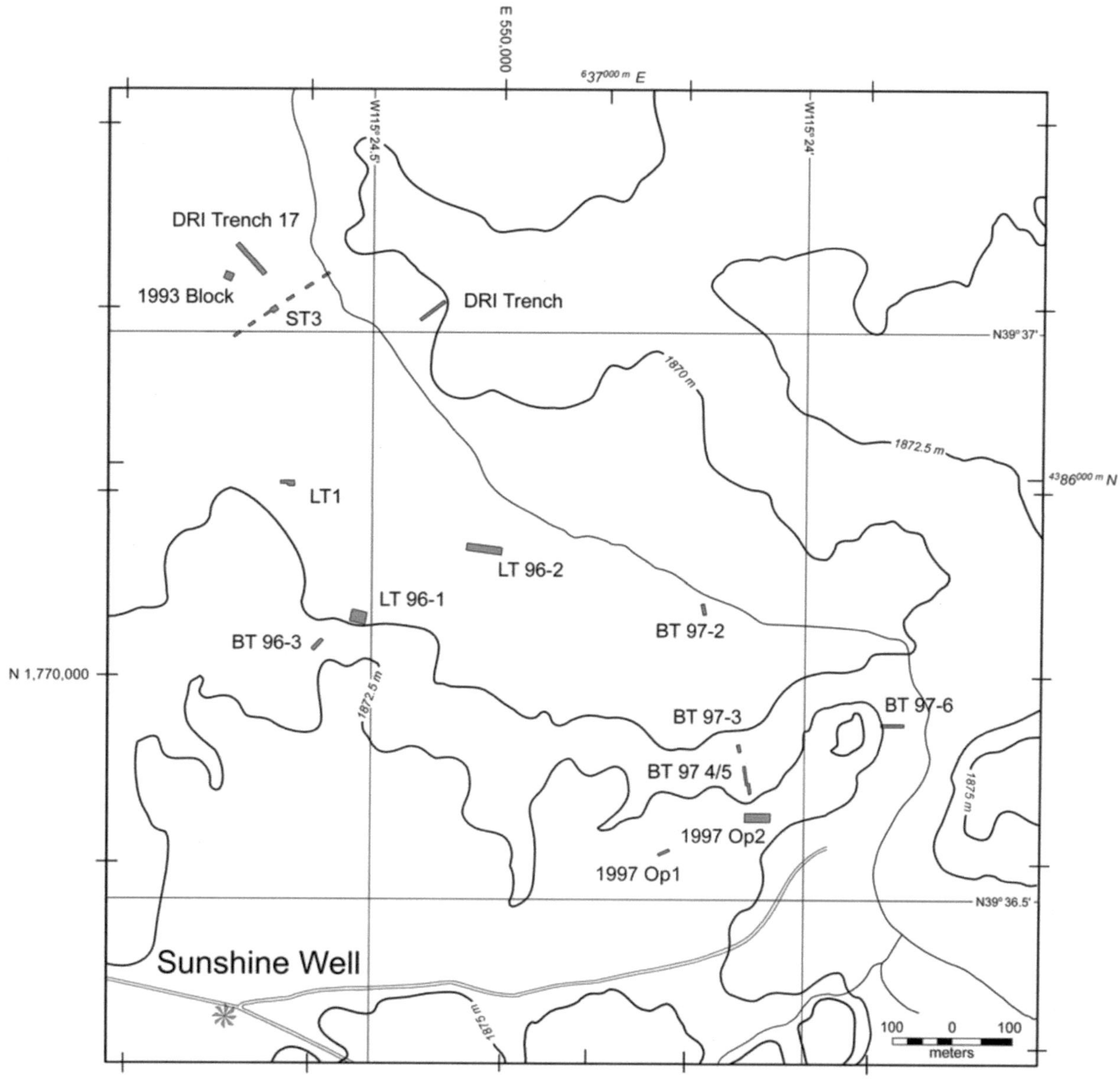

FIGURE 3.1. Locations of excavation units at the Sunshine Locality from 1988 (Nevada State Museum–Desert Research Institute) through 1997 (Hamilton College).

2-m section between TP 1 and TP 2 was excavated (TP 4), joining the first two test pits into a 6-m-long trench, which became known as the Strat Trench (Figure 3.3). A 4-×-6-m area was laid out adjacent to the Strat Trench on its southwest side (Figure 3.2) and divided into 2-×-2-m grid squares. Finally, a fifth 1-×-2-m test pit was excavated (TP 5) adjacent to TP 3, the northeastern edge of which was along the same east–west lines as TPs 1, 2, and 4 (Figure 3.2).

We began excavation of the 2-×-2-m squares within the 4-×-6-m grid simultaneously, with two students assigned to each unit. Level provenience was maintained within 1-×-1-m units within each grid square. Crews were randomized and changed on a weekly basis in an effort to minimize bias that could be introduced in the excavation due to differing abilities of the students.

As with testing in the Strat Trench, excavation in the 4-×-6-m block proceeded in 10-cm levels within the natural strata. Natural strata were assigned letters, and levels were numbered consecutively throughout the excavation. Excavation in the trench proceeded ahead of that in the large grid, so that the stratigraphy could be observed and anticipated by the excavators in the grid excavation (Figure 3.4). By the conclusion of our excavations,

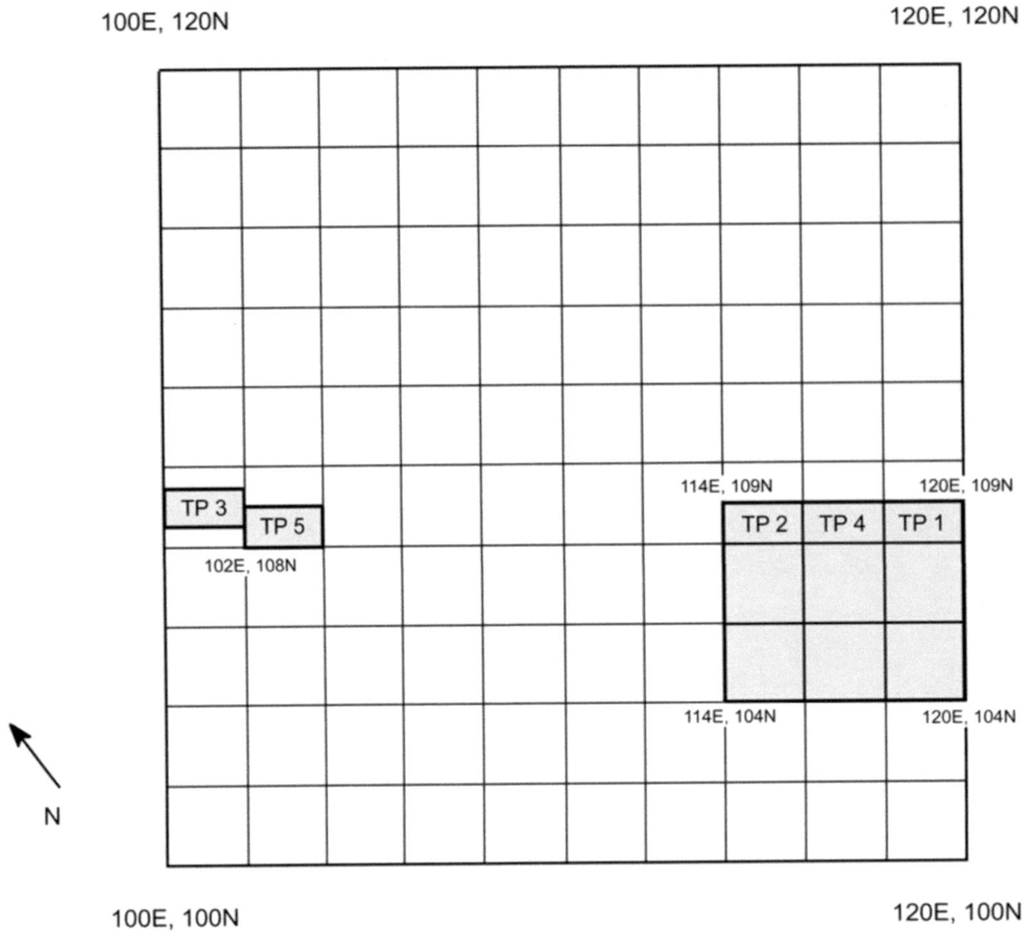

FIGURE 3.2. Schematic showing the 20-×-20-m surface grid, five test pits (TPs), and the final 5-×-6-m excavation pit.

39 levels, contained within seven natural strata, were excavated (Figure 3.5).

In addition to entries in field notebooks, excavators completed excavation records for each level, including descriptions of sediment type and level contents. These records include a plan drawing of the floor of each 10-cm level (or of the bottom of the stratum, whichever came first) and record any disturbances, such as krotovina. Materials were screened using ⅛-in mesh screen. All artifacts and bones were collected; charcoal was picked from the screens and bagged separately in aluminum foil. These practices were continued in subsequent years.

Sandy eolian sediments cap the terraces running along Sunshine Wash, which contain dense surface artifact scatters in many locations. Dune hummocks and deflated areas are common on these terraces, giving rise to concerns over the stratigraphic integrity of the artifact-bearing deposits. Moreover, based on information from testing within the wash proper, we suspected that as much as the uppermost 2 m of the channel deposits may not have any stratigraphic integrity, as they probably were derived from slope wash and strongly affected by rodent burrowing. These suspicions were heightened by what we found in the test pits: unconsolidated sediments, many krotovinas, and primarily small flakes. In order to demonstrate that this was the case, however, we proceeded in the primary excavation as if there was stratigraphic integrity, keeping precise vertical and horizontal provenience and screening all material. We could, then, evaluate our results later based on a size-sorting analysis of both sediments and artifacts as well as documentation of animal burrows.

Combined, the Strat Trench and the block excavation covered an area of 5 × 6 m. This unit was excavated to a depth of 2.4 m below the surface datum (7.6 m), at which point we stepped in three sides of the block for safety reasons (Figure 3.6). The 4-×-4-m area thus created was excavated simultaneously to maintain a level floor across the block. Excavation of this floor was continued through level 39, reaching a depth of 4 m below datum. Even at this depth we did not penetrate the base of the alluvial gravels (see chapter 4). With the help of Brian Amme

FIGURE 3.3. Arianne Pinson working in the Strat Trench, 1993 (photograph by Tom Jones).

from the BLM, we spent several more days excavating a 1-×-1-m unit in the southeast corner to a depth of 5.0 m below the surface (Figure 3.7), and still having not passed out of gravel, we cored another .7 m. In all, our probes reached 5.7 m below the surface but did not reach the base of the gravels.

A total of 6,738 artifacts were recovered by the excavation. Most (n = 5,922) came from the uppermost stratigraphic unit (Stratum A), which is sheet-wash colluvium. Artifacts were rare between Stratum A and the coarse alluvial basal deposit. The most important exception is a complete large stemmed projectile point recovered in situ (Figure 3.8) just superior to a pair of charcoal lenses that produced dates of 8560 ± 100 (not ^{13}C corrected) and 9800 ± 60 rcy BP (see chapter 4). Over 2,000 faunal elements were also recovered, 801 of which are identifiable at least to family. Not surprising, the majority of these are burrowing rodents and came from the upper 2 m of sediment (see chapter 7).

Stratigraphy. Figure 3.5 illustrates the profile of the southern wall of the excavation block, showing the seven strata identified during excavation. Stratigraphic distinctions were based on differences in sediment texture, sorting, and color that could be traced laterally over the entire excavation block. Letter designations (A–G) were assigned sequentially to strata as excavation proceeded downward from the surface. The stratigraphic conventions developed in 1993 were used in subsequent field seasons as

FIGURE 3.4. Ongoing work in the 1993 excavation block. The Strat Trench, visible on the right, was excavated ahead of the other units to provide stratigraphic control (photograph by Tom Jones).

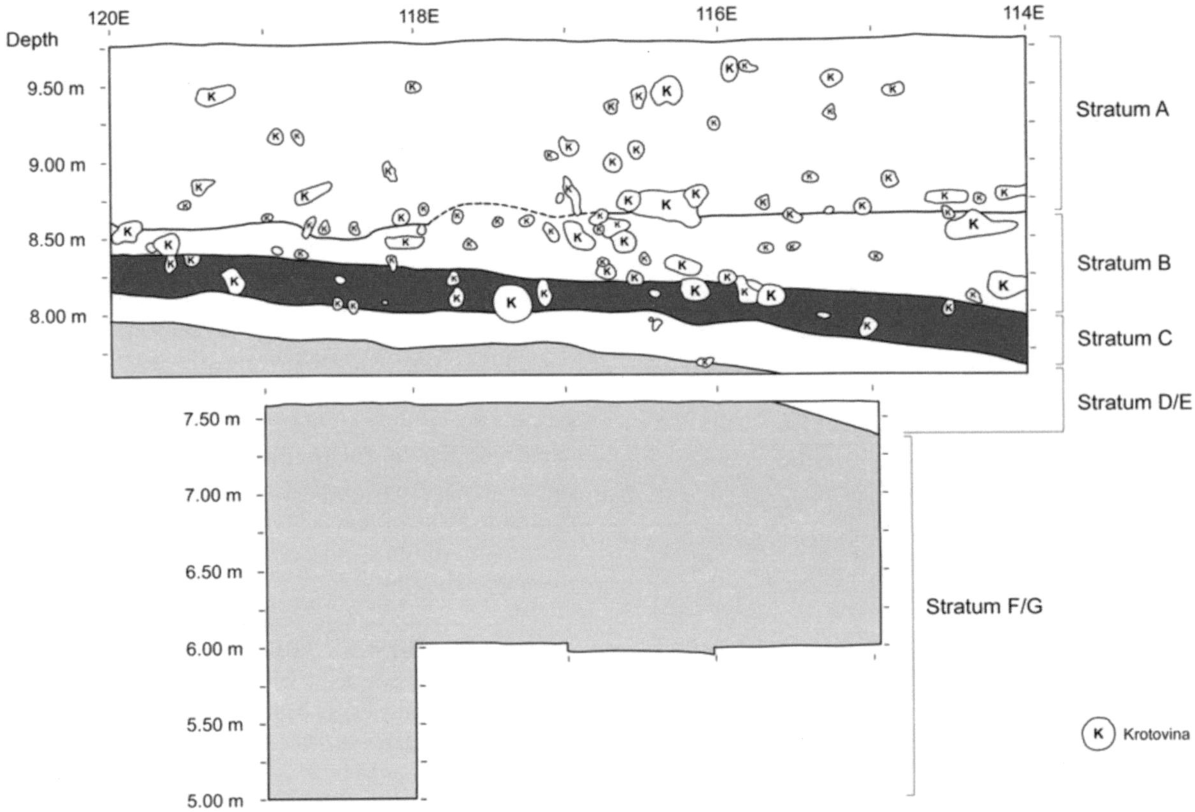

FIGURE 3.5. Stratigraphy of the south wall of the 1993 excavation block.

FIGURE 3.6. The 1993 excavation block after it was stepped in on three sides for safety purposes (photograph by Tom Jones).

FIGURE 3.7. Brian Amme screening sediment from a 1-x-1-m unit at the base of the 1993 excavation block. This attempt to expose the base of the alluvial gravels was unsuccessful (photograph by Tom Jones).

FIGURE 3.8. Large stemmed point found in situ at the boundary of Strata B and C. The point is lying on an ash couplet at the top of Stratum C (note the ash near the stem in the insert; photograph by Tom Jones).

well. More detailed stratigraphic analysis by Holmes and Huckleberry refined the sequence and reduced the number of analytic strata to five (chapter 4; Holmes 1998; Huckleberry et al. 2001). A concordance between field stratigraphic units (as reported in Jones et al. 1996) and analytic units (as reported in chapter 4; see also Huckleberry et al. 2001) is shown in Table 3.1. For the remainder of this chapter we discuss the testing with reference to the field stratigraphic units; analytic results presented in later chapters use Holmes and Huckleberry's analytic strata.

The base of the stratigraphic sequence in the 1993 excavation block consisted of complexly bedded lenses of sand and gravel, which reached a combined thickness of more than 3 m (Figures 3.5, 3.7, and 3.9). Fine and medium sand lenses were encountered at the top of this unit and were designated Stratum F. Gravel lenses were encountered at greater depth; these were assigned to Stratum G. Throughout the excavation, we maintained a distinction between sand (Stratum F) and gravel (Stratum G) facies of the alluvium, and each textural class was excavated and screened separately. As both are facies of channel-fill alluvium, they have been combined for this and subsequent descriptions and referred to as Stratum F/G.

The F/G alluvium fills channels of a braided stream that incised lacustrine and shoreline deposits following the recession of Lake Hubbs. The 1993 excavation failed to reach the base of the alluvium, but later testing in other locations in the paleochannel revealed this contact. Lenses of the alluvium are moderately to well sorted and are dominated by sand (Figures 3.5, 3.7, and 3.9). The lower section of this unit contains numerous lenses of gravel. These are well rounded, sometimes exhibiting

TABLE 3.1. Concordance Between 1993 Field and Analytic Stratigraphy

FIELD STRATUM	ANALYTIC STRATUM	DESCRIPTION
A	A	Silty and fine sandy alluvium.
B	B	Well-sorted eolian sediment with calcic soil.
C	C	Organic silty clay (paludal or pedogenic) topped by a series of thin burned layers. Referred to as the cienega paleosol throughout the discussion of the Hamilton College excavations.
D/E	D/D_{df}	Both D and E are thin lenses of fine sand that are strongly indurated; the sediments that are more strongly cemented were designated as Stratum E, and those less cemented sediments overlying Stratum E sediments were designated Stratum D. In Huckleberry et al.'s (2001) reclassification D represents cross-bedded alluvial sands and D_{df} represents horizontally bedded alluvial fine sands and silts (see Figure 4.1).
F/G	E	Channel-fill alluvium: In 1993 the sand lenses were designated Stratum F, and the gravel lenses, Stratum G.

FIGURE 3.9. Tom Jones removing sediment samples from the south wall of the 1993 excavation block (photograph by Phil LeTourneau).

oblate shapes. Gravel clasts likely were derived from beach deposits breached by the Sunshine stream. Small subangular blocks of clay also occur in some gravel lenses and indicate that the stream periodically eroded lacustrine sediments within the channel or that formed the bank of the paleochannel. Moving up the stratigraphic column, the alluvium generally grades to finer textures, suggesting that stream flow and transport energy diminished over time. The stratum generally dips to the west and exhibits cut-and-fill bedding.

Stratum E consists of thin lenses of fine sand and, like Stratum F/G, dips to the west (Figure 3.5). It is strongly indurated, exhibiting platy structure and oxidation and reduction colors. Stratum D, which overlies E, has similar textural properties but is less strongly cemented. The zone of cementation that encompasses both strata lies on a horizontal plane and does not follow the westwardly dipping contour of these beds. Thus it seems quite clear that pedogenic processes probably associated with the development of Stratum C above influenced these alluvial sands. We have combined these strata (D/E) for description.

Stratum C is a distinctive horizon found in every stratigraphic section we have explored in the paleochannel (especially visible in Figure 3.9). In the 1993 excavation block it consists of well- to poorly sorted loam that exhibits a very dark brown (10YR 2/2) color. It, too, dips to the west, though less strongly than the underlying strata. The unit contains lenses of different colors, but these cannot be easily traced across the profile; in other exposures, discrete lenses are easily differentiated. This very friable deposit is strongly affected by bioturbation.

Stratum B in the 1993 block is composed of two massive beds of generally well-sorted eolian sediment (Figures 3.5, 3.7, and 3.9). Like Strata A and C, it contains numerous krotovinas. The small artifact assemblage that it yielded probably was intruded from Stratum A as the result of bioturbation. Near the base of Stratum B, and in places nearly merging with the top of Stratum C, is a pair of thin charcoal lenses (see Figure 3.8). These lenses do not contain coherent pieces of charcoal but are composed of rather friable, ashy material. They presumably represent prairie fires that swept across Sunshine Wash. Rodent burrows locally disturb the lenses, and in some places along the profile the lenses nearly merge into a

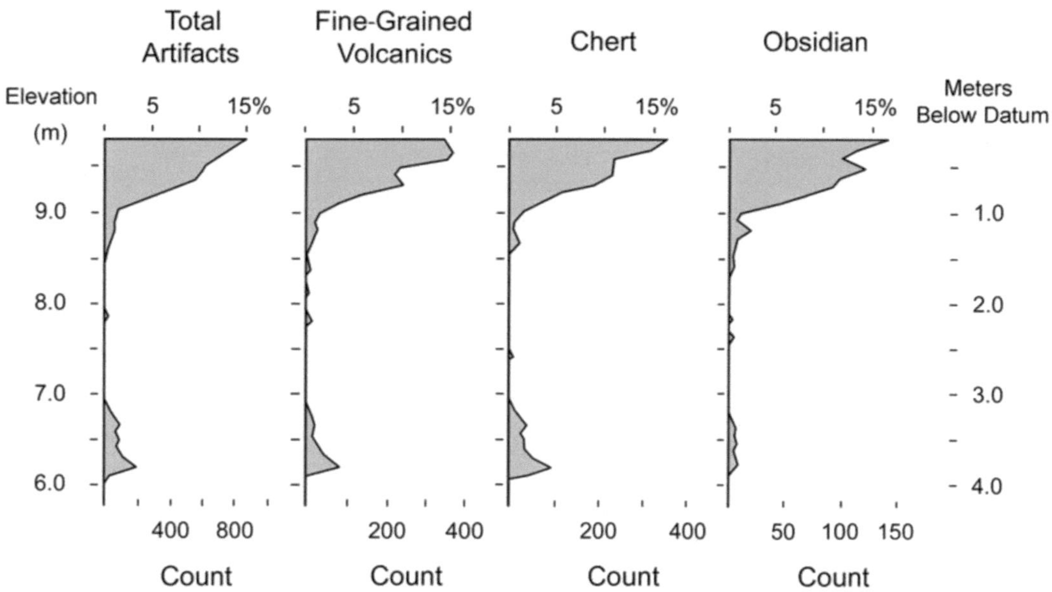

FIGURE 3.10. Vertical distribution of artifacts from the 1993 excavation block. Proportional representation by 10-cm levels is calculated on the basis of the total count of artifacts and the count within each major material category (after Jones et al. 1996:54, Figure 4).

single layer. Although they could be traced across the entire profile of the excavation block, they were not represented in most of the other stratigraphic exposures examined in the paleochannel (but see the description of Loader Trench 96-3 below). As stated above, the charcoal lenses were associated with a Great Basin Stemmed Series projectile point (Figure 3.8).

The stratigraphic sequence is capped by Stratum A, which reaches a maximum depth of ca. 1.2 m below the surface (Figure 3.5). This unit exhibits loamy texture and is believed to represent sheet-flood alluvium and colluvium derived from terraces adjacent to, and up-channel from, the excavation block. Stratum A contains a weakly developed soil (see chapter 4). Numerous artifacts were recovered in this unit, but these apparently lie in secondary context. This unit also contains numerous rodent borrows.

Artifacts. A total of 6,738 artifacts were recovered in the excavation of the 1993 block.[1] Additionally, 2,045 faunal elements were collected during this season's excavations. The artifact inventories of each excavation level are reported in chapter 5 (Table 5.3); the faunal inventories of each level are presented in chapter 7 and in the Appendix (Table A.1). Artifacts were recovered from 32 of the 39 levels. The highest frequencies are recorded in Strata A and F/G, whereas a number of levels within Stratum D/E were sterile. The assemblage is dominated by interior flakes (60.0 percent), most quite small, and undiagnostic shatter (38.6 percent; Table 3.2). Retouched artifacts represent only about .5 percent of the inventory (see chapters 5 and 6 for detailed analysis of the artifacts).

In Stratum A, which yielded by far the largest number of artifacts (n = 5,922), frequency diminished more or less continuously from the surface to the base of the stratum, and, indeed, this trend effectively continued to the top of Stratum F/G (Figure 3.10). This trend persists, as well, when the artifact sample is broken down into raw material categories (Figure 3.10). From this pattern it is difficult to judge whether the vertical distribution of artifacts, at least in the upper half of the column, more strongly reflects a temporal pattern in the redeposition of artifacts from adjacent terraces or is a result of bioturbation. There is, however, a pattern of increasing artifact frequency from the northeastern to the southwestern side of the excavation block within every level of Stratum A. This strongly suggests that the bulk of the artifacts at this location were derived from terrace deposits farther up the channel that once contained a primary cultural record, indicating that the input of artifacts to this location increased over time. The presence of artifacts in Strata B and C, in decreasing frequencies with greater depth, suggests there is a bioturbation imprint here as well.

The numbers of artifacts begin to increase again in Level 31, at a point where coarse sands and gravels begin to appear in Stratum F/G (Figure 3.10). In general, artifact frequency rises throughout the rest of the stratum in parallel with the coarsening of sediment texture. No artifacts

TABLE 3.2. Distribution of Artifacts by Type and Raw Material in the 1995 and 1996 Excavation Units

Assemblage	Raw Material	Tool Type							
		Cortex Flake	Interior Flake	Uniface	Biface	Projectile Point	Core	Shatter	Total
1993—Surface									
	Chert	3	147		1	1		72	224
	Obsidian	1	35			1		23	60
	Fine-Grained Volcanics (FGV)	17	197		1	3		112	330
	Quartzite								
	Other								
	Total	21	379		2	5		207	614
1993—Excavation									
	Chert	9	1,605	3	4	2	2	823	2,448
	Obsidian	2	643		2			309	956
	FGV	6	1,519	1	7	3	1	1,339	2,876
	Quartzite		3				1	1	5
	Other		281					172	453
	Total	17	4,051	4	13	5	4	2,644	6,738
1995—Surface									
	Chert	14	202	12	12	5	3	16	264
	Obsidian		29	1	1	3		2	36
	FGV	21	191	7	6	8	1	9	243
	Quartzite		8			1		2	11
	Total	35	430	20	19	17	4	29	554
1995—Excavation									
Strat Trench (ST) 3-95	Chert	1	50	1	2			8	62
	Obsidian		4						4
	FGV		35		2			6	43
	Other		9		1			1	11
	Total	1	98	1	5			15	120
Loader Trench 95-1	Chert	1	52	1	1	1		4	60
	Obsidian		6		2			1	9
	FGV		9					2	11
	Other		4						4
	Total	1	71	1	3	1		7	84
1996—Surface									
	Obsidian					1			1
	FGV					1			1
	Total					2			2
1996—Excavation									
ST 3-96	Chert		37	3		1		15	56
	Obsidian		6					9	15
	FGV		45					27	72
	Total		88	3		1		51	143
1997—Surface									
	Chert	4	21	1			1	9	36
	Obsidian		3					3	6
	FGV	1	42	1				16	60
	Quartzite								
	Other								
	Total	5	66	2			1	28	102

TABLE 3.2. (cont'd.) Distribution of Artifacts by Type and Raw Material in the 1995 and 1996 Excavation Units

		Tool Type							
Assemblage	Raw Material	Cortex Flake	Interior Flake	Uniface	Biface	Projectile Point	Core	Shatter	Total
1997—Excavation									
Operation 1	Chert	4	35	1				26	66
	Obsidian		14					21	35
	FGV	4	28					54	86
	Quartzite	1				1			2
	Total	9	77	1		1		101	189
Operation 2	Chert	3	73	3	1		1	63	144
	Obsidian		26					18	44
	FGV	1	142	1				177	321
	Total	4	241	4	1		1	258	509
2004—Surface									
	Chert				6	1			7
	Obsidian				1				1
	FGV				1				1
	Total				8	1			9

FIGURE 3.11. Artifacts from the 1993 excavation: (A) stemmed point found in situ between Strata B and C, 114.05E, 104.55N; (B) multiple-spurred graver found in situ, 188.80E, 105.45N, Level 34, Stratum F/G; (C) fragment of a triangular spurred end scraper, 102E, 108N, Stratum A; (D) polyhedral core, 114E, 106N, Stratum F/G; (E) amorphous core, 114E, 106N, Stratum F/G.

from this stratum were clearly contained within sand lenses (Stratum F); rather, all appear to come from gravel lenses, suggesting they were transported to this location as part of the stream's bed load. A controlled sampling of Stratum F/G to evaluate the correspondence between sediment texture and artifact size confirmed the pattern evident from the general excavation (Jones et al. 1996).

Interestingly, artifact recovery from the lowest level (39) was dramatically lower than that in the levels superior to it. Our excavation of a 1-×-1-m square to Level 50 at the southeastern corner of the block (see Figure 3.7) also failed to yield any artifacts. It is not clear why the lowest part of the alluvium contains no artifacts, although we might speculate that these deposits represent a somewhat earlier channel deposit, perhaps coeval with a pre–11,000 rcy BP unit represented in Loader Trench 96-2 (see below) and thus effectively predating human occupation of the locality. The occurrence of strong oxidation skins on gravels below Level 39, but not above, is consistent with this interpretation.

Although the artifact assemblage from the 1993 excavation is covered in detail in later chapters, mention will be made here of a particularly important discovery. As fortune would have it, the only classifiable projectile point recovered in this excavation was found in situ (Figure 3.8), a Great Basin Stemmed Series (GBSS) point made of dacite (Figure 3.11A). The point was discovered near the base of Stratum B, lying virtually on top of the upper band of the charcoal/ash couplet. It was separated from this charcoal by no more than 1–2 mm of sediment and appears to have been dropped on this surface without disturbing the underlying charcoal band.

We carefully evaluated the relationship between the point and the charcoal couplet in the field. The lens of charcoal is very fragile, and yet, except where it was disturbed by krotovinas, it was continuous across the profile. This indicates that the eolian dust that capped the charcoal couplet fell shortly after the second fire. Thus, the close association of the point and the charcoal couplet suggests that the age of the charcoal provides a very close estimate of the age of the projectile point. Radiocarbon assay returned two dates on the charcoal couplet. One date, an AMS assay of charcoal fragments, gave an age of 9800 ± 60 rcy BP. A conventional assay of a bulk sediment sample containing the charcoal gave a more recent age of 8560 ± 100 rcy BP. Of the two dates, the former is less susceptible to contamination and probably is a more accurate estimate of the fire and thus the point's age. Both dates are, however, consistent with the two other radiocarbon dates obtained from the 1993 excavations, both from Stratum F/G: 10,240 ± 80 and 10,250 ± 60 rcy BP.

Very few other retouched artifacts were recovered from the excavation. Three unifaces (two end scrapers [Figure 3.11C], one graver), 11 bifaces (five production, five amorphous [see chapter 5 for definitions], and one bifacial scraper), and two unclassifiable projectile points were recovered from Stratum A. A single multiple-spurred graver found in situ (Figure 3.11B), two amorphous bifaces, two blade sections of GBSS points, and four cores (Figure 3.11D–E) were recovered from Stratum F/G. The graver from Stratum F/G is particularly noteworthy as it is one of the few in the Sunshine assemblage manufactured from fine-grained volcanic (FGV) toolstone (see chapter 5).

An additional 614 artifacts were collected from the surface. Most of these came from the controlled collection surrounding the excavation block. These artifacts are predominantly debitage and shatter (Table 3.2), although there are two bifaces and three projectile points; of the latter, two are stems of GBSS points and one is the blade section of an Archaic point. Ten additional artifacts were located by Phil Hutchinson, who visited the site while we were there, and we obtained their provenience with our transit and collected them.[2] These include one fluted (Figure 3.12A) and five unfluted (Figure 3.12C–G) Great Basin Concave Base points, a fluted point preform (Figure 3.12B), a Parman point (Figure 3.12H), a Windust point (Figure 3.12I), and a bifacial hafted graver (Figure 3.12J).

Of the 2,045 faunal specimens recovered from the 1993 excavation black, 801 (39.2 percent) have been identified (see chapter 7). Most are burrowing rodents that live in the area today, but several elements of fish and waterbirds were found in Stratum F/G as well as one element of a red fox (*Vulpes vulpes*); these taxa are not presently found in the area. These are discussed more fully in chapter 7.

The 1995 and 1996 Field Seasons

The 1995 Field Season

As was the case in 1993, the 1995 fieldwork was conducted in conjunction with the Hamilton College field school. The crew consisted of 11 students and a camp assistant. Phil LeTourneau returned as our teaching assistant.

The stratigraphic sequence revealed by our 1993 excavation was very similar to the sequence reported by Nials and Davis (1990) based on the NSM-DRI testing. We entered the field in 1995 with plans to evaluate other locations within Sunshine Wash to determine if this sequence typified those areas as well. As before, we hoped to recover datable materials to refine the chronology and hoped our efforts would identify occupational surfaces within the wash.

Gary Huckleberry (then at Washington State University) joined us at the beginning of the season, overseeing geoarchaeological investigations for the project. He recommended that we begin by creating additional exposures of the paleochannel and channel margin stratigraphy. Thus we began by excavating six backhoe trenches perpendicular to the channel axis a short distance upchannel (south) from our 1993 test (Figure 3.1). Each trench was approximately 10 m in length and was excavated to depths in excess of 3 m. Most of these exposures revealed a familiar stratigraphic profile, a sequence we now recognize to be represented throughout the paleochannel. The most eastern trenches, however, encountered lacustrine sediments near the surface, indicating that this part of the channel was incised recently.

Large mammal bones were uncovered by the backhoe from the third trench. Also, embedded in the wall of this trench was a tooth, at an elevation of 1863.4 m (approximately 3.6 m below the surface; Figures 3.13–3.14). The tooth was removed along with a piece of charcoal ca. 30 cm above it. The tooth was sent to Donald Grayson, who identified it as *Camelops* sp. Grayson sent it to Russell Graham, who confirmed the identification; he added that it was likely *Camelops hesternus.* Based on the

FIGURE 3.12. Artifacts collected from the surface in 1993: (A) FS 2, fluted point; (B) FS 4, fluted point preform; (C–G) FSs 9, 11, 1, 10, 6, unfluted lanceolate points; (H) FS 3, Parman point; (I) FS 5, Windust point; (J) FS 8, hafted bifacial graver.

FIGURE 3.13. The south wall of Backhoe Trench 3, which was extended and excavated as Strat Trench 3-95 (photograph by Phil LeTourneau).

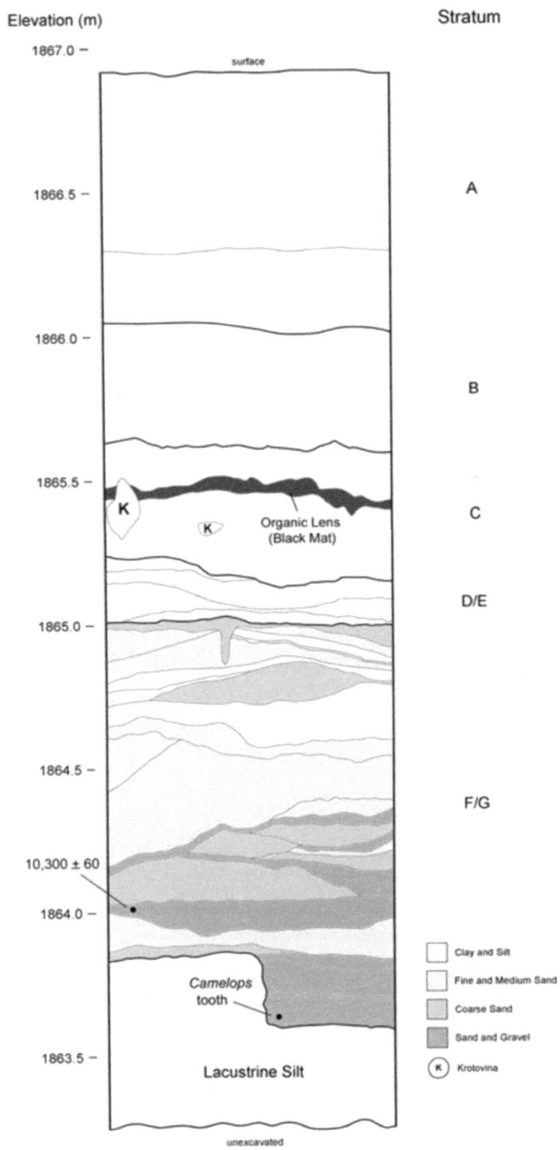

FIGURE 3.14. Profile showing the location of a *Camelops* tooth; locations of dated charcoal samples are approximate.

presence of the large faunal remains and charcoal in this trench, we decided to continue with hand-testing at this location. As we had demonstrated by our excavations in 1993 and subsequent analyses (see Jones et al. 1996) that artifacts in the upper strata (A and B) were in secondary context and further disturbed by burrowing animals, we used a front-end loader to strip these sediments (ca. 2 m) from an 8-×-6-m area at the eastern end of Strat Trench (ST) 3 to just above the contact with the cienega deposit (Stratum C; Figure 3.15). The eastern end of the exposure was ramped to the surface for easier access. From this point on, excavations in ST3 were carried out by hand.

Farther up the channel, about 230 m south/southeast of the skip trenches, we excavated a second area using a front-end loader (Figure 3.1). Loader Trench (LT) 1 consisted of a ramp cut into the terrace, which was then extended eastward into the wash. In the wash, the ramp was expanded into a pit measuring about 8 × 10 m. This pit became the focus of further excavation. As with ST3, the uppermost beds (Strata A–B) in LT1 were stripped mechanically to just above Stratum C. Controlled excavations were centered in a 4-×-6-m area within the pit (Figure 3.16).

Strat Trench 3 Excavation. The mechanical stripping of ST3 created a pit nearly 2 m deep that sloped to the surface on the eastern side. Our first task was to hand-strip the sandy sheet-wash alluvium (Strata A–B) from the ramp to produce a flat excavation surface just above the contact with the cienega unit (Stratum C). Once this was completed, a grid of 2-×-2-m units covering a 4-×-6-m area was centered in the pit. Excavation proceeded by a combination of hand-troweling and skim shoveling in 10-cm levels until Stratum C was revealed across the floor of the grid. Thereafter, we hand-troweled the sediments, maintaining provenience within 1-×-1-m quadrants in each 2-×-2-m unit. Vertical control was maintained within strata using 10-cm levels. All sediments were passed through ⅛-in mesh screen.

As the sediments dried and hardened, our excavation of ST3 slowed. While still in the process of removing Stratum C we decided to reduce the size of our excavation unit to a 2-×-6-m unit centered in the original 4-×-6-m pit. Our progress improved, but it was clear we could not expect to penetrate the F/G alluvium by the close of the season. So after we completed excavation of six levels (.60 m), the excavation unit was narrowed again, and work continued in a 1-×-6-m trench (Figure 3.17). This trench was ultimately excavated to a depth of about 1.5 m below the top of Stratum C (about 3.5 m below the surface), where basal lacustrine beds were encountered (Figure 3.18).

The strata (C–E) above the alluvial gravels did not contain any artifacts. Once we encountered coarse alluvium (Stratum F/G), however, small numbers of artifacts appeared, and their numbers increased the more deeply we dug. Compared with our 1993 results, the alluvial beds at ST3 were less artifact rich, which probably reflects the fact that ST3 lies nearer the axis of the channel and farther from artifact sources. But the alluvium also produced a large number of faunal remains, most notably several elements identified as genus *Camelops* (see chapter 7). These bones, including a complete scapula and phalanx (Figure 3.19), lay in close proximity to several artifacts including a large biface (see discussion below). Unfortunately, the

FIGURE 3.15. Strat Trench 3 being prepared for excavation in 1995 (photograph by Tom Jones).

FIGURE 3.16. Phil LeTourneau at the beginning of the excavation of Loader Trench 1 in 1995 (photograph by Tom Jones).

FIGURE 3.17. Strat Trench 3 after it was narrowed. Josh Allen is removing the camel bones in 1995 (photograph by Tom Jones).

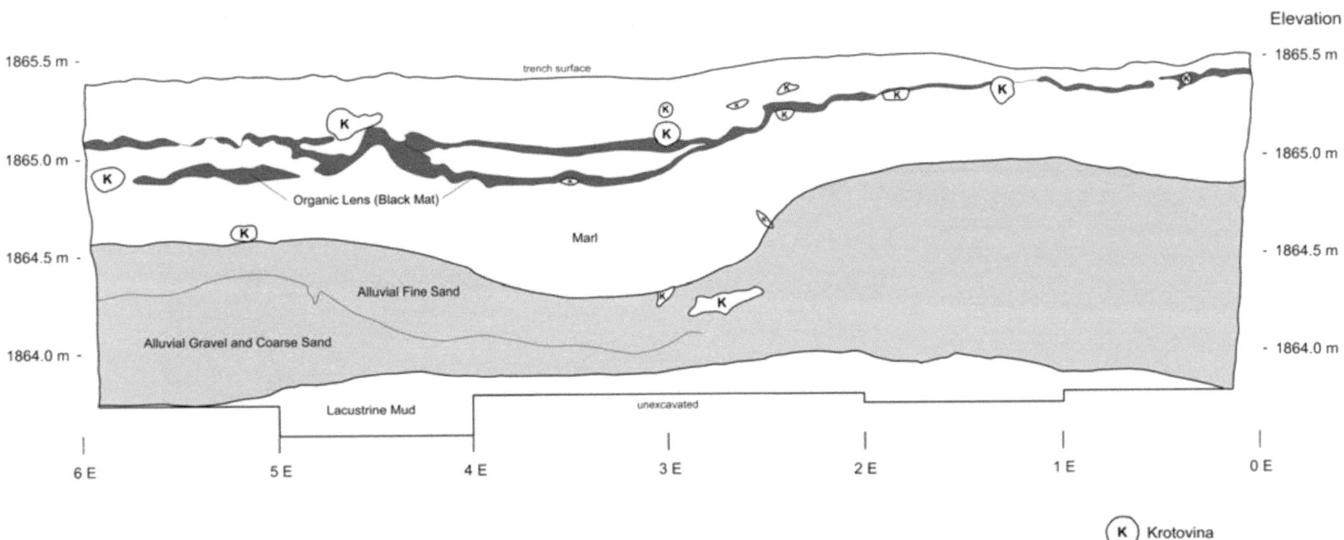

FIGURE 3.18. Profile of the south wall of Strat Trench 3 in 1995.

context of the bones and artifacts made it nearly impossible to evaluate whether they co-occurred for other than geologic reasons. It was the case, certainly, that the bones and artifacts rested in alluvium, which argued for transport from their primary contexts to this location. The alluvium surrounding them, however, was much smaller than the bones, leading us to wonder if this stream had sufficient energy to transport such large items as the scapula of a camel, as they rested parallel to the alluvial structures in essentially a horizontal plane. Still, inadequate stream energy did not rule out the possibility that both bones and artifacts were derived from a terrace that had collapsed into the stream. If not, the stones and bones might have been deposited together by humans or were derived from very nearby deposits that had collapsed into the stream channel. Neither the bones nor the artifacts exhibited rounding due to water transport, suggesting that if they were moved, they did not travel far in the bed load of the stream.

As fate would have it, the discovery of the camel bones and artifacts was made near the corner of unit 4E, 0N, about 2.13 m below the top of Stratum C on the last day

FIGURE 3.19. Bones of *Camelops* found in the gravels of Strat Trench 3 in 1995. Bones identified as *Camelops*: scapula and carpal. Bones of camel-sized mammal not identified as *Camelops*: mandible and unidentifiable fragment (upper photograph by Charlotte Beck; lower photograph by Phil LeTourneau).

of the field project. This precluded opening up an adjacent unit to see if more bones and artifacts lay nearby. We were forced to backfill but made plans to return the following summer.

Loader Trench 1 Excavation. Excavations at LT1 proceeded in much the same fashion as in ST3. A 4-×-6-m area was centered within the pit excavated at the base of the LT1 ramp. We leveled this area by shoveling to the top of the cienega (Stratum C); except for a small sample, these sediments were not screened. A grid of 2-×-2-m squares was placed over the unit to provide horizontal control. Excavation proceeded in 10-cm levels within geologic strata, referenced to 1-×-1-m quadrants within each 2-×-2-m grid unit. For the most part, sediments were removed by hand-troweling and passed through ⅛-in mesh screening. All artifacts and organic remains, including bones, gastropod shells, and charcoal, were collected.

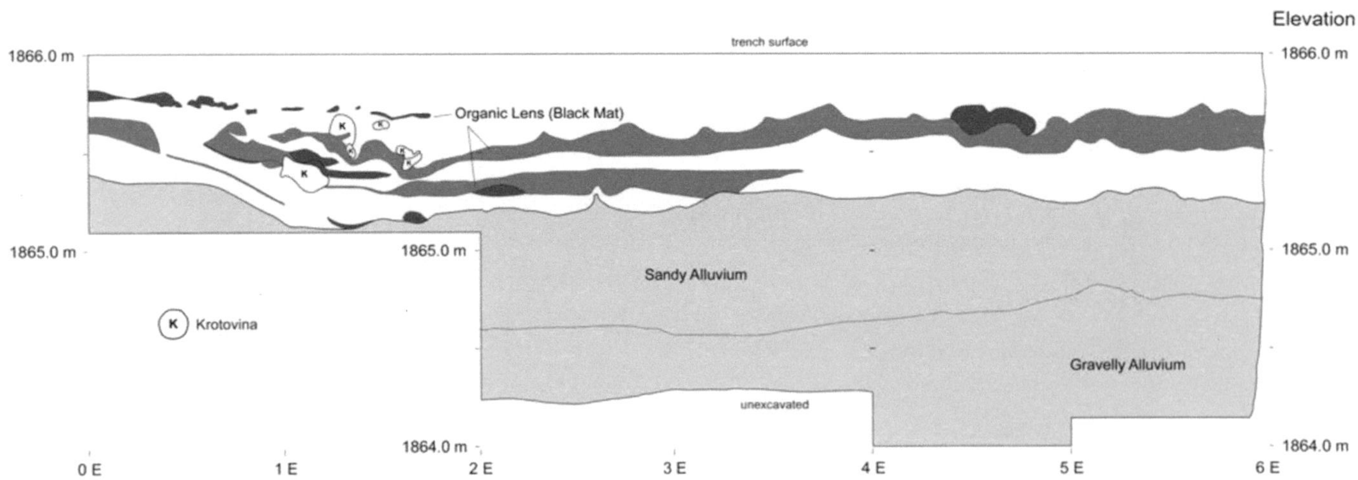

FIGURE 3.20. Profile of the north wall of Loader Trench 1 in 1995.

TABLE 3.3. The 1995 Field Strata for Loader Trench 1 and Strat Trench 3 as Compared with the 1993 Field Strata and the Final Strata Devised by Huckleberry and Holmes

1995 FIELD STRATUM	1993 FIELD STRATUM	FINAL STRATUM
Loader Trench 1		
A	A	A
B_1	C	C
B_2	C	C
B_3	C	C
C_1	F/G	E
C_{2a}	F/G	E
C_{2b}	F/G	E
Strat Trench 3		
B	C	C
C_1	F/G	E
C_2	not represented	E

Three stratigraphic units provided general vertical control (Figure 3.20). The uppermost of these, identified for excavation purposes as "A" (Table 3.3), consisted of silt loam. Most of it was removed mechanically before hand-excavation began, but nearly 20 cm of "A" was sampled on the western side of the grid. The next unit, identified as "B," represents the cienega paleosol (Stratum C). At LT1 this unit reached a thickness of about 80 cm and is complexly stratified. Oxidation mottling from wetting/drying episodes is evident throughout the paleosol. A distinct zone of marl or indurated loam corresponding to Stratum D/E is not evident at LT1. Instead the cienega paleosol rests directly on friable alluvial sand, which corresponds to the top of the F/G alluvium. This local expression of Stratum F/G was identified as "C" and contains two components. The upper unit (C_1) is a silty sand, which ranges between 20 and 75 cm in thickness. The lower component consists of lenses of coarse sand (C_{2a}) or sandy gravel (C_{2b}). At LT1 this stratum contains numerous lenses of different textures, all of which gently dip to the west.

As was the case at ST3, we overestimated how quickly LT1 could be excavated. We began by carefully removing Stratum C, which proved to be much thicker in LT1 than in ST3 or our 1993 unit (Figure 3.20). Although artifact recovery from Stratum C was at best modest, we did find two conjoinable pieces of a biface (Figures 3.21 and 3.22D). The pieces were found in adjacent grid squares but nearly 2 m apart. This find clearly indicated that the cienega paleosol contained an in situ archaeological deposit, however ephemeral it might be.

Because of the time required to thoroughly excavate Stratum C, we were forced to revise our schedule and to reduce the size of the excavation unit to 2 × 6 m (Figure 3.23). Then, as we approached the end of the field season we concentrated efforts at the eastern end of the trench in order to penetrate the alluvial sediments as deeply as possible. Our excavation at LT1 failed to reach the base of the alluvial beds.

The Stratum F/G alluvium at LT1 contained more beds of sand and fewer gravel lenses. Artifact recovery from the sands was low. When they could clearly be associated with a particular bed or lens, artifacts were predominantly located in gravels, paralleling our 1993 findings. Although the LT1 alluvium produced little in the way of faunal remains, it did offer up several important artifacts, including a segment of a crescent, a large curved blade,

Figure 3.21. The larger of two segments of a biface found in situ in unit 2E, 0N, Stratum C, of Loader Trench 1 (photograph by Tom Jones).

Figure 3.22. Artifacts from Loader Trench 1, 1995: (A) Clovis blade, 3.43E, 3.33N, 1,864.5 m, Stratum F/G; (B) fluted point, 4E, 2N, Stratum F/G; (C) crescent, 2E, 2N, Stratum F/G; (D) biface, 2.68E, 1.00N, 1,865.22 m, Stratum C; (E) graver, 2E, 4N, Stratum F/G; (F) combination graver/notch, 4E, 2N, Stratum F/G.

FIGURE 3.23. Loader Trench 1 after it was narrowed (photograph by Tom Jones).

and the base of a fluted point (Figure 3.22). Additionally, we recovered a number of pieces of charcoal from the excavation walls that subsequently were submitted for radiocarbon dating.

Controlled Surface Collection. In addition to the excavation at ST3 and LT1, a controlled surface collection was made of a small area south of ST3. We had collected a fluted point from this area in 1993 and had noticed a relatively dense distribution of artifacts, a number of which were retouched tools. Upon reexamination of this area in 1995, we decided to make a complete collection of the area. The provenience of each artifact was obtained using the transit, and each was given its own Field Specimen (FS) number; 554 artifacts were collected (Table 3.2).

The 1996 Field Season

During a brief field session in the summer of 1996 we continued excavations at ST3 where camel bones and artifacts had been found the previous year.[3] Although earlier work had demonstrated that both the cienega and alluvial beds within Sunshine Wash contained artifacts, in no instance had we been able to show that the artifacts from the lowest strata lay in primary archaeological context. Thus the first goal of our testing in 1996 was to explore places within the wash where lower-energy deposits—for example, point and lateral bars—might be preserved. We hoped to improve our chances of finding undisturbed cultural deposits by locating such landforms. Our second goal was to expand our probes of the alluvial beds in ST3, hoping not only to increase the faunal and artifact sample but also to achieve a more detailed picture of depositional processes and to obtain datable material for better control of the age of the deposits.

Work began by reopening the ST3 excavation unit (Figure 3.24), which had been backfilled at the end of the 1995 season, and by mechanically excavating a new set of stratigraphic exposures elsewhere in Sunshine Wash. Figure 3.1 shows the locations of the latter, which were sited by Gary Huckleberry in an effort to expose low-energy deposits. To ensure the safety of the testing team, we excavated large exposures at Loader Trenches 96-1

A

B

FIGURE 3.24. Reopening Strat Trench 3 in 1996: (A) Stephanie Livingston digging while Tom Jones and Don Grayson direct; (B) Don Grayson and Tom Jones hard at work (photographs by Mike Cannon).

FIGURE 3.25. Gary Huckleberry (far right) describing the stratigraphy of Loader Trench 96-1 while Mike Cannon records. Others, from left to right: Gene Hattori (Nevada State Museum), Arianne Pinson (University of New Mexico), Carolyn Sherve (Bureau of Land Management [BLM], Ely Field Office), Pat Barker (BLM, Nevada State Office; photograph by Tom Jones).

TABLE 3.4. Field Strata for Strat Trench 3-96 as Compared with the 1993 Field Strata and the Final Strata Devised by Huckleberry and Holmes

LAYER(S)	1996 FIELD STRATUM	1993 FIELD STRATUM	FINAL STRATUM
1–11	A	F/G	E
1–2	B	F/G	E
A–D 3	C	F/G	E
4 A and B 5			
1 A and B 2–3	D	F/G	E
1	E	not represented	F

(Figure 3.25) and 96-2 using both front-end loader and backhoe. These excavations were stepped after every 2 m of depth. Backhoe Trench 96-3 was excavated using only a backhoe. The stratigraphic profiles from these excavations match very closely the succession of strata revealed in 1993 and 1995. Unfortunately, we were unable to identify low-energy alluvium or stable surfaces in any of the test profiles. Samples of alluvial charcoal recovered from these tests, however, provided additional radiocarbon dates on the stratigraphic sequence.

After exposing the eastern end of the 1995 excavation trench at ST3, we hand-shoveled backfill to reestablish the stratigraphic profiles within the trench. Three 1-×-1-m units were targeted for excavation. These were located adjacent to the excavation unit where camelid bones had been recovered in 1995 (Figure 3.26). Our goal was to establish more conclusively how these bones were distributed through the alluvial beds and what, if any, relationship they had with artifacts in the same deposit. Vertical control was maintained using natural strata; the F/G alluvium was excavated in 31 separate strata (Figure 3.27, Table 3.4).

It became clear from stratigraphic testing between 1993 and 1996 that Sunshine Wash contains basically the same sequence of depositional units over 600 m of distance. We concluded the 1996 season by auger sampling wash-margin topography about 500 m down-channel (north) from our 1993–1995 tests. These tests proved inconclusive as we were not able to clearly resolve the edges of the paleochannel, nor were we able to determine if the terraces paralleling the wash were capped by alluvium or by lacustrine deposits that had been weathered and reworked by wind action. We also examined a dune ridge lying on the south side of the wash about 500 m up-channel of our 1996 tests. A deflated surface on the windward side (west) of the ridge contained a dense arti-

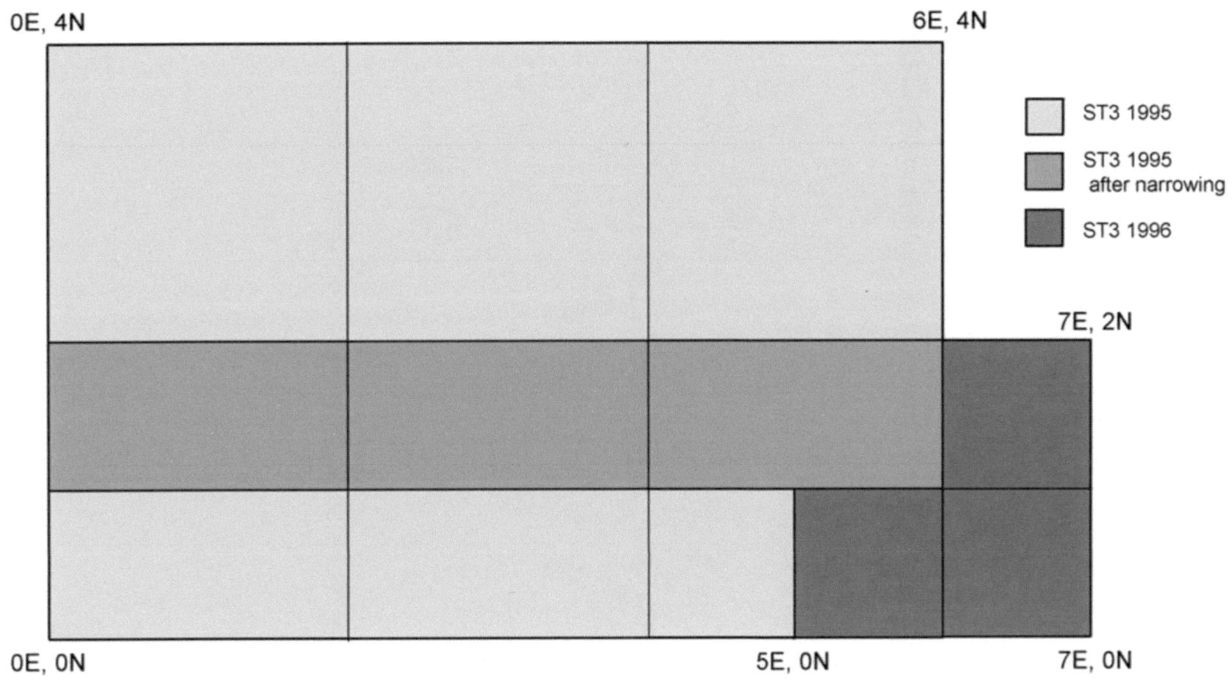

FIGURE 3.26. Schematic showing the original size of Strat Trench 3, the narrowed trench that was excavated to 3.5 m below the surface, and the three 1-x-1-m units excavated in 1996.

fact lag, but we were not able to determine if that surface continued beneath the dune or if the dune sealed undisturbed artifact-bearing deposits. Testing this deposit became a focus of our 1997 field studies (see Figure 3.1).

Results of Testing in 1995 and 1996

Strat Trench 3 Stratigraphy. The stratigraphic sequence at ST3 mirrors that in the 1993 excavation block. Minor differences arise from the positions of the test units in relation to the main axis of the paleochannel and the unique history of cut and fill at both locations.

Figure 3.18 illustrates the stratigraphy of the south wall of the 1995 trench. At this location, Stratum C (Strata A and B were not excavated) exhibits lighter sediment colors generally but includes several narrow layers of darker sediment. The latter appear to be ephemeral A horizons and contrast markedly in their development compared with Stratum C soils at LT1. Stratum C contained no artifacts.

Several layers of medium to fine alluvial sand underlie Stratum C, reaching a combined thickness of about 30 cm. Below these sands is a silty clay. The uppermost part of this unit exhibits a strong blocky structure and represents a fine-textured channel fill or marl. It is quite thick at the midpoint of the profile, where it rests in an obvious channel that intrudes coarser F/G alluvium. The silty clay rests on fine sand, which represents the basal unit of the channel fill. The sand and clay beds appear to represent a midchannel facies of Stratum D/E.

The F/G alluvium comprises complexly bedded sand and gravel lenses. This unit is generally thinner in ST3 than in the 1993 excavation block. It is most fully exposed at the eastern end of the 1995 trench, where cut-and-fill stratigraphy is quite evident. Bones of *Camelops* and a small artifact sample were recovered from this alluvium, primarily near its base.

Stratum F/G rests on gravelly silt, which, presumably, is a lacustrine deposit laid down by Lake Hubbs. The contact, which is quite irregular, is represented by a lag of coarse gravel and fine cobbles that are cemented by carbonates to a fine silty matrix.

The profile at the eastern end of the 1995 trench was expanded by additional excavation in 1996. Our work focused on the F/G alluvium in an effort to improve the stratigraphic record and to tighten our control of artifact and bone recovery. Additional bones of *Camelops* were recovered from this excavation (Figure 3.28). Figure 3.29 shows the stratigraphy exposed by the 1996 excavation.

This work more clearly revealed that the basal lacustrine unit consists of alternating beds of fine sand and blocky silt. Above the contact, the F/G alluvium reaches a thickness of about 1 m. Four major units (A–D) were identified within the alluvium, and each of these was in turn subdivided further on the basis of sediment texture

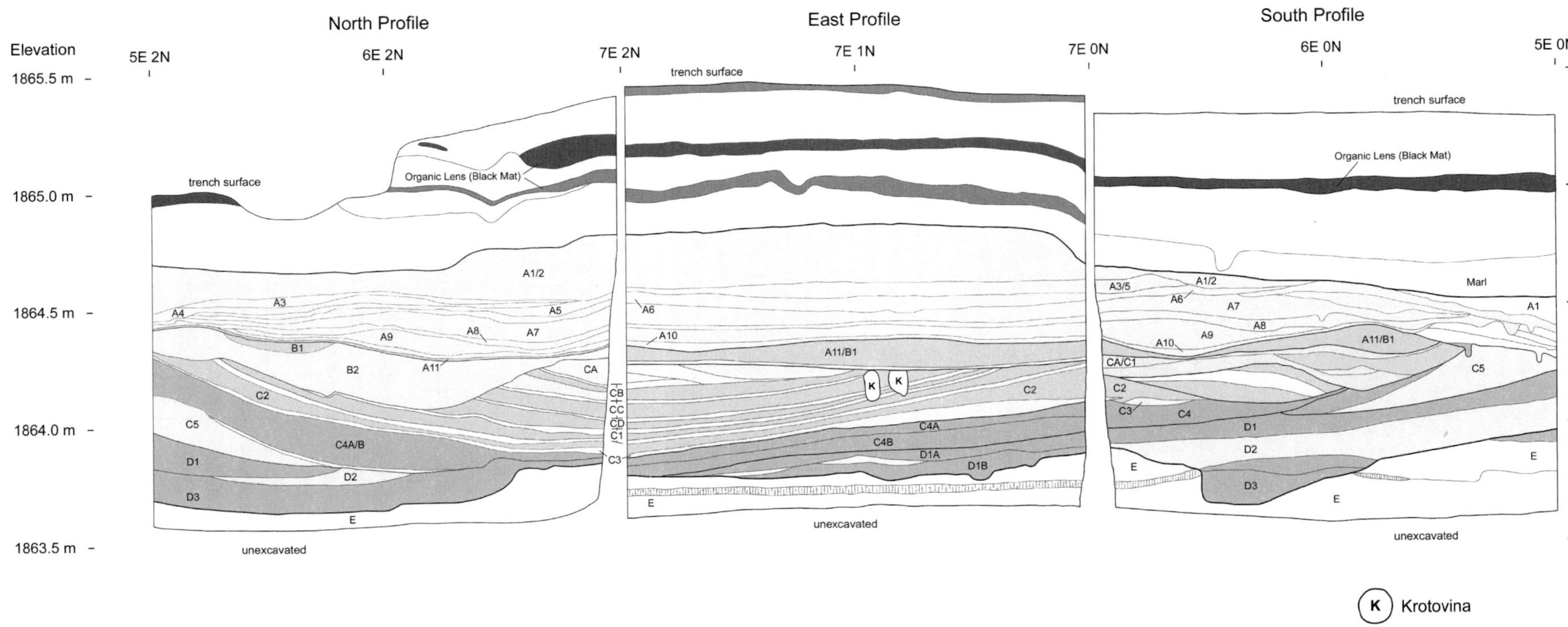

Figure 3.27. Stratigraphy of the south, east, and north walls of the 1996 Strat Trench 3 excavation unit. A rib of *Camelops hesternus,* exposed in the south wall, was recovered from D2 (see Figures 3.28–3.29).

A

B

FIGURE 3.28. Rib of *Camelops hesternus* in Strat Trench 3, 1996: (A) a partially exposed rib with head inside the south wall; (B) the completely exposed rib (photograph by Tom Jones).

A

B

FIGURE 3.29. Stratigraphy of Strat Trench 3, 1996: (A) south wall showing the hole where the *Camelops* rib was removed; (B) east wall: Unit D, incised into the basal lacustrine unit, is visible on the floor of the excavation (photographs by Tom Jones).

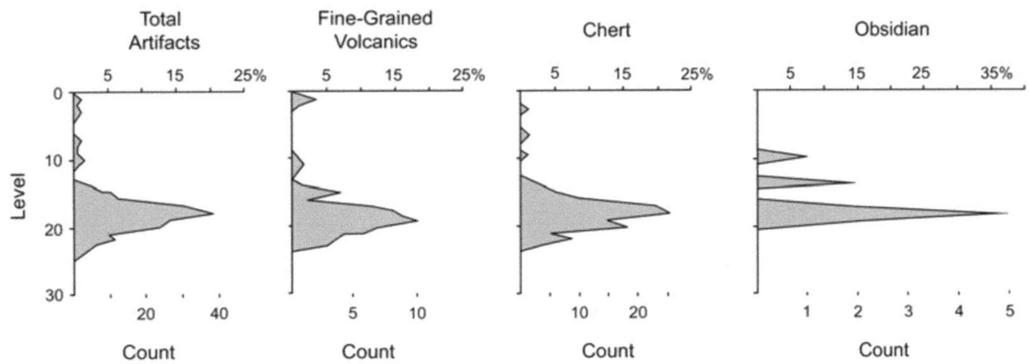

FIGURE 3.30. Vertical distribution of artifacts from the 1995 excavations of Strat Trench 3. Proportional representation by 10-cm levels is calculated on the basis of the total count of artifacts and the count within each major material category. Compare with Figure 3.10.

(Table 3.4). Thirty-one discrete layers were excavated and screened (Figures 3.27 and 3.29). Unit A, the uppermost set of beds, consists of 11 layers, which alternate between fine sand and coarse sand and gravel. The layers dip gently to the southeast, vary in thickness, and are difficult to trace across the entire profile. The contents of all of the layers except the upper two (A1 and A2) were screened. Bones and artifacts were recovered from layers with coarse texture, consistent with alluvial transport.

Unit B consists of two beds. The lowermost, B2, is a thick sandy layer, which is best exposed in the profile of the northern wall of the trench (Figure 3.27). B fills a shallow channel that was cut into the underlying unit, Unit C. As seen in the profile of the southern wall (Figure 3.27), Unit C contains five layers, but these can be further divided into additional discrete layers. It is evident from the profile that Unit C encompasses three cut-and-fill episodes. The profile of the eastern wall (Figure 3.27) shows that the upper section of Unit C comprises a series of alternating coarse and fine beds. These couplets have very uniform thickness and textural properties. These characteristics suggest deposition during floods and periods of slack water, perhaps related to storm events or seasonal stream discharge.

The lowest alluvial unit, D, rests in a channel incised into the basal lacustrine unit. Unit D was divided into three layers based on sediment texture (Figure 3.29). D3 rests unconformably on the pebbly, silty Unit E. The stream peeled away Unit E along bedding planes leaving an irregular, "plucked" surface. In places the stream left vertical and undercut faces.

Strat Trench 3 Artifact and Faunal Remains. Two hundred sixty-three flaked-stone artifacts were recovered in the F/G alluvium (N = 120 in 1995; N = 143 in 1996) in ST3. Most of the assemblage was represented in excavation units at the eastern end of the trench, where coarse alluvium is common. The vertical distribution of artifacts within the alluvium parallels that of the 1993 excavation. That is, the number of artifacts increases with greater depth, following the increase in texture class of the alluvium. This is evident in the distribution of artifacts by excavation level recorded in both the 1995 and 1996 excavation units. Figure 3.30 shows sample size as a function of depth (level) in the 1995 ST3 excavation for all artifacts as well as for each of the primary raw material. The increase in artifact recovery moving downward in the alluvium is clearly evident in all four graphs.

Like the alluvial assemblage from the 1993 block excavation, the ST3 assemblage is dominated by interior flakes and shatter (Table 3.2), mainly made from chert and FGV toolstone. Artifact size increases with depth, reflecting transport energy.

The assemblage contains a small number of unifacially and bifacially flaked artifacts. Several of these artifacts were recovered in close proximity to one another and to camel bones in the 1995 excavation unit. These came from deep in grid 4E, 0N. In Level 21, at 5.8E, 1.95N, and 2.06 m below the surface of Stratum C, a large chert biface (FS 11) was found in situ (Figures 3.31 and 3.32A). Seven centimeters deeper, at 5.3E, 1.4N, a phalanx of *Camelops* (FS 5) was exposed (Figures 3.31 and 3.33C), and 3 cm below the phalanx, an unciform of *Camelops* was recovered (Figures 3.31 and 3.33D). Within a 50-×-50-cm area, between 5.5 m and 6 m east and 1 m and 1.5 m north, an additional four bones were found (FS numbers 4, 7, 8, and 9), all between 2.16 and 2.20 m below the top of Stratum C (Figures 3.31, 3.33A–B, E–F). Only the scapula could be identified as *Camelops.* All bones and the biface were pedestaled, and the surrounding sediments

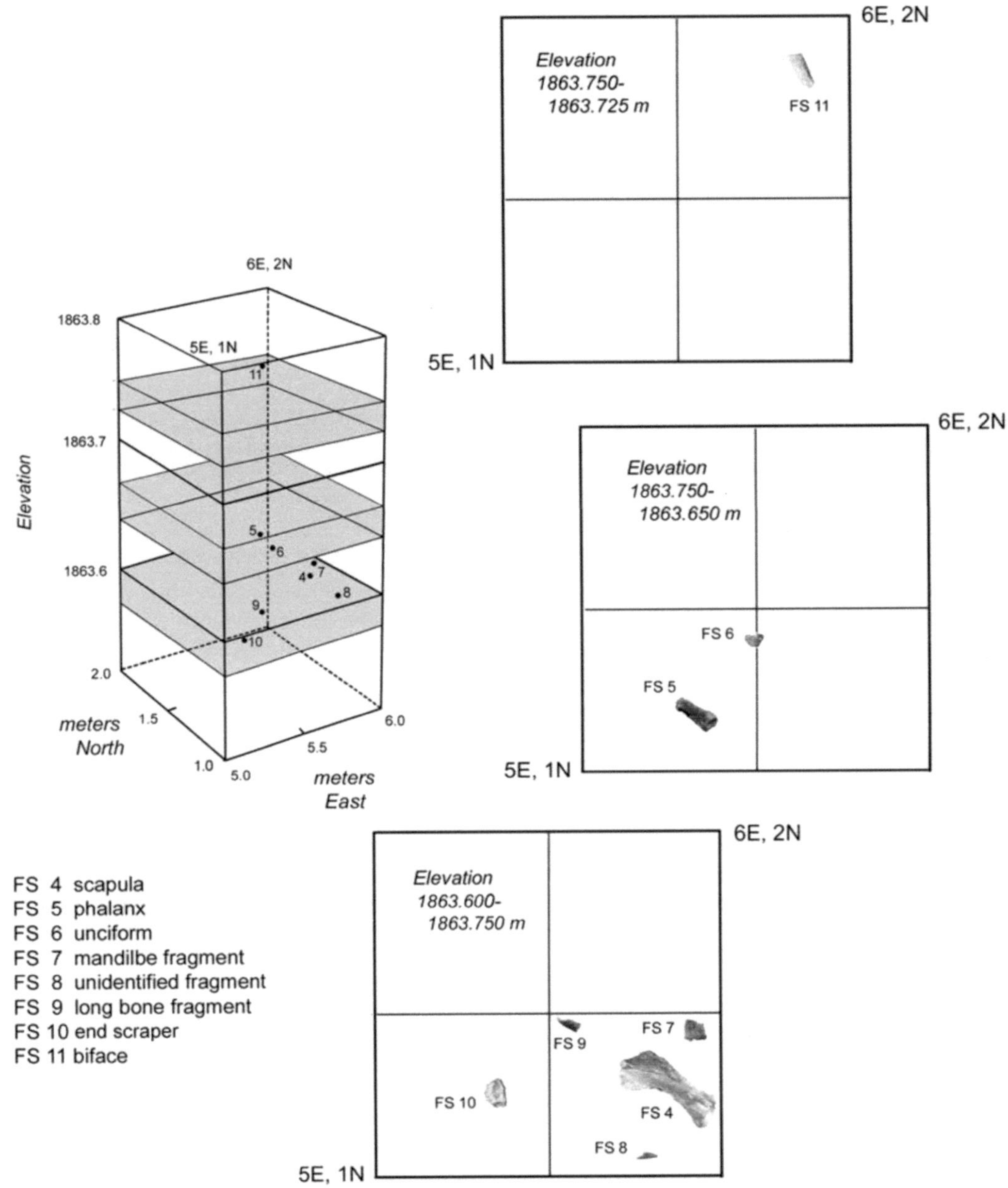

FIGURE 3.31. In situ locations of the bones and artifacts found in the northeastern quarter of unit 4E, 0N, in Strat Trench 3, 1995. FSs 4–6 have been identified as *Camelops hesternus*; FS 7 is from a camel-sized animal; FSs 8–9 are unidentifiable taxa. Vertical dimension is exaggerated.

were excavated and screened; the screening yielded five flakes and several small bone fragments. FS 9 was located beneath the pedestal for FS 6. Finally, a large chert end scraper (FS 10; Figures 3.31 and 3.32B) was located 5 cm north of and 10 cm below the phalanx. A date of 11,330 ± 60 rcy BP was obtained on the phalanx (see chapter 4). An FGV biface (Figure 3.32C) was also found in the same level (21) and vicinity of the chert biface (FS 11) but was recovered in the screen. The other piece of this biface was found in Level 19.

Additional bones of *Camelops* and a tooth of *Equus* were found in the 1996 ST3 unit (Figures 3.28 and 3.34). Artifacts were found in the same unit as well, but none was in apparent association with the bones.

The F/G alluvium in ST3 also produced bones of mammals and birds, although the majority (84.4 percent) are

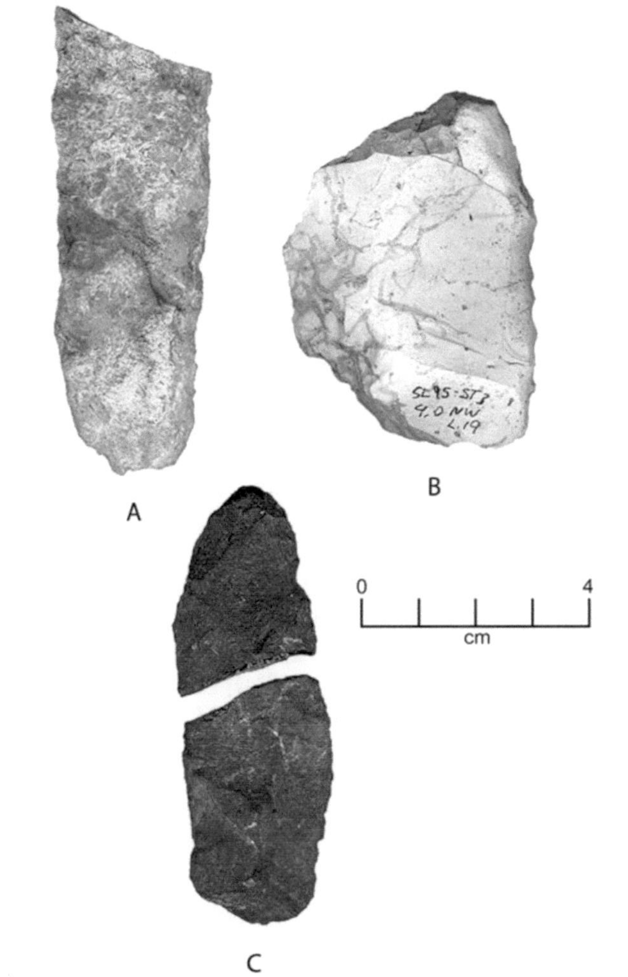

FIGURE 3.32. The artifacts found in close proximity to the camel bones in Strat Trench 3, 4E, 0N, Level 21: (A) FS 11, Stage 2 production biface (stemmed point preform); (B) FS 10, triangular end scraper; (C) broken biface found in screen, from two levels (19 and 21) in the northeast quadrant of 4E, 0N, near FS 11.

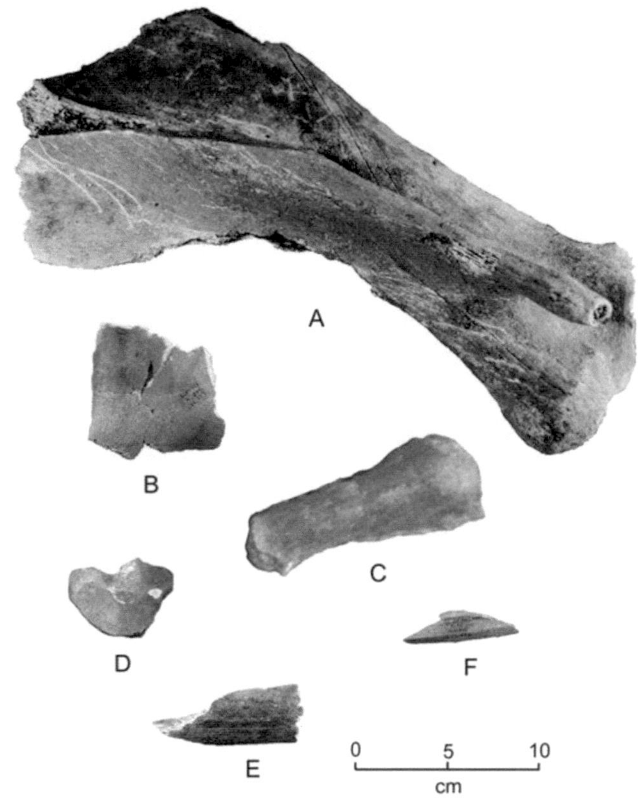

FIGURE 3.33. Bones found in the gravels of Strat Trench 3 in close proximity to artifacts. *Camelops hesternus*: (A) FS 4, scapula; (C) FS 5, phalanx; (D) FS 6, unciform. Camel sized: (B) FS 7, mandible; (E) FS 9, long bone shaft fragment; (F) FS 8, unidentifiable fragment.

unidentifiable (see chapter 7). In addition to the cluster of camel bones near the base of this deposit, nine specimens of waterfowl are represented, including swans, geese, and ducks. Our detailed stratigraphic tests in 1996 confirmed that bones occurred throughout the alluvium, in each of the substrata defined during that work.

Loader Trench 1 Stratigraphy. While the stratigraphy of LT1 reflects the general sequence previously outlined, it contains several distinctive facies expressions. The eastern end of the trench contained a 1-m-thick section of Stratum F/G, but excavations did not penetrate the contact at the base of this layer. The lowest part of the exposed unit comprises numerous interleaved beds of well-sorted sand and poorly sorted sand and gravel (Figure 3.20). These are capped by a thick zone of alluvial fine sand that reaches about .5 m in thickness. In addition to detrital charcoal, this unit contains poorly preserved fish bones. We were not able to determine if these remains represented contemporaneous fish populations or had been redeposited. The beds of Stratum F/G dip westward, indicating that they fill a channel that appears to have rested against the terrace.

Stratum F/G grades upward to finer alluvium that was influenced by pedogenic processes associated with Stratum C. As a result, while bedding is evident in the boundary zone, it is difficult to identify with certainty a clear boundary between the two strata (Figure 3.35). We have placed the boundary at a point where oxidized colors give way to reduced olive gray coloration.

The cienega paleosol at LT1 approaches 1 m in thickness, is complexly layered, and exhibits much darker colors than in other stratigraphic exposures (Figure 3.35). Unfortunately, dating control does not indicate if the stratum had a longer period of development at LT1

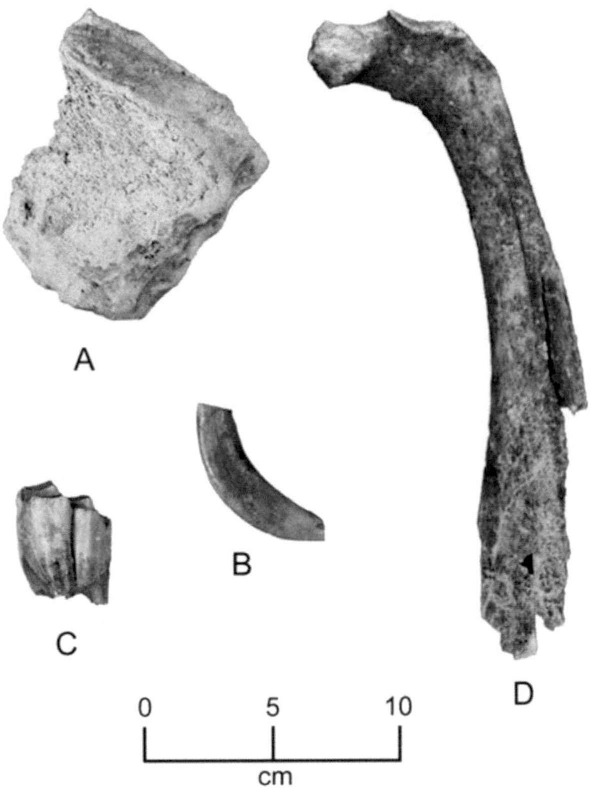

FIGURE 3.34. Elements of extinct fauna in Strat Trench 3, 1996. *Camelops hesternus*: (A) radio-ulna; (C) molar; (D) rib. *Equus* sp.: (B) incisor.

than at other locations in Sunshine Wash. At best, we can speculate that the thickness of Stratum C was partly controlled by sediment flux from the adjacent terrace and perhaps by an absence of erosion. Sediment colors at LT1 lead us to suggest as well that a seep emerging at the terrace edge supported dense vegetation at this location. At the western end of the LT1 trench, individual lenses within Stratum C exhibit very wavy, disturbed boundaries or are discontinuous. These features probably are attributable to bioturbation. Localized, generally ovate pockets of looser sediments are probably krotovinas, but these were more difficult to identify in the field because color differences were less distinct.

Loader Trench 1 Artifacts and Fauna. A significant artifact collection was made from LT1 (Table 3.2), primarily from the F/G alluvium. The identifiable faunal collection, however, was quite small (14 of 158 elements, 8.9 percent). Five pieces of debitage were recovered from Stratum A, and two conjoinable pieces of a biface (counted as a single artifact in chapter 5; Figure 3.22D) and a flake were found in Stratum C. The remaining 77 artifacts were recovered from the F/G alluvium. The upper silty sand component of the F/G alluvium was practically devoid of artifacts. At the base of this component, in Level 17, in a lens of medium sand, a long, curved chert blade was discovered in situ (Figure 3.22A). This artifact, which is discussed more fully in chapter 5, is very similar in morphology to Clovis blades (Collins 1999a, 1999b). The blade was resting horizontally with no apparent dip. It edges are very sharp, showing no retouch or damage of any kind. The surrounding sands appeared to be overbank sands with fine laminations resting horizontally. It is difficult to conceive of how this blade might have been transported to this location except by people. The sediments do not have the character of a sediment pulse, nor do they slope in a manner consistent with colluvial deposition. We believe the blade was most likely in primary context.

A basal section of a chert fluted point (Figure 3.22B) was recovered at a slightly greater depth. It was found while screening, and its precise provenience was not recovered, but it clearly came from the lower component of the F/G alluvium and probably from a gravel lens rather than a sand lens. Also recovered in the same level and unit was a combination graver/notch (Figure 3.22F), which was made from the same raw material as the fluted point. Finally, in preparing the wall for profile drawing, we discovered a section of a chert crescent (Figure 3.22C). This artifact also came from the lower component of the F/G alluvium.

Except in the case of the blade, the stratigraphic circumstances of the artifacts in the F/G alluvium at LT1 are consistent with fluvial transport. The conjoinable biface fragments (Figure 3.22D) from the Stratum C cienega, in contrast, were more likely to be in primary context. This stratigraphic unit probably developed under a thick wetland or marsh vegetation, which would have inhibited movement of artifacts once deposited. But as the assemblage is limited to just two fragments, there is little more that can be inferred about their use or circumstances of deposition. No use-wear was observed on the biface edges.

Only 14 identifiable faunal specimens were recovered from LT1, six from Stratum C and eight from Stratum F/G (see Table A.2). None of these elements, however, is from extinct Pleistocene mammals.

Surface Artifacts. The assemblage from the surface clearly differs from those collected from the excavations and from the surface in 1993, in that nearly 11 percent of these artifacts are retouched tools. This percentage increases slightly with the addition of the concave base point collected from this area in 1993. Examples from this assemblage are shown in Figure 3.36. This figure also shows two projectile points collected from the surface in 1996 (Figure 3.36S–T).

FIGURE 3.35. South wall of Loader Trench 1, 1995. Note the thickness of Stratum C (photograph by Phil LeTourneau).

Summary. The stratigraphic sections at ST3 and LT1 indicate that, just as today, these locations lie in different positions in relation to the stream channel. During the terminal Pleistocene/early Holocene transition, ST3 was located midchannel, while LT1 was at the channel edge. ST3 contains a complex cut-and-fill alluvial sequence, which is inset into lacustrine or nearshore deposits of Lake Hubbs. Bones and artifacts were recovered in the F/G alluvium, primarily from coarsely textured layers (granules and gravels). Their context is consistent with having been fluvially transported and entrained in channel fill, but their condition is not consistent with transport over a long distance. Although the close proximity of artifacts and bones is intriguing, there is no indication of cut marks on the bone suggesting a direct association between bones and artifacts related to cultural processes (Dorenbosch 2000). At LT1 the F/G alluvium contained artifacts but yielded no large mammal bone. Like their counterparts at ST3, coarsely textured rather than sandy layers at LT1 produced the majority of the artifacts.

One important outcome of the 1995 excavations concerns several of the artifacts recovered. A Clovis-like blade, probably in primary context, a fluted point, and a crescent fragment were all found in the lowest levels of LT1. These lay stratigraphically below the in situ stemmed point recovered in 1993 from the contact between Stratum B and the Stratum C cienega. This would suggest that fluted points predate stemmed points at this locality but are temporally associated with crescents. However, the chert biface found quite near the camel bones in ST3 is a stage 2 production biface, on its way to becoming a GBSS point, most likely of the Cougar Mountain type (see chapters 5–6). We cannot say that this biface is in primary context, but the fact that it was also found in the lowest levels of Stratum F/G is suggestive of *similar* age with the Sunshine fluted point recovered from LT1. We discuss this issue in more detail in the final chapter.

At ST3, finer alluvial sands directly overlie coarse alluvium, and silty clay deposits having the character of marl overlie these. The latter imply much lower stream energy and, perhaps, indicate that this segment of the channel contained deep standing, or at least very slow-moving, water prior to the development of Stratum C. These deposits, the local expression of Stratum D/E, contained no artifacts. Comparable deposits are poorly represented at LT1; their presence may be obscured by soil development associated with the cienega deposit at this location.

Stratum C is a complex organic horizon, which rests on the alluvial sequence. Unlike its expression in the 1993 block, Stratum C at ST3 contains several discrete dark lenses separated by lighter-colored loamy sediments. This midchannel location shows that the cienega soil developed in several episodes, although precisely how much time elapsed during and between these episodes is unclear. At LT1, this stratum attains a thickness of nearly 1 m and is complexly bedded. Dark brown soil A horizons

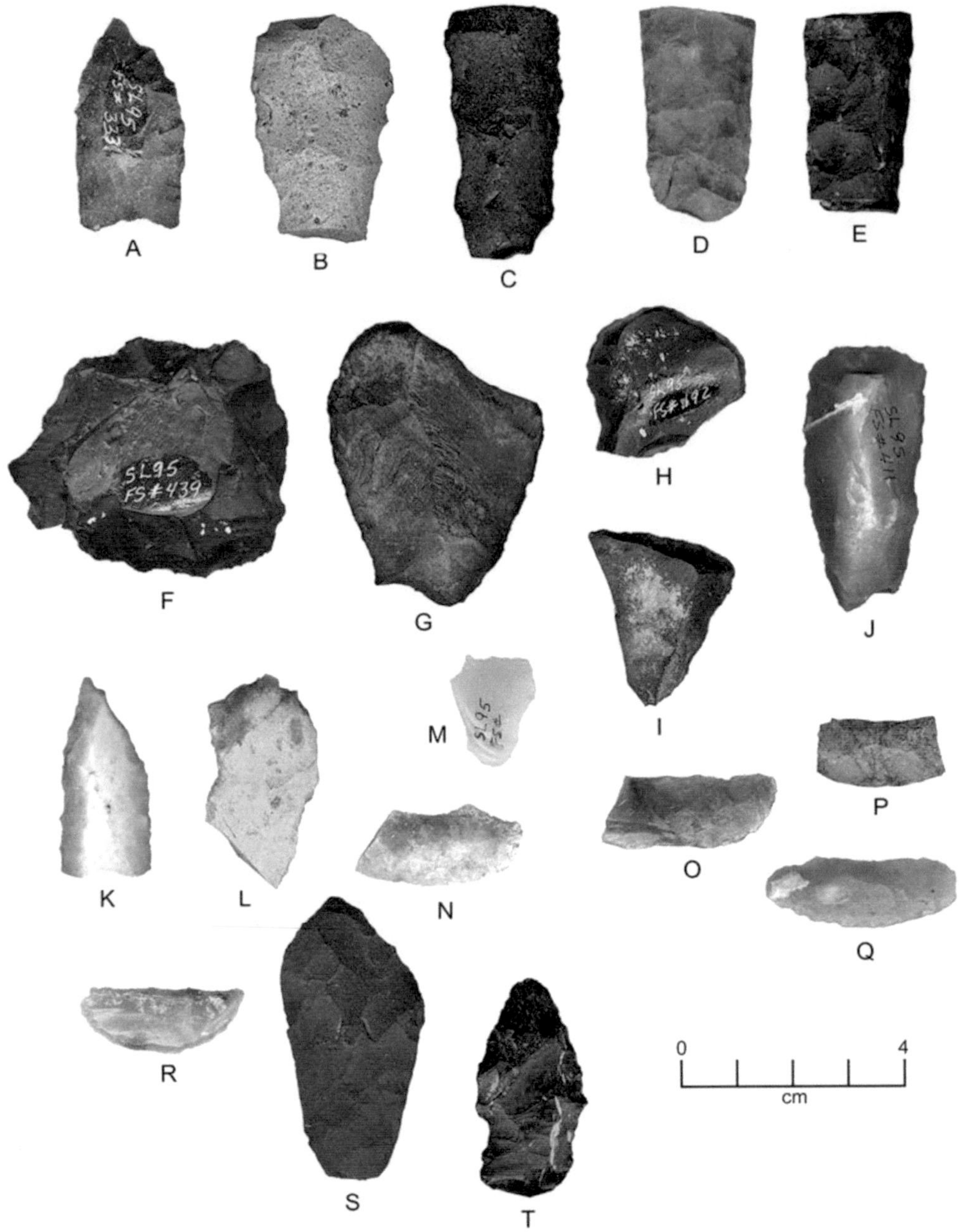

FIGURE 3.36. Retouched tools from the 1995 (A–R) and 1996 (S–T) surface collections: (A) Great Basin Concave Base point (FS 333); (B–E) Great Basin Stemmed Series points (FS 231, 350, 170, 175); (F–K) scrapers (FS 439, 165, 92, 257, 411, 214); (L–M) gravers (FS 218, no #); (N–R) crescents (FS 161, 228, 133, 153, 416); (S) Lake Mohave point (1996, FS1); (T) Windust point (1996, FS2).

separate very dark organic lenses, which, though not fibrous, have a peaty character. Faunal remains were recovered at LT1, but there is no indication that these are cultural in origin. A single blade section of an obsidian biface, broken in two pieces at the time of deposition, was the only artifact recovered in Stratum C at LT1.

Additional Stratigraphic Explorations

In addition to excavation at ST3 in 1996, we excavated several stratigraphic exposures in the Sunshine channel. This was accomplished using a backhoe and front-end loader. Figure 3.1 shows the locations of these exposures. Each location was selected in the hope that testing would expose

FIGURE 3.37. Gary Huckleberry (right) and Mike Cannon inspecting the stratigraphy in Loader Trench 96-1 (photograph by Tom Jones).

surfaces developed under low-energy depositional regimes, for example, overbank sedimentation on lateral or point bars or eolian deposition. Thus, we not only sought to assess the variety of depositional contexts developed at the site but hoped to locate archaeological deposits that were more or less in situ. Regarding this final goal, these tests were unsuccessful.

Loader Trench 96-1 Stratigraphy. LT 96-1 was sited about 600 m southeast of ST3 (Figure 3.1), along the southern edge of the Sunshine channel where the entrance of a small side channel creates an "embayment" in the main wash. A stratigraphic exposure was excavated just to the east of the mouth of the channel to determine if this was an ancient tributary channel and how it might articulate with sediments in the main channel. A front-end loader exposed an area measuring roughly 15 × 25 × 2 m. The center of the pit was excavated to a depth of about 3.5 m (Figure 3.25).

Gravels in a silt loam matrix (Stratum H) were exposed at the base of the trench (Figure 3.37). Holmes (1998) suggests that the oblate shape of the gravels in this deposit represent a nearshore environment. Following recession of Lake Hubbs from this position a stream incised Stratum H and deposited sand and gravel. From this point the stratigraphy follows the sequence discussed above. The profile provides a clear exposure of calcic soil development in Stratum B. Holmes (1998) estimates that this soil formed over several millennia and probably dates to the mid-Holocene. No artifacts were found in this exposure.

Loader Trench 96-2 Stratigraphy. This test excavation was sited in relation to a prominent hummock lying near the center of the modern channel (Figure 3.1). We believed the hummock was probably an erosional feature, which contained a core of lacustrine sediments, and we reasoned that it might have "protected" areas immediately down-channel from major downcutting events and have consequently protected primary archaeological deposits at this location. As we learned, however, the hummock is a dune that was deposited in the channel sometime during the middle or late Holocene.

The trench ran from the hummock in roughly a westerly direction for about 40 m, paralleling the modern channel (Figure 3.1). To create the exposure, a front-end loader excavated a 5-m-wide trough to a depth of about 2 m below the modern channel surface. This was followed by backhoe excavation in the center of the trough (Figure 3.38). A 1-m-wide trench was excavated to a depth of about 2.5 m. Combined, the testing reached a maximum depth of about 4.5 m below the surface of the modern channel surface. Even at this great depth, however, the trench did not penetrate the contact between channel alluvium (Stratum F/G) and underlying lacustrine deposits.

Figure 3.39 shows the stratigraphic sequence on the north wall of the trench. LT 96-2 contained the same

FIGURE 3.38. Mike Cannon examining the stratigraphy in Loader Trench 96-2 (photograph by Tom Jones).

stratigraphic sequence observed in other exposures in the paleochannel, with variation of a local nature. For example, Stratum C and the underlying clay marl are not nearly so thick or well developed as they are in other locations, and they are interrupted by small channels in several places.

This location contains a thick section of Stratum F/G alluvium. Although numerous small-scale cut-and-fill events are evident, the alluvium is divided into two principle units by a significant erosional surface. The lowest unit contains numerous sand and gravel layers but exhibits generally coarser texture than the upper unit. The lower unit also contains layers with strong oxidation colors and others with dark manganese staining. The upper alluvial unit, by contrast, exhibits much less oxidation and, in this regard, is similar to F/G exposures in other tests. The erosion event that cut through the lower alluvial unit at this location may well have stripped contemporaneous deposits from the main axis of the channel, and, as a consequence, we do not find them at locations like ST3. Two radiocarbon dates of 10,930 ± 60 and 10,640 ± 70 rcy BP on a cluster of charcoal pieces from a sandy layer in the lower alluvial unit indicate that the basal alluvial unit here is considerably older than F/G alluvium in other locations. Such an event may also explain why the date on camel bone at ST3 (11,390 ± 60 rcy BP) is earlier than dates for alluvial charcoal from this location but similar to the date for the older alluvium at LT 96-2.

Both the D/E alluvium/marl and the C cienega soils are evident at LT 96-2, but neither forms as deep a section as in other test locations. Stratum D/E rests unconformably on sandy F/G alluvium and varies from several centimeters to 30 cm in thickness. Stratum C is about 30 cm thick and has the same general appearance as it does at ST3. In some sections of the LT 96-2 profile, this unit resolves into two or three discrete dark bands, but these bands are discontinuous in other places. Erosion channels cut into Strata D/E and C at several places along the profile. They are covered by about 2 m of eolian and sheet-wash sandy silt. The profile was carefully inspected for artifacts, but none was found.

Backhoe Trench 96-3 Stratigraphy. BT 96-3 is a 23-m-long trench, excavated by backhoe along the western edge of the paleochannel, about 310 m up the channel from LT1 (Figure 3.1). It rests in a similar context to that of LT1, stretching from the paleochannel into the adjacent terrace. The trench exposes sediments to a depth of about 2.25 m, to a point just beneath the contact between channel alluvium (Stratum F/G) and overlying silty clay/marl (Stratum D/E). A short perpendicular trench was excavated on the north side of the main trench to establish the orientation of the strata at this location.

As shown in Figure 3.40, the profile of the north wall of the trench reveals a stratigraphic sequence consistent with other locations in the paleochannel. That is, the lowest unit is the Stratum F/G alluvium. It is succeeded by marl (Stratum D/E), which in turn is overlain by the Stratum C cienega. Stratum B does not occur at this location; the sequence is capped by 1.2–1.4 m of sandy sheetflood or colluvial deposit (Stratum A).

Stratum C at this location consists of alternating organic zones and calcic horizons. The uppermost of these organic zones is very faintly colored but resolves itself near the eastern end of the trench into a charcoal couplet. Presumably this couplet is correlative with the couplet at the base of Stratum B in the 1993 block. At the western end of the trench the organic zones begin to ascend the terrace. These zones—soil A horizons—are separated by wedges of sediment that originate from the terrace. Because this zone is strongly bioturbated, it is difficult to trace the beds.

Sediment samples from Stratum C were examined by Robert Thompson (U.S. Geological Survey, Denver) for

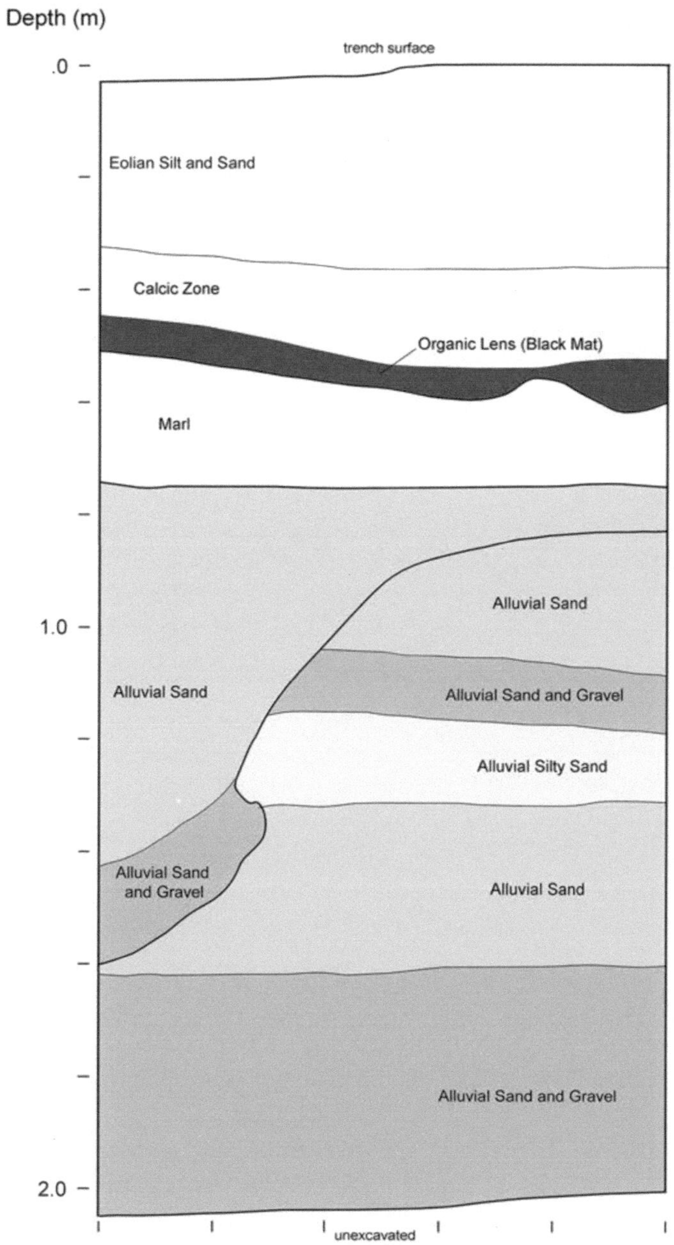

FIGURE 3.39. Profile of Loader Trench 96-2.

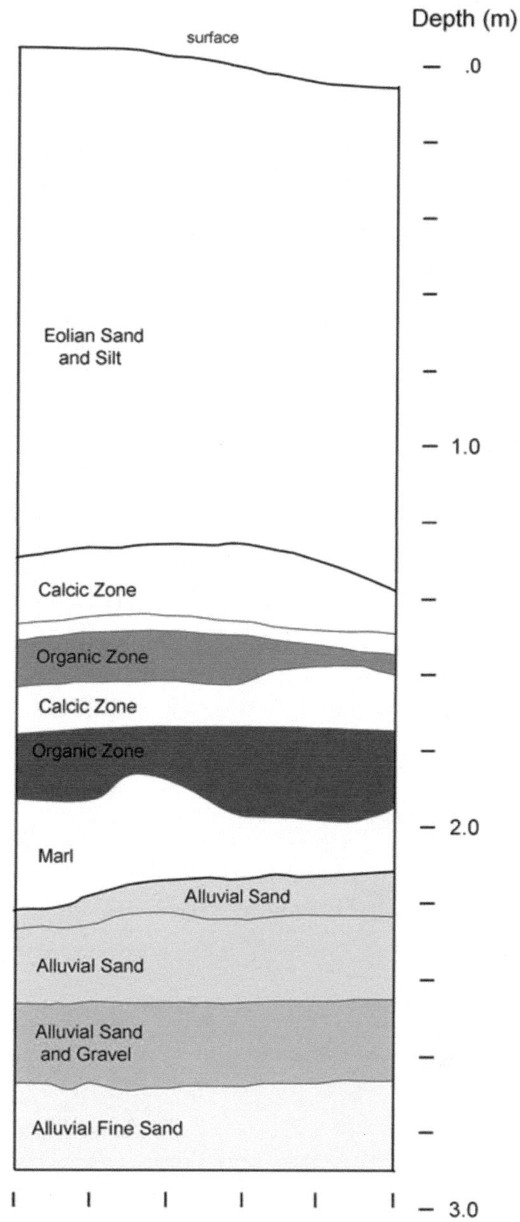

FIGURE 3.40. Profile of Backhoe Trench 96-3.

the presence of pollen, but none was detected (personal communication 1996). No artifacts or bones were recovered during excavation or field evaluation at BT 96-3.

The 1997 Field Season

Field studies during the 1997 season were once again accomplished with a field school: six undergraduate students and two graduate student teaching assistants, Amy Holmes (Washington State University) and Mike Cannon (University of Washington). This season's work combined further stratigraphic testing and two controlled excavations. The latter involved trenching the dune deposit mentioned above and a series of tests east of the dunes to evaluate the integrity of deposits beneath the sand sheet that caps the terraces on the south side of the wash. Figures 3.1 and 3.41 show the locations of the 1997 operations.

Operation 1

The first test excavation, referred to as Operation 1, was located at a dune ridge. Three 1-×-2-m test units were placed approximately perpendicular to the axis of the ridge

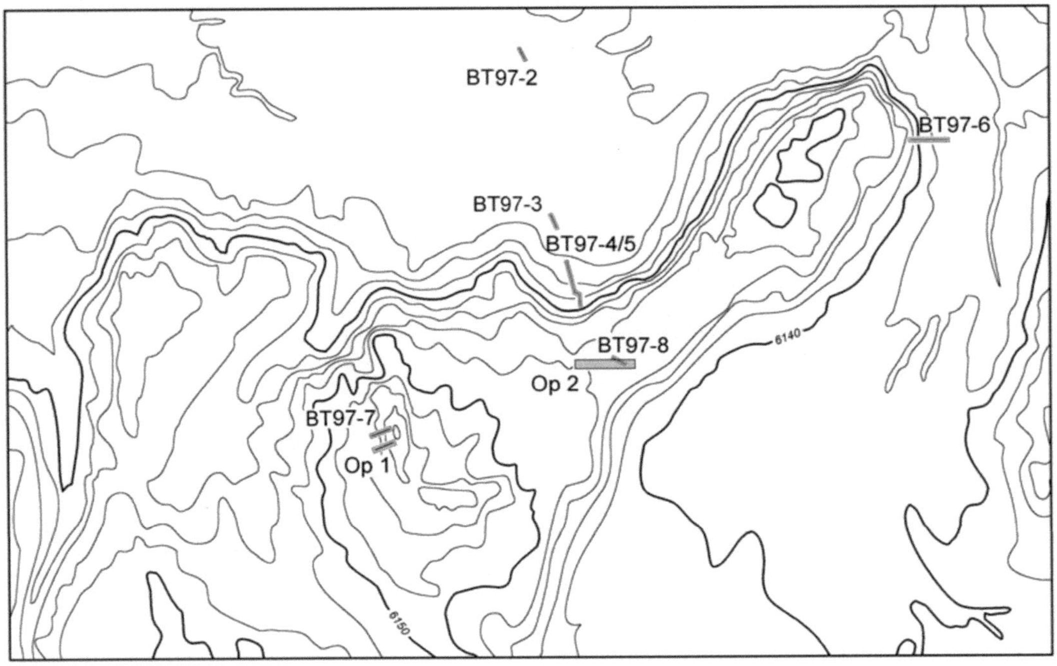

FIGURE 3.41. The 1997 excavation units. BT = Backhoe Trench; OP = Operation.

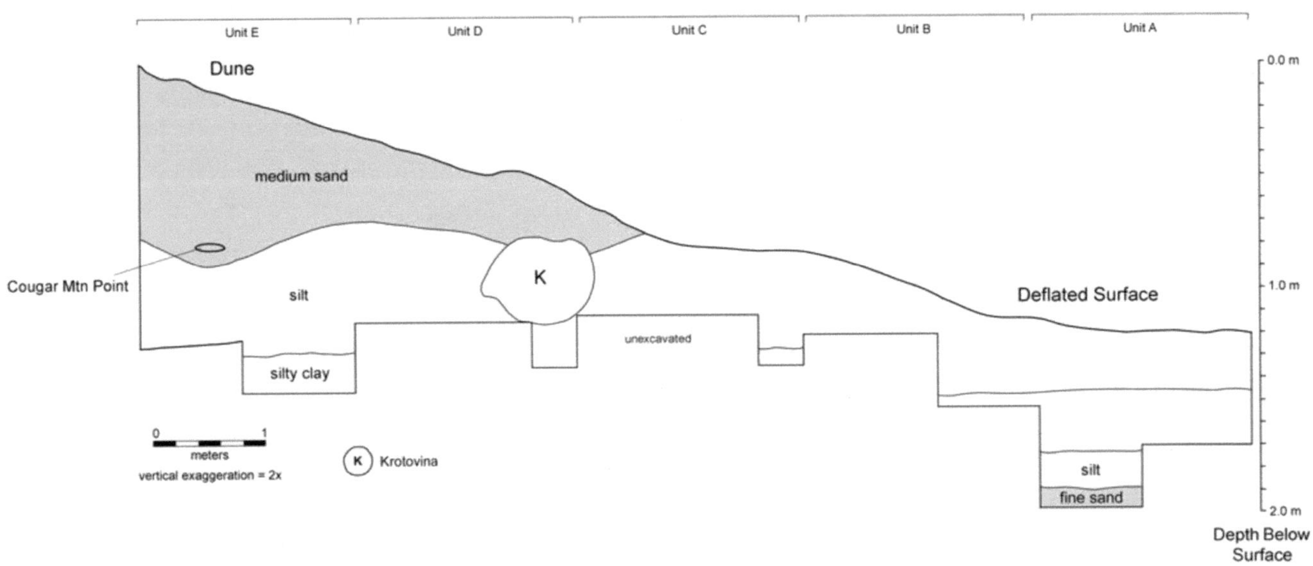

FIGURE 3.42. Stratigraphy of the south wall of the 1997 Operation 1 excavation unit.

(Figures 3.41–3.42). Intervening units were subsequently excavated to create a 10-m-long trench. The west–east trench ran from the deflated surface on the windward side of the dune to the crest of the dune ridge. Trowels and shovels were used to excavate 10-cm levels; sediments were passed through ⅛-in mesh screen, and all artifacts and faunal remains were collected.

Stratigraphy. The excavations at Operation 1 revealed two stratigraphic units (Figure 3.42, Table 3.5). The lowest levels contain alternating beds of silty and sandy alluvium. (This unit was subsequently identified as Stratum D_{df}—see chapter 4.) The deflated surface on the west side of the dune is eroded into this unit. As revealed in auger cores and a backhoe trench (BT 97-7 [Figure 3.41]) that

FIGURE 3.43. Artifacts from the 1997 excavations. Operation 1: (A) FS 8, Cougar Mountain midsection, Unit E. Operation 2: (B) graver, Unit A, 6.91E, 1.60N, Level 9; (C) side scraper, Unit A, 0E, 4N, Level 3; (D) triangular end scraper, Unit H, 0E, 4N, Level 3.

paralleled the Operation 1 trench, these fine alluvial beds pass downward into coarser sands and gravels, giving the entire sequence a general upward-fining character. Although a few artifacts were recovered from this unit, they cannot be attributed as in situ with certainty. Gastropod (*Psillium* sp.) shells are numerous throughout the beds.

A sandy eolian unit, which forms the dune ridge at Operation 1 as well as other dune hillocks in the vicinity, unconformably overlies the bedded alluvium. The base of this deposit is strongly bioturbated, making it difficult to provide stratigraphic attributions to artifacts lying at the contact between the alluvium and eolian sand.

Artifacts. A total of 189 artifacts, dominated by debitage and shatter, were recovered from Operation 1 (Table 3.2). The lower alluvial units appear to contain a cultural record, as artifacts were discovered well below the contact with overlying dune sand. Nevertheless, because of the high degree of bioturbation at the boundary between these units, we are hesitant to state confidently that these artifacts were in situ. The majority of artifacts were recovered in the eolian unit. These, too, may have been in secondary contexts, perhaps derived from an artifact lag developed on an older deflated surface, which subsequently were incorporated in the dune by rodent activity. The majority of artifacts are small interior flakes. One artifact of note, the midsection of a Cougar Mountain point (Figure 3.43A) was recovered near the base of the dune at the eastern end of the trench (Figure 3.42); its stratigraphic relations are complicated by bioturbation.

TABLE 3.5. Field Strata for Operations 1 and 2 in 1997 as Compared with the 1993 Field Strata and the Final Strata Devised by Huckleberry and Holmes

Excavation Unit	Test Unit	1997 Field Stratum	1993 Field Stratum	Final Stratum
Operation 1	A	1–2	D/E	D_{df}
	B	1	B/D/E	B–D_{df}
		2–4	D/E	D_{df}
	C	1	B	B
		2	B/D/E	B–D_{df}
		3–5	D/E	D_{df}
	D	1–4	B	B
		5	B/D/E	B–D_{df}
		6–7	D/E	D_{df}
	E	1–4	B	B
		5	D/E	D_{df}
		6–7	B	B
		8	B/D/E	B–D_{df}
		9–11	D/E	D_{df}
Operation 2		A	B	B
		A/B	B	B
		B	B	B
		B/C	B/D/E	B–D_{df}
		C	D/E	D_{df}

FIGURE 3.44. Excavation of Operation 2 at the beginning of the 1997 field season (photograph by Tom Jones).

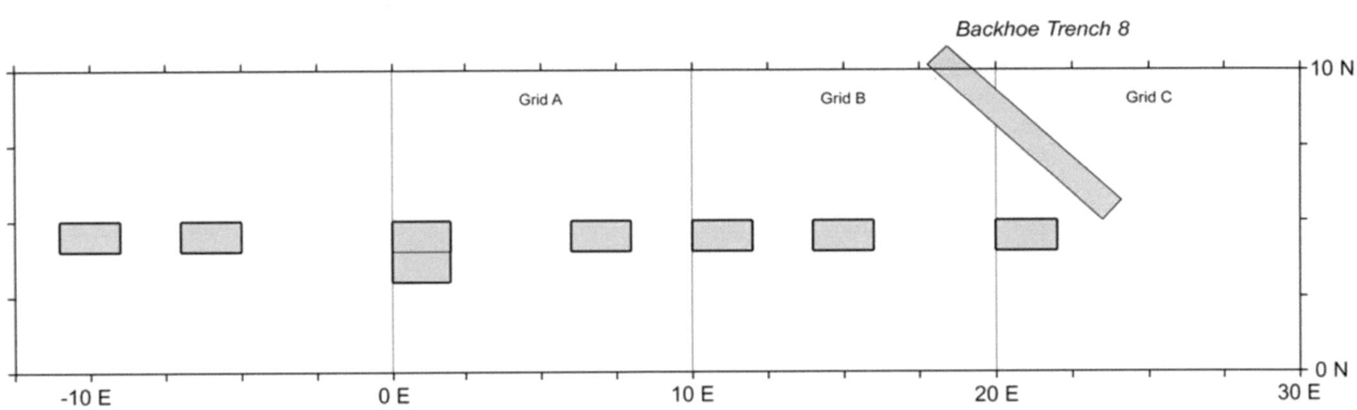

FIGURE 3.45. Schematic of the Operation 2 test units, 1997.

Operation 2

The southwestern corner of Operation 2 was established about 225 m east-northeast of Operation 1 and adjacent to Backhoe Trench 97-8 (Figures 3.41 and 3.44). Our work in Operation 2 consisted of surface collection and test excavation. This area contained a surface artifact scatter resting on a thin sheet of loose eolian sand. The artifacts consist mainly of dacite and chert flakes, but there are also a core and two unifaces. Excavations were conducted to determine if artifacts lay below the surface and their relation to the stratigraphic sequence at this location. Shovel testing was combined with mechanical trenching to reveal stratigraphic relationships.

Work began at Operation 2 by collecting surface artifacts from a 10-×-30-m area. The collection area was broken into three 10-×-10-m grids (Figure 3.45: 0E, 30N; see also Figure 3.46), which incorporated most of BT 97-8, and the provenience of each artifact was tied to these grids. All artifacts within this area were collected. An east–west baseline bisecting the collection was established, and six test units measuring 1 × 2 m were placed along the baseline (Figure 3.44). Stratum B extended much deeper

FIGURE 3.46. Amy Holmes directing stratigraphy mapping at Operation 2 (photograph by Tom Jones).

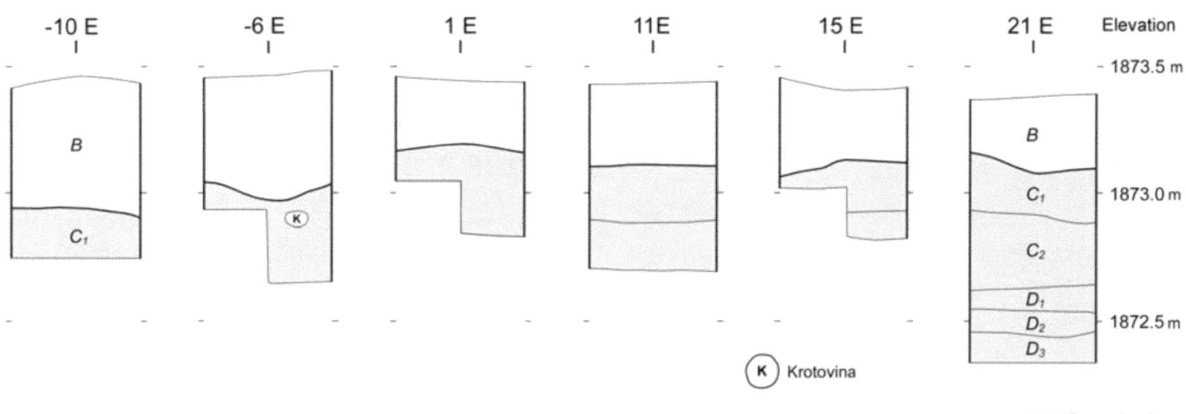

FIGURE 3.47. Stratigraphy of the 1997 Operation 2 test units.

in the western unit, and the artifacts were larger than in the upper levels. In the hope of finding an in situ deposit at the base of Stratum B, we extended Operation 2 westward another 10 m, and two additional units were excavated (Figure 3.45), but no in situ deposit was found.

Stratigraphy. Four primary stratigraphic units were identified at Operation 2 (Figure 3.47). For purposes of field description these were sequentially lettered A–D (Table 3.1). Stratum A consists of a thin layer of unconsolidated sand at the surface. It is underlain by Stratum B, a layer of well-sorted coarse sand of eolian origin. Stratum B, a widely distributed sand sheet on the terraces bordering the southern edge of Sunshine Wash, reaches a thickness of ca. 30 to 50 cm at Operation 2. Stratum B is massive but at its base contains a moderately cemented zone. Holmes and Huckleberry (chapter 4) consider this calcic horizon as correlative with soil horizons in their Stratum B elsewhere at the Sunshine Locality.

Stratum C was subdivided into two components: an olive-colored fine sandy loam (Holmes 1998) containing many cicada burrows underlain by a coarser unit.

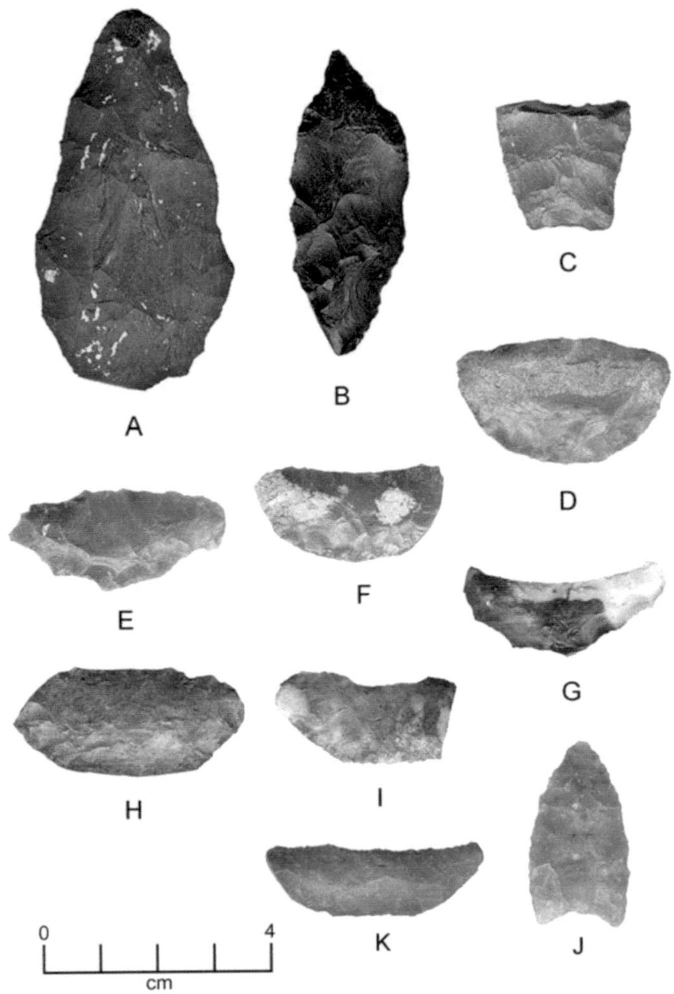

FIGURE 3.48. Artifacts collected during 2004 (A–I) and 2007 (J–K) visits to the Sunshine Locality: (A) FS 2; (B) FS 9; (C) FS 7; (D) FS 1; (E) FS 3; (F) FS 4; (G) FS 5; (H) FS 6; (I) FS 8; (J) 2007-1; (K) 2007-2.

Stratum C rests on alternating fine and coarse layers that we termed Stratum D. The layers making up Strata C and D are sheet-flood alluvium and, as in the case of similar deposits at Operation 1, represent the distal segment of an alluvial fan that interdigitates with alluvium in Sunshine Wash. Although only about 1 m of this alluvium was exposed by hand-excavations, trenching in BT 97-8 showed that these beds persist to a depth of more than 3 m below the surface.

The undulating surface of Stratum C suggests that it was deflated before eolian sand was deposited. Artifact numbers rise near the boundary of C and B and suggest that an artifact lag was created on this surface. Subsequent bioturbation (by cicadas and rodents) is probably responsible, in part at least, for the distribution of artifacts through the upper levels of Stratum B. Similarly, artifacts within Stratum C may have been introduced from the lag by bioturbation; however, the age of Strata C and D, estimated to be about 10,000 rcy old, does not preclude an in situ cultural record in these deposits.

Artifacts and Fauna. Stone tools were recovered from the surface and by excavation at Operation 2; 102 artifacts were collected from the surface, and 509 were collected from the excavation units (Table 3.2). The surface assemblage is dominated by debitage and shatter but also contains a core and two unifaces, one of which is a multiple-spurred graver. This pattern is reflected in the subsurface assemblage as well; of the 509 artifacts collected, 503 are either debitage or shatter. The remaining six specimens are represented by a biface, three scrapers, a graver, and a core (Figure 3.43). One of the scrapers is a triangular, spurred end scraper (Figure 3.43D), believed by some (e.g., Frison 1991; Morrow 1997; Shott 1995) to be diagnostic of Paleoindian assemblages. None of these artifacts, however, was found in situ.

A number of faunal specimens were recovered from the 1997 excavations, but they have not yet been analyzed. As Cannon and colleagues state in chapter 7, however, field observations during the excavation process suggest a similar faunal profile to those of the previous years, with the exception of extinct mammals.

Additional Stratigraphic Explorations

As test excavations were conducted at Operations 1 and 2, evaluations of stratigraphy in a number of backhoe trenches in the vicinity were undertaken by Amy Holmes (1998). Trenches within Sunshine Wash exposed a stratigraphic sequence identical to that seen in other trenches excavated between 1993 and 1996. Investigation of the terraces where Operations 1 and 2 were situated revealed an alluvial fan facies corresponding to the wash alluvium (Stratum F/G).

Subsequent Visits

Since our final field season in 1997, we have made several visits to the Sunshine Locality. BLM archaeologists have encouraged us to record and collect diagnostic artifacts when there is a possibility that those artifacts might be removed by relic collectors. We have therefore collected an additional 11 artifacts, nine in 2004 and two in 2007 (Figure 3.48). These artifacts are discussed in chapter 5.

Summary

Test excavations at the Sunshine Locality between 1993 and 1997 were conducted to evaluate stratigraphic succession in the paleowash and to provide artifact and paleoenvironmental samples for study. Stratigraphic exposures were developed by mechanical and hand-excavation along a 1.6-km stretch of the upper section of

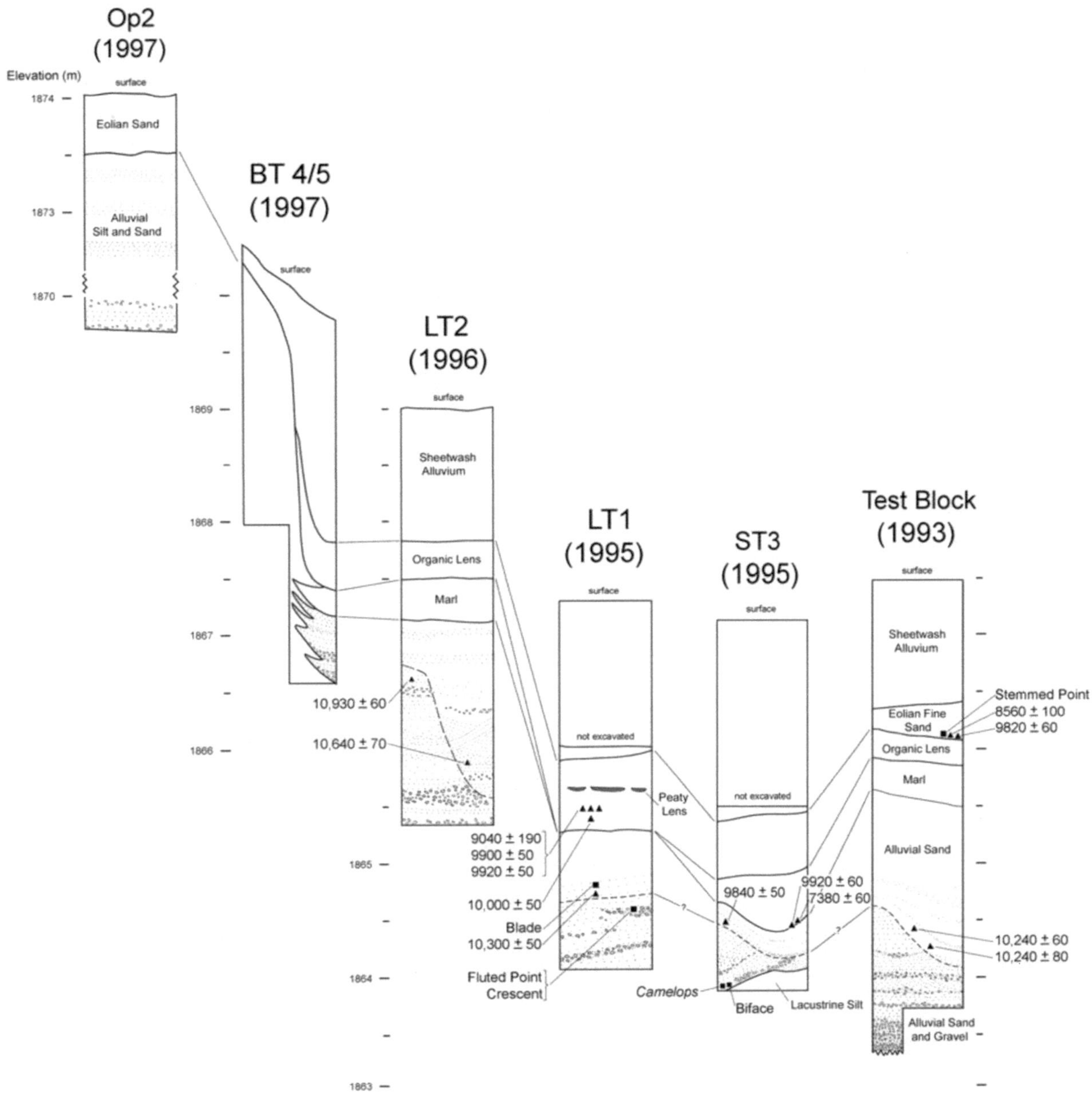

FIGURE 3.49. Composite profile of the Hamilton College excavation units. Stratigraphic locations of radiocarbon-dated material, the 1995 *Camelops* bone recovery location, and the locations of several artifacts are indicated.

Sunshine Wash. Figure 3.49 presents a composite of the hand-excavations and two of the mechanical excavations. Locations of radiocarbon dates, selected artifacts, and the 1995 camel bone recovery are also shown. Twenty radiocarbon dates have been obtained by Hamilton College; one, by the DRI; and two, by the NSM (see Table 4.4). These dates are discussed in chapter 4.

The exposures in Figure 3.49 reveal a consistent depositional sequence of an upward-fining alluvium, capped by eolian and sheet-wash sediments, which fill a channel(s) incised into late glacial lacustrine and deltaic sediments. Faunal remains, including extinct mammals, fish, and birds, and artifacts were introduced to the alluvium, presumably as a result of erosion of the channel edges. Artifacts and extinct fauna, including a number of elements of *Camelops hesternus,* were discovered in close spatial proximity to one another near the base of the coarse alluvial deposits. Their association appears to be fortuitous, and a cultural association between them, if any once existed, was lost in the redeposition of the artifacts and bones. The possible association is intriguing, nonetheless, as neither the bones nor the artifacts exhibit any evidence of water transport, suggesting that, if they traveled, it was not far.

Hand-excavations at several localities produced sizable artifact samples. The 1993 excavation produced the largest artifact sample by far. The majority of the nearly 7,000 artifacts were recovered in the uppermost 1.5 m in sheet-wash colluvium. The colluvium, along with the artifacts it contains, most likely was derived from the channel margins immediately west of the excavation area, an area that today contains a dense surface scatter of artifacts. The sources of artifacts contained at depth in terminal Pleistocene alluvium are less clear. No doubt as the braided stream migrated within the wash, it undercut the banks of the channel and eroded cultural surfaces as a result. Artifacts on these surfaces were introduced into the stream, although, as noted above, their conditions do not suggest they were transported very far.

A silty sandy organic zone—Stratum C—is a prominent stratigraphic marker everywhere in Sunshine Wash where we have tested. This "black mat" (see Huckleberry et al. 2001) appears to represent a time of restricted stream flow but high water table, which probably encouraged vegetation growth especially along the edges of the wash. This stratum contains an ephemeral artifact record but one that is clearly in situ.

Notes

1. This total differs from that reported by Jones et al. (1996; $n = 5{,}872$), which is often the case when analysis results (and computer files) are "revisited."
2. We actually located and collected the fluted point, the preform, two Great Basin Concave Base points, and one Windust point. Phil Hutchinson located and collected the remaining artifacts, although we recorded their locations by transit. He later gave these artifacts to us, but because he collected them, we include them in the Hutchinson collection in our analyses in chapters 5 and 6.
3. We did not have a field school in 1996, but several good friends volunteered to come out and help us. Donald Grayson, Gary Huckleberry, Stephanie Livingston, and Mike Cannon were invaluable in their determination and perseverance to find those camel bones, and we will be eternally grateful to them. We also had a lot of fun!

4

Stratigraphy and Paleoenvironment

Amy M. Holmes and Gary A. Huckleberry

The stratigraphy at the Sunshine Locality is complex in that it includes lacustrine, alluvial, and eolian deposits, some of which contain buried paleosols. It is also remarkably consistent across the 37 units excavated over a period of 10 years, first by the Nevada State Museum (NSM) and the Desert Research Institute (DRI; 1989–1990) and then by Hamilton College (1993–1997). The latter excavations are described in chapter 3, along with detailed descriptions of a number of stratigraphic profiles, and thus these descriptions will not be repeated here. Instead, this chapter presents an overview of the Sunshine stratigraphy, based on overall comparisons and mechanical and chemical analyses of sediments. This is followed by a discussion of the depositional history of Sunshine Wash and its implications for terminal Pleistocene/early Holocene paleoenvironmental interpretations in this region. Finally, a discussion of the radiocarbon dates is presented.

Analytic Protocol

During the 1996 and 1997 field seasons, 11 backhoe trenches were excavated at the southern end of the Sunshine Locality specifically for geoarchaeological study (see Figure 3.1 for locations of most of these trenches). Sediment samples were taken from each stratigraphic horizon represented in one wall of each trench.

The sediment and soil samples were subjected to mechanical and chemical tests in order to further characterize the strata. Mechanical analyses of sediment and soil samples determined texture and particle sizes expressed as frequency of grain sizes in a deposit (Table 4.1). The coarse fraction was dry-sieved through the following series of mesh sieves: -2φ, -1.51φ, $-.75\varphi$, 0φ, $.5\varphi$, 1φ, 2.5φ, 3.25φ. The fine fraction (e.g., $>1\varphi$) was pretreated to remove soluble salts, carbonates, and organic matter and analyzed using the hydrometer method (Bouyoucos 1962; Gee and Bauder 1986; Janitsky 1986). Chemical analyses performed included tests for soil organic carbon (Walkley and Black 1934), phosphorus (Olsen and Sommers 1982), pH, and calcium carbonate (Jackson 1975; Table 4.2).

Stratigraphy and Geochronology of Sunshine Wash

Seven stratigraphic units are recognized in the generalized profile (Figure 4.1, Table 4.3); these have been adapted from Jones et al. 1996.[1]

Unit F

Unit F is composed of lacustrine deposits from pluvial Lake Hubbs (Figure 4.1, Table 4.3); it is divided into Subunits F_1 and F_2. Subunit F_1 consists of indurated subrounded gravels in a silt loam matrix (Table 4.1). These sediments are dark greenish gray with olive and brownish yellow mottles caused by iron oxidation and reduction resulting from water table fluctuations. The oblate-shaped gravels in this stratum are indicative of beach processes and are similar to gravels found on higher beach ridges that flank the margins of Long Valley. These beach gravels also contrast with the overlying alluvial gravels that are spherical. Subunit F_2 is composed of clay, silt, and fine sand. Like Subunit F_1, these fine sediments also exhibit mottling. The Unit F lacustrine deposits were observed in the central Sunshine Wash area (see, e.g., Figure 3.29B). An upper limiting age for this unit is the 17,520 ± 570 rcy BP on high-stand shoreline mollusks (Young and McCoy 1984).

Unit E

This stratum consists of coarse fluvial sands and gravels inset into Unit F strata that reaches a maximum thickness of more than 3 m (Figure 4.1, Table 4.3). The trough cross-bedded sands are referred to as Unit E_1 (corresponding to Jones et al.'s [1996] Stratum F), and the subrounded gravels are referred to as Unit E_2 (corresponding to Jones et al.'s [1996] Stratum G). These high-energy stream deposits record conditions when Sunshine Wash supported a more competent braided channel. Sediments are mottled olive and orange and contain fluvially transported bones of *Camelops, Equus,* small mammals, fish, and birds, as well as artifacts. Overall the alluvium generally grades to finer textures with decreasing depth, suggesting that stream flow and transport energy diminished over time. Five

TABLE 4.1. Particle Size Data for 1996 and 1997 Samples

Trench	Sample Number	% Gravel	% Sand	% Silt	% Clay	U.S. Department of Agriculture Texture	Deposit or Stratigraphic Unit
Loader Trench (LT) 96-1							
Upper Tier	122	0	61	25	14	sandy clay loam	B
	123	0	34	53	13	silt loam	B
	124	0	46	36	18	loam	B (calcic soil)
	125	0	36	57	7	silt loam	B (calcic soil)
	126	0	59	38	3	sandy loam	C
	127	0	32	57	11	silt loam	D
Lower Tier	128	0	39	51	12	silt loam	C
	129	0	42	52	6	silt loam	C
	130	0	47	48	5	sandy loam	C
	131	0	52	43	5	sandy loam	D
	132	31	28	68	4	medium gravelly silt loam	F_1
LT 96-2							
Column A	135	0	61	26	13	sandy loam	B
	136	0	45	53	2	silt loam	C (marl)
	137	0	42	54	4	silt loam	D
	138	0	59	34	7	sandy loam	D
	139	0	73	19	8	loamy sand	D
	140	0	37	62	1	silt loam	F_2
Column B	141	0	42	55	3	silt loam	C
	142	0	72	25	3	loamy sand	D
	143	0	15	80	5	silt	F_2
	144	60				very gravelly sand	F_1
Column C	145	0	39	54	7	silt loam	C
	146	0	46	58	6	silt loam	C
	147	0	18	72	10	silt loam	D
	148	0	90	2	8	fine sand	D
Backhoe Trench (BT) 96-3							
Column A	156	0	60	34	6	sandy loam	B
	149	0	64	20	16	sandy loam	C (marl)
	150	0	55	29	16	sandy loam	C (marl)
	151	0	33	58	9	silt loam	C
	152	0	44	48	8	loam	C (marl)
	153	0	40	55	5	silt loam	C
	154	0	29	61	10	silt loam	C (marl)
	155	0	42	44	14	loam	D
Column C	157	0	69	23	8	sandy loam	C (marl)
	158	0	48	46	6	loam	C
	159	0	45	50	5	sandy loam	D
	160	0	32	60	8	silt loam	C
BT 97-4	181	0	23	63	14	silt loam	D_{df}
	182	10	83	2	5	gravelly loamy sand	E
	183	1	71	24	4	gravelly sandy loam	D_{df}
	184	0	27	63	10	silt loam	D_{df}
	185	0	13	80	7	silt loam	D_{df}
	186	0	10	72	18	silt loam	D_{df}
	187	2	68	24	6	gravelly sandy loam	D_{df}
	188	0	9	81	10	silt	D_{df}
	189	0	80	12	8	loamy sand	D_{df}
	190	0	57	39	4	sandy loam	D_{df}
BT 97-7	191	0	10	75	15	silt loam	D_{df}
	192	0	78	14	8	loamy sand	D_{df}
	193	0	9	76	15	silt loam	D_{df}
	194	0	81	4	15	sandy loam	B
	195	0	20	60	20	silt loam	D_{df}
	196	0	85	4	11	loamy sand	D_{df}
	197	2	92	1	5	gravelly sand	D

TABLE 4.2. Chemical Data for 1996 and 1997 Samples

Trench	Sample Number	% Organic Matter	% Organic Carbon	% Phosphorus	% Calcium Carbonate	pH	Deposit or Stratigraphic Unit
Loader Trench (LT) 96-1							
Upper Tier	122	.34	.2	.17	1.21	8	B
	123	.23	.17	.29	6.94	7.68	B
	124	.13	.07	.03	11.88	7.82	B (calcic soil)
	125	.38	.22	.12	11.48	8.18	B (calcic soil)
	126	.3	.17	.08	17.06	8.2	C
	127	.07	.04	.04	6.92	8.94	D
Lower Tier	128	.29	.17	.56	2.93	7.82	C
	129	.05	.03	.06	.17	8.14	C
	130	.37	.22	.21	3.36	7.89	C
	131	.07	.04	1.12	5.19	7.07	D
	132	.18	.1	.09	5.84	8.22	F_1
LT 96-2							
Column A	135	.61	.35	.17	13.41	8.07	B
	136	.86	.5	.04	31.31	7.92	C (marl)
	137	.17	.01	.39	5.59	8.22	D
	138	.17	.01	.16	3.46	8.33	D/E
	139	.29	.17	.05	5.95	8.28	D/E
	140	.18	.11	.1	6.12	8.07	F_2
Column B	141	.07	.04	.02	2.17	8.43	C
	142	.06	.03	.05	11.09	8.9	D
	143	.08	.05	.4	6.0	7.91	F_2
	144	.2	.15	.4	10.59	8.08	F_1
Column C	145	.45	.26	.42	2.09	8.54	C
	146	.18	.11	1.36	.27	8.57	C
	147	.12	.07	.15	8.05	8.65	D
	148	.17	.10	.15	10.28	8.77	D
Backhoe Trench (BT) 96-3							
Column A	156	.59	.34	.16	5.25	7.06	B
	149	.9	.52	.15	8.74	8.19	C (marl)
	150	.72	.42	.04	10.97	8.24	C (marl)
	151	.81	.47	.43	6.63	8.11	C
	152	1.40	.81	.13	8.76	8.21	C (marl)
	153	1.9	1.14	.17	5.97	8.3	C
	154	.26	.15	.01	.3	8.2	C (marl)
	155	.5	.61	.18	2.85	8.0	D
Column C	157	.28	.16	.05	2.51	7.35	C (marl)
	158	.28	.16	.01	3.19	7.58	C
	159	.39	.22	.25	.75	6.9	D
	160	.1	.06	.17	20.1	7.87	C
BT 97-4	181	1.37	.79	.45	13.07	7.87	D_{df}
	182	1.34	.78	.28	11.31	7.94	E
	183	1.38	.80	.15	5.54	8.16	D_{df}
	184	1.7	.98	.18	10.88	7.78	D_{df}
	185	1.41	.82	.18	11.80	7.18	D_{df}
	186	1.77	1.0	.12	8.46	8.14	D_{df}
	187	1.39	.79	.21	11.62	8.05	D_{df}
	188	1.43	.83	.27	8.78	8.78	D_{df}
	189	1.69	.98	.27	10.17	8.22	D_{df}
	190	1.33	.77	.22	9.12	8.24	D_{df}
BT 97-7	191	1.73	1.0	.26	18.99	7.77	D_{df}
	192	1.73	1.0	.41	18.33	7.88	D_{df}
	193	2.55	1.48	.24	25.73	7.93	D_{df}
	194	2.0	1.17	.38	19.64	7.77	B
	195	2.18	1.27	.33	24.93	7.97	D_{df}
	196	1.28	.74	.5	14.4	8.12	D_{df}
	197	1.25	1.25	.44	10.99	8.10	D

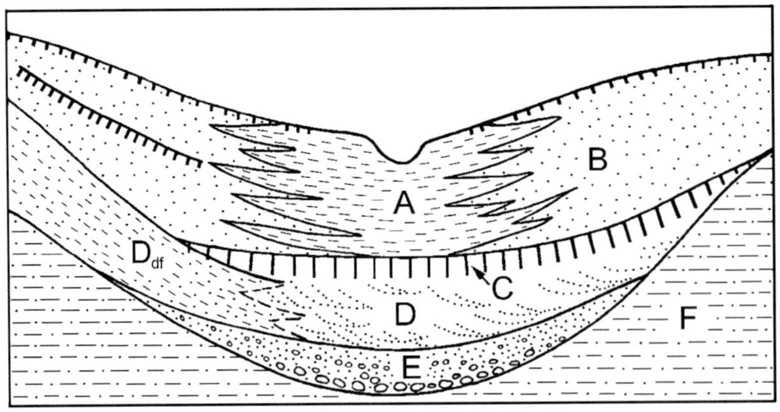

FIGURE 4.1. Generalized schematic of the stratigraphy at the Sunshine Locality (after Huckleberry et al. 2001:Figure 2).

radiocarbon dates have been obtained from this stratum, ranging from 9860 to 13,550 rcy BP (Table 4.4).

Units D and Ddf

Unit D overlies E and has two facies, the primary of which (D) is a channel facies marked by channel cut-and-fill stratigraphic boundaries and cross-bedded sands (Figure 4.1, Table 4.3). Jones et al. (1996) originally differentiated this unit into two (E overlain by D) based on greater cementation toward the top. Several channel cut-and-fill sequences were observed in these trough cross-bedded sands. The second facies (D_{df}) occurs in the southern part of the Sunshine Locality where distal alluvial fan deposits interfinger with the channel deposits of Sunshine Wash. The D_{df} deposits are characterized by fine sand and silty thin beds that extend laterally over several meters. Presumably, they were formed by predominant sheet flow on the distal ends of fans flanking the southern margin of Long Valley. Small freshwater shells (*Psillium* sp.) are abundant in the silt loam beds of this stratum. A lag concentration of artifacts resting on a silt bed was noted during 1997 test unit excavations, suggesting fluvial or eolian erosion of the deposits. Three radiocarbon dates were obtained for Stratum D, ranging between 9840 and 7380 rcy BP (Table 4.4).

Unit C

Unit C is a .5- to 1.0-m-thick, dark silty clay organic zone (Figure 4.1, Table 4.3). A whitish marl commonly occurs either above or below the organic zone and can be traced from the center of Sunshine Wash onto its margins, where it gradually pinches out. This unit contains numerous cylindrical (ca. 2-×-4-cm) burrow structures, suggesting extensive bioturbation by cicadas (*Magicicada* sp.). Unit C contains a pedogenic structure ranging from massive to subangular blocky, with its structure best expressed near the modern Sunshine Wash channel (Table 4.1). Except in the case of Loader Trench (LT) 95-1, where it reaches a meter in thickness (see discussion in chapter 3), the pedogenic structure diminishes toward the channel margin area where Unit C grades onto adjacent terraces (Figure 4.2). Here, Unit C is a faint, dark zone at the upper contact of pluvial lake deposits (Unit F_2). Excavations by the DRI and NSM in 1989 revealed the presence of decomposed peat in several of their backhoe trenches that is likely a facies of Unit C (Nials 1990); these deposits, however, were not observed in any of the excavations conducted in 1996 and 1997. Several flaked lithic artifacts were recovered from this stratum in the modern channel area (see chapter 3). Six radiocarbon dates were obtained for Unit C (Table 4.4), ranging from 8560 to 10,000 rcy BP.

Units A and B

The uppermost deposits at Sunshine consist of interfingering well-sorted eolian sands (Unit B) and silty to fine sandy alluvium (Unit A) and reflect drier conditions and ephemeral stream flow (Figure 4.1, Table 4.3).

TABLE 4.3. Summary of Sunshine Stratigraphy

STRATIGRAPHIC UNIT	RADIOCARBON YEARS BP	DEPOSITIONAL ENVIRONMENT	LITHOLOGY	COLOR	STRUCTURE OR BEDDING	MAXIMUM OBSERVABLE THICKNESS (cm)	LOCATION
F	17,520 ± 570	pluvial lake	indurated fine sand and silt and oblate beach gravels	light greenish gray (10GY 7/1 m), mottled olive (5Y 5/3 m), and brownish yellow (10YR 6/8 m)	massive to angular blocky, ripple cross-laminated sands	150	north and central Sunshine Wash
E	11,910–9800	braided stream	subrounded fluvial sands and gravels	pale brown (10YR 6/3 m), mottled olive (5Y 5/3 m), and brownish yellow (10YR 6/8 m) and strong brown (7.5YR 4/6 m)	trough cross-bedded sands and indurated gravel beds	50	north, center, south Sunshine Wash
D	10,000–9800	channel	subrounded medium to coarse fluvial sands	pale yellow (5Y 7/3 m), mottled light olive brown (2.5Y 5/6 m)	channel cut-and-fill cross-bedded sands	150	north, center, south Sunshine Wash
D_{df}	10,000–9800	distal alluvial fan; sheet flow	subrounded fine sand and coarse silty loam	very pale brown (10YR 8/2 m) sand; light yellowish brown (2.5Y 6/3 m)	interbedded, thin silt and sand beds	100	southern Sunshine Wash and channel–dune interface
C	9800–9000	organic zone	silty clay and marl	very dark grayish brown (10YR 3/2 m) and white (10YR 8/1 m)	moderate coarse angular blocky and subangular blocky	100	north, central, southern Sunshine Wash; pinches out on the southern channel margin
B	ca. 7500–4000	eolian sands	well-sorted, subrounded coarse sand	light yellowish brown (2.5Y 6/3 m)	weak fine subangular blocky parting to coarse granular; calcic soil: moderate medium subangular blocky, Stage II morphology, bioturbated	200	ubiquitous for Sunshine Wash
A	<4000	alluvial silts; sheet flow	silty clay and loam	very pale brown (10YR8/3 m)	moderate medium subangular blocky structure; modern soil has cambic B horizon	100	ubiquitous for Sunshine Wash

Source: Young and McCoy 1984.

Unit A is commonly found adjacent to the modern Sunshine Wash channel, whereas Unit B is located on the channel margin and extends onto higher terraces (Figure 4.2). Unit B was exposed by all of the 1997 trenches and is the most ubiquitous Holocene deposit at the Sunshine Locality. A calcic soil with Stage II carbonate morphology (Gile et al. 1966) was observed in Unit B during the 1995 and 1996 testing efforts. Based on regional soil chronosequences (Harden et al. 1991; Machette 1985), the calcic soil dates to the mid-Holocene or between approximately 4000 and 7500 rcy BP. This age range is supported by a single radiocarbon date of 8120 ± 70 rcy BP from the lower part of Unit B, providing a maximum age for the calcic soil that overlies it. Units A and B are highly bioturbated by small rodents, and lithic tools are associated with numerous krotovina.

TABLE 4.4. Radiocarbon Dates from the Sunshine Locality

Excavation Unit	Stratum	Lab Number	Radiocarbon Age (^{14}C Years BP)	δ^{13}C Corrected Age[a]	δ^{13}C[b]	Calibrated Years BC[c]	^{14}C Method	Sample Type	Matrix
LT 1-96	B	Beta-105660	8120 ± 70	8120 ± 70	−25.0	7288–7056	Conventional	OS	ES
1993 Ex	C	Beta-69781	8560 ± 100	not given	—	7674–7538	Conventional	OS	TOZ
LT 1-95	C	Beta-86200	9040 ± 190	9040 ± 190	−25.0	8452–7965	Conventional	OS	COZ
1993 Ex	C	Beta-69782	9820 ± 60	9800 ± 60	−26.0	9282–9230	AMS	CH	TOZ
LT 1-95	C	Beta-86202	9910 ± 50	9900 ± 50	−25.5	9386–9277	AMS	CH	COZ
LT 1-95	C	Beta-86203	9940 ± 60	9920 ± 50	−25.9	9597–9281	AMS	OS	COZ
LT 1-95	C	Beta-86204	10,060 ± 50	10,000 ± 50	−28.4	9948–9392	AMS	OS	COZ
ST 3-95	D	Beta-86199	7420 ± 60	7380 ± 60	−27.9	6383–6223	AMS	OS	SCF
ST 3-95	D	Beta-86201	9880 ± 50	7840 ± 50	−27.2	9346–9253	AMS	CH	SCF
ST 3-95	D	Beta-86198	9940 ± 60	9920 ± 60	−26.7	9586–9278	AMS	CH	SCF
ST 3-95	E	Beta-86206	9880 ± 50	9860 ± 50	−26.1	9346–9253	AMS	CH	GCF
LT 1-96	E	Beta-105659	9890 ± 60	9860 ± 60	−26.9	9384–9253	AMS	CH	GCF
1993 Ex	E	Beta-69779	10,240 ± 80	10,240 ± 80	−25.2	10,365–9753	AMS	CH	GCF
1993 Ex	E	Beta-69780	10,250 ± 60	10,240 ± 60	−25.7	10,363–9813	AMS	CH	GCF
ST 3-95	E	Beta-83090	10,340 ± 60	10,300 ± 60	−27.4	10,620–9999	AMS	CH	GCF
LT 1-95	E	Beta-86205	10,320 ± 50	10,300 ± 50	−26.6	10,398–9993	AMS	CH	GCF
DRI[d]	E	Beta-37515	10,700 ± 430	10,690 ± 430	−25.6	11,193–10,011	Conventional	CH	GCF
LT 2-96	E	Beta-105658	10,760 ± 70	10,640 ± 70	−33.0	10,998–10,701	AMS	CH	GCF
LT 2-96	E	Beta-105657	11,020 ± 60	10,930 ± 60	−30.6	11,192–10,955	AMS	CH	GCF
ST 3-95	E	Beta-105662	11,330 ± 60	11,390 ± 60	−21.6	11,487–11,207	AMS	BC	GCF
NSM[e]	E	UCR-3934	11,340 ± 50	not given	−16.0	11,376–11,230	AMS	TO	GCF
NSM[e]	E	UCR-3933	11,910 ± 50	not given	−16.5	12,121–11,945	AMS	TO	GCF
ST 3-96	E	Beta-105661	13,550 ± 70	13,450 ± 70	−31.5	14,564–14,090	AMS	CO	GCF

Note: BC = bone collagen from camel phalanx; CH = charred material; CO = calcic concretion; COZ = center of organic zone; DRI = Desert Research Institute; ES = eolian sands; Ex = excavation; GCF = gravelly channel fill; LT = Loader Trench; NMS = Nevada State Museum; OS = organic sediment; SCF = sandy channel fill; ST = Strat Trench; TO = camel tooth; TOZ = top of organic zone.

[a] All ages are $^{13}C/^{12}C$ corrected except for Beta-69781, UCR-3933, and UCR-3934, which were reported only in uncorrected ^{14}C years BP. All radiocarbon samples but the camel bones and teeth received standard acid (HCl)/alkali (NaOH)/acid pretreatment by Beta Analytic prior to analysis. Collagen extraction from the camel phalanx (Beta-105662) was done by first applying cold HCl acid repeatedly until the mineral fraction (bone apatite) was eliminated and second applying alkali (NaOH) to ensure the absence of secondary organic acids.

[b] $^{13}C/^{12}C$ values are estimated based on material type.

[c] Calendar ages were determined with the program CALIB 4.3 for Macintosh (Stuiver and Reimer 1993).

[d] Date was obtained by DRI on the charcoal collected from Backhoe Trench 10 in 1989 (see Figure 2.10).

[e] Dates were obtained on two Camelops teeth from the mandible extracted from Backhoe Trench 17 by the NSM-DRI crew in 1990 (see Figure 2.12).

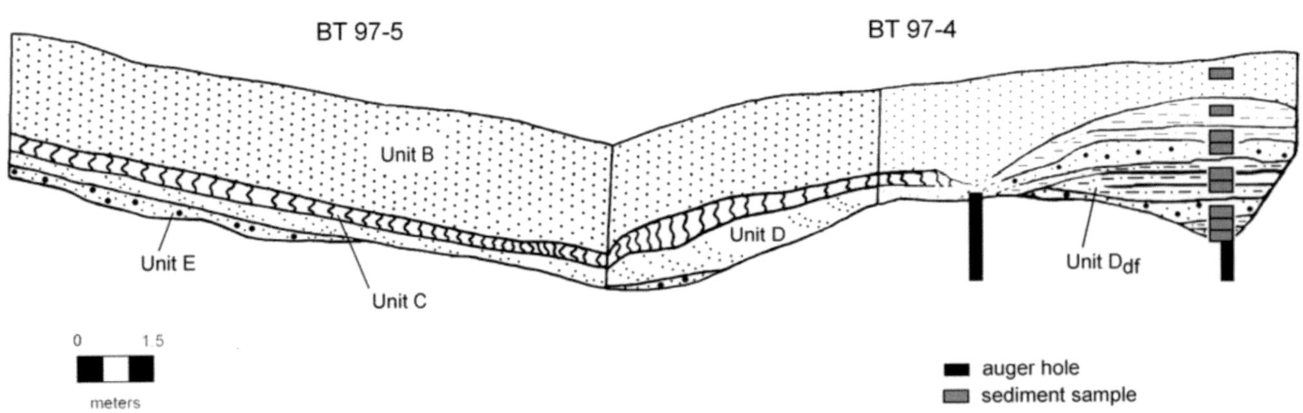

FIGURE 4.2. Profile of Backhoe Trenches 97-4 and 97-5.

Depositional History and Paleoenvironment

The Sunshine Locality contains a lacustral/alluvial/eolian stratigraphic record that reflects environmental changes since the late Pleistocene. Figure 4.3 is a schematic showing the major environmental changes in Long Valley from the late Pleistocene to the early Holocene (i.e., 18–9 thousand years ago [ka]). In general, pluvial Lake Hubbs was present in Long Valley at 18 ka. By 12 ka, the lake had desiccated, and the valley floor was open for plant and animal habitation. Sunshine Wash continued to incise the valley floor at this time. An increase in moisture and available sediment load by 10 ka created a braided Sunshine Wash channel. The braided stream environment transformed into a wetland marsh by 9 ka, with high water tables and a low-energy stream flow. After 9 ka, the marshland desiccated as the climate became drier. Sunshine Wash continues to be an ephemeral stream in southern Long Valley.

The oldest sediments at the Sunshine Locality are beach gravels, sands, silts, and clays from pluvial Lake Hubbs (Unit F, ca. 18,000–11,000 rcy BP; Figure 4.1). Transgressions and regressions of the lake periodically deposited and eroded beach sands and gravels along the lake margins, creating numerous beach ridges in eastern and southern Long Valley upslope from the Sunshine Locality. Climatic conditions during pluvial lake times were characterized by cooler-than-modern temperatures and greater effective moisture. These were the dominant climatic factors responsible for the formation of pluvial lakes throughout the Great Basin in the late Pleistocene (Benson et al. 1990). Although there is no age control on the final desiccation event, it is clear that the lake receded before 11,910 rcy BP, which is the oldest date for the overlying Sunshine Wash alluvium (Table 4.4).

After the recession of pluvial Lake Hubbs, Sunshine Wash incised the valley floor and began to aggrade with the deposition of Units E and D (Figure 4.1). Rain and snowmelt from surrounding uplands and spring discharge from groundwater recharge fed this paleochannel. Sediment textures and bedforms of Units E and D suggest Sunshine Wash was a braided stream at this time (Table 4.1). Thus, the climate was moist enough to support adequate discharge to maintain a perennial stream environment for upward of 2,000 years (i.e., from 11,910 to 9800 rcy BP). Adjacent to the main Sunshine Wash channel there were smaller ephemeral streams on the distal parts of alluvial fans that extended from the south to the main braided stream channel. Unit D_{df}, with its thin and horizontally extensive sandy beds, represents sheet flow on these distal fan areas. The sheet-flow sediments interfinger with the channel sediments along the channel margins. Small shells found within this stratum

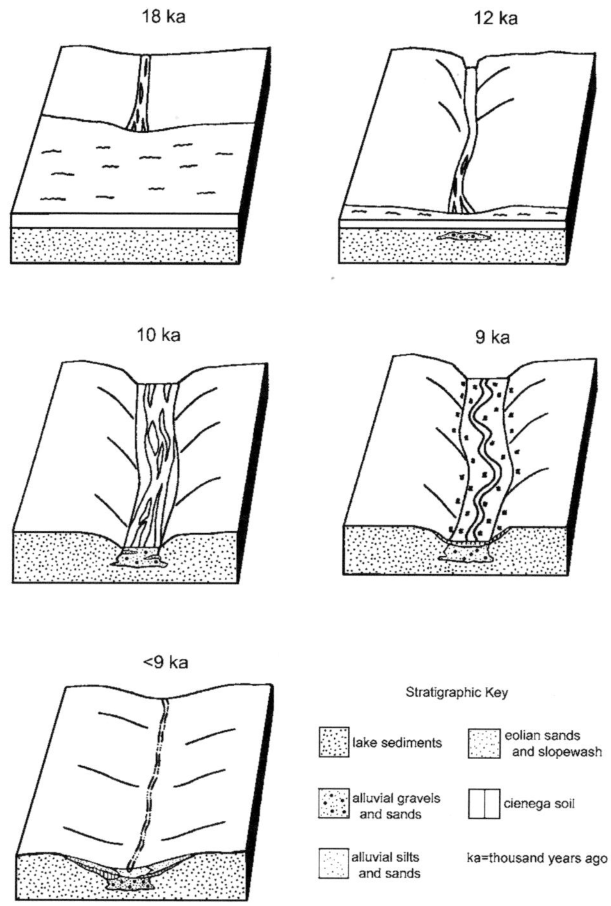

FIGURE 4.3. Late Quaternary geomorphic reconstruction of Sunshine Wash.

suggest that standing water was common in this environment, although it is possible that these shells were reworked from older pluvial lake sediments. The overall upward decrease in alluvial grain size in Units E and D (Holmes 1998) indicates that the stream competence of Sunshine Wash decreased through time (Table 4.1). It is likely that this textural trend reflects less effective moisture, assuming that there was no change in the size of sediments available for entrainment and transport. The drying trend in Long Valley is also seen in valleys in southern Nevada (Quade et al. 1998) and is the hallmark of the early Holocene in the Great Basin.

Despite reduced stream competence and gradual xerification, the presence of an organic zone (Unit C) suggests persistent shallow water tables in Long Valley between 9800 and 9000 rcy BP (Figure 4.1). Field observations in 1997 indicate that this dark organic zone was a wetland soil or cienega containing pedogenic structure and burrow features (Holmes 1998). However, stratigraphic investigations in 1989 revealed a peaty deposit associated with the organic zone, suggesting it is likely indicative of a wetland environment (Nials 1990). The presence of marl was commonly observed above and below the organic zone, suggesting that a shallow pond was present, perhaps in some of the topographically low areas. A preliminary analysis of microfossils from Unit C where it occurs along the channel margin (see Figure 4.2) indicates that algal spores dominate the sediment deposit, lending further support that this was a paludal environment (Holmes 1998). The organic zone at Sunshine is similar to deposits described by Quade (1986; Quade et al. 1998) in southern Nevada (Huckleberry et al. 2001). According to Quade et al. (1998), these organic zones vary in origin but all developed in microenvironments related to spring discharge (e.g., wet meadows and shallow ponds). In sum, the organic zone at the Sunshine Locality formed by paludal or pedogenic processes.

In the southern Great Basin, organic zones like Unit C, whether referred to as "black mats" (Haynes 1967; Quade 1986; Quade et al. 1998) or "cienega soils" (Huckleberry et al. 1997), range in age between 11,800 and 6300 rcy BP and 2300 rcy BP to the present (Quade et al. 1998). Many date to 11,000–10,000 rcy BP, possibly correlating with the Younger Dryas event. The organic zone at the Sunshine Locality is bracketed between 9800 and 9000 rcy BP and thus represents a mesic period that is later than the Younger Dryas. Because hydrologic systems respond differently to major climatic events, they can contain different response lag times to changes in moisture (Bull 1991: 10–13). Hence, it is conceivable that the organic zone at the Sunshine Locality formed in response to the Younger Dryas cooling event. Although Sunshine Wash did not support adequate discharge to maintain its braided channel at this time, the water table was elevated allowing periodic ponding and wetland soil formation.

After the formation of Unit C, sedimentary deposition was relatively continuous (Figure 4.1). Sand dune deposits (Unit B) directly overlying Unit C indicate the onset of eolian activity soon after the shallow pond/wet meadow environment desiccated at roughly 9000 rcy BP (Figure 4.3). Since then, Sunshine Wash has aggraded with fine-textured alluvium and coarse eolian sands. The fine texture of Unit A suggests the presence of an ephemeral stream and lends further support to increasing xeric conditions in Long Valley during the late Holocene. The Sunshine stratigraphy indicates that an active sand dune field dominated the landscape, but it was stable enough at times to permit the development of a calcic soil. It is uncertain what climatic significance, if any, can be attributed to this period of dune stability. Eolian action continued after the formation of the calcic paleosol until the modern soil containing a weak cambic horizon formed. Today, the modern surface of Long Valley supports many large shrubs and grasses, indicating a relatively stable landscape. Active dunes are limited to the northern margins of the modern Long Valley playa.

The Sunshine Radiocarbon Dates

A total of 23 radiocarbon dates have been obtained from deposits at the Sunshine Locality, 20 by Hamilton College, two by the Nevada State Museum, and one by the Desert Research Institute.[2] These are shown in Table 4.4, and their calibrated ranges are shown in Figure 4.4. The dates are discussed by stratum, beginning with Unit E.

Unit E

Thirteen dates are associated with Unit E. The first (Beta-37515), 10,690 ± 430 rcy BP, was obtained on charcoal from the alluvial gravels in Backhoe Trench 10, excavated by the NSM–DRI field crew in 1989 (see Figure 2.9 for the location of this trench). Eight other dates on detrital charcoal were obtained by Hamilton College between 1993 and 1996 (Table 4.4), which range between 10,930 ± 60 and 9860 ± 50 rcy BP. Figure 3.49 shows the locations of these dates in each of the units from which the charcoal was retrieved. As evident in this figure, the dates are in good chronological order from the base to the top of the unit.

Four additional dates are associated with Unit E, three of which are on the *Camelops* specimens found here. Two (11,910 ± 50 and 11,340 ± 50 rcy BP) were obtained on collagen extracted from teeth recovered by the NSM–DRI crew in 1990; the third (11,330 ± 60 rcy BP) was obtained from collagen extracted from a *Camelops* phalanx discovered at the end of the 1995 field season in Strat Trench (ST) 3. The fourth date (13,450 ± 70 rcy BP) was obtained on a calcitic concretion retrieved in 1996 from the lower gravels in ST3.

Although the majority of these dates come from detrital charcoal, the precise relationship between the burning events producing the charcoal and the depositional events is uncertain. We note, however, that the dates occur in the proper stratigraphic order. The dates on detrital charcoal from Unit E suggest that the stream alluvium was deposited over a period of ca. 1,200 radiocarbon years, encompassing all of the Younger Dryas; calibration of these dates expands the period to a maximum range of ca. 2,000 years (Figure 4.4). As can be seen from Figure 4.4, the bone and teeth dates fall well outside this range, making it all but certain that these faunal elements were redeposited.

Unit D

Three dates are associated with Unit D. Two of these dates, 9920 ± 60 rcy BP (from LT 95-1) and 9840 ± 50 rcy BP (from ST 3-95) are consistent with the other dates below and above them (see Figure 3.49). The date of 7380 ± 60 rcy BP,

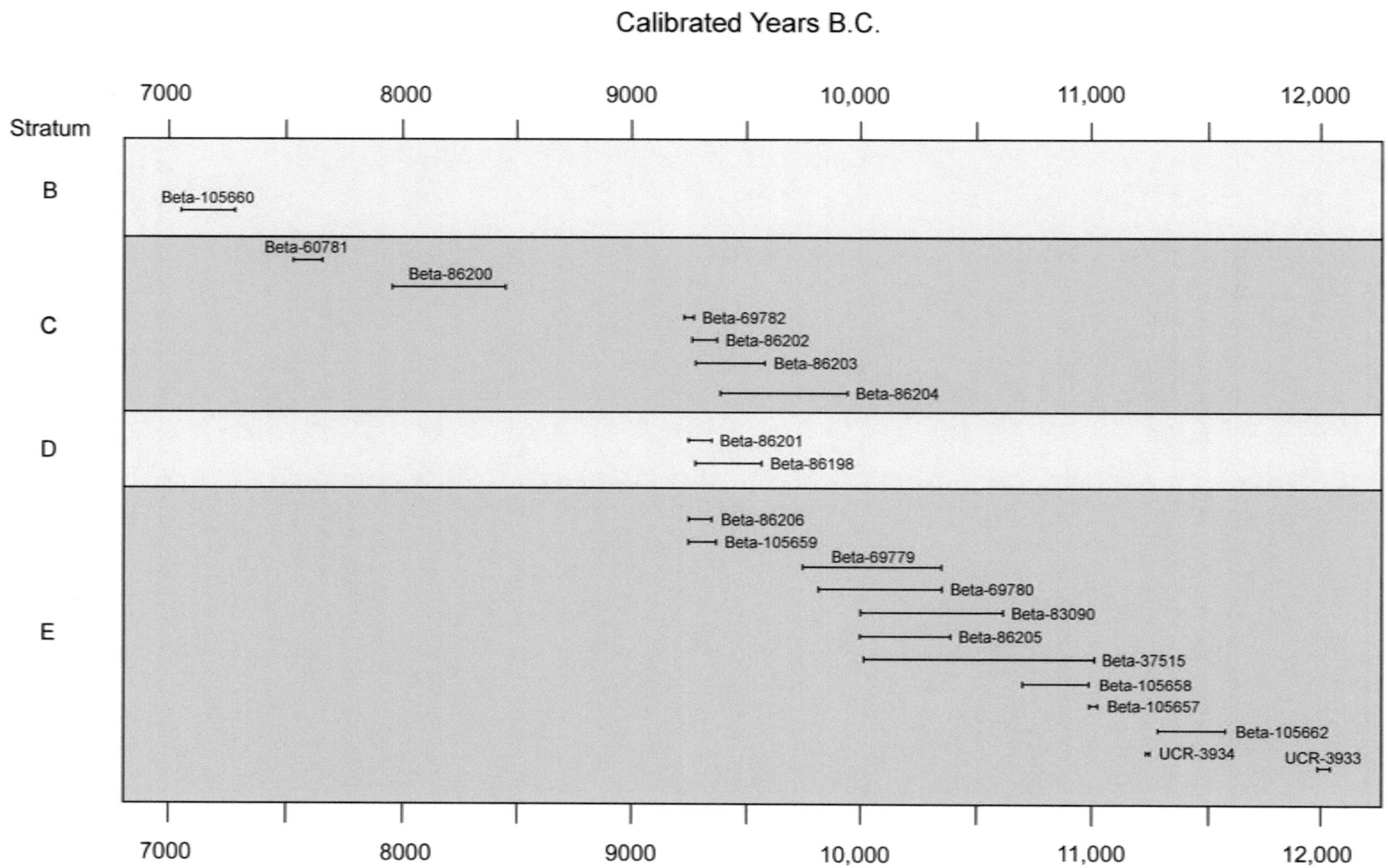

FIGURE 4.4. Calibrated radiocarbon dates by stratum from the Sunshine Locality. Range reflects standard deviation as reported by dating laboratories (see Table 4.4). (Two dates, Beta-86199, calibrated range of 6383 to 6223, and Beta-105661, calibrated range of 14,564 to 14,090, are not included.)

however, is not. This latter date is a conventional date obtained on organic sediment, whereas the other two are AMS dates on charcoal. Conventional dates obtained on organic sediment are more subject to contamination than those on charred material (Hedges and van Klinken 1992; Quade et al. 1998), and thus the latter are more reliable. We are inclined, then, to accept the first two dates as the most reliable of the three.

Unit C

The six radiocarbon dates associated with Unit C range from 10,000 ± 50 to 8560 ± 100 rcy BP. Two of these dates are conventional dates on organic sediments, two are AMS dates on organic sediments, and two are AMS dates on charcoal. The four AMS assays give consistent ages between ca. 9800 and 10,000 rcy BP, while the conventional dates (Beta-69781 and -86200) are substantially younger. As there is no stratigraphic indication of a break in the deposition of Unit C, we regard the latter dates as less certain.

Unit B

A single date of 8120 ± 70 rcy BP exists for Unit B, from LT 96-1. This conventional assay on organic sediments, which contained numerous fine charcoal particles, may be too young, as is the case for the two in Unit C and the one in Unit D discussed above.

Notes

1. The stratigraphic units used in Huckleberry et al. 2001 were adapted from those used by Jones et al. (1996). Based on chronological and lithologic similarity, Jones et al.'s Strata D and E (both sandy alluvium) were combined into Unit D and Strata F and G (both gravely sandy alluvium) were combined into Unit E here.
2. Unless otherwise indicated, all dates in the text are ^{13}C corrected years BP.

5

Artifact Analysis

Charlotte Beck and George T. Jones

Over the last 45 years many thousands of artifacts have been collected from the Sunshine Locality, from both surface and subsurface contexts. The first known collections were made by Tadlock in 1962. Tadlock collected 11 crescents (Table 5.1), supposedly from the surface of the Long Valley playa, but as noted in chapter 2, note 1, York believes that these artifacts more likely came from one of the "beaches" within the Sunshine Locality. Because their provenience is unclear, however, Tadlock's crescents are not included in our analyses.

Tadlock's work was followed in the early 1970s by that of Phil Hutchinson and Gary Noyes, whose collections are also from the surface. Hutchinson and Noyes eventually donated their collection, totaling 4,501 artifacts (Table 5.1), to the Nevada State Museum (NSM). One of the primary goals of this monograph is to present the results of our analysis of the Hutchinson–Noyes (H–N) collection. Although their primary collecting activities at the Sunshine Locality occurred in the early to mid-1970s, Hutchinson continued to visit the site over the years and collected small numbers of artifacts that eventually were curated by the museum. In our analysis of the H–N collection at the NSM, we attempted to examine every artifact; however, given that some artifacts were late accessions and not necessarily combined with the earlier collections, we may have missed a small number of objects.

Also noted in chapter 2, Robert York made both surface and subsurface collections for the NSM between 1972 and 1978. Although York did not report analyses of these artifacts, Gigi York (1995) analyzed his collection, totaling 8,558 artifacts (Table 5.1), for her master's thesis. Therefore, we did not analyze the York collection but occasionally use some of these data in our comparisons. We did, however, conduct analyses of 16 crescents that were collected by York and thus include those results in our discussions.

The NSM and DRI conducted two short field seasons in 1989 and 1990, during which 14 flakes were collected from the backhoe trenches (Table 5.1). These artifacts also are not included in our analyses.

During the course of our work at the Sunshine Locality, from 1993 through 1997, a total of 9,059 artifacts were collected from seven separate locations, 7,787 from excavation and 1,272 from the surface. In subsequent visits to Sunshine in 2004 and 2007, an additional 10 artifacts were collected, bringing the total to 9,069 (Table 5.1).[1] We do include these artifacts in our analyses.

In total, then, 22,158 artifacts have been collected from the Sunshine Locality since the early 1960s. Because the H–N and Hamilton College (HC) assemblages were collected quite differently, the analytic protocol for each differed. The H–N assemblage, for instance, is not in any way a representative sample of artifacts from the Sunshine Locality; it is, instead, a haphazard sample that is heavily weighted toward formal tools, such as projectile points, crescents, gravers, and scrapers. Hutchinson and Noyes collected debitage less often, and when they did, they generally did not note its provenience. Because of the size of the collection, however, we believe it to represent a fairly good sample of formal tools. We examine this further below.

Although the locations of the HC collections were also not chosen randomly but selected according to where backhoe excavations had revealed possible depth (see Figure 3.1), collection was always conducted systematically within standard 2-×-2-m grid units (1993–1996) or 1-×-2-m grid units (1997); further, all artifacts were collected. Thus, as Table 5.1 shows, the *majority* of the HC assemblage is composed of debitage. Most of the debitage was collected in 1993 from analytical Unit A, which we

TABLE 5.1. Summary of Artifacts Found at the Sunshine Locality

COLLECTION	FORMAL TOOLS/CORES	DEBITAGE	TOTAL
Tadlock	11 (100.0%)		11
Hutchinson and Noyes	2,725 (60.7%)	1,765 (39.3%)	4,490
York	5,588 (65.3%)	2,970 (4.7%)	8,558
Nevada State Museum–Desert Research Institute		14 (100.0%)	14
Hamilton College	131 (1.4%)	8,938 (98.6%)	9,069
Total	8,455	13,687	22,142

now know to be redeposited sediments related to slope wash. Even so, the large number of artifacts combined with those from other units and other seasons are likely a fairly representative sample of the debitage as well as the raw materials used at Sunshine.

This chapter presents the analysis results for both collections. We begin with a general analysis of the collections followed by more detailed treatment of particular tool categories, such as bifaces, crescents, scrapers, gravers, notches, and drills. The analysis of projectile points is presented separately in chapter 6.

General Artifact Analysis Protocol and Results

We used several different protocols in our analysis of the HC and H–N assemblages. In our analyses of the HC assemblage we followed a basic protocol used in our previous work in Butte and Jakes valleys. This general protocol consists of metric measures of size (maximum length, maximum width, maximum thickness, and actual weight); a set of standard technological distinctions, based on the kind and extent of subtractive modification evident (Table 5.2); a set of raw material categories; and a set of 13 size categories. The raw material categories are chert, obsidian, fine-grained volcanics (andesite, dacite, basalt, rhyolite), quartzite, and "other." The size categories are based on plan area (cm^2), the smallest having an area of .296 cm^2 and the area of each successive category being 1.5 times that of the previous one (Figure 5.1). The largest (Size 12) has an area of 25.630 cm^2; anything larger than this was given a designation of 13. Areas are drawn as squares and rectangles, and each artifact was identified with the drawing most appropriate to its size and shape. Because this variable represents plan area only, it may not always correspond with other measures of size, such as weight. Two artifacts of the same weight, for instance, one thick and one thin, may identify with different size categories.

Tables 5.3 through 5.6 summarize the technological categories and raw material represented by stratigraphic unit for the 1993, 1995, 1996, and 1997 artifact assemblages, respectively. Table 5.7 summarizes these same variables by stratigraphic unit for the assemblages from all four years combined, and Table 5.8 summarizes the total assemblage.

As Tables 5.3–5.6 show, raw material proportions, although they vary slightly from year to year, are roughly similar except for in the 1995 assemblage, where chert proportions are somewhat larger and obsidian proportions are smaller. Overall, however, fine-grained volcanic (FGV) toolstone constitutes the largest proportion (48.6 percent), followed by chert (37.1 percent) and obsidian (12.9 percent). These proportions contrast somewhat with those from assemblages we have collected from adjacent Butte Valley to the east (Beck and Jones 1993), specifically with respect to chert and obsidian. Although the percentage of artifacts manufactured from FGV (49.1 percent) is similar to that at Sunshine, the percentage of chert artifacts in the Butte Valley assemblages is approximately 31 percent, and that of obsidian artifacts is 19.1 percent. This may be related in part to the availability of a small pebble obsidian source (Butte Mountain [see Jones et al. 2003]), but it also may be related to the difference in technological composition between the Butte Valley sites and the Sunshine Locality, which we address at various points in this chapter.

As discussed in chapter 3, our initial explorations in 1993 led us to question the stratigraphic integrity of artifact samples from the upper strata (Units A–B). Nials (1990) notes that eolian sands and fine sandy alluvium exhibited extensive bioturbation. Additionally, as Hutchinson (1993) points out, he and Noyes had noticed on several occasions that artifacts gradually moved downslope during rainstorms. To make this assessment we believed that these strata had to be carefully excavated and screened, as if the sediments were not deflated or mixed. We also proceeded with the analysis in the same vein. Each artifact, whether a shaped object or debitage, was examined microscopically (generally 10× to 50×), and several variables, in addition to those in Table 5.2, were recorded for debitage (Table 5.9). Finally, the degree of rounding was recorded for all artifacts in an effort to determine how much sandblasting or water wear was evident. The results of the debitage analysis from the 1993 excavation will be discussed with the bifaces.

Sediment analyses of samples taken during the 1993 excavation supported our contention that the artifacts in the upper two stratigraphic units (A–B) were redeposited (Jones et al. 1996). As noted in chapters 3 and 4, Units A and B represent an interfingering of well-sorted eolian sands (Unit B) and fine sandy alluvium consistent with slope wash (Unit A). Both exhibit extreme bioturbation. Further, an examination of artifact frequencies along the primary axes of the excavations revealed a uniform decrease in artifact number from west to east, that is, toward the center of the channel, in each level from the surface down to 1 m (Jones et al. 1996). Although there is no corresponding size gradation within the upper meter of sediments, Figure 5.2 shows that there is a difference in the proportion of larger artifacts in the upper and lower units (see also Table 5.10).[2] As these data indicate, the proportions of size 1 and 2 artifacts are much greater in Units A, B, and C (particularly B and C) than in the lower units (D and E). As studies have shown that smaller artifacts are more likely to be redeposited by slope wash than larger ones (Michie 1990), we believe the

TABLE 5.2. General Technological Categories Used to Identify the Hamilton College Collection

TECHNOLOGICAL CATEGORY	DEFINITION
Unmodified Cortical Flake	A flake that exhibits cortex on its dorsal surface and no edge retouch. The distinction between primary and secondary cortical flakes is not made here given the ambiguity of this distinction.
Unmodified Interior Flake	A flake that exhibits no cortex and no edge retouch.
Uniface	An artifact with retouch on only one face.
Biface	An artifact (not a projectile point) with retouch on two opposing faces.
Projectile Point	A biface that possesses consistent manufacturing properties of "point," "haft," and "bilateral symmetry." These items were analyzed separately because of their chronological significance.
Core	An irregularly shaped mass bearing negative flake scars originating from one or more platforms.
Split Pebble	A core or core fragment produced by the bipolar technique (Crabtree 1972), as distinct from other kinds of cores and core fragments.
Shatter	Debitage produced during the manufacturing process that exhibits no classic attributes of a flake.
Chunk	A thick, angular piece produced during the manufacturing process that exhibits no classic attributes of a flake or core.

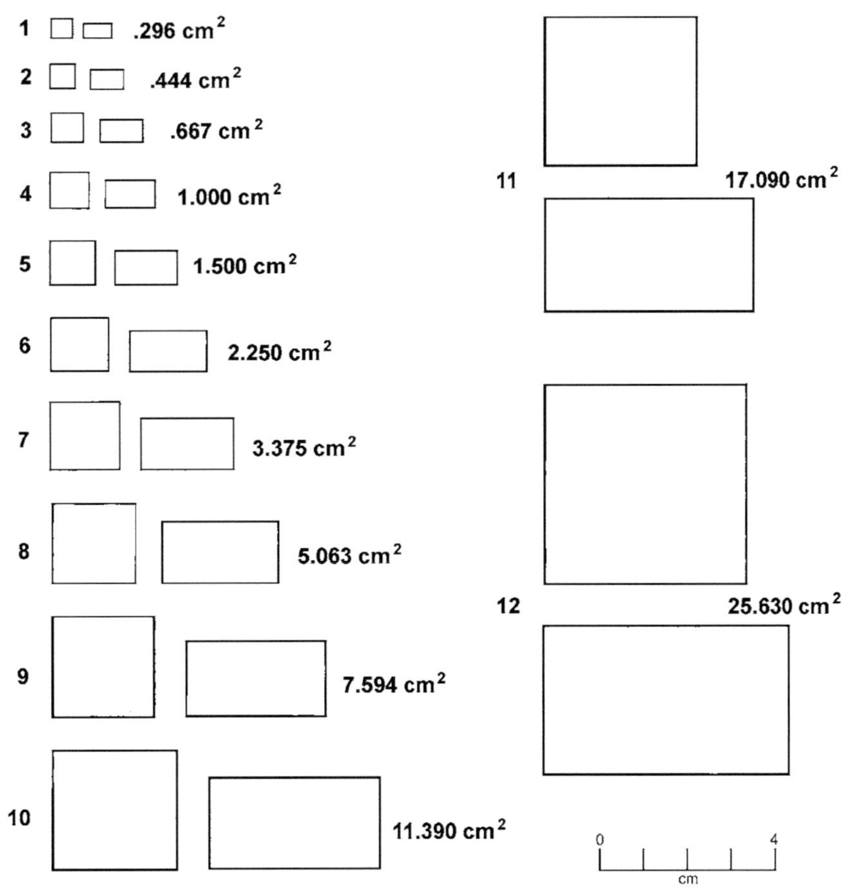

FIGURE 5.1. Size categories used in the artifact analysis.

TABLE 5.3. Distribution of Raw Material Across Technological Categories by Stratum in the 1993 Hamilton College Collection

Stratum	Technological Category	Raw Material: Chert	Obsidian	Fine-Grained Volcanics	Quartzite	Other	Total
Surface	Cortical Flake	3	1	17			21
	Interior Flake	147	35	197			379
	Biface	1		1			2
	Projectile Point	1	1	3			5
	Shatter	66	22	107			195
	Chunk	6	1	5			12
	Subtotal	224	60	330	0	0	614
A	Cortical Flake	5	1	2			8
	Interior Flake	1,357	601	1,307	2	203	3,470
	Uniface	3					3
	Biface	3	1	7			11
	Projectile Point	1		1			2
	Shatter	722	297	1,221	1	140	2,381
	Chunk	30	3	14			47
	Subtotal	2,121	903	2,552	3	343	5,922
B	Interior Flake	11	3	13		2	29
	Shatter	7	3	15		6	31
	Subtotal	18	6	28	0	8	60
B–C	Projectile Point			1			1
	Subtotal	0	0	1	0	0	1
C	Interior Flake	4	8	14		2	28
	Shatter	1		8			9
	Subtotal	5	8	22	0	2	37
D	Interior Flake	6	1	1		5	13
	Shatter			2		1	3
	Subtotal	6	1	3	0	6	16
E	Cortical Flake	4	1	4			9
	Interior Flake	227	30	184	1	69	511
	Uniface			1			1
	Biface	1	1				2
	Projectile Point	1		1			2
	Core	2		1	1		4
	Shatter	63	6	78		25	172
	Chunk			1			1
	Subtotal	298	38	270	2	94	702
Total		2,672 (36.3%)	1,016 (13.8%)	3,206 (43.6%)	5 (<.01%)	453 (6.2%)	7,352 (100.0%)

TABLE 5.4. Distribution of Raw Material Across Technological Categories by Stratum in the 1995 Hamilton College Collection

Stratum	Technological Category	Raw Material: Chert	Obsidian	Fine-Grained Volcanics	Quartzite	Other	Total
Surface	Cortical Flake	14		21			35
	Interior Flake	202	29	191	8		430
	Uniface	12	1	7			20
	Biface	12	1	6			19
	Projectile Point	5	3	8	1		17
	Core	3		1			4
	Shatter	10	1	6			17
	Chunk	6	1	3	2		12
	Subtotal	264	36	243	11	0	554
A	Interior Flake			1		1	2
	Shatter	1		2			3
	Subtotal	1	0	3	0	1	5
C	Interior Flake					1	1
	Biface		2				2
	Subtotal	0	2	0	0	1	3
E	Cortical Flake	2					2
	Interior Flake	104	10	43		11	168
	Uniface	2					2
	Biface	4		2[a]			6
	Projectile Point	1					1
	Shatter	12	1	7		1	21
	Subtotal	125	11	52	0	12	200
Total		390 (51.2%)	49 (6.4%)	298 (39.1%)	11 (1.4%)	14 (1.8%)	762 (100.0%)

[a] These two specimens are fragments of the same biface and are considered a single object in the biface analysis and Tables 5.13–5.17.

TABLE 5.5. Distribution of Raw Material Across Technological Categories by Stratum in the 1996 Hamilton College Collection

Stratum	Technological Category	Raw Material: Chert	Obsidian	Fine-Grained Volcanics	Quartzite	Other	Total
Surface	Projectile Point		1[a]	1[b]			2
	Subtotal		1	1			2
E	Interior Flake	37	6	45			88
	Uniface	3					3
	Projectile Point	1					1
	Shatter	15	9	27			51
	Subtotal	56	15	72			143
Total		56 (38.6%)	16 (11.0%)	73 (50.3%)	0 (.0%)	0 (.0%)	145 (100.0%)

[a] In the channel on the surface 2 m south of the south edge of the loader trench.

[b] On a sand terrace above the wash, 10 m southeast of the loader trench.

TABLE 5.6. Distribution of Raw Material Across Technological Categories by Stratum in the 1997 Hamilton College Collection

STRATUM	TECHNOLOGICAL CATEGORY	RAW MATERIAL					TOTAL
		CHERT	OBSIDIAN	FINE-GRAINED VOLCANICS	QUARTZITE	OTHER	
Surface	Cortical Flake	4		1			5
	Interior Flake	21	3	42			66
	Uniface	1		1			2
	Core	1					1
	Shatter	5	3	15			23
	Chunk	4		1			5
	Subtotal	36	6	60			102
B	Cortical Flake	4		2			6
	Interior Flake	81	33	146			260
	Uniface	4		1			5
	Biface	1					1
	Core	1					1
	Shatter	74	22	196			292
	Subtotal	165	55	345			565
B–D_{df}	Interior Flake	10	1	9			20
	Projectile Point			1			1
	Shatter	6	2	10			18
	Subtotal		16	3	20		39
D_{df}	Cortical Flake	3		3	1		7
	Interior Flake	17	6	15			38
	Shatter	9	15	25			49
	Subtotal	29	21	43	1		94
Total		246 (30.8%)	85 (10.6%)	468 (58.5%)	1 (.2%)	0 (.0%)	800 (100.0%)

TABLE 5.7. Summary of Raw Material Across Technological Categories Represented in the Hamilton College Collection

STRATUM	TECHNOLOGICAL CATEGORY	RAW MATERIAL					TOTAL
		CHERT	OBSIDIAN	FINE-GRAINED VOLCANICS	QUARTZITE	OTHER	
Surface	Cortical Flake	21	1	39			61
	Interior Flake	370	67	430	8		875
	Uniface	13	1	8			22
	Biface	13	1	7			21
	Projectile Point	7	5	11	1		24
	Core	4		1			5
	Shatter	81	26	128			235
	Chunk	16	2	9	2		29
	Subtotal	525	103	633	11		1,272
A	Cortical Flake	5	1	2			8
	Interior Flake	1,357	601	1,308	2	204	3,472
	Uniface	3					3
	Biface	3	1	7			11
	Projectile Point	1		1			2
	Shatter	723	297	1,223	1	140	2,384
	Chunk	30	3	14			47
	Subtotal	2,122	903	2,555	3	344	5,927

TABLE 5.7. (cont'd.) Summary of Raw Material Across Technological Categories Represented in the Hamilton College Collection

		Raw Material					
Stratum	**Technological Category**	**Chert**	**Obsidian**	**Fine-Grained Volcanics**	**Quartzite**	**Other**	**Total**
B	Cortical Flake	4		2			6
	Interior Flake	92	36	159		2	289
	Uniface	4		1			5
	Biface	1					1
	Core	1					1
	Shatter	81	25	211		6	323
	Subtotal	183	61	373		8	625
B_{df}	Interior Flake	10	1	9			20
	Projectile Point			1			1
	Shatter	6	2	10			18
	Subtotal	16	3	20			39
B–C	Projectile Point			1			1
	Subtotal			1			1
C	Interior Flake	4	8	14		3	29
	Biface		2				2
	Shatter	1		8			9
	Subtotal	5	10	22		3	40
D	Interior Flake	6	1	1		5	13
	Shatter			2		1	3
	Subtotal	6	1	3		6	16
D_{df}	Cortical Flake	3		3	1		7
	Interior Flake	17	6	15			38
	Shatter	9	15	25			49
	Subtotal	29	21	43	1		94
E	Cortical Flake	6	1	4			11
	Interior Flake	368	46	272	1	80	767
	Uniface	5		1			6
	Biface	5	1	2			8
	Projectile Point	3		1			4
	Core	2		1	1		4
	Shatter	90	16	112		26	244
	Chunk			1			1
	Subtotal	479	64	394	2	106	1,045
Total		3,365 (37.1%)	1,166 (12.9%)	4,044 (44.6%)	17 (.2%)	467 (5.2%)	9,059 (100.0%)

TABLE 5.8. Summary of Technological Categories by Raw Material Represented in the Hamilton College Collection

	Raw Material					
Technological Category	**Chert**	**Obsidian**	**Fine-Grained Volcanics**	**Quartzite**	**Other**	**Total**
Cortical Flake	39 (41.9%)	3 (3.2%)	50 (53.8%)	1 (1.1%)		93
Interior Flake	2,224 (40.4%)	766 (13.9%)	2,208 (40.1%)	11 (.2%)	294 (5.3%)	5,503
Uniface	25 (69.4%)	1 (2.8%)	10 (27.8%)			36
Biface	22 (51.2%)	5 (11.6%)	16 (37.2%)			43
Projectile Point	11 (34.4%)	5 (15.6%)	15 (46.9%)	1 (3.1%)		32
Core	7 (70.0%)		2 (20.0%)	1 (10.0%)		10
Shatter	991 (30.3%)	381 (11.7%)	1,719 (52.7%)	1 (<.1%)	173 (5.3%)	3,265
Chunk	46 (59.7%)	5 (6.5%)	24 (31.2%)	2 (2.6%)		77
Total	3,365 (37.1%)	1,166 (12.9%)	4,044 (44.6%)	17 (.2%)	467 (5.2%)	9,059 (100.0%)

TABLE 5.9. Analytic Protocol for Debitage Collected by Hamilton College During the 1993 Season

CATEGORY	DEFINITION
Edge Damage	Evidence along the flake edge of regular chipping, crushing, stacked micro–step fractures, or abrasion; recorded only as present or absent.
Platform Configuration	The faceting evident on the striking platform (if platform is present); recorded as cortex, single faceted, multiple faceted, or abraded facet.
Platform Crushing	The presence or absence of crushing on the platform.
Platform Lipping	The presence or absence of a lip where the platform meets the bulb on the ventral side of the flake.
Platform Angle	The angle between the platform edge and the dorsal surface of the flake; measured as near 90° or acute.
Dorsal Scars	The number of previous flake scars present on the dorsal surface; measured as 0, 1, 2, 3, >4.
Retouch	Presence or absence of retouch along the flake edge; measured as unifacial, bifacial, or none.
Termination	Termination of the distal flake edge; measured as feather, hinge, or step/snap.

TABLE 5.10. Distribution of Size Categories by Stratum for the Artifacts from the 1993 Hamilton College Excavation

	STRATUM											
	A		B		C		D		E		TOTAL	
SIZE	*N*	%	*N*	%	*N*	%	*N*	%	*N*	%	*N*	%
1	2,842	48.0	31	51.7	23	62.2	2	12.5	131	18.7	3,029	45.0
2	1,223	20.7	18	30.0	7	18.9	1	6.2	81	11.5	1,330	19.7
3	920	15.5	8	13.3	5	13.5	4	25.0	123	17.5	1,060	15.7
4	449	7.6			1	2.7	3	18.8	97	13.8	550	8.2
5	263	4.4	3	5.0			3	18.8	79	11.3	348	5.2
6	120	2.0					3	18.8	70	10.0	193	2.9
7	62	1.0							52	7.4	114	1.7
8	21	.4							32	4.6	53	.8
9	14	.2							17	2.4	31	.5
10	4	.1			1	2.7			10	1.4	15	.2
11	3	.1							8	1.1	12	.2
12	1	<.1							2	.3	3	<.1
Total	5,922		60		37		16		702		6,738	

majority of small artifacts in Unit A were derived from upslope sources. Those few artifacts in Unit B were likely the result of bioturbation (Jones et al. 1996). The results for Unit C, however, are surprising because bioturbation is less pronounced. The one artifact found in the interface between Units B and C is a large stemmed projectile point (see Figure 3.8) lying on the thin layer of ash that overlies Unit C. This ash appears undisturbed, and the radiocarbon date obtained on this ash is 9820 ± 60 rcy BP, which is consistent with its depth as well as the other radiocarbon dates in the column (see chapter 4). These facts suggest to us that the large proportion of small artifacts in Unit C lay in primary context.

Because the artifacts in Units A and B appeared to lie in secondary context, the subsequent 1995 and 1996 excavations began at the top of Unit C, and thus the results in Tables 5.4 and 5.5 do not include artifacts from Units A and B. The 1997 excavations, however, were located far to the south of the earlier units and not in the wash (Figure 3.1); consequently, during this season the upper strata were once again examined, as reflected in Table 5.6.

The analysis of the H–N collection followed several different protocols. The primary H–N collection, which comprises 1,680 formal tools, was stored by Phil Hutchinson (and subsequently by the NSM) in long, open trays, with artifacts lying on cotton batting. Among these are the artifacts that are described in chapter 2 as having been given point provenience with Hutchinson's two homemade transits and photographed individually.

When we first visited the NSM in 1995 to analyze the H–N collection, we believed that the artifacts stored in the open trays constituted the entire collection.[3] We

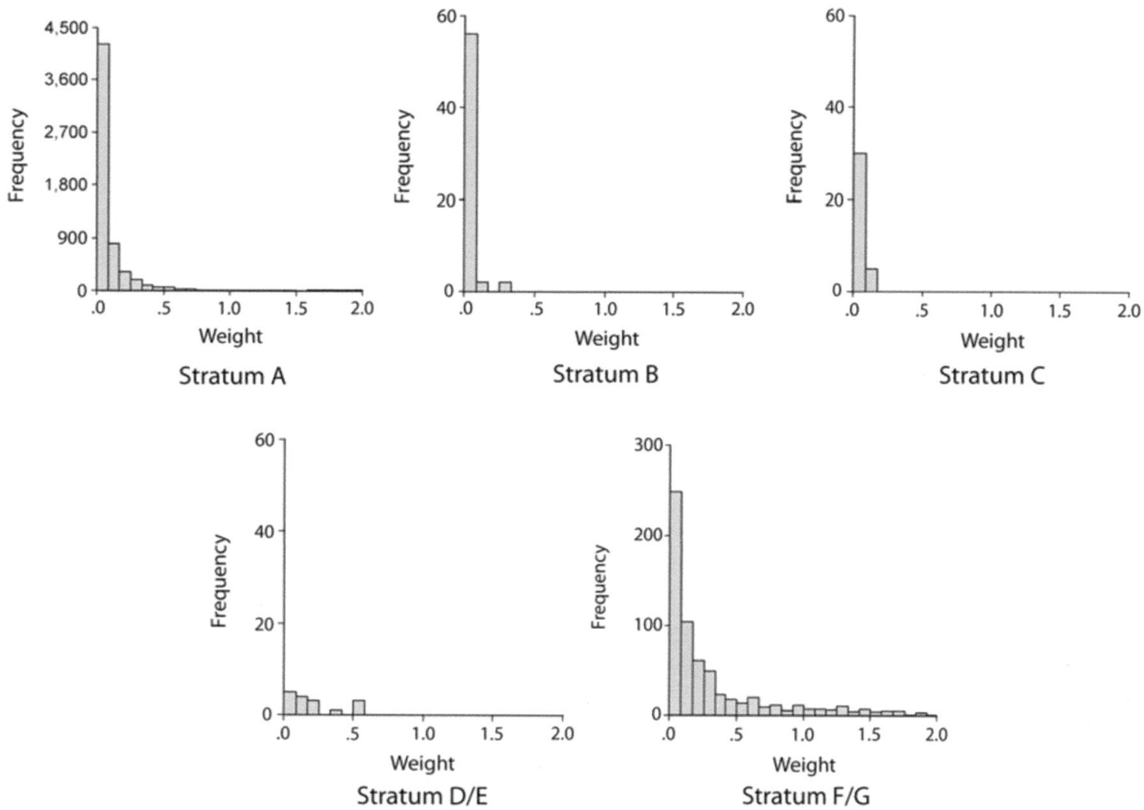

FIGURE 5.2. Distribution of artifact weight (g) by stratum in the 1993 assemblage.

began our analysis by identifying each artifact with the analytic protocol used in our analysis of the Hamilton collections (i.e., Table 5.2), but because we would not have ready access to the artifacts after leaving the museum, each artifact was drawn, and additional measurements were recorded on its own individual (e.g., uniface, biface, or projectile point) form. For example, the uniface form included additional variables such as blank type, hafting information, overall shape, and the shape of the worn edge. Thus, although we intended to follow the same protocol as used for the Butte Valley assemblages and with our own Sunshine collections, we subsequently found that this was not the most parsimonious procedure.

Analysis of North American Paleoindian assemblages generally focuses on formal tools and retouched flake tools, for the most part, because these assemblages are usually small and debitage constitutes a relatively small component. Also, the formal tool component is often quite rich. General categories, such as "scrapers," are subdivided into subcategories, such as "end scraper," "side scraper," "circular scraper," and so on, which are most often associated with particular uses by the analyst. We initially devised our general analysis protocol to avoid using terms like *scraper* that often have functional connotations. We instead employed terms that reflect only the type of retouch present, with the exception of projectile points. Thus, instead of *scraper* we used *uniface.* Tools such as scrapers, however, are not necessarily all unifacial, and certainly not all unifaces are scrapers. In our Butte Valley studies the more general approach did not seem problematic because the nondebitage component of the assemblages is composed almost completely of bifaces and finished points. The H–N collection, however, is quite different with respect to the formal tool component. After our analysis of the provenienced H–N assemblage, we decided to revise our analytic protocol, using formal categories, such as "scraper," "graver," "drill," and so on, which was possible because we had drawn each artifact and recorded its measurements on individual forms. These categories are defined in Table 5.11.

Toward the end of our second visit to the museum, which took place in 1996, we discovered that the H–N collection was much larger than we had originally thought. We discovered that there were at least two large boxes of artifacts, many of which were loose in large plastic bags, with just site location or no provenience at all. We arranged to have these sent to us at Hamilton College, but

TABLE 5.11. Definitions of Formal Tool Categories Recognized in the Sunshine Assemblage

TOOL CATEGORY	DEFINITION
Amorphous Uniface	An artifact with retouch on only one face. Many of the tools defined below are unifacial, including gravers and scrapers, but these tools can also be bifacial. Thus we have called all unifaces that cannot be identified as these tools amorphous unifaces.
Biface	An artifact with retouch on two opposing faces. Three types of bifaces are recognized: *production*—identifiable with the production sequence for large stemmed points; *amorphous*—has no particular or standardized form; *indeterminate*—recognizable as a biface but too fragmentary to categorize.
Point Blade	The tip or blade section of a projectile point. Three types are recognized: *Western Stemmed Tradition*—recognizable as part of a Western Stemmed Tradition point but not necessarily the particular type; *Archaic*—identifiable as part of an Archaic point but not to a particular type; *indeterminate*—recognizable only as a point blade.
Core	A mass bearing negative flake scars originating from one or more platforms. Three types of cores are recognized: *amorphous*—shape is irregular, and flake scars originate from various locations on the surface; *bifacial*—bifacially shaped, and flakes generally originate from margins; *polyhedral blade*—conically shaped, source of prismatic blades.
Chisel	An artifact with a long, narrow projection ending in a rounded or blunt point.
Combination Tool	An artifact exhibiting two or more different tools. A number of different combination tools are recognized, including various combinations of scrapers and gravers (see definitions below) and single examples of a graver and notch and a graver and production biface blade.
Crescent	A biface [or uniface] of crescentic shape. The edges often exhibit grinding at the midpoint (Gramly 1990:18).
Drill	Implement with a projection that is used for perforating. Identified by edge beveling on alternating faces (Gramly 1990:20).
Graver	A flake or blade with a small, sharp projection (sometimes called a spur) created by unifacial retouch. Often exhibits multiple spurs (Gramly 1990:26).
Ground Stone	A slab or cobble that has been smoothed by grinding (mano or metate [Gramly 1990:27]).
Hammer Stone	A piece of stone, usually a cobble of tough material, that exhibits evidence of percussion (i.e., crushing [Gramly 1990:28]).
Notch	A small, narrow concavity on the edge of a flake or shaped tool, usually unifacial (Gramly 1990:34).
Preform	A biface that was destined to have become a particular type of tool, especially a specific type of projectile point (Gramly 1990:42).
Prismatic Blade	A removal from a core (blade core) that has a length at least twice its width. A pronounced single or double arris runs parallel to the main axis making the cross section triangular or quadrilateral (Gramly 1990:44).
Projectile Point	A biface that possesses consistent manufacturing properties of "point," "haft," and "bilateral symmetry." These items were analyzed separately from other bifaces because of their chronological utility.
Scraper	A flaked-stone tool, generally made on a flake or blade, having bold unifacial retouch on one or more margins (Gramly 1990:49).

the loan period was very brief. We applied the revised protocol in the analysis, but because of time limitations specific analyses were not applied to most categories in portions of this assemblage. Approximately 59 percent of this assemblage is debitage, collected by Hutchinson and Noyes to obtain what they deemed a sample of material types; the remaining artifacts are formal tools and tool fragments. But because of limitations on our time spent with the material, every artifact was not drawn individually, as was done for the primary assemblage contained in trays, with the exception of projectile points (n = 68) and crescents (n = 17). Consequently, only these latter two artifacts could be examined more fully in our special analyses.

An additional 510 artifacts were collected and donated during the late 1980s and early 1990s by Hutchinson. These were housed in a different location in the museum and thus were not found by us until several years later, during another trip to photograph artifacts. We were able to borrow these for a longer period and thus able to draw each of the formal tools individually so that they could be included in the special analyses.

Therefore, we refer to the assemblage of 2,275 that were subjected to special analyses as the *specific assemblage,* whereas the remaining 2,215 artifacts for which only general information was recorded are referred to as the *general assemblage.* The results of the general analyses are presented in Table 5.12 for both the general and formal H–N assemblages combined. We subsequently identified the formal artifacts from the Hamilton College collections with these categories as well, and these results are shown in Table 5.13.

TABLE 5.12. Technological Categories Represented in the Hutchinson–Noyes Collection

TECHNOLOGICAL CATEGORY	RAW MATERIAL					
	CHERT	OBSIDIAN	FINE-GRAINED VOLCANICS	QUARTZITE	OTHER	TOTAL
Fluted Lanceolate Point	11	3				14
Unfluted Lanceolate Point	61	3	3			67
Great Basin Stemmed Series Point[a]	120	98	465	3		686
Early Holocene Point[b]	8	11	10			29
Archaic Point[c]	39	25	20	2		86
Unclassifiable Point	16	8	23	1		48
Projectile Point Preform	3					3
Crescent[d]	220	7	6	1		234
Production Biface	156	43	244			443
Amorphous Biface	154	6	10	2		172
Unique Biface	4					4
Scraper	456	5	27	1		489
Graver	153	3	4			160
Notch	7					7
Drill	10	2				12
Chisel	1					1
Combination Tool						
Scraper/Graver	119		5		1	125
Graver/Notch	7					7
Scraper/Notch	5					5
Scraper/Graver/Notch	10					10
Chisel/Scraper/Graver	2					2
Crescent/Graver	17		3			20
Drill/Scraper	1					1
Point Blade/Notch	1					1
Amorphous Uniface	88	6	6			100
Flake with Platform	655	36	7			698
Flake Without Platform	875	54	18	1	1	949
Core	11	1				12
Chunk	115	2		1		118
Ground Stone					2	2
Hammer Stone	1					1
Total	3,326	313	851	12	4	4,506

Note: Includes artifacts from both general and specific assemblages.

[a] Includes points of the Cougar Mountain, Ovate, Lake Mohave, Parman, and Silver Lake types and fragments identified only as Western Stemmed Tradition blade, midsection, or stem.

[b] Includes points of the Windust, Pinto, and Butte Valley Corner Notched types.

[c] Includes points of the Elko, Gatecliff, Humboldt, and Rosegate series.

[d] Includes 16 crescents collected by York.

TABLE 5.13. Technological Categories Represented in the Hamilton College Collection

TECHNOLOGICAL CATEGORY	RAW MATERIAL					TOTAL
	CHERT	OBSIDIAN	FINE-GRAINED VOLCANICS	QUARTZITE	OTHER	
Fluted Lanceolate Point[a]	3					3
Unfluted Lanceolate Point[b]	5					5
Great Basin Stemmed Series Point[c]	6	2	13	1		22
Early Holocene Point[d]		1	1			2
Archaic Point[e]			1			1
Unclassifiable Point[f]	2	1	1			4
Projectile Point Preform	1					1
Crescent[g]	11					11
Production Biface	5	1	9			15
Amorphous Biface[h]	9	3	5		1	18
Scraper[i]	11		6			17
Graver	7		2			9
Notch	1					1
Combination Tool						
Scraper/Graver	1					1
Graver/Notch	1					1
Scraper/Notch	2					2
Scraper/Graver/Notch	1		1			2
Amorphous Uniface	3	1	2			6
Cortical Flake	39	3	50	1		93
Interior Flake	2,224	766	2,208	11	294	5,503
Core	7		2	1		10
Chunk	46	5	24	2		77
Shatter	991	381	1,719	1	173	3,265
Total	3,376	1,164	4,044	17	468	9,069

[a] One of these points was actually collected just outside of the Sunshine Locality in a survey of Long Valley conducted in 1991. We include it here because it is included in the fluted point analysis in chapter 6.
[b] Includes one lanceolate unfluted point collected during our visit to the site in 2004.
[c] Includes points of the Cougar Mountain, Ovate, Lake Mohave, Parman, and Silver Lake types and fragments identified only as Western Stemmed Tradition blade, midsection, or stem.
[d] Includes points of the Windust, Pinto, and Butte Valley Corner Notched types.
[e] Includes points of the Elko, Gatecliff, Humboldt, and Rosegate series.
[f] Includes one unclassifiable projectile point collected during our visit to the site in 2004.
[g] Includes five crescents collected during our visit to the site in 2004.
[h] Includes one biface collected during our visit to the site in 2004.
[i] Includes one bifacial scraper collected during our visit to the site in 2004.

Special Artifact Analyses

Several kinds of artifacts such as bifaces, crescents, scrapers, and gravers were subjected to more detailed analyses. In doing this we have made use of the technological categories described in Gramly's *Guide to the Palaeo-Indian Artifacts of North America* (1990). We begin with a discussion of bifaces.

Bifaces

Exclusive of projectile points, 934 bifaces were analyzed from the Sunshine assemblage, 887 from the H–N collection and 47 from the HC collection (Table 5.14). We discuss only production bifaces, point preforms, unique bifaces, and amorphous bifaces in this section. All others (i.e., crescents, scrapers, etc.) will be discussed in subsequent sections.

Production Bifaces and Biface Reduction. One of the characteristic aspects of most Paleoarchaic assemblages that we have studied in the central Great Basin (e.g., Beck et al. 2002; Jones et al. 2003) is a biface reduction sequence for the production of large contracting-stem

TABLE 5.14. Bifaces by Raw Material in the Hutchinson–Noyes and Hamilton College Collections

Collection Category	Raw Material: Chert	Obsidian	Fine-Grained Volcanics	Quartzite	Other	Total
Hutchinson–Noyes						
Production Biface	156	43	244			443
Crescent[a]	185	6	5	1		197
Scraper	45		1			46
Concave Base Preform	3					3
Graver	5					5
Scraper/Graver	3					3
Scraper/Notch	1					1
Unique	4					4
Drill	11	2				13
Amorphous	154	6	10	2		172
Subtotal	567	57	260	3		887
Hamilton College						
Production Biface[b]	5	1	9			15
Crescent[c]	10					10
Scraper[d]	2	1	1			4
Amorphous[e]	9	3	5		1	18
Subtotal[f]	26	5	15		1	47
Total	593	62	275	3	1	934

[a] Includes 16 crescents collected by York.
[b] There are actually two obsidian biface fragments that have been refitted. Although they are counted separately in the previous summary tables, they are treated as a single biface in our analysis of production bifaces.
[c] The total contains five crescents collected during our visit to the site in 2004.
[d] The total contains one bifacial scraper collected during our visit to the site in 2004.
[e] The total contains one limestone biface collected during our visit to the site in 2004.
[f] The total of 48 shown here (less the five crescents and one biface mentioned above) is one less than that in Table 5.8 because two biface fragments collected in 1995 are from the same specimen (see Table 5.4) and are thus considered here as a single object.

points (Figure 5.3), such as Cougar Mountain, Lake Mohave, and Parman. The bifaces produced in this sequence are so standardized that they are readily recognizable, even in the absence of finished points. A total of 458 bifaces in the Sunshine assemblage can be identified with this sequence, 443 from the H–N collection and 15 from the HC collection. The majority of the H–N bifaces (374), however, are in the general collection that were not drawn individually, so specific analyses could not be done on them. Consequently, in our discussions we will, for the most part, concentrate on the 15 HC specimens and the 69 H–N specimens that were subjected to further analysis.

Only five production bifaces are complete; the remaining artifacts were categorized according to the portion of the biface represented (Table 5.15). Table 5.16 provides the metric attributes for all 84 bifaces. In Paleoarchaic assemblages across the central Great Basin, these bifaces are most commonly manufactured from FGV toolstone, but in areas where obsidian is common, such as the northern Great Basin (e.g., Amick 1995a), this material often predominates. These tools, however, are less often manufactured from chert (but see Graf 2001). In the assemblages we have examined from Butte Valley just to the east, for example, over 90 percent of production bifaces are manufactured from FGV (Beck and Jones 1990b). In the Sunshine assemblage, however, a much smaller proportion of these tools is made from FGV (n = 55, 65.5 percent); 33.3 percent (n = 28) are manufactured from chert (Table 5.15). Similar proportions are evident in the other 374 production bifaces from the H–N general assemblage, with only 52.9 percent (n = 198) manufactured from FGV and 35.6 percent (n = 133) made from chert. We emphasize once again, however, that the H–N collection is *not* a representative sample; chert may have been more visible or desirable to collect than FGV, and Hutchinson and Noyes may have unconsciously focused on finished tools, such as projectile points and crescents, rather than unfinished

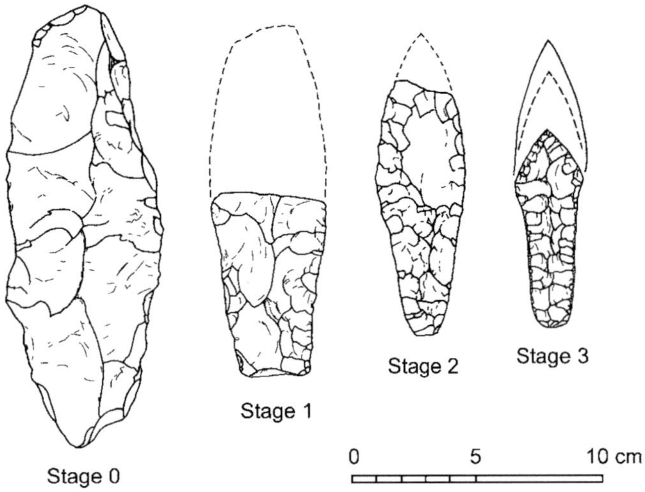

FIGURE 5.3. Biface reduction sequence used to produce large, contracting-stem points in Paleoarchaic assemblages across the Great Basin (after Jones et al. 2003:11, Figure 3).

TABLE 5.15. Sunshine Production Bifaces by Raw Material

	Raw Material			
Fragment	Chert	Obsidian	Fine-Grained Volcanics	Total
Complete	1		4	5
Tip	2			2
Blade	3		12	15
Tip/Blade	9	1	12	22
Stem/Blade	9		15	24
Midsection	4		11	18
Tip/Blade + Midsection			1	
Total	28 (33.3%)	1 (1.2%)	55 (65.5%)	84

TABLE 5.16. Quantitative Data for the Sunshine Production Bifaces

Statistic	Total Length (mm)	Maximum Width (mm)	Maximum Thickness (mm)	Actual Weight (g)
N	5	31	73	84
Range	70.2–83.5	19.8–49.2	6.00–18.8	1.6–62.0
Mean	76.58	35.80	10.54	19.41
SD	6.335	7.707	2.315	10.767

bifaces. If we consider only the HC bifaces, which *can* be considered a representative sample, although very small, the proportions are similar to those of the H–N collection, with nine (60 percent) specimens manufactured from FGV and five (33.3 percent) from chert. Thus, use of raw material for biface manufacture appears somewhat different at Sunshine than in many other Paleoarchaic assemblages.

Two of the complete production bifaces exhibit use-wear on the blade. A majority (n = 22, 61.1 percent) of the 36 fragmentary blades and tips for which use-wear could be determined are also worn (Table 5.17). Several of these show extensive use-wear, but for most, the blade is too fragmentary to evaluate the extent of the wear. These data suggest that production bifaces, although not "finished tools" (i.e., finished stemmed points), were used as tools themselves. Very few production bifaces have been resharpened (n = 2; Table 5.17), however.

One of the defining characteristics of large stemmed points is broad collateral flaking (see Table 6.12 and Figure 6.5 in chapter 6). This type of flaking is also evident on the majority of production bifaces for which flaking type was discernable (n = 62, 88.6 percent).

Focusing once again on the HC bifaces, it is notable that fewer than 32 percent (15 of 48) identify with the stemmed point reduction sequence; more often they are specialized tools or amorphous bifaces (Table 5.14). On the other hand, 59.5 percent of the classifiable projectile points in the HC collection result from this reduction sequence (Table 5.13). In the H–N collection, 49.9 percent (n = 443) of the bifaces are production bifaces that can possibly be identified with the reduction sequence (Table 5.14), whereas 78.2 percent (n = 686) of the classifiable points can be identified with the sequence (Table 5.12). These results suggest that although the use of stemmed points was likely a primary activity at Sunshine, their manufacture was not, and biface manufacture was focused toward more varied goals than at the sites we have studied in Butte and Jakes valleys. We turn to the results of the HC collection debitage analysis for further information concerning lithic reduction at Sunshine.

Shott (1994:74) suggests that debitage gives a more accurate picture of prehistoric activities at a particular location because unretouched flakes are not generally curated by prehistoric inhabitants and they are of little interest to modern collectors. A number of researchers have successfully revealed both type of reduction (e.g., Ingbar et al. 1989; Patterson 1990; Sullivan and Rozen 1985; Teltser 1991) and stage of reduction (e.g., Ingbar et al. 1989; Magne and Pokotylo 1981) through debitage analysis. For instance, although several studies have shown that particular kinds of flakes can occasionally be produced through various kinds of reduction (e.g., Ahler 1989:87; Magne 1985:94;

TABLE 5.17. Use-Wear and Resharpening on the Sunshine Production Biface Blades

	BIFACE FRAGMENT					
					TOTAL	
TYPE OF SCARS	COMPLETE	TIP/BLADE	TIP/BLADE + MIDSECTION	MIDSECTION	*N*	%
Use-Wear[a]						
None	3	14		2	19	31.7
Minimal		8			8	13.3
Moderate	1	1			2	3.3
Extensive	1	3			4	6.7
Present/Fragment		10			10	16.7
Indeterminate		3	1	13	17	28.3
Total	5	39	1	15	60	100.0
Resharpening						
Not Present	5	33	1	4	43	71.7
Present		1		1	2	3.3
Indeterminate		5		10	15	25.0
Total	5	39	1	15	60	100.0

[a] Minimal = less than half the blade; moderate = half the blade, extensive = more than half the blade; Present/Fragment = present, but blade is fragmentary.

Patterson 1982:56–57), flakes derived from biface reduction, in general, exhibit platform faceting, abrasion, and crushing; an acute exterior platform angle; pronounced interior platform lipping; a diffuse bulb of percussion; and multiple flake scars on the dorsal surface (e.g., Newcomer 1971:89–90; Odell 1996:382; Whittaker 1994:185–187). As Whittaker notes, however, "not all of these traits are present on every flake" (1994:185). For example, multifaceted platforms are most indicative of late-stage reduction, and thus flakes resulting from earlier-stage biface reduction may have single-faceted platforms. Also, as reduction of a biface proceeds, the exterior platform angle becomes increasingly acute, and thus at an earlier stage this angle may be closer to 90°.

In most cases, researchers refer to biface *thinning* rather than biface *reduction* flakes. The former is a more specific category within the latter, referring to later-stage biface thinning, shaping, and resharpening. The presence of lipping on biface thinning flakes is a function of the use of soft hammer percussion in later-stage reduction as well as the fact that these flakes are removed from a bifacial edge, usually by a bending fracture. In fact, Whittaker (1994:187) states that lipping is the most characteristic attribute of soft hammer thinning of bifaces. Here, however, we use the more general category of biface reduction flake, which includes flakes resulting from earlier-stage reduction as well. We must determine, therefore, which attribute combination(s) defines these flakes in the Sunshine assemblage.

As Table 5.9 shows, in the analysis of the Sunshine debitage in the HC collection we measured several of the variables that can be indicative of biface reduction flakes, including platform configuration, the presence of crushing on the platform, exterior platform angle, the presence of interior platform lipping, and the number of dorsal scars. Because the number of dorsal scars is relevant only to complete flakes, however, we begin with the first four variables.

Among the 9,069 artifacts collected by Hamilton College, 5,596 have been identified as flakes, but only 1,847 (33.0 percent) have complete platforms. An additional 2,634 flakes have partial platforms, but as one or more of the four variables were not measurable on these flakes, we focus on those for which the platform is complete.

Table 5.18 shows the number of flakes for which different combinations of acute exterior platform angle, platform crushing, and interior platform lipping appear on flakes with different platform configurations by raw material. For example, there are 34 chert flakes with single-faceted platforms on which all three attributes are present. In contrast, there are 50 chert flakes with single-faceted platforms on which none of these attributes occurs. Table 5.19 shows resulting probabilities of chi-square tests performed on attribute pairs, again for each platform configuration and raw material type. As stated above, multifaceted platforms are, in general, characteristic of biface reduction flakes, but these flakes can also have single-faceted platforms, especially in the earlier stages of

TABLE 5.18. Presence of Acute Angles, Crushing, and Lipping on Sunshine Flakes of Different Platform Configurations and the Three Predominant Raw Materials

PLATFORM CONFIGURATION	COMPARISON	RAW MATERIAL			TOTAL
		CHERT	OBSIDIAN	FINE-GRAINED VOLCANICS	
Cortex Platform	Acute Angle, Lipping, and Crushing	1		2	3
	Acute Angle and Lipping	1		2	3
	Acute Angle and Crushing			1	1
	Lipping and Crushing				
	Acute Angle	6		2	8
	Lipping	1		1	2
	Crushing				
	None	5		9	14
	Subtotal	14	0	17	31
Single-Faceted Platform	Acute Angle, Lipping, and Crushing	34	15	38	87
	Acute Angle and Lipping	115	16	103	234
	Acute Angle and Crushing	5	2	8	15
	Lipping and Crushing	1		1	2
	Acute Angle	80	11	55	146
	Lipping	7		1	8
	Crushing	4	2	2	8
	None	50	3	28	81
	Subtotal	296	49	236	581
Multifaceted Platform	Acute Angle, Lipping, and Crushing	148	109	202	459
	Acute Angle and Lipping	250	55	276	581
	Acute Angle and Crushing	18	11	20	49
	Lipping and Crushing	4		1	5
	Acute Angle	35	7	35	77
	Lipping	5	2	6	13
	Crushing	6	7	4	17
	None	18	2	14	34
	Subtotal	484	193	558	1,235
Total		794	242	811	1,847

TABLE 5.19. Chi-Square Probabilities for Two-by-Two Comparisons of Flakes by the Three Predominant Raw Materials

PLATFORM CONFIGURATION	COMPARISON	RAW MATERIAL		
		CHERT	OBSIDIAN	FINE-GRAINED VOLCANICS
Cortex Platform	Acute Angle and Lipping	.707	—	**.036**
	Acute Angle and Crushing	.369	—	**.023**
	Lipping and Crushing	**.047**	—	.119
Single-Faceted Platform	Acute Angle and Lipping	**<.001**	**.002**	**<.001**
	Acute Angle and Crushing	.102	.953	.088
	Lipping and Crushing	**<.001**	.070	**.002**
Multifaceted Platform	Acute Angle and Lipping	**<.001**	**<.001**	**<.001**
	Acute Angle and Crushing	.453	.876	**.010**
	Lipping and Crushing	.301	.919	.100

Note: Significant values in bold.

TABLE 5.20. Biface Reduction Flakes by Raw Material in the Hamilton College Collection

	Raw Material							
	Chert		Obsidian		Fine-Grained Volcanics		Total	
Flake Type	*N*	%	*N*	%	*N*	%	*N*	%
Biface Reduction Flake	547	70.1	195	80.6	618	77.9	1,360	74.9
Non–Biface Reduction Flake	233	29.9	47	19.4	176	22.1	456	25.1
Total	780	100.0	242	100.0	794	100.0	1,816	100.0

reduction. It is doubtful, however, that they would have cortex platforms, and thus even though there are several significant results in the comparisons of attribute pairs, it is unlikely that any of these flakes came from a bifacial edge. We focus, then, on the other two platform configurations.

As can be seen from Table 5.19, the combination of acute angle and platform lipping is significant for all material types within both single- and multifaceted platforms. There are only two significant results for the lipping/crushing comparison (chert and FGV single-faceted platforms) and for the acute angle/crushing comparison (FGV multifaceted platforms). This suggests that crushing is most likely not highly characteristic of biface reduction in this assemblage and that acute angle and lipping are characteristic only in combination. Therefore, we consider only those flakes with single- or multiple-faceted platforms on which this combination occurs to be biface reduction flakes. In Table 5.18, for example, there are 34 chert flakes with single-faceted platforms on which all three attributes occur and 115 on which only acute angle and lipping occur; for chert flakes with multifaceted platforms, these numbers are 148 and 250, respectively. Therefore, there is a total of 547 chert biface reduction flakes. As Table 5.20 shows, biface reduction flakes represent 70.1 percent of chert flakes with platforms, as compared with 80.6 percent of obsidian and 77.9 percent of FGV flakes with platforms. These results certainly suggest that considerable biface reduction occurred at the Sunshine Locality.

We did not analyze the majority of the H–N debitage in detail because it does not constitute a representative sample. For a small number ($n = 74$) of flakes with platforms, however, we did note (using the above criteria) that 58 (78.4 percent) are biface reduction flakes (57 chert, one obsidian).

To guard against the possibility that focusing only on flakes with platforms may give a biased picture of reduction at Sunshine, we turn to another approach that considers all debitage. Patterson has shown that "bifacial reduction gives an exponential curve form for flake-size distribution, which seems to be unique to the bifacial reduction process" (1990:551). In other words, when flake frequencies are plotted against size, the resulting curve is characteristically concave downward, whereas that for general core reduction has an irregular form. Figure 5.4 shows flake-size distributions for all chert, obsidian, and FGV flakes; all three distributions conform to Patterson's model for biface reduction. This figure, however, includes not only complete flakes but those that are fragmentary as well. Figure 5.5 shows flake-size distributions only for complete chert, obsidian, and FGV flakes. As is evident, there is little difference in the curves in this figure compared with those in Figure 5.4. Therefore, we conclude that biface reduction was the dominant type of reduction in all three raw materials at the Sunshine Locality.

These data indicate that biface reduction *was* a primary activity at Sunshine, but as we noted earlier, the focus of this reduction appears to have been somewhat different from that at sites we have studied in Butte Valley (e.g., Beck and Jones 1990a, 1990b). Regarding these latter assemblages, 72.8 percent of the Butte Valley bifaces can be identified with the stemmed point reduction sequence, compared with only 47.9 percent of Sunshine bifaces. In addition, 44.7 percent are unclassifiable biface fragments, most of which we believe to be production bifaces as well. Only 25 (15 percent) of the 167 identifiable bifaces from the Butte Valley sites are tools other than production bifaces, including drills, crescents, bifacial scrapers, and preforms.

An examination of the biface reduction flakes from the Butte Valley sites shows that the percentage of chert flakes is similar to that at Sunshine, but the percentages of those made from FVG and obsidian are quite different, especially with respect to obsidian (Table 5.21). The obsidian data reflect the use of a local source of obsidian pebbles too small for the manufacture of stemmed points (Beck and Jones 1994; Jones and Beck 1990), but these flakes cannot be separated out at this point, as all the flakes represented in Table 5.21 have not been analyzed as to source.

The assemblage from another site, however, Limestone Peak Locality 1 (LPL1), located in Jakes Valley to the south of the Sunshine Locality, appears more similar to

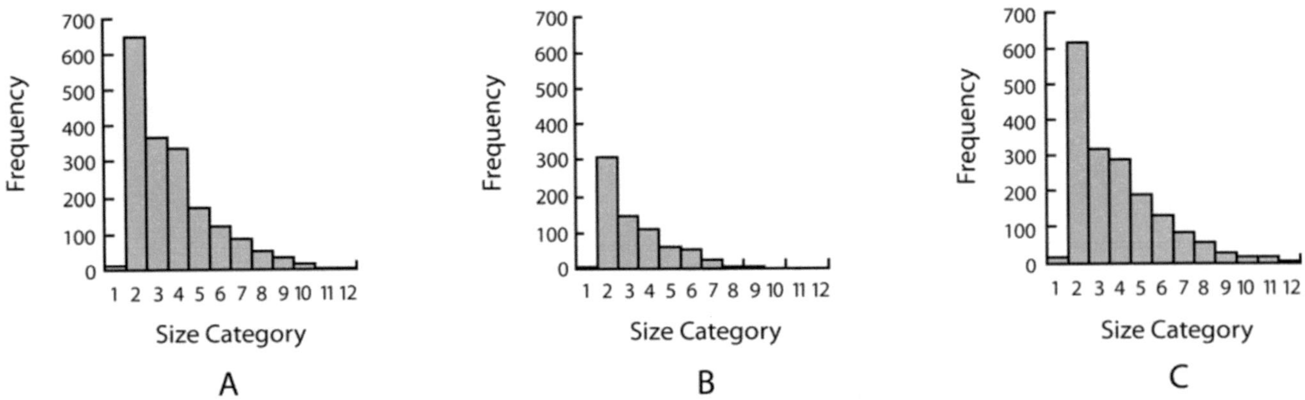

FIGURE 5.4. Histograms showing the distribution of all (A) chert, (B) obsidian, and (C) fine-grained volcanic flakes in the Hamilton College collection.

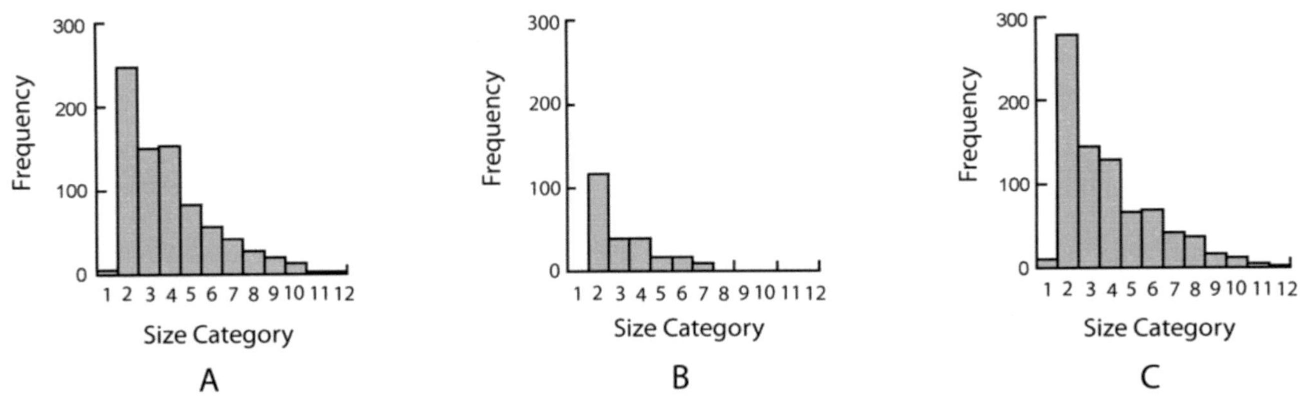

FIGURE 5.5. Histograms showing the distribution of only complete (A) chert, (B) obsidian, and (C) fine-grained volcanic flakes in the Hamilton College collection.

TABLE 5.21. Biface Reduction Flakes Represented in the Butte Valley and Jakes Valley Collections

		RAW MATERIAL									
		CHERT		OBSIDIAN		FINE-GRAINED VOLCANICS		OTHER		TOTAL	
SAMPLE	FLAKE TYPE[a]	*N*	%	*N*	%	*N*	%	*N*	%	*N*	%
Butte Valley	Biface Reduction Flake	890	74.3	306	46.0	1,698	88.6	7	63.6	2,901	76.5
	Non–Biface Reduction Flake	308	25.7	359	54.0	218	11.4	4	36.4	889	23.5
	Total	1,198	100.0	665	100.0	1,916	100.0	11	100.0	3,790	100.0
Jakes Valley	Biface Reduction Flake	599	71.1	76	85.4	837	88.9	1	100.0	1,513	80.7
	Non–Biface Reduction Flake	244	28.9	13	14.6	104	19.3			361	19.3
	Total	843	100.0	89	100.0	941	100.0	1	100.0	1,874	100.0

[a] Does not include flakes that could not be classified (n = 12,271 from Butte Valley sites, and n = 5,057 from the Jakes Valley site Limestone Peak Locality 1).

that at Sunshine. At LPL1, 233 of the 238 projectile points are Western Stemmed Tradition points that are made predominantly from FGV (60.1 percent) and obsidian (27.9 percent). Of the 236 bifaces, 142 (60.2 percent) of these are production bifaces; these artifacts are also made predominantly from FGV (n = 107, 75.4 percent), but 20.4 percent (n = 29) are made from chert, whereas only 4.3 percent (n = 6) are made from obsidian. The remaining 94 (39.8 percent) bifaces comprise tools such as scrapers, gravers, and crescents, as well as amorphous bifaces and unidentifiable biface fragments. Only 54.7 percent (n = 52) of these are made from FGV; whereas 31.6 percent (n = 30) are made from chert, and 13.7 percent (n = 13) are made from obsidian. Further, unlike the Butte Valley assemblages, LPL1 contains a large number of scrapers, most of which are manufactured from chert and some of which are bifacial. These data are much more similar to those from the Sunshine Locality than to the data from the Butte Valley sites. Finally, the proportions of biface reduction flakes by material, also shown in Table 5.21, come closer to those from Sunshine than those from the Butte Valley site assemblages. Consequently, we believe that biface reduction at the Sunshine Locality was directed at slightly different goals than those at the Butte Valley sites but may have been similar to biface reduction at LPL1. That is, biface reduction, especially in chert, was not carried out primarily for the manufacture of stemmed points but, rather, was focused toward more diverse end products. Further, at both Sunshine and LPL1, more production bifaces were manufactured from chert. Whether or not this reflects raw material availability or nodule size (see Jones and Beck 1999) is yet unknown.

A greater proportion of the reduction in obsidian and FGV toolstone at Sunshine, however, does seem to have been focused toward stemmed point manufacture or refurbishment. It appears that reduction was mid- to late stage, judging by the small proportion of cortex flakes represented (see below). As we have done elsewhere (e.g., Beck and Jones 1988, 1990b; Beck et al. 2002; Jones et al. 2003), we employ two measures of reduction stage in order to evaluate the reduction being carried out at Sunshine. The first is a traditional stage classification based on that devised by Callahan (1979; see Figure 5.3), and the second is a biface thinning index proposed by Johnson (1981). Traditional stage classifications can be problematic in that they segment what is believed to be a theoretical continuum (Teltser 1991:366). There is some indication, however, that there are sometimes empirical disjunctions in this continuum, especially as the knapper changes from hard to soft hammer percussion (see Pecora 2001), but these disjunctions do not necessarily occur at the same point in every case. The advantage of stage classifications is that they are based on multiple criteria, and

Table 5.22. Biface Reduction Stage Definitions

Stage	Definition
0	Overall plan (shape) is highly irregular and amorphous, few flake scars are present and are widely spaced, and offset (sinuosity of edge) is extremely wide or nonexistent.
1	Overall plan is irregular, flake scars are widely and/or variably shaped, and offset is wide.
2	Overall plan is semiregular and semisymmetrical, flake scars are somewhat closely and/or semiregularly spaced (pressure flaking may appear but is not common), and offset is moderate.
3	Finished point. Overall plan is regular and symmetrical, flake scars are closely and/or quite regularly spaced, and offset is close; lateral edge grinding is evident on the stem.

Source: After Callahan 1979.

thus assignment of an artifact to a stage is not based on a single variable. The Johnson Thinning Index has the advantage of measuring reduction along a continuum but is based on only two criteria: weight and plan area. These two independent approaches complement one another and act to limit bias that may be introduced by simply using one or the other.

We have revised the stage classification several times, most recently in our discussion of two Paleoarchaic quarries and associated residential sites (e.g., Beck et al. 2002). The stages are defined in Table 5.22. Table 5.23 shows the reduction stages represented by the Sunshine bifaces, separated by collection and raw material. Examples of each stage are shown in Figure 5.6. Examining the HC bifaces first, only eight can be assigned to reduction stage, but of these, six (80.0 percent) are stage 2, two (20.0 percent) are stage 1, and none is stage 0 (Table 5.23). This biface sample, admittedly, is extremely small. We can consider the production bifaces from the H–N assemblage, keeping in mind, however, that they do not represent a statistical sample and therefore the information may be somewhat biased. That is, when Hutchinson and Noyes were collecting they may have unconsciously focused on more finished-looking (and thus later-stage) bifaces, ignoring the "rougher-looking" objects. This said, as Table 5.23 shows, the majority of those that are identifiable as to stage (43 of 64, 67.72 percent) are stage 2, supporting the findings in the Hamilton assemblage.

The Johnson Thinning Index (JTI) is computed as weight divided by plan area. As a biface is thinned, its weight diminishes faster than its plan area, and therefore the index decreases as reduction proceeds. Table 5.24 shows the descriptive JTI statistics from two Paleoarchaic dacite quarries, Cowboy Rest Creek Quarry in

FIGURE 5.6. Production bifaces in the Sunshine assemblage. Stage 0: (A) 2766. Stage 1: (B) 2772; (C) 2771; (D) 2792; (E) 2778; (F) 2775. Stage 2: (G) 2773; (H) 2776; (I) 2779; (J) 2777; (K) 2774; (L) 2770; (M) SW95, 4E, 0N, Final Stratum E; (N) 2328.

TABLE 5.23. Reduction Stages Represented in the Hamilton College and Hutchinson–Noyes Collections

		RAW MATERIAL							
		CHERT		OBSIDIAN		FINE-GRAINED VOLCANICS		TOTAL	
COLLECTION	REDUCTION STAGE	*N*	%	*N*	%	*N*	%	*N*	%
Hamilton College[a]	0								
	1	1	50.0			1	5.6	2	20.0
	2	1	50.0	1	100.0	4	22.2	6	80.0
	Total	2		1		5		8	100.0
Hutchinson–Noyes[b]	0	1	5.3			1	2.2	2	3.1
	1	5	26.3			14	30.4	19	29.2
	2	13	68.4			30	67.4	43	67.7
	Total	19				45		64	100.0

Note: Does not include Stage 3, which is a finished point.
[a] Stage could not be determined for seven specimens.
[b] Stage could not be determined for four specimens.

Grass Valley and Little Smoky Quarry in Little Smoky Valley, and their associated residential sites, the Knudtsen site in Grass Valley and LPL1 in Jakes Valley (Beck et al. 2002). (JTI values for LPL1 are based only on the bifaces made from Little Smoky Quarry dacite. Although an additional 67 bifaces from LPL1 have been identified as production bifaces, JTI has not yet been computed for them.) This table also shows the descriptive JTI statistics for the Sunshine bifaces, both separated by collection and combined. The values for the H–N and HC collections are not significantly different ($t = -.643, df = 17.3, p = .528$), and thus the 83 cases can be considered as a single assemblage; the JTI distribution for the combined assemblage is shown in Figure 5.7. A comparison between the Sunshine values and those from the two quarries reveals that the mean for the Sunshine bifaces is much smaller than that for the quarry bifaces but slightly larger than those from Knudtsen and LPL1. *T*-tests confirm that the differences are significant between the Sunshine values and those from both quarries ($p < .001$ in both cases) as well as both residential sites ($p < .001$ for Knudtsen; $p = .049$ for LPL1). Beck et al. (2002) argue that reduction at Knudtsen and LPL1 is later in the continuum than at the two quarries. The JTI values for the Sunshine bifaces suggest that reduction at this site lies somewhere between the early-stage reduction at the quarries and the late-stage reduction at the residential sites.

A comparison of biface stages, however, suggests later reduction at Sunshine than at Knudtsen and LPL1 (Table 5.25). In this case, all LPL1 bifaces that could be assigned to stage ($n = 122$) are included. Although early-stage bifaces (stage 0) are few in all three assemblages, Knudtsen and LPL1 assemblages have much higher percentages of stage 1 than the Sunshine assemblage, in which 68.1 percent are stage 2. These data suggest that middle- to late-stage reduction predominated at Sunshine.

TABLE 5.24. Johnson Thinning Index Statistics for Two Paleoarchaic Quarries and Their Associated Residential Sites Compared with Those for the Hutchinson–Noyes and Hamilton College Collections

	STATISTIC			
SITE	*N*	RANGE	MEAN	SD
Cowboy Rest Creek Quarry	659	.15–27.86	2.97	2.25
Little Smoky Quarry	301	.14–11.02	2.23	1.28
Knudtsen Site	752	.29–8.39	1.25	.51
Limestone Peak Locality 1[a]	52	.51–3.61	1.38	.47
Sunshine Locality				
Hutchinson–Noyes	68	.87–2.85	1.54	.34
Hamilton College	15	.92–2.75	1.44	.47
Combined	83	.87–2.85	1.51	.36

Note: Values for Stage 3 (finished point) not included.
[a] Values are computed only for production bifaces manufactured from Little Smoky Quarry dacite (includes two Stage 3 points).

Biface reduction flake size at Sunshine tends to support late-stage reduction. First, biface reduction flakes overall are smaller than non-biface reduction flakes (Figure 5.8), although this difference is not significant, for either weight ($t = -.301, p = .082$) or size category ($\chi^2 = 12.821, p = .305$). Table 5.26 shows that nearly 70 percent of chert and FGV and over 80 percent of obsidian

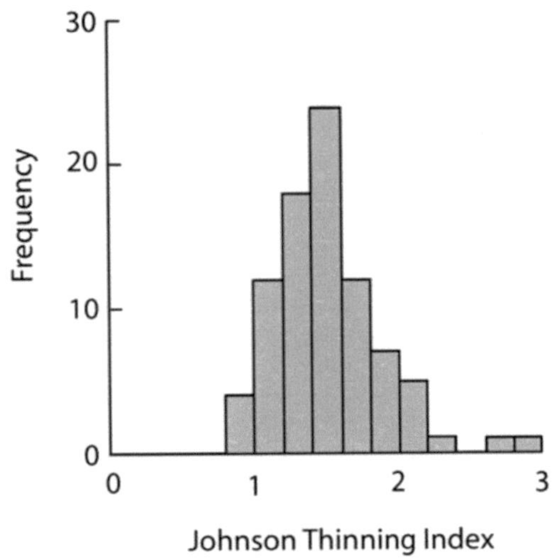

FIGURE 5.7. Distribution of Johnson Thinning Index values for the Sunshine bifaces.

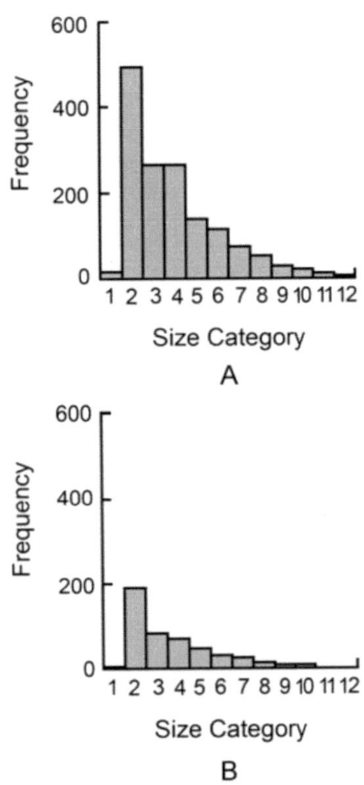

FIGURE 5.8. Histograms showing the distribution of (A) biface reduction flakes and (B) non–biface reduction flakes across size categories.

biface reduction flakes are of sizes 1–3. Of course, flake size is a function not only of reduction stage but also of original core size. The large majority of these flakes (86.1 percent), however, weigh .5 g or less, which is nearly twice the proportion of biface reduction flakes of this size in the Butte Valley assemblage (Beck and Jones 1990a). Further, an analysis of variance indicates that there is a significant difference in the average size of obsidian biface reduction flakes (mean weight = .09 g) and that of chert (mean weight = .34 g; p = .001) and FGV (mean weight = .35 g; p = .001) but no significant difference between the latter two (p = .996). This difference is consistent with our arguments elsewhere (e.g., Beck and Jones 1990b, 1993) that obsidian tools were brought into the study area as late-stage bifaces or finished points and the debitage is primarily the result of resharpening. However, given that the mean weights of chert and FGV biface reduction flakes are substantially smaller than those from the Butte Valley sample, where we have argued early- to middle-stage reduction in FGV toolstone, we believe that reduction in these materials at the Sunshine Locality is late stage and/or refurbishment as well.

The amount of cortex present on debitage also suggests late-stage reduction. Only 92 (1.8 percent) of the HC debitage specimens exhibit cortex, which is much lower than in the assemblages from Butte Valley (n = 1,178, 10.5 percent). This latter percentage, however, reflects the presence of the local obsidian source of small pebbles, mentioned above; eliminating obsidian flakes from consideration, the percentage is reduced to 7.3 percent (n = 622), still considerably higher than at Sunshine. The percentage of cortex flakes from LPL1 in Jakes Valley is more in line with the Butte Valley sites, at 6.1 percent (n = 384). These data suggest less early-stage reduction at Sunshine than at the Butte and Jakes valley sites.

Finally, an examination of the number of dorsal scars supports late-stage reduction. Table 5.27 shows the number of biface reduction flakes with one, two, three, or four or more flake scars present on the dorsal surface. The number of dorsal scars increases, on average, as reduction continues (Teltser 1991; Whittaker 1994). Table 5.27 shows that 64.1 percent of chert, 67.4 percent of obsidian, and 62.3 percent of FGV flakes exhibit three or more dorsal scars, strongly suggesting late-stage reduction.

In sum, biface reduction at the Sunshine Locality appears to have been directed at more diverse end products than at Paleoarchaic sites in Butte Valley and more in line with reduction at LPL1 in Jakes Valley. Further, chert was used for the manufacture of production bifaces more often than is typical for most central Great Basin Paleoarchaic assemblages. The manufacture of production bifaces was primarily late stage at Sunshine, as evidenced by both biface and biface reduction flake analyses.

TABLE 5.25. Biface Stages for Two Paleoarchaic Quarries and Their Associated Residential Sites Compared with Those for the Hutchinson–Noyes and Hamilton College Collections

	Stage						
	0		1		2		
Site	*N*	%	*N*	%	*N*	%	Total
Cowboy Rest Creek Quarry	164	24.9	360	54.7	134	20.4	658
Little Smoky Quarry	32	10.6	148	48.8	123	40.6	303
Knudtsen	12	1.6	413	54.8	329	43.6	754
Limestone Peak Locality 1[a]	3	5.8	31	59.6	18	34.6	52
	4	3.2	54	44.3	64	52.5	122
Sunshine Locality							
Hutchinson–Noyes	2	3.1	19	30.0	43	67.2	64
Hamilton College			2	20.0	6	80.0	8
Combined	2	2.8	21	29.2	49	68.1	72

Note: Does not include Stage 3, which is a finished point.
[a] First line shows only those production bifaces manufactured from Little Smoky Quarry dacite; second line shows all production bifaces.

TABLE 5.26. Size Categories of Biface Reduction Flakes by Raw Material in the Hamilton College Collection

	Raw Material						
	Chert		Obsidian		Fine-Grained Volcanics		
Size Category	*N*	%	*N*	%	*N*	%	Total
1	163	29.8	95	48.7	220	35.6	478
2	109	19.9	32	16.4	105	17.0	246
3	108	19.7	34	17.4	106	17.2	248
4	56	10.2	14	7.2	51	8.3	121
5	43	7.9	14	7.2	50	8.1	107
6	29	5.3	5	2.6	31	5.0	65
7	17	3.1	1	.5	30	4.9	48
8	12	2.2			14	2.3	26
9	7	1.3			7	1.1	14
10	2	.4			4	.6	6
11	1	.2					1
Total	547	100.0	195	100.0	618	100.0	1,360

TABLE 5.27. Dorsal Scar Counts by Raw Material for Complete Flakes in the Hamilton College Collection

	Raw Material										
	Chert		Obsidian		Fine-Grained Volcanics		Quartzite		Other		
Number of Scars	*N*	%	*N*	%	*N*	%	*N*	%	*N*	%	Total
0			1	.1	3	.1			1	1.7	5
1	86	13.2	16	12.4	72	13.8			10	17.2	184
2	147	22.5	25	19.4	122	23.3			15	25.9	309
3	106	16.2	22	17.1	151	28.9			13	22.4	292
≥4	313	47.9	65	50.4	175	33.5	1	100.0	19	32.8	573
Indeterminate	1	<.01									
Total	653	100.0	129	100.0	523	100.0	1	100.0	58	100.0	1,364

FIGURE 5.9. Examples of concave base point preforms in the Sunshine assemblage: (A) 2130; (B) 2129; (C) 1830; (D) surface 1993, FS 4.

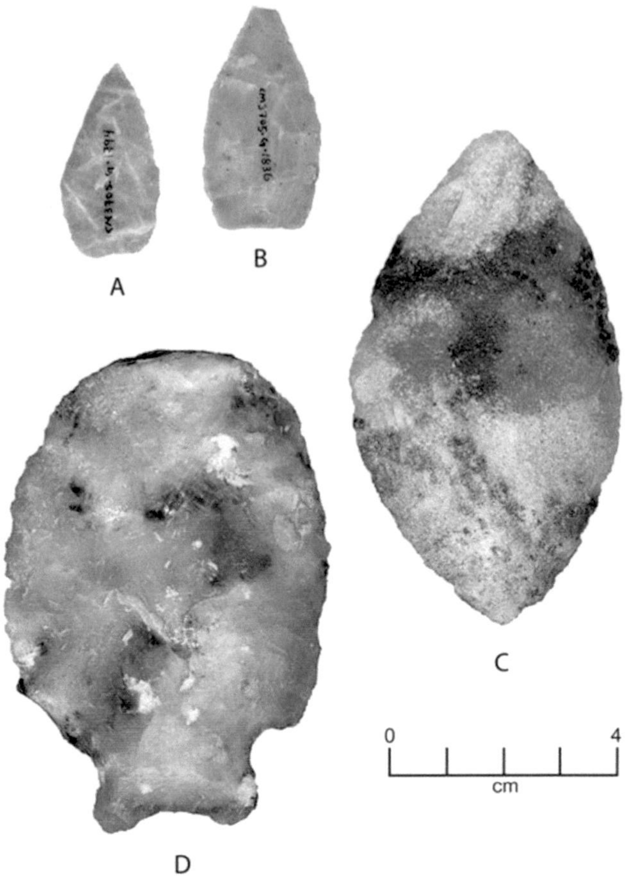

FIGURE 5.10. Unique bifaces in the Sunshine assemblage: (A) 1794; (B) 1836; (C) 1889; (D) 1887.

Concave Base Preforms. The H–N collection contains four concave base preforms, all manufactured from chert (Figure 5.9). One (Figure 5.9B) exhibits broad collateral flaking on both faces, whereas the other three have broad collateral flaking on one face and parallel oblique flaking on the other (see Figure 6.5 for flaking types). Use-wear could not be determined for any of these artifacts because all are missing the blade sections. None is ground on the lateral edges or in the basal concavity (see also Figure 2.5). Figure 5.9D is a fluted preform that still retains the fluting platform in the basal concavity (see also Figure 2.5). This artifact is discussed in more detail in chapter 6. Table 5.28 shows the quantitative data for these artifacts.

Unique Bifaces. The H–N collection contains four artifacts we have called "unique bifaces" because they fit into no other category (Figure 5.10). All are made from chert. These specimens exhibit quite different shapes, but three share abraded blade edges. Specimen 1794 (Figure 5.10A) is so heavily abraded on one side that it is almost polished, and the object has been rendered asymmetrical. Specimen 1836 is almost a carbon copy of 1794 but is not abraded in the same way. Neither exhibits lateral edge grinding. Figure 5.10D has a fashioned haft element, but the lateral and basal edges are not ground. The quantitative data for these three artifacts are also shown in Table 5.28.

Amorphous Bifaces. Amorphous bifaces are those that are irregularly shaped and cannot be identified with any other biface category. There are 166 of these tools in the Sunshine assemblage, 149 from the H–N collection and 17 from the HC collection (Figure 5.11). The majority (n = 119) of those from the H–N collection, however, are in the general collection and were not subjected to special analysis; thus discussion will focus on the 17 HC bifaces and the 30 H–N bifaces available for detailed analysis.

The majority of these tools are manufactured from chert, but as Table 5.29 shows, the proportion is quite different between the two collections. This suggests that Hutchinson and Noyes were biased toward the collection

TABLE 5.28. Quantitative Data for the Sunshine Concave Base and Ovate Preforms and Unique Bifaces

TYPE	PROVENIENCE	MAXIMUM LENGTH (mm)	MAXIMUM WIDTH (mm)	MAXIMUM THICKNESS (mm)	ACTUAL WEIGHT (g)
Concave Base Preforms	2129	—	38.8	7.4	16.84
	2130	—	35.6	5.5	7.41
	1830	—	28.6	6.8	—
	Surface 1993, FS4	—	29.1	6.7	7.23
Unique Bifaces	1794	34.5	17.7	5.7	3.02
	1836	39.8	21.2	4.5	—
	1889	87.0	48.7	9.3	39.82
	1887	—	58.1	8.1	52.80

of chert, but sampling uncertainty precludes evaluation of this difference. Use-wear was indeterminate for 26 specimens; of the worn bifaces, 10 show abrasion, five show crushing, one shows both, and five show none. Table 5.30 provides the descriptive statistics for amorphous bifaces by collection.

Crescents

Probably the most enigmatic tools found in Paleoarchaic assemblages are crescents. These tools are most often bifacially flaked, but they also occur in the form of unifacially retouched flakes. They range widely in size, are almost always made from chert (Amick 1995a, 1998), and are most often ground along the medial segment of the lateral edges.

Crescents are found almost exclusively in the Great Basin but have been occasionally found outside that province as well. A single crescent, for instance, was found in the Fenn cache, which is believed to have been discovered "somewhere in the three corners area where Utah, Wyoming, and Idaho meet" (Frison and Bradley 1999:22). Daugherty (1956; see also Craven 2003:45) recovered three crescents from the Lind Coulee site in north-central Washington, 11 crescents were found by Harrington (1948:94) at the Borax Lake site in north-central California, and at least seven of these tools were collected from the surface of the Witt site in the San Joaquin Valley of California (Riddell and Olsen 1969; Wallace and Riddell 1988). Far to the south, a single crescent was found in the San Dieguito component at the C. W. Harris site, which lies only several miles inland from the Pacific Ocean (Rogers 1939; Warren and True 1961). But these occurrences are rare, and for the most part, crescents are associated with Paleoarchaic assemblages from the Great Basin. They do not, however, occur in all, or even most, of these assemblages. In fact, crescents are found in large numbers only in a few areas within the Great Basin, such as the Black Rock Desert (Amick 1998, 1999; Clewlow 1968a), Coyote

FIGURE 5.11. Amorphous bifaces in the Sunshine assemblage. None has provenience.

TABLE 5.29. Amorphous Bifaces by Raw Material in the Hutchinson–Noyes and Hamilton College Collections

	Raw Material								
	Chert		Obsidian		Fine-Grained Volcanics		Quartzite		
Collection	*N*	%	*N*	%	*N*	%	*N*	%	Total
Hutchinson–Noyes	135	90.6	5	3.4	8	5.4	1	.7	149
Hamilton College	9	52.9	3	17.6	5	29.4	—	—	17
Total	144	86.7	8	4.8	13	7.8	1	.6	166

TABLE 5.30. Quantitative Data for the Sunshine Amorphous Bifaces

Collection	Statistic	Total Length (mm)	Maximum Width (mm)	Maximum Thickness (mm)	Actual Weight (g)
Hutchinson–Noyes	*N*	6	6	30	30
	Range	48.20–68.50	24.80–41.50	2.30–17.80	.62–37.76
	Mean	55.37	32.73	10.92	15.58
	SD	7.1	5.75	3.54	8.86
Hamilton College	*N*	1	1	7	17
	Range	44.50	28.30	4.90–14.70	.07–28.36
	Mean	—	—	10.43	7.83
	SD	—	—	3.87	8.35

Flat (Butler 1970), and the Alvord Desert (Pettigrew 1984) in the northern Great Basin and in the southern Mojave Desert near Pleistocene Lakes Mojave (Amsden 1935) and China (Davis 1978a) and in the vicinity of Pleistocene Lake Tonopah (Phil Hutchinson, personal communication 1995; Pendleton 1979). They are notably rare, however, at the Nevada Test Site in the southern part of the state (Amick 1993; Haynes 1996) and at Fort Irwin in the northern Mojave Desert (Basgall 1993a, 1993b; Basgall and Hall 1993; Hall 1993; Warren 1990), where numerous stemmed, and some fluted, points are prevalent. At the Dietz site in central Oregon, where one of the largest assemblages of fluted and stemmed points has been collected, only five crescents have been recovered (Willig 1988:439). This makes the Sunshine assemblage all the more remarkable, as it contains 245 of these artifacts.

The assemblages in which large numbers of crescents occur also contain substantial numbers of both fluted and stemmed points, and thus the specific dating of crescents remains unclear. Although they are generally believed to be associated with stemmed points (e.g., Fagan 1988:404; Grayson 1993:238–239; Willig 1988:439), the occurrence of crescents in the Fenn cache and in the same subsurface context as a fluted point at the Sunshine Locality (see chapter 3) suggests that they may have been associated with fluted points as well. Of course, the relative timing of fluted and stemmed points also remains problematic, which we address in the concluding chapter.

Speculation as to the purpose of crescents has been ongoing since the early part of the twentieth century (e.g., Wardle 1913), but their function(s) continues to elude us. Davis states that crescents occur "*only in one context*: proximity to water, particularly lakes and marshes" (1978a:57; emphasis in the original). If this is, in fact, the case, then this association would explain the lack of crescents in some areas but not necessarily in others. For example, in Butte Valley, where we have located and collected nearly 13,000 artifacts from site and off-site contexts, only three crescents have been found. Yet most of the Paleoarchaic sites in this valley are adjacent to what would have been extensive marshes. Thus, the function of crescents, which may have been in an activity that was performed adjacent to lakes and marshes, was not performed in all of these contexts where Paleoarchaic foragers camped.

The first systematic study of crescents was published by Tadlock in 1966, in which he defines three different types based on morphology (Figure 5.12). This publication has been used for years as the "definitive" study of crescents. If a specimen does not fit into one of Tadlock's three types, then it is considered an "aberrant" form (e.g., Beck and Jones 1997:205; Davis 1978a:61; Riddell and Olsen 1969:126). As pointed out in chapter 2, however,

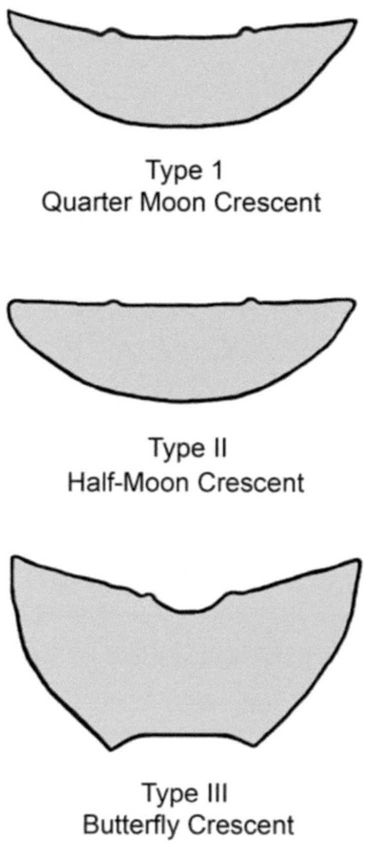

FIGURE 5.12. Three types of crescents defined by Tadlock (1966:663, Figure 1).

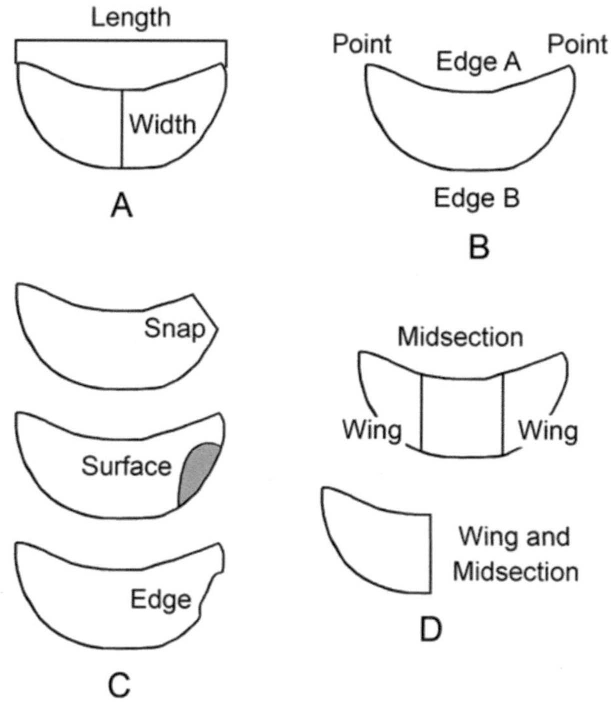

FIGURE 5.13. Protocol for Sunshine crescent analysis: (A) length and width measurements; (B) location of edge grinding; (C) breakage type; (D) portion represented.

Tadlock based his analysis on a sample of only 29 artifacts from the Long Valley playa. Since that time thousands of crescents have been collected and examined. In a paper presented at the 1998 Great Basin Anthropological Conference in Bend, Oregon, for example, Amick reported on the analysis results of 563 crescents from the Black Rock Desert in northwestern Nevada, all of which are in private collections (see also Amick 1999). This study, which is of the largest sample to date, indicates that crescents are considerably more variable along a number of formal and technological dimensions than Tadlock's initial study suggests. Amick (1999:162–164) argues, and we agree, that the traditional formal analysis of crescents is limited and yields no information concerning the use of these objects; only through analysis of such variables as use-wear, breakage, and resharpening patterns are we likely to shed light on this question. In our analysis of the Sunshine crescents, therefore, we focused on these as well as a number of other technological variables.

Several metric attributes were measured, including length, width at the midsection (see Figure 5.13A), thickness, and actual weight. Type of raw material and size category were measured as previously described for the general artifact analysis. Cortex and haft wear (e.g., arris abrasion) were recorded as present or absent. Edge grinding was recorded for both concave and convex edges (Figure 5.13B) as "none," "light," "medium," or "heavy." Use-wear, resharpening, and breakage were recorded as indicated in Table 5.31. Breakage types are shown in Figure 5.13C. Use-wear and resharpening locations were recorded as indicated in Figure 5.13B. The fragment represented (that is, whether it is complete or partial) was recorded as indicated in Figure 5.13D and Table 5.31. Flaking pattern was determined as shown in Figure 5.14.

A total of 218 crescents and crescent fragments were analyzed from the H–N collection, a small sample of which are shown in Figure 5.15. We also analyzed 16 crescents that were collected by York. Six crescents were collected by the Hamilton College field project, five from the surface in 1995 and one from the 1995 loader trench excavation. The latter artifact was collected during wall cleaning and is associated with Unit E (see chapter 3). As noted above, a fluted point was also found in the Loader Trench Unit E. Finally, five crescents were collected in 2004 (see note 3). In total, then, 245 crescents from the Sunshine Locality have been analyzed, and these are considered together below in the discussion of results.

TABLE 5.31. Analytic Protocol for the Sunshine Crescents

VARIABLE	ALTERNATIVE STATES
Fragment (Figure 5.13D)	1. Complete/Nearly Complete 2. Midsection 3. Wing 4. Midsection + Wing 5. Half Midsection + Wing 6. Resharpened into Another Tool
Burin Fracture	1. Present, One Wing 2. Present, Both Wings 3. Present, Edge A Adjacent to Point 4. Present, Edge B Adjacent to Point 5. Absent 6. Indeterminate
Bending Fracture	1. Present, Midsection 2. Present, One Wing 3. Present, Both Wings 4. Present, Midsection and One Wing 5. Present, Midsection and Both Wings 6. Absent 7. Indeterminate
Other Breaks (Figure 5.13C)	1. Snap on Tip of Wing 2. Surface 3. Edge 4. Combination of 1, 2, and/or 3 5. None 6. Indeterminate
Use-Wear	1. Crushing/Stacked Microfractures 2. Abrasion on High Points of Edge 3. Abrasion on Arris + 1 and/or 2 4. Crushing and Abrasion 5. None
Location of Wear (cont.)	1. None 2. One Point 3. Both Points 4. Edge A 5. Edge B 6. Both Edges 7. One Point + Edge A 8. One Point + Edge B 9. One Point + Both Edges 10. Both Points + Edge A 11. Both Points + Edge B 12. Both Points + Both Edges 13. Resharpened and Worn as Another Tool 14. Indeterminate
Location of Resharpening (Figure 5.13B)	1. None 2. One Point 3. Both Points 4. Edge A 5. Edge B 6. Both Edges 7. One Point + Edge A 8. One Point + Edge B 9. One Point + Both Edges 10. Both Points + Edge A 11. Both Points + Edge B 12. Both Points + Both Edges 13. Resharpened into Another Tool 14. Indeterminate

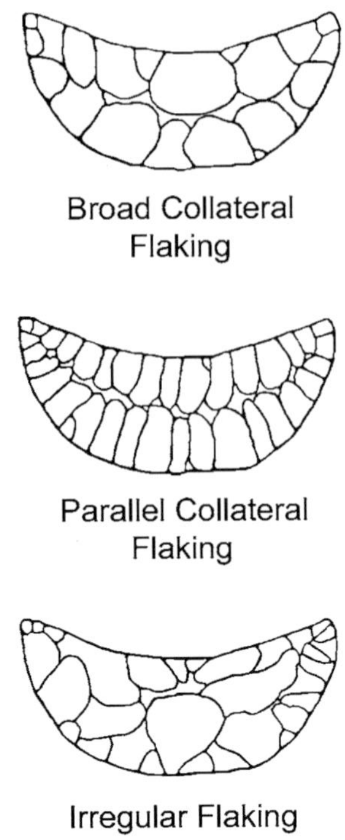

FIGURE 5.14. Flaking patterns recorded for the Sunshine crescents.

In his 1998 paper, Amick states that 92 percent of the 563 Black Rock crescents are made from cherts and chalcedonies. We have previously noted the preference for chert when manufacturing these artifacts (Beck and Jones 1990b; see also Amick 1998, 1999), using data from Coyote Flat (Butler 1970), the Black Rock Desert (Clewlow 1968a), and Steens Mountain (Beck 1984; Jones 1984), all in the northern Great Basin. This trend, however, is prevalent in the Sunshine crescents as well; 94.3 percent of these artifacts are manufactured from chert (Table 5.32).

Nearly all of the Sunshine crescents are bifacially flaked (i.e., exhibit complete bifacial shaping), but 37 (15.1 percent) are made on what Amick (1998) refers to as edged flakes or flake blanks. Some of these are simply flakes with retouched edges, whereas others exhibit slightly more unifacial or bifacial shaping. In the Black Rock sample, Amick (1998) found that crescents made on flake blanks were, on the average, smaller than crescents that were completely bifacial. This appears to be the case for the Sunshine crescents as well. Table 5.33 shows the distribution across size categories of all complete/nearly complete bifacial specimens ($n = 61$) and those made on flake blanks ($n = 17$). In both cases the range of size categories is the same (with the exception of a single bifacial specimen in category 11), but about 21 percent of bifacial specimens are in the smallest two size categories (7 and

Table 5.32. Raw Material Represented in the Sunshine Crescents

Raw Material	N	%
Chert	231	94.3
Obsidian	7	2.9
Fine-Grained Volcanics	6	2.3
Quartzite	1	.4
Total	245	100.0

Table 5.33. Distribution of Complete Sunshine Bifacial and Unifacial Crescents Across Size Categories

Size Category	Bifacial Crescents		Crescents on Flake Blanks	
	N	%	N	%
7	4	6.6	3	17.6
8	9	14.8	5	29.4
9	29	47.5	8	47.1
10	18	29.5	1	5.9
11	1	1.6		
Total	61	100.0	17	100.0

Table 5.34. Quantitative Data for the Sunshine Crescents by Facial Flaking

Crescent Type	Statistic	Total Length (mm)	Maximum Width (mm)	Maximum Thickness (mm)	Actual Weight (g)
Bifacial	N	56	159	206	206
	Range	33.60–67.50	9.30–30.60	3.40–18.0	.71–21.01
	Mean	44.12	16.30	5.97	4.15
	SD	6.86	3.63	1.57	2.43
Flake Blank	N	18	30	36	37
	Range	29.30–62.00	9.90–26.50	2.60–9.00	.76–13.95
	Mean	40.64	14.21	4.91	3.16
	SD	9.14	3.32	1.31	2.31

8), whereas 47 percent of the crescents on flake blanks are of those sizes. It is difficult to draw a conclusion from this difference, however, given the small number of crescents made on flake blanks.

Although there is a range in size categories, the majority of specimens are in categories 9 and 10. There is a wide distribution in length, whereas the distributions are tighter for width and thickness (Table 5.34).

Many uses have been suggested for crescents, namely, as surgical instruments (Amsden 1937:51; Wardle 1913:656), cutting implements (Cressman et al. 1942; Daugherty 1956; Davis 1978a:61; Gifford and Schenck 1926), ornaments or amulets (Davis 1978a:61; Warren 1967), and "composite tools used by women for scraping, pealing, trimming, incising, gouging, and sawing" (Davis 1978a:61–62). Probably the most prevalent suggestion is that crescents were hafted transversely (as shown in Figure 5.16B) and used as weapons for waterside hunting of large birds (Clewlow 1968a; Davis 1973, 1978a; Tadlock 1966). Davis has argued that

> if the projectile hypothesis is correct, then a haft (a foreshaft or handle), was lashed into the deeper concavity, and the missile was launched at a swimming goose, let us say, with the two wings pointed backward. In this position, the wings would allow this unique projectile to glance or skip should it touch the water before striking the bird [1978a:60].

Amick (1999:164) suggests that some of the use-wear, resharpening, and breakage patterns he has observed are consistent with a transversely hafted projectile (but more likely as depicted in Figure 16C because the burin breaks extend from the point down Edge B). For example, he states that "use-damage on finished crescents commonly involves bending breaks or burination of the tips," which is "consistent with the wear and damage expected from transverse hafting and projectile impact, as well as cutting and slotting activities" (1999:164). On the other hand, Amick also observes that other of the manufacturing, resharpening, and breakage patterns, such as burin fractures on the tips, resharpening of the tips into sharp projections, and bending fractures, are consistent with handheld or possibly longitudinally hafted tools (Figure 5.16A) used for cutting, slotting, and wedging of soft (e.g., animal hides and flesh, plant fiber) as well as hard material. Our results are similarly ambiguous.

The most convincing evidence of hafting is the fact that the inner and outer margins of crescents (Edges A and B) most often exhibit edge grinding. As Table 5.35

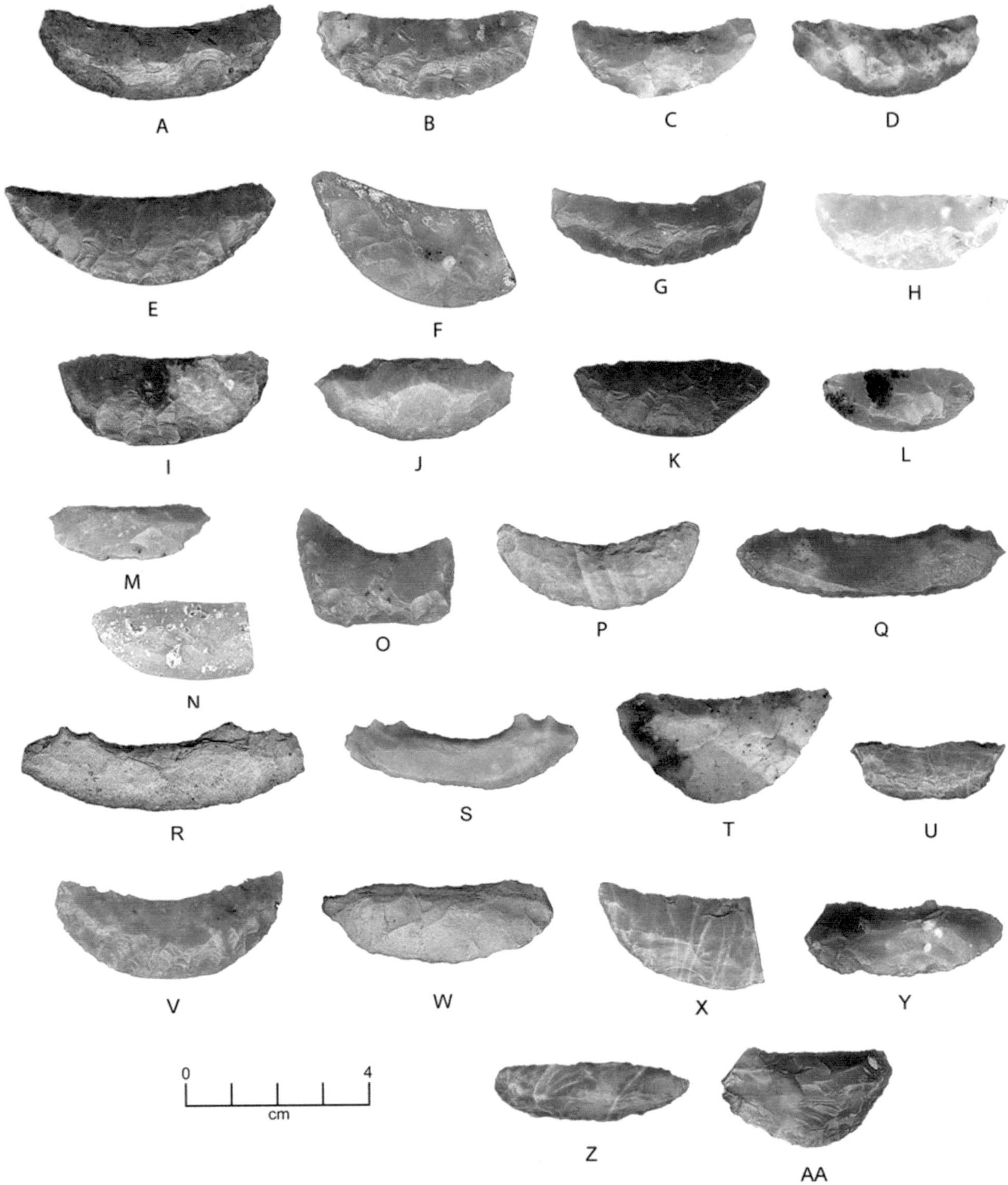

FIGURE 5.15. Examples of crescents from the Sunshine Locality: (A) 2471; (B) 2478; (C) 2463; (D) 2517; (E) 2475; (F) 2512; (G) 2468; (H) 2484; (I) 2488; (J) 2510; (K) 2511; (L) 2554; (M) 2513; (N) 2533; (O) 2508; (P) 3536; (Q) 2477; (R) 2469; (S) 2467; (T) 2532; (U) 2518; (V) 3535; (W) 2473; (X) 2534; (Y) 2515; (Z) SW93-1; (AA) 2523.

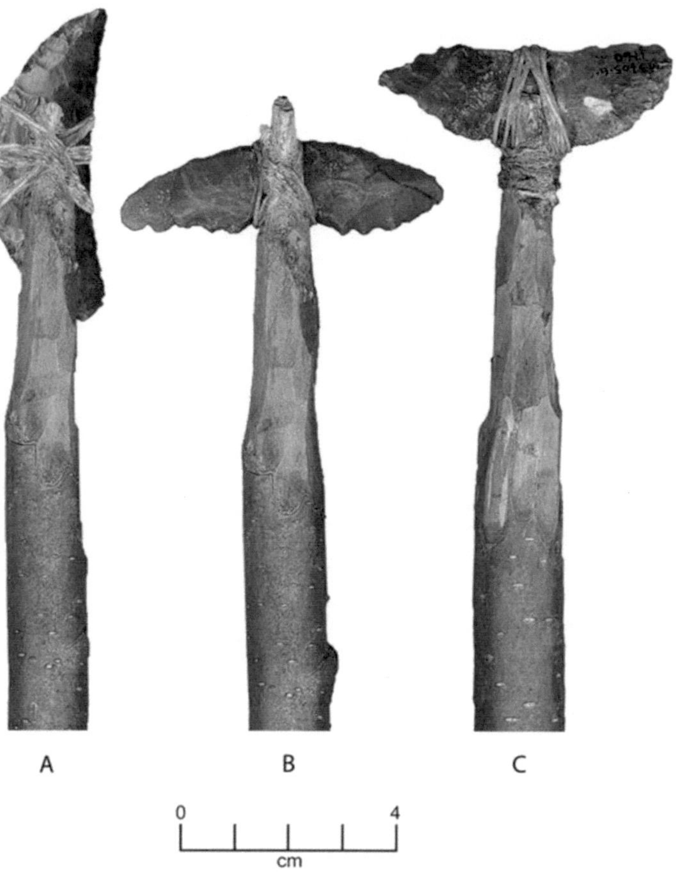

FIGURE 5.16. Possible hafting modes of crescents: (A) a composite created for our discussion of hafting; (B–C) Sunshine crescents that were hafted by Phil Hutchinson.

TABLE 5.35. Edge Grinding on Individual Edges of the Sunshine Crescents

	EDGE A		EDGE B	
EDGE GRINDING	*N*	%	*N*	%
None	51	20.8	47	19.2
Light	33	13.5	28	11.4
Medium	53	21.6	43	17.6
Heavy	78	31.8	95	38.8
Indeterminate	30	12.2	32	13.1
Total	245	100.0	245	100.0

TABLE 5.36. Edge Grinding on Both Edges of the Sunshine Crescents

EDGE A	EDGE B	*N*	%
Not Ground	Not Ground	37	15.1
Not Ground	Ground	15	6.1
Ground	Not Ground	10	4.1
Ground	Ground	145	59.2
Ground	Indeterminate	1	.4
Indeterminate	Indeterminate	37	15.1
Total		245	100.0

shows, approximately 21 percent of the Sunshine crescents have no grinding on the concave edge (Edge A), and 19 percent show no grinding on the convex edge (Edge B). If the specimens for which edge grinding could not be determined are excluded, then 75.7 percent of the Sunshine crescents exhibit grinding on Edge A, and 77.9 percent exhibit grinding on Edge B. As Table 5.36 shows, however, only 37 specimens exhibit no grinding on either edge. Again, excluding those for which grinding could not be determined, 82.2 percent of the Sunshine crescents show grinding on at least one edge, supporting the suggestion that these tools were hafted. In contrast, however, only a *single* specimen shows any arris abrasion on the surface of the midsection. This suggests that either these tools were not hafted or, if they were, the pressure they experienced in the haft during use was not great enough to cause abrasive damage to the crescent surface.

Of the 37 specimens without edge grinding, 26 are fragmentary and may have broken during manufacture. Eighteen of these fragments exhibit a single bending fracture, supporting this suggestion; the remaining eight, however, exhibit either burin fractures or other types of breaks (such as surface impacts or snapped tips) in addition to bending fractures, suggesting they broke during use. If this is the case, they were likely not hafted. Seventy of the 78 complete/nearly complete specimens have no breaks, but the remaining eight exhibit combinations of burin, bending, and other types of breaks on the wings or tips, again suggesting breakage during use. Together, these data support hafting but suggest that some crescents may have been handheld.

Of the 194 crescents for which the presence of use-wear could be determined, 143 are worn. Table 5.37 shows the locations of wear on these tools. The location of use-wear, however, is, in part, a function of breakage. If a specimen consists only of a midsection and wing, use-wear can only be observed on that midsection and wing. Therefore, Table 5.37 also shows the location of use-wear on only complete/nearly complete specimens. Because of the difference in use-wear patterns, we consider only the complete specimens in our discussion.

Of the 78 complete specimens, the presence of use-wear could be evaluated for 66; 48 (72.7 percent) are worn. The majority of these ($n = 32$, 66.7 percent) are worn only on the points. An additional 12 (25.0 percent) are worn on at least one point and one or both edges. Only four

TABLE 5.37. Location of Use-Wear on the Sunshine Crescents

LOCATION OF USE-WEAR	ALL CRESCENTS		COMPLETE CRESCENTS ONLY	
	N	%	*N*	%
None	51	20.8	18	23.1
One Point	73	29.8	21	26.9
Both Points	14	5.7	11	14.1
Edge A	3	1.2	1	1.3
Edge B	7	2.9	3	3.8
Both Edges	1	.4		
One Point + Edge A	5	2.0	1	1.3
One Point + Edge B	26	10.6	5	6.4
One Point + Both Edges	7	2.9	3	3.8
Both Points + Edge A	2	.8	1	1.3
Both Points + Edge B	2	.8		
Both Points + Both Edges	3	1.2	2	2.6
Indeterminate	51	20.8	12	15.4
Total	245	100.0	78	100.0

TABLE 5.38. Location of Resharpening on the Sunshine Crescents

LOCATION OF RESHARPENING	ALL CRESCENTS		COMPLETE CRESCENTS ONLY	
	N	%	*N*	%
None	148	60.4	31	39.7
One Point	29	11.8	13	16.7
Both Points	8	3.3	8	10.3
Edge A	7	2.9	3	3.8
Edge B	15	6.1	6	7.7
Both Edges	1	.4		
One Point + Edge A	7	2.9	5	6.4
One Point + Edge B	8	3.3	3	3.8
Both Points + Edge B	3	1.2	3	3.8
Both Points + Both Edges	7	2.9	3	3.8
Resharpened into Another Tool	2	.8	1	1.3
Indeterminate	10	4.1	2	2.6
Total	245	100.0	78	100.0

artifacts (8.7 percent) are worn only on an edge. Therefore, it appears that whatever the function of these artifacts, it had to do with the points rather than the edges. Resharpening and breakage patterns are consistent with the use-wear results (Table 5.38). Also once again, the patterns for complete specimens differ from those of the entire assemblage, and thus we focus on the results for the latter. Nearly 40 percent ($n = 31$) of complete/nearly complete specimens exhibit no resharpening; but among those that do, all but nine are resharpened on at least one point, supporting the suggestion that the points were the focus of use. Amick's (1998) data indicate that 40 percent of bifacial crescents show resharpening, whereas only 20 percent of those made on flake blanks are resharpened. Our data show no significant difference in these two types of crescents with respect to resharpening ($\chi^2 = 13.175$, $df = 12$, $p = .356$), but they do with respect to use-wear ($\chi^2 = 10.737$, $df = 5$, $p = .057$).

Interestingly, the points of a number of these tools have been refashioned into gravers (see, e.g., Figure 5.15B, D, J, M, Q) and in two cases, into beaked scraper bits (see below). In addition, (graver?) points have been fashioned along Edge A (Figure 5.15Q–S), or this edge is serrated (Figure 5.15I), usually near one or both points. For some specimens, such as those in Figure 5.15Q–S, this appears to have been done during the manufacturing process, whereas for others, it seems to be the product of resharpening. The high points of the projections are either broken or abraded. We have called these specimens crescent/gravers and include them in the graver section below.

Although the data indicate that the crescent points were heavily used and resharpened, whether these tools were handheld or hafted is unclear. Breakage patterns, however, support the former more than the latter. Table 5.39 shows the fragments represented in the crescent assemblage (see Figure 5.13D). As this table shows, breakage is more often between the wing and midsection than at the center of the midsection. That is, the fragments of single wing, midsection, and midsection and wing all show this breakage pattern. Only 61 (24.9 percent) were broken in half. This pattern supports hafting in which bending forces are concentrated at the edge of the haft rather than inside it.

All but seven of these fragments exhibit bending breaks. In addition, 68 (28.5 percent) of the 239 specimens that exhibit point breakage show burin breaks on at least one point. Four specimens have burin breaks on Edge A adjacent to the point: there are none with burin breaks on Edge B adjacent to the point. Finally, 106 (43.3 percent) specimens have other types of breaks, such as snapped tips and/or surface or edge impact fractures. The overall breakage patterns contrast in some ways with Amick's (1998) assemblage but are similar in others. For instance, 80 percent of the 563 specimens he examined are complete, but this is true for just over 30 percent of the Sunshine crescents. On the other hand, about 30 percent exhibit bending fractures, and about 25 percent show burin breaks on at least one point, similar to the percentages in the Sunshine assemblage.

In summary, the Sunshine crescents are manufactured

TABLE 5.39. Fragments Represented in the Sunshine Crescents

FRAGMENT	*N*	%
Complete/Nearly Complete	78	31.8
Midsection + Wing	28	11.4
Midsection Only	12	4.9
Wing Only	65	26.5
Half of Midsection + Wing	61	24.9
Resharpened into Another Tool	1	.4
Total	245	100.0

Note: See Figure 5.13D.

almost exclusively from chert, which is a pattern that has been observed elsewhere. Further, use-wear, resharpening, and breakage patterns suggest that the points of these artifacts constituted the tool. Breakage patterns also suggest they were hafted. These patterns overall, however, are more consistent with hafting exhibited in Figure 5.16A or 5.16C rather than Figure 5.16B. If Davis and others are correct in hypothesizing that these tools were used to stun birds (hafted as in Figure 5.16B), it is hard to imagine how the points would have been damaged in the way they are, especially by burin fractures that appear to originate at the point and extend down Edge B. We might even ask, Why the points at all? Our data are more consistent with the use of these points in cutting activities.

The grinding evident on the lateral edges of the midsections of these tools is consistent with hafting as suggested in Figure 5.16B or 5.16C. This grinding may not, however, have been done to dull the edges but, rather, to strengthen them, as argued by Woods and Titmus (1985) for fluted points. This would also argue against Davis's suggestion and in support of the use of these tools whereby considerable pressure resulted at the midsection or between the midsection and the wings.

Crescents may not have been the most efficient means of accomplishing the task at hand. If hafted sideways (as in Figure 5.16A), the shape of the tool would cause "work" to focus at the point of bending, reducing the effectiveness of the tool. A more efficient means of hafting, of course, would be notching, which we do not see in the Great Basin until ca. 8500–8000 rcy BP. Crescents, though, seem to disappear at this time, and thus perhaps they were replaced by a more efficient notched tool.

Scrapers

Scrapers are defined by Gramly as flaked-stone tools "often made on a flake or blade, having bold unifacial retouch on one or more margins" (1990:49). A total of 659 of these tools have been identified from Sunshine, 631 from the H–N collection and 28 from the Hamilton collection. Nearly a quarter (n = 156, 23.7 percent) of these scrapers occur as combination tools, such as scraper/gravers and scraper/notches (see Tables 5.12–5.13). Of the 631 scrapers from the H–N collection, 385 were subjected to special analyses.

Several quantitative measurements were taken on each specimen, including length, width, maximum thickness, and weight. In addition, several qualitative variables were recorded, including raw material, the type of blank on which the scraper was made (biface reduction flake, non–biface reduction flake, indeterminate flake, or indeterminate), and the presence or absence of cortex. Overall shape was recorded as shown in Figure 5.17A.

The question of whether scrapers were hafted is often raised. Upon reviewing the ethnographic evidence regarding end scrapers, for example, Shott states that these tools were likely most often hafted, "and some effort invested in their modification probably was intended to facilitate hafting" (1995:58). Such prehafting modification might involve trimming the distal end with lateral retouch (Gallagher 1977; Hayden 1979) or thinning the proximal end (Clark 1958:149). Once it is placed in the haft, the force exerted often leaves behind evidence in the form of arris abrasion or polish, which sometimes extends two-thirds of the length of the scraper (Beyries 1988:219–220). Further evidence of hafting is a bending break just proximal to the functional edge (Shott 1995:58). In their discussion of hafted flake shavers (slug scrapers), Grimes and Grimes state that "during use the combination of compressive force through the major axis of the tool and bending force perpendicular to it periodically results in a transverse snap. In a rigid haft, this failure generally occurs at the point where the tool emerges from the socket" (1985:41). In an effort to determine whether the Sunshine scrapers were hafted, three additional variables were recorded: the presence or absence of haft wear, of proximal thinning, and of a transverse break near the working edge (Figure 5.17B).

Finally, it has been noted that Paleoindian end scrapers often have a triangular shape with a spur at the intersection of the working and lateral edges, as shown in Figure 5.17C. Some researchers have suggested that this type of end scraper is actually diagnostic of Paleoindian assemblages (e.g., Frison 1991; Morrow 1997; O'Brien 1984; Rogers 1986; Shott 1995; but see Morris and Blakeslee 1987). Therefore, the presence or absence of a spur was recorded as well.

In our analysis of scrapers, as well as that of gravers, notches, chisels, and drills, we have used the concept of "employable unit," or EU. This concept was first used by Knudson (1973:17) to refer to the portion of a continuous edge or projection deemed appropriate for use in performing a specific task (see also Knudson 1979, 1983). The

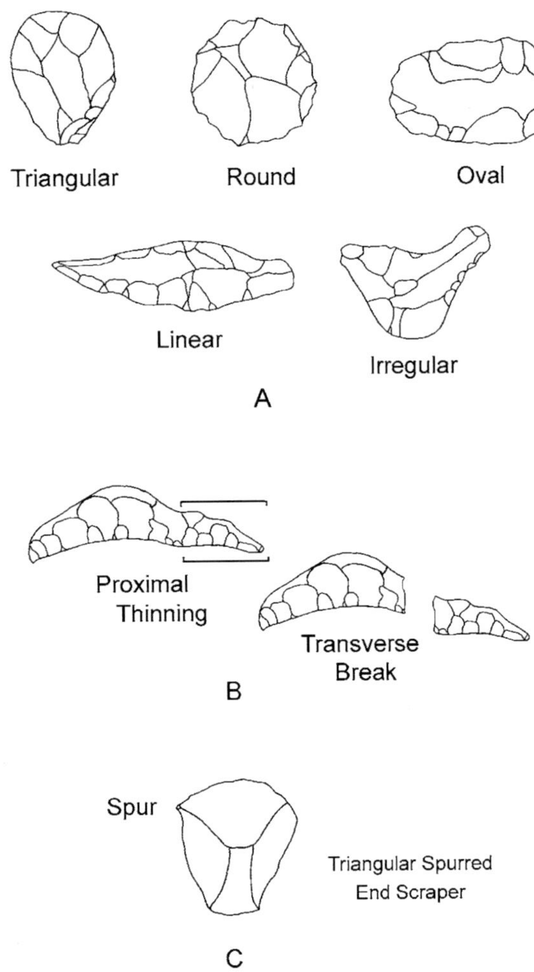

FIGURE 5.17. Qualitative attributes recorded for the Sunshine scrapers: (A) shape; (B) evidence of hafting; (C) presence of a spur.

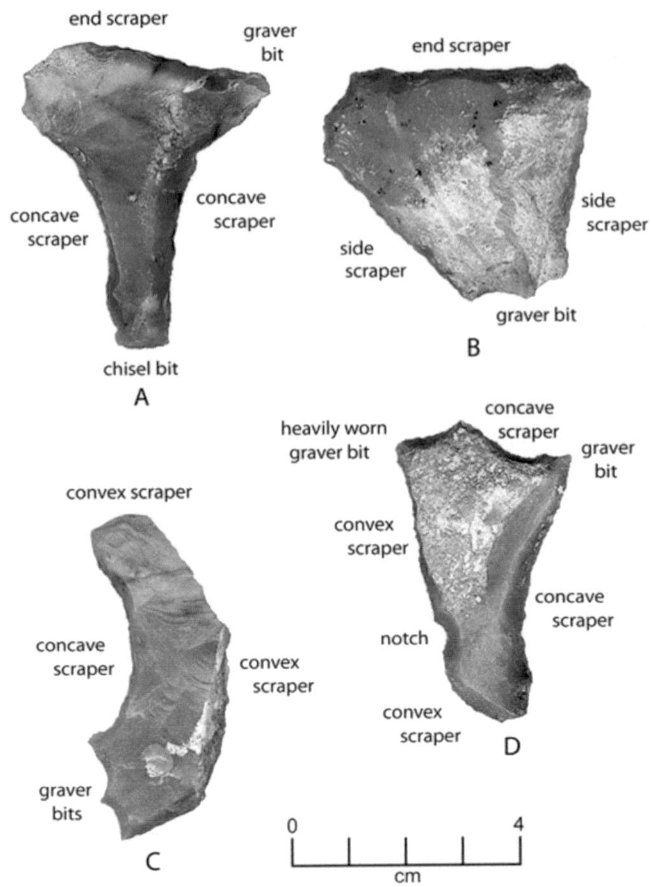

FIGURE 5.18. Artifacts with multiple employable units (EUs). (A) 1746, end/side scraper-graver-chisel; (B) 1679, end/side scraper-graver; (C) 1701, concave/convex scraper-graver; (D) 1745, concave/convex scraper-graver-notch.

concept of EU is reminiscent of the functional classification developed over a series of studies in the Lower Columbia River Valley (e.g., Dunnell and Beck 1979; Dunnell and Campbell 1977; see also Beck 1984; Jones 1984), which specifies the utilized edge or surface rather than the object as the tool. This concept has more recently been used by Marshall (1985), Frison (1987, 1991), and Shott (1996). For each specimen, the number and type of EUs were recorded; the type of EU was determined based on the variables shown in Table 5.40. A single object will often have more than one EU (Figure 5.18). Further, the EUs can be related to different kinds of activities and thus different types of tools. For example, an object may have one EU that is straight in shape with a steep angle and another that is shaped as a continuous notch–point–notch that has a medium angle (Figure 5.18B). The use-wear for each may be quite different as well. These two EUs would be characterized in Gramly's terms as a scraper edge in the first case and a graver bit in the second. Thus, the overall object is identified as a scraper/graver. We have used the EUs to assign objects to specific technological categories. In our discussions below, we refer to the scraper portions of these combination tools. For example, when discussing a side scraper/graver in the section on side scrapers, we discuss use-wear and edge angle only of the side scraper EU, leaving the discussion of use-wear and edge angle of the graver EU to the section on gravers. If, however, an object has two or more side scraper EUs, we still count only a single object; that is, in a table showing the number of side scrapers, that number will reflect the number of artifacts exhibiting side scraper EUs.

Gramly describes a number of different types of scrapers commonly found in Paleoindian assemblages, six of which we have identified in the Sunshine assemblage (Table 5.41). In addition to these categories, we have added a seventh that we refer to as "beaked scrapers" (Storck 1997:65). As is evident from Table 5.42, about a quarter of the Sunshine scrapers (n = 10, 24.2 percent)

TABLE 5.40. Variables Measured for Employable Units on the Sunshine Scrapers

VARIABLE	VARIABLE STATE
Shape	1. Convex 2. Straight 3. Concave 4. Notched 5. Point 6. Notch–Point–Notch (graver edge)
Angle (°)	1. 1–10 2. 11–20 3. 21–30 4. 31–40 5. 41–50 6. 51–60 7. 61–70 8. 71–80 9. 81–90
Use-Wear	1. Crushing/Micro–Step Fractures 2. Minor Abrasion 3. Heavy Abrasion 4. Crushing and Minor Abrasion 5. Crushing and Heavy Abrasion 6. Minor + Heavy Abrasion 7. Crushing/Micro–Step Fractures + Minor and Heavy Abrasion 10. Indeterminate

occur in combination with other tools (we do not include end/side scrapers as combination tools here). Although scrapers are generally referred to as being unifacial, they may sometimes occur in bifacial form. Few of the Sunshine scrapers, however, are bifacial, with the exception of beaked scrapers; 35 of 118 (29.7 percent) of the latter are bifacial, whereas only 25 of 294 (8.5 percent) of the remaining scrapers are bifacial. Therefore, for all but beaked scrapers, we combine bifacial and unifacial specimens for discussion. In the section on beaked scrapers, the difference between unifacial and bifacial specimens is examined. Table 5.42 shows the scraper categories represented in the Sunshine assemblage by raw material.

End Scrapers. Counting those occurring as combination tools, there are 98 end scrapers in the Sunshine assemblage (91 from the H–N collection and seven from the Hamilton collection), about a quarter of the scraper assemblage (Figures 5.19 and 5.20E–P). Although nearly all of the Sunshine end scrapers are manufactured from chert, 12 (12.2 percent) are manufactured from FGV, and one (1.0 percent) is manufactured from quartzite.

The Sunshine end scrapers do not vary considerably in size, as Tables 5.43 and 5.44 show. Size categories range from 7 to 13, but the majority are of size 9 or greater (Table 5.43). Of those specimens for which the original blank could be determined ($n = 66$), all are flakes, but only a small number ($n = 22$) still have platforms. Ten (45.5 percent) of these are biface reduction flakes, and 12 (54.5 percent) are not, an interesting split given that the majority of debitage in the Sunshine assemblage (74.9 percent) resulted from biface reduction (Table 5.20).

TABLE 5.41. Scraper Categories Used in the Sunshine Analysis

SCRAPER CATEGORY[a]	DEFINITION
End Scraper	A unifacial tool, usually made on a flake blade or blade, with a broad working edge opposite the bulbar scar (Gramly 1990:21).
Side Scraper	A unifacial tool, usually made on a flake, with removals (scraper retouch) on one or both lateral edges (Gramly 1990:50).
Combination End/ Side Scraper	A unifacial tool, usually made on a flake blade or blade, with a broad working edge opposite the bulbar scar as well as scraper retouch on one or both lateral edges (Gramly 1990:16).
Concave Scraper	Usually unifacial, this artifact exhibits one or more broad concavities on its edge that have been created by scraper retouch (Gramly 1990:16). Also called spokeshaves.
Combination Concave/Convex Scraper	A tool with no set form, exhibiting both concave and straight to convex scraper edges. Cannot be identified as an end scraper or side scraper.
Circular Scraper	A uniface, usually based on a flake, that has a circular shape and scraper retouch completely around its periphery. Also termed a discoidal scraper (Gramly 1990:14).
Slug Scraper	A narrow, slug-shaped, unifacial, flaked-stone tool having steep edge angles and a high dorsal surface that is often rounded. Also commonly referred to as a limace or flake shaver; less commonly referred to as a groover, bar, narrow side scraper, unifacially flaked drill, or awl (Gramly 1990:32).
Beaked Scraper	Artifact type varying greatly in form, having a cutting or scraping tip that is plano-convex in cross section, usually steeply retouched, and frequently quite thick (Storck 1997:65).

[a] Although many of these definitions specify unifacial tools, scrapers are sometimes bifacial, which is the case in the Sunshine assemblage (see Table 5.14).

As discussed above, a number of researchers have argued that most end scrapers were probably hafted tools. Table 5.45 shows the presence/absence of haft wear, proximal thinning, and transverse breaks as measured on the Sunshine end scrapers. Interestingly, in no case where

TABLE 5.42. Scraper Categories by Raw Material Represented in the Sunshine Assemblage

	Raw Material				
Category	Chert	Obsidian	Fine-Grained Volcanics	Quartzite	Total
Single Tools					
End Scraper	35		4	1	40
Side Scraper	9		1		10
End/Side Scraper	40		7		47
Concave Scraper	25		1		26
Circular	10		6		16
Slug	55		1		56
Beaked	115	1	3		119
Subtotal	289	1	23	1	314
Scraper/Gravers					
End Scraper	3		1		4
Side Scraper	43		1		44
End/Side Scraper	6				6
Concave Scraper	19				19
Circular	4				4
Slug	2		1		3
Subtotal	77		3		80
Scraper/Notches					
Side Scraper	3				3
Concave Scraper	3				3
Slug Scraper	1				1
Subtotal	7				7
Scraper/Graver/Notches					
Side Scraper	5		1		6
Concave Scraper	3				3
Subtotal	8		1		9
Scraper/Graver/Chisels					
End/Concave Scraper	1				1
Concave Scraper	1				1
Subtotal	2				2
Scraper/Drill					
Concave Scraper	1				1
Subtotal	1				1
Total	384	1	27	1	413

Note: Includes only those from the Hutchinson–Noyes Collection that were subjected to special analyses.

FIGURE 5.19. Examples of end scrapers in the Sunshine assemblage: (A) 1727; (B) 1730; (C) 1731; (D) 2739; (E) no provenience; (F) 1651; (G) 1675; (H) 2729.

TABLE 5.43. Distribution of the Sunshine End Scrapers Across Size Categories

SIZE CATEGORY	END SCRAPER	END/SIDE SCRAPER	END SCRAPER/ GRAVER	END/SIDE SCRAPER/GRAVER	END SCRAPER/ CHISEL/GRAVER	TOTAL	
						N	%
7		1				1	3.3
9	3	2				5	8.2
10	2	4	3	1	1	11	18.0
11	8	13	1	3		25	41.0
12	7	9				16	26.2
13	2	1				3	4.9
Subtotal	22	30	4	4	1	61	100.0
Indeterminate	18	17		2		37	
Total	40	47	4	6	1	98	

FIGURE 5.20. Examples of side scrapers and end/side scrapers in the Sunshine assemblage. Side scrapers: (A) 1997 Operation 2, 100E, 104N, Level 3; (B) 714; (C) 2802; (D) 2734. End/side scrapers: (E) 1680; (F) 1678; (G) 1657; (H) no provenience; (I) 1846; (J) 1842; (K) 1718; (L) SW3, no #; (M) 1660; (N) SW3, no #; (O) 1657; (P) no provenience.

TABLE 5.44. Quantitative Data for the Sunshine End Scrapers

CATEGORY	STATISTIC	TOTAL LENGTH (mm)	MAXIMUM WIDTH (mm)	MAXIMUM THICKNESS (mm)	ACTUAL WEIGHT (g)
End Scraper	*N*	16	23	40	40
	Range	38.7–74.4	32.4–75.9	5.8–22.5	4.1–71.0
	Mean	53.28	45.22	12.63	26.94
	SD	8.246	11.811	4.431	16.223
End/Side Scraper	*N*	18	34	47	47
	Range	40.4–64.8	20.2–56.3	5.9–31.7	5.7–94.1
	Mean	50.13	36.81	11.70	23.58
	SD	6.826	8.149	5.293	18.375
End Scraper/Graver	*N*	1	2	3	3
	Range	63.6	22.5–27.6	5.8–15.2	5.5–34.7
	Mean		25.05	10.73	19.44
	SD		3.606	4.717	14.676
End/Side Scraper/Graver	*N*	1	3	6	6
	Range	33.7	34.8–49.4	5.5–16.7	6.4–30.6
	Mean		40.67	10.15	16.47
	SD		7.711	4.013	8.709
End Scraper/Chisel/Graver	—	—	6.20	11.65	
	N	1	1	1	1
	Value	53.8	43.8	6.0	11.7

haft wear and proximal thinning are both measurable ($n = 34$) do they occur together. Five of these show haft wear, eight show proximal thinning, and 21 show neither. One additional specimen for which proximal thinning was indeterminate shows haft wear and four for which haft wear was indeterminate show proximal thinning. For 26 of those 28 specimens with transverse breaks, neither of the other two variables could be measured, which is not surprising as the break will in most cases obliterate both haft wear and proximal thinning. It would seem that haft wear or a transverse break alone is more definitive of hafting than proximal thinning alone, and thus we can say that 34 end scrapers were likely hafted and an additional 13 may have been (Table 5.45). Twenty-one specimens show no evidence of haft wear or proximal thinning and are not broken; these, we conclude, were not hafted. We are unable to determine hafting for the remaining 30 specimens. Considering only the 68 specimens for which a determination could be made, 69.1 percent were likely (or may have been) hafted.

All of the 98 end scrapers show evidence of use-wear (Table 5.46). There is evidence of both crushing ($n = 31$, 31.6 percent) and abrasion ($n = 36$, 36.7 percent), sometimes in combination ($n = 31$, 31.6 percent). There are 32 (32.7 percent) specimens on which the abrasion is extremely heavy. The majority of end scrapers have more than a single EU (Table 5.47), but of course this is obvious because 58 of the 98 are combination tools of some sort (e.g., end/side scrapers, end scraper/gravers, and so forth). However, a number of these ($n = 28$, 28.6 percent) have three or more EUs, and one specimen has six. As will be evident in the discussion of different tool types, especially gravers, multiple use of a single object is fairly common in the Sunshine assemblage.

Considerable debate has taken place regarding the function of end scrapers. The common assumption is that prehistoric end scrapers were used for hide working (Shott 1995:54). Experimental work performed by McDevitt (1994) produced similar use-wear patterns on experimental specimens used for scraping both fresh and dry white-tailed deer hides and several archaeological specimens. Although a range of uses has been documented ethnographically, Hayden (1986:66–68) argues that these uses were the exception rather than the rule and that hide working was likely the dominant activity. After a brief review of the ethnographic record, Shott (1995:54) suggests this is probably the case but argues that "hide working" is a broad class of activity and end scrapers may have been put to more specific actions within that class.

TABLE 5.45. Presence of Haft Wear, Proximal Thinning, and Transverse Breaks on the Sunshine End Scrapers

Variable									
Haft Wear	Proximal Thinning	Transverse Break	End Scraper	End/Side Scraper	End Scraper/Graver	End/Side Scraper/Graver	End Scraper/Chisel/Graver	Total	Hafting
A	A	A	9	10	1		1	21	NH
P	A	A	2	3				5	H
A	P	A	2	6				8	PH
A	I	A	2	1				3	I
A	I	P	1					1	H
P	I	A	1					1	H
I	P	A	2		1	1		4	PH
I	A	A				1		1	I
I	P	P	1					1	H
I	P	I				1		1	PH
I	I	P	10	13	1	2		26	H
I	I	A	4	5				9	I
I	I	I	6	9	1	1		17	I
Summary									
Total Hafted			19	22				47	
Total Not Hafted			9	10	4	6	1	21	
Total Indeterminate			12	15				30	
Overall Total			40	47	4	6	1	98	

Note: A = absent; H = hafted; I = indeterminate; NH = not hafted; P = present; PH = possibly hafted.

TABLE 5.46. Use-Wear Present on the Sunshine End Scrapers

Type of Use-Wear	End Scraper	End/Side Scraper	End Scraper/Graver	End/Side Scraper/Graver	End Scraper/Chisel/Graver	Total *N*	Total %
Crushing/Micro–Step Fractures	10	16	1	4		31	31.6
Minor Abrasion	8	1	1		1	11	11.2
Heavy Abrasion	11	13		1		25	25.5
Crushing/Micro–Step Fractures + Minor Abrasion	10	11	2	1		24	24.5
Crushing/Micro–Step Fractures + Heavy Abrasion		3				3	3.1
Crushing/Micro–Step Fractures + Minor and Heavy Abrasion	1	3				4	4.1
Total	40	47	4	6	1	98	100.0

TABLE 5.47. Number of Employable Units Present on the Sunshine End Scrapers

Number of Employable Units	*N*	%
1	40	40.8
2	30	30.6
3	22	22.4
4	4	4.1
5	1	1.0
6	1	1.0
Total	98	

TABLE 5.48. Maximum Edge Angles Represented on the Sunshine End Scrapers

MAXIMUM EDGE ANGLE (°)	END SCRAPER	END/SIDE SCRAPER	END SCRAPER/ GRAVER	END/SIDE SCRAPER/GRAVER	END SCRAPER/ CHISEL/GRAVER	TOTAL	
						N	%
11–20				1		1	1.1
21–30	1	2		1		4	4.3
31–40	1	1				2	2.1
41–50	1	2				3	3.2
51–60	5	6			1	12	12.8
61–70	5	9	3	1		18	19.2
71–80	9	11	1	3		24	25.5
81–90	16	14				30	31.9
Subtotal	38	45	4	6	1	94	100.0
Indeterminate	2	2				4	
Total	40	47	4	6	1	98	

The attribute of end scrapers that makes them so useful for activities related to hide working is their steep-angled working edge. In the cleaning and working of hides, constant and repeated motion in a single direction requires a strong, durable edge, and a steep edge angle provides this. Table 5.48 shows the maximum edge angle (represented in 10° increments) represented on the Sunshine end scrapers, and as can be seen from these data, 76.6 percent ($n = 72$) have edge angles greater than 60°, with 31.9 percent ($n = 30$) having angles greater than 80°. Also contributing to the durability of end scrapers, as well as other types of scrapers, is the choice of material from which they are made. Most of the Sunshine specimens are made from chert. Even though obsidian constitutes between 7 (H–N) and 13 percent (Hamilton) of the Sunshine assemblage, there is only one scraper made from this material (Table 5.42). We have made the argument elsewhere (Beck and Jones 1990b:286) that chert was preferred for the manufacture of scrapers as well as crescents, gravers, and drills for functional purposes, because it is a tough, durable material. Obsidian, however, although it is preferred for some types of tools, such as projectile points or knives, because it provides such a sharp edge, is brittle and would dull much more quickly when put to use scraping hides.

It has been argued that a particular form of end scraper—triangular in shape with at least one spur at the intersection of the working and lateral edges—is diagnostic of Paleoindian assemblages. Morrow (1997), for example, compared 229 Paleoindian and Early Archaic end scrapers from three sites in the Mississippi–Missouri–Illinois rivers confluence area. She found that Paleoindian end scrapers are generally smaller and more extensively shaped (triangularly) than Early Archaic end scrapers. Alternatively, the latter tend to more closely resemble the original flake blank and thus exhibit a wider variety of shapes than the former. Morrow states, however, "Of all the differences among these Paleoindian and Early Archaic end scrapers, outline morphology (triangular) and the presence of angular or spurred corners are the most prevalent" (1997:75). As Table 5.49 shows, there are 31 triangular end scrapers in the Sunshine assemblage, but only seven of these have spurs; these are shown in Figure 5.21A–G. There are three fragmentary specimens that were likely triangular before they were broken that also have spurs (Figure 5.21H–J). Finally, on our latest trip to the museum for photographing artifacts (May 2007), we came across two other triangular spurred specimens, which are shown in Figure 5.21K–L. These occur in the general assemblage, but they are so classic in form that we decided to include them in Figure 5.21.

TABLE 5.49. Shape and Presence of Spurs on the Sunshine End Scrapers

SHAPE	SPUR		INDETERMINATE	TOTAL	
	PRESENT	ABSENT		*N*	%
Circular		5	1	6	6.2
Oval		17		17	17.3
Triangular	7	22	2	31	31.6
Irregular	1	5	1	7	7.1
Fragment	5	24	8	37	37.8
Total	13	73	12	98	100.0

It could be, given Morrow's (1997) results, that these few end scrapers constitute the earlier, terminal Pleistocene record at Sunshine and the other 49 (excluding the

FIGURE 5.21. Examples of triangular spurred end scrapers in the Sunshine assemblage: (A) SW3, no #; (B) SW3B, no #; (C) 2641; (D) 2745; (E) 1710; (F) 1997 Operation 2, 100E, 104N, Final Stratum B; (G) 1993 excavation, 102.82E, 108.02N, Final Stratum A; (H) surface 1995, FS 257; (I) 1993 excavation, 102E, 108N, Final Stratum A; (J) SW3B, no #; (K) 484; (L) no provenience.

35 fragmentary specimens) constitute the early Holocene component. Unfortunately we cannot separate the terminal Pleistocene and early Holocene components of the Sunshine assemblage, except in a few cases. One of the triangular spurred scrapers, for example, was recovered from Unit B in the 1997 Hamilton excavation (Figure 5.21F). We have only a single radiocarbon date from Unit B (8120 ± 70 rcy BP) and two dates from the top of Unit C (8560 ± 100 and 9820 ± 60 rcy BP). We have argued that the first of the latter two dates was obtained on contaminated charcoal and that the latter date is more likely correct (Huckleberry et al. 2001). In any event, if the date on Unit B is correct, then the specimen in Figure 5.21F, a classic triangular spurred end scraper, dates to the late early Holocene rather than to the terminal Pleistocene.

The meaning of spurs is unknown but debated. Some believe the spur to be a functional component of the tool for use as a graver (e.g., Rogers 1986; Wilmsen 1968), whereas others suggest spurs are fortuitous, simply resulting from breakage and/or resharpening (Collins 1999a; Nissen and Dittemore 1974:71; see Andrefsky 1998:35 for a schematic of this process). We point out that a large number of Sunshine scrapers in general occur as combination tools with gravers (n = 131 if we include those for which special analyses were not done; Table 5.12). In fact, several of these combination tools exhibit classic gravers at the intersection of the working and lateral edges (see, e.g., Figure 5.21C). Thus, it is not out of the question that spurs were meant to be used as gravers.

Side Scrapers. Side scrapers often occur in combination with end scrapers, but Gramly (1990:16) notes that when this occurs they are generally identified as one or the other. The combination of end and side scraper was formerly defined by Ellis and Deller (1988:115–116) for Paleoindian industries in the Great Lakes region. As Table 5.42 shows, only 10 side scrapers occur as single tools (see Figure 5.20A–D), whereas 47 occur in combination with end scrapers (Figure 5.20E–P). The majority of side scrapers occur in combination with gravers (n = 50), notches (n = 3), and graver/notch combinations (n = 6; see, e.g., Figure 5.18B), which brings the total number of side scrapers in the Sunshine assemblage to 116 (108 from the H–N collection and eight from the HC collection). Many of the combination tools identified here as side scrapers, as well as those identified as concave scrapers discussed in the following section, may be what others have referred to as "retouched flake tools" rather than "formal tools" (e.g.,

TABLE 5.50. Distribution of the Sunshine Side Scrapers Across Size Categories

SIZE CATEGORY	SIDE SCRAPER	END/SIDE SCRAPER	SIDE SCRAPER/ GRAVER	END/SIDE SCRAPER/ GRAVER	SIDE SCRAPER/ NOTCH	SIDE SCRAPER/ GRAVER/NOTCH	TOTAL	
							N	%
7		1	4				5	6.4
8			3			1	4	5.1
9		2	10		1		13	16.7
10		4	11	1	1	3	20	25.6
11	4	13	4	3			24	30.8
12	1	9					10	12.8
13	1	1					2	2.6
Subtotal	6	30	32	4	2	4	78	100.0
Indeterminate	4	17	12	2	1	2	38	
Total	10	47	44	6	3	6	116	

Frison 1987:235–245). Frison (1987:251) suggests, however, that the difference between these two categories is quite arbitrary. In the assemblage from Horner I, a Cody Complex site in the Big Horn Basin of Wyoming, Frison distinguishes six side scrapers from other retouched flake tools, as he says, "rather arbitrarily," on the basis of "thickness, steep percussion, and pressure-flaked EUs that are straight to slightly convex in outline" (1987:251). In most cases, "formal" unifacial tools are simply retouched flakes, and therefore we have assigned all flake tools to categories rather than attempting to decide at what point a flake is more than retouched and should be called a "formal tool."

As is the case for end scrapers, side scrapers are manufactured almost entirely from chert, although three (ten counting the end/side scrapers already discussed) of these are manufactured from FGV (Table 5.42). Of the 116 side scrapers, the original blank could be determined for 83. With the exception of a single specimen, all are made on flake blanks; the exception is made on a chunk. Only a small number ($n = 24$) of these, however, still have platforms, 15 (62.5 percent) of which are biface reduction flakes and nine (37.5 percent) of which are not.

Side scrapers vary slightly more in size than do end scrapers (Tables 5.50–5.51). But this difference is related to the greater number of side scrapers in combination with gravers, which are smaller on the average than side and end/side scrapers.

Table 5.52 shows the presence/absence of haft wear, proximal thinning, and transverse breaks for side scrapers. Approximately half (51.2 percent) for which data are available ($n = 84$) appear to have been hafted or possibly hafted, fewer overall than in the case of end scrapers.

Whereas the majority of nonfragmentary end scrapers are triangular in shape, the shape of side scrapers is much more varied (Table 5.53), most likely because the majority occur as combination tools. The shape of side scrapers on such tools appears to conform to the shape of the dominant tool; that is, if they occur in combination with end scrapers, the shape is most often triangular, but if they occur in combination with gravers, the shape is more often irregular.

Because side scrapers often occur in combination with end scrapers, their functions are assumed to be similar. In the Sunshine assemblage, however, end and side scrapers differ considerably in both use-wear patterns and edge angle. Table 5.54 shows the use-wear evident on side scrapers by tool category. As in the case of end scrapers, all show evidence of use-wear, with the exception of one specimen for which this variable could not be determined. A greater proportion of side scrapers exhibits only crushing/micro–step fractures (42.6 percent) than is the case for end scrapers (31.6 percent; see Table 5.46). As Table 5.54 shows, the predominance of crushing/micro–step fracturing is not determined by any single category. Frison (1987:251) finds a similar pattern on the six side scrapers from the Horner I assemblage, stating that the high incidence of breakage along with crushing (step fractures) on EUs is suggestive of tasks common in bison butchering.

Overall, edge angles of side scrapers are somewhat lower than those of end scrapers (Table 5.55), with 63.3 percent ($n = 72$) having maximum angles greater than 60°, as compared with 76.6 percent of end scrapers. Only 10.5 percent ($n = 12$) have maximum angles greater than 80°, as compared with 31.9 percent of end scrapers.

What do these data suggest about the function of side scrapers? Gramly states that "the role of sidescrapers in the Palaeo-Indian tool-kit is a mystery. They might have worked wood or shaved away fat and tissue from hides"

TABLE 5.51. Quantitative Data for the Sunshine Side Scrapers

SCRAPER TYPE	STATISTIC	TOTAL LENGTH (mm)	MAXIMUM WIDTH (mm)	MAXIMUM THICKNESS (mm)	ACTUAL WEIGHT (g)
Side Scraper	*N*	4	6	10	10
	Range	49.4–80.7	29.4–50.2	5.8–11.8	8.9–55.8
	Mean	59.00	38.40	8.77	21.21
	SD	14.568	8.94	2.013	13.483
End/Side Scraper	*N*	18	34	47	47
	Range	40.4–64.8	20.2–56.3	5.9–31.7	5.7–94.1
	Mean	50.13	37.81	11.70	23.58
	SD	6.826	8.149	5.293	18.375
Side Scraper/Graver	*N*	—	—	43	44
	Range	—	—	31.0–17.50	1.25–30.84
	Mean	—	—	6.59	7.46
	SD	—	—	2.75	6.28
End/Side Scraper/Graver	*N*	1	3	6	6
	Range	33.7	34.8–49.4	5.5–16.7	6.4–30.6
	Mean	—	40.67	10.15	16.47
	SD	—	7.711	4.013	8.709
Side Scraper/Notch	*N*	1	1	3	3
	Range	43.0	24.7	6.6–11.3	5.7–10.1
	Mean	—	—	8.97	8.50
	SD	—	—	2.350	2.422
Side Scraper/Graver/Notch	*N*	1	1	5	5
	Range	51.2	23.4	4.6–16.7	3.6–22.6
	Mean	—	—	9.04	11.81
	SD	—	—	4.85	8.357

TABLE 5.52. Presence of Haft Wear, Proximal Thinning, and Transverse Breaks on the Sunshine Side Scrapers

VARIABLE										
HAFT WEAR	PROXIMAL THINNING	TRANSVERSE BREAK	SIDE SCRAPER	END/SIDE SCRAPER	SIDE SCRAPER/ GRAVER	END/SIDE SCRAPER/ GRAVER	SIDE SCRAPER/ NOTCH	SIDE SCRAPER/ GRAVER/ NOTCH	TOTAL	HAFTING
A	A	A	2	10	25		1	3	41	NH
P	A	A	1	3	1				5	H
A	P	A		6	1				7	PH
A	I	A	1	1					2	I
I	P	A				1			1	PH
I	A	A				1			1	I
I	P	I				1			1	PH
I	I	P		13	12	2		2	29	H
I	I	A	1	5	1				7	I
I	I	I	5	9	4	1	2	1	22	I
Summary										
Total Hafted			1	22	14	4		2	43	
Total Not Hafted			2	10	25		1	3	41	—
Total Indeterminate			7	15	5	2	2	1	32	
Overall Total			10	47	44	6	3	6	116	

Note: A = absent; H = hafted; I = indeterminate; NH = not hafted; P = present; PH = possibly hafted.

TABLE 5.53. Shape of the Sunshine Side Scrapers

SHAPE	SIDE SCRAPER	END/SIDE SCRAPER	SIDE SCRAPER/ GRAVER	END/SIDE SCRAPER/GRAVER	SIDE SCRAPER/ NOTCH	SIDE SCRAPER/ GRAVER/NOTCH	TOTAL	
							N	%
Round		3	3				6	5.2
Oval	3	9	5	1		1	19	16.4
Triangular		19	1	2			22	19.0
Linear	1		2				3	2.6
Irregular	4	1	22	1	3	2	33	28.4
Fragment	2	15	11	2		3	33	28.4
Total	10	47	44	6	3	6	116	100.0

TABLE 5.54. Use-Wear Present on the Sunshine Side Scrapers

TYPE OF WEAR	SIDE SCRAPER	END/SIDE SCRAPER	SIDE SCRAPER/ GRAVER	END/SIDE SCRAPER/ GRAVER	SIDE SCRAPER/ NOTCH	SIDE SCRAPER/ GRAVER/ NOTCH	TOTAL	
							N	%
Crushing/Micro–Step Fractures	5	21	20	2		1	49	42.6
Minor Abrasion	1	2	14		2	1	20	17.4
Heavy Abrasion	1	10	2	1		2	16	13.9
Minor + Heavy Abrasion		1				1	2	1.7
Crushing/Micro–Step Fractures + Minor Abrasion	2	8	4	3	1		18	15.7
Crushing/Micro–Step Fractures + Heavy Abrasion	1	4	2				7	6.1
Crushing/Micro–Step Fractures + Minor and Heavy Abrasion		1	2				3	2.6
Subtotal	10	47	44	6	3	5	115	100.0
Indeterminate						1	1	
Total	10	47	44	6	3	6	116	

TABLE 5.55. Maximum Edge Angles Represented on the Sunshine Side Scrapers

MAXIMUM EDGE ANGLE (°)	SIDE SCRAPER	END/SIDE SCRAPER	SIDE SCRAPER/ GRAVER	END/SIDE SCRAPER/GRAVER	SIDE SCRAPER/ NOTCH	SIDE SCRAPER/ GRAVER/NOTCH	TOTAL	
							N	%
11–20	1		1				2	1.8
21–30		2	2				4	3.5
31–40	1	1	4				6	5.3
41–50	1	7	3				11	9.7
51–60	3	5	8			3	19	16.7
61–70	2	12	8	1	1	1	25	21.9
71–80	1	15	11	5	1	2	35	30.7
81–90		4	7		1		12	10.5
Subtotal	9	46	44	6	3	6	114	100.0
Indeterminate	1	1					2	
Total	10	47	44	6	3	6	116	

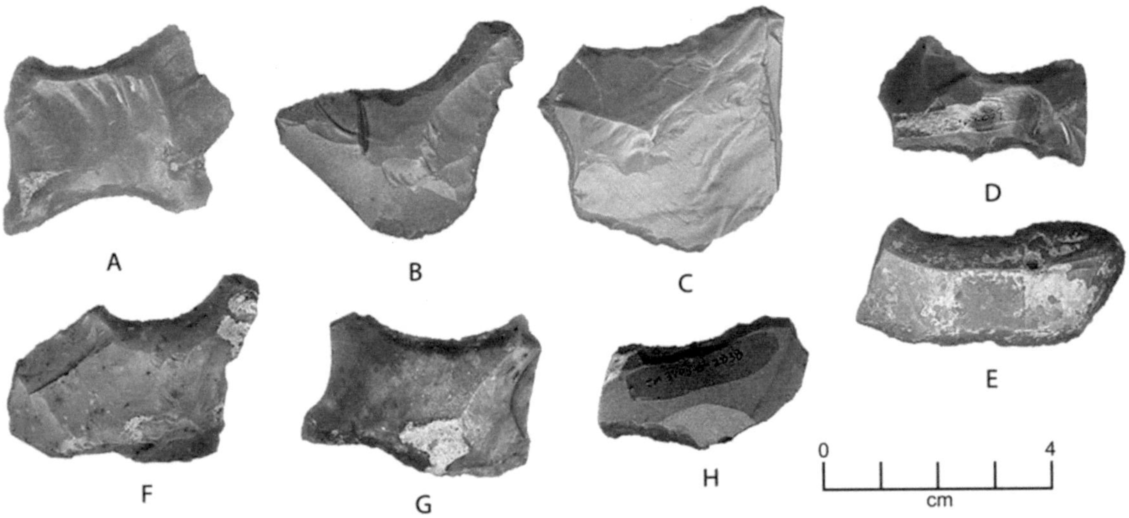

FIGURE 5.22. Examples of concave scrapers in the Sunshine assemblage: (A) 2833; (B) 2836; (C) 2830; (D) 2839; (E) 2832; (F) 2837; (G) 2837; (H) 2838.

TABLE 5.56. Quantitative Data for the Sunshine Notch–Concave Scraper Comparison

Tool Type	Statistic	Width (mm)	Depth (mm)	Notch Ratio (Width/Depth)
Notch	*N*	20	20	20
	Range	4.30–23.20	0.80–8.50	2.60–8.56
	Mean	8.30	1.96	4.98
	SD	4.38	1.75	1.71
Concave Scraper	*N*	57	57	57
	Range	7.10–48.20	0.90–7.90	3.52–20.62
	Mean	27.00	3.51	8.86
	SD	9.22	1.66	3.78

Note: Some artifacts contain more than one notch or concave scraper employable unit (see, e.g., Figure 5.22G–I). Two notches were not measurable.

(1982:37). He goes on to say that because there is considerable evidence for the use of bone implements in Mesolithic and Paleolithic sites in the Old World for scraping hides, he "favors the idea that chert sidescrapers were used on wood" (1982:37). As stated above, Frison (1987:251) believes that the side scrapers from Horner I were probably used in butchering. Frison states, however, that "the normal carcass-reduction process used in butchering large animals requires a continual interplay of cutting and scraping actions" (1987:238). It makes sense, then, that two or three different types of cutting and scraping tools might occur on the same object. Further, different combinations may have been used for slightly different actions at different stages in the process. That is, a side scraper/graver with an edge angle of, say, 40° would likely be used at a different point in the process than an end scraper/graver with an angle close to 90°. Frison goes on to say that these tools "need not be restricted to a context of animal butchering and processing" (1987:238) but could also have been used in other activities, such as wood- and hide working.

It seems clear that side scrapers, as defined here, are very generalized tools and were likely used to perform a variety of tasks, probably related to butchering and meat, hide, and bone (and possibly wood) processing. A side scraper that occurs in combination with another tool likely served in complementary actions to that tool.

Concave and Concave/Convex Scrapers. Concave scrapers, also commonly called spokeshaves, and combination concave/convex scrapers are defined primarily on the basis of edge shape and the fact that they do not identify with either the end or side scraper categories. There are 29 concave scrapers in the Sunshine assemblage; an additional 25 occur in combination with convex scraper edges (Figure 5.22). We consider all 54 together here and refer to them simply as "concave scrapers." Only one specimen is from the HC collection; all others are from the H-N collection.

Discussion of spokeshaves is often combined with that of notches (e.g., Frison 1987:240), and in fact, the difference between them is simply size. Gramly (1990:16) points out that the cavities of notches are smaller than those of concave scrapers but there are no "hard-and-fast" rules for distinguishing one from the other. Table 5.56 shows descriptive statistics for the width and depth of the concavity for both the concave scraper and the notch EUs in the Sunshine assemblage. As these data demonstrate, there is overlap for both attributes, especially depth. This table also shows the statistics for the ratio of width to

TABLE 5.57. Distribution of the Sunshine Concave Scrapers Across Size Categories

Size Category	Concave Scraper[a]	Concave Scraper/ Graver	Concave Scraper/ Notch	Concave Scraper/Graver/ Notch	Concave Scraper/ Chisel/Graver	Concave Scraper/ Drill	Total	
							N	%
8	1		2				3	8.8
9	4	4		1	1		10	29.4
10	5	7	1	1	1	1	16	47.1
11	1	2		1			4	11.8
12	1						1	2.9
Subtotal	12	13	3	3	2	1	34	100.0
Indeterminate	14	6					20	
Total	26	19	3	3	2	1	54	

[a] Concave and concave/convex scrapers are combined.

TABLE 5.58. Quantitative Data for the Sunshine Concave Scrapers

Scraper Type	Statistic	Total Length (mm)	Maximum Width (mm)	Maximum Thickness (mm)	Actual Weight (g)
Concave Scraper[a]	*N*	5	6	24	25
	Range	37.40–68.40	21.10–47.80	3.70–12.50	2.93–40.10
	Mean	55.40	33.80	6.91	10.26
	SD	13.81	8.66	2.28	8.08
Concave Scraper/Graver	*N*	1	1	19	16
	Range	48.90	30.8	3.70–12.00	1.68–16.93
	Mean	—	—	6.49	7.73
	SD	—	—	2.24	5.06
Concave Scraper/Notch	*N*	1	1	3	3
	Range	43.70	15.30	6.30–9.00	5.09–9.75
	Mean	—	—	7.80	6.66
	SD	—	—	1.38	2.68
Concave Scraper/Graver/Notch	*N*	—	—	3	3
	Range	—	—	4.70–8.40	3.71–18.02
	Mean	—	—	6.40	10.50
	SD	—	—	1.86	7.19
Concave Scraper/Chisel	*N*	—	1	1	1
	Value	—	34.80	4.90	4.91
Concave Scraper/Drill	*N*	—	—	1	1
	Value	—	—	8.10	12.42

[a] Concave and convex/concave scrapers are combined.

depth. Although there is overlap here as well, a *t*-test indicates that there is a significant difference in ratio means ($t = 6.153, df = 70, p < .001$).

About half ($n = 28$, 52.7 percent) of the concave scrapers occur in combination with other tool types, particularly gravers (e.g., Figure 5.22B, D, G), and all but one are manufactured from chert (Table 5.42). The original blank could be determined for 21 of the 55 specimens. All are flakes, but only 10 have platforms, of which six are biface reduction flakes.

Concave scrapers are similar in size to other scraper forms (Tables 5.57–5.58). Unlike end and side scrapers, however, very few ($n = 5$) of these tools appear to have been hafted (Table 5.59).

FIGURE 5.23. Examples of circular scrapers in the Sunshine assemblage: (A) 1676; (B) 1663; (C) 1670; (D) 1669; (E) 1681; (F) 1664; (H) surface 1995, FS 439; (I) 1674; (J) surface 1995, FS 192.

All 54 concave scrapers show use-wear (Table 5.60). Nearly half (48.2 percent) exhibit only crushing and micro–step fractures, and another 31.5 percent exhibit only abrasion; the remaining 20.3 percent exhibit both of these use-wear types. A large proportion (62.3 percent) of these tools have edge angles over 60° (Table 5.61).

The function of concave scrapers (or spokeshaves) is assumed to be the shaving and smoothing of weapon shafts or tool handles (Judge 1973:107–108), although Irwin and Wormington (1970:29) have suggested that their use might have been extended to the shredding of plant fibers. Judge notes that "in order to be used efficiently, spokeshaves must have been made for the final rounding process, and should be reliable indicators of shaft sizes if an adequate sample can be obtained" (1973: 108). Given the large range in size of the Sunshine specimens, however, this does not seem a likely prospect.

Circular Scrapers. Gramly suggests that circular scrapers are, in most instances, "resharpened and reworked endscrapers with their bulbs of percussion flaked away" (1990:14). This does not appear to be the case for most of the Sunshine specimens. There are 20 circular scrapers in the Sunshine assemblage (16 from the H–N collection and four from the HC collection; Figure 5.23). Unlike the other scraper forms, they do not often occur in combination with other tools; only four occur as combination tools with gravers (Table 5.42; see Figure 5.23D). Further, six of the 20 (30 percent) are manufactured from FGV.

By definition circular scrapers are round or oval in shape and exhibit retouch around the entire edge, which precludes hafting. Use-wear on circular scrapers differs somewhat from that of other scraper categories, in that seven (35 percent) exhibit only crushing and micro–step fractures and eight (40 percent) exhibit only abrasion (Table 5.62). The remaining five (25 percent) show both types of use-wear.

Edge angles, however, are consistent with those of end scrapers, with 14 (73.7 percent) having angles greater than 60° (Table 5.63); however, only four (20 percent) have angles greater than 80°. These tools are also consistent with other scraper categories with respect to their range in size (Tables 5.64–5.65).

Slug Scrapers. A total of 60 artifacts have been identified as slug scrapers, 58 from the H–N collection and two from the HC collection. These tools have also been referred to as "limaces" (Gramly 1982:37–38, 1990:32) and "flake shavers" (Grimes and Grimes 1985:40). In his discussion of tools from the Vail site in Maine, Gramly states that "the *limace* or slug-shaped uniface (scraper) is an unfamiliar tool to most North American archaeologists" (1982:37; emphasis in the original). He goes on to say that these tools are well known in the Old World. Old World limaces, however, as defined by Bordes, are made on blades that are "retouched along both sides to form a 'slug-shaped' object" (1968:245). Similar tools found in Paleoindian assemblages are generally made on flakes, and the retouch resembles that on end scrapers; thus the similarity between Old World limaces and North American Paleoindian "slug scrapers" has to do with their "sluglike

TABLE 5.59. Presence of Haft Wear, Proximal Thinning, and Transverse Breaks on the Sunshine Concave Scrapers

Variable										
Haft Wear	Proximal Thinning	Transverse Breaks	Concave Scraper	Concave Scraper/ Graver	Concave Scraper/ Notch	Concave Scraper/ Gravers/ Notch	Concave Scraper/ Chisel	Concave Scraper/ Drill	Total	Hafting
A	A	A	3	12		3	2	1	21	NH
I	I	I	21	2	3				26	I
I	A	I	2						2	NH
I	I	P		5					5	H
Summary										
Total Hafted				5					5	
Total Not Hafted			5	12		3	2	1	23	
Total Indeterminate			21	2	3				26	
Overall Total			26	19	3	3	2	1	54	

Note: A = absent; H = hafted; I = indeterminate; NH = not hafted; P = present.

TABLE 5.60. Use-Wear Present on the Sunshine Concave Scrapers

Type of Use-Wear	Concave Scraper	Concave Scraper/ Graver	Concave Scraper/ Notch	Concave Scraper/ Graver/Notch	Concave Scraper/ Chisel	Concave Scraper/ Drill	Total	
							N	%
Crushing/Micro–Step Fractures	13	11	1	1			26	48.1
Minor Abrasion	5	4	1				10	18.5
Heavy Abrasion	2	1		1			4	7.4
Minor + Heavy Abrasion	1			1			2	3.7
Crushing/Micro–Step Fractures + Minor Abrasion	5	1	1				7	13.0
Crushing/Micro–Step Fractures + Heavy Abrasion		2			2	1	5	9.3
Total	26	19	3	3	2	1	54	100.0

TABLE 5.61. Maximum Edge Angles Represented on the Sunshine Concave Scrapers

Maximum Edge Angle (°)	Concave Scraper	Concave Scraper/ Graver	Concave Scraper/ Notch	Concave Scraper/ Graver/ Notch	Concave Scraper/ Chisel	Concave Scraper/ Drill	Total	
							N	%
21–30	3						3	5.7
31–40	2	2					4	7.6
41–50	1	2					3	5.7
51–60	5	4					9	17.0
61–70	6	5		1	2		14	26.4
71–80	5	5	2	2			14	26.4
81–90	3	1	1			1	6	11.3
Subtotal	25	19	3	3	2	1	53	100.0
Indeterminate	1						1	
Total	26	19	3	3	2	1	54	

Table 5.62. Use-Wear Present on the Sunshine Circular Scrapers

Type of Use-Wear	Circular Scraper	Circular Scraper/ Graver	Total *N*	Total %
Crushing/Micro-Step Fractures	4	3	7	35.0
Minor Abrasion	4		4	20.0
Heavy Abrasion	2	1	3	15.0
Minor + Heavy Abrasion	1		1	5.0
Crushing/Micro-Step Fractures + Minor Abrasion	5		5	25.0
Total	16	4	20	100.0

Table 5.63. Maximum Edge Angles Represented on the Sunshine Circular Scrapers

Maximum Edge Angle (°)	Circular Scraper	Circular Scraper/ Graver	Total *N*	Total %
11–20		1	1	5.0
21–30				
31–40				
41–50	3		3	15.0
51–60	1		1	5.0
61–70	1	2	3	15.0
71–80	6	1	7	35.0
81–90	4		4	20.0
Subtotal	15	4	19	100.0
Indeterminate	1		1	
Total	16	4	20	

Table 5.64. Distribution of the Sunshine Circular Scrapers Across Size Categories

Size Category	Scraper Type: Circular Scraper	Scraper Type: Circular Scraper/ Graver	Total *N*	Total %
8	1	1	2	11.8
9	1	1	2	11.8
10	1	2	3	17.6
11	9		9	52.9
12	1		1	5.9
Subtotal	13	4	17	100.0
Indeterminate	3		3	
Total	16	4	20	

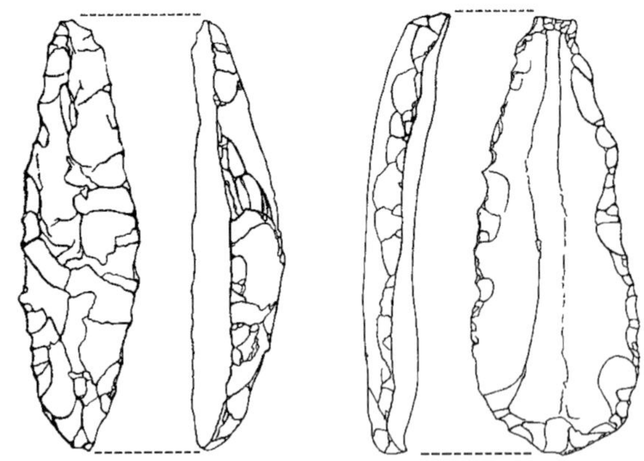

Figure 5.24. Drawings of slug scrapers (limaces) from the (A) Vail and (B) Bull Brook sites (after Gramly 1990:32). The majority of slug scrapers in the Sunshine assemblage resemble the bipointed example from the Vail site rather than the rounded example from the Bull Brook site.

shape" rather than their technology. The limaces from the Vail site in Maine (Gramly 1982), for example, are, for the most part, bipointed with thinning of the proximal end, such as that shown in Figure 5.24A.

Grimes and Grimes (1985:40), in their analysis of 41 similar artifacts from the Bull Brook site in Massachusetts, conclude that these tools were used to shave or gouge hard materials, referring to them as flake shavers. Although bipointed specimens are present, the majority have at least moderate rounding of the distal (working) end, with this end being wider than the proximal end. In some cases this rounding is pronounced (Figure 5.24B), resulting presumably from considerable resharpening. Grimes and Grimes argue that these tools were hafted in socket hafts, based on the narrow range of variation for measurements on the proximal end. Further, some specimens are asymmetrical, which they argue is the result of intentional thinning to fit the haft.

The majority of the Sunshine specimens resemble the Vail example (Figure 5.25A–E), with a pointed working (distal) end; only in five cases is this end rounded (see, e.g., Figure 5.25F), and in two, just moderately so. It is logical that the pointed and rounded specimens would be put to different uses; however, because of their overall sluglike form, we have placed them in the same general category, which we continue to refer to as slug scrapers. We distinguish within this group between rounded and pointed specimens. Only four slug scrapers occur as combination tools, one with a notch and the other three with gravers.

Slug scrapers vary a little more in size than other scraper forms (Tables 5.66–5.67), ranging between categories 6 and 11, but the majority ($n = 40$, 90.9 percent) are

TABLE 5.65. Quantitative Data for the Sunshine Circular Scrapers

SCRAPER TYPE	STATISTIC	MAXIMUM LENGTH (mm)	MAXIMUM WIDTH (mm)	MAXIMUM THICKNESS (mm)	ACTUAL WEIGHT (g)
Circular Scraper	*N*	10	14	16	16
	Range	35.0–60.8	28.2–48.1	4.2–19.1	3.9–56.6
	Mean	47.3	39.9	11.1	23.0
	SD	7.55	5.61	4.85	14.93
Circular Scraper/ Graver	*N*	—	—	4	3
	Range	—	—	4.0–9.5	3.1–10.1
	Mean	—	—	7.0	5.84
	SD	—	—	2.77	3.76

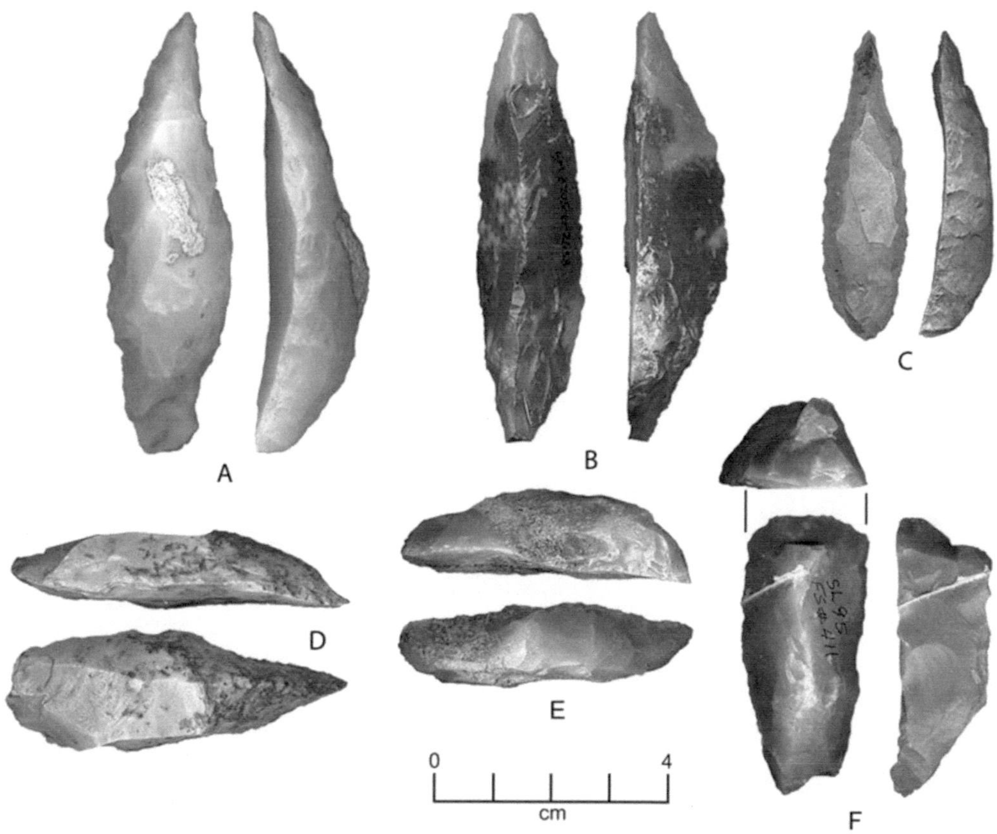

FIGURE 5.25. Examples of slug scrapers in the Sunshine assemblage: (A) 2602; (B) 2658; (C) 2620; (D) 2601; (E) 2606; (F) surface 1995, FS 411.

size 8 or greater (Table 5.66). Grimes and Grimes (1985) argue that size variation in the flake shavers from Bull Brook is related to resharpening, but this does not appear to be the case for the Sunshine specimens. Few exhibit evidence of extensive resharpening.

Only two slug scrapers are not manufactured from chert; these are made from FGV (Table 5.42). The blank was observable for 25 of the 60 slugs, all of which are flakes, but the platform remains on only nine. Four of these are biface reduction flakes, and five are generalized core flakes. Interestingly, one of the tools with a rounded distal end exhibits a small spur (Figure 5.25F).

Table 5.68 shows that of the 59 slug scrapers for which the distal end is present, all exhibit use-wear, primarily in the form of crushing alone. Much like end and side scrapers, the maximum angles for these tools are steep, with 44 of 56 (78.6 percent) having angles greater than 70° (Table 5.69).

TABLE 5.66. Distribution of the Sunshine Slug Scrapers Across Size Categories

Size Category	Slug Scraper	Slug Scraper/ Graver	Slug Scraper/ Notch	Total N	Total %
6	1			1	2.3
7	3			3	6.8
8	10	1		11	25.0
9	18		1	19	43.2
10	7	2		9	20.4
11	1			1	2.3
Subtotal	40	3	1	44	100.0
Indeterminate	16			16	
Total	56	3	1	60	

TABLE 5.67. Quantitative Data for the Sunshine Slug Scrapers

Scraper Type	Statistic	Maximum Length (mm)	Maximum Width (mm)	Maximum Thickness (mm)	Actual Weight (g)
Slug Scraper	*N*	29	44	54	55
	Range	16.1–82.0	8.1–29.2	3.8–20.7	1.7–27.5
	Mean	47.74	17.34	9.35	8.34
	SD	13.170	4.504	3.725	5.29
Slug Scraper/Graver	*N*	3	3	3	3
	Range	39.4–58.5	14.7–22.2	5.8–17.5	3.4–19.4
	Mean	48.70	18.80	10.43	10.51
	SD	9.560	3.799	6.218	8.169
Slug Scraper/wNotch	*N*	—	—	1	1
	Value	—	—	5.6	4.5

TABLE 5.68. Use-Wear Present on the Sunshine Slug Scrapers

Use-Wear Category	Slug Scraper	Slug Scraper/ Graver	Slug Scraper/ Notch	Total N	Total %
Crushing/Micro–Step Fractures	42	1	1	44	74.6
Minor Abrasion	1	1		2	3.4
Heavy Abrasion	2			2	3.4
Crushing/Micro–Step Fractures + Minor Abrasion	8	1		9	15.3
Crushing/Micro–Step Fractures + Major Abrasion	2			2	3.4
Subtotal	55			59	100.0
Indeterminate	1			1	
Total	56	3	1	60	

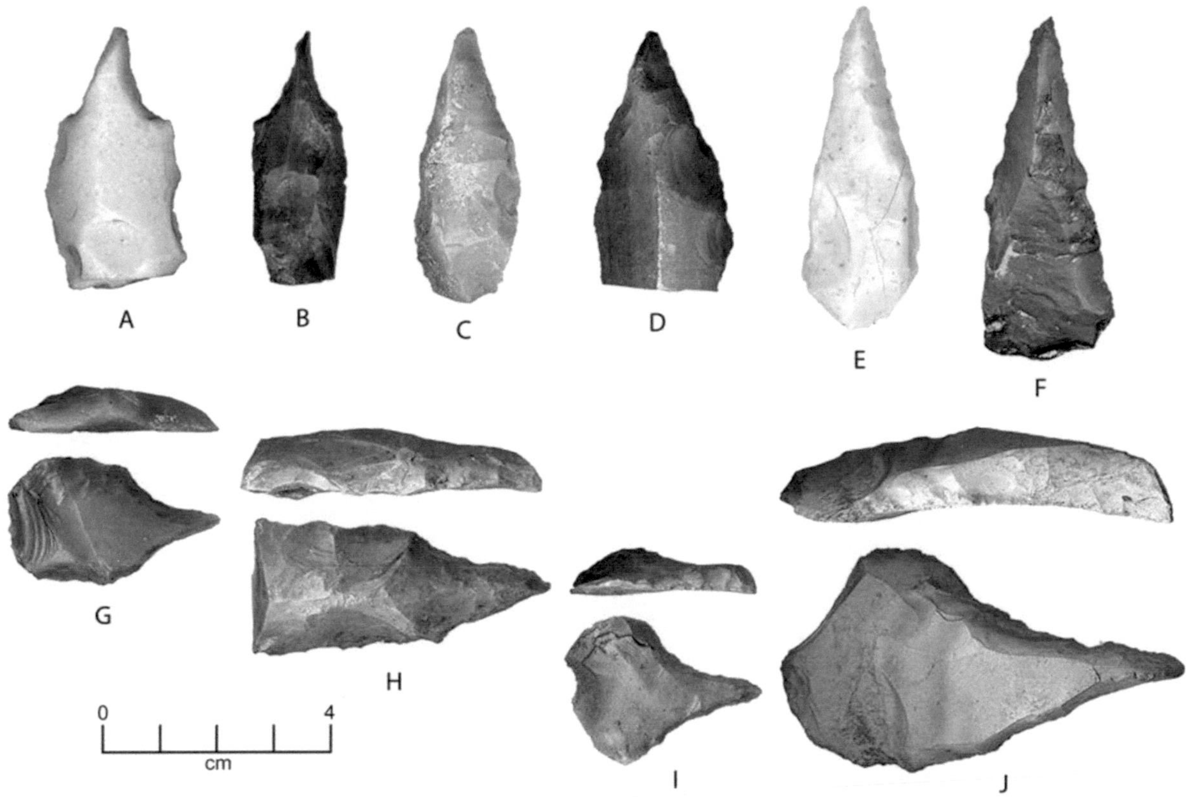

FIGURE 5.26. Examples of beaked scrapers in the Sunshine assemblage. Type A: (A) 1739; (B) 1754; (C) 1802; (D) 1740; (E) 1751. Type B: (F) 1755; (G) 2685; (H) 2673; (I) 2689; (J) 2958.

Finally, the data suggest that most of these tools were probably hafted (Table 5.70). Of the 60 slug scrapers, hafting attributes could be determined for 46, of which 41 (89.1 percent) are believed to have been hafted or possibly hafted. Whether or not these objects were inserted into a socket, as Grimes and Grimes suggest for the Bull Brook flake shavers, is difficult to determine. Their (1985:40–41) argument is based on the high degree of consistency in size and shape of the proximal end as well as transverse breaks where the tool emerges from the haft. Few of the Sunshine slugs have transverse breaks (n = 14, 23.3 percent), and there is little consistency in size and shape.

TABLE 5.69. Maximum Edge Angles Represented on the Sunshine Slug Scrapers

Maximum Edge Angle (°)	Slug Scraper	Slug Scraper/ Graver	Slug Scraper/ Notch	Total	
				N	%
51–60	2			2	3.6
61–70	10			10	17.9
71–80	14	1		15	26.8
81–90	27	2		29	51.8
Subtotal	53	3		56	100.0
Indeterminate	3		1	4	
Total	56	3	1	60	

Beaked Scrapers. The tools referred to as "beaked scrapers" in this analysis have been referred to variously as "narrow end scrapers" (Deller and Ellis 1992:60–63; Ellis and Deller 1988:117–118), "groovers" (Deller 1980:67), "chisels" (Mason 1962:96, Plate 3.2) or "chisel-gravers" (Judge 1973:104–106), "awls" (Gramly 1990:4), and "beaks" or "beaked scrapers" (Ellis and Deller 1988; Storck 1997). As in the case of slug scrapers, this difference in terminology is likely related to the variation in form, size, and possibly function of these objects. Recognizing this wide variation, we use the term *beaked scrapers* loosely and distinguish these tools from "chisels." As defined by Storck, beaked scrapers have a "cutting or scraping tip which is plano-convex in cross-section, usually steeply retouched, and frequently quite thick, hence the term 'beaked'" (1997:65). Two forms of beaked scrapers are recognized in the Sunshine assemblage: (1) those for which the focus of use appears to have been limited to the tip or "beak," which we refer to as Type A "beaks" (n = 52; 51 from the H–N collection and one from the HC collection; Figure 5.26A–E), and (2) those in which retouch occurs around the circumference to create scraper edges, which we refer

TABLE 5.70. Presence of Haft Wear, Proximal Thinning, and Transverse Breaks on the Sunshine Slug Scrapers

	Variable						
Haft Wear	Proximal Thinning	Transverse Break	Slug Scraper	Slug Scraper/ Graver	Slug Scraper/ Notch	Total	Hafting
A	A	A	4	1		5	NH
A	P	A	31			31	PH
P	P	A	2			2	H
I	P	P	1			1	H
A	I	A		1		1	I
I	I	A	6		1	7	H
I	I	P	12	1		13	I
Summary							
Total Hafted						41	
Total Not Hafted						5	
Total Indeterminate						14	
Overall Total						60	

Note: A = absent; H = hafted; I = indeterminate; NH = not hafted, P = present; PH = possibly hafted.

to as Type B "beaks" ($n = 67$; 65 from the H–N collection and two from the HC collection; Figure 5.26F–J). The latter are called "combination narrow/wide end scrapers" by Deller and Ellis (1992:63). Only four specimens are not manufactured from chert; three of these are made from FGV, and the fourth is made from obsidian (Table 5.42).

As is the case for all of the Sunshine scrapers, the beaked scrapers occur in both unifacial and bifacial form, but where over 90 percent of end and side scrapers are unifacial, over 30 percent ($n = 36$) of beaked scrapers are bifacial. To assess if facial flaking determined differences in function, we examined all variables separately for the two. There appears to be an association between scraper type and facial retouch ($\chi^2 = 3.643, df = 1, p = .056$), with a greater number of unifacial Type B beaks (77.6 percent) than unifacial Type A beaks (61.5 percent), but unifacial and bifacial specimens do not differ significantly, either as to size category ($\chi^2 = 4.334, df = 6, p = .632$) or in metric measures (Table 5.71). Unifacial and bifacial specimens also do not differ with respect to maximum edge angle, but they do with respect to use-wear (Table 5.72). Type A and Type B beaks also do not differ in size categories ($\chi^2 = 1.560, df = 5, p = .905$) or length, width, or weight, but they do differ in thickness (Table 5.71). Size categories and descriptive statistics are shown by type in Tables 5.73 and 5.74.

The two scraper types also differ with respect to both use-wear and maximum edge angle (Table 5.72). Concerning use-wear, Type B specimens exhibit both crushing/micro-step fractures and abrasion more often than do Type A specimens (Table 5.75). But, in fact, this difference

TABLE 5.71. Results of *T*-Test Comparisons Between Size Measures of the Sunshine Beaked Scrapers with Respect to Facial Flaking and Scraper Type

Comparison	Variable	*t*	*df*	*p*
Facial Flaking	Maximum Length	.973	12.9	.070
	Maximum Width	−.153	11.1	.881
	Maximum Thickness	.531	59.3	.598
	Actual Weight	.297	64.0	.767
Scraper Type	Maximum Length	.258	12.9	.800
	Maximum Width	−1.151	16.0	.267
	Maximum Thickness	−1.833	112.8	.062
	Actual Weight[a]	−.955	10.0	.362

[a] Calculated using complete specimens only ($n = 15$).

TABLE 5.72. Results of Chi-Square Comparisons of Use-Wear and Maximum Edge Angle of the Sunshine Beaked Scrapers with Respect to Facial Flaking and Scraper Type

Comparison	Variable	χ^2	*df*	*p*
Facial Flaking	Use-Wear	13.746	7	**.056**
	Maximum Angle	10.471	6	.160
Scraper Type	Use-Wear	14.473	7	**.043**
	Maximum Angle	17.789	6	**.007**

Note: Significant probabilities are in bold.

TABLE 5.73. Distribution of the Sunshine Beaked Scrapers Across Size Categories

	Scraper Type			
	A		B	
Size Category	*N*	%	*N*	%
7	1	3.5	2	4.8
8	7	24.1	8	19.1
9	11	37.9	18	42.8
10	7	24.1	9	21.4
11	3	10.3	5	11.9
Subtotal	29	100.0	42	100.0
Indeterminate	23		25	
Total	52		67	

TABLE 5.74. Quantitative Data for the Sunshine Beaked Scrapers

Scraper Type	Statistic	Maximum Length (mm)	Maximum Width (mm)	Maximum Thickness (mm)	Actual Weight (g)
Type A	*N*	7	7	49	50
	Range	37.6–66.7	10.2–24.8	3.3–13.9	1.42–19.59
	Mean	48.97	18.44	8.47	8.21
	SD	9.249	4.616	2.501	4.895
Type B	*N*	8	10	66	66
	Range	34.90–66.20	14.20–34.30	4.80–22.10	2.67–63.11
	Mean	47.56	21.32	9.53	11.2
	SD	11.842	5.986	3.528	9.499

TABLE 5.75. Use-Wear Present on the Sunshine Beaked Scrapers

	Scraper Type											
	Type A						Type B					
	Unifacial		Bifacial		Total		Unifacial		Bifacial		Total	
Type of Use-Wear	*N*	%	*N*	%	*N*	%	*N*	%	*N*	%	*N*	%
Crushing/Micro–Step Fractures	25	78.1	15	83.3	40	80.0	28	53.8	11	73.3	39	58.2
Minor Abrasion	4	12.5	1	5.6	5	10.0	6	11.5			6	9.0
Heavy Abrasion	2	6.3	1	5.6	3	6.0	2	3.8	1	6.7	3	4.5
Crushing/Micro–Step Fractures + Minor Abrasion	1	3.1			1	2.0	10	19.2			10	14.9
Crushing/Micro–Step Fractures + Heavy Abrasion							2	3.8	1	6.7	3	4.5
Minor + Heavy Abrasion			1	5.6	1	2.0	3	5.8	2	13.3	5	7.5
Crushing/Micro–Step Fractures + Minor and Heavy Abrasion							1	1.9			1	1.5
Subtotal	32	100.0	18	100.0	50	100.0	52	100.0	15	100.0	67	100.0
Indeterminate	2				2							
Total	34				52						67	

is driven by the unifacial Type B specimens, which relates back to the significant association between scraper type and facial flaking, as noted above. It makes sense that Type B scrapers exhibit more varied use-wear because they are combination tools, with a pointed bit on one end and a rounded scraper edge either at the other end or along one or both sides. Why there is more variation in the use-wear on unifacial and bifacial Type B specimens, however, is unclear. Type B specimens also have larger edge angles than do Type A specimens, with nearly 75 percent having angles greater than 70° (Table 5.76) as compared with 58.0 percent for Type A specimens. Again, this difference appears to be attributable to the unifacial specimens, which overall have larger edge angles than bifacial specimens, but, as Table 5.72 shows, this difference is not significant.

In sum, there is no size difference between unifacial and bifacial specimens, nor is there any significant difference in maximum edge angle, although unifacial specimens appear to have slightly larger angles than bifacial specimens. The only significant difference between unifacial and bifacial beaks is with respect to use-wear. On the other hand, there is a difference in thickness, maximum edge angle, and use-wear between Type A and Type B beaks. This is in some part likely related to the fact that Type B beaks are combination tools, with a point and one or more scraper EUs, whereas Type A beaks are not. With respect to Type B beaks, however, the difference in use-wear is exhibited by the unifacial rather than bifacial specimens, which constitute over 77 percent of this tool type. It appears, then, that both facial flaking and tool type bear a relation to function.

Table 5.77 shows hafting attributes for both Type A and Type B beaks. Of 51 Type A beaks, haft could be determined for 43 specimens, and of 67 Type B beaks, for 47 specimens. In his examination of 48 beaked scrapers from the Fisher site in southern Ontario, Storck (1997:72) describes two forms, similar to the two types described here from Sunshine. He notes that those that resemble our Type A beaks are often irregular in shape and quite thick at the proximal end. He argues that "the absence of any attempt to thin or otherwise shape this area suggests that the tool was not intended to be hafted but hand-held" (1997:72). On the other hand, those that resemble our Type B specimens may have been hafted; Storck notes that one specimen had actually been notched for this purpose. No similar pattern exists in the Sunshine beaks. Interestingly, the two types differ little in the proportions of unhafted (30.2 and 31.9 percent, respectively), hafted (55.8 and 48.9 percent, respectively), and possibly hafted specimens (14.0 and 19.1 percent, respectively).

Storck (1997:74) concludes, based on use-wear studies, that the beaked scrapers he examined were used in either pulling or pushing motions or in both. Judge, in his examination of "chisel-gravers" from the central Rio Grande Valley, suggests "hand-held gouging of wood or bone in deep, narrow places such as that necessary to hollow out the distal end of a main shaft to receive the pointed foreshaft." He also suggests that use in this way is similar to that of a drill and "that it was the lateral edges rather than the tip [of the bit] that were the important functional components of the tool" (1973:104–106). In the Sunshine sample it does appear that with respect to the beak, the lateral edges were heavily used, but there is also sometimes heavy abrasion on the tips as well. Rarely, however, are the tips broken. This may be related to the fact that the lateral edge angles of the beak are almost always greater than 70° and often between 80 and 90° (Table 5.76), which would provide strength for the bit. Lateral edge angles of the scraper edges, when present, are generally lower.

The original blank is preserved on 40 Type A specimens and 43 Type B specimens. All are flakes except for two, which are chunks. Of the flakes, only 16 have platforms (eight Type A and eight Type B); four (50 percent) of the Type A specimens and three (37.5 percent) of the Type B specimens are made on biface reduction flakes.

Gravers

A total of 351 artifacts have been identified as gravers, 329 from the H–N collection and 22 from the Hamilton College collection. Of the H–N specimens, 153 have been subjected to special analysis (Table 5.78). A graver is defined by Gramly in the strictest sense as "a flake or blade with a small, sharp projection that has been created by unifacial retouch" (1990:26); he points out, however, that the term is "loosely applied to a broad range of flake artifacts with spurs" (1990:26). These artifacts are variously referred to as "graving spurs" (Moeller 1980:60–61), "piercers" (Deller and Ellis 1992:70), "perforators" (Goebel et al. 1991:54), or simply "spurs" (Deller and Ellis 1992; Irwin and Wormington 1970). Almost all of the Sunshine gravers identify with Gramly's strict definition (Figure 5.27); only 45 are bifacial, and 29 of these occur as combination tools with either crescents ($n = 20$) or scrapers ($n = 9$).

As Table 5.78 shows, nearly all of the Sunshine gravers ($n = 164$, 93.7 percent) are made from chert. Also, the majority of these tools are fairly large, as 88.1 percent ($n = 118$) of the 134 specimens for which size could be measured are size 8 or larger (Table 5.79). Not surprisingly, all of the smallest gravers (size 5 or smaller) are from the HC excavations rather than either the H–N or HC surface collections. One in particular, the size 2 specimen, was only recognized as a graver once it was viewed under the microscope (Figure 5.28). It is only 10.8 mm in length! We find it hard to imagine how this tool was actually used.

TABLE 5.76. Maximum Edge Angles Represented on the Sunshine Beaked Scrapers

	Scraper Type											
	Type A						Type B					
	Unifacial		Bifacial		Total		Unifacial		Bifacial		Total	
Maximum Edge Angle (°)	*N*	%	*N*	%	*N*	%	*N*	%	*N*	%	*N*	%
21–30			1	5.6	1	2.0	1	2.0			1	1.5
31–40	1	3.1			1	2.0						
41–50	2	6.3	4	22.2	6	12.0						
51–60	2	6.3	2	11.1	4	8.0	5	9.8	1	6.7	6	9.1
61–70	7	21.9	2	11.1	9	18.0	6	11.8	4	26.7	10	15.2
71–80	17	53.1	3	16.7	20	40.0	16	31.4	2	13.3	18	27.3
81–90	3	9.4	6	33.3	9	18.0	23	45.1	8	53.3	31	46.9
Subtotal	32	100.0	18	100.0	50	100.0	51	100.0	15	100.0	66	100.0
Indeterminate			2		2		1				1	
Total	32		20		52		52		15		67	

TABLE 5.77. Presence of Haft Wear, Proximal Thinning, and Transverse Breaks on the Sunshine Beaked Scrapers

Variable					
Haft Wear	Proximal Thinning	Transverse Break	Type A Scraper	Type B Scraper	Hafting
A	A	A	14	15	NH
A	P	A	6	8	PH
P	A	A	1	1	H
P	P	A	2	2	H
A	I	A	1		I
P	I	A	1		H
I	A	A	3	13	I
I	I	A	2	3	I
P	I	P	1	1	H
I	I	P	18	19	H
A	I	I	1	1	I
I	I	I	2	3	I
I	P	A		1	PH
Summary					
Total Hafted			29	32	
Total Not Hafted			14	15	
Total Indeterminate			9	20	
Overall Total			52	67	

Note: A = absent; H = hafted; I = indeterminate; NH = not hafted; P = present; PH = possibly hafted.

FIGURE 5.27. Examples of gravers in the Sunshine assemblage. Single spurred: (A) 1729; (B) 2044; (C) 1721, (D) surface 1993, FS 8, (E) 2585; (F) 1848. Multispurred: (G) 325; (H) 1997 Operation 2, 6.91E, 1.60N, Level 9; (I) 2590; (J) 2027; (K) 2053; (L) 607; (M) 2589.

TABLE 5.78. Gravers from the Sunshine Locality by Raw Material

	RAW MATERIAL		TOTAL	
TOOL TYPE	CHERT	FINE-GRAINED VOLCANICS	*N*	%
Graver	53	4	57	32.6
Scraper/Graver	77	3	80	45.7
Crescent/Graver	17	3	20	11.4
Graver/Notch	7		7	4.0
Scraper/Graver/Notch	8	1	9	5.1
Chisel/Scraper/Graver	2		2	1.1
Total	164	11	175	100.0

Edge angles for the graver spurs are, on the average, fairly large (Table 5.80). For single-spurred gravers, about half (n = 43, 53.8 percent) are over 60°. For multispurred gravers, 76.8 percent (n = 53) have at least one spur with an edge angle over 60°. All of the graver spurs for which use-wear could be determined (n = 162) show evidence of use (Table 5.81). A number of spurs have some sort of break, often a snapped tip or a burin-like break originating at the tip on either the ventral or dorsal side of the tool. Breakage, however, was not systematically recorded.

A number of functions have been proposed for gravers, such as tattooing (e.g., MacDonald 1985; Painter 1985; Roberts 1936), piercing (e.g., Deller and Ellis 1992), and engraving (e.g., MacDonald 1985; Roberts 1936). As Tomenchuck and Storck (1997:509) have recently pointed out, however, these hypothesized functions remain largely untested. Gravers come in a variety of shapes (Table 5.82), and if the length of the spurs, number of spurs per object, and proximity of spurs to one another on an object were considered, we would likely see a good deal of variation there as well. We have recorded only the number of spurs, which can be seen in Table 5.83. Nearly half (n = 80, 45.7 percent) of the Sunshine gravers exhibit more than a single spur, and one tool has eight. Johnson (1989:113) has suggested that multiple spurs represent serial replacement; that is, when one spur breaks or is worn out, the object can be turned slightly to engage another. This is a reasonable suggestion, especially in cases where spurs occur in various, not necessarily patterned, locations on the artifact.

Tomenchuck and Storck (1997; see also Tomenchuck 1997) have proposed two particular types of gravers, which they term compass gravers and coring gravers. Although these tools were proposed as part of the northeastern Paleoindian tool kit, they may also exist in western and Alaskan Paleoindian sites as well (see Tomenchuck and Storck 1997:518, Table 2). We were intrigued by their analysis and decided to examine the Sunshine data for

TABLE 5.79. Distribution of the Sunshine Gravers Across Size Categories

Size Category	Graver	Scraper/ Graver	Crescent/ Graver	Graver/ Notch	Scraper/ Graver/Notch	Chisel/ Scraper/Graver	Total *N*	Total %
2	1						1	.8
3			1				1	.8
4	1						1	.8
5	1						1	.8
6	2						2	1.5
7	4	5		1			10	7.5
8	15	5	3	3	1		27	20.1
9	13	16	4	1	1	1	36	26.9
10	8	25	4	1	3	1	42	31.3
11	1	9	1		1		12	9.0
12	1						1	.8
Subtotal	47	60	13	6	6	2	134	100.0
Indeterminate	10	20	7	1	3		41	
Total	57	80	20	7	9	2	175	

TABLE 5.80. Edge Angles Represented on the Sunshine Gravers

Edge Angle (°)	Single-Spurred Gravers	Multiple-Spurred Gravers: Minimum	Multiple-Spurred Gravers: Maximum
11–20		3	
21–30	1	3	
31–40	9	8	2
41–50	12	5	6
51–60	15	14	8
61–70	20	16	17
71–80	18	19	32
81–90	5	1	4
Indeterminate	3	2	2
Total	83	71	71

Note: Angles for points on crescent/gravers are not included because they were not systematically measured.

TABLE 5.81. Use-Wear Present on the Sunshine Graver Spurs

Type of Use-Wear	*N*	%
Crushing/Micro–Step Fractures	80	49.4
Minor Abrasion	42	25.9
Major Abrasion	10	6.2
Minor + Major Abrasion	2	2.5
Crushing/Micro–Step Fractures + Minor Abrasion	13	8.0
Crushing/Micro–Step Fractures + Major Abrasion	10	6.2
Crushing/Micro–Step Fractures + Major and Minor Abrasion	3	1.9
Subtotal	162	100.0
Indeterminate	13	
Total	175	

such tools. Unfortunately, Tomenchuck and Storck's article came to our attention long after we began the analysis of the H–N collection, and thus we were only able to examine those items still in our possession (that is, without yet another trip to the museum!); so our results are preliminary but interesting nonetheless. We concentrate here only on compass gravers.

Tomenchuck and Storck suggest that these tools were used to create a circular groove, much the same way as a draftsman's compass is used to draw a circle (Figure 5.29). Compass gravers can have either two (Figure 5.29A) or three spurs (Figure 5.29B) as a single tool unit. On a

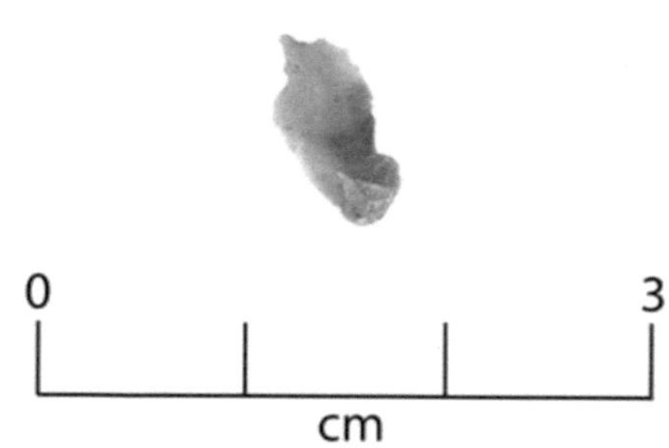

FIGURE 5.28. Small graver found in Test Unit E, Level 3, of the 1997 excavation by Hamilton College.

TABLE 5.82. Shape of the Sunshine Gravers

Shape	Graver	Scraper/ Graver	Crescent/ Graver	Graver/ Notch	Scraper/ Graver/Notch	Chisel/ Scraper/Graver	Total	
							N	%
Circular	10	7		2			19	10.9
Oval	7	9			1		17	9.7
Irregular	29	39		4	5	2	79	45.1
Triangular		4					4	2.3
Linear	1	5					6	3.4
Crescentic		2	20				22	12.6
Fragment	10	14		1	3		28	16.0
Total	57	80	20	7	9	2	175	100.0

TABLE 5.83. Number of Spurs Represented on the Sunshine Gravers

Number of Spurs	Graver	Scraper/ Graver	Crescent/ Graver	Graver/ Notch	Scraper/ Graver/Notch	Chisel/ Scraper/Graver	Total	
							N	%
1	29	48	12	1	3	2	95	54.3
2	16	22	4	2	2		46	26.3
3	7	4	1	2	3		17	9.7
4	4	4	1	2	1		12	6.9
5		2					2	1.1
6								
7			2				2	1.1
8	1						1	.8
Total	57	80	20	7	9	2	175	100.0

tool with two spurs, one spur serves as the pilot, and the other, as the scribe (Figure 5.29C). On the three-spurred graver, the middle spur serves as the pilot, while the other two both serve as scribes. Describing these tools in their assemblage from the Fisher site in southern Ontario, Tomenchuck and Storck state:

> The spurs and interspur notches were produced by fine, abrupt secondary retouch originating on the ventral flake surface (the cutting edge, or attack surface) and terminating on the dorsal face (the clearance surface). The axes of the spurs that are presumed to have functioned in pairs or triads tend to be parallel or slightly divergent (i.e., <5 degrees) [1997:510].

The two different types of spurs exhibit contrasting types of use damage (Tomenchuck and Storck 1997:511). The pilot spur tends to have microchip scars that radiate out from the tip, suggesting stationary, rotary movement. The scribe shows microchip scars also originating from the tip but parallel to one another, suggesting a pulling or pushing motion. The use-wear is generally more intensive on the inside edges of both spurs. Finally, the notch between pilot and scribe exhibits polish.

Of the 80 multiple-spurred Sunshine gravers subjected to special analysis, we were able to reexamine only 21. Of these, four gravers definitely exhibit the three types of use-wear described above; three of these are single-scribe gravers (Figure 5.30A–C), and the fourth (Figure 5.30D) is a double-scribe graver (with the pilot in the center). Another three gravers exhibit some but not all of the proposed types of use-wear described by Tomenchuck and Storck (Figure 5.30E–G). For example, it was difficult to tell whether there was abrasion in the notch when the entire tool appears slightly abraded; or a broken spur prohibited examining the microchip wear on the tip. Two of the "possibles" have a single scribe, and one may have two scribes. Therefore, we conclude that there are four compass gravers (Figure 5.30A–D) and another three tools that could be (Figure 5.30E–F), representing 35 percent of the gravers examined. Of course these results are

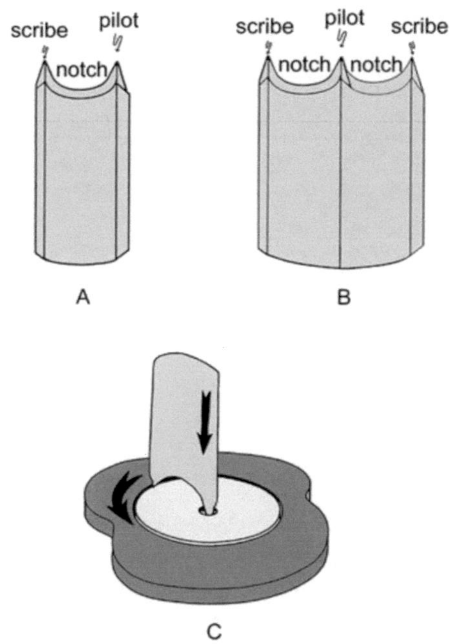

FIGURE 5.29. Schematic diagram of (A) single- and (B) double-scribe compass gravers and (C) the suggested manner of their use (after Tomenchuck and Storck 1997:516, Figure 5).

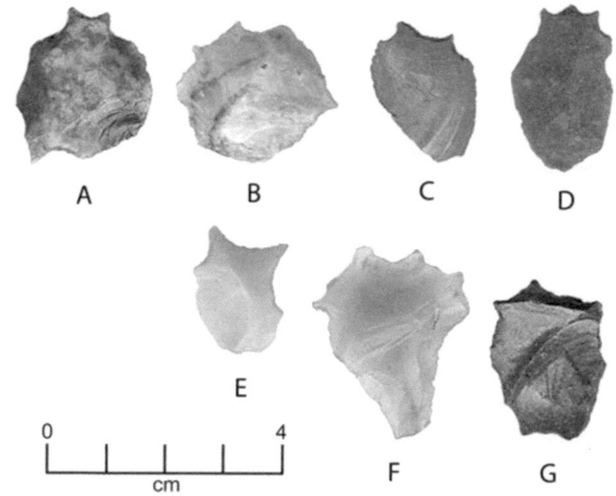

FIGURE 5.30. Examples of compass gravers in the Sunshine assemblage. Definite: (A) 1853; (B) 1800; (C) SW3, no #; (D) SW3, no #. Possible: (E) 1804, (F) 1722; (G) SW3, no #.

tentative because we were able to examine fewer than a quarter of the multiple-spurred gravers, but they do suggest that compass gravers may be an important component of the Sunshine graver assemblage. On a recent trip to the NSM (summer 2005) to pull artifacts for photographing, we came across a number of gravers that, at least to the naked eye, appeared to be compass gravers (see, e.g., Figure 5.27E), which would add weight to this conclusion.

Notches

Thirty-five artifacts were identified as exhibiting notches, 29 from the H–N collection (22 of which were subjected to special analysis) and six from the HC collection (Figure 5.31). Thus a total of 28 notches were analyzed, 24 of which occur in combination with other tools (Table 5.84). All but one combination graver/scraper/notch (which is made from FGV) are made from chert. Of the 23 for which use-wear could be determined, nine exhibit crushing and micro–step fractures, 10 are lightly abraded, and four exhibit both crushing and abrasion (Table 5.84). Edge angles for notches, like those of gravers, are generally large (Table 5.85). Of the 23 artifacts that exhibit a single notch, 14 (63.6 percent) are greater than 60° (one is indeterminate). All of the five multiple-notched tools have at least one notch with edge angles greater than 70°.

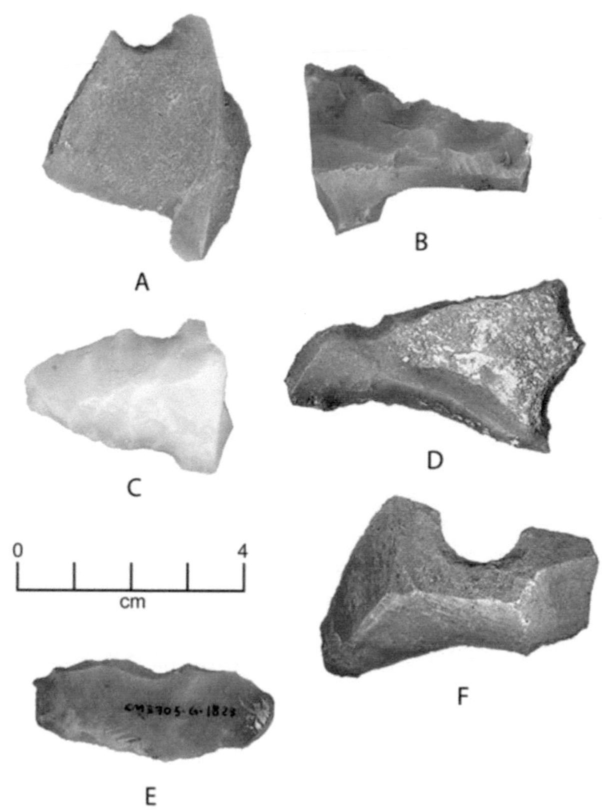

FIGURE 5.31. Examples of notches in the Sunshine assemblage: (A–B) no provenience; (C) SW3, no #; (D) 1745; (E) 1823; (F) 231.

TABLE 5.84. Use-Wear Present on the Sunshine Notches

TYPE OF USE-WEAR	NOTCH	GRAVER/ NOTCH	SCRAPER/ NOTCH	POINT BLADE/ NOTCH	GRAVER/ SCRAPER/NOTCH	TOTAL N	TOTAL %
Crushing/Micro–Step Fractures		5	2		2	9	39.1
Minor Abrasion	2	1	3	1	3	10	43.5
Crushing/Micro–Step Fractures + Minor Abrasion					1	1	4.4
Crushing/Micro–Step Fractures + Major Abrasion			2		1	3	13.0
Subtotal	2	6	7	1	7	23	100.0
Indeterminate	2	1			2	5	
Total	4	7	7	1	9	28	

TABLE 5.85. Edge Angles Represented on the Sunshine Notches

EDGE ANGLE (°)	SINGLE-NOTCHED TOOLS N	SINGLE-NOTCHED TOOLS %	MULTIPLE-NOTCHED TOOLS MINIMUM N	MINIMUM %	MAXIMUM N	MAXIMUM %
31–40			1	20.0		
41–50	3	13.6	1	20.0		
51–60	5	22.7	1	20.0		
61–70	3	13.6	2	40.0		
71–80	8	36.4			1	20.0
81–90	3	13.6			4	80.0
Subtotal	22	100.0	5	100.0	5	100.0
Indeterminate	1					
Total	23		5		5	

Drills

Thirteen artifacts in the Sunshine assemblage have been identified as drills (Figure 5.32), all from the H–N collection. These artifacts are recognized less on the basis of morphology than on edge beveling and the pattern of use-wear. Beveling and use-wear occur on alternate margins of the drill bit, indicating a rotary motion (Gramly 1990:20; see Figure 5.32I–J). All of these artifacts are made from chert, with the exception of two (Figure 5.32G, I), which are made from obsidian. As Figure 5.32 shows, the Sunshine drills vary considerably in size and morphology (see also Table 5.86), and because there are so few, they are discussed individually rather than as a group.

Three artifacts (specimens 1886, 1750, 2848; Figure 5.32 A–C) are long and cylindrical in shape. All three exhibit bending breaks, one (1886) only at the distal end and the other two at both ends. Specimen 1886 (Figure 5.32A) is heavily abraded on alternate margins, presumably resulting from use. The proximal end is also abraded, but the damage here extends to surface arrises as well, suggesting haft wear. Specimen 1750 (Figure 5.32B) also exhibits haft wear at the proximal end, although part of the haft element is missing. Surface abrasion on this specimen is extreme, suggesting great or extended pressure on the haft area. The distal end exhibits two successive burin breaks, which appear to have resulted from the bending break on that end. The third specimen is just a small section of the drill bit and exhibits heavy abrasion on alternate margins.

Specimen 1783 (Figure 5.32D) was originally believed to be a projectile point, based on its morphology. However, it exhibits a small amount of abrasion along the alternate edges of the distal end, which is not consistent with use as a projectile point. Because of the pattern of use, we have identified it as a possible drill. The tip of this specimen has been snapped off. The lateral edges of the proximal end are lightly ground, suggesting it was hafted, but this grinding extends only about .6 cm up each edge.

Specimens 1888, 1890, and 1858 (Figure 5.32E–G) show haft abrasion on their proximal ends. Specimens in Figure 5.32I–J likely were hafted but are broken; and thus this cannot be definitely determined. The artifact in Figure 5.32H as well as Sunshine Well 2, no # (which is of the same shape but was not photographed) are obviously broken, but on the basis of form we have categorized them as possible drills. There is use-wear along the edges of what would have been the drill bit on both, but there is not enough of the bit to determine whether the wear would have been on alternate margins. No haft wear was observed on either artifact.

Finally, the artifact in Figure 5.32K is a concave/convex scraper with a small drill bit at one corner. The artifact is unifacial except for the drill bit, which is bifacially retouched. The bit is beveled and worn on alternate margins.

TABLE 5.86. Quantitative Data for the Sunshine Drills and Chisels

PROVENIENCE	MAXIMUM LENGTH (mm)	MAXIMUM WIDTH (mm)	MAXIMUM THICKNESS (mm)	ACTUAL WEIGHT (g)	FIGURE REFERENCE
Drills					
1886	—	14.0	8.0	10.97	5.32A
1750	—	—	8.0	5.26	5.32B
2848	—	—	3.1	1.46	5.32C
1783	63.4	13.7	6.0	4.68	5.32D
2699	—	—	9.2	6.76	5.32J
SW3A, 47	—	—	8.4	6.18	Not photographed
1888	41.9	30.4	8.0	5.99	5.32E
1890	25.3	23.7	5.2	2.25	5.32F
1843	—	—	6.4	3.15	5.32I
1858	22.1	8.2	3.8	.61	5.32G
SW2, no #	—	—	8.8	—	Not photographed
SW3, no #	—	31.0	9.2	12.20	5.32H
SW3B, 10M	—	—	8.1	12.42	5.32K
Chisels					
1746	53.8	43.8	6.0	11.70	5.33A
1757	—	34.8	4.9	4.91	5.33B
1799	37.6	10.2	6.2	2.52	5.33C

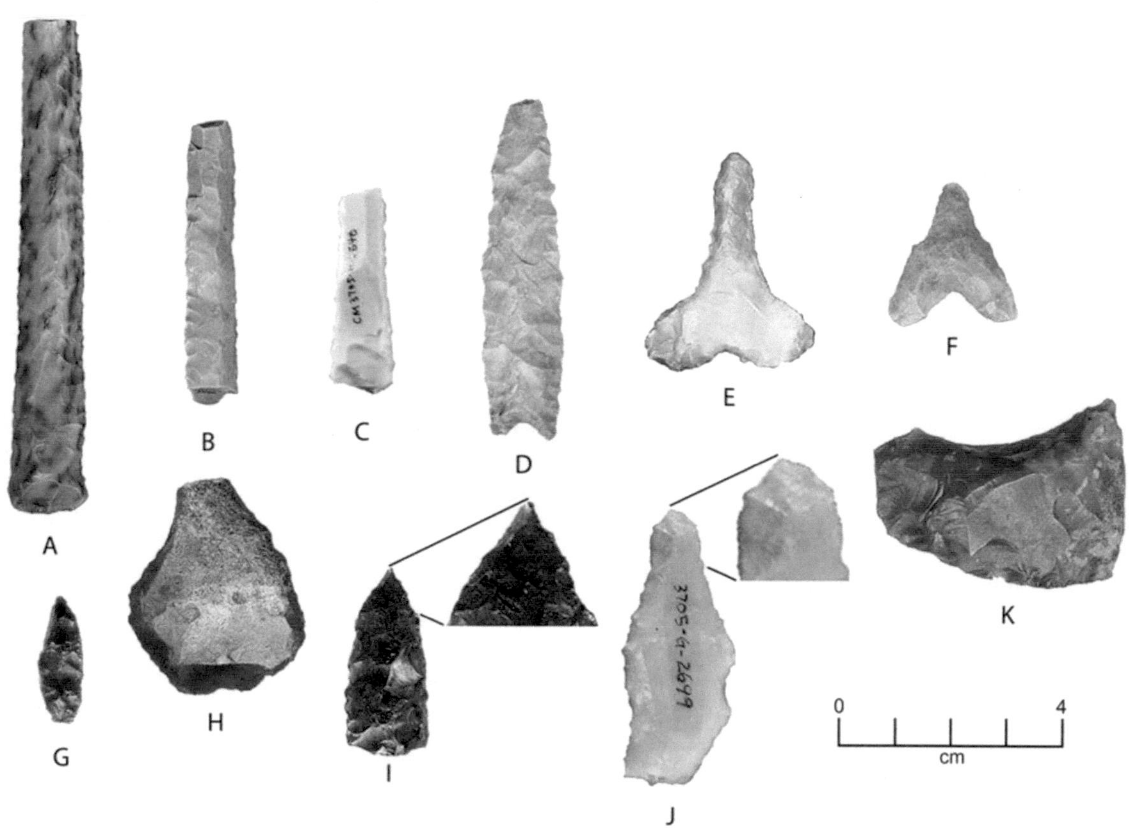

FIGURE 5.32. Drills in the Sunshine assemblage: (A) 1886; (B) 1750; (C) 2848; (D) 1783; (E) 1888; (F) 1890; (G) 1858; (H) SW3, no #; (I) 2699; (J) 1843; (K) SW3B, 10M. (SW3A, 47, and SW2, no #, were not photographed.)

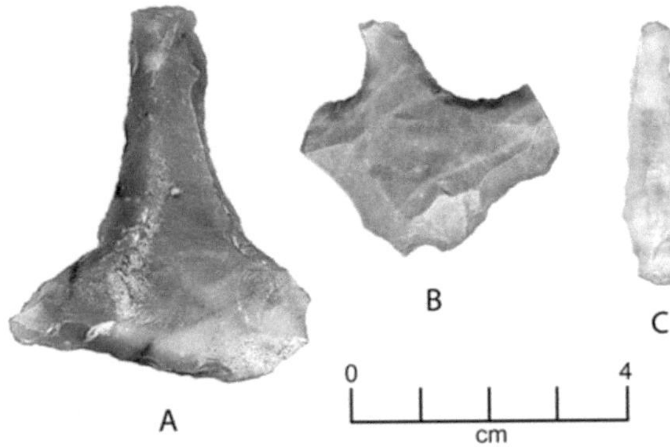

FIGURE 5.33. Chisels in the Sunshine assemblage: (A) 1746, chisel/scraper/graver; (B) 1757, chisel/scraper/graver; (C) 1799, hafted chisel.

FIGURE 5.34. Examples of amorphous unifaces in the Sunshine assemblage. None has provenience.

TABLE 5.87. Quantitative Data for the Sunshine Amorphous Unifaces

Statistic	Maximum Length (mm)	Maximum Length (mm)	Maximum Thickness (mm)	Actual Weight (g)
N	2	7	48	49
Range	29.5–41.9	5.7–35.1	3.3–17.2	1.2–21.7
Mean	35.70	20.97	6.63	6.69
SD	8.768	9.185	2.706	4.663

Given the variation in size and morphology, these artifacts were likely used for several different kinds of tasks, all of which required rotary motion to penetrate the median. We will not speculate as to the functions these artifacts might have served.

Chisels

Three artifacts have been identified as possible chisels (Figure 5.33, Table 5.86). These tools are identified by a long, narrow projection that ends in a rounded or blunt point. All three of the Sunshine chisels are made from chert; two are unifacial combination tools, and the third is a bifacial chisel. Specimen 1746 (Figure 5.33A) is a chisel/scraper/graver. The chisel bit occurs at the end of the long projection. The bit is actually on the original striking platform of the flake blank (a non–biface reduction flake), but this area also appears to be abraded from use as well. This artifact is the ultimate combination tool in that there are also two concave scrapers and an end scraper with a spur (which we have categorized as a graver—see Figure 5.18A). Specimen 1757 (Figure 5.33B) is also a chisel/scraper/graver. The chisel tip is heavily abraded, as are the scraper edges. There was another projection, which has been snapped off, but it may have been a second chisel bit.

Specimen 1799 (Figure 5.33C) is a bifacial chisel that appears to have been hafted. The lateral edges of the lower third of the artifact are heavily abraded, although there is little in the way of surface arris abrasion. The chisel bit is also heavily abraded on the end.

Amorphous Unifaces

Amorphous unifaces are those specimens that cannot be identified with any of the other categories. There are 106 amorphous unifaces in the Sunshine assemblage (Figure 5.34), 100 from the H–N and six from the Hamilton collection. Forty-three of the H–N specimens and all of the HC specimens were subjected to special analyses, for a total of 49. Most ($n = 44$) of these artifacts are manufactured from chert; four of the remaining five are FGV, and the fifth is obsidian.

All of these artifacts are either irregular in shape ($n = 21$) or fragmentary ($n = 28$). The original blank could be determined for all but six specimens; 12 are made on chunks, and 31 are made on flakes, nine of which retain their platforms. Five of these are biface reduction flakes.

Use-wear could be determined on all of the 49 amorphous unifaces, nearly half ($n = 24$) of which exhibit only crushing/micro–step fractures; 20 have only abrasion. The remainder exhibit both types of use-wear. Table 5.87 shows the quantitative data for these tools.

Cores and "Clovis Blade"

Twenty-two cores have been identified in the Sunshine assemblage, 12 from the H–N collection and 10 from the HC collection; five of the latter are from the excavations (Figure 5.35). As Table 5.88 shows, all but four are manu-

FIGURE 5.35. Examples of cores in the Sunshine assemblage: (A) no provenience; (B) 1997 Operation 2 (97-Op2), 114.7E, 105.5N, surface; (C) 97-Op2, 106E, 104N, FS 1; (D) SW3, no #; (E) SW3B, no #; (F) surface 1995, FS 290; (G) 1993 excavation, 114E, 106N, Final Stratum E; (H) SW3B, no #; (I) SW3, no #; (J) 1993 excavation, 114E, 106N, Final Stratum E.

factured from chert, and all but one (Figure 5.35A) are relatively small. Thirteen of the 15 that were subjected to special analysis are amorphous cores, but one is a possible polyhedral core (Figure 5.35I), similar to that shown in Gramly's Figure 14a (1990:9), and the other (from Stratum E of the 1993 excavation) is a possible wedge-shaped core (Figure 5.35J), similar to that shown in Gramly's Figure 57 (1990:57).

Several of the cores exhibit battering or abrasion of the edges, suggesting they served as more than just cores. One in particular exhibits a point that is heavily abraded like that of a large graver bit.

A large blade was recovered from Stratum E of the 1995 loader trench excavation (Figure 5.36A). It is manufactured from a white and tan banded chert. Although it was collected from the alluvial gravels, as were the camel bones, the fluted point, and the crescent, the edges show no abrasion, suggesting it did not travel far after deposition. In his study of Clovis blades, Collins (1999b:97–100) recorded 13 measurements and indexes for blades from 12 Clovis and probable Clovis contexts. We recorded nine of these measurements/indexes for the Sunshine blade, and a comparison with Collins's data indicates that this blade is indistinguishable from classic Clovis blades. This find is all the more remarkable because not a single blade or core from which such blades could have been removed was ever mentioned by Hutchinson or Noyes. On our most recent trip to the museum to take final photographs, however, we came across two artifacts that we believe to be blades (Figure 5.36B–C). Neither has the extreme curvature of the specimen in Figure 5.36A, but the artifact in Figure 5.36B is broken, it appears at the midpoint, and thus may have been not only as large (or larger) but also as curved. It is not surprising that these artifacts did not appear unusual to Hutchinson and Noyes, but Clovis blade cores are another matter. These cores are especially spectacular for their size and form, and thus there is no doubt that had they found one, they would have collected it, and the fact that there are none in the H–N assemblage strongly suggests they were (are) not present. We will address this issue in more detail in the concluding chapter.

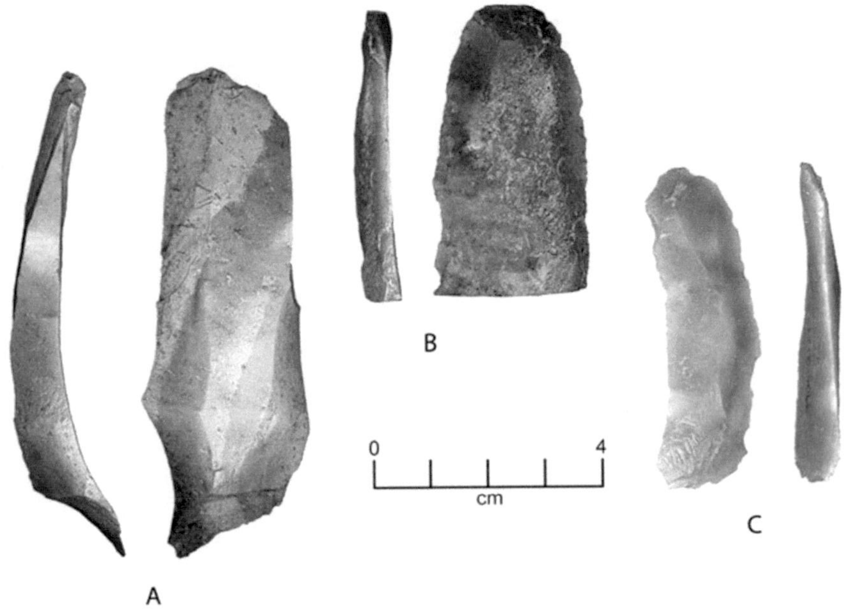

FIGURE 5.36. Blades from the Sunshine Locality: (A) Clovis blade found in situ in Loader Trench 1, 1995, 3.43E, 3.33N, 1,864.5 m; (B) possible blade, no provenience; (C) 2720, possible blade.

TABLE 5.88. Quantitative and Qualitative Data for the Sunshine Cores

Provenience	Final Stratum	Raw Material	Actual Weight (g)	Size Category	Core Type	Abrasion/ Battering	Figure Reference
SW3B/C[a]		Obsidian	8.75	8	—	—	Not shown
Surface 1995		Chert	10.31	8	AM	No	Not shown
SW3		Chert	13.65	9	PO	Yes	5.35I
Surface 1995		Chert	16.76	9	AM	No	Not shown
SW3B		Chert	17.53	9	AM	Yes	5.35H
SW3B		Chert	20.02	10	AM	No	5.35E
SW3		Chert	23.15	10	AM	Yes	5.35D
SW3C[a]		Chert	26.32	10	—	—	Not shown
SW3C[a]		Chert	30.24	10	—	—	Not shown
SW3C[a]		Chert	34.67	10	—	—	Not shown
SW2B[a]		Chert	37.28	11	—	—	Not shown
SW3B[a]		Chert	37.76	11	—	—	Not shown
SW3		Chert	39.54	10	AM	No	Not shown
Excavation 1993	E	Chert	48.57	11	PO	No	5.35J
Surface 1995		Chert	49.02	11	AM	No	5.35F
Surface 1997		Chert	51.63	9	AM	No	5.35B
Excavation 1997	B	Chert	61.12	10	AM	No	5.35C
Surface 1995		FGV	61.84	13	AM	Yes	Not shown
Excavation 1993	E	Quartzite	67.77	11	AM	No	Not shown
Excavation 1993	E	FGV	87.88	12	AM	Yes	5.35G
Excavation 1993	E	Chert	102.90	12	AM	No	Not shown
SW[a]		Chert	363.8	13	—	—	5.35A

Note: AM = amorphous; PO = polyhedral.
[a] Not subjected to special analyses.

FIGURE 5.37. Ground stone in the Sunshine assemblage: (A) 1294, hammer stone; (B) 1826, possible metate fragment; (C) 71, possible metate fragment.

Ground Stone and Hammer Stone

Two pieces of "ground stone" were collected from the Sunshine Locality by Hutchinson and Noyes. Both are fragmentary (Figure 5.37B–C) and are natural cobbles that exhibit light abrasion on one surface and crushing around the edges. Neither is large, but they may have served as small metates. The note accompanying one of these artifacts (Figure 5.37B), written by Phil Hutchinson, states that "this artifact was collected during site surveys to study how artifacts are exposed (revealed) through the action of weather, [or] trampling by bovine and wild horses." He also notes that "groundstone is rare at Sunshine Well. No pestles, mortars, and few shaped [ground-]stone tools [have been] found over a period of more than 15 years" (1979). This is an important, and we believe accurate, statement. We have spent many hours walking over the surface of this site, although not nearly as much time as Phil Hutchinson and Gary Noyes, and we have occasionally seen what might be a fragment of metate, but essentially there does not appear to be much of a ground stone component at Sunshine.

One hammer stone (specimen 1294) was also recovered by Hutchinson and Noyes (Figure 5.37A). It is made from chert and weighs 66.34 g. Because it is part of the general assemblage we did not subject it to special analyses; we did not record any other information concerning this tool.

Notes

1. We returned to the Sunshine Locality in June 2004, meeting Mike Cannon and several of his students. Mike brought a ground-penetrating radar that he wanted to try out at Sunshine to see if we could locate other buried deposits. As we walked around the site, we located five crescents, a concave base point, and three additional bifaces, which we drew, photographed, and shot in with a handheld GPS. When we informed the Bureau of Land Management archaeologist of our discoveries, he suggested that as we had a GPS, we should collect these artifacts. Therefore, when we returned to the site the following day, we relocated the artifacts found the previous day and collected them, giving them Field Specimen numbers 1–9. These are included in Table 5.13 and were included in the special analyses.

   During summer 2007 the Hamilton field school students visited the site, at which time a complete fluted point and a crescent were collected. Because the fluted point was a significant find and adds important information to our discussion, we reexamined the data with this point included. Because of the time involved in reexamining the crescent data and the likelihood that inclusion of this newest specimen would not change the results, we did not include it in our analyses or in the tables.

2. Figure 5.2 includes 6,622 of the 6,738 (98.3 percent) artifacts from the 1993 excavation. Because the weights of 98.3 percent of the assemblage are less than or equal to 2.0 g but maximum weights exceed 100 g, we eliminated the larger artifacts in order to demonstrate the difference in size distributions of the majority of artifacts by stratum. Of the remaining artifacts, 52 occurred in Stratum A (weights range from 2.01 to 50.31 g, with 11 above 10.0 g), two in Stratum C (7.14 g, 18.17 g), and 62 in Stratum F/G (weights range between 2.01 and 102.9 g, with 15 above 15.0 g). These numbers underscore the differences in artifact size across strata.

3. We made a number of visits to the NSM to analyze the H–N collection. In 1995, when we first visited the museum, only a small portion of the artifacts had been accessioned and given museum catalog numbers. For those artifacts not yet accessioned, we recorded Hutchinson and Noyes's catalog numbers, which consist of their site number (1–8) and a Field Specimen number within that site (e.g., Sunshine Well 3, 1). Over the years more of the collection was accessioned, but at the submission of this monograph the process was still incomplete. We have attempted to replace the H–N numbers with the museum numbers during each of our visits, but this had been done for only about half of the collection the last time we visited the museum.

6

Projectile Points

Charlotte Beck and George T. Jones

The Sunshine assemblage contains a sizable number of projectile points, which for the purpose of this study are those bifaces that possess consistent manufactured properties of point, haft, and bilateral symmetry. A total of 967 artifacts have been identified as projectile points, 933 from the Hutchinson and Noyes (H–N) collection and 34 from the Hamilton College (HC) collection. One of the important aspects of the Sunshine point assemblage is the relatively large number of fluted and unfluted lanceolate points, a rarity in the Great Basin, as we discuss below. It is generally believed that fluted points represent Clovis and date the earliest significant occupation of the Great Basin as they do elsewhere in North America (e.g., ca. 11,500–10,800 rcy BP), but there are so few instances in which they have been found in buried contexts and dated that this belief remains conjecture. Further, no comprehensive study has ever been undertaken of either the morphology or the spatial distribution of these points (but see Taylor 2002, 2003), and thus their identification with Clovis is simply an assertion. Here we address two issues with respect to these points. First, we examine the morphology of the Sunshine fluted points and compare them with Clovis and Folsom in order to establish similarities and differences that may exist. Second, we compare the morphology of fluted and unfluted lanceolates in an attempt to evaluate their relation to one another.

The majority of points from Sunshine, however, represent types of the Great Basin Stemmed Series (GBSS). We address two questions concerning these points. A number of types have been defined that date to the terminal Pleistocene/early Holocene (TP/EH), and the first issue we address regards the validity of these types. To date there has been no systematic attempt, comparable to that of Thomas (1981) for Archaic points, to evaluate the typology applied to points of this early period. In spite of the fact that at least seven different stemmed point types have been defined, there is a great deal of similarity among them; this similarity has prompted some researchers to argue that the differences used to distinguish the so-called types are simply the result of breakage and resharpening, a hypothesis that we examine below.

A second issue we address in this chapter regards the actual function of these points; that is, were they, in fact, used as components of projectiles, either javelins or atlatl darts, or did they serve some other purpose? We evaluate these possibilities in detail below.

In addition to lanceolate and GBSS points, there are a small number of early Holocene and Archaic points representative of the Windust (which we do not include in the GBSS), Pinto, Humboldt, Gatecliff, Elko, and Rosegate series. The Gatecliff Series was defined by Thomas (1981, 1983) in an attempt to deal with the "Pinto problem." This problem, however, is still with us (see below), in that confusion remains as to whether all split-stemmed points in areas north of the Mojave Desert are similar morphologically and represent the same time period as those from Gatecliff Shelter. There are several points in the H–N and HC collections, for example, that are quite similar to those from the Pinto Basin site in the Mojave Desert. Thus the Pinto problem is discussed in more detail below.

Finally, there are points in the Sunshine assemblage that do not identify with any previously defined type. We attempt, through an examination of various attributes, to establish categories for these points.

Analytic Protocol

Metric Attributes

All points were measured on the set of attributes standardized by Thomas (1970, 1981; Thomas and Bettinger 1976; see Table 6.1, Figures 6.1–6.2), with two exceptions. First, we differed from Thomas (1981) in the way in which proximal shoulder angle (PSA) and distal shoulder angle (DSA) were measured (Figure 6.2). In his examination of PSA and DSA for the Monitor Valley points Thomas selected the largest angle, between that on the left and that on the right, for measurement. Here, if both left and right angles were measurable, they were averaged for the specimen. If only one side was measurable, that side was considered representative of the specimen.

Second, instead of L_M, which measures the distance from the widest point to the base, we took two separate measurements, L_B (blade length) and L_S (stem length; Figure 6.1). The points in the Sunshine assemblage that are attributable to four of the five GBSS types—Lake Mohave, Silver Lake, Cougar Mountain, and Parman—

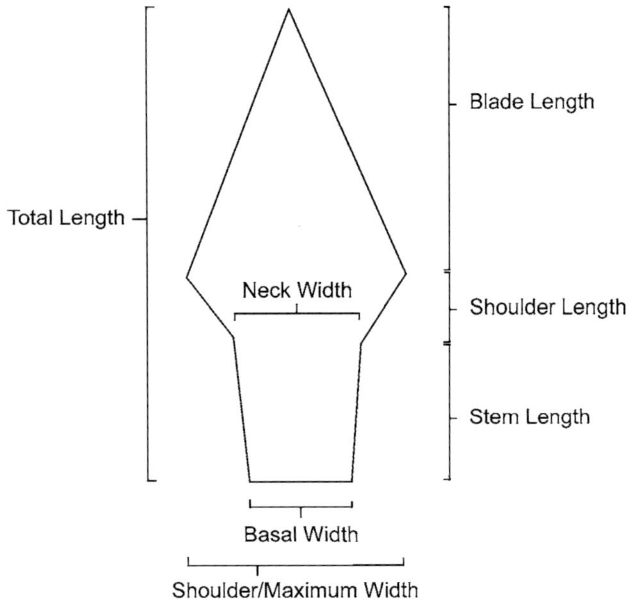

FIGURE 6.1. Metric variables measured on the Sunshine projectile points (after Thomas 1981:14).

are shouldered and have stems that often are equal to or longer than the length of the blade. The DSA on all of these points is greater than 180°, creating a relatively large area between the point of maximum width and the neck, which we refer to as the shoulder (SH). In these cases, $SH = L_T - (L_B + L_S)$, where L_T is total length. Whereas DSA measures the *angle* of the shoulder, SH measures the *portion that the shoulder contributes to overall length.* We believed it might be possible to differentiate points of some types on the basis of stem, shoulder, and blade length. Thus, for these points, the length measurements taken are those shown in Figure 6.1. Actual thickness and actual weight were measured for all specimens.

Qualitative Attributes

A number of qualitative attributes were also measured on all points (Table 6.1). These include material type, presence and location of use-wear, presence and location of resharpening, number of breaks, kind of breakage, location of breakage, flaking pattern, presence and degree of edge grinding, and beveling (on either blade or stem).

Material Type. As discussed in chapter 5, raw material types include chert, obsidian, fine-grained volcanics (FGV), and quartzite; to these we add quartz for the projectile points. The most predominant of these materials are FGV, chert, and obsidian, in that order. As in the general analysis, no attempt was made to distinguish chalcedonies, agates, and so on; all microcrystalline silicates were categorized as chert. An attempt was made, however, to distinguish obsidians by color because in some cases color corresponds fairly well with source (see Jones et al. 2003).

Breakage and Resharpening. Nearly 20 years ago, Flenniken and Raymond (1986) published a controversial article concerning the reliability of projectile points as chronological indicators (see also Flenniken 1985; Flenniken and Wilke 1989). Flenniken and Raymond's argument is based on the fact that projectile points are often broken during use and resharpened for reuse, which can alter considerably a point's morphology. Further, breakage and resharpening most often occur on the proximal end of the point, that is, the base and barbs, the result being that an expanding stem might be resharpened into a parallel-sided stem. This resharpening, they argue, could alter the type assignment of a particular specimen. For example, a point identified with the Elko Eared type before use might, after breakage and resharpening, be identified with the Gatecliff Split-Stem type. This article stimulated a good deal of controversy (e.g., Bettinger et al. 1991; Flenniken and Wilke 1989; Thomas 1986), but several authors have demonstrated that, even if resharpening is a factor, Great Basin Archaic projectile point types are good chronological indicators at a broad scale (Basgall and Hall 2000; Beck 1995, 1998; O'Connell and Inoway 1994). Even so, breakage and resharpening are important factors that should be considered in any projectile point analysis (e.g., Titmus and Woods 1986). Bamforth, in a discussion of sources of variation in Paleoindian projectile point morphology, states that "once a tool is produced, other factors may alter its appearance over the course of its useful life. In the case of projectile points, the most important of these is likely to be the process of resharpening or rejuvenation which occurs after the point breaks" (1991:310). Resharpening has long been recognized as a factor affecting the morphology of lanceolate points, both fluted and unfluted (e.g., Ahler and Geib 2000; Bamforth 1991; Bradley and Frison 1987; Wheat 1979; Wormington 1979). Also, a number of researchers (Amick 1993, 1996; Basgall 1993b; Basgall and Hall 1991; Beck and Jones 1993; Simms and Isgreen 1984) have noted that points of the GBSS quite often exhibit resharpening, which may indeed result in an alteration of their morphologies.

Thus we examined all points for the type of breakage (Figure 6.3) and the location of both breakage and resharpening (Figure 6.4). Whether or not a point has been resharpened is often quite difficult to evaluate and must be done on a case-by-case basis, considering other factors as well. For instance, a bifacial edge typically forms a continuous curve; resharpening because of breakage creates irregularities in this curve. Resharpening can also result

TABLE 6.1. Variables Measured on the Projectile Points from the Sunshine Locality

VARIABLE TYPE	VARIABLE	COMMENTS/STATES
Quantitative	Total Length	As shown in Figure 6.1
	Blade Length	As shown in Figure 6.1
	Stem Length	As shown in Figure 6.1
	Shoulder	(Total Length – [Blade Length + Stem Length])
	Neck Width	As shown in Figure 6.1
	Maximum Width	As shown in Figure 6.1 (same as Blade Width for Great Basin Stemmed Series Points)
	Basal Width	As shown in Figure 6.1
	Actual Weight	
	Proximal Shoulder Angle	As shown in Figure 6.2
	Distal Shoulder Angle	As shown in Figure 6.2
Qualitative	Raw Material	Chert, Obsidian, Fine-Grained Volcanics (dacite, rhyolite, basalt), Quartzite, Quartz
	Breakage Type	As shown in Figure 6.3
	Breakage Location	As shown in Figure 6.4
	Resharpening Location	As shown in Figure 6.4
	Lateral Edge Grinding	Absent, Light, Medium, Heavy, Extreme
	Flaking Pattern	As shown in Figure 6.5
	Beveling	Absent, Blade, Stem, Blade and Stem
	Blade Wear	None, Minimal (less than half of the blade), Moderate (about half of the blade), Extreme (more than half of the blade)
	Haft Wear	Absent, Present
	Fragment	Complete, Tip/Blade, Midsection, Stem/Base, Combination
	Serration	Absent, Present (on Archaic points only)

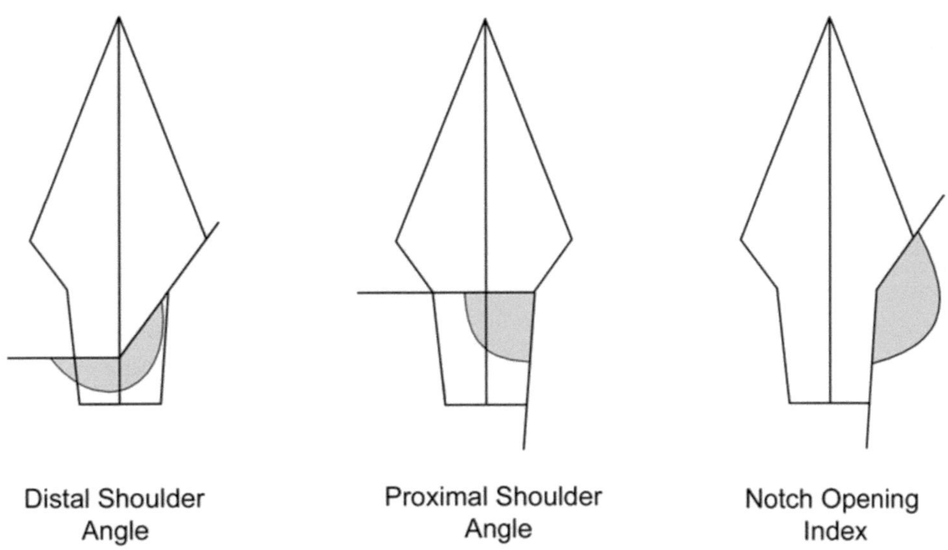

FIGURE 6.2. Angles measured on the Sunshine projectile points (after Thomas 1981:14).

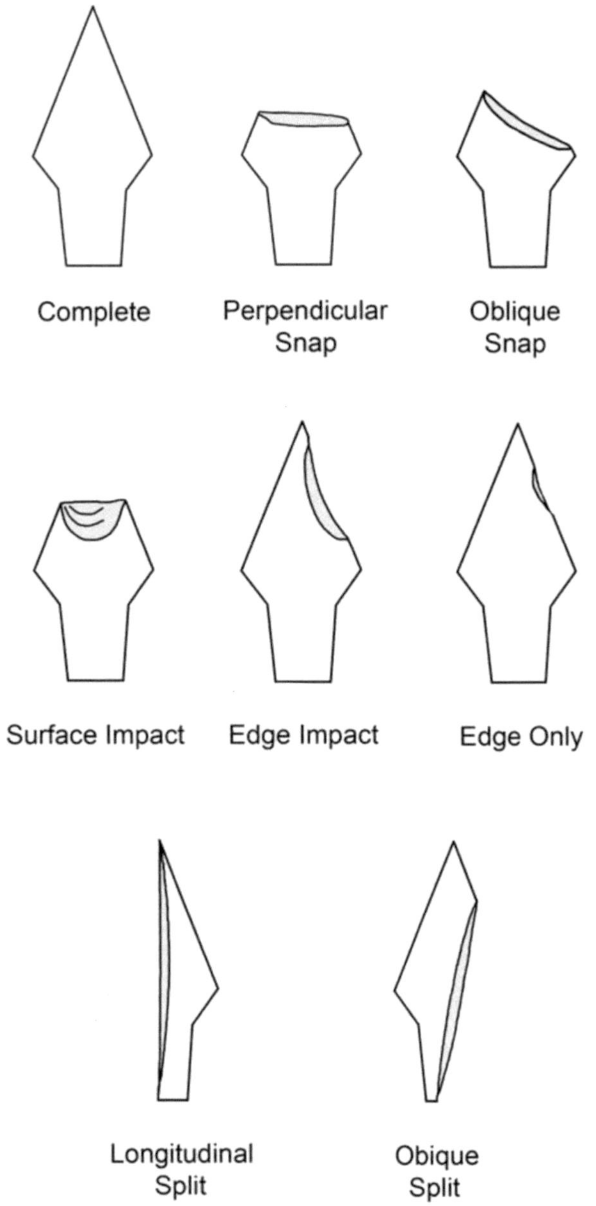

FIGURE 6.3. Breakage types recorded for the Sunshine projectile points.

in step fractures and create flake scars that are generally less invasive than the original flake scars; these scars often occur in conjunction with a steeper edge profile than existed after initial manufacture. Resharpening is most evident, however, when it interrupts the original flaking pattern, when it is associated with an obvious break, or when it truncates use-wear.

Flaking Pattern. Flaking patterns (Figure 6.5) were also recorded for all points, as some researchers have suggested that particular patterns are associated with certain morphologies. For example, points of the Cougar Mountain type most often exhibit broad collateral flaking, as do points of other GBSS types.

Beveling, Use-Wear, and Haft Wear. In our analysis of points of the GBSS we noticed that a number of these points appeared to be beveled on alternate margins ("different edges of opposite faces" [Storck 1997:47]) of the blade, although we also noticed occasional beveling on the stem. Beveling is believed by some to be the result of unifacial resharpening (e.g., Deller and Ellis 1992:49). Tuohy has suggested that beveling was part of the process of the burination of point tips, in the creation of what he calls a "squared-off chisel bit" (1969:139). We discuss this further in the section on GBSS points. Because it was unclear during the artifact analysis whether the observed beveling was part of the resharpening sequence or used to enhance the function of a hafted biface tip, we recorded it separately from data on resharpening so that we might examine (1) if beveling occurs on one type more frequently than it does on others and (2) if it might be an important aspect of point function (as Tuohy suggests).

In addition to beveling, a large number of points of the GBSS exhibit use-wear on their blades (Beck and Jones 1993), and in some cases, the use-wear is pronounced. Point blade sections were examined under 10–70× magnification for evidence of crushing and abrasion. Because most of these points are manufactured from FGV, however, it was often difficult to distinguish the type of use-wear (e.g., crushing, abrasion, etc.), and thus use-wear was recorded in terms of how much of the blade edge is worn (i.e., none, <50 percent, ca. 50 percent, >50 percent).

Almost all items exhibit arris abrasion on at least one side; this abrasion is generally greater on the side that is covered with a calcium carbonate film. We believe that this abrasion may be the result of chemical weathering (see Jones et al. 1997), and thus only when abrasion was extreme along blade edges or at the point did we consider it the result of use. When such extreme abrasion occurred along the high points of the stem and blade, it was considered haft wear.

Other. The fragment represented (see Table 6.1) was recorded for all points. The presence or absence of serration was recorded for Archaic points.

Projectile Point Analysis: Fluted and Unfluted Lanceolate Points

Fluted and unfluted lanceolate points occur throughout the Great Basin, primarily in surficial contexts. Unfluted lanceolate points, including those examples referred to as "Black Rock Concave Base" (Clewlow 1968a), exhibit

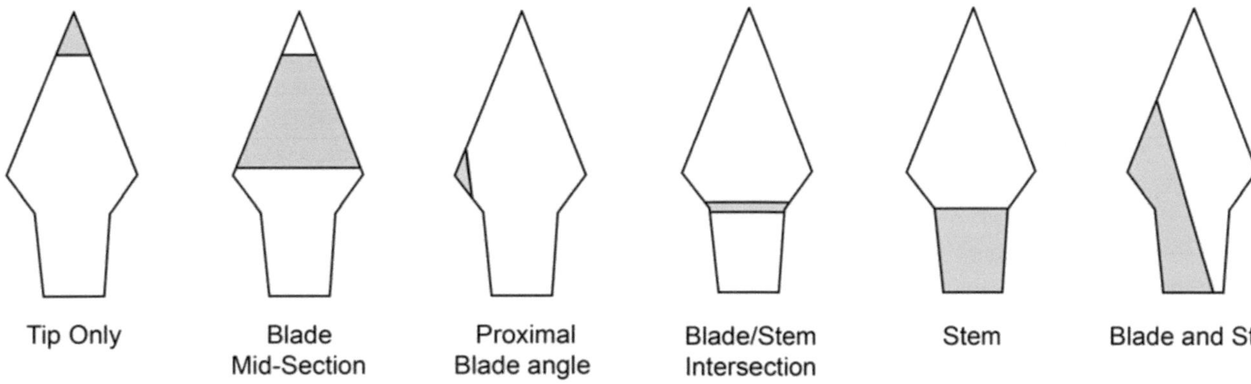

FIGURE 6.4. Locations of breakage and resharpening on the Sunshine projectile points.

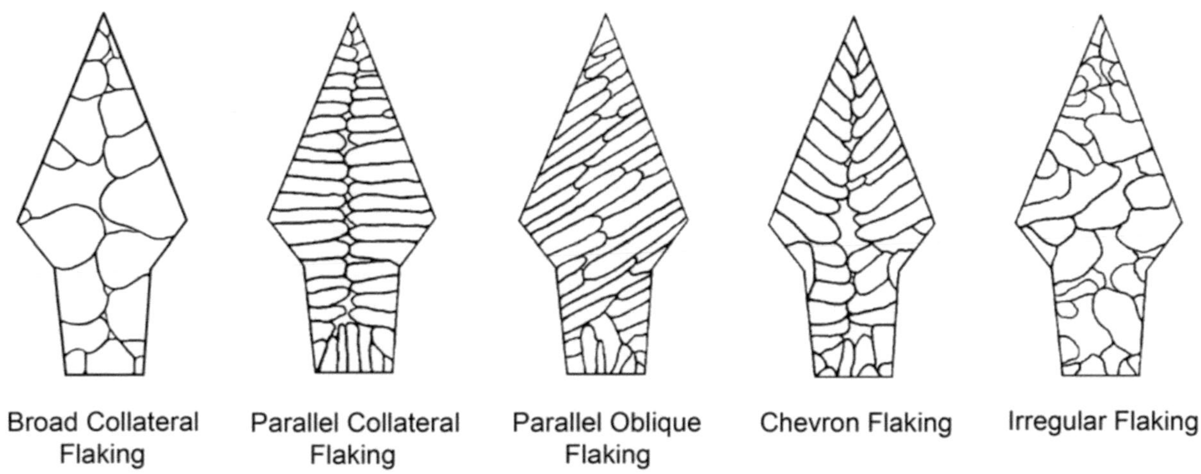

FIGURE 6.5. Flaking patterns recorded for the Sunshine projectile points.

varying degrees of basal thinning but are not truly fluted (sensu Warren and Phagan 1988, see below), although this basal preparation is often mistaken for fluting. Fluted and unfluted lanceolate points are sometimes found together in the Great Basin, rather like Folsom and Midland points on the Plains (e.g., Hofman 1992), which led Pendleton (1979) to combine these two forms into the Great Basin Concave Base (GBCB) Series, a procedure that has been followed by others as well (e.g., Basgall 1988, 1993a, 1993b). Collapsing these two forms can be problematic, however, because of the almost complete lack of knowledge concerning their technological association and temporal placement. Thus, although we follow suit in combining them within the GBCB Series, we treat them separately in our analysis.

Great Basin Fluted points share with classic "Clovis" points the fact that they are generally manufactured from either good-quality microcrystalline silicates or obsidian (Amick 1995a; Beck and Jones 1990b). Also like Clovis, Great Basin Fluted points vary a great deal in size and form (see, e.g., photographs in Davis and Shutler 1969 and Tuohy 1969). Much of this size variation is likely related to resharpening (see Fagan 1988), but some of the variation, such as that represented by the much more gracile forms at the Sunshine Locality, may represent a difference in age. As stated earlier, however, the dating of these points is problematic in the Great Basin. The most reliable date comes from the Sunshine Locality (discussed in chapter 4), a date of 10,320 ± 50 rcy BP, which provides a minimum age for the single buried fluted point. Depending on how *much* older the point is than the dated charcoal, it could be contemporaneous with *either* Clovis *or* Folsom, which date to 11,600–10,800 rcy BP and 10,900–10,200 rcy BP, respectively, in the Plains (Frison 1991; Haynes 1992; Taylor et al. 1996; but see Waters and Stafford 2007). Because their temporal position in the Great Basin is still unknown and because no systematic analysis of these points has ever been done across this region, some researchers prefer not to use the term *Clovis* but to refer to these points as Western fluted (Willig and Aikens 1988) or Great Basin Fluted (Grayson 1993). We use the latter term here.

Although fluted points are found in most parts of the Great Basin (e.g., Copeland and Fike 1988; Davis and Shutler 1969; Schroedl 1991; Tuohy 1985, 1986; Warren and Phagan 1988; Willig and Aikens 1988), they are not numerous, and they are almost exclusively surface finds. Outside the Sunshine Locality, they have been found in buried contexts in only three instances (see Beck and Jones 1997 for discussion). One additional case has recently been raised, that of a point from Connley Cave No. 5, but this case is debated (see Beck et al. 2004). Fluted points also occur primarily as isolates but are found in larger numbers in a few areas, including the Sunshine Locality. The others are the Alkali Lake Basin of north-central Oregon (Fagan 1988; Pinson 1999; Willig 1988, 1989, 1991), China Lake in southeastern California (Davis 1978a, 1978b), and the vicinity of Pleistocene Lake Tonopah in southern Nevada (Campbell and Campbell 1940; Pendleton 1979; Tuohy 1988). None of these areas contains exclusively fluted point assemblages, however, but also large numbers of stemmed points, giving rise to the argument of some researchers (e.g., Bedwell 1973; Bryan 1980, 1988, 1991; Davis et al. 1969) of contemporaneity between the two technologies.

Unfluted concave base points occur in somewhat larger numbers than do fluted ones, but we know even less about them. Clewlow (1968a), in his work in the Black Rock Desert, found a number of these points, to which he gave the name Black Rock Concave Base. These points are also poorly dated, and their relation to fluted points is unknown. For instance, how do they compare technologically with fluted points? Could the case of fluted/unfluted points in the Great Basin be similar to that of Folsom/Midland on the Plains? A good deal of discussion has taken place concerning the relation between Folsom and Midland (see, e.g., Amick 1995b; Hofman 1992). A number of researchers have suggested that these two forms are part of the same technology. Amick suggests that "large-scale patterns of variation indicate these two types may represent equivalent alternatives in the production of functional weapon tips by Folsom hunters. The decision to flute may depend on several variables including regional strategies of land use and mobility and the availability of tool stone" (1995b:23).

Hofman (1992) makes a similar argument, more specifically focused on the size of the flake blank, which in turn depends on the distance traveled since retooling at a quarry combined with the number of use events. In other words, Midland points are not fluted because the flake blanks on which they were made were too thin to begin with. Of course Folsom and Midland are associated with specialized bison hunting, a subsistence strategy that likely never developed in the Great Basin. Arguably, hunting of large game was an important component of the more generalized Great Basin Paleoarchaic subsistence, but we cannot assume the same technological relationships between fluted and unfluted points in this region as existed in the specialized strategy on the Plains. Thus, the relation between Great Basin fluted and unfluted points is examined below.

The unfluted lanceolate category is also problematic because other forms, notably examples of the Humboldt Series believed to date to the mid- and late Holocene, can have similar morphologies. Much less attention has been focused on unfluted lanceolates, and thus from site to site, points identified as such may represent wholly different entities.

Fluted Lanceolate Points

Assignment to the fluted or unfluted category depends on how we define fluting as distinct from general basal thinning. Bradley, citing a 1988 personal communication from J. B. Sollberger, defines a flute as "any basal thinning flake(s) that traveled past the area of the hafting element" (1993:254). Warren and Phagan (1988:121), however, suggest that the term *fluted* has been increasingly applied to points that are simply basally thinned. Callahan appears to be in at least some agreement with this statement, having written:

> I feel that the term "flute" should be restricted to the last flake or series of flakes intended to become the actual hafting accommodation scar. Accordingly, the term "flute" should not be used for end-thinning flake removal prior to this final stage. There are major differences in knapping approach between the two [1979:15].

Crabtree provides a more technical definition of the term flute:

> A negative semi-concave flake scar having parallel sides. The result of force applied to the objective piece which has previously had special preparation of the surface and platform area to accomplish fluting. A concave trough on the artifact from the proximal toward the distal end. Generally related to blademaking and basal thinning of projectile points. Produced to allow special hafting [1972:66].

In an effort to restrict the term *fluting* to a more specific type of basal thinning, Warren and Phagan suggest a relatively simple set of criteria to distinguish fluting from

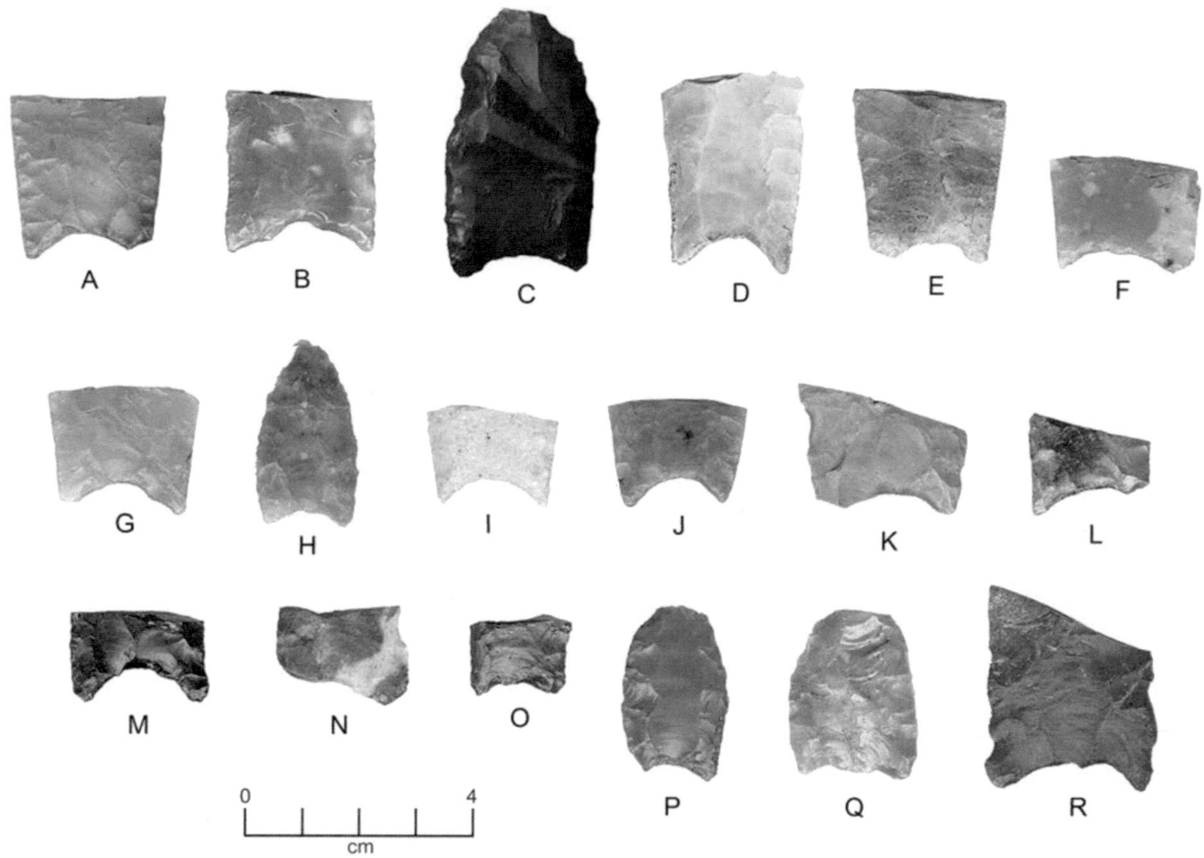

FIGURE 6.6. Fluted points from the Sunshine Locality: (A) 1879; (B) 2157; (C) 1881; (D) LVS, U10-103; (E) 1911; (F) 2207; (G) 2122; (H) 2007-1; (I) Loader Trench 95; (J) surface 1993, FS 3; (K) 1838; (L) 1894; (M) 1891; (N) 2123; (O) 1893; (P) 1885; (Q) 1905; (R) surface 1993, FS 4 (fluted point preform).

basal thinning, which embodies aspects of the above definitions and which we have used here. They suggest that the term *fluting* be

> restricted to a particular kind of basal thinning characterized by flake scars that:
> 1. are produced by base-to-tip directed force, and
> 2. are at least ¼ the length of the point, and/or
> 3. are at least ⅓ the width of the point, and
> 4. are removed relatively late in the production sequence, such that they truncate at least some of the lateral edge—producing flake scars [1988:121].

Warren and Phagan go on to say that "such a definition requires that fluting flakes be few (usually one, but never more than three per face), large, removed late in the production sequence, and producing major section alteration of the haft element" (1988:121–122).

Phil Hutchinson (1988) reports 20 fluted points in his and Noyes's collection. Following Warren and Phagan's narrow definition of *fluting*, however, we changed the type assignment of several of these points, reducing the number in the H–N collection to 13. We believe for our purposes here, especially as we compare fluted and unfluted points both morphologically and technologically, that to err on the conservative side is best. We have collected an additional four fluted points from the Sunshine Locality (two from the surface in 1993, one from the excavation in 1995, and one from the surface in 2007) as well as a fifth from Long Valley just outside of the Sunshine Locality boundary. One of the specimens from 1993 is unfinished and thus is slightly larger and more irregular than the others, but it has been fluted on both sides. G. York (1995) reports two fluted points collected by R. York (1974, 1978) in his work for the Nevada State Museum in the 1970s. Thus, to date, a total of 20 fluted points have been documented from the Sunshine Locality or its vicinity.

For the current analysis we use 17 of these points (Figure 6.6A–Q), excluding the unfinished specimen (preform) collected in 1993 (Figure 6.6R) and the two points collected by York. We exclude the preform because it cannot be expected to fulfill all of the criteria of a finished point, but it is discussed in detail later in this section with respect to the fluting technique used for the Sunshine points. We also do not include the two points from the York collection because we did not personally analyze them.

As stated earlier, we follow Grayson (1993) in using the term *Great Basin Fluted* rather than *Clovis* for two reasons. First, fluted points in the Great Basin have not been demonstrated to date to the Clovis period, for example, 11,600–10,900 BP, and second, no systematic morphological or technological comparisons have been made among Great Basin Fluted points or between Great Basin Fluted points and classic Clovis points (but see Beck and Jones 2007; Beck and Jones 2008; Taylor 2002, 2003). The question we address here is: Are the Sunshine fluted points representative of a Clovis technology?

Clovis technology has received a great deal of attention over the years, but there has not yet been a precise definition of the Clovis point type, perhaps because there is such a great deal of variation in these points, and no one feature appears to be distinctive, always present, and thus diagnostic. For example, in distinguishing between Elko Eared and Gatecliff Split-Stem types, it is primarily the proximal shoulder angle that is the diagnostic feature; points of these types vary considerably in almost all other features but can almost always be distinguished using PSA. But for Clovis, every distinguishing feature (other than "fluted/not fluted") varies so much that it has proven difficult to write a precise definition of the type.

Criteria for Evaluation

The original discovery of Clovis was, of course, at the Blackwater Draw site near Clovis, New Mexico (Howard 1935, 1936), and the only radiocarbon dates come from the Southwest and the Plains (e.g., Haynes 1992; Taylor et al. 1996; but see Waters and Stafford 2007). "Clovis" points are reported, however, from coast to coast across North America. But what precisely is Clovis? Adding to the confusion is the fact that the term *Clovis*, as is so true of many archaeological terms, means many things; it can refer to a morphology, a technology, a time period, or a lifeway. There seems, however, to be no general agreement concerning any but the time period, and even this has been debated recently (e.g., Haynes et al. 2007; Waters and Stafford 2007).

We are interested here, for the moment at least, in what constitutes Clovis morphology and technology. Because Folsom was the first Paleoindian point to be discovered (Figgins 1927), all fluted points subsequent to that discovery were referred to as Folsom, that is, until Clovis was discovered several years later. Because Clovis appeared to be the more general of the two forms, Clovis became the "catchall" term for fluted points that were not identified as Folsom (see Roosa, in Mason 1962:263).

In 1957 Wormington offered the following description of Clovis points:

> Fluted lanceolate points with parallel or slightly convex sides and concave bases. They range in length from one and a half to five inches, but are usually some three inches or more in length and fairly heavy. The flutes sometimes extend almost the full length of the point but usually they extend no more than half way from the base to the tip. Normally one face will have a longer flute than the other. The fluting was generally produced by the removal of multiple flakes. In most instances the edges of the basal portion show evidence of smoothing by grinding. Certain points found in the eastern United States resemble the Clovis type, but they have a constriction at the base, which produces a fish-tail effect [1957:263].

Of Folsom Wormington states:

> A more specialized type, of excellent workmanship, thought to be derived from the Clovis type. There is some overlap in size between Clovis and Folsom points, but the latter are lighter and usually smaller. They range in length from three-quarters of an inch to three inches with an average of about two inches. They are lanceolate in outline and have concave bases usually marked by ear-like projections. There is frequently a small central nipple in the basal concavity. The points were fluted through the removal of longitudinal flutes. The flutes usually extend over most of the length of the point. In most cases one major channel flake was removed from each face but sometimes only one face was fluted. Most specimens have a fine marginal retouch. The lower edges usually bear evidence of grinding [1957:263].

In comparing these two descriptions, without a mental image of Clovis or Folsom points, the differences between the two appear to be

1. size
2. flute extension on the blade
3. number of flute flakes per face
4. whether or not both faces are fluted
5. fineness of flaking
6. presence of the remnant of the fluting striking platform in the concavity

Of course no one today would confuse a Clovis point with a Folsom point, for the most part because, as Wormington originally stated, Folsom represents a "more specialized form" (1957:263). But the term *Folsom,* like *Clovis,* represents not only a morphology but a technology, a time period, and a lifeway and in addition, a specific area. Folsom occurs primarily on the Plains and in the Rio Grande Valley, although it is also found on the Columbia Plateau (Titmus and Woods 1991a) and occasionally in the Great Basin (see Davis and Shutler 1969:166, Figure 4d).

But in looking east and west from the Plains, fluted points deviate from the "Clovis" description given by Wormington. Eastern fluted points, such as Barnes (Deller and Ellis 1992; Roosa 1977a, 1977b), Gainey (Deller and Ellis 1988), and others (see Anderson et al. 1996:10, Figure 1.2), often have a distinctive "fishtail." In the Southeast, there are several later forms, including Simpson, Cumberland, and Dalton, all of which are often fluted (e.g., Anderson et al. 1996:10, Figure 1.2; Futato 1996:304, Figure 15.2; Ledbetter et al. 1996:279, Figure 13.4; Wycoff 1999:53, Figure 7). In the West, especially in the Great Basin, we have not documented such a sequence, but there is every reason to believe that it would exist here as it does in the eastern United States and on the Plains. We just cannot seem to find any in buried context to tell us if this is so. And, because the "definition" of Clovis is actually composed of many "descriptions" (sensu Dunnell 1970), it is difficult to isolate Clovis in the Great Basin from "other" fluted point morphologies (see, e.g., photographs in Davis and Shutler 1969 and Tuohy 1969). *Clovis* is still a catchall term for non-Folsom fluted points. Therefore, we begin our analysis in an attempt to define criteria that can be used to isolate Clovis from other fluted points in the Great Basin.

In an effort to create a general type description for the Clovis point, Howard (1990) reviewed a number of the original descriptions of these points (e.g., Cox 1986; Hester 1972; Prufer and Baby 1963; Roosa 1965; Wormington 1957). He also conducted a review of published morphological and technological attributes of Clovis points. This review resulted in the following type description:

> Clovis is a comparatively large and heavy bifacially flaked fluted lanceolate point, lenticular to near oval in cross-section with parallel to moderately convex lateral edges, a majority having the latter. Maximum width is usually at or slightly below the midpoint, frequently resulting in rather long sharp tips. Bases are normally only slightly concave, the depth usually ranging from 1 mm to 4 mm and arching completely across basal width. Basal corners range from nearly square to slightly rounded without forming eared projections. Length range is considerable, with a majority between 75 mm and 110 mm. Maximum width range is 25 mm to 50 mm, a majority near the former. Maximum thickness range, 5 mm to 10 mm. They are normally fluted on both faces. Flutes are most often produced by multiple flake removals. Length and quality of flutes is greatly variable, with length usually 30% to 50% of overall point length, and the majority near the former. Base of flutes is often widened by subsequent removals of additional channel flakes or short wide flakes. There is minimal post-fluting retouch of basal areas. Overall flaking frequently irregular in both size and orientation, often including large facet remnants of early stage reduction processes. There is very moderate evidence of pressure flaking. Lower lateral and basal edges are smoothed by grinding, often resulting in slight tapering of the base.
>
> Clovis points do not have recurved (fishtail) lateral edges, or pronounced basal constrictions. Neither do they have convex (Folsom-type) channel flake platform remnants [Howard 1990:259].

Taking this description apart, we essentially have that list of differences between Clovis and Folsom originally observed by Wormington but with a few specifics added. Howard's description can be broken down into the following set of criteria:

1. Parallel to moderate convex lateral edges, mostly the latter.
2. A maximum width usually slightly below the midpoint.
3. Basal indentation between 1 and 4 mm, arching completely across basal width.
4. Basal corners range from nearly square to slightly rounded, without forming ears.
5. Length most often ranges between 75 and 110 mm.
6. Maximum width ranges between 25 and 50 mm, with the majority nearer the former.
7. Fluting generally occurs on both sides.
8. Flutes are most often produced by multiple flake removals.
9. Length of flutes is usually 30 to 50 percent of overall point length, with the majority near the former.
10. Base of flutes often widened by subsequent removals of additional channel flakes or short, wide flakes.
11. Minimal postfluting retouch of basal area.
12. Overall flaking frequently irregular in both size and orientation.
13. Very moderate evidence of pressure flaking.
14. Lower lateral edges are smoothed by grinding.

15. Do not have fishtail lateral edges.
16. Do not have convex (Folsom-type) channel flake platform remnants.

In reviewing this list of criteria, some are more definitive than others. For example, a number of these criteria can be applied to Folsom as well as to Clovis, and thus they are not distinctive of Clovis only. Certainly Great Basin Fluted points are not Folsom points, but in determining criteria that can be used to apply specifically to Clovis, Folsom, the only other recognized fluted point type in the West, provides a means for comparison. In other words, if a criterion describes both Clovis and Folsom, it is not very useful for us in attempting to answer the question of whether the Sunshine points could represent Clovis. We examine each of the criteria with this in mind.

We have assembled data on both Clovis and Folsom points for comparison. The Clovis data (Table 6.2) come from several sources: 287 points from Texas (Meltzer and Bever 1995), 26 points from the Rio Grande Valley (Judge 1973), 20 points from the Fenn cache (Frison and Bradley 1999), and 69 points from 13 Clovis sites from the Plains and Southwest analyzed by Tompkins (1993). Folsom data (Table 6.3) include eight points from the Shifting Sands site (Hofman et al. 1990), 64 points from the southwestern Plains (Amick 1995b), 33 points from Judge's (1973) Rio Grande Survey, 10 points from the Mitchel Locality of Blackwater Draw (Boldurian 1990), 30 additional points from Blackwater Draw (Broilo 1971, in Boldurian 1990), and 16 from Idaho (Titmus and Woods 1991a). The Clovis data are much more complete because we have access to the data recorded by Tompkins, thanks to C. Vance Haynes. Tompkins presents measurements for, and drawings of, each individual point. Also, the data on each of the Fenn points are presented individually by Frison and Bradley (1999). This gives us measurements on 89 individual points from various locations that can be considered in different ways. The Texas and Rio Grande data, however, as well as all of the Folsom data are presented in their respective sources as summary statistics, and in the case of Folsom, only some of the variables we are interested in are summarized.

Criteria 1 and 14 can easily be applied to Folsom as well as Clovis, and this needs no elaboration. With respect to criterion 3, the range of basal indentation (BI) specified for Clovis can incorporate a majority of Folsom points as well. As Tables 6.2 and 6.3 show, the values for BI, although reported only for two of the Folsom assemblages (Table 6.3), overlap completely with those reported for Clovis points (Table 6.2); thus this criterion cannot discriminate between Clovis and Folsom.

In an examination of basal corner shape of the 89 Clovis points for which we have drawings or photos, the number of points having "ears" is roughly equal to those that do not, and thus we exclude criterion 4. Criterion 7 is also somewhat problematic, because most Folsom points are also fluted on both sides. In his examination of Midland and Folsom points, Amick (1995b) identified 173 unfluted (Midland), 112 fluted on one side (Folsom), and 515 fluted on both sides (Folsom). If only the Folsom points are considered, then 82.1 percent are fluted on both sides.

Criterion 13, regarding pressure flaking, is debated. Frison, in discussing Paleoindian weaponry, states, "The Goshen projectile point is smaller than the Clovis point and demonstrates a change from percussion to pressure flaking in its manufacture" (1991:241). Callahan, however, believes that pressure flaking was used in the manufacture of Clovis points:

> Close examination of numerous authentic Eastern and Western Clovis fluted points and comparison of these with experimental replicas has removed any doubt in my mind that Paleo workers used pressure flaking. Though there may have been exceptions from point to point, the Williamson and Flint Run examples show unmistakably that the technique was used, usually after billet preforming and before and after fluting [1979:84].

Bradley agrees with Callahan, stating of Clovis points on the High Plains, "In some cases the projectile points were mostly percussion finished with only minimal pressure retouch. In other cases, the projectile points underwent substantial pressure thinning and shaping, and on other points substantial marginal pressure retouch followed the pressure flaking" (1993:253).

Titmus and Woods (1991a:125) have observed pressure flaking on Clovis points from Idaho, stating that the pressure flake scars are generally spaced irregularly, except on the points from the Simon cache; on these, the pressure flake scars are more evenly spaced. It appears that points from Clovis caches are generally larger (see Table 6.3, for example) and more finely made, which suggests to some (e.g., Bonnichsen 1977; Butler 1963; Lahren 1969) that they are mortuary items.

Thus, the presence or absence of pressure flaking is not as distinctive as Howard suggests. *Degree and consistency* of pressure flaking may be more informative. For example, in the manufacture of Folsom points pressure flaking becomes dominant very early in the manufacturing process. Bradley (1982:186–188) presents a nine-stage reduction sequence represented by the points found at the Agate Basin site in Wyoming. In this sequence, following the initial shaping and thinning of the blank by "percussion bifacing" (Stage 2) is pressure shaping and thinning (Stage 3). Pressure flaking then becomes the predominant mode of manufacture in all succeeding stages (see also Boldurian 1990; Nami 1999:90–92). Although both Callahan and Bradley suggest that this can sometimes be the case for Clovis, it is not *consistently* so. In Folsom this process produces finely flaked and very stylized products for which the range of morphological variation is much smaller than for Clovis (see Ahler and Geib 2000). Thus, in evaluating pressure flaking, the criterion should be *the degree of pressure flaking on the point and the consistency with which it is used from point to point within an assemblage.*

Criterion 15 refers most specifically to eastern fluted points and is rarely observed on fluted points in the West. Finally, criterion 16, the absence of channel flake platform remnants *is* likely indicative of Clovis, but this platform is sometimes missing on Folsom as well (see, e.g., Boldurian 1990:73, Figure 39F; Hofman et al. 1990:221, Figure 4b). When this is the case the basal arch is continuous, as specified for Clovis in criterion 3. This is an important point because even though we know that no specialized Folsom technology developed in the Great Basin, we do suspect that perhaps a sequence of Clovis-aged and Folsom-aged fluted points *did* develop in that region. If this is the case, we cannot assume that a Folsom-like fluting technology was used in the latter part of the sequence just because it was on the Plains and possibly in the East (see Howard 1990). The absence of such a platform on later, non-Clovis fluted points could simply mean a continuation or modification of the same type of fluting process. The remaining criteria, 2, 5–6, and 8–12, we believe likely do refer exclusively to Clovis.

Criterion 5 specifies that, although length ranges considerably among Clovis points, most are between 75 and 100 mm in length. Length ranges for the small sample of Folsom points (Table 6.3) are all below 75 mm, but the lengths of many of the Clovis points (Table 6.2) are as well. Mean length in all cases, however, is vastly different, although we are unable (because of the nature of the data) to test for significance.

Much of the variation in Clovis point length is likely the result of resharpening, but we should keep in mind that small points without evidence of resharpening do sometimes occur in Clovis assemblages. In their discussion of the Blackwater Draw Clovis points, for example, Boldurian and Cotter (1999:56) note that four of the 10 specimens are less than 40.0 mm in length. They state that the small examples are not all related to resharpening and refer to other small points from Naco and Lehner. In fact, Hester (1972:97) has proposed a separate category for small (ca. 30–50 mm) Clovis points. In our comparative assemblage for which we have data on individual points, 11 are less than 50 mm in length. The elimination of these, however, still does not put the majority between 75 and 110 mm in length, although without these points there is no overlap in Clovis and Folsom length ranges, except for one of the Shifting Sands specimens. Aside from the 32 points from caches (Drake, Fenn, and Simon), which are generally larger than noncache points, 23 are between 50 and 75 mm long and 23 are longer than 75 mm. Consequently, we place the lower value in Howard's criterion 5 at 50 mm for our comparisons.

Criterion 6 specifies a maximum width for Clovis between 25 and 50 mm. Again, some of the Clovis ranges have lower values than 25 mm, and there is more overlap with Folsom ranges. Also again, however, the means for Clovis are considerably higher than those for Folsom. Without the 11 small points mentioned above, all of the remaining specimens (with the exception of the Texas and Rio Grande assemblages) have maximum widths greater than 25 mm, and there is no overlap with the Folsom ranges.

These data indicate that at times there is overlap in size between Clovis and Folsom points but, on average, they differ considerably. We therefore will use criteria 2, 4, 6, 8–12, and 5 with our modification for our evaluation of the Sunshine points. Also, we examine the presence, extent, and consistency of pressure flaking (criterion 13) in conjunction with the fineness of flaking and general morphological variation within the assemblage.

Evaluation of the Sunshine Fluted Points

Before discussing the Sunshine fluted points with respect to these criteria, we need to make several statements concerning the data. First, all but four of the specimens in this assemblage are basal fragments (Figure 6.6), and thus certain quantitative measurements, such as total length and to some extent, maximum width, could be measured on only a few points. Second, this same fragmentary nature limited our assessment of where on the blade the maximum width occurred (criterion 2) and flute length (criterion 9). Finally, as discussed in chapter 5, the analysis of the specific H–N collection, which contains the majority of both fluted and unfluted lanceolate points, took place in the Nevada State Museum during two successive five-day visits in 1996 and 1997. Table 6.4 shows each point with its corresponding score on criteria 2, 5–6, and 8–12. We discuss each in turn.

Criterion 2. Of the four points for which this criterion could be evaluated (Figure 6.6C, H, P, Q), the maximum width occurs at the midpoint on one, below the midpoint on the second, and above the midpoint on the other two. Specimens 1881 (Figure 6.6C) and 1905 (Figure 6.6Q), however, show extensive breakage and resharpening and were likely considerably longer when they were

TABLE 6.2. Summary of Quantitative Data for Clovis Projectile Points

LOCALITY	STATISTIC	LENGTH	MAXIMUM WIDTH	BASAL WIDTH	MAXIMUM THICKNESS	BASAL INDENTATION
Texas[a]	*N*	285	287	260	269	177
	Range	11.0–164.0	17.1–48.9	13.8–45.0	3.0–12.0	0–8.0
	Mean	61.4	27.5	23.6	7.3	2.8
	SD	27.8	4.9	4.6	1.5	1.7
Fenn Cache[b]	*N*	20	20	20	20	20
	Range	76.8–212.5	26.6–53.8	24.7–45.7	6.6–11.7	0–11.8
	Mean	112.8	37.5	32.9	7.9	4.3
	SD	35.6	6.3	4.9	1.2	2.9
Rio Grande Valley[c]	*N*	—	26	26	26	26
	Range		22.0–32.2	19.1–29.2	4.1–9.0	1.5–7.1
	Mean		26.4	23.9	5.8	3.5
	SD		2.7	2.7	1.2	1.3
Blackwater Draw[d]	*N*	15	15	15	15	15
	Range	26.6–108.8	15.8–35.6	14.0–32.4	3.9–9.8	.8–3.9
	Mean	62.30	24.96	22.52	6.85	2.42
	SD	27.195	5.888	5.137	1.650	.872
Colby[d]	*N*	4	4	4	4	4
	Range	56.0–92.2	28.0–37.2	22.6–31.1	5.5–7.6	3.3–9.3
	Mean	74.76	33.07	26.79	6.68	5.34
	SD	19.092	4.827	3.499	.960	2.706
Dent[d]	*N*	2	2	2	2	2
	Range	90.3–114.3	30.5–36.0	30.5–30.5	7.2–9.5	3.6–4.2
	Mean	102.32	33.29	30.54	8.36	3.90
	SD	16.942	3.882	.000	1.598	.445
Domebo[d]	*N*	3	3	3	3	3
	Range	55.7–76.4	20.3–26.2	19.0–24.1	5.4–8.6	1.0–1.8
	Mean	65.89	23.25	21.72	7.14	1.45
	SD	10.347	2.956	2.585	1.643	.396
Drake Cache[d]	*N*	7	7	7	7	7
	Range	88.7–162.8	29.9–39.9	25.1–35.8	6.7–8.7	2.8–4.9
	Mean	120.68	35.12	31.19	7.77	4.14
	SD	30.870	3.124	3.170	.634	.863
Escapule[d]	*N*	2	2	2	2	2
	Range	89.3–96.0	30.0–33.8	25.4–28.6	6.8–8.9	4.1–4.5
	Mean	92.63	31.87	27.02	7.81	4.34
	SD	4.738	2.715	2.242	1.492	.283
Casper[d]	*N*	1	1	1	1	1
	Value	69.4	27.8	23.9	7.6	4.1
Lehner[d]	*N*	10	10	10	10	10
	Range	30.9–94.8	16.4–30.5	15.2–26.5	4.5–9.5	1.2–4.9
	Mean	60.53	25.28	22.19	7.23	2.72
	SD	20.732	5.530	3.924	1.291	1.061

TABLE 6.2. (cont'd.) Summary of Quantitative Data for Clovis Projectile Points

LOCALITY	STATISTIC	LENGTH	MAXIMUM WIDTH	BASAL WIDTH	MAXIMUM THICKNESS	BASAL INDENTATION
Miami[d]	*N*	3	3	3	3	3
	Range	73.6–115.1	24.4–29.8	20.6–23.8	7.4–8.6	2.0–2.7
	Mean	99.93	27.99	22.28	7.85	2.23
	SD	22.865	3.135	1.593	.637	.413
Murray Springs[d]	*N*	6	6	6	6	6
	Range	41.6–81.9	21.9–33.8	15.7–29.8	5.6–9.6	2.5–5.2
	Mean	59.65	28.69	23.00	8.14	4.00
	SD	14.655	4.708	4.859	1.772	1.231
Naco[d]	*N*	8	8	8	8	8
	Range	57.2–116.9	22.8–34.3	19.7–28.3	7.3–9.7	2.5–6.0
	Mean	81.20	28.35	24.61	8.43	3.87
	SD	19.775	3.711	3.050	.905	1.371
Wyoming[d]	*N*	3	3	3	3	3
	Range	70.3–81.4	21.1–70.3	26.3–36.4	8.2–8.7	3.55–3.64
	Mean	76.03	46.29	30.15	8.50	3.607
	SD	5.563	20.909	5.474	.265	.047
Simon Cache[d]	*N*	5	5	5	5	5
	Range	93.7–182.4	33.9–38.6	30.1–35.1	7.8–9.0	1.7–3.4
	Mean	142.53	36.86	32.41	8.22	2.75
	SD	44.506	1.976	2.240	.498	.775
Noncache Points[d]	*N*	57	57	57	57	57
	Range	26.6–116.9	15.8–70.3	14.0–36.4	3.9–9.8	.8–9.3
	Mean	70.72	28.23	23.92	7.52	3.19
	SD	23.227	7.842	4.547	1.420	1.452
Cache Points[d]	*N*	32	32	32	32	32
	Range	76.8–212.5	26.6–53.8	24.7–45.7	6.6–11.7	.0–11.8
	Mean	119.14	36.90	32.46	7.93	4.01
	SD	36.491	5.269	4.191	.977	2.372

Note: Measurements in millimeters.

[a] Meltzer and Bever 1995:68.

[b] Frison and Bradley 1999:107; basal indentation and width not given, measurements taken on photographs.

[c] Judge 1973:249.

[d] Tompkins 1993:17–18.

manufactured. Specimen 1905 is resharpened on the blade and the base; the blade of specimen 1881 is resharpened down below the original maximum width. Thus it is impossible to say one way or another where the maximum width originally occurred on these specimens.

Criterion 5. Length was measurable only on three points, specimens 1885 (35.2 mm; Figure 6.6P), 1881 (45.8 mm; Figure 6.6C), and 2007-1 (32.4 mm; Figure 6.6H). Specimen 1881, as mentioned above, shows extensive resharpening along the blade and likely was considerably longer when manufactured, which would conceivably put it at least within the lower portion of the specified Clovis range. This may also be true of the 2007 specimen, as much of the blade has been resharpened. Specimen 1885, however, exhibits no resharpening, and thus 35.2 mm is likely a realistic measurement of its length, well below the specified Clovis range.

Criterion 6. Maximum width was measurable (or estimated) for eight points (Figure 6.6A–E, H, P–Q), five of which fall within the specified Clovis range.

TABLE 6.3. Summary of Quantitative Data for Folsom Projectile Points

LOCALITY	STATISTIC	LENGTH	MAXIMUM WIDTH	BASAL WIDTH	MAXIMUM THICKNESS	BASAL INDENTATION
Shifting Sands[a]	*N*	8	12	9	14	—
	Range	16.3–52.8	13.1–24.7	12.3–21.5	2.9–7.1	—
	Mean	35.7	18.8	16.3	3.7	—
	SD	—	—	—	—	—
Southwest Plains[b]	*N*	64	—	295	521	—
	Range	—	—	—	—	—
	Mean	32.8	—	18.5	3.7	—
	SD	—	—	—	—	—
Rio Grande Valley[c]	*N*	—	33	33	33	33
	Range	—	18.5–25.0	17.2–22.0	3.1–5.0	2.0–6.0
	Mean	—	21.5	19.4	3.8	2.9
	SD	—	1.5	1.1	.5	1.2
Mitchell Locality[d]	*N*	—	—	10	—	10
	Range	—	—	17.5–22.0	—	1.7–6.0
	Mean	—	—	19.6	—	3.3
	SD	—	—	1.7	—	1.4
Blackwater Draw[e]	*N*	—	—	30	—	—
	Range	—	—	16.0–22.0	—	—
	Mean	—	—	18.8	—	—
	SD	—	—	1.3	—	—
Idaho[f]	*N*	2	3	4	16	3
	Range	37.0–39.0	23.0–27.0	15.0–23.0	4.0–17.0	2.0–6.0
	Mean	38.0	24.7	19.8	6.7	4.0
	SD	1.4	2.1	3.9	3.6	2.0

Note: Measurements in millimeters.
[a] Hofman et al. 1990:241.
[b] Amick 1995b:31.
[c] Judge 1973:165.
[d] Boldurian 1990:78.
[e] Broilo 1971, cited in Bouldarian 1990:165.
[f] Titmus and Woods 1991a:122–123.

Criterion 8. Nine of the 17 points had multiple flutes on at least one face; the remaining eight (Figure 6.6A, D, G–H, L, N–P) have only a single flute on each face (or for those that are fluted on only one face, on that one face).

Criterion 9. Flute length could be evaluated for only seven points (Figure 6.6A–E, H, P); for five of these the flute scar(s) extended less than 50 percent of the length of the point, and for the remaining two, the flute scar(s) extended farther than 50 percent (Figure 6.6H, P). The flute scars on an additional specimen, 1905 (Figure 6.6Q), also extend above 50 percent of the length of the point, but as stated above, its blade has been heavily resharpened, which has likely severely reduced its length; for this reason flute length on this specimen is categorized as indeterminate.

Criterion 10. On only six (Figure 6.6A, I–K, M, Q) of the 17 points is there evidence of widening of the flute scar from further basal thinning.

Criterion 11. All of the 17 points were evaluated for post-fluting basal retouch. Eleven show evidence of such retouch, three show none (Figure 6.6B, G, Q), and three are indeterminate (Figure 6.6E, N–O).

Criterion 12. We believe this criterion is especially telling; it states that Clovis points exhibit irregular flaking

TABLE 6.4. Data Relative to Howard's Clovis Criteria for 17 Fluted Points from Eastern Nevada

	Criterion											
Provenience	2: Maximum Width Location	5: Total Length	6: Maximum Width	8: Number of Flutes	9: Flute Length	10: Basal Flute Widening	11: Postfluting Retouch	12: Type of Flaking	13: Pressure Flaking	Thickness	Basal Width	Basal Indentation/ Basal Width
SW-1893	—	—	—	single	—	absent	indeterminate	parallel	extensive	5.4	16.1	.161
SW-1885	at midpoint	35.2	18.9	single	>50%	absent	present	parallel	extensive	4.2	15.2	.230
SW3-6N	—	—	—	multiple	—	absent	present	parallel	extensive	4.1	24.2	.165
SW-1911	—	—	28.3	multiple	0–30%	absent	indeterminate	parallel	extensive	5.3	21.7	.207
SW-1838	—	—	—	multiple	—	present	present	parallel	extensive	6.1	26.2	.179
SW-1894	—	—	—	single	—	absent	present	parallel	extensive	4.2	20.9	.220
SW-1881	above midpoint	45.8	26.1	multiple	0–30%	absent	present	irregular	extensive	6.0	22.1	.231
SW93-2	—	—	—	multiple	—	present	present	parallel	extensive	3.7	18.0	.206
SW-1879	—	—	28.2	single	30–50%	present	present	parallel	extensive	4.7	22.2	.252
SW-54	—	—	—	single	—	absent	absent	—	extensive	4.7	22.5	.253
SW95-11	—	—	—	multiple	—	present	present	parallel	extensive	4.4	20.2	.287
LVS-103	—	—	26.2	single	30–50%	absent	present	parallel	extensive	5.4	21.4	.349
SW3-89	—	—	27.1	multiple	30–50%	absent	absent	parallel	extensive	6.3	26.8	.243
SW-1891	—	—	—	multiple	—	present	present	—	extensive	5.9	24.8	.290
SW1-1905	above midpoint	—	24.1	multiple	—	present	absent	parallel	extensive	6.0	22.8	.088
SW4-56	—	—	—	single	—	absent	indeterminate	parallel	extensive	5.1	—	—
SW-SURF 2007	below midpoint	32.4	18.5	single	>50%	absent	present	parallel	extensive	5.1	16.6	.157

Note: Measurements in millimeters. See Howard 1990.

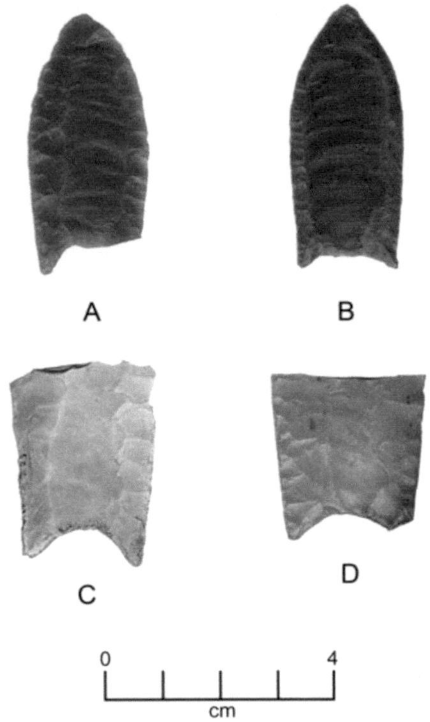

FIGURE 6.7. Comparison of (A–B) Folsom and (C–D) Sunshine fluted points: (A) Folsom site; (B) Lindenmeir; (C) Long Valley Survey, U10-103; (D) 1879.

in both size and orientation. For the 15 points for which flaking could be evaluated (Figure 6.6G and M could not be evaluated), only one shows irregular flaking (although this may be related to extensive resharpening; Figure 6.6C); 14 exhibit carefully executed parallel collateral flaking. In fact, Figure 6.7 shows two of the Sunshine fluted points together with casts of two Folsom points (from Folsom and Lindenmeier). The flaking patterns are remarkably similar among them.

Although not mentioned by Howard (1990), two additional variables, maximum thickness and basal width, are relevant to this comparison. We reserve the discussion of pressure flaking (criterion 13) until after we discuss these two variables. Regarding thickness, Clovis points are, on the average, much larger than Folsom points, and thus it would seem that an examination of maximum thickness would be relevant to a comparison between the two. Tables 6.2 and 6.3 show the mean maximum thickness for both Clovis and Folsom points from the assemblages already discussed; these averages range from 5.8 to 8.5 mm for Clovis and from 3.7 to 3.8 mm for Folsom. The overall mean for noncache Clovis points (Table 6.2) is 7.5 mm. Thickness values for the Sunshine points, shown in Table 6.4, range between 3.7 and 6.3 mm, with a mean thickness of 5.1 mm. As these data show, the Sunshine points lie midway between Clovis and Folsom in terms of maximum thickness.

Basal width has long been deemed important in defining Folsom points. Judge (1973) has argued that standardization in basal width was a result of an attempt to manufacture points to fit existing hafts (see also Ahler and Geib 2000; Boldurian 1990). Although basal width has not figured greatly in past descriptions of Clovis points, we examine this variable in relation to what published data we can find. Again, consistency in basal width, resulting in a small range of variation, may be the important factor, as stated by Judge (1973).

As is evident from Tables 6.2 and 6.3, Folsom points exhibit not only considerably smaller means than do Clovis but, with the exception of the Idaho and Blackwater Draw points, a much smaller range of values, conforming to Wormington's (1957) description of Folsom as a more standardized form. As Table 6.4 shows, the basal width of the Sunshine points ranges between 15.2 and 26.8 mm (mean = 22.1 mm). Although this mean is only slightly below that of Clovis, the range of values is much narrower (11.6 mm as compared with 31.2 mm for the Texas survey points, 21.0 mm for the Fenn cache, and 22.4 mm for the Tompkins data), suggesting that the Sunshine points represent a somewhat more standardized form than Clovis, although not so much as Folsom.

Because of the large range in size of Clovis points, Morrow and Morrow (1999) suggest the use of ratios in order to standardize comparisons. One ratio they believe to be pertinent to fluted point comparison is the ratio between basal indentation and basal width (BI/BW), which they suggest should be less than .150 for Clovis points. Earlier we discussed basal indentation (Howard's criterion 3) and excluded it because of the overlap with Folsom. In ratio to basal width, however, which we have just demonstrated differs somewhat between Clovis and Folsom, it might be useful. A comparison between Great Basin Fluted and Clovis values for this ratio shows that they are statistically different ($t = -5.168$, $df = 180.8$, $p < .001$).[1] Although the range for both is similar, nearly all Clovis values are below .175, whereas fully one-third of Great Basin Fluted point values are above this number.

The basal width of another lanceolate type—Goshen—actually comes closer to those in our assemblage. Goshen points, which are on average smaller than Clovis points, are unfluted and occur in the Northern Plains during the transition between the Clovis and Folsom periods. Some have argued that Goshen points are the same as those that have been called Plainview (e.g., Krieger 1947) points to the south (e.g., Pitblado 1998, 2003), but this issue is not resolved. At the Mill Iron site, Bradley and Frison (1996) report a range for the basal

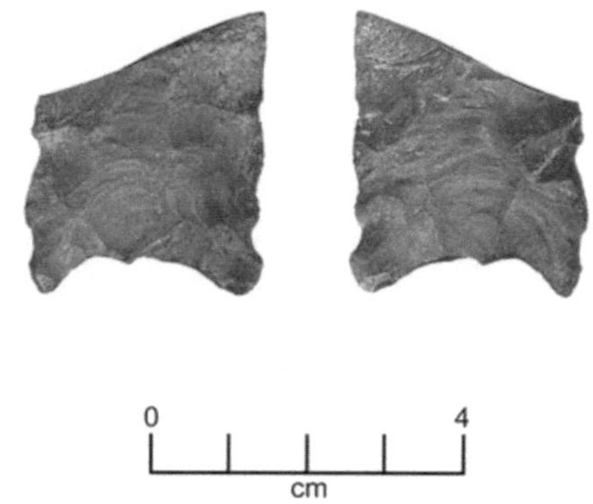

FIGURE 6.8. Fluted preform collected from the surface at the Sunshine Locality (surface 1993, FS 4).

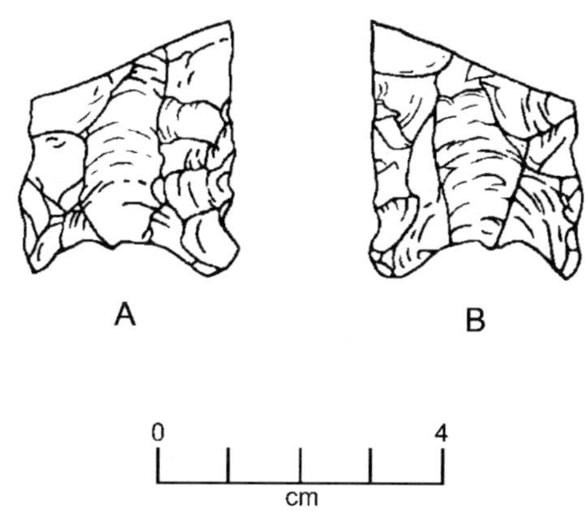

FIGURE 6.9. Drawing of the fluted preform collected from the surface at the Sunshine Locality (surface 1993, FS 4).

widths for 31 Goshen points of 13.5 to 25.6 mm, with a mean of 22.6 mm. Goshen points bear resemblance to the Sunshine fluted points in another way. Although the relation between Goshen and Clovis/Folsom is still unclear, Bradley and Frison state that

> to us, there is a greater resemblance in form to Folsom points than there is to Clovis points. Flaking technology is fairly consistent, but flake scar patterns are variable. Characteristically, the points exhibit well controlled and evenly spaced flake scars that include comedial and transmedial terminations. Flake scar orientations are mainly perpendicular to the point axis, except for the basal thinning flakes, which are parallel with it [1996:43].

This brings us to a discussion of pressure flaking, criterion 13. All of the Sunshine fluted points exhibit more than moderate pressure flaking. An examination of Figure 6.6 confirms that the statement quoted above concerning the Goshen points from the Mill Iron site could easily be applied to these points, with one change: the flake scar patterns are not variable but quite regular. And, of course, the flute scar obliterates the comedial terminations. The points in the Sunshine assemblage *consistently* exhibit pressure flaking, and, with the exception of specimen 1881 (and the three for which flaking could not be measured), they *consistently* exhibit fine parallel flaking.

Table 6.5 summarizes these findings. For those attributes of each point that meet the Clovis criteria, there is a "C"; for those that do not, there is an "NC." The final column shows the total number of attributes that qualify the point as Clovis and those that do not over the number of measurable criteria for that point. For 12 points, fewer than 50 percent of the Clovis criteria are satisfied. Only for two are more than 50 percent satisfied, with an equal number satisfied for the remaining three. Overall, these data suggest that only two of the Sunshine fluted points could, in fact, be characterized as Clovis, but at least 12 (and possibly 15) are likely not. The most telling of these criteria are the regularity of flaking patterns and the consistent and extensive pressure flaking.

Fluting Technology

One final variable we address is fluting technology. Although the specimens we have evaluated up to this point are all at the end of their use-lives, we are lucky enough to have a preform from the Sunshine Locality that has the base intact. Figure 6.8 shows a photograph of this preform, and Figure 6.9 shows a line drawing. This specimen is the proximal segment of a fluted biface, which is truncated by an obliquely oriented facet that represents a bending fracture. The specimen is 35.7 mm long, has a maximum width of 20.1 mm, and weighs 6.78 g. It has parallel stem margins and a concave base. The basal concavity, which has a maximum depth of 4.8 mm, does not extend across the entire width of the base and thus leaves rounded, earlike projections at the corners. Only one side of one face exhibits aligned, regular flake scars indicating pressure thinning (Figure 6.9). These flake scars originate from an edge prepared by abrasion. The opposing margin is more irregular, with several steep facets reflecting damage sustained at the time of the snap or from thinning blows that caused the edge to collapse.

The fluting procedure is similar to that described by Boldurian (1990) for Folsom points. Each side of the preform exhibits one fluting scar. These scars are oriented along the long axis of the preform and originate at the center of the basal cavity. The platform from which the first flute flake (Figure 6.9, side B) was removed has been

TABLE 6.5. Evaluation of Clovis Type Assignment for 18 Fluted Points Based on the Data in Table 6.4

	Criterion									
Provenience	2: Maximum Width Location	5: Total Length	6: Maximum Width	8: Number of Flutes	9: Flute Length	10: Basal Flute Widening	11: Postfluting Retouch	12: Type of Flaking	13: Pressure Flaking	Basal Indentation/ Basal Width[a]	Clovis/ Not Clovis[b]
SW-1893	—	—	—	NC	—	NC	NC	NC	NC	<1sd C	1:5
SW-1885	C	NC	NC	NC	NC	NC	NC	NC	NC	>1sd I	1:8
SW3-6N	—	—	—	C	—	NC	NC	NC	NC	<1sd C	2:4
SW-1911	—	—	C	C	C	NC	—	NC	NC	>1sd I	3:3
SW-1838	—	—	—	C	—	C	NC	NC	NC	<1sd C	3:3
SW-1894	—	—	—	NC	—	NC	NC	NC	NC	>1sd I	0:5
SW-1881	NC?	C?	C	C	C	NC	NC	C	NC	>1sd I	5:4
SW93-2	—	—	—	C	—	C	NC	NC	NC	>1sd I	2:3
SW-1879	—	—	C	NC	C	C	NC	NC	NC	>2sd NC	3:5
SW-54	—	—	—	NC	—	NC	C	—	NC	>2sd NC	1:4
SW95-11	—	—	—	C	—	C	NC	NC	NC	>2sd NC	2:4
LVS-103	—	—	C	NC	C	NC	NC	NC	NC	>3sd NC	2:6
SW3-89	—	—	C	C	C	NC	C	NC	NC	>1sd I	4:3
SW-1891	—	—	—	C	—	C	NC	—	NC	>2sd NC	2:3
SW1-1905	NC?	—	NC	C	—	C	C	NC	NC	<1sd C	4:4
SW4-56	—	—	—	NC	—	NC	—	NC	NC	—	0:4
SW-Surf 2007	C	NC	NC	NC	NC	NC	NC	NC	NC	<1sd C	2:8

Note: C = Clovis; I = inconclusive; NC = not Clovis.

[a] Values less than one standard deviation (.059) are designated as <1sd; values between two and one standard deviations are designated as >1sd, between two and three standard deviations, >2sd, etc. Values below one standard deviation are considered Clovis; between one and two standard deviations, inconclusive; and greater than two standard deviations, not Clovis.

[b] Ratio of the number of criteria indicative of Clovis to the number not indicative of Clovis. For blade indentation/blade width, values between one and two standard deviations are considered inconclusive and thus are not included in the ratio.

eliminated by preparing the central concavity for removal of the opposing flute flake. The proximal end of the first flute flake is about 5.4 mm wide and diverges distally, reaching a maximum width of ca. 12.5 mm. The fluting scar, which is ca. 24.0 mm long, nearly reaches the fracture facet; it truncates previous scars on the left side but is impinged upon by scars originating on the right side. The flute scar on side A originates from an edge in the center of the basal cavity that has been steepened in the opposite direction. A slight protrusion of the edge on the left side of the flake scar is a remnant of a prepared platform. To either side of the platform the edge of the base is abraded and rounded, producing concave areas that isolate the platform in the center of the concavity. The platform area exhibits a sharp edge, indicating that no additional marginal grinding was performed after removal of this flute, presumably because the preform broke at this point. The flute scar interrupts flake scars from the lateral margin and is truncated by the facture facet.

In summary, only two of the 17 points evaluated according to Howard's criteria could be considered Clovis. The thickness of both (6.0 and 6.1 mm) and the basal width of one (22.1 mm) are both slightly below the Clovis means but certainly are within the Clovis ranges. But both points, as is the case for the remaining Sunshine fluted points, consistently exhibit pressure flaking; one of these (Figure 6.6C) is the specimen that is irregularly flaked. As we pointed out earlier, however, this may be related to extensive resharpening. Overall, these data suggest to us that the fluted points in the Sunshine assemblage are not representative of the Clovis type. This is not to say that Clovis points do not exist in the Great Basin; we believe they do (Beck and Jones 2007; Beck and Jones 2008). For instance, a number of those presented by Davis and Shutler (1969) fulfill all or most of the Clovis criteria. We believe, however, that the Sunshine fluted points examined here are more likely a derivative of Clovis, which would put them slightly later in time. We discuss this more fully in the concluding chapter.

Fluted vs. Unfluted Lanceolates

The second issue we address concerns the morphological and technological relation between the fluted and unfluted lanceolate points in the Sunshine assemblage. Although the latter points are often found in the same site assemblages with both fluted and stemmed points, we know much less about them. Clewlow (1968a) was the first to define an unfluted lanceolate type for the Great Basin—Black Rock Concave Base—based on points he found in the Black Rock Desert of northwestern Nevada. Although Clewlow does not give a specific description of these points, he notes their resemblance to Plainview points, a type that had been defined by Krieger (1947) to describe an assemblage of 16 unfluted lanceolate points from the Plainview, Texas, area (see Haynes 1991; Knudson 1983). (Some researchers believe that Plainview is virtually indistinguishable from Goshen, discussed earlier [Pitblado 1998:336].) In describing the Black Rock specimens, however, Clewlow also states that

> the absence of fluting is a problem which involves certain technological aspects of stone tool manufacturing. Specifically, the critical consideration of unfluted points which are shaped very much like types which are often fluted is whether or not the unfluted examples are *thick enough* to have been fluted had the manufacturing artisan so desired [1968a:14; emphasis in the original].

This statement, of course, is reminiscent of the discussion of Midland and Folsom points, which Clewlow actually mentions. He goes on to say that although the Black Rock specimens *resemble* Plainview points, the latter *are* thick enough to have been fluted whereas those from the Black Rock Desert are not. Further, as the Black Rock specimens were surface finds, their chronological position is unknown. For these two reasons, he proposes the new Black Rock Concave Base type.

Clewlow (1968a:15, Table 5) presents length, width, thickness, and weight measurements for eight Black Rock Concave Base points. The length measurements are somewhat larger than those of the Sunshine unfluted points (Table 6.6), ranging from 50 to 75 mm (mean = 63.4 mm), but the width range is quite similar, ranging between 19 and 29 mm (mean = 24.6 mm). The range of thickness values is somewhat smaller than that of the Sunshine specimens, ranging from 3.0 to 5.0 mm (mean = 4.1 mm). Clewlow does not give the basal widths, but this measurement was extrapolated from his photographs and ranges between 18 and 24.3 mm (mean = 19.8 mm), very similar once again to those in the Sunshine assemblage. The difference in length simply could be a reflection of resharpening of the Sunshine specimens, but the difference in thickness is another matter. Granted, the data from the Black Rock Desert are based on only eight points, but given the difference in thickness, we believe that the Sunshine points are inappropriately described as Black Rock Concave Base.

The question, then, is: Do we have a situation comparable to Clovis and Goshen/Plainview, which no one has ever argued are fluted and unfluted alternatives of the same entity, or to Folsom and Midland (as argued by Hofman 1992)? This question may be impossible to answer

TABLE 6.6. Summary of Quantitative Data for Fluted and Unfluted Points in the Sunshine Assemblage

CATEGORY	STATISTIC	TOTAL LENGTH	MAXIMUM WIDTH	BASAL WIDTH	THICKNESS
Fluted	*N*	4	6	16	17
	Range	35.4–45.8	18.5–28.7	15.2–26.8	3.7–6.3
	Mean	36.44	22.37	21.06	5.07
	SD	6.347	4.314	3.651	.789
Unfluted	*N*	15	31	65	72
	Range	34.0–57.3	10.9–31.6	13.4–27.8	3.7–7.4
	Mean	42.83	23.17	20.15	5.40
	SD	7.070	4.423	3.229	.838

Note: Measurements in millimeters.

TABLE 6.7. Summary of Qualitative Data for Fluted and Unfluted Points in the Sunshine Assemblage

	FLUTED		UNFLUTED	
VARIABLE	*N*	%	*N*	%
Raw Material				
Chert	15	88.2	66	91.7
Obsidian	2	11.8	3	4.2
Fine-Grained Volcanics			3	4.2
Flaking Pattern				
Collateral			12	16.7
Parallel	14	82.4	26	36.1
Oblique			13	18.1
Irregular	1	5.9	4	5.6
Combination[a]			13	18.1
Indeterminate	2	11.8	4	5.6
Blade Wear				
Present	3	17.6	1	1.4
Absent			15	20.8
Indeterminate	17	82.4	56	77.8
Lateral Edge Grinding				
Absent	1	5.9	10	13.9
Light	4	23.5	12	16.7
Medium	4	23.5	32	44.4
Heavy	7	41.2	17	23.6
Indeterminate	1	5.9	1	1.4

[a] A combination of flaking patterns, such as collateral on one face and parallel on the other.

given the lack of dating for both Great Basin Fluted and Great Basin unfluted points, but we can make comparisons between these forms nonetheless.

A total of 73 unfluted lanceolate points are represented in the Sunshine assemblage (Figure 6.10), with 63 in the H–N collection and seven from the HC collection. One of the H–N points (1834; Figure 6.10UUU), however, could not be analyzed because it is hafted; therefore, our discussion focuses on only 72 of the 73 points. An examination of Table 6.6 shows that in terms of the quantitative attributes, Great Basin Fluted and Great Basin unfluted points are virtually identical. Although visual inspection of the qualitative attributes (Table 6.7) suggests differences in some variables, chi-square tests suggest that the only significant difference is in flaking type ($\chi^2 = 92.719$, $df = 8.0, p < .001$). Fluted points most often exhibit parallel collateral flaking on both sides (82.4 percent), where unfluted points exhibit much greater variation in this attribute—only 36.1 percent are parallel flaked, and the remaining specimens show broad collateral (16.7 percent), oblique (18.1 percent), irregular (5.6 percent), or a combination (e.g., broad collateral on one face and parallel collateral on the other—18.1 percent). Interestingly, it is this particular variable that might argue against a Folsom/Midland-like relation between Great Basin fluted and unfluted points. If, for instance, points are fluted only when blanks are large enough, all other manufacturing techniques should be the same—that is, if fluted points are predominantly parallel flaked, unfluted points should be also. Considering this factor, in combination with the fact that there is no significant difference in overall size (particularly thickness) between the two, the relation between Great Basin fluted and unfluted appears more like that of Clovis and Plainview/Goshen than that between Folsom and Midland.

FIGURE 6.10. Unfluted lanceolate points from the Sunshine Locality: (A) 1882; (B) 2134; (C) 2137; (D) 1708; (E) 1705; (F) 2143; (G) 1837; (H) 1883; (I) 2145; (J) 1883; (K) 2144; (L) 2200; (M) 2156; (N) 2205; (O) 2208; (P) 1851; (Q) 1909; (R) 2132; (S) 2136; (T) 2131; (U) 2133; (V) 2140; (W) 2142; (X) 2135; (Y) 2006; (Z) 1903; (AA) 1906; (BB) 2120; (CC) 2122; (DD) 2126; (EE) 2118.

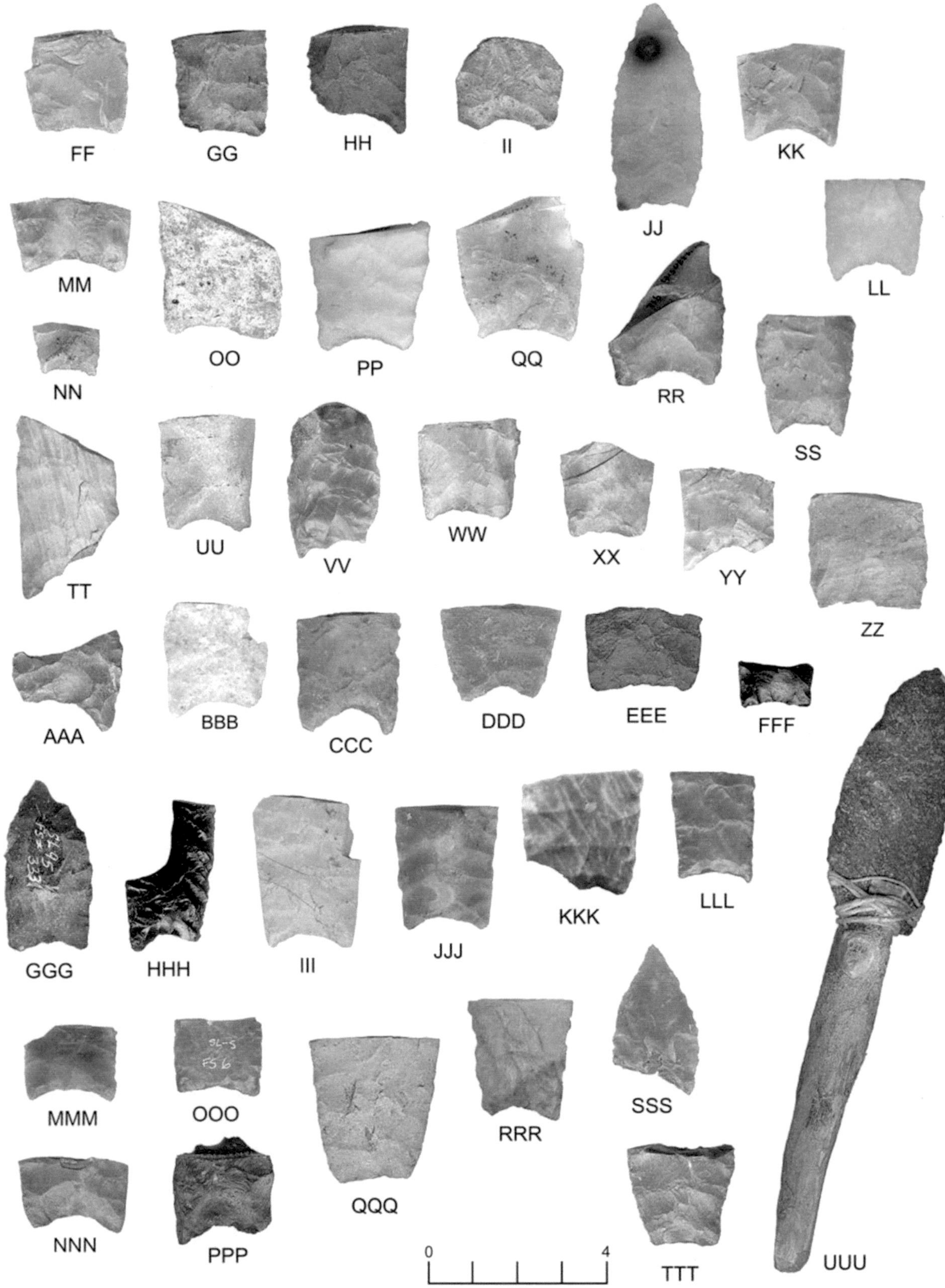

FIGURE 6.10. (cont'd.) Unfluted lanceolate points from the Sunshine Locality: (FF) 2117; (GG) 2116; (HH) 2115; (II) 2119; (JJ) 2152; (KK) 2209; (LL) 1873; (MM) 2212; (NN) 2127; (OO) 1914; (PP) 1910; (QQ) 1913; (RR) 1912; (SS) 1904; (TT) 1902; (UU) 1908; (VV) 1907; (WW) 2211; (XX) 1896; (YY) 1895; (ZZ) 1897; (AAA) 2129; (BBB) 1832; (CCC) 1633; (DDD) 1586; (EEE) 1827; (FFF) 2894; (GGG) surface 1995, FS 333; (HHH) 1623; (III) surface 1993, FS 9; (JJJ) surface 1993, FS 11; (KKK) 705; (LLL) 1775; (MMM) surface 1993, FS 1; (NNN) surface 1993, FS 10; (OOO) surface 1993, FS 6; (PPP) 2004, FS7; (QQQ) 1840; (RRR) 1804; (SSS) 1903; (TTT) 2004, FS 6; (UUU) 1834, hafted by Phil Hutchinson.

Summary of Lanceolate Points

In sum, the comparison of Sunshine fluted points with Clovis and Folsom points strongly suggests that the Sunshine points are not representative of Clovis. They are generally smaller, have deeper basal concavities relative to their basal widths, and more often exhibit single flute scars. All but one are finely parallel flaked, and all exhibit extensive and consistent pressure flaking. Finally, based on our analysis of the fluted point preform recovered, the fluting technology of the Sunshine points is more similar to that of Folsom than to that of Clovis.

The comparison between fluted and unfluted lanceolates suggests that they are *not* "two sides of the same coin" so to speak. In other words, they are not representative of a Folsom–Midland situation as suggested by Hofman (1992) but, rather, more like a Clovis–Goshen/Plainview situation. Because of the poor dating control with regard to both forms, it is impossible to say what their temporal relation might be, but we can speculate that the unfluted form follows the fluted form in time, as is the case for Clovis and Goshen/Plainview.

Projectile Point Analysis: Great Basin Stemmed Series

A number of different stemmed projectile point types, all generally attributed to the TP/EH period, have been formulated in different parts of the Desert West. Similarities among points of these different types prompted Tuohy and Layton (1977) to combine them into the Great Basin Stemmed Series (GBSS). Point types that have been included in this series include Cougar Mountain (Layton 1970, 1972), Silver Lake, Lake Mohave (Amsden 1937), Parman (Layton 1970), Lind Coulee (Daugherty 1956), Haskett (Butler 1965), and Windust (Rice 1972). The latter was originally included in the GBSS by Tuohy and Layton, but we treat it separately here because it is quite different morphologically (see Beck and Jones 1997).

We also add a type to the GBSS, which we call Ovate. These points strongly resemble points of the Cascade type, defined by Butler (1961), that are found in the Northwest and Columbia Plateau. They also are quite similar to those of the Cougar Mountain type except that there is no inflection point between the stem and blade. Because points of this type occur in other early assemblages in the Great Basin (e.g., Bedwell 1973; Connolly and Jenkins 1999) and are well represented in the Sunshine assemblage, we include the Ovate type in our discussion of the GBSS types.

Figure 6.11 shows examples of these types redrawn from the publications where each was originally defined. Most of these examples have counterparts in the Sunshine assemblage, as Figure 6.12 shows. A comparison of the examples in this figure would suggest significant differences in a number of traits, such as size, stem shape, shouldering, and blade shape. These examples, however, represent the "ideals" and are rare, with reality looking more like what is represented in Figure 6.13.

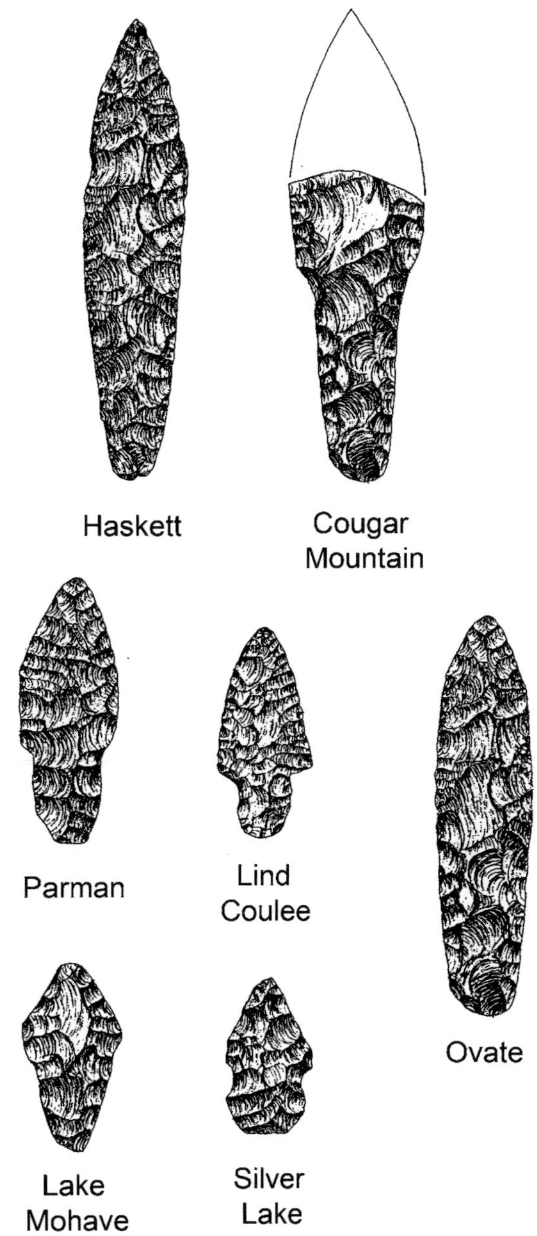

FIGURE 6.11. Projectile point types included in the Great Basin Stemmed Series.

Figure 6.13A shows a recognizable Cougar Mountain point in the center, with gradations to the right toward less pronounced shoulders, resulting eventually in an Ovate point, and to the left toward more pronounced shoulders, resulting in a Parman. Figure 6.13B shows similar gradations emanating from a Silver Lake form, resulting in Lake Mohave to the right and Pinto to the left. As

FIGURE 6.12. Examples of Great Basin Stemmed Series types. Cougar Mountain from Jakes Valley, all others from the Sunshine Locality.

is evident from this figure, the distinction between types is not that easily defined, and points do not separate by type on the basis of metric variables, as is often the case for Archaic types (see, e.g., O'Connell and Inoway 1994). Consequently, we proceed in a somewhat different fashion than does Thomas (1981) in his analysis of Archaic points. We first assign specimens to types using the original type definitions. We then make between-type comparisons in an attempt to establish a set of distinctive features for each type.

Although most of the Sunshine GBSS points are in the form of stem fragments, there are a number of fairly complete specimens; we use these as a comparative collection to address the morphological and functional questions mentioned at the beginning of this chapter. In order to increase the sample size of the comparative collection, we have added several specimens from other eastern Nevada assemblages, points collected from Butte and Jakes valleys, as well as Long Valley outside the boundaries of the Sunshine Locality. We subsequently refer to this assemblage as the eastern Nevada comparative collection.

Exacerbating the problem of type assignment is the fact that the imprecise definitions of these early types have been expanded by many authors to include other forms. For example, the Silver Lake type as defined by Amsden (1937) characterizes a distinctive morphology with a relatively short blade, a slightly expanding and then contracting stem that is about equal in length to the blade, and a rounded base. Brott (1966), however, has suggested that there may be at least four varieties of the Silver Lake type. Tuohy (1969), although recognizing the several morphologies that had been defined as Cougar Mountain, Haskett, and Lind Coulee types, collapses all points with long, tapering stems into the Lake Mohave type. Thus, much confusion has arisen in the discussion of points of the GBSS analogous to that experienced in the discussion of Archaic points (see Thomas 1981). For this reason, we begin by presenting the original definition for each type. Because the Sunshine assemblage contains no specimens that identify with the Haskett type, we do not include the Haskett definition here.

Great Basin Stemmed Series Type Definitions

Lake Mohave Type. The Lake Mohave type (Figure 6.11) was first defined by Amsden based on points collected from the beaches of Pleistocene Lake Mojave. According to Amsden,

> The Lake Mohave type is characterized by a long, tapering stem, produced by shouldering the point (usually very slight), just below the center of its vertical axis. This results in a generally diamond-shape form, with more shoulder than blade. The form is not highly standardized, wavering frequently between the oval on the one hand and the Silver Lake type on the other [1937:80].

Amsden includes 12 specimens in this group, and it can be seen from his Plate XLI (1937:81) that although there is a good deal of variation among the points represented, there is a distinctive morphology represented.

Silver Lake Type. The Silver Lake type (Figure 6.11) was also defined by Amsden (1937). Points assigned to this type were found with other artifactual material, which was named the "Silver Lake Culture" by William H. Campbell

FIGURE 6.13. Morphological gradations of Great Basin Stemmed Series projectile points: (A) from Cougar Mountain to Parman and Ovate; (B) from Silver Lake to Pinto and Lake Mohave.

(Campbell 1936), on an old shoreline of Pleistocene Lake Mojave. According to Amsden, points of this type "have more definition of shoulder and less basal taper than the Lake Mohave type. The base comprises never more than half the whole length, usually about a third. It is always somewhat rounded at the butt" (1937:84).

Lind Coulee Types. Daugherty describes three types ("styles") of Lind Coulee points in his report on the excavation of the Lind Coulee site in Washington State (Figure 6.11):

> *Style 1,* based on two specimens, is defined as having a "tapered stem, rounded shoulders, and convex base" (Daugherty 1956:246). The one complete specimen from this site is 66 mm long, 21 mm wide, and 4 mm thick. Both specimens were made by percussion and pressure flaking, and "the flaking scars indicate pressure flaking for the final shaping. In some cases the scars extend completely across the face; in others, flakes struck from opposing sides meet at the midline" (Daugherty 1956:246).
>
> "*Style 2* points may be distinguished from those of *Style 1* by their sharp lateral shoulders.... The complete specimens are long and slender in shape, the larger of these two measuring 70 mm. in length, 21 mm. in width, and 5 mm. in thickness, whereas the other measures 63 mm. in length, 18 mm. in width, and 5 mm. in thickness.... The flaking techniques are identical to *Style 1,* with the flaking scars forming an even more symmetrical ribbon-like pattern" (Daugherty 1956:246).
>
> *Style 3* is represented by only one point: "It is shorter and broader than styles 1 and 2, being more triangular in shape the length is 57 mm., the width 24 mm., and the thickness 6 mm." (Daugherty 1956:246). Also, this point exhibits much more pronounced shouldering than that of the other two styles.

Cougar Mountain Type. The Cougar Mountain type (Figure 6.11) was defined by Layton (1970, 1972) based on the analysis of points excavated by John Cowles (1959) from Cougar Mountain Cave in south-central Oregon. Layton describes points of the Cougar Mountain type as

> lanceolate in form with prominent sloping shoulders. The stem contracts with straight sides to a convex base. The edges of the stem are heavily ground or blunted for their entire length; however, the base is not ground. The specimens vary from lenticular

> to diamond-shaped in cross section; however, stems generally approach a lenticular cross section and the blades a diamond-shaped cross section. Flake scars on the blade are large, steep and invasive forming a medial ridge. Fine secondary flaking is found only along the edges of the stem. Although none of the six specimens are complete, a maximum length range of 13.0 to 13.5 cm. has been extrapolated. The stem length, measured from shoulders to base, is approximately 5/13 of the projected total specimen length [1970:2–3].

Points of this type bear a strong resemblance to Lind Coulee Style 1, but we use the Cougar Mountain designation here.

Parman Types. Six Parman types were defined by Layton (1970, 1972) based on points collected from the surface around the margins of pluvial Lake Parman as well as specimens excavated at Hanging Rock Shelter and Silent Snake Springs, all located in the northeastern corner of Nevada. According to Layton, points of the Parman types

> generally range from 3 cm. to 7 cm. in length and they represent a distinctly shorter length mode than Cougar Mountain specimens. Parman points also manifest considerably more variation in form and flaking than do Cougar Mountain specimens. Parman points usually have broad blades and square to sloping shoulders. A few are single-shouldered. Flaking is irregular. Stems are generally proportionally shorter than blades, and stem bases vary from rounded to square. Edge grinding is usually less pronounced than on Cougar Mountain specimens [1979:48].

In examining Layton's (1972) drawings of the six types of Parman points one is struck by the wide variety in form of points from one type to another and sometimes even points within the same type. The most coherent form is that of Type 1 points, which bear a strong resemblance to Lind Coulee Style 3. Layton (1972:3) recognized this resemblance but notes that the Parman points are thicker than those of the Lind Coulee type. Parman Type 2 points resemble Windust Groups 1 and 2 points (discussed below).

In his 1972 presentation of an obsidian hydration chronology for the Fort Rock Valley, Layton (1972:3, Figure 1f–i) pictures seven points from Cougar Mountain Cave, which he designates as Parman Type 1. One of these, however, bears more resemblance to his original Type 6 (1972:3, Figure 1i). In 1979 Layton collapsed the six Parman types into two, distinguished simply by whether the base of the stem is rounded or square. The Sunshine points identified as Parman most resemble those classified as Parman Type 1 (Figure 6.11) originally (Layton 1970:195, Figure 21 i–k) and those identified later as Parman Style 1 (Layton 1979:52, Figure 4g–l) when the six types were collapsed into two, as well as Lind Coulee Style 3. We use the Parman designation here.

Ovate Type. The points of this type are similar to points of the Cougar Mountain type in overall size and shape, except that they exhibit no definite intersection between the stem and blade but simply a widening from the base to the point of maximum width (which is most often at the midpoint, whereas that of Cougar Mountain points is in the upper third of the point) and then a narrowing to the tip. They are also similar in some respects to points of the Haskett type (Butler 1965), in that there is no well-defined shoulder region. Haskett points, however, are, in general, more finely made, in that they are symmetrical and also generally exhibit a well-defined point, but this is not the case for the Sunshine Ovate points. Instead, as mentioned earlier, these points are more like points of the Cascade type, defined by Butler (1961), but we do not use this designation here because we do not know if the Sunshine Ovate points represent the same entity, in form, function, or temporal occurrence.

Analysis of the Eastern Nevada Comparative Collection

The majority of points that identify with GBSS types are fragmentary, making it difficult to identify them with a specific type. For example, many of the point fragments are midsections, blade sections, or stems that might possibly be identifiable with a particular type, given a set of definitive criteria. One of our aims here is to attempt to establish standardized measures for each type, which is difficult to do using fragments. There are a number of fairly complete specimens in this assemblage that we use here, with the addition of several specimens from our collections in Butte, Long, and Jakes valleys, as the eastern Nevada comparative collection (ENCC). The ENCC contains a total of 101 points identified with five GBSS types: Cougar Mountain (n = 18; Figure 6.14), Ovate (n = 22; Figure 6.15), Lake Mohave (n = 30; Figure 6.16), Silver Lake (n = 17; Figure 6.17), and Parman (n = 14; Figure 6.18).

Quantitative Attributes. The quantitative data for 10 metric variables and two ratios (stem length/total length and neck width/maximum width) measured on the 101 points in the ENCC are summarized in Table 6.8. Because there is no obvious break between the stem and blade on Ovate points, variables relating to one or the

TABLE 6.8. Summary of Quantitative Data for Five Great Basin Stemmed Series Types from the Eastern Nevada Comparative Collection

VARIABLE	STATISTIC	POINT TYPE				
		COUGAR MOUNTAIN	OVATE	PARMAN	LAKE MOHAVE	SILVER LAKE
Total Length (mm)	*N*	10	21	5	23	14
	Range	66.9–111.7	47.0–89.5	45.9–77.3	33.4–64.0	28.7–42.5
	Mean	81.69	61.83	61.87	49.16	36.06
	SD	12.963	9.763	14.000	9.005	5.007
Blade Length (mm)	*N*	13	—	7	30	16
	Range	22.3–50.0		23.3–42.25	10.7–32.3	11.5–26.3
	Mean	35.69		30.61	20.30	17.92
	SD	11.037		6.050	5.068	4.767
Shoulder Length (mm)	*N*	15	—	12	30	17
	Range	3.8–29.7		1.5–12.7	.0–14.7	.0–6.3
	Mean	16.12		6.06	4.90	3.20
	SD	6.041		3.452	3.328	1.573
Stem Length (mm)	*N*	10	—	10	23	14
	Range	22.8–48.0		16.2–32.6	13.8–33.0	11.9–18.3
	Mean	33.56		24.48	24.31	14.92
	SD	9.291		5.371	5.612	1.928
Maximum Width (mm)	*N*	18	22	12	30	17
	Range	20.0–34.1	17.1–25.9	21.1–37.0	16.0–28.6	19.0–26.9
	Mean	28.29	21.09	28.07	23.27	22.60
	SD	3.694	2.129	5.089	3.110	2.096
Thickness (mm)	*N*	16	22	13	29	17
	Range	6.8–11.4	6.3–9.7	5.40–8.40	4.9–11.3	5.7–8.4
	Mean	9.09	8.24	6.90	6.86	6.99
	SD	1.307	.902	.915	1.583	.841
Basal Width (mm)	*N*	10	18	11	22	12
	Range	10.6–19.2	9.3–16.7	9.8–17.4	8.0–20.4	14.6–18.7
	Mean	15.00	11.67	14.30	15.52	16.86
	SD	2.440	1.951	2.784	3.093	1.448
Neck Width (mm)	*N*	18	—	14	30	17
	Range	16.4–29.4		11.7–26.4	14.4–23.8	13.6–19.7
	Mean	21.27		19.60	19.88	16.90
	SD	2.974		3.579	2.468	1.864
Proximal Shoulder Angle (°)	*N*	18	—	14	25	17
	Range	80.5–90.0		81.0–90.0	78.5–90.0	93.0–104.5
	Mean	85.58		84.82	85.58	99.50
	SD	2.528		2.614	2.835	3.432
Distal Shoulder Angle (°)	*N*	18	—	13	30	17
	Range	229.5–262.5		206.0–247.0	198.0–258.5	193.5–245.0
	Mean	252.11		225.39	241.12	215.94
	SD	9.150		15.783	15.443	13.515
Neck Width/Maximum Width Ratio	*N*	17	—	12	30	17
	Range	.63–1.00		.63–.87	.71–1.04	.57–.89
	Mean	.753		.724	.862	.745
	SD	.088		.068	.070	.090
Stem Length/Total Length Ratio	*N*	9	—	5	23	14
	Range	.30–.56		.35–.46	.34–.64	.3–.52
	Mean	.419		.381	.495	.419
	SD	.091		.047	.077	.064

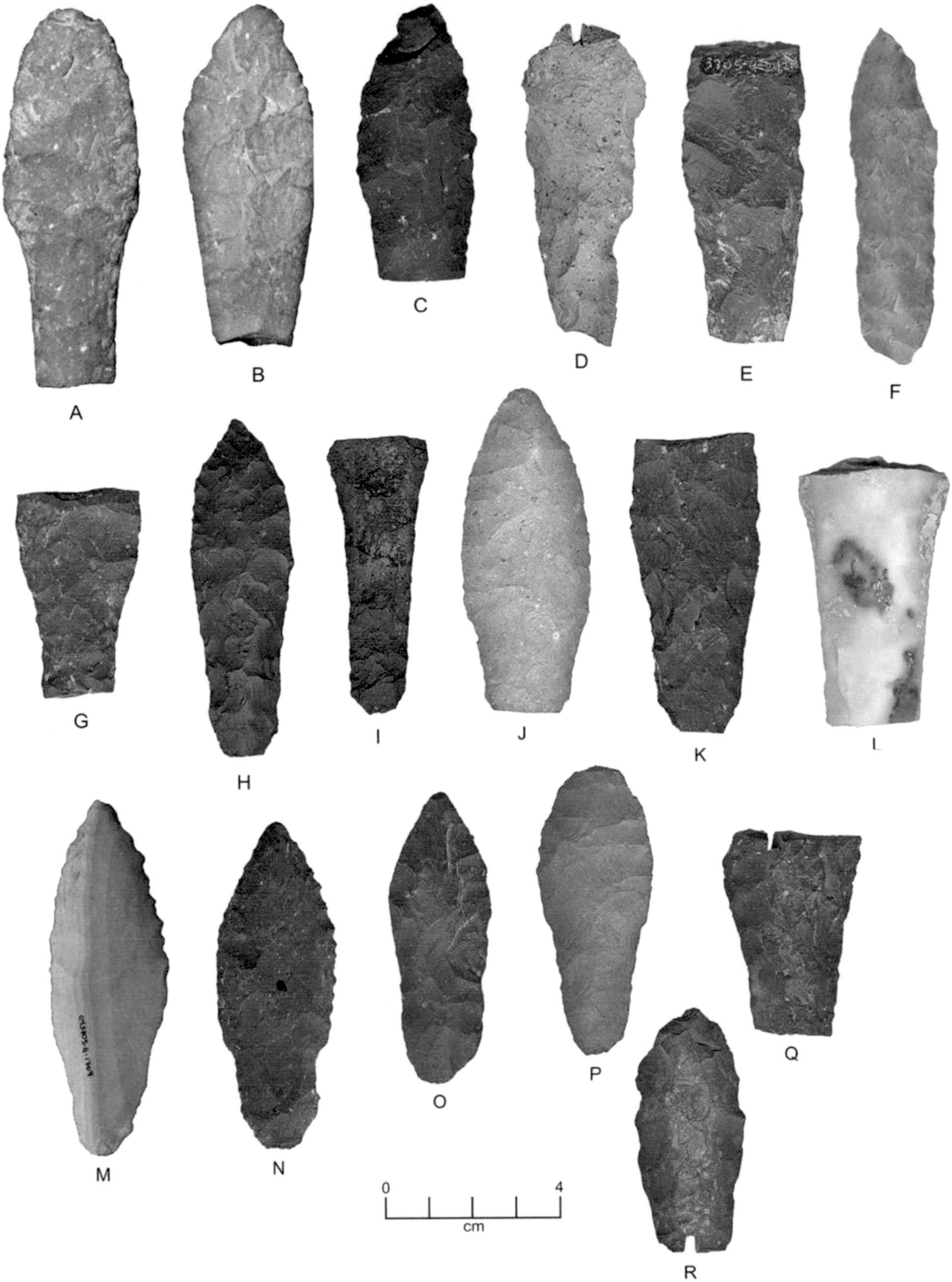

FIGURE 6.14. Points of the Cougar Mountain type in the eastern Nevada comparative collection: (A–B) Jakes Wash, Jakes Valley, no provenience; (C) 1790; (D) CCL7, FS 2 (Butte Valley); (E) 1789; (F) 2421; (G) 1874; (H) 1876; (I) 2313; (J) 2179; (K) 2182; (L) LPL1, 320E, 292N (Jakes Valley); (M) 1709; (N) SW93, 114.05E, 104.44N, Final Stratum C/D; (O) 1784; (P) 2178; (Q) CCL6/CCL8, FS 1 (Butte Valley); (R) HPL1, FS 107 (Butte Valley).

FIGURE 6.15. Points of the Ovate type in the eastern Nevada comparative collection: (A) 2198; (B) 2192; (C) 2200; (D) 2204; (E) 1985; (F) 2195; (G) 2202; (H) 2203; (I) 2196; (J) 2218; (K) 2221; (L) 2219; (M) 2214; (N) 2213; (O) 2216; (P) 2217; (Q) 2447; (R) 2215; (S) 2222. (1997, SW1, 2N, not photographed.)

FIGURE 6.16. Points of the Lake Mohave type in the eastern Nevada comparative collection: (A) 1875; (B) 1884; (C) 2150; (D) 2148; (E) 2160; (F) 2161; (G) 3504; (H) 2149; (I) 2157; (J) 2159; (K) 2146; (L) 2147; (M) 2174; (N) LPL1, 368E, 382N; (O) LPL1, 362E, 342N; (P) HPL1, FS 146; (Q) LPL1, 230E, 262N; (R) HPL5, 290E, 110N (Butte Valley); (S) surface 1996, FS 1; (T) no provenience; (U) 2893; (V) 2138; (W) 2895; (X) 2199; (Y) HPL3, 190E, 244N (Butte Valley); (Z) 1791; (AA) LPL1, 370E, 326N; (BB) Jakes Pond Survey, Q2, FS 2; (CC) 1782; (DD) LPL1, 322E, 366N.

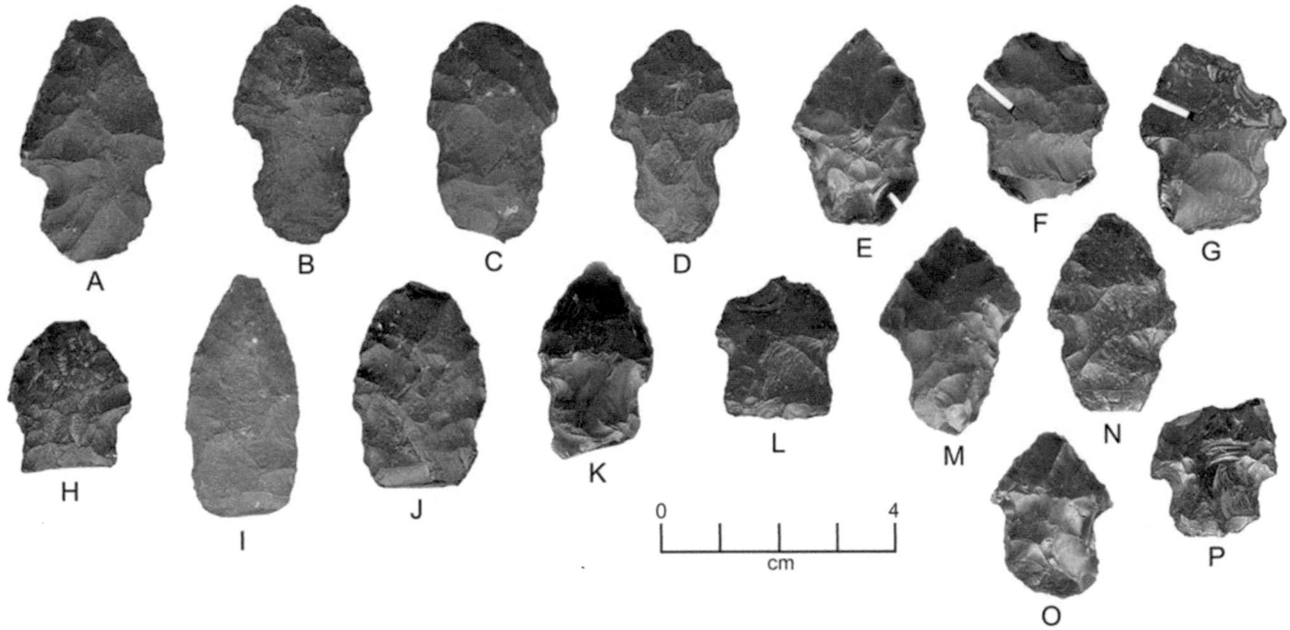

FIGURE 6.17. Points of the Silver Lake type in the eastern Nevada comparative collection: (A) 2163; (B) 2171; (C) 2170; (D) 2172; (E) HPL2, FS 217 (Butte Valley); (F) LPL1, 270E, 244N; (G) LPL1, 320E, 252N; (H) 2168; (I) 1748; (J) 1898; (K) 2897; (L) 2898; (M) 2880; (N) 2879; (O) 2903; (P) 2900. (SW3A, 31, not photographed.)

FIGURE 6.18. Points of the Parman type in the eastern Nevada comparative collection: (A) 1792; (B) 2183; (C) 2185; (D) 2124; (E) 2892; (F) 2187; (G) surface 1993, FS 3; (H) 2194; (I) 2896; (J) no provenience; (K) Butte Valley Survey, Q10, FS 1; (L) LPL1, 302E, 384N; (M) 2153; (N) 2330.

TABLE 6.9. Results of Analysis of Variance Comparisons Between Pairs of Point Types on 12 Quantitative Variables

		PAIR									
VARIABLE	STATISTIC	CM & LM	CM & P	CM & SL	CM & O	P & SL	P & LM	P & O	SL & LM	SL & O	LM & O
Blade Length	*f*	−15.385	−5.077	−17.077	—	−12.688	10.307	—	−2.381	—	—
	df	62	62	62		62	62		62		
	p	**<.001**	.667	**<.001**		**<.001**	**.003**		1.000		
Total Length	*f*	−32.522	−19.815	−45.628	−19.854	−25.813	12.707	.039	−13.106	−25.774	12.668
	df	68	68	68	68	68	68	68	68	68	68
	p	**<.001**	**.004**	**<.001**	**<.001**	**<.001**	.094	1.000	**.002**	**<.001**	**<.001**
Shoulder	*f*	−11.227	−10.065	−12.926	—	−2.861	1.162	—	−1.700	—	—
	df	70	70	70		70	70		70		
	p	**<.001**	**<.001**	**<.001**		.293	1.000		.861		
Stem Length	*f*	−9.247	−9.080	−18.642	—	−9.562	.167	—	−9.395	—	—
	df	53	53	53		53	53		53		
	p	**.001**	**.006**	**<.001**		**.001**	1.000		**<.001**		
Maximum Width	*f*	−5.027	−.225	−5.495	−7.205	−5.270	4.802	6.980	−.468	1.711	−2.179
	df	94	94	94	94	94	94	94	92	92	92
	p	**<.001**	1.000	**<.001**	**<.001**	**<.001**	**<.001**	**<.001**	1.000	1.000	.172
Thickness	*f*	−2.227	−2.184	−2.093	−.848	.090	.044	−1.335	.134	−1.245	1.379
	df	92	92	92	92	92	92	92	92	92	92
	p	**<.001**	**<.001**	**<.001**	.352	1.000	1.000	**.021**	1.000	**.019**	**.001**
Basal Width	*f*	.541	−.675	1.879	−3.308	2.554	−1.216	2.633	1.338	5.188	−3.849
	df	68	68	68	68	68	68	68	68	68	68
	p	1.000	1.000	.818	**.012**	.163	1.000	.072	1.000	**<.001**	**<.001**
Neck Width	*f*	−1.389	−1.676	−4.372	—	−2.696	−.287	—	−2.983	—	—
	df	75	75	75		75	75		75		
	p	.536	.518	**<.001**		**.043**	1.000		**.003**		
Proximal Shoulder Angle	*f*	.003	−.762	13.917	—	14.679	−.759	—	13.920	—	—
	df	70	70	70		70	70		70		
	p	1.000	1.000	**<.001**		**<.001**	1.000		**<.001**		
Distal Shoulder Angle	*f*	−10.994	−26.726	−36.170	—	−9.443	−15.732	—	−25.175	—	—
	df	74	74	74		74	74		74		
	p	**.058**	**<.001**	**<.001**		.413	**.006**		**<.001**		
Stem Length/Total Length Ratio	*f*	.077	−.038	.000	—	.038	−.114	—	−.076	—	—
	df	47	47	47		47	47		47		
	p	.070	1.000	1.000		1.000	**.018**		**.023**		
Neck Width/ Maximum Width Ratio	*f*	.109	−.029	−.008	—	.021	−.138	—	−.116	—	—
	df	72	72	72		72	72		72		
	p	**<.001**	1.000	1.000		1.000	**<.001**		**<.001**		

Note: Significant probabilities are shown in bold. CM = Cougar Mountain; LM = Lake Mohave; O = Ovate; P = Parman; SL = Silver Lake.

TABLE 6.10. Summary of Significant Analysis of Variance Comparisons

VARIABLE	PAIR									
	CM & LM	CM & P	CM & SL	CM & O	P & SL	P & LM	P & O	SL & LM	SL & O	LM & O
Blade Length	S	NS	S	—	S	S	—	NS	—	—
Total Length	S	S	S	S	S	NS	NS	S	S	S
Shoulder	S	S	S	—	NS	NS	—	NS	—	—
Stem Length	S	S	S	—	S	NS	—	S	—	—
Maximum Width	S	NS	S	S	S	S	S	NS	NS	NS
Thickness	S	S	S	NS	NS	NS	S	NS	S	S
Basal Width	NS	NS	NS	S	NS	NS	NS	NS	S	S
Neck Width	NS	NS	S	—	S	NS	—	S	—	—
Proximal Shoulder Angle	NS	NS	S	—	S	NS	—	S	—	—
Distal Shoulder Angle	S	S	S	—	NS	S	—	S	—	—
Stem Length/Total Length Ratio	NS	NS	NS	—	NS	S	—	S	—	—
Neck Width/Maximum Width Ratio	S	NS	NS	—	NS	S	—	S	—	—

Note: CM = Cougar Mountain; LM = Lake Mohave; NS = not significant; O = Ovate; P = Parman; S = significant; SL = Silver Lake.

other (e.g., blade length, stem length, etc.) were not measured for these points; consequently, only four variables are shown in Table 6.8 for Ovate points.

Table 6.9 shows the results of one-way analysis of variance comparisons between pairs of points of each type on all of these variables except weight. (Weight was not included in the comparisons because we measured the actual weight of each specimen, which was most often fragmentary, rather than estimating the weight of the complete point.) The results are summarized in Table 6.10. When all variables are considered, Cougar Mountain points show the greatest number of differences with points of the other types, whereas Parman points show the fewest.

On some variables, points of one type differ significantly from points of all other types with which they were compared. For example, Cougar Mountain points differ from points of all other types in total length, shoulder, stem length, and DSA (we consider DSA significant even though $p = .058$); Lake Mohave points differ from points of all other types in DSA and the neck width/maximum width (NW/MW) ratio; and Silver Lake points differ from all other types in total length, stem length, neck width, and PSA. We consider these variables "distinctive features" for these types, and they are indicated with an "X" in Table 6.11. In the case of the Parman and Ovate types, however, there is not a single distinctive feature when compared with all other types. Ovate points are significantly different from all but Parman in total length and basal width (the two types differ on this variable at a p of .072) and from all but Cougar Mountain in thickness; Parman points differ from all but Cougar Mountain points on blade length, all but Lake Mohave points on stem length and all but Silver Lake on DSA. These we consider "possible distinctive features" of these two types, and they are designated by question marks in Table 6.11. Possible distinctive features, that is, variables for which a type differs from all but one other type, are also designated for the other types in Table 6.11.

These differences can be seen more clearly using box plots. The great difference in overall size between Cougar Mountain and all other points is evident in Figure 6.19, which shows total length, shoulder, stem length, and maximum thickness. There is almost no overlap in total length and shoulder between Cougar Mountain points and those of the other types and only slight overlap in stem length. Stem length among Cougar Mountain points is about twice that, on the average, of Parman and Lake Mohave points and over three times that of Silver Lake points. Figure 6.19A and C also illustrates the significant difference in total length and stem length of Silver Lake points from points of the other four types. Points of the different types vary less in thickness (Figure 6.19D), which is a possible distinctive feature for Cougar Mountain and Ovate types (Table 6.11).

The two other distinctive features of the Silver Lake type are neck width and PSA, which are shown in Figure 6.20A and B, respectively. Whereas points of the Cougar Mountain, Lake Mohave, and Parman types have almost identical PSA values, the values for Silver Lake points are drastically different (Figure 6.20B). Going back to the original definition of these points, Amsden states that

TABLE 6.11. Distinctive Features and Possible Distinctive Features of Five Great Basin Stemmed Series Types

	TYPE				
VARIABLE	COUGAR MOUNTAIN	PARMAN	LAKE MOHAVE	SILVER LAKE	OVATE
Blade Length	?	?	?	?	
Total Length	X		?	X	?
Shoulder	X				
Stem Length	X	?	?	X	
Maximum Width	?	?			
Thickness	?				?
Basal Width					?
Neck Width				X	
Proximal Shoulder Angle				X	
Distal Shoulder Angle	X	?	X	?	
Stem Length/Total Length Ratio			?		
Neck Width/Maximum Width Ratio			X		
Total Distinctive Features	4	0	2	4	0
Total Possible Distinctive Features	3	4	4	2	3

Note: X = distinctive feature; ? = possible distinctive feature.

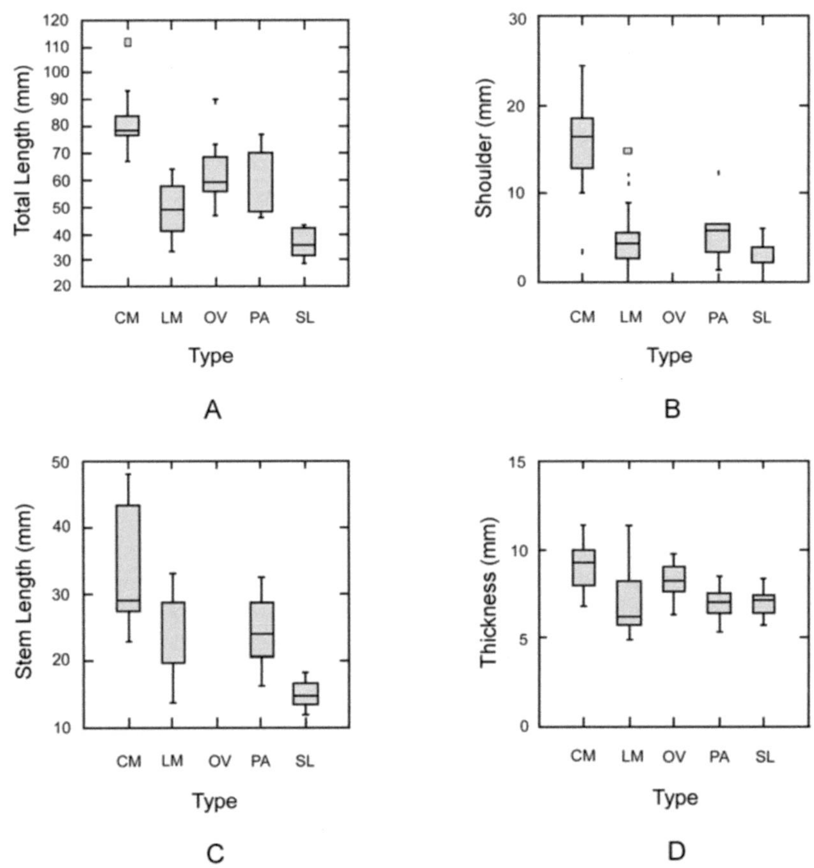

FIGURE 6.19. Box plots of (A) total length, (B) shoulder length, (C) stem length, and (D) thickness for Great Basin Stemmed Series points in the eastern Nevada comparative collection. CM = Cougar Mountain; LM = Lake Mohave; OV = Ovate; PA= Parman; SL = Silver Lake.

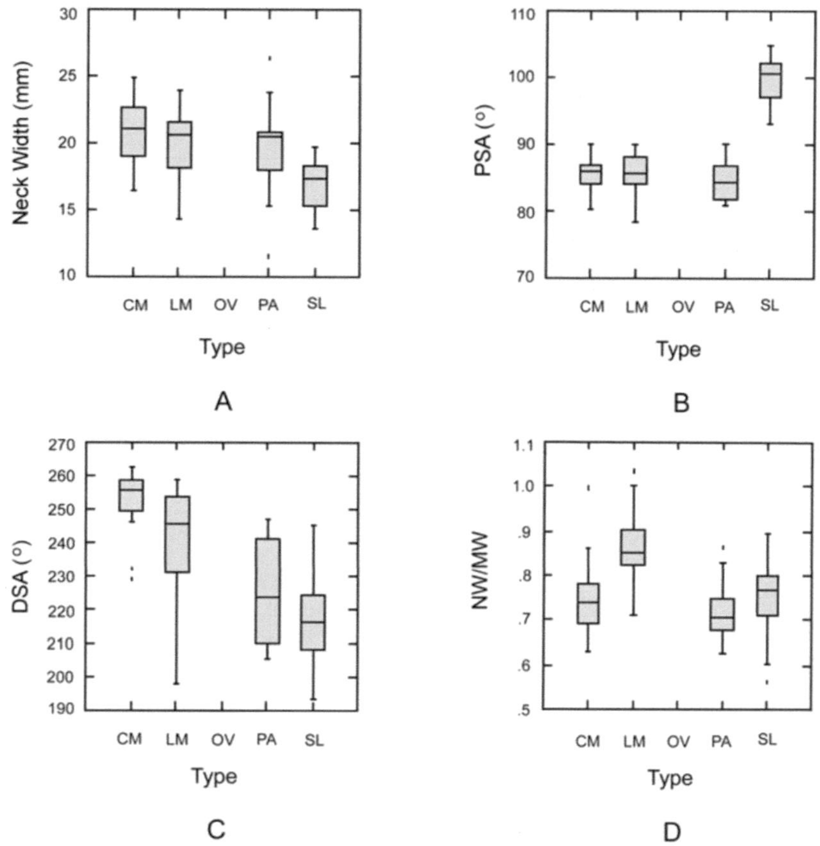

FIGURE 6.20. Box plots of (A) neck width, (B) proximal shoulder angle (PSA), (C) distal shoulder angle (DSA), and (D) neck width/maximum width ratio (NW/MW) for Great Basin Stemmed Series points in the eastern Nevada comparative collection. CM = Cougar Mountain; LM = Lake Mohave; OV = Ovate; PA= Parman; SL = Silver Lake.

Silver Lake points "have more definition of shoulder and less basal taper than the Lake Mohave type" (1937:84). In fact, the stems of these points actually expand initially before contracting to what Amsden refers to as a "somewhat rounded butt" (1937:84), thus accounting for the difference in PSA. As discussed below, this difference, together with the short stem of these points, indicates a haft morphology for Silver Lake points that is very different from that of the other four types.

Figure 6.20C and D shows plots for DSA and NW/MW. These two variables are indicated in Table 6.11 as distinctive features of the Lake Mohave type. As Figure 6.21 shows, the range of values for DSA among Lake Mohave points is extremely wide, although the majority of values (n = 22, 73.3 percent) are greater than 239°. The mean DSA with all 30 values is 241.1° ± 15.44°; without the lowest eight values the mean increases to 249° and the standard deviation is reduced to 6.38°. Even so, the large range of DSA limits the utility of this variable as a distinctive feature for the Lake Mohave type. NW/MW is somewhat more promising, although its values also overlap with those of the other types.

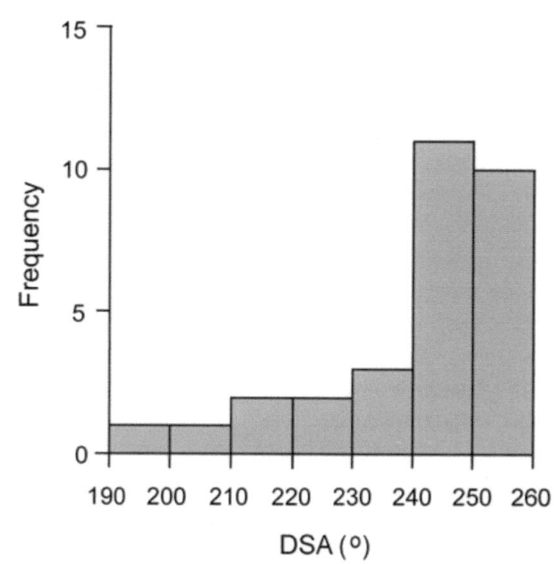

FIGURE 6.21. Histogram of distal shoulder angle (DSA) for Lake Mohave points in the eastern Nevada comparative collection.

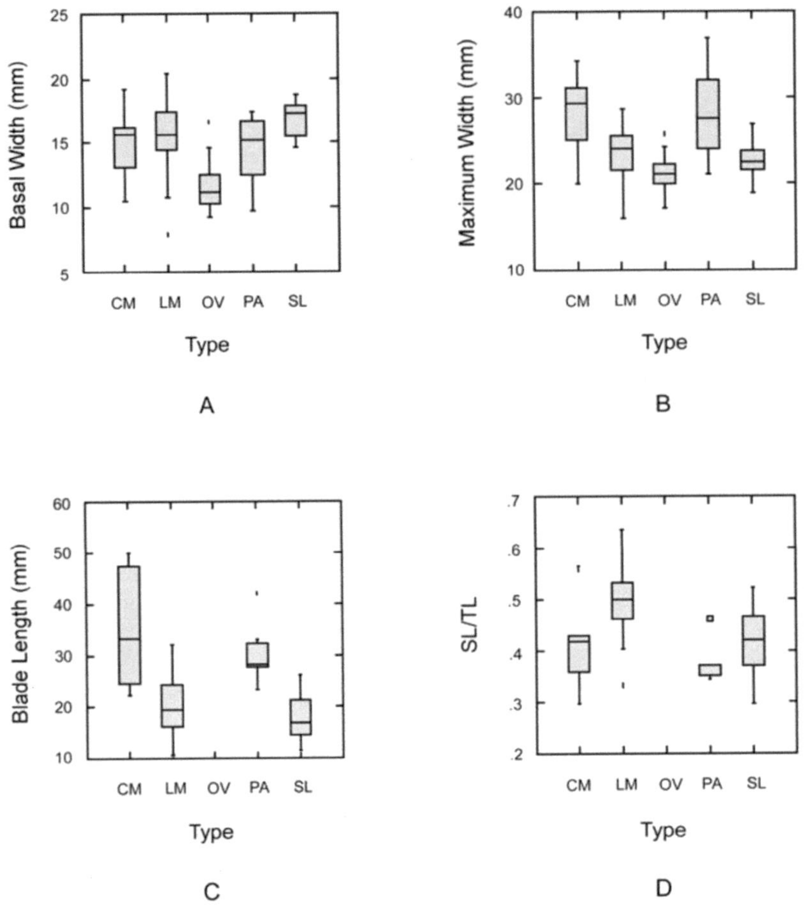

FIGURE 6.22. Box plot of (A) basal width, (B) maximum width, (C) blade length, and (D) stem length/total length (SL/TL) ratio for Great Basin Stemmed Series points in the eastern Nevada comparative collection. CM = Cougar Mountain; LM = Lake Mohave; OV = Ovate; PA= Parman; SL = Silver Lake.

Also evident in Figure 6.20C is the small range and high value of DSA for Cougar Mountain points, which have the least pronounced shoulders of all four types shown (Ovate, of course, has no observable shouldering). Finally, Figure 6.22 shows basal width, a possible distinctive feature for Ovate points; maximum width, a possible distinctive feature for Cougar Mountain and Parman points; blade length, a possible distinctive feature for all but the Ovate type; and stem length/total length (SL/TL), a possible distinctive feature for the Lake Mohave type.

These data make clear that most variables exhibit a wide range of values, and, as a result, there is a good deal of overlap among points of the different types. In fact, most of these metrics when graphed bivariately are continuous across the entire assemblage. Even in the case of the "distinctive features," there is often considerable overlap among points of different types. This makes it difficult to use metric variables to distinguish among these types as Thomas (1981) has done for Archaic points. There is, nevertheless, a subset of variables that can be used to differentiate among them.

First, points of the Cougar Mountain type are fairly distinct from those of the other types on the basis of their large size, specifically measures of length, and their slight shouldering, as represented by the variable shoulder. Shoulder values for Cougar Mountain points range from 3.8 to 29.7 mm, but all but one specimen have a value of 10.0 mm or greater (Table 6.8). Cougar Mountain points exhibit little overlap in shoulder values with Parman and Lake Mohave points. The highest value for Parman is 12.7 mm, and the highest for Lake Mohave is 14.7 mm. Therefore, we can safely identify a large blade section with a shoulder value of 15 mm or greater as a Cougar Mountain blade. Similarly, even though there is greater overlap in stem length among Cougar Mountain, Parman, and Lake Mohave points, we can confidently identify those stem sections of 35 mm or greater in length (greater than the highest stem length value for either Parman or Lake Mohave) as Cougar Mountain stems.

Points of the Silver Lake type can be distinguished on the basis of their short stem length and distinctive stem shape, as measured by PSA. A stem with a PSA of 91° or greater and a length of 13.5 mm (less than the smallest stem length for points of any of the other types) is characteristic of Silver Lake. These stems can be distinguished from Archaic stems of similar length or with similar PSA values by a combination of neck width and thickness.

Ovate points can be distinguished only by their lack of shouldering and thus no obvious break between the blade and stem. Parman points can sometimes be distinguished on the basis of low values of DSA, at least those specimens that have very distinct shoulders, even though they overlap considerably on this variable with Silver Lake points; the latter, as stated above, can be distinguished on the basis of other variables. Otherwise, metrics prove to be of little use. Isolated stem fragments, for instance, which make up the majority of the Sunshine point assemblage, are virtually identical except in the case of those from Silver Lake points. Therefore, we turn to the qualitative variables in an attempt to identify other distinguishing features to aid in type definition.

Qualitative Attributes. All points of the GBSS were examined on eight qualitative attributes: type of material, flaking pattern, lateral edge grinding, beveling, use-wear, breakage type, breakage location, and resharpening. Table 6.12 shows the distribution of the ENCC points of each type across all but breakage type and location. Beginning with raw material, 90.9 percent of Ovate points and 77.8 percent of Cougar Mountain points are made from FGV, whereas points of the other types are less frequently made of this material. Fewer than 6 percent of these points are manufactured from obsidian, but nearly 59 percent of Silver Lake points are made from this material, followed by 35.7 percent of Parman points and 36.7 percent of Lake Mohave points. Chert is rare among points of all types except for Cougar Mountain and Lake Mohave, where it constitutes ca. 17 and 23 percent of the raw material, respectively.

Except in the case of Ovate points, all but three points show at least light lateral edge grinding on the stem. Between 71 and 77 percent of Cougar Mountain, Parman, and Lake Mohave points show medium to heavy lateral edge grinding; an additional 10.0 percent of Lake Mohave points are extremely heavily ground, the edge appearing almost polished. In marked contrast, only 36.4 percent of Ovate points show medium to extreme lateral edge grinding, whereas the majority (63.6 percent) exhibit light or no edge grinding.

As in the case of lateral edge grinding, flaking pattern is broadly similar across the types, but differences are evident. The majority of Cougar Mountain, Ovate, and Parman points exhibit broad collateral flaking (72.2, 68.2, and 64.3 percent, respectively); fewer Lake Mohave and Silver Lake points show this pattern (53.3 and 41.2 percent, respectively).

Very little beveling exists on any but points of the Lake Mohave type, where 16 (53.3 percent) are beveled on the blade. One specimen (3.3 percent) has a beveled stem, and another point (3.3 percent) is beveled on both the blade and the stem. A chi-square test demonstrates that the differences in this variable across types are significant ($\chi^2 = 51.447, df = 16, p < .001$).

Finally, Table 6.12 shows the presence of use-wear and resharpening on points of all five types. Ovate and Cougar Mountain points show the least amount of resharpening (36.4 and 37.5 percent, respectively [resharpening could not be measured on two Cougar Mountain points]). Over half of Parman points (57.2 percent) show resharpening, and almost all of the Lake Mohave and Silver Lake points are resharpened (86.7 and 82.4 percent, respectively). In general, there is an inverse relationship between resharpening and use-wear, as might be expected. Ovate and Cougar Mountain points show the least amount of resharpening, but 63.6 percent of Ovate and 74.1 percent of the 14 Cougar Mountain points for which this variable could be evaluated show use-wear. Six of the nine (66.6 percent) measurable Parman points, 23 of the 29 (79.3 percent) Lake Mohave points, and 10 of the 17 (58.8 percent) Silver Lake points are worn. Thus, Cougar Mountain and Parman points show less resharpening but more extensive use-wear, whereas Silver Lake points show more extensive resharpening but less use-wear. Lake Mohave points, however, are heavily resharpened and heavily worn.

Summarizing the qualitative results (Table 6.13), points of the Ovate and Cougar Mountain types are distinct on almost all attributes, as they are on metric variables. They are made predominantly from FGV and exhibit broad collateral flaking, and few are beveled. They are worn about two-thirds of the time but are resharpened only about a third of the time. Parman points are manufactured less often from FGV and more often from obsidian. They are also more often beveled. Lake Mohave points, on the other hand, although predominantly collaterally flaked, exhibit more of a variety of flaking patterns, are heavily resharpened and heavily worn, and are most often beveled. These points are made equally from FGV and obsidian, but a quarter of them are made from chert. Finally, Silver Lake points are the most variable in flaking pattern, are heavily resharpened but less heavily worn, and are made most often from obsidian and somewhat

Table 6.12. Distribution of Five Great Basin Stemmed Series Types Across Six Qualitative Variables

	Type											
	Cougar Mountain		Ovate		Parman		Lake Mohave		Silver Lake		Total	
Variable	*N*	%	*N*	%	*N*	%	*N*	%	*N*	%	*N*	%
Raw Material												
Chert	3	16.7	1	4.5	1	7.1	7	23.3			12	11.9
Obsidian	1	5.6	1	4.5	5	35.7	11	36.7	10	58.8	28	27.7
Fine-Grained Volcanics	14	77.8	20	90.9	8	57.1	12	40.0	7	41.2	61	60.4
Total	18	100.0	22	100.0	14	100.0	30	100.0	17	100.0	101	100.0
Flaking Pattern												
Broad Collateral	13	72.2	15	68.2	9	64.3	16	53.3	7	41.2	60	59.4
Parallel Collateral			1	4.5			2	6.7	2	11.8	5	5.0
Oblique							3	10.0			3	3.0
Irregular	1	5.6	3	13.6	2	14.3	3	10.0	3	17.6	12	11.9
Collateral/Parallel	2	11.1	1	4.5	1	7.1	2	6.7			6	5.9
Parallel/Oblique	1	5.6	1	4.5	2	14.3			2	11.8	6	5.9
Collateral/Oblique									1	5.9	1	1.0
Collateral/Irregular			1	4.5			4	13.3			5	5.0
Oblique/Irregular											1	1.0
Indeterminate	1	5.6							1	5.9	2	2.0
Total	18	100.0	22	100.0	14	100.0	30	100.0	17	100.0	101	100.0
Beveling												
Absent	16	88.9	20	90.9	8	57.1	12	40.0	15	88.2	71	70.3
Blade			2	9.1	2	14.3	16	53.3	2	11.8	22	21.8
Stem					1	7.1	1	3.3			2	2.0
Blade/Stem							1	3.3		1	1.0	
Indeterminate	2	11.1			3	21.4				5	5.0	
Total	18	100.0	22	100.0	14	100.0	30	100.0	17	100.0	101	100.0
Lateral Edge Grinding												
Absent			9	40.9			2	6.7	1	5.9	12	11.9
Light	4	22.2	5	22.7	2	14.3	3	10.0	6	35.3	20	19.8
Medium	12	66.7	4	18.2	5	35.7	11	36.7	6	35.3	38	37.6
Heavy	2	11.1	2	9.1	6	42.9	10	33.3	4	23.5	23	22.8
Extreme			2	9.1	1	7.1	3	10.0			6	5.9
Indeterminate							1	3.3			2	2.0
Total	18	100.0	22	100.0	14	100.0	30	100.0	17	100.0	101	100.0
Resharpening												
Absent	10	55.6	14	63.6	6	42.9	4	13.3	3	17.6	37	36.6
Tip/Blade	6	33.3	7	31.8	6	42.9	14	46.7	10	58.9	43	42.6
Stem			1	4.5	2	14.3	2	6.7			5	5.0
Tip/Blade and Stem							10	33.3	4	23.5	14	13.9
Into Another Tool											2	2.0
Indeterminate	2	11.1										
Total	18	100.0	22	100.0	14	100.0	30	100.0	17	100.0	101	100.0
Blade Wear												
Absent	4	22.2	8	36.4	3	21.4	6	20.0	7	41.2	28	27.7
Minimal	3	16.7	5	22.7	2	14.3	9	30.0	3	17.5	22	21.8
Moderate	2	11.1	6	27.3			5	16.7			13	12.9
Extensive	2	11.1	3	13.6			9	30.0	7	41.2	21	20.8
Present/Fragment	3	16.7			4	28.6					7	6.9
Indeterminate	4	22.2			5	35.7	1	3.3			10	9.9
Total	18	100.0	22	100.0	14	100.0	30	100.0	17	100.0	101	100.0

TABLE 6.13. Summary of Qualitative Data for Five Great Basin Stemmed Series Types in the Eastern Nevada Comparative Collection

	Point Type				
Variable	Cougar Mountain	Ovate	Parman	Lake Mohave	Silver Lake
Raw Material					
Fine-Grained Volcanics	78	91	57	40	41
Obsidian	6	9	36	37	59
Chert	17		7	23	
Flaking Pattern					
Broad Collateral	72	68	64	53	41
Collateral/Other	11	9	7	13	5
Other	17	23	29	34	54
Beveled	0	9	27	60	12
Resharpened	38	36	57	87	82
Worn	71	64	67	79	59

Note: Data are in percentages, rounded to the nearest whole number, based only on those specimens that could be measured for a particular variable; "indeterminates" are not included.

less often from FGV; none is made from chert. Unfortunately, however, none of these attributes can be used to exclusively identify fragmentary specimens with a particular type. If a blade section is beveled, for instance, it is most likely a Lake Mohave blade, but given the data in Table 6.13, it could also be anything but a Cougar Mountain blade. Beveling, however, might be used in conjunction with other attributes, both quantitative and qualitative, to identify fragmentary specimens. We return to this below.

Discussion

We address two questions here concerning these five GBSS types. The first concerns whether the five types actually represent distinct stylistic or functional categories. Could they represent instead a morphological continuum that arises from breakage and resharpening as Flenniken and Raymond (1986; see also Flenniken and Wilke 1989) have suggested for Archaic points? For example, it is not difficult to envision a Lake Mohave form resulting from the reworking of a Cougar Mountain form. In fact, there are several examples in the H–N collection of points identifiable with the Lake Mohave type that were constructed from stems that likely came from Cougar Mountain points because of their large size (Figure 6.23). These stems were resharpened at their distal ends to remove the transverse fracture facets; the distal end was then shaped into a triangular blade and completed by creating a chisel tip (see below). A morphological continuum related to resharpening would certainly account, at least in part, for the difficulty in creating reliable type definitions.

FIGURE 6.23. Lake Mohave points manufactured on Cougar Mountain stems.

The second question concerns the function(s) of these tools. Are they projectile points, or do they represent other types of tools? The scale of use-wear and resharpening suggests that even if they did serve as projectiles, they served in other capacities as well, as knives, for instance. We address these questions in the context of our previous work.

TABLE 6.14. Raw Material Represented in Other Eastern Nevada Paleoarchaic Assemblages

	RAW MATERIAL										
	CHERT		OBSIDIAN		FINE-GRAINED VOLCANICS		QUARTZITE		OTHER		
ASSEMBLAGE	*N*	%	*N*	%	*N*	%	*N*	%	*N*	%	TOTAL
Butte Valley Sites	3,846	31.2	2,442	19.8	6,003	48.7	26	.2	3	<.1	12,320
Butte Valley Survey	22	16.9	49	37.7	57	43.8	2	1.5	—	—	130
Jakes Valley Site (Limestone Peak Locality 1)	2,572	37.1	532	7.7	3,822	55.1	5	<.1	1	<.1	6,932
Jakes Valley Survey	139	64.4	25	11.6	52	24.1	—	—	—	—	216
Total	6,579	33.6	3,048	15.6	9,934	50.7	33	.2	4	<.1	19,598

TABLE 6.15. Eastern Nevada Production Bifaces by Stage and Raw Material

	STAGE 0		STAGE 1		STAGE 2		STAGE 3[a]		
RAW MATERIAL	*N*	%	*N*	%	*N*	%	*N*	%	TOTAL
Chert	1	2.2	11	23.4	13	27.7	22	46.8	47
Obsidian			1	1.1	2	2.1	91	96.8	94
Fine-Grained Volcanics	24	8.3	42	14.5	49	17.0	174	60.2	289

Note: Sunshine bifaces not included.

[a] Stage 3 is the finished point that exhibits lateral edge grinding.

Validity of the Five Great Basin Stemmed Series Types. Judging on the basis of their similarity in form but difference in size, GBSS projectile point types may actually reflect differences resulting from breakage and resharpening rather than stylistic/functional differences. That is, they may not represent distinctive forms of types. If this is indeed the case, for a highly mobile population, such as we believe existed in this region during the TP/EH (Jones et al. 2003), certain patterns concerning size progression, raw material representation, resharpening, and use-wear might be expected. We discuss these patterns in the context of the larger picture of Paleoarchaic territorial range and mobility using material representation in TP/EH assemblages we have collected from eastern Nevada (Jones et al. 2003). Briefly, about half (50.7 percent) of the raw material represented in the eastern Nevada (EN) assemblages is FGV, followed by chert (33.6 percent) and obsidian (15.6 percent; Table 6.14). Most of the chert is in the form of debitage; the manufactured tools represented are primarily scrapers and Archaic projectile points, although there are three crescents and occasional drills and gravers. Points of the GBSS are manufactured almost entirely from FGV or obsidian; only about 10 percent are manufactured from chert. Source analysis indicates that there are 40 geochemical obsidian types represented in the EN assemblages (Jones et al. 2003), an incredible diversity given the paucity of obsidian in the study area. Of the 21 chemical types that have been identified with source areas, all but one lie between 100 and 250 km distant, to the north, south, and east (see Jones et al. 2003:18, Figure 6). Source analysis of the FGV material suggests that this toolstone is "local," from sources that range between 10 and 90 km from the Sunshine Locality (Jones et al. 1996; Jones et al. 1997; Jones et al. 2003:19, Figure 7).

Further, the obsidian tools in the EN assemblages are predominantly late-stage bifaces and expended stems, whereas the FGV tools are bifaces of all stages (Table 6.15), and except for Stage 3 (finished points), most show little resharpening. It is also notable that, although few production bifaces are manufactured from chert, all stages are also represented in this material, which we return to below. We have elsewhere proposed that Paleoarchaic people traveled into our EN study area carrying obsidian tools in all states of repair, some only partially used, others nearly at the end of their use-lives (Beck and Jones 1990a, 1990b, 1992, 1994; Jones and Beck 1990, 1992; Jones et al. 2003). The latter were discarded, replaced by tools made from local FGV. That obsidian was a preferred material for the manufacture of stemmed points is supported by assemblages from areas where both obsidian and FGV are plentiful, such as the Black Rock Desert

TABLE 6.16. Expectations of Variable Progression Based on the Resharpening Model

VARIABLE	SEQUENCE				
	COUGAR MOUNTAIN	OVATE	PARMAN	LAKE MOHAVE	SILVER LAKE
Size	largest	decreasing →	→	→	smallest
Raw Material	local	decreasing →	→	→	exotic
	exotic	increasing →	→	→	local
Resharpening	low	increasing →	→	→	high

TABLE 6.17. Actual Variable Progression

VARIABLE	SEQUENCE				
Size	Cougar Mountain →	Ovate →	Parman →	Lake Mohave →	Silver Lake
Raw Material	Ovate →	Cougar Mountain →	Parman →	Silver Lake →	Lake Mohave
Resharpening	Cougar Mountain →	Ovate →	Parman →	Silver Lake →	Lake Mohave

and southern Oregon (see Amick 1996; Beck and Jones 1990b; Butler 1970; Clewlow 1968a). In our earlier studies of these material use patterns we combined all stemmed points for analysis and made no attempt to examine raw material representation, use-wear, or resharpening within separate type categories, which we do here.

If we take as a working hypothesis that all stemmed points brought into the study area were manufactured originally to a Cougar Mountain (the largest) morphology but were exhausted through a combination of use, breakage, and resharpening and then replaced in local material, we might expect several patterns. The logical progression in the use–resharpening–reuse process would be a reduction in overall size, from the largest (Cougar Mountain) to the smallest (Silver Lake). If each type is derived from the resharpening of the next largest type, then the Cougar Mountain form represents the beginning of a point's use-life, and the Silver Lake form represents the end, with the Ovate, Parman, and Lake Mohave forms in between. Consequently, the greatest amount of resharpening should be evident on Silver Lake points, and the least, on Cougar Mountain points. The extent of use-wear, however, is less predictable. On the one hand, a point can be used extensively and discarded without ever being resharpened. On the other hand, it could be resharpened, in which case at least some, if not most, of the use-wear scars would be obliterated. Then it might be used extensively once again, making the points in either case appear the same in terms of the extent of resharpening. Therefore, use-wear is not particularly useful for our present purpose. Finally, Silver Lake points should most often be made from exotics (obsidian in this case), whereas Cougar Mountain points should be only minimally represented in this material; the latter should be represented more often in local material (i.e., FGV). In both cases, Ovate, Parman, and Lake Mohave points should lie in between. The progression we would expect in terms of these three variables is shown in Table 6.16. This scenario, however, does not preclude a Cougar Mountain point fragment being resharpened into a Parman or Lake Mohave form. The important components are the beginning (Cougar Mountain—the largest) and the end (Silver Lake—the smallest) of the trajectory. The actual trajectory is shown in Table 6.17.

The progression from Cougar Mountain to Parman to Lake Mohave to Silver Lake in Table 6.16 is based on the size progression already demonstrated. Although none of these types differs significantly from the next adjacent one in the progression in *all* size measures, in general, the progression holds. For instance, Cougar Mountain and Parman points do not differ *significantly* from one another on blade length, maximum width, basal width, or neck width, but Cougar Mountain means are *greater* than Parman means for all of these variables (see Tables 6.8–6.9). In the case of Parman and Lake Mohave, for all measurements of size except stem length, basal width, and neck width (the means for stem length and neck width are virtually identical), Parman means exceed Lake Mohave means, although these differences are significant only in the case of blade width and maximum width. Therefore, in this hypothetical production–maintenance continuum, Parman precedes Lake Mohave based on size progression in Table 6.17.

With the size progression established, we turn to raw material. As can be seen from Table 6.17, there is a deviation from the expected sequence in two ways. First, Ovate

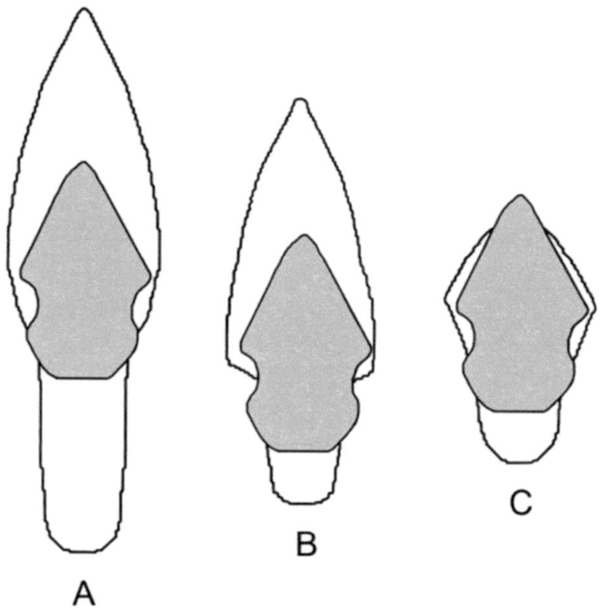

FIGURE 6.24. Schematic showing the difficulty of resharpening points of the (A) Cougar Mountain, (B) Parman, and (C) Lake Mohave types into points of the Silver Lake type.

points are more often made from local material than are Cougar Mountain points, and second, Lake Mohave points are more often made from exotic material than are Silver Lake points. However, 23 percent of Lake Mohave points and 17 percent of Cougar Mountain points are also made from chert, a factor that sets them apart from points of the other three types. If these cherts are local, the positions within each pair are switched, and the progression is as predicted. If the cherts are exotic, the positions of Ovate as first and Lake Mohave as last in the sequence are underscored. We have not done any chemical source analysis of the cherts but have attempted to identify them based on color, texture, and inclusions. In the end, however, the task proved to be overwhelming as we discovered time and again that colors we had considered as separate sources appeared together in a single piece. We have established source locations for several local chert types represented in our assemblages and believe that, in all likelihood, the majority of the chert is from local sources, but this cannot be demonstrated conclusively. The fact that all stages of production bifaces are present in this material (Table 6.15), as is the case for FGV, supports a local origin. Regarding resharpening, Ovate and Cougar Mountain points are virtually identical; otherwise the progression mirrors that of raw material with respect to Lake Mohave points, which show the greatest amount of resharpening.

In both cases where there is deviation from the predicted pattern, it is Silver Lake that is most often out of sequence. If these points are removed from consideration, the sequence for the four variables is consistent, with the exception of Ovate and Cougar Mountain, and if our notion is correct that most of the chert is local, Ovate and Cougar Mountain are really quite similar. The patterns of biface reduction discussed in chapter 5 support a local origin for this material That is, all reduction stages are represented in chert (as well as FGV), but only the latest stage is represented in obsidian. Based on the stem size and morphology of Silver Lake, we believe that they represent a quite different entity from the other four types. First, Silver Lake stems are significantly shorter than those of the other point types (except in the case of Ovate points, for which stem length was not measured). Second, Silver Lake stems are very different in shape (expanding then contracting) from those of the other four types. Cougar Mountain, Ovate, Parman, and Lake Mohave points are all large, *contracting-stemmed* points that can all be accommodated by a socketed haft (see discussion below); the short, expanding/contracting stem of Silver Lake points, however, precludes fitting them into a socketed haft. Further, the expanding stem of these points would make it virtually impossible for them to have resulted from the resharpening of any of the four contracting-stemmed types (Figure 6.24). Thus, we believe that Silver Lake points are *not* the result of resharpening of any of the other four types and remove them from consideration in the remainder of this discussion.

Returning to the discussion of the other four types, the data considered thus far (size, raw material, and degree of resharpening) all support the possibility that the Cougar Mountain–Ovate–Parman–Lake Mohave sequence could simply be the result of breakage and resharpening of largest to smallest. There are, however, two factors that do not support this hypothesis. The first regards *where* the resharpening occurs on the point. The greatest difference in the four forms is in stem length; as discussed earlier, Cougar Mountain points differ significantly from all others with respect to this attribute. Taking as a given that the Cougar Mountain type is the beginning of the progression, if breakage occurred at the neck, then the upper stem would have to be resharpened into a blade (Figure 6.25A). The average neck width of points of the Cougar Mountain type is 21.5 mm; the average blade widths for points of the Ovate, Parman, and Lake Mohave types for which blades could be measured (Table 6.18) are 21.1, 28.1, and 23.3 mm, respectively (blade width = maximum width for those contracting-stem points complete enough for measurement). Given that the new blade would have to be fashioned from the widest end of the broken stem, which is at the neck, there would not be enough width to create these blades. Although, as mentioned earlier, there are several cases in the

Sunshine assemblage in which a Lake Mohave blade has been fashioned on a broken Cougar Mountain stem (Figure 6.23), the majority of the Ovate, Parman, and Lake Mohave points did not result from the resharpening of Cougar Mountain stems.

If breakage occurred only on the blade, there would be little shortening of the stem as a result of resharpening, only of the blade (Figure 6.25B). The primary way in which a shorter stem would result from resharpening but at the same time allow for the maximum width of the Parman and Lake Mohave blades would be if breakage occurred toward the proximal end (base) of the stem (Figure 6.25C). It is a fact that the fragment of GBSS points most often recovered from the archaeological record is some portion of the stem. Over 50 percent of the Sunshine GBSS points are stem sections (see below), most of which are too fragmentary to be identified with a type. Many of these stem fragments are short basal sections, which could have been broken from the original point before it was resharpened into another form. If this is the case, then the greatest amount of resharpening of Ovate, Parman, and Cougar Mountain points should occur on the stem. As Table 6.12 shows, however, this is not the case; for each of the four types the greatest amount of resharpening occurs on the tip and blade. Interestingly, a breakdown by raw material (Table 6.19) shows that there is little difference in resharpening on points of different raw materials; that is, within type (with the exception of Cougar Mountain), resharpened points made of obsidian show roughly equal numbers to resharpened points of FGV and chert. Within-type chi-square analysis reveals no significant differences except for Cougar Mountain, for which there is a difference at a probability of .06.

A second argument against the working hypothesis concerns the mechanics of resharpening. As Table 6.9 shows, Cougar Mountain and Ovate points differ significantly in thickness from Parman and Lake Mohave points (but not from one another), but the difference in thickness is not significant between Parman and Lake Mohave. Cougar Mountain cross sections are more often biconvex, whereas the cross sections of the Parman and Lake Mohave forms are more often lenticular (Ovate points are variable in their cross sections). It is quite difficult to remove thinning flakes that carry across the centerline of a thick, biconvex point, a process that is necessary to achieve the thinner, lenticular cross section. Further, as Table 6.12 shows, 77.8 percent of Cougar Mountain stems show medium to heavy edge grinding. Titmus and Woods (1991b) suggest that edge grinding on fluted points serves to strengthen the edge rather than prevent cutting of the haft binding, as has been suggested by others (e.g., Wormington 1957; Young and Bonnichsen 1995:119). If this is the case for fluted points, then it may also be the case for stemmed points. Once an edge is strengthened in this way, it is difficult to use the edge as a platform from which to remove percussion or pressure thinning flakes.

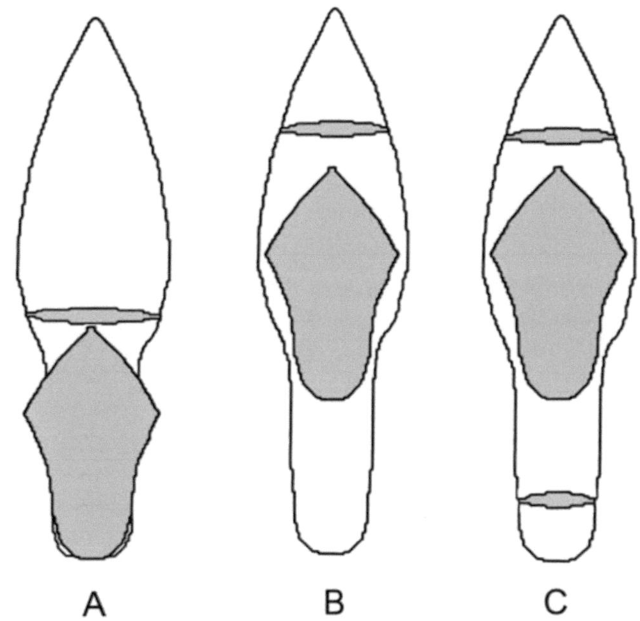

FIGURE 6.25. Schematic showing three hypothetical ways in which a point of the Lake Mohave type might be obtained by resharpening a broken point of the Cougar Mountain type: (A) breakage at the neck; (B) breakage on the blade; (C) breakage on both the blade and stem.

TABLE 6.18. Statistics for Maximum Blade Width of Points of the Ovate, Parman, and Lake Mohave Types

	Type		
Statistic	Ovate	Parman	Lake Mohave
N	22	12	30
Range	17.1–25.9	21.1–37.0	16.0–28.6
Mean	21.09	28.07	23.27
SD	2.129	5.089	3.110

Note: Measurements in millimeters.

This review of the patterns in size, raw material, use-wear, breakage, and degree of resharpening suggests that it may be entirely possible that many types of the GBSS represent segments of a production–maintenance continuum. The extent to which many metric variables overlap would seem to support this sequence. The location and mechanics of resharpening, however, argue against this hypothesis. Thus for our next discussion, that of

TABLE 6.19. Presence of Resharpening by Type and Raw Material for Five Great Basin Stemmed Series Types

	Point Type									
	Cougar Mountain		Parman		Lake Mohave		Silver Lake		Ovate	
Raw Material	P	A	P	A	P	A	P	A	P	A
Fine-Grained Volcanics	4	8	4	4	10	2	5	2	7	13
Obsidian	1		3	2	11		9	1		1
Chert	1	2	1		5	2			1	
Total	6	10	8	6	26	4	14	3	8	14

Note: A = absent; P = present.

function, we continue to treat all five types as separate entities, because even if one form might in some cases result from another through reworking, it still may represent a different and distinct function.

Functions of the Five Great Basin Stemmed Types. We begin with the question of whether these artifacts were components of a projectile system; that is, did they tip spears or atlatl darts, or did they serve some other function? We begin with what we see as the simplest possibility, that all of these tools served as projectile points exclusively. (Parts of this discussion rely heavily on a similar discussion we have presented elsewhere [Beck and Jones 1997:202–204].) Musil (1988:374) outlines four criteria to assess whether projectile points perform efficiently as piercing tools while conserving lithic material and preserving the wooden shaft: (1) a sharp point, (2) sharp blade edges, (3) a haft element that will absorb the force caused by impact while doing minimal damage to the shaft, and (4) an overall haft design that minimizes point damage and allows for the reworking of the point after breakage. The importance of criteria 1 and 2 is elaborated by Frison:

> In order for a projectile point to be effective on larger animals, it must penetrate more than the length of the point. The tip must be sharp enough to penetrate the hide and the blade edges must be sharp enough to widen the cut and allow the projectile and shaft to continue on into the carcass and reach a vital spot.... One noticeable attribute of projectile points from bison kills is the care taken to sharpen the point to obtain the best possible penetration of the hide [1991:293].

Points of the Cougar Mountain, Ovate, Parman, Lake Mohave, and Silver Lake types rarely conform to these criteria (e.g., Amick 1993, 1996; Basgall 1993b; Basgall and Hall 1991; Beck and Jones 1993; Tuohy 1969). A perusal of Figures 6.14 through 6.18 reveals few sharp points or edges. When compared with dart points, such as those of the Elko, Gatecliff, and Northern Side-Notched types, GBSS points are often more poorly made, excessively thick, and asymmetrical. Further, as shown above, points of the GBSS almost always exhibit extensive use-wear. Sixty-nine percent of the 91 points in the ENCC for which use-wear on the blade could be assessed are worn. In contrast, Archaic points are rarely worn. For example, among 115 Archaic points from Butte, Jakes, and Long valleys (outside the Sunshine Locality), only 18 (15.7 percent) exhibit any use-wear on the blade. Only one member of the GBSS—Haskett—does appear to satisfy Musil's first two criteria. These points, which are similar in form to Hell Gap and Agate Basin forms (Frison and Stanford 1982), consistently have sharp tips and edges and may represent a function quite distinct from that represented by the other members of the series (Amick 1996). The Haskett type, however, is not represented in the Sunshine assemblage and is not dealt with further here.

The last two of Musil's criteria refer to hafting techniques. Musil, following Bryan (1980), suggests that Paleoarchaic people used three different hafting technologies. The first, and earliest, is the fluted or basally thinned point that is inserted into a split shaft. According to Musil, because the shaft takes more time and effort to manufacture than does the stone tip, it is prudent to manufacture a stone point to fit an existing shaft, and fluting is viewed as a thinning technique used in order to accomplish this (see also Ahler and Geib 2000). The second hafting technology relates to stemmed points, and Musil refers here to two subtechnologies. The first is the square-based point (such as Windust A, see below) inserted into a split shaft; the second is the large, contracting-stemmed point (such as Cougar Mountain) inserted into a socketed shaft. Musil argues that both stemmed hafts have an advantage over lanceolate hafts in that the bindings are removed from the blade edges of the stone point. A further advantage of long-stemmed socketed hafts is that the stem, which is completely contained within the socket, absorbs more force upon impact of a thrust.

The final, and latest, hafting technology is the notching of a point for insertion into a split shaft. Musil suggests that the notched haft "renders all others obsolete" (1988:382), its major advantage being that damage usually occurs at the notch, which is close to the base, allowing the blade to be reworked and rehafted (but see Beck 1995). This argument seems to apply equally to the square-based forms like Windust.

Musil takes as a given that all of the point forms discussed are components of projectiles and thus each successive technology followed and replaced the former. The changes in point form through time are viewed as functional and resulted in (1) increased efficiency as killing instruments, (2) increased efficiency in the prevention of shaft damage, and (3) the increasing ability to rehaft reworked points into undamaged shafts after breakage (Musil 1988:385). As we have argued elsewhere (Beck and Jones 1997:203–204), Musil may be incorporating two different functional forms within the same technological model. The two types of stemmed hafts, the square-based split shaft and the contracting-stemmed socketed haft, are, in fact, quite different from one another. For example, Musil portrays both as roughly the same in overall size, but Cougar Mountain points are generally longer and considerably thicker than Windust points. Further, the morphology of these two point forms is different. In the case of square-based points, the stem can constitute as little as one-fifth, but never more than half, of the overall length. In the case of long contracting-stemmed points, the stem generally constitutes *at least* one-third and sometimes *more than half* the overall length of the point. Thus, on the one hand, considerably more of the blade is exposed in a hafted square-based point than in a hafted contracting-stemmed point, and on the other, a great deal more of the overall contracting-stemmed point is inserted in the haft to receive the force of use than is the case for the square-based point. As a result, contracting-stemmed points make contact with the foreshaft/socket along more of the point's edge and thus dissipate energy more effectively. These factors suggest different functions for the two forms.

The extreme battering evidenced by many contracting-stemmed points (e.g., Cougar Mountain, Ovate, Lake Mohave, Parman) suggests that these items received considerable use in contexts where axial as well as impact forces obtained. As already discussed, use-wear analysis of contracting-stemmed points in the comparative collection shows damage at the tips and along the edges; these points also often show abrasion on the surface of

FIGURE 6.26. Heavy polish on the surface of a Cougar Mountain point midsection caused by haft abrasion.

the stem and the portion of the blade that was confined within the socket, such as that shown in Figure 6.26. Such damage is not consistent with exclusive use as projectile tips but, rather, with a variety of motions such as cutting and scraping and perhaps thrusting with considerable force. The morphology of the haft tends to support this contention. A long contracting stem inserted into a socket provides, as Musil notes, resistance to breakage by absorbing force over a large portion of the point while reducing damage to the shaft. But it is noteworthy that breakage is most common at midblade, which would be where the blade emerges from the socket, and at the proximal end of the stem (as in Figure 6.26), suggesting a "twisting" motion within the haft that exerts force on both blade and stem.

Musil's argument of socketed hafts is easiest to make for points of the Cougar Mountain and perhaps the Ovate types because of the overall large size of these points. This argument is more difficult to make for points of the Lake Mohave and Parman types, which are smaller overall and have shorter stems. It is especially difficult to make for points of the Silver Lake type (and we do not), which have not only short but slightly expanding stems. As Tables 6.8 and 6.9 show, average stem length for Cougar Mountain points is significantly greater than that of Parman and Lake Mohave points. Further, Cougar Mountain points are significantly thicker than the other two types (Tables 6.8–6.9), whereas thickness for Parman and Lake Mohave points is statistically equal. As discussed above, Cougar Mountain points more often have a biconvex cross section, but Parman and Lake Mohave points most often have a lenticular cross section. DSA (measuring the degree of shouldering) differs among all three, with an increase in shouldering from Cougar Mountain to Lake Mohave and Parman. There is no difference, however, in PSA among the three types (Tables 6.8–6.9). Finally, there is no significant difference in basal width among the three types. Ovate points, however, differ significantly from Cougar Mountain and Lake Mohave points in basal width, and the difference with Parman is significant at a probability of .072 (Table 6.9). Overall, though, these patterns suggest that, on the one hand, stem plan is similar among the four types, with the exception of cross-sectional shape for Cougar Mountain points and basal width for Ovate points. The contracting shape of the stems suggests that all four forms could have been hafted in socketed shafts. On the other hand, the lenticular cross-sectional shape as well as the shorter stem length of Parman and Lake Mohave points argue against socketing and more for split-shaft hafting. In addition, blade morphology differs among the three (not measured for Ovate points) with respect to the distinctiveness of the shoulder, relative size, and in the case of Lake Mohave points, shape, as discussed below. This variation may indicate differences in function.

These factors strongly suggest that points of the GBSS were not used exclusively as projectile points, although their use in this capacity is not precluded altogether. One or more of them may, in fact, have been used as projectiles in some way, say as spear tips, or more likely, as thrusting spears, while serving other functions as well (Beck and Jones 1997). There is no reason to believe, however, that they were all used in the same way, given their morphological differences. It is possible that points of one category were designed for a specific task or set of tasks, and others were designed for a more general purpose. Summarizing once again the morphological differences, Cougar Mountain and Ovate points are large, made almost exclusively of FGV toolstone, and are resharpened less often than points of the other three types. As stated earlier the material composition and lack of resharpening may simply indicate tools that were manufactured from local material and were still early in their use-lives. The size of these points, however, sets them apart from those of the four other categories. Silver Lake points are the smallest, are more often made from obsidian, and show extensive resharpening. Again, their small size and their distinctive stem shape set them apart from points of the other four categories, especially those of the Cougar Mountain and Ovate types. There is no association between material type and resharpening, except possibly for Cougar Mountain, as discussed above (Table 6.19); that is, it is not the obsidian points that are mostly resharpened, and thus the extensive resharpening more likely relates to the function of the points.

Parman points exhibit more varied morphology and, as a consequence, overlap in some respects with points of each of the other types. The most distinctive aspect of these points is their wider blade and more pronounced shoulders. Whereas the blade widths (which is the same as maximum width for these points; see Table 6.9) of Lake Mohave and Silver Lake points differ statistically from that of Cougar Mountain points, the blade width of Parman points does not, although they are smaller points overall.

Aside from the diamond-shaped form described by Amsden in the original definition, the most obvious attributes that differentiate points of the Lake Mohave type from those of the other types are material type, flaking pattern, and beveling. We have already pointed out that 36.7 percent of the Lake Mohave points in the comparative collection are made from obsidian, with 23.3 percent made from chert and 40 percent made from FGV. Both the obsidian (except in the case of Silver Lake points) and the chert components are larger for points of this type than for points of any of the other types. Although these points exhibit broad collateral flaking just over half of the time, all other patterns are evident as well. The final attribute, beveling, is almost exclusively found on Lake Mohave points, where it occurs on 56.6 percent of the blades. Although we have not examined points of this form in other collections, beveling can be observed in photographs of these points in various assemblages (e.g., Amsden 1937:81, Plate XLIc, f; Tuohy 1969:Figure 3k–l, t, w–x).

Beveling on alternate margins is often argued to be a by-product of resharpening of the point while still in the haft (e.g., Deller and Ellis 1992:44). If true, it follows that points of the other types should show beveling as well, relative to the amount of resharpening. As Table 6.12 shows, points of all but the Cougar Mountain type exhibit some degree of beveling on the blade. In fact, the data in Table 6.20 indicate a general correspondence between the proportions of resharpening and beveling, although a chi-square test indicates no significant association ($\chi^2 = 5.415$, $df = 4$, $p = .242$). Silver Lake points, for example, should exhibit considerably more beveling given the large number of specimens that are resharpened. If, however, beveling *is* related to resharpening, we must explain why beveling is most common on Lake Mohave blades (Table 6.20).

The answer to this question may lie in the distinctive diamond-shaped blade. Obviously some specimens were manufactured in this form to begin with, but others have been resharpened into this form: those that were manufactured on Cougar Mountain stems, for instance (see

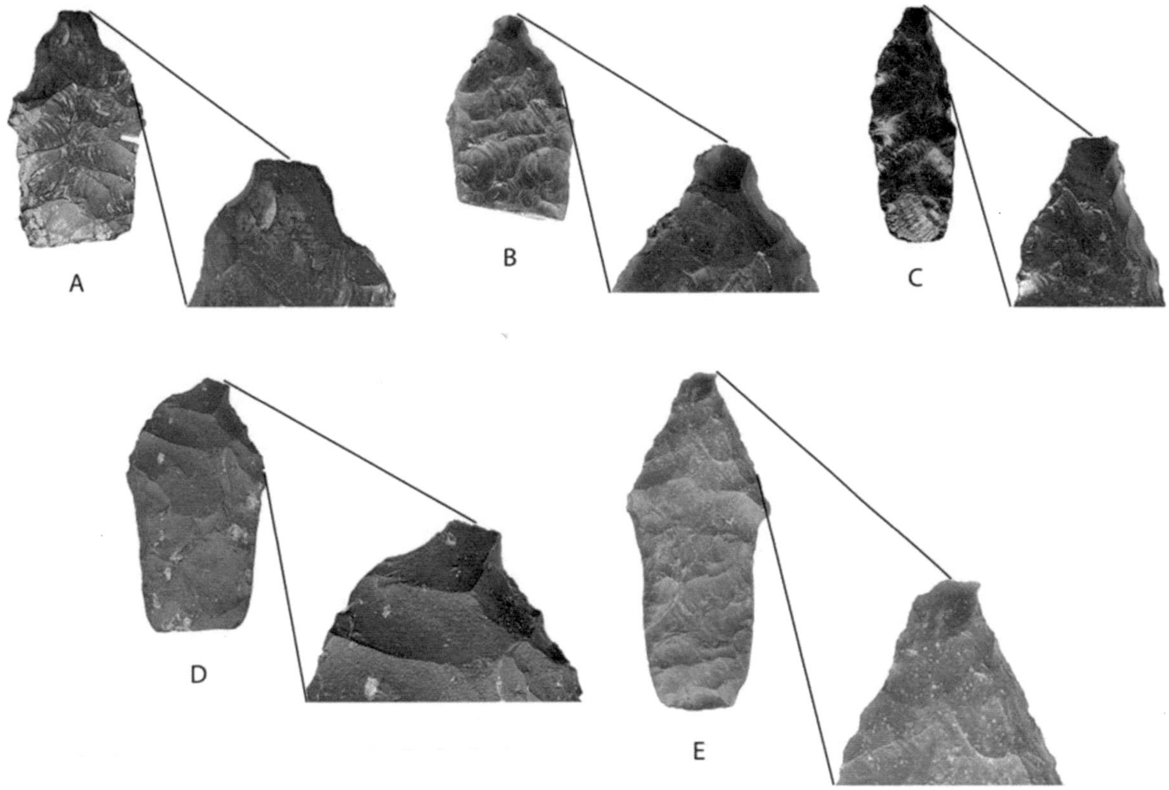

FIGURE 6.27. Examples of chisel tips on Lake Mohave points in the eastern Nevada comparative collection: (A) HPL5, 290E, 110N; (B) 3504; (C) 2157; (D) 1791; (E) 1875.

Figure 6.23). Perhaps it is this particular blade form that is directly related to the point's function, and beveling is simply the by-product of producing this form. An additional morphological feature that is often present on Lake Mohave points and which may shed light on this issue is a tip that is squared rather than pointed (Figure 6.27). This feature, which occurs on 13 of the 25 Lake Mohave points on which the tip is present, has not been observed on points of any other category, with the exception of a single Cougar Mountain blade (see Figure 6.28D). Tuohy (1969) was intrigued by this pattern and has suggested that this morphology results from the removal of burin spalls. Tuohy calls these forms "burin-faceted point tips," which he defines as "flake removals at point tips in such a manner as to create the typical squared-off chisel bit" (1969:140). The "bit" often exhibits striations running perpendicular to its squared-off end (Figure 6.27B). In our study of the lithic assemblage from the Old Riverbed area of western Utah, we examined a Lake Mohave point with a chisel tip that exhibits extreme abrasion, again with the striations running perpendicular to its squared-off end (see Jones et al. 2002). These striations and their orientation certainly suggest that these points could have been used as chisels, but the tips are often quite thin, making them rather fragile, especially those made from obsidian. In addition, many of these squared tips are associated with constrictions proximal to the tip (see, for instance, Figure 6.27A–B).

TABLE 6.20. Resharpening and Beveling on the Sunshine Great Basin Stemmed Series Points by Type

Point Type	% Resharpened	% Beveled on Blade or Blade and Stem	% Beveled on Stem Only
Cougar Mountain	37.5		
Ovate	36.3	9.1	
Parman	57.1	18.2	9.1
Silver Lake	82.4	11.8	
Lake Mohave	86.7	56.7	3.3

Note: Percentages based only on those specimens for which resharpening and beveling could be determined.

The squared tip morphology often occurs in combination with the beveled blade edges (Table 6.21) and, in fact, is significantly associated with this feature (χ^2 = 13.268, *df* = 6.0, *p* = .039). That is, when a blade is beveled, it

TABLE 6.21. Co-Occurrence of Beveling and Chisel Tip on Points of the Lake Mohave Type

	Beveling			
Chisel Tip	None	Blade	Stem	Blade and Stem
Absent	8	3	1	
Present	3	10		
Tip Missing	1	3		1
Total	12	16	1	1

almost always has a chisel tip, complicating the situation once again. If beveling is a by-product of resharpening an existing blade or stem fragment into a diamond-shaped blade for a specific purpose, why don't those blades made originally in this form have a chisel tip? For that matter, why don't resharpened points of other types have beveled blades? Whatever the answer, we believe that the Lake Mohave form, whether or not it sometimes results from the resharpening of another form, is a goal for a specific set of functions, one of which requires a chisel tip. We do not believe those specimens with these tips were used as projectiles, although those without certainly could have been.

In summary, we conclude that none of the five GBSS point types we examined was used exclusively as projectile tips. We cannot, however, eliminate their use in this capacity as one of the many functions they served. This function is least likely for Silver Lake and Lake Mohave points, which appear to have been used for specific tasks or sets of tasks. Cougar Mountain points appear to have served as more generalized tools and could conceivably have served as tips for thrusting spears. Thrusting spears are not uncommon in ethnographic and historic hunting kits (e.g., Alcock 1987; Ellis 1984; Gould 1970) and are generally used to finish off a kill (Hughes 1998). Parman points may also have served a more generalized function, as their heavily worn blades suggest. The significance of the wider blade and pronounced shoulder in a generalized function, however, is unclear. Wide shoulders on projectile points allow for better penetration of the intended target (Frison and Zeimens 1980), but to penetrate the target the point must have a sharp tip and edges, which is often not the case for Parman points.

Type Assignment of the Remaining Great Basin Stemmed Series Points. Table 6.22 summarizes the defining criteria for the Cougar Mountain, Ovate, Parman, Lake Mohave, and Silver Lake types. These features certainly are not as definitive as those Thomas proposed for Archaic types, but they add some objectivity to the original definitions.

TABLE 6.22. Criteria Used to Identify Fragmentary Specimens in the Sunshine Assemblage with the Five Great Basin Stemmed Series Types

Type	Criteria
Cougar Mountain	Stems that are ≥35 mm in length. Blades that have shoulder values ≥15 mm. Midsections that have distal shoulder angles ≥240° and neck widths ≥20 mm.
Lake Mohave	Blades that are triangular in shape with beveling and/or chisel tip.
Parman	Pronounced shoulders, lenticular cross section, and parallel to contracting stem (overlaps completely with Lake Mohave but can be used after Lake Mohave has been distinguished as above).
Silver Lake	Stems that are ≤13.5 mm in length, with a proximal shoulder angle ≥91°.
Ovate	Midsection with no discernable inflection point between the stem and blade.

Table 6.23 shows the distribution of points of the GBSS by type in both the H–N (n = 674) and HC (n = 22) collections. The numbers in this table include the Sunshine points examined in the ENCC. The criteria in Table 6.22 were used to identify some of the fragmentary specimens with the five types discussed. In most cases these fragments were identified with one of the five GBSS types only if portions of both stem and midsection or blade and midsection were present. In some cases, however, blade sections, midsections, or stems could be identified with a type. Six blade sections and 55 stems were identified with the Cougar Mountain type based on their large size. Seventeen midsections were identified as Cougar Mountain based on DSA and shoulder. One blade/stem section was identified with the Lake Mohave type, based on DSA and overall morphology. In addition, three blades were identified with the Lake Mohave type because of their DSA and possession of a chisel tip. As noted above, one of the Cougar Mountain blades also has a chisel tip (Figure 6.28D), but it is definitely not a Lake Mohave blade. Twenty-four specimens were identified as Ovate midsections because they lack an inflection point between blade and stem. The tip is present on five of these, and the base of the stem is present on one. Two stem sections and one blade/midsection were identified with Parman; one of the stems, which has a partial shoulder, and the blade/midsection were identified based on their DSA. The other stem was assigned to the Parman type based on its overall morphology. Finally, four blade/midsections and one stem were identified with the Silver Lake type based on DSA and PSA, respectively. Figures

Figure 6.28. Additional points of the Cougar Mountain type in the Sunshine assemblage: (A) 2181; (B) 2180; (C) 1781; (D) SW3, no #; (E) 1109; (F) 408; (G) SW3, no #; (H) 2423; (I) SW 1997, Operation 1, FS 8; (J) 1943; (K) 2416; (L) SW3A/3B, no #; (M) 1733; (N) 2189; (O) SW3A/3B, no #; (P) 905; (Q) 1930; (R) 2188; (S) 2190; (T) 2191; (U) surface 1995, FS 403; (V) surface 1995, FS 231; (W) surface 1995, FS 350, (X) surface 1995, FS 170; (Y) surface 1995, FS 175.

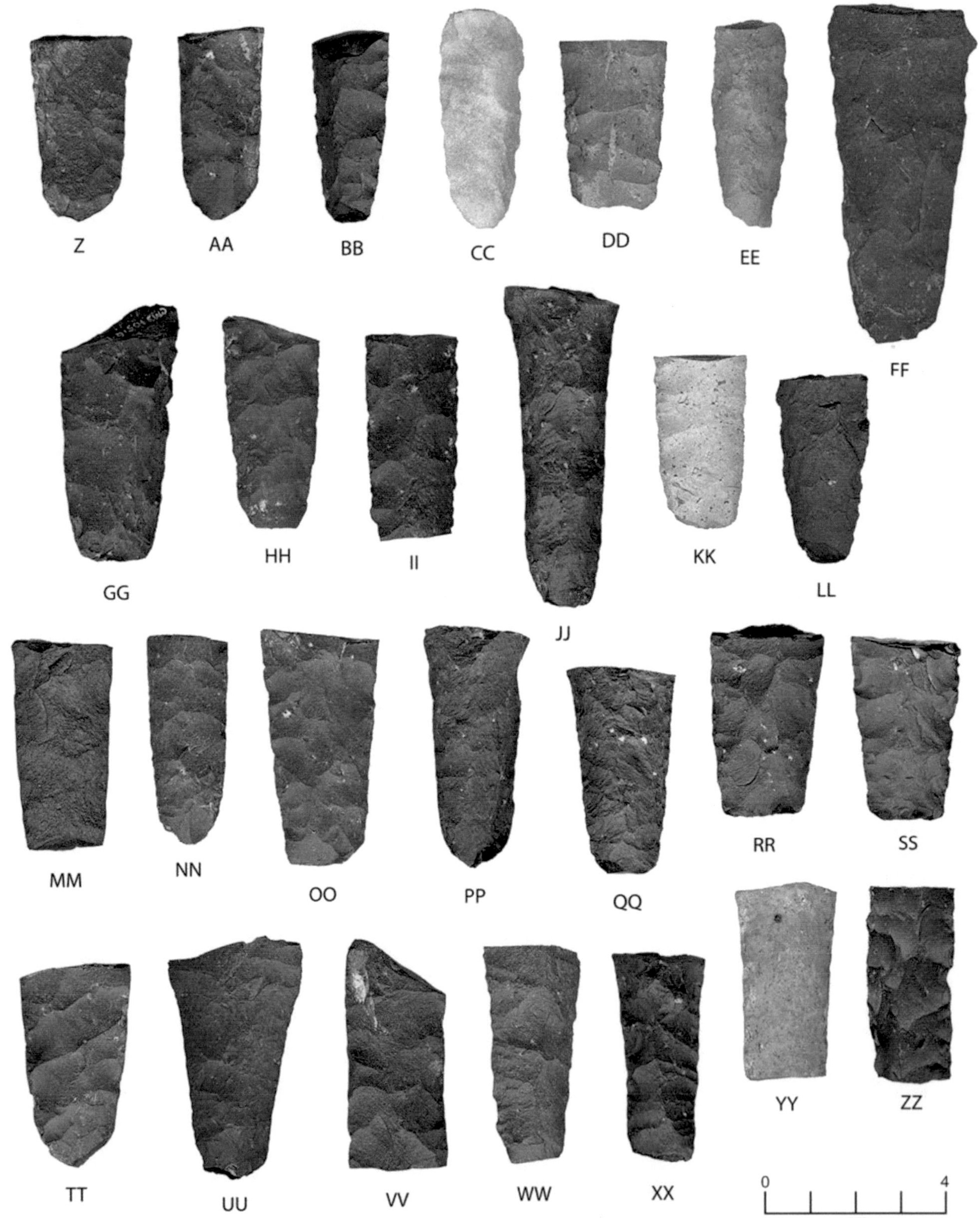

Figure 6.28. (cont'd.) (Z) SW3, no #; (AA) SW3, no #; (BB) SW3, no #; (CC) 1712; (DD) SW2, 104; (EE) 1817; (FF) 1861; (GG) 1577; (HH) 1317; (II) 1941; (JJ) 3023; (KK) 778; (LL) 800; (MM) 798; (NN) 2318; (OO) 2317; (PP) 2315; (QQ) 2319; (RR) 2314; (SS) 2316; (TT) 2320; (UU) 2186; (VV) 2414; (WW) SW3, FS4, 15; (XX) 2411; (YY) 2408; (ZZ) 2412.

Figure 6.28. (cont'd.) (AAA) 2333; (BBB) 2336; (CCC) 2334; (DDD) 2332; (EEE) 2337; (FFF) 890; (GGG) 2432; (HHH) 2340; (III) 3030; (JJJ) SW3, no #; (KKK) 49; (LLL) 3409; (MMM) 487; (NNN) 2782; (OOO) 913; (PPP) 2384; (QQQ) 2386; (RRR) 2428; (SSS) 2418: (TTT) 2431; (UUU) 3003; (VVV) 3194; (WWW) 139; (XXX) 350; (YYY) 2253; (ZZZ) surface 1995, FS 440.

TABLE 6.23. Points of the Great Basin Stemmed Series Represented in the Sunshine Assemblage

	Portion						
Collection and Type	Blade/ Midsection/ Stem	Blade/ Midsection	Midsection/ Stem	Blade Only	Midsection Only	Stem Only	Total
Hutchinson–Noyes							
Cougar Mountain	14	5	2	2	12	59	94
Ovate[a]	22	5	1		18		46
Parman	13		1		1		15
Lake Mohave	22	1		4			27
Silver Lake	16	2	1				19
Western Stemmed Tradition			6	130	29	316	481
Mini Great Basin Stemmed Series	4						4
Subtotal	91	13	11	136	60	375	686
Hamilton College							
Cougar Mountain	2				2	2	6
Lake Mohave	1						1
Western Stemmed Tradition			1	5		9	15
Subtotal	3		1	5	2	11	22
Total	94	13	12	141	62	386	708

Note: Includes Sunshine points in the eastern Nevada comparative collection.
[a] Because there is no break between the stem and blade on Ovate points, most fragments are referred to only as "midsections." "Blade/Midsection" refers to those where the tip is present, and "Midsection/Stem," to one in which the base of the stem is present.

6.28 through 6.32 illustrate the points assigned to particular types that are not part of the ENCC (illustrated in Figures 6.14 through 6.18). Points identified as Western Stemmed Tradition (WST) blade sections, midsections, and stems are not illustrated.

One final group of four points is included as "Mini GBSS" in Tables 6.23–6.25. All four of these resemble the Cougar Mountain form (Figure 6.33). We hesitate to speculate as to what these points represent. The situation may be analogous to that of the small Clovis points discussed previously.

Table 6.24 provides a summary of the quantitative data for these points; Table 6.25 summarizes the qualitative data. We note the general similarity of patterns in both quantitative and qualitative data between the ENCC collection and the remaining GBSS points.

Projectile Point Analysis: Early Holocene and Archaic Types

Windust

In defining the Windust Phase in the Lower Snake River region of Idaho, Rice (1972) describes 24 different projectile point forms, two of which are relevant here, Groups 1 and 2. Group 1 points are defined by Rice as those with "convex sides; acute tip; small but well defined shoulders; stem slightly contracting with straight sides; stem edges and base are ground; straight base; lenticular cross section; well controlled percussion and pressure flaking" (1972:36). Group 2 points are virtually identical to those of Group 1, except that the stems are described as slightly expanding to slightly contracting. We consider Group 1 and 2 points together and designate this category as Windust A.[2] These points bear some morphological similarity to points of the Cody Complex (e.g., Eden, Scottsbluff; see Frison and Todd 1987) and have been reported from the Black Rock Desert of northwestern Nevada (Clewlow 1968a; Wallman and Amick 1991), Coyote Flat in southeastern Oregon (Butler 1965), and the Paulina Lake site in central Oregon (Connolly and Jenkins 1999:113, Figure 9.26).

The Sunshine points assigned to this category ($n = 14$) are large with parallel-sided stems; 13 are from the H–N collection and one is from the HC collection (Figure 6.34). These points are comparable in total length to Silver Lake points (Table 6.26); however, where the stem constitutes an average of two-fifths of the overall length among Silver Lake points (mean SL/TL = .403), the stem of Windust A points constitutes just over one-quarter of overall length (mean SL/TL = .282). Neck width between the two is also very similar, as is thickness.

FIGURE 6.29. Additional points of the Ovate type in the Sunshine assemblage: (A) 1431; (B) 1931; (C) 1934; (D) 1932; (E) 2101; (F) 1919; (G) 782; (H) 2076; (I) 2098; (J) 2356; (K) 2304; (L) 2434; (M) 2422; (N) 2426; (O) 2425; (P) 2420; (Q) 2425; (R) 2426; (S) 3A/3B, no #; (T) 2332a; (U) 2409; (V) 2433. (1825, SW38, no #, not photographed.)

FIGURE 6.30. Additional points of the Lake Mohave type in the Sunshine assemblage: (A) 2176; (B) 2175; (C) 1423; (D) 2365. (SW3, 32, not photographed.)

FIGURE 6.31. Additional points of the Silver Lake type in the Sunshine assemblage: (A) 2165; (B) 2156; (C) 2886; (D) 991; (E) 1057.

FIGURE 6.32. Additional point of the Parman type (2177) in the Sunshine assemblage. (512, SW2A, 33, not photographed.)

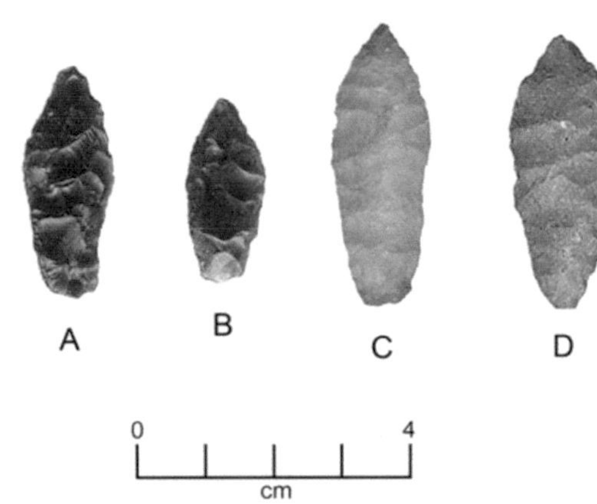

FIGURE 6.33. "Mini" Great Basin Stemmed Series points in the Sunshine assemblage: (A) SW3, 61; (B) SW3B, 159; (C) 3405; (D) 3227.

The similarity with Silver Lake can be extended to qualitative variables as well, including raw material composition, flaking patterns, resharpening, and to some extent, use-wear patterns (Table 6.27). They differ, however, in that the majority of Windust A points (n = 10, 71.4 percent) show medium lateral edge grinding, whereas a large number of Silver Lake points (n = 8, 42.1 percent) have only light edge grinding.

In addition to similarity in form, Windust A points are similar to Alberta/Cody points in size as well. The 21 Alberta/Cody points from the Horner II assemblage, for example, average 59.6 mm in length, 20.8 mm in width, and 6.3 mm in thickness (Bradley and Frison 1987:205) as compared with 45.5, 23.6, and 7.1 mm for the Sunshine Windust A points (Table 6.26). The range in length for the Alberta/Cody points, however, is much wider than that for the Sunshine Windust A points, the longest Alberta/Cody being 86.0 mm as compared with 59.0 mm for Windust A.

Table 6.24. Summary of Quantitative Data for All Sunshine Great Basin Stemmed Series Points

		Point Type								
Variable	Statistic	Cougar Mountain	Ovate	Parman	Lake Mohave	Silver Lake	Western Stemmed Tradition (WST) Blade	WST Midsection	WST Stem	Mini Great Basin Stemmed Series
Total Length (mm)	*N*	9	21	6	19	13	—	—	—	4
	Range	66.9–83.8	11.9–89.5	45.9–77.3	33.4–64.0	28.7–42.5				27.1–41.6
	Mean	75.51	60.16	59.98	50.93	37.70				35.83
	SD	5.660	14.354	13.354	8.977	4.621				6.660
Blade Length (mm)	*N*	17	—	9	23	17	3	—	—	4
	Range	23.7–72.6		23.3–57.7	10.7–26.2	11.5–30.5	24.6–72.1			11.8–17.9
	Mean	40.59		35.78	20.57	19.11	42.647			15.84
	SD	12.944		12.437	4.596	4.899	25.844			2.741
Shoulder Length (mm)	*N*	12	—	4	7	9	—	—	—	4
	Range	3.8–24.4		3.8–6.0	.0–8.9	2.1–4.4				4.6–7.5
	Mean	15.92		4.58	5.06	3.10				5.89
	SD	5.797		1.040	2.954	.915				1.486
Stem Length (mm)	*N*	18	—	10	20	14	—	—	4	4
	Range	11.6–65.5		16.6–32.6	13.8–33.0	10.0–19.3			29.2–39.0	10.7–16.1
	Mean	37.53		23.41	25.01	15.30			33.88	12.79
	SD	15.149		5.789	5.556	2.563			4.047	2.556
Maximum Width (mm)	*N*	27	36	12	23	16	31	—	—	4
	Range	20.0–37.0	16.1–32.5	21.1–37.0	16.0–28.6	19.0–28.5	12.1–34.9			11.5–15.2
	Mean	28.40	21.77	28.23	22.64	22.87	25.53			13.84
	SD	3.678	3.302	5.301	3.272	2.451	4.980			1.645
Thickness (mm)	*N*	91	45	14	26	18	125	30	305	4
	Range	5.8–11.4	4.6–10.2	5.4–9.1	4.8–11.3	5.0–8.4	4.4–12.9	4.6–12.7	3.7–10.7	4.3–6.4
	Mean	8.40	8.06	7.18	6.84	6.83	8.13	8.03	7.04	5.49
	SD	1.306	1.199	1.078	1.747	.927	1.595	2.116	1.266	.950
Basal Width (mm)	*N*	58	21	11	20	12	—	—	179	4
	Range	10.0–19.2	9.3–16.7	9.8–18.5	10.8–20.0	10.3–18.7			7.8–20.9	6.3–17.8
	Mean	14.73	12.08	13.60	15.43	15.90			13.93	9.58
	SD	2.434	2.080	2.794	2.370	2.243			2.457	5.497

TABLE 6.24. (cont'd.) Summary of Quantitative Data for All Sunshine Great Basin Stemmed Series Points

		Point Type								
Variable	Statistic	Cougar Mountain	Ovate	Parman	Lake Mohave	Silver Lake	Western Stemmed Tradition (WST) Blade	WST Midsection	WST Stem	Mini Great Basin Stemmed Series
Neck Width (mm)	*N*	38	—	14	24	19	—	10	6	4
	Range	15.2–28.6		15.4–26.4	14.4–33.8	13.6–19.7		12.6–25.2	16.2–28.2	9.5–12.3
	Mean	21.14		20.54	20.27	16.88		22.05	22.28	10.86
	SD	3.370		3.349	3.950	1.724		3.625	4.468	1.260
Proximal Shoulder Angle (°)	*N*	89	10	14	23	17	—	6	128	4
	Range	80.5–90.0	83.0–90.0	81.0–90.0	77.5–90.0	87.0–110.0		84.5–88.0	79.5–90.0	77.5–85.0
	Mean	85.97	86.50	84.46	84.59	99.06		86.00	85.89	82.63
	SD	2.162	2.494	2.635	3.088	6.400		1.483	2.284	3.449
Distal Shoulder Angle (°)	*N*	32	—	14	24	18	2	3		4
	Range	210.0–262.5		206.0–247.0	209.0–258.5	168.5–248.0	243.0–251.0	193.0–248.5		254.5–266.0
	Mean	249.42		227.64	243.94	217.53	247.00	226.17		260.0
	SD	11.576		14.616	13.684	19.210	5.657	29.293		5.845
Neck Width/ Maximum Width Ratio	*N*	26	—	12	23	16	—	—	—	4
	Range	.57–1.00		.67–.87	.71–1.29	.57–.89				.68–.88
	Mean	.73		.73	.893	.737				.79
	SD	.096		.061	.118	.097				.086
Stem Length/ Total Length Ratio	*N*	8	—	6	19	13	—	—	—	4
	Range	.14–.56		.33–.46	.34–.64	.26–.52				.32–.40
	Mean	.33		.38	.491	.402				.358
	SD	.134		.046	.083	.075				.038

Note: Includes all Sunshine points including those from the eastern Nevada comparative collection.

Table 6.25. Distribution of the Sunshine Great Basin Stemmed Series Points Across Six Qualitative Variables

	Point Type																			
	Cougar Mountain		Ovate		Parman		Lake Mohave		Silver Lake		Western Stemmed Tradition (WST) Blade		WST Midsection		WST Stem		Mini Great Basin Stemmed Series		Total	
Variable	*N*	%	*N*	%	*N*	%	*N*	%	*N*	%	*N*	%	*N*	%	*N*	%	*N*	%	*N*	%
Raw Material																				
Chert	8	8.0	7	15.2	2	13.3	5	17.9	1	5.3	36	26.9	8	26.7	58	17.5	1	25.0	126	17.8
Obsidian	3	3.0	2	4.3	4	26.7	10	35.7	10	52.6	17	12.7	4	13.3	48	14.5	2	50.0	100	14.1
Fine-Grained Volcanics	86	86.0	37	80.4	9	60.0	13	46.4	8	42.1	81	60.4	18	60.0	226	68.1			478	67.5
Quartzite	3	3.0															1	25.0	4	.6
Total	100	100.0	46	100.0	15	100.0	28	100.0	19	100.0	134	100.0	30	100.0	332	100.0	4	100.0	708	100.0
Flaking Pattern																				
Collateral	85	85.0	29	63.0	6	40.0	13	46.4	8	42.1	103	76.9	25	83.3	273	82.2	2	50.0	544	76.8
Parallel	2	2.0	3	6.5	4	26.7	2	7.1	2	10.6	8	5.9	1	3.3	12	3.6			34	4.8
Oblique	2	2.0	1	2.2			3	10.7			3	2.2			7	2.1			16	2.3
Irregular	7	7.0	3	6.5	3	20.0	4	14.3	4	21.1	12	9.0			17	5.1	1	25.0	51	7.2
Collateral/Parallel	3	3.0	5	10.9			2	7.1			4	3.0	2	6.7	10	3.0	1	25.0	27	3.8
Collateral/Oblique			1	2.2					1	5.3	1	.7			2	.6			5	.7
Collateral/Irregular			2	4.3			4	14.3			2	1.5	1	3.3	2	.6			11	1.6
Parallel/Oblique			1	2.2	2	13.3			2	10.5					1	.3			6	.8
Irregular/Oblique									1	5.3									1	.1
Indeterminate	1	1.0	1	2.2					1	5.3	1	.7	1	3.3	8	2.4			13	1.8
Total	100	100.0	46	100.0	15	100.0	28	100.0	19	100.0	134	100.0	30	100.0	332	100.0	4	100.0	708	100.0
Beveling																				
Absent	29	29.0	33	71.7	8	53.3	13	46.4	16	84.2	130	97.0	3	10.0	10	3.1	4	80.0	246	34.7
Blade			2	4.3	2	13.3	14	50.0	2	10.5	3	2.2	1	3.3	1	.3			25	3.5
Stem	1	1.0			1	6.7	1	3.6							3	.9			6	.8
Blade/Stem																				
Indeterminate	70	70.0	11	23.9	4	26.7			1	5.3	1	.7	26	86.7	318	95.8		20.0	431	60.9
Total	100	100.0	46	100.0	15	100.0	28	100.0	19	100.0	134	100.0	30	100.0	332	100.0	4	100.0	708	100.0

Table 6.25. (cont'd.) Distribution of the Sunshine Great Basin Stemmed Series Points Across Six Qualitative Variables

	Point Type																			
	Cougar Mountain		Ovate		Parman		Lake Mohave		Silver Lake		Western Stemmed Tradition (WST) Blade		WST Midsection		WST Stem		Mini Great Basin Stemmed Series		Total	
Variable	*N*	%	*N*	%	*N*	%	*N*	%	*N*	%	*N*	%	*N*	%	*N*	%	*N*	%	*N*	%
Lateral Edge Grinding																				
Absent	9	9.0	13	28.3	1	6.7	2	7.1	1	5.3			3	10.0	15	4.5			44	6.5
Light	12	12.0	6	13.0	3	20.0	2	7.1	8	42.1			4	13.3	53	16.0	3	75.0	91	12.9
Medium	46	46.0	14	30.4	4	26.7	10	35.7	5	26.3			12	40.0	162	48.8	1	25.0	254	35.9
Heavy	23	23.0	6	13.0	5	33.3	7	25.0	4	21.1			8	26.7	91	27.4			144	20.3
Extreme	1	1.0	2	4.3	1	6.7	2	7.1					1	3.3	6	1.8			13	1.8
Indeterminate	9	9.0	5	10.9	1	6.7	5	17.9	1	5.3	134	100.0	2	6.7	5	1.5			162	22.9
Total	100	100.0	46	100.0	15	100.0	28	100.0	19	100.0	134	100.0	30	100.0	332	100.0	4	100.0	708	100.0
Resharpening																				
Absent	69	69.0	30	65.2	7	46.7	7	25.0	6	31.6	94	70.1	4	13.3	76	22.9	4	100.0	297	42.0
Tip/Blade	8	8.0	8	17.4	3	20.0	14	50.0	9	47.4	33	24.6	1	3.3					76	10.7
Stem	3	3.0	4	8.7	2	13.3							4	13.3	14	4.2			27	3.8
Tip/Blade and Stem	1	1.0			1	6.7	6	21.4	4	21.1									12	1.7
Into Another Tool	1	1.0	1	2.2	1	6.7							1	3.3	1	.3			5	.7
Indeterminate	18	18.0	3	6.5	1	6.7	1	3.6			7	5.2	20	66.7	241	72.6			291	41.1
Total	100	100.0	46	100.0	15	100.0	28	100.0	19	100.0	134	100.0	30	100.0	332	100.0	4	100.0	708	100.0
Use-Wear																				
Absent	11	11.0	12	26.1	3	20.0	8	28.6	8	42.1	19	14.2	3	10.0					64	9.0
Minimal	5	5.0	8	17.4	3	20.0	9	32.1	4	21.1	28	20.9							57	8.1
Moderate	3	3.0	7	15.2			4	14.3			27	20.1							41	5.8
Extensive	2	2.0	4	8.7			4	14.3	5	26.3	27	20.1							42	5.9
Present/Fragment	7	7.0	4	8.7	4	26.7	1	3.6			22	16.4	1	3.3					39	5.5
Indeterminate	72	72.0	11	23.9	5	33.3	2	7.1	2	10.6	11	8.2	26	86.6	332	100.0	4	100.0	465	65.7
Total	100	100.0	46	100.0	15	100.0	28	100.0	19	100.0	134	100.0	30	100.0	332	100.0	4	100.0	708	100.0

Note: Includes Sunshine points from the eastern Nevada comparative collection.

FIGURE 6.34. Points of the Windust type in the Sunshine assemblage: (A) 2151; (B) 2166; (C) 2164; (D) SW7, 1N; (E) 1713; (F) 1878; (G) SW1, no #; (H) surface 1993, FS 5; (I) 2899; (J) 1864; (K) surface 1996, FS 2; (L) SW2, 48; (M) 2902; (N) 1571.

Even though there are slight differences, particularly in flaking and raw material (the Horner II points are all made from chert), we believe that they may be related technologically (Beck et al. 2008). As is the case for Alberta/Cody points, the Windust A points, we believe, functioned as projectiles as opposed to the variety of functions served by GBSS points (see Beck and Jones 1997). The Alberta/Cody Complex dates to between 10,000 and 8000 rcy BP (Frison 1991:26–27, Tables 2.2–2.4). Two radiocarbon dates (10,810 ± 275 rcy BP, 10,750 ± 90 rcy BP) are associated with Windust A points at Marmes Rockshelter in Washington state (Rice 1972) and one (10,740 ± 220 rcy BP) at the Coopers Ferry site in Idaho (Davis 2001). These dates suggest that the basic square-based form is earlier on the Columbia Plateau than on the Plains, and we have suggested elsewhere (Beck et al. 2008) that it may have actually diffused from the Columbia Plateau to the Plains.

The only dates associated with Windust A points in the Great Basin are from the Paulina Lake site in central Oregon (Connolly and Jenkins 1999).[3] Thirteen radiocarbon dates were obtained from three pre-Mazama components, all of which contained both Windust A and Cougar Mountain points: a single date of 9920 ± 470 rcy BP from Component 1; nine dates from Component 2, ranging from 9060 ± 80 to 7930 ± 80 rcy BP;

TABLE 6.26. Summary of Quantitative Data for Windust A Points

	STATISTIC			
VARIABLE	*N*	RANGE	MEAN	SD
Total Length (mm)	9	38.5–59.0	45.54	6.144
Blade Length (mm)	10	24.1–47.9	31.54	7.205
Stem Length (mm)	12	9.7–17.7	13.18	2.753
Maximum Width (mm)	11	19.7–27.3	23.56	2.135
Thickness (mm)	14	5.7–8.5	7.14	.784
Basal Width (mm)	11	15.6–21.2	18.18	2.011
Neck Width (mm)	13	13.8–20.9	17.64	2.387
Proximal Shoulder Angle (°)	13	86.0–105.0	93.35	6.790
Distal Shoulder Angle (°)	12	161.0–235.5	210.83	19.803
Neck Width/Maximum Width Ratio	11	.60–.83	.73	.070
Stem Length/Total Length Ratio	9	.19–.37	.28	.053

TABLE 6.27. Summary of Qualitative Data for Windust A Points

VARIABLE	*N*	%
Raw Material		
Chert	1	7.1
Obsidian	7	50.0
Fine-Grained Volcanics	6	42.9
Subtotal	14	100.0
Flaking Pattern		
Broad Collateral	6	42.9
Parallel Collateral	1	7.1
Oblique	1	7.1
Chevron	1	7.1
Irregular	4	28.6
Oblique/Parallel	1	7.1
Subtotal	14	99.9
Beveling		
None	11	78.6
Blade	1	7.1
Stem	2	14.3
Subtotal	14	100.0
Lateral Edge Grinding		
None	2	14.3
Light	2	14.3
Medium	10	71.4
Subtotal	14	100.0
Resharpening		
None	5	35.7
Tip/Blade	5	35.7
Tip/Blade and Stem	2	14.3
Stem	1	7.1
Indeterminate	1	7.1
Subtotal	14	99.9
Blade Wear		
None	7	50.0
Minimal	1	7.1
Moderate	2	14.3
Extensive	1	7.1
Present/Fragment	1	7.1
Indeterminate	2	14.3
Subtotal	14	99.9
Total	14	100.0

and two dates from Component 3, 7560 ± 90 and 7080 ± 150 rcy BP. These dates suggest the Windust A dates to about the same time in the Great Basin as on the Plains, perhaps having diffused from the Columbia Plateau.

Butte Valley Corner Notched

Points assigned to the Butte Valley Corner Notched category are among those we earlier referred to as untyped. We have named this form Butte Valley Corner Notched because we first encountered it in 1986 on a Paleoarchaic surface site in Butte Valley. Ten examples have been collected; six are from our Butte and Long valley collections, and four are from the H–N collection (Figure 6.35). Because we are defining a new type, we include all ten in our discussion.

These specimens are large, corner-notched points with expanding stems that have generally convex bases and exhibit very large neck widths. As Table 6.28 shows, they are fairly uniform in size, especially in neck width, basal width, and total length, with the exception of specimen Sunshine Well 3B-2022, which has seen considerable resharpening on the tip and blade (Figure 6.35C). If this specimen is removed, there is very little variation in total length (mean = 46.02, SD = 2.335). As Table 6.29 shows, all three primary raw materials are represented, with a preference shown for FGV. Flaking is primarily irregular, most exhibit resharpening, and about half are worn.

Butte Valley Corner-Notched points tend to co-occur with GBSS, Windust A, and Pinto points, suggesting similar or overlapping age. Several are made from obsidian of two different geochemical types. Two points are made from Tempiute Mountain obsidian (from southeastern Nevada—previously called "unknown B" [see Beck and Jones 1994; Jones et al. 2003]), for which the range of hydration readings on the projectile points is 2.6 to 7.1 μm (Table 6.30). As Table 6.30 shows, however, the range of hydration values for all point types, including Elko, Humboldt, and Gatecliff, overlap. The two Butte Valley Corner Notched readings (4.5 μm, 5.2 μm) could fit within any of these ranges.

The third point is made from Panaca Summit obsidian, also from southeastern Nevada. The range of hydration readings for projectile points made from this obsidian is 3.4 to 8.8 μm (Table 6.30), but the majority of readings are above 5.0 μm. Once again the points of the different types (except for the single Pinto) have overlapping ranges, and the Butte Valley Corner-Notched point, with a reading of 6.3 μm, could fit within the ranges of Elko, Humboldt, or Cougar Mountain. All we can really say, then, is that these points likely date to the early Holocene.

Points of similar morphology are rarely reported in the Paleoarchaic literature, but three can be seen in

Figure 6.35. Points of the Butte Valley Corner-Notch type. Sunshine assemblage: (A) 2019; (B) 2022; (C) 2902; (D) 166. Butte Valley assemblage: (E) JP, FS 57; (F) LVS-91, FS 48-46; (G) WSWL1, FS 66; (H) HPL5, 344E, 236N; (I) HPL5, 318E, 246N; (J) CCL7, 162E, 122N.

Table 6.28. Quantitative Data for Butte Valley Corner-Notched Points

Provenience	Total Length (mm)	Stem Length (mm)	Neck Width (mm)	Basal Width (mm)	Maximum Width (mm)	Maximum Thickness (mm)	Actual Weight (g)	Proximal Shoulder Angle (°)	Distal Shoulder Angle (°)
SW3-10[a]	—	11.7	18.1	23.5 (est.)	23.5 (est.)	8.6	5.87	146.0	216.0
SW3B-2019[a]	42.2	9.3	20.4	25.3	37.9	8.1	9.79	116.0	151.0
SW3B-2022[a]	29.6	6.8	18.2	—	25.8	5.6	4.39	128.0	148.0
SW-166[a]	—	—	25.8	—	—	—	—	105.0	230.0
CCL7, 162N, 122E	46.6 (est.)	12.3	20.0	22.0	25.6	6.2	6.51	99.5	185.0
HPL5, 318N, 246E	—	—	25.3	—	—	6.9	2.50	96.5	—
HPL5, 344N, 236E	—	9.6	19.0	22.2	—	6.6	3.75	113.0	—
Johns Point, FS 57	47.1 (est.)	10.7	21.3	22.9	29.7	6.7	6.00	99.0	176.0
LVS, U48, FS 46	45.8	13.3	21.2	24.0 (est.)	27.7	8.8	10.40	99.0	183.0
WSWL1B, FS 66	48.4	9.8	22.4	25.2	29.5	6.2	7.52	115.0	203.0
Mean	43.28	10.44	21.33	23.80	28.53	7.08	6.30	111.70	186.50
SD	7.021	2.034	2.870	1.373	4.693	1.143	2.631	15.708	29.037

[a] Points from the Sunshine Locality.

Table 6.29. Qualitative Data for Butte Valley Corner-Notched Points

Provenience	Raw Material	Flaking Pattern	Lateral Edge Grinding	Resharpening	Blade Wear
SW3-10	Obsidian	Semicollateral	Light	Tip/Blade and Barb	Minimal
SW3B-2019	Chert	Irregular	None	Tip/Blade and Barb	None
SW3B-2022	Chert	Irregular	None	Tip/Blade, Barb, and Stem	None
SW-166	Fine-Grained Volcanics (FGV)	Semicollateral	Indeterminate	Tip/Blade	Indeterminate
CCL7, 162N, 122E	FGV	Irregular	Medium	Blade and Barb	Extensive
HPL5, 318N. 246E	Obsidian	Indeterminate	Medium	Indeterminate	Indeterminate
HPL5, 344N, 236E	Obsidian	Indeterminate	Medium[a]	Barb and as Another Tool	Indeterminate
Johns Point-57	Obsidian	Semiparallel	Light	Light	None
LVS, U48, FS 46	FGV	Semicollateral	None	None	Minimal
WSWL1B, FS 66	FGV	Irregular	Light	Light	Extensive

[a] Also heavily ground on the base of the stem.

Pendleton's 1979 report on the Campbell collection from southern Big Smoky Valley, west of Tonopah, Nevada. Two occur in a group she terms "GBSS, Untypable Points" (1979:212, Figure 22). These points appear to be similar in size to those discussed here (see Pendleton 1979:214, Table 25). For example, basal width values are 20.8 and 20.9 mm, thickness values are 7.4 and 9.4 mm, and neck width values are 20.0 and 20.2 mm. Pendleton illustrates another example among those she calls "Silver Lake, Flat Base" (1979:197, Figure 18).

Pinto, Gatecliff, and Elko

The Pinto type was first defined by Amsden based on the points from the Pinto Basin site in the Mojave Desert. Amsden describes Pinto points as

> having a definite although narrow shoulder and usually an incurving base. Frequently there are side nocks just below the shoulder, producing most often three serrations at each edge. The points are thickish, well rounded on each face, as if made from a thick flake by trimming down to its core. Proportionally expressed, maximum thickness often equals 30 per cent of total length and probably averages 20 to 25 per cent [1935:44].

The most often cited typology for these points, however, is that presented by Harrington (1957) from the Stahl site in Owens Valley. Harrington defines five Pinto subtypes—Shoulderless, Sloping Shoulders, Square Shoulders, Barbed Shoulder, and One-Shoulder:

> *Shoulderless Sub-Type*: among the shoulderless Pintos there is considerable variation in outline, from the almost triangular and the straight-sided to those with edges bulging slightly above the base. Five only fall into the "broad notch" class, the others all being "deep notch." The longest is a spearhead a little more than 2¾ inches long; the shortest, not resharpened, is 1½ inch. Much resharpening is evident.
>
> *Sloping Shoulders Sub-Type*: the name covers various shapes from shoulders hardly noticeable to those well developed, but all distinctly sloping. The largest specimen in this sub-class, properly a spearhead, measures 2⅝ inches in length; the smallest well-formed example, 1¼ inch. A few are still shorter, but as their shortness is plainly the result of resharpening (down to a ⅞-inch stub in one case), this cannot be called normal length.
>
> *Square Shoulders Sub-Type*: these are characterized first of all by the broad shallow basal notch instead of the deep variety; the shoulders are formed by rather shallow side-notches; they are usually flat, broad in proportion to length, thinner than most Pinto points, and the chipping, often well-done, appears to be by pressure rather than by percussion.... These points average 1¼ inch to 1½ inch in length, with a width of about an inch.
>
> *Barbed Shoulder Sub-Type*: many of the barbed type of Pinto points found at the Stahl Site seem to be merely a further development of the square shoulder.... Among the barbed points also is a special group...points which are longer, averaging about 2¼ inches, symmetrical, serrated, deep-notched, distinctly barbed, very well made for Pinto points.... In general the barbed Pinto points measure in

TABLE 6.30. Obsidian Hydration Values for Projectile Points of Late Pleistocene/Early Holocene and Archaic Point Types in the Eastern Nevada Comparative Collection

	OBSIDIAN SOURCE	
PROJECTILE POINT TYPE	TEMPIUTE MOUNTAIN	PANACA SUMMIT
Great Basin Concave Base	4.6, 6.6	
Cougar Mountain		6.5. 7.2
Lake Mohave	4.2	
Silver Lake	7.1	7.7
Western Stemmed Tradition Stem	4.6, 4.9, 5.3, 5.7, 6.1	5.2, 6.3, 6.8, 7.0, 8.8
Western Stemmed Tradition Blade	4.5, 6.1	5.5, 5.9, 7.0, 8.3
Butte Valley Corner Notched	4.5, 5.2	6.3
Pinto	4.2, 6.5	5.0
Elko	4.5, 4.5, 4.7, 4.7, 5.0, 5.5	6.1, 6.5, 6.7
Gatecliff	4.6, 4.7	
Humboldt	4.2, 4.4	6.8

Note: Hydration values are in microns.

length from 1½ inch to 2½ inches, excluding some shorter ones that had been obviously resharpened.

> *One-Shoulder Sub-Type*: because of their resemblance to the notched-based type of Sandia points, our 14 one-shoulder points are listed separately... lengths range from 1⅜ inch to a broken spear-head still measuring 2⅜ inches, which originally must have exceeded 3 inches long [1957:51–53].

Upon publication, Harrington's type definitions were used throughout the Great Basin to categorize all split-stemmed points (e.g., Aikens 1970; Clewlow 1968a, 1968b; Heizer and Clewlow 1968; Heizer et al. 1968). Confusion, however, began to arise concerning the dating of the type; as a result, considerable debate has taken place concerning the definition of the Pinto type and its placement in time. A number of researchers have suggested that the points from the Stahl site are not of the same type as those from the Pinto Basin site (e.g., Beck and Jones 1990a; Bettinger and Taylor 1974; Heizer and Hester 1978; Hester 1973; Layton 1970; O'Connell 1975) but are more similar to split-stemmed points from farther north. Green (1975) has proposed the name "Little Lake Series" for the more northern group. Thomas (1981) attempted to solve the problem by designating the more "gracile" split-stemmed form "Gatecliff Split Stem." He suggests that an earlier, more robust form might exist to the south but did not pursue the issue further.

Vaughn and Warren (1987) address the north–south difference in a comparison of 21 points of the Pinto type from the Awl site in the Mojave Desert with the points from Gatecliff Shelter identified by Thomas as Gatecliff Split Stem. First, they applied Thomas's key to the Awl site points; 15 keyed out as Elko, four as Gatecliff, and two were "out-of-key." They then compared the Awl points with those from Gatecliff Shelter (of both Gatecliff and Elko series) in terms of a number of metric variables and found that there were significant differences in mean thickness, distal shoulder angle, and shoulder extension. Thus Vaughn and Warren conclude that there are, indeed, morphological differences between points termed Pinto in the Mojave Desert and points called Gatecliff to the north but that the key as it stands cannot distinguish the former from the latter or from points of the Elko Series.

Although the study by Vaughn and Warren demonstrated that the points from the Awl site differ morphologically from the Gatecliff points, two issues still remained unclear. First, do the points from the Stahl and Pinto Basin sites represent the same morphological form? Second, if they are the same, do these points represent a different form not only from that at Gatecliff but also from those found in other parts of the Great Basin as well? Basgall and Hall (2000) attempt to answer these questions with a detailed analysis of 688 split-stemmed points from several southern (Fort Irwin, Stahl, Pinto Basin, Alabama Gates), western (Hidden Cave), central (Monitor Valley), and northern (Surprise Valley, Silent Snake Springs) Great Basin sites/regions. They also include analysis of, and comparison with, 62 points of the Elko type from Fort Irwin and Alabama Gates in the Mojave Desert. All points were measured on 12 metric attributes, most of which are used in Thomas's (1981) key. In comparing the southern points with those from the central and northern Great

Basin, Basgall and Hall find "at least two morphological expressions in the western Great Basin, a northern pattern consistent with the more gracile morphology that Thomas (1981, 1983) termed Gatecliff Split-stem, and a southern pattern characterized by the robust Pinto/Little Lake forms" (2000:248). Though there is some variation among the northern specimens, they are indistinguishable statistically on nearly all attributes measured. Variation among the southern specimens, however, does prove to be statistically significant. Among other things, points from the Pinto Basin and Stahl sites differ on all but stem length and maximum thickness. Basgall and Hall find, however, that this variation in size is likely related to access to raw material: small points occur in "material-poor" areas, whereas larger points occur in "material-rich" areas. Thus, they conclude that "levels of morphological/temporal convergence in point samples from localities in the southwestern Great Basin are consistent with a single, Pinto series, repudiating the claim that Stahl site variants are somehow different than artifacts from the deeper desert" (2000:271).

Based on statistical comparisons of 11 metric variables, Basgall and Hall (2000:261) present revised class definitions for distinguishing Pinto and Elko points in the southern Great Basin:

Pinto Series: BW > 10.0 mm; PSA ≤ 100° or NOA ≥ 80°
Elko Series: BW > 10.0 mm; 110° ≤ PSA ≤ 150° or NOA < 80°

NOA stands for notch opening angle, which is the same as Thomas's (1981) notch opening index (NOI). We use these definitions to distinguish the Sunshine Pinto and Elko points. Unfortunately, the definition for the Pinto Series does not distinguish between Pinto and Gatecliff unless the NOA is less than 80° (Thomas's 1981 key specifies NOI ≥ 60° for the Gatecliff Series).

In their analysis of split-stemmed points, Basgall and Hall do not analyze points from anywhere east of Monitor Valley. If they had, they likely would have found a more complex picture in that area because there are both Pinto *and* Gatecliff points represented in our collections from Butte, Jakes, and Long valleys as well as in the H–N collection from Sunshine. Because of the controversy concerning split-stemmed points, we consider Pinto, Elko, and Gatecliff points together for type assignment.

Type Assignment of the Sunshine Pinto, Elko, and Gatecliff Points

Using Basgall and Hall's criteria to distinguish between Pinto and Elko, we identified 13 Pinto Series points (12 from the H–N collection and one from the HC collection; Figure 6.36) and 49 Elko Series points (all from the H–N collection; Figure 6.37) in the Sunshine assemblage. Unfortunately, the results also include two points that we believe are better identified as Gatecliff points, and thus based on morphology and other metric criteria, we have assigned these two specimens to the Gatecliff type and consider them later in this section.

Table 6.31. Basal Width, Notch Opening Angle, and Proximal Shoulder Angle for the Sunshine Pinto Points

Specimen Number	Basal Width (mm)	Notch Opening Angle (°)	Proximal Shoulder Angle (°)
762	18.3	—	91.0
1694	18.2	120.0	106.0
1690	—	—	102.5
1696	18.7	—	90.0
1778	—	—	105.0
1863	19.8	126.0	104.0
1872	13.9	121.5	97.5
2011	18.5	—	96.0
2014	13.3	—	104.0
2007	—	—	106.0
2169	19.5	95.0	103.0
2909	15.6	147.5	86.0
SW2, no # (GO)	23.5	127.0	105.0

Table 6.31 shows basal width, PSA, and NOA for the 13 Pinto points. As this table shows, nine of the 13 points are consistent with Basgall and Hall's definition; in these cases either the PSA is less than 100° or the NOA is greater than 80°. There are four cases, however, in which the PSA is greater than 100° but where NOA could not be calculated because DSA was not measurable. In three cases, identification was based on general morphology, thickness (which is discussed as a defining attribute by Vaughn and Warren [1987]), and neck width. Table 6.32 summarizes the metric data for points of the Pinto type, and Table 6.33 summarizes the qualitative data.

Table 6.34 shows basal width, PSA, and NOA for the 49 Elko points. Here, all but six are consistent with Basgall and Hall's definition. In two cases, PSA was not measurable because of extensive resharpening on the stem (Figure 6.37U, VV). In the case of the other four, PSA is less than 110°. One specimen (Figure 6.37D) has a PSA value of 104° but is resharpened on one side of the stem and broken on the other. The other three specimens (Figure 6.37RR–TT) have PSA values just under 110°, but NOA could not be calculated for any of these. As in the case of the Pinto examples, these six points were identified with the Elko Series based on other criteria, including morphology, thickness, and neck width. Tables 6.32 and 6.33 show the quantitative and qualitative data, respectively, for the 49 Sunshine Elko points.

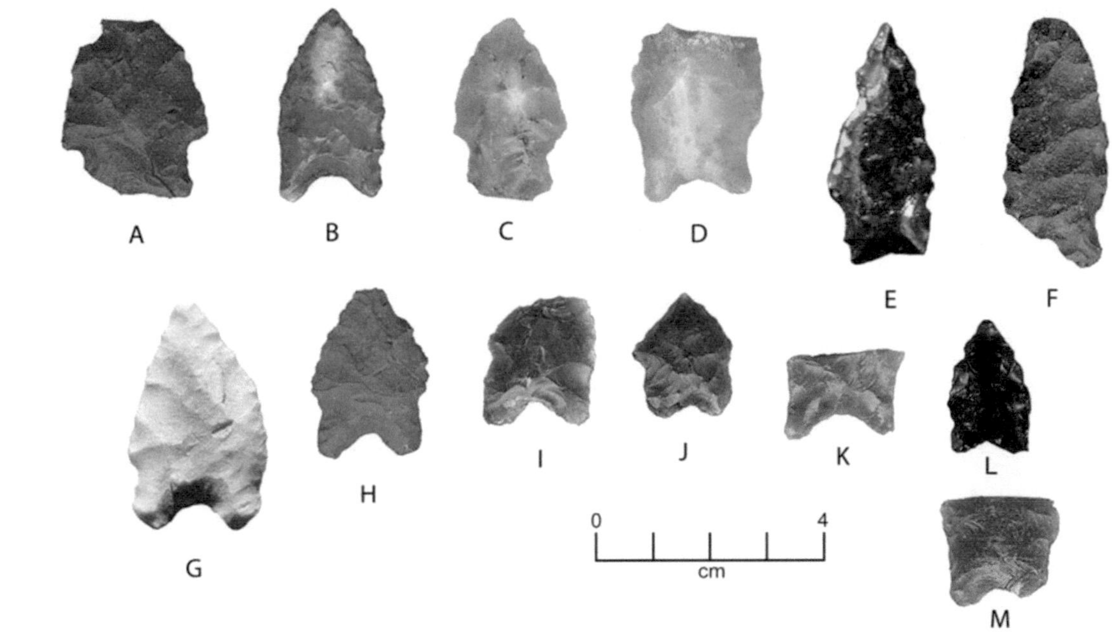

FIGURE 6.36. Points of the Pinto type in the Sunshine assemblage: (A) 2169; (B) 2001; (C) 1872; (D) 1863; (E) 2909; (F) 1778; (G) SW2, no #; (H) 1694; (I) 1696; (J) 1690; (K) 1833; (L) 2014; (M) 762.

FIGURE 6.37. Points of the Elko Series in the Sunshine assemblage: (A) 2004; (B) SW2, FS 70; (C) 2008; (D) 2002; (E) 2011; (F) 2010; (G) 1859; (H) 1865; (I) 1860; (J) 1972; (K) 1965; (L) 2025; (M) 2023; (N) 2026; (O) 1966; (P) 2024.

FIGURE 6.37. (cont'd.) (Q) 2018; (R) 1967; (S) 1971; (T) 2003; (U) 1961; (V) 2016; (W) 1959; (X) 1963; (Y) 2005; (Z) 2017; (AA) 1976; (BB) 1974; (CC) 1979; (DD) 1977; (EE) 1973; (FF) 1978; (GG) 1981; (HH) 1982; (II) 1983; (JJ) 1975; (KK) 1984; (LL) 1704; (MM) 1693; (NN) 1692; (OO) 1701; (PP) 1700; (QQ) 1699; (RR) 1698; (SS) 1702; (TT) SW3, no #; (UU) 3235; (VV) 1980; (WW) 2382.

TABLE 6.32. Summary of Quantitative Data for Pinto, Elko, and Gatecliff Series Points

VARIABLE	STATISTIC	PINTO SERIES	ELKO SERIES	GATECLIFF SERIES
Total Length (mm)	*N*	7	30	4
	Range	32.1–49.5	27.2–58.0	34.6–43.6
	Mean	38.64	40.59	38.95
	SD	6.497	7.944	3.852
Blade Length (mm)	*N*	5	7	—
	Range	19.0–35.5	23.7–32.5	
	Mean	28.05	28.55	
	SD	6.280	2.926	
Stem Length (mm)	*N*	9	37	4
	Range	7.6–13.9	4.8–10.2	8.0–10.7
	Mean	9.77	7.79	9.03
	SD	2.262	1.472	1.190
Maximum Width (mm)	*N*	5	6	
	Range	19.6–26.3	20.3–29.2	
	Mean	23.25	23.83	
	SD	2.913	3.512	
Thickness (mm)	*N*	13	48	4
	Range	4.7–7.4	3.4–8.4	5.2–6.9
	Mean	5.92	6.12	6.23
	SD	.844	1.111	.763
Basal Width (mm)	*N*	11	25	3
	Range	13.3–23.5	12.3–23.0	12.4–15.0
	Mean	18.16	16.85	13.37
	SD	2.946	2.892	1.422
Neck Width (mm)	*N*	11	45	4
	Range	14.5–21.1	8.6–18.9	11.3–16.0
	Mean	17.84	13.74	13.08
	SD	2.268	2.599	2.188
Proximal Shoulder Angle (°)	*N*	12	47	4
	Range	86.0–106.0	104.0–136.5	82.0–102.5
	Mean	99.17	118.4	94.63
	SD	6.903	8.529	8.845
Distal Shoulder Angle (°)	*N*	6	9	3
	Range	198.0–233.5	120.0–201.5	168.0–186.0
	Mean	223.08	160.00	176.20
	SD	13.343	23.029	9.106

It is obvious from Figure 6.37 that most of the points identified as Elko do not fit the classic form. In fact, several (such as Figure 6.37OO, VV–WW) might, at first glance, be considered Humboldt points. This is because of the high degree of resharpening evident on these points. As Table 6.33 shows, of the 46 specimens for which this variable could be evaluated, 42 (91.3 percent) have been resharpened; 36 of these have been resharpened on the barb, obliterating it in some cases. We have found this to be the case in other Elko assemblages we have examined as well (e.g., Steens Mountain [Beck 1995] and Butte Valley). The Elko points in the Butte Valley assemblage, for instance, especially those made from obsidian, bear almost no resemblance to the classic Elko form,

TABLE 6.33. Summary of Qualitative Data for Pinto, Elko, and Gatecliff Series Points

	PINTO SERIES		ELKO SERIES		GATECLIFF SERIES	
VARIABLE	*N*	%	*N*	%	*N*	%
Raw Material						
Chert	5	38.5	19	38.8	1	25.0
Obsidian	4	30.8	15	30.6	2	50.0
Fine-Grained Volcanics	4	30.8	13	26.5	1	25.0
Quartzite			2	4.1		
Total	13	100.0	49	100.0	4	100.0
Flaking Pattern						
Collateral	1	7.7	2	4.1		
Parallel	2	15.4	3	6.1		
Oblique			14	28.5	2	50.0
Chevron			5	10.2	2	50.0
Irregular	8	61.5	11	22.4		
Indeterminate	2	15.4	14	28.6		
Total	13	100.0	49	100.0	4	100.0
Serration						
Absent	10	76.9	43	87.8	4	100.0
Present	3	23.1	4	8.1		
Indeterminate			2	4.1		
Total	13	100.0	49	100.0	4	100.0
Beveling						
Absent	10	76.9	47	95.9	4	100.0
Indeterminate	3	23.1	2	4.1		
Total	13	100.0	49	100.0	4	100.0
Lateral Edge Grinding						
Absent	4	30.8	35	71.4	3	75.0
Light	3	23.1	10	20.4	1	25.0
Medium	1	7.7	1	2.0		
Heavy	3	23.1	3	6.1		
Indeterminate	2	15.4				
Total	13	100.0	49	100.0	4	100.0
Resharpening						
Absent	2	15.4	6	12.2		
Tip/Blade	1	7.7	4	8.2		
Barb			1	2.0	1	25.0
Tip/Blade and Barb	4	30.8	25	51.0	2	50.0
Barb and Stem			1	2.0		
Tip/Blade and Stem			1	2.0		
Tip/Blade, Barb, and Stem	3	23.1	9	18.4	1	25.0
Into Another Tool	1	7.7	1	2.0		
Indeterminate	2	15.4	1	2.0		
Total	13	100.0	49	100.0	4	100.0
Blade Wear						
Absent	6	46.2	37	75.5	4	100.0
Minimal			5	10.2		
Moderate	1	7.7	4	8.2		
Extensive	2	15.4	1	2.0		
Indeterminate	4	30.8	2	4.1		
Total	13	100.0	49	100.0	4	100.0

TABLE 6.34. Basal Width, Notch Opening Angle, and Proximal Shoulder Angle for the Sunshine Elko Points

SPECIMEN NUMBER	BASAL WIDTH (mm)	NOTCH OPENING ANGLE (°)	PROXIMAL SHOULDER ANGLE (°)
1692	16.4	—	110.0
1693	14.3	—	136.5
1698	—	—	109.0
1699	—	—	130.0
1700	—	—	119.5
1701	17.5	—	110.5
1702	15.0	—	108.0
1704	16.8	—	135.0
1859	15.0	58.0	105.0
1860	—	—	120.0
1865	14.2	56.0	114.0
1959	—	—	132.0
1961	13.9	—	121.0
1963	21.1	—	125.5
1965	16.1	—	120.5
1966	—	—	121.0
1967	—	—	132.0
1971	—	—	120.0
1972	—	65.0	113.0
1973	—	—	115.5
1974	17.5	32.5	109.5
1975	—	—	127.0
1976	—	—	114.5
1977	16.8	15.0	105.0
1978	17.6	—	104.5
1979	22.5	—	112.0
1980	—	—	—
1981	—	—	113.0
1982	—	—	114.0
1983	16.5	28.5	133.5
1984	—	—	121.0
2002	12.3	—	104.0
2003	13.2	—	122.5
2004	14.2	—	110.0
2005	—	—	114.0
2008	16.3	—	118.0
2010	—	—	119.0
2011	—	—	118.0
2016	18.6	27.0	126.0
2017	—	—	—
2018	14.0	19.0	131.0
2023	23.0	—	117.0
2024	14.3	—	118.5
2025	21.9	—	122.0
2026	18.1	—	111.5
2382	18.4	—	121.0
3235	—	—	131.0
SW3, no #	—	—	109.0
SW2, FS 70	—	86.5	115.0

TABLE 6.35. Weight, Proximal Shoulder Angle, and Notch Opening Angle for the Sunshine Gatecliff Points

SPECIMEN NUMBER	WEIGHT (g)	PROXIMAL SHOULDER ANGLE (°)	NOTCH OPENING ANGLE (°)
1691	4.57	98.5	—
1697	4.08	98.0	76.6
1866	2.59	96.0	72.0
2015	4.57	82.0	104.0

FIGURE 6.38. Points of the Gatecliff type in the Sunshine assemblage: (A) 1691; (B) 1697; (C) 1866; (D) 2015.

TABLE 6.36. Remaining Archaic Points by Raw Material

	RAW MATERIAL							
	CHERT		OBSIDIAN		FINE-GRAINED VOLCANICS		TOTAL	
PROJECTILE POINT TYPE	*N*	%	*N*	%	*N*	%	*N*	%
Humboldt	14	63.6	4	18.2	4	18.2	22	100.0
Large Side Notched			1	100.0			1	100.0
Large Corner Notched	1	100.0					1	100.0
Rosegate			1	50.0	1	50.0	2	100.0
Archaic Blade	4	50.0	2	25.0	2	25.0	8	100.0

except for the stem (note that only 11 of the 42 points show resharpening on the stem [Table 6.33]). This underscores the arguments made by many Great Basin archaeologists regarding the Flenniken and Raymond (1986) hypothesis concerning resharpening and type change mentioned at the beginning of this chapter.

Finally, four points, all from the H–N collection, were identified with the Gatecliff Series using Thomas's (1981) definition from his key (Figure 6.38):

Weight > 1.0 g; PSA ≤ 100° or NOI ≥ 60°

Table 6.35 shows these variables for the four Sunshine Gatecliff points. All four are consistent with Thomas's definition. As noted above, two of these specimens were initially identified as Pinto points using the Basgall and Hall definition; however, their definition was not written to distinguish Pinto from Gatecliff but Pinto from Elko, as points of Pinto and Gatecliff types were not both found in any of the areas they examined. Basgall and Hall found significant differences between Pinto and Gatecliff points in thickness, stem length, basal width, neck width, PSA, and DSA. In the Sunshine assemblage, however, separate variance t-tests indicate significant differences only in basal width ($t = 4.245$, $df = 12$, $p = .001$), neck width ($t = 4.106$, $df = 8.6$, $p = .013$), and DSA ($t = 7.169$, $df = 8.0$, $p < .001$). This may be related to small sample size, the Sunshine Pinto points being less robust than those from the southern Great Basin, the Gatecliff points being more robust than those tested by Basgall and Hall, or any combination of these factors. We feel confident that the four points we identified as Gatecliff are distinct from those identified as Pinto. Tables 6.32 and 6.33 show the quantitative and qualitative data, respectively, for the Sunshine Gatecliff points.

Remaining Archaic Points

Table 6.36 shows the remaining 34 Archaic points, identified using Thomas's (1981) key, by type and raw material. These include 22 Humboldt points (Figure 6.39), one Large Side-Notched point (Figure 6.40A), two Rosegate points (Figure 6.40B–C), and nine Archaic blades (not illustrated). Archaic blades are blade sections that almost certainly represent Archaic projectile points. In two cases the neck was present but type identification was still not possible. Thirty-three of these remaining points are from

FIGURE 6.39. Points of the Humboldt Series in the Sunshine assemblage: (A) 1877; (B) 1835; (C) 2139; (D) 2012; (E) 1900; (F) 1715; (G) 2009; (H) 1870; (I) 1960; (J) 1828; (K) 1694; (L) 1985; (M) 1703; (N) 3418; (O) 2007; (P) 1638; (Q) 2088; (R) 2293; (S) 3705; (T) 2297; (U) 763; (V) 777.

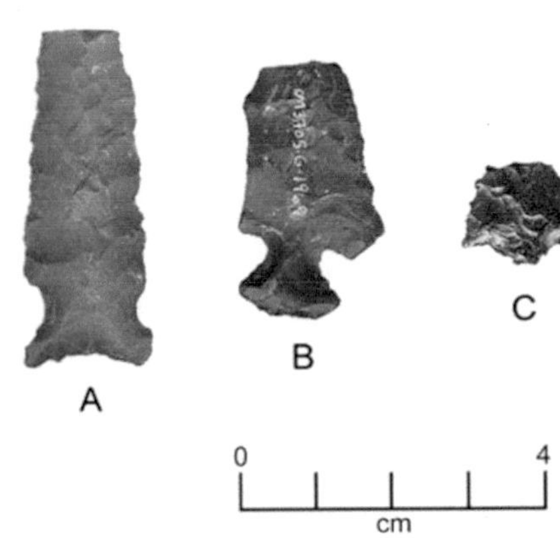

FIGURE 6.40. Other Archaic points in the Sunshine assemblage: (A) 1964, Large Side Notched; (B) 1969, Rosegate; (C) 754, Rosegate.

TABLE 6.37. Summary of Quantitative Data for the Remaining Archaic Projectile Points

		POINT TYPE			
VARIABLE	STATISTIC	HUMBOLDT	LARGE SIDE NOTCHED	ROSEGATE	ARCHAIC BLADE
Total Length (mm)	*N*	13	1	1	—
	Range	28.6–64.3	56.7	43.9	
	Mean	42.75			
	SD	12.402			
Blade Length (mm)	*N*	—	—	—	2
	Range				33.8–34.7
	Mean				34.23
	SD				.601
Stem Length (mm)	*N*	—	1	1	—
	Value		7.0	8.5	
Maximum Width (mm)	*N*	17	—	1	—
	Range	13.8–22.5		16.5	
	Mean	18.52			
	SD	2.745			
Thickness (mm)	*N*	22	1	2	7
	Range	4.4–9.0	8.20	4.3–4.8	4.8–7.3
	Mean	5.74		4.53	5.96
	SD	1.210		.389	.964
Basal Width (mm)	*N*	21	1	—	—
	Range	12.0–20.7	14.4		
	Mean	15.16			
	SD	2.315			
Neck Width (mm)	*N*	—	1	2	2
	Range		11.9	6.3–6.9	9.6–12.6
	Mean			6.58	11.10
	SD			.389	2.121
Proximal Shoulder Angle (°)	*N*	—	1	1	—
	Value		179.5	134.0	
Distal Shoulder Angle (°)	*N*	—	1	1	1
	Value		199.0	161.0	166.5

the H–N collection; one Archaic blade is from the HC collection. Tables 6.37 and 6.38 summarize the quantitative and qualitative data, respectively, for these points.

Indeterminate Blades and Unclassifiable Points

There are 39 blade sections that could not be identified as coming from a particular group of points, such as WST or Archaic. An additional 13 points were too fragmentary to identify with any category.

Summary

A total of 967 artifacts in the Sunshine assemblage were identified as projectile points; 410 of these were classifiable to type. An additional 496 were identifiable with the GBSS in general, and nine, as Archaic points. The remaining 52 specimens are too fragmentary for identification. By far, the greatest number of the identifiable points represent TP/EH diagnostics: Great Basin fluted and unfluted lanceolates (9.7 percent); GBSS (77.4 percent); and

TABLE 6.38. Summary of Qualitative Data for the Remaining Archaic Projectile Points

	POINT TYPE							
	HUMBOLDT		LARGE SIDE NOTCHED		ROSEGATE		ARCHAIC BLADE	
VARIABLE	*N*	%	*N*	%	*N*	%	*N*	%
Flaking Pattern								
Collateral	1	4.5						
Parallel	8	36.4					3	33.3
Oblique	9	40.9					1	11.1
Chevron	1	4.5	1	100.0			1	11.1
Irregular	1	4.5			1	50.0	2	22.2
Collateral/Parallel							1	11.1
Parallel/Oblique	1	4.5						
Indeterminate	1	4.5			1	50.0	1	11.1
Total	22	100.0	1	100.0	2	100.0	9	100.0
Resharpening								
Absent	11	50.0	1	100.0	2	100.0	7	77.8
Tip/Blade	5	22.7					2	22.2
Tip/Blade and Base/Stem	3	13.6						
Into Another Tool	1	4.5						
Indeterminate	2	9.1						
Total	22	100.0	1	100.0	2	100.0	9	100.0
Blade Wear								
Absent	14	63.6	1	100.0	2	100.0	8	88.9
Moderate								
Medium								
Heavy	1	4.5						
Present/Fragment							1	11.1
Indeterminate	7	31.8						
Total	22	100.0	1	100.0	2	100.0	9	100.0

Windust, Butte Valley Corner Notched, and Pinto (3.4 percent). Less than 10 percent represent Archaic types. Table 6.39 shows these points by type and raw material. The paucity of Archaic points at the Sunshine Locality underscores the drop-off in visitation to the site following the early Holocene, as suggested by the radiocarbon dates.

We have concentrated our discussions in this chapter on issues surrounding lanceolate and stemmed points. A comparison of the Sunshine fluted points with those of Clovis and Folsom suggests that most are not similar morphologically to either but, rather, represent a different fluted form. We believe, given the radiocarbon dates from the site, that the Sunshine fluted points date somewhat later than Clovis. A comparison of fluted and unfluted lanceolates from the Sunshine Locality indicates that these differ as well and that unfluted lanceolates are not unfluted simply because they were too thin to begin with. We have suggested here that unfluted lanceolates possibly follow fluted lanceolates in time, but there are no associated dates to support this suggestion.

Two general issues were examined with respect to stemmed points. First, are the five different GBSS types represented at the Sunshine Locality valid types, or do they simply reflect morphological differences resulting from breakage and resharpening? The latter possibility is supported to some extent by the data but not completely. We have concluded that, although the resharpening of one form into another did occur, most examples were not created in this way. We believe that a particular form is directly related to its function, which is the second issue examined.

Although these points have been regarded by most researchers to have functioned as projectile points, the Sunshine data do not support this conclusion. Use-wear, hafting, and breakage patterns indicate a variety of mo-

TABLE 6.39. Summary of Projectile Point Types Represented in the Sunshine Assemblage

	Raw Material				
Type	Chert	Obsidian	Fine-Grained Volcanics	Quartzite	Total
Lanceolate					
Great Basin Fluted	15[a]	2			17
Great Basin Unfluted	66	3	3		72[b]
Subtotal	81	5	3		89
Great Basin Stemmed Series (GBSS)					
Cougar Mountain	8	3	86	3	100
Ovate	7	2	37		46
Parman	2	4	9		15
Lake Mohave	5	10	13		28
Silver Lake	1	10	8		19
Mini GBSS	1	2		1	4
Western Stemmed Tradition	102	69	325		496
Subtotal	126	100	478	4	708
Early Holocene					
Windust A	1	7	6		14
Butte Valley Corner Notched	2	1	1		4
Pinto	5	4	4		13
Subtotal	8	12	11		31
Archaic					
Elko	19	15	13	2	49
Gatecliff	1	2	1		4
Humboldt	14	4	4		22
Large Side Notched		1			1
Rosegate		1	1		2
Archaic Blade	5	2	2		9
Subtotal	39	25	21	2	87
Unclassifiable	18	9	24	1	52
Total	272	151	537	7	967

[a] Includes a fluted point from just outside the boundary of the Sunshine Locality.
[b] Does not include the hafted point in Figure 6.10UUU.

tions, such as cutting and sawing, thrusting, and in the case of some Lake Mohave points, chiseling. Thus we have concluded that the five types likely had different functions. Some, such as Cougar Mountain, may have served as projectile points, but they more likely served a variety of functions. We return to a discussion of these findings in our final chapter.

Notes

1. Comparison was made between the Clovis data presented in Table 6.2 and a data set of Great Basin Fluted points originally compiled by Amanda Taylor (2002, 2003), which we then supplemented.
2. We use the designation "Windust A" because we have identified another form of Windust in the Butte Valley assemblages, which we call "Windust B." This form is similar to Windust A but has a concave base (see Beck and Jones 1988:284, Figure 3r).
3. Bryan (1988:55, Figure 1) reports a square-based point from Handprint Cave. Charcoal "from immediately below the point" yielded a date of 10,740 ± 70 rcy BP, but it is difficult to know how much older this date is than the point. Also, it is difficult to tell from the drawing if this point actually represents the Windust A type or a broken Cougar Mountain on which basal resharpening has occurred. The shape of the blade suggests the latter, but because there is no scale, the size of the point is unknown.

7

Faunal Remains from the Sunshine Locality

Michael D. Cannon, Stephanie D. Livingston, and Jack M. Broughton

This chapter describes the vertebrate faunal materials collected during the 1993, 1995, and 1996 field seasons of the Hamilton College field project at the Sunshine Locality, as well as those collected at Sunshine in 1990 by the Nevada State Museum (NSM) and the Desert Research Institute (DRI).[1] These excavations have recovered specimens of numerous taxa of mammals, birds, and fishes, which date to as early as the terminal Pleistocene.

Though it is possible that people may have played a role in the deposition of some of the animal remains described here, it is not possible to unambiguously associate any of the faunal specimens from the Sunshine Locality with human activity. Nevertheless, this assemblage is important for a variety of reasons. Terminal Pleistocene deposits at Sunshine have produced specimens of *Camelops hesternus*, the extinct yesterday's camel, that are among the youngest known from the Great Basin, and a specimen from an extinct American horse (*Equus* sp.) has also been recovered. In addition, bird, fish, and small mammal remains from terminal Pleistocene contexts add to our knowledge of environmental conditions at the Sunshine Locality during this time. The significance of the Sunshine fauna as regards these issues is considered in greater detail following a description of the material and a discussion of its taphonomic history.

Descriptive Summary: Hamilton College Assemblage

In this section we describe the faunal materials collected during the Hamilton College excavations. We list the number of identified specimens of each element of each taxon recovered, and we discuss the criteria used for identification where appropriate. For mammals, scientific and common names follow Wilson and Reeder (1993) and Wilson and Cole (2000), and discussions of geographical ranges are based on the maps in Hall 1946, 1981, and Zeveloff and Collett 1986; for fishes and birds, see Sigler and Sigler 1987 and Ryser 1985, respectively. Table 7.1 presents numbers of identified specimens per stratigraphic unit, and Tables A.1, A.2, and A.3 provide a more detailed listing of specimens recovered by year and provenience.

Class Osteichthyes (Bony Fishes)

Order Salmoniformes (Trouts and Pike)
Family Salmonidae (Trouts)
Material: 1 basioccipital: 1 specimen

Order Cypriniformes (Carps, Minnows, and Suckers)
Material: 9 vertebrae: 9 specimens

Family Cyprinidae (Carps and Minnows)
Material: 1 pterotic, 1 basioccipital, 1 dentary, 1 pharyngeal, 6 cleithra, 2 first vertebrae, 1 second vertebra: 13 specimens
Discussion: The pterotic matches closely in size and morphology with *Gila atraria* (Utah chub), and one of the cleithra also matches well in size with this species.

Family Catostomidae (Suckers)
Material: 1 parietal, 1 scapula: 2 specimens

Class Aves (Birds)

Order Podicipediformes (Grebes)
Family Podicipedidae (Grebes)
cf. *Podiceps* sp. (Eared, Red-Necked, and Horned Grebes)
Material: 1 ulna, 1 tibiotarsus: 2 specimens

Order Anseriformes (Waterfowl)
Family Anatidae (Waterfowl)
Material: 1 coracoid, 1 humerus, 1 carpometacarpus, 1 flat wing phalanx, 1 tibiotarsus: 5 specimens
Discussion: The humerus specimen is the size of a small duck. The coracoid, carpometacarpus, and tibiotarsus are the size of a medium-sized duck.

Cygnus sp. (Swans)
Material: 1 humerus: 1 specimen

Branta sp. (Geese)
Material: 1 cervical vertebra, 1 radius, 1 phalanx: 3 specimens
Discussion: The cervical vertebra specimen was identified as cf. *Branta* sp.

Table 7.1. Identified Faunal Specimens Recovered During the Hamilton College Excavations at the Sunshine Locality, 1993–1996

	Stratum						
Taxon	**A**	**B**	**C**	**D/E**	**F/G**	**N.A.**[a]	**Total**
Fishes							
Salmonidae (Trout)					1		1
Cypriniformes (Minnows and suckers)					9		9
Cyprinidae (Minnows)					13		13
Catostomidae (Suckers)					2		2
Birds							
Podiceps sp. (Grebes)					2		2
Anatidae (Waterfowl)			1		4		5
Cygnus sp. (Swans)					1		1
Branta sp. (Geese)					3		3
Anas sp. (Dabbling ducks)				3	7		10
Aythya sp. (Diving ducks)			2		10	1	13
Accipiter striatus (Sharp-shinned hawk)			1				1
Scolopacidae (Shorebirds)					1		1
Passeriformes (Perching birds)					2		2
Pica pica (Black-billed magpie)					1		1
Oreoscoptes montana (Sage thrasher)	1						1
Mammals							
Leporidae (Rabbits and hares)	30		8	2	26		66
Brachylagus idahoensis (Pygmy rabbit)	11				8		19
Sylvilagus sp. (Cottontails)	4		1		7		12
Lepus sp. (Jackrabbits)	6				6		12
Sciuridae (Squirrels)	211	29	11		9		260
Tamias sp. (Chipmunks)	1						1
Spermophilus sp. (Ground squirrels)	16		1				17
Spermophilus mollis (Piute ground squirrel)	107	19	14				140
Thomomys sp. (Pocket gophers)	134	20	25	1	4		184
Thomomys bottae (Botta's pocket gopher)	19	1	4				24
Dipodomys sp. (Kangaroo rats)	5				2		7
Dipodomys ordii (Ord's kangaroo rat)	3						3
Peromyscus sp. (Deer mice)	3		1				4
Neotoma cinerea (Bushy-tailed wood rat)				1			1
Arvicolinae (Voles)	18	2	2		11		33
Microtus sp. (Meadow voles)			1	1	7	1	10
Lemmiscus curtatus (Sagebrush vole)	6				2		8
Canidae (Dogs)					1		1
Canis latrans (Coyote)					1		1
Vulpes vulpes (Red fox)					1		1
Mustela vison (American mink)					1		1
Equus sp. (Horses)					1		1
Artiodactyla (Even-toed ungulates)	1				5	2	8
Camelops hesternus (Yesterday's camel)					11	2	13
Total number of identified specimens	576	71	72	8	159	6	892
Total unidentified	433	52	151	29	1,089[b]	33[c]	1,787

[a] Stratigraphic provenience is not available for these specimens.
[b] Sixteen of these specimens are from very large, camel- or horse-sized mammals.
[c] Three of these are from camel- or horse-sized mammals.

Anas sp. (Dabbling Ducks)
Material: 1 furculum, 2 coracoids, 1 scapula, 1 humerus, 1 radius, 1 scapholunar, 2 cuneiforms, 1 flat wing phalanx: 10 specimens
Discussion: All of these specimens are the size of a large *Anas.*

Aythya sp. (Diving Ducks)
Material: 1 sternum, 2 coracoids, 1 scapula, 1 humerus, 1 ulna, 1 radius, 2 carpometacarpi, 1 wing phalanx, 2 tibiotarsi, 1 tarsometatarsus: 13 specimens
Discussion: The sternum, coracoids, tibiotarsi, tarsometatarsus, and one of the carpometacarpi are the size of a small *Aythya.* The scapula, humerus, ulna, radius, wing phalanx, and one of the carpometacarpi are the size of a large *Aythya.*

Order Falconiformes (Diurnal Birds of Prey)
Family Accipitridae (Eagles, Hawks, and Relatives)
Accipiter striatus (Sharp-Shinned Hawk)
Material: 1 tibiotarsus: 1 specimen

Order Charadriiformes (Shoreline Birds)
Family Scolopacidae (Shorebirds)
Material: 1 ulna: 1 specimen

Order Passeriformes (Perching Birds)
Material: 1 mandible, 1 ulna: 2 specimens
Discussion: Both of these specimens are from small passerines.

Family Corvidae (Jays, Crows, and Relatives)
Pica pica (Black-Billed Magpie)
Material: 1 tarsometatarsus: 1 specimen

Family Mimidae (Mockingbirds, Thrashers, and Catbirds)
cf. *Oreoscoptes montana* (Sage Thrasher)
Material: 1 humerus: 1 specimen

Class Mammalia (Mammals)
Order Lagomorpha (Rabbits, Hares, and Pikas)
Family Leporidae (Rabbits and Hares)
Material: 2 frontals, 2 temporals, 4 auditory bullae, 1 sphenoid, 2 maxillae, 5 mandibles, 7 upper cheek teeth, 2 lower incisors, 1 first cervical vertebra, 2 lumbar vertebra, 5 thoracic vertebrae, 1 sacrum, 1 rib, 1 scapula, 1 humerus, 3 ulnae, 1 carpal, 1 indeterminate metacarpal, 3 radii, 1 femur, 1 astragalus, 1 second metatarsal, 2 indeterminate metatarsals, 4 indeterminate metapodials, 4 first phalanges, 7 second phalanges, 1 phalangeal sesamoid: 66 specimens
Discussion: Genus-level identifications of leporid specimens were based primarily on size; specimens identified only to the family Leporidae were too fragmentary to determine the size of the animal from which they came or fell within the range of overlap in size between two genera.

Brachylagus idahoensis (Pygmy Rabbit)
Material: 1 maxilla, 2 mandibles, 3 upper cheek teeth, 1 lower cheek tooth, 1 innominate, 1 tibia, 2 calcanei, 1 second metatarsal, 7 first phalanges: 19 specimens
Discussion: These specimens were distinguished from *Sylvilagus* based on their small size, though the upper cheek teeth were also identified based on the presence of few or no crenulations in the enamel of the reentrant (e.g., Green and Flinders 1980; Ruedas 1998).

Sylvilagus sp. (Cottontails)
Material: 1 maxilla, 1 mandible, 1 upper second premolar, 4 upper cheek teeth, 1 ulna, 1 innominate, 1 tibia, 2 first phalanges: 12 specimens
Discussion: The only *Sylvilagus* species that currently occurs in Long Valley is *S. nuttallii* (mountain cottontail), though *S. audubonii* (desert cottontail) can be found within approximately 100 km to the south and east. None of the specimens that was recovered could be identified to species.

Lepus sp. (Hares and Jackrabbits)
Material: 1 temporal, 3 upper cheek teeth, 1 lower cheek tooth, 1 femur, 1 tibia, 1 calcaneus, 1 indeterminate metatarsal, 2 first phalanges, 1 third phalanx: 12 specimens
Discussion: None of these specimens was identifiable to species. Both *L. townsendii* (white-tailed jackrabbit) and *L. californicus* (black-tailed jackrabbit) can be found in the area today.

Order Rodentia (Rodents)
Family Sciuridae (Squirrels)
Material: 2 partial crania, 13 frontals, 5 parietals, 20 temporals, 1 malar, 9 occipitals, 16 auditory bullae, 7 sphenoids, 6 nasals, 14 premaxillae, 3 maxillae, 15 mandibles, 1 lower cheek tooth, 1 clavicle, 8 scapulae, 27 humeri, 23 ulnae, 12 radii, 16 innominates, 26 femora, 28 tibiae, 7 calcanei: 260 specimens
Discussion: All of these specimens are from ground squirrel-sized sciurids.

Tamias sp. (Chipmunks)
Material: 1 mandible: 1 specimen

Spermophilus sp. (Ground Squirrels)
Material: 5 premaxillae, 1 maxilla, 11 mandibles: 17 specimens

Spermophilus mollis (= townsendii) (Piute Ground Squirrel)
Material: 8 partial crania, 26 maxillae, 36 mandibles, 30 upper fourth premolars or first or second molars, 4 upper third molars, 3 lower fourth premolars, 15 lower first or second molars, 9 lower third molars: 131 specimens
Discussion: Of the *Spermophilus* species that inhabit the region today, *S. elegans* (Wyoming ground squirrel), *S. beldingi* (Belding's ground squirrel), and *S. variegatus* (rock squirrel) can be excluded as the source of these specimens on the basis of size. They can be distinguished from *S. lateralis* (golden-mantled ground squirrel) based on these dental characteristics (e.g., Hall 1946, 1981): on the upper fourth premolars and upper first and second molars, the metaloph is continuous with the protocone and the parastylar ridge joins the protocone at an abrupt angle; the lower fourth premolars have broad protoconids; the lower first and second molars have a narrow parallelogram shape in occlusal surface outline; and the upper and lower third molars are relatively narrow buccal-lingually in occlusal surface outline. Maxillae were also distinguished from *S. lateralis* based on the width of the infraorbital foramen relative to its height (e.g., Hall 1946, 1981).

Family Geomyidae (Pocket Gophers)
Thomomys sp. (Pocket Gophers)
Material: 4 frontals, 6 temporals, 2 auditory bullae, 1 sphenoid, 2 nasals, 7 premaxillae, 6 maxillae, 38 mandibles, 22 upper incisors, 11 upper fourth premolars, 6 upper first or second molars, 1 upper third molar, 18 lower incisors, 12 lower first or second molars, 3 lower third molars, 1 indeterminate incisor, 1 indeterminate fourth premolar, 4 scapulae, 10 humeri, 4 ulnae, 2 radii, 11 femora, 9 tibiae, 3 calcanei: 184 specimens

Thomomys bottae (= umbrinus) (Botta's Pocket Gopher)
Material: 7 partial crania, 1 premaxilla, 4 maxillae, 12 lower fourth premolars: 24 specimens
Discussion: *T. talpoides* (northern pocket gopher) can be excluded as the source of these specimens either because the incisive foramen is located posterior to the infraorbital foramen or because the anterior enamel plate on the lower fourth premolar is round in occlusal outline and is located on the anterior-most portion of the tooth (e.g., Thaeler 1980). The size of these specimens is more consistent with *T. bottae* than with the larger *T. townsendii* (Townsend's pocket gopher). According to Hall (1946, 1981), only *T. talpoides* is currently present in western White Pine County (where Long Valley is located), whereas *T. bottae* occurs to the east in Steptoe Valley, and *T. townsendii* occurs to the west in central Eureka County. However, all of the archaeofaunal *Thomomys* specimens recovered at the Sunshine Locality that were identifiable to species were identified as *T. bottae.* There is little reason to think that these specimens from Sunshine are very old because most are from the upper strata, and the few that are from deeper contexts may be the result of burrowing by recent animals. It is thus probable that the pocket gopher species identification used for this area by Hall, who lists no specimens actually collected in Long Valley in his publications, is incorrect.

Family Heteromyidae (Pocket Mice, Kangaroo Rats, and Kangaroo Mice)
Dipodomys sp. (Kangaroo Rats)
Material: 1 premaxilla, 1 maxilla, 1 upper incisor, 1 humerus, 1 ulna, 1 innominate, 1 tibia: 7 specimens

Dipodomys ordii (Ord's Kangaroo Rat)
Material: 2 mandibles (both with lower fourth premolar), 1 lower fourth premolar: 3 specimens
Discussion: *D. microps* (chisel-toothed kangaroo rat) can be excluded as the source of these specimens because the lower fourth premolars have rounded anterior loops and gaps in the enamel on the buccal and lingual sides of the posterior loop. In addition, the morphology of the masseteric ridge on the mandibles is inconsistent with identification as *D. microps* (e.g., Grayson 2000a).

Family Muridae (Rats, Mice, Voles, and Relatives)
Subfamily Sigmodontinae (Deer Mice, Wood Rats, and Relatives)
Peromyscus sp. (Deer Mice)
Material: 1 premaxilla, 2 maxillae, 1 mandible: 4 specimens

Neotoma cinerea (Bushy-Tailed Wood Rat)
Material: 1 humerus: 1 specimen
Discussion: This distal humerus is distinguishable from that of a similarly sized sciurid based on the medial–lateral length of the medial epicondyle relative to its proximal–distal height. The specimen was identified as *N. cinerea* as opposed to *N. lepida* (desert wood rat), the other wood rat species that presently occurs in the region, based on its large size, which is well within the range of *N. cinerea.*

Subfamily Arvicolinae (Voles, Lemmings, and Muskrats)
Material: 4 partial crania, 1 frontal, 1 occipital, 7 maxillae, 12 mandibles, 2 alveolus fragments, 2 upper first molars, 1 upper second molar, 2 lower second molars, 1 femur: 33 specimens
Discussion: All of these specimens are from vole-sized arvicolines (e.g., *Microtus* or *Lemmiscus*).

Microtus sp. (Meadow Voles)
Material: 5 mandibles (4 with lower first molar), 5 lower first molars: 10 specimens
Discussion: These specimens were distinguished from *Lemmiscus curtatus* based on the presence of a seventh triangle on the lower first molar (e.g., Barnosky and Rasmussen 1988) or by the location of the mandibular foramen on the lingual surface of the incisive capsule. None of these specimens was identifiable below the genus level because of the lack of dental variation among the *Microtus* species that are present in the area today or that were likely to have been present here in the past.

Lemmiscus (= Lagurus) curtatus (Sagebrush Vole)
Material: 4 mandibles (all with lower first molar), 1 upper third molar, 3 lower first molars: 8 specimens
Discussion: The upper third molar was distinguished from *Microtus* based on the absence of an infold on the buccal side of the posterior loop (e.g., Barnosky and Rasmussen 1988).

Order Carnivora (Carnivores)
Family Canidae (Dogs)
Material: 1 upper second premolar: 1 specimen
Discussion: This specimen is comparable in size to *Vulpes vulpes.*

Canis sp., cf. *C. latrans* (Coyote)
Material: 1 fifth metacarpal: 1 specimen
Discussion: This proximal fifth metacarpal is the size of *C. latrans,* but the slight possibility that it is from a domestic dog cannot be ruled out.

Vulpes vulpes (Red Fox)
Material: 1 lower first molar: 1 specimen
Discussion: This specimen is distinguishable from *Urocyon cinereoargenteus* (gray fox) based on the lack of an accessory cusp on the posterio-buccal surface of the protoconid. Its size is inconsistent with identification as either *V. velox* (kit fox) or *Canis latrans.*

Family Mustelidae (Weasels, Badgers, Skunks, and Otters)
Mustela vison (American Mink)
Material: 1 tibia: 1 specimen

Order Perissodactyla (Odd-Toed Ungulates)
Family Equidae (Horses and Relatives)
Equus sp. (Horses and Relatives)
Material: 1 incisor: 1 specimen

Order Artiodactyla (Even-Toed Ungulates)
Material: 8 tooth fragments: 8 specimens

Family Camelidae (Camels and Relatives)
Camelops hesternus (Yesterday's Camel)
Material: 1 indeterminate premolar, 1 upper second molar, 1 upper third molar, 2 indeterminate molars, 1 indeterminate tooth fragment, 1 rib, 1 scapula, 3 radio-ulnae, 1 unciform, 1 first phalanx: 13 specimens
Discussion: These specimens were identified by comparison to specimens of *Camelus bactrianus* (Bactrian camel) and *Lama glama* (llama) held in the mammalogy collection of the Burke Museum at the University of Washington, in addition to consultation with Webb 1965, which discusses osteological variability among living and extinct camelid genera. One of the indeterminate molars, which consists only of a portion of the tooth enamel, was identified as cf. *Camelops hesternus*; the size of this specimen, the fact that it is rooted, and the depth of the infold all suggest *Camelops,* but this identification is not conclusive. The three radio-ulna specimens may all be from the same individual: one is a proximal right, one is a proximal left, and one is a distal left.

Descriptive Summary: Nevada State Museum–Desert Research Institute Assemblage

This section describes the mammal and bird remains recovered from terminal Pleistocene deposits at the Sunshine Locality by the Nevada State Museum and the Desert Research Institute in 1990. A list of all vertebrate specimens in this assemblage by provenience is provided in Table 7.2.[2]

Class Aves (Birds)

Order Anseriformes (Waterfowl)
Family Anatidae (Waterfowl)
Material: 1 quadrate, 1 humerus, 1 radius: 3 specimens
Discussion: No attempt was made to identify these specimens, which are all from duck-sized anatids, below the family level. As discussed above, however, specimens of both duck genera *Anas* and *Aythya* were recovered in the Hamilton College excavations.

Class Mammalia (Mammals)

Order Lagomorpha (Rabbits, Hares, and Pikas)
Family Leporidae (Rabbits and Hares)
Brachylagus idahoensis (Pygmy Rabbit)
Material: 1 radius: 1 specimen

Lepus sp. (Hares and Jackrabbits)
Material: 1 auditory bulla, 1 tibia, 1 first phalanx: 3 specimens

Order Rodentia (Rodents)
Family Sciuridae (Squirrels)
Material: 1 mandible: 1 specimen

Discussion: This specimen is from a ground squirrel–sized sciurid.

Family Muridae (Rats, Mice, Voles, and Relatives)
Subfamily Sigmodontinae (Deer Mice, Wood Rats, and Relatives)
Material: 1 mandible: 1 specimen
Discussion: This edentulous specimen is from a mouse-sized sigmodontine.

Subfamily Arvicolinae (Voles, Lemmings, and Muskrats)
Material: 1 mandible, 2 lower second molars, 1 lower third molar: 4 specimens
Discussion: These specimens are all from vole-sized arvicolines.

Microtus sp. (Meadow Voles)
Material: 4 lower first molars: 4 specimens

Lemmiscus curtatus (Sagebrush Voles)
Material: 1 mandible (with lower first molar): 1 specimen

Family Camelidae (Camels and Relatives)
Camelops hesternus (Yesterday's Camel)
Material: 3 mandibles, 1 upper third molar, 1 lower first incisor, 2 lower second incisors: 7 specimens
Discussion: The two lower second incisors are both from right mandibles, and two of the mandible specimens overlap substantially along the left diastemal crest, indicating that the remains of at least two different animals are present in this assemblage.

Taphonomy of the Sunshine Faunal Materials

Given the geologic context in which they were found, there is good reason to think that most or all of the bones recovered from the terminal Pleistocene fluvial strata at the Sunshine Locality were deposited by water. Within these deposits, the size of both faunal specimens and lithic artifacts correlates roughly with the size of the rest of the clasts in the strata in which they were found; that is, larger bones and artifacts are usually found in strata indicative of higher energies of deposition, which suggests that fluvial action was important in the deposition of these objects (Jones et al. 1996). In addition, several of the faunal specimens from the fluvial sediments exhibit surface rounding suggestive of water transport (Table 7.3); these include three unidentified leporid specimens, one pygmy rabbit specimen, one vole specimen (Arvicolinae), two *Camelops* specimens, and 14 unidentified specimens (five of which are from very large, horse- or camel-sized mammals).[3] An analysis of edge abrasion on lithic artifacts from these deposits suggests that many of

TABLE 7.2. Identified Faunal Specimens Recovered by the Nevada State Museum and the Desert Research Institute at the Sunshine Locality in 1990

TAXON	PROVENIENCE: TRENCH 10	TRENCH 17	TOTAL
Unidentified fishes	15		15
Anatidae (Waterfowl)	3		3
Mammals			
Brachylagus idahoensis (Pygmy rabbit)	1		1
Lepus sp. (Jackrabbits)	3		3
Sciuridae (Squirrels)	1		1
Sigmodontinae (Deer mice and relatives)	1		1
Arvicolinae (Voles)	4		4
Microtus sp. (Meadow voles)	4		4
Lemmiscus curtatus (Sagebrush vole)	1		1
Camelops hesternus (Yesterday's camel)		7	7
Total number of identified specimens	33	7	40
Total unidentified	ca. 230[a]	1[b]	ca. 231

Note: All specimens are from Stratum F/G (Analytic Stratum E).
[a] Two of these specimens are from a very large, camel- or horse-sized mammal.
[b] From a camel- or horse-sized mammal.

TABLE 7.3. Faunal Specimens from the Sunshine Locality with Macroscopically Visible Surface Polishing or Rounding, Such as Might Occur in Fluvial Transport

TAXON	HAMILTON COLLEGE: STRATUM F/G	NEVADA STATE MUSEUM–DESERT RESEARCH INSTITUTE: TRENCH 10, "BOTTOM OF TRENCH"	TOTAL
Leporidae (Rabbits and hares)	3		3
Brachylagus idahoensis (Pygmy rabbit)		1	1
Arvicolinae (Voles)	1		1
Camelops hesternus (Yesterday's camel)	2[a]		2
Unidentified	13[b]	1	14
Total	19	2	21

[a] These include the *Camelops* scapula and the molar enamel fragment identified as cf. *C. hesteruns.*
[b] Five of these specimens are from camel- or horse-sized mammals.

TABLE 7.4. Faunal Specimens from the Sunshine Locality with Evidence of Burning

TAXON	HAMILTON COLLEGE STRATUM						NEVADA STATE MUSEUM–DESERT RESEARCH INSTITUTE	TOTAL
	A	B	C	D/E	F/G	N.A.[a]		
Unidentified Fishes							2[b]	2
Anatidae (Waterfowl)					1			1
Leporidae (Rabbits and hares)					1			1
Brachylagus idahoensis (Pygmy rabbit)					1			1
Lepus sp. (Jackrabbits)					3[c]		1[d]	4
Sciuridae (Squirrels)					1			1
Microtus sp. (Meadow voles)					1			1
Canis latrans (Coyote)					1			1
Unidentified	16[e]		2		36[f]	1	ca. 20[g]	ca. 75
Total	16	0	2	0	45	1	ca. 23	ca. 87

[a] Stratigraphic provenience is not available for this specimen.
[b] Trench 10, Level 6A, sand.
[c] One of these is calcined.
[d] Trench 10, "Level 6?, bottom of trench."
[e] Ten of these are calcined.
[f] Four of these are calcined.
[g] Trench 10, Level 6, various.

these were also affected by stream transport (Jones et al. 1996).

However, this does not necessarily mean that most or all of the faunal specimens from the fluvial deposits were transported by water over very great distances. By far the majority of the faunal specimens from these deposits show no macroscopically visible evidence of fluvial transport, as is also the case microscopically for about 30 percent of the lithic artifacts analyzed (Jones et al. 1996). It thus appears that if these bones were redeposited by water, which is likely, they did not move very far. Furthermore, in some instances the orientation and size of the bones and artifacts within the fluvial strata did not correspond to that of the surrounding sediments, and a few tight clusters of lithic artifacts of the same rare raw material were also found (Jones et al. 1996). These observations also suggest that stream transport may not have involved very long distances in at least some cases. As discussed elsewhere in this monograph, however, efforts to find nearby areas of low-energy deposition in which bones or artifacts might have been buried and preserved more or less in primary context have proven unfruitful (see chapter 3).

Almost 90 of the faunal specimens from Sunshine have been burned (Table 7.4); the majority of these specimens are merely blackened, though 15 of them are calcined. Specimens from the fluvial deposits that were identified as burned include two unidentified fish, one duck (Anatidae), one unidentified leporid, one pygmy rabbit, four jackrabbit, one ground squirrel–sized sciurid, one vole (*Microtus* sp.), one canid (probably a coyote), and approximately 56 unidentified specimens. Two additional burned unidentified specimens were recovered from the cienega layer, and 16 were recovered from the upper eolian deposits. Of course, people may have had something to do with the burning of these specimens, but the possibility that natural fires were responsible cannot be ruled out. None of the camel, horse, or unidentified large mammal specimens is burned, nor do any of the bones from Sunshine exhibit unambiguous evidence of human activity such as cut marks. One of the duck specimens in the NSM–DRI assemblage (a radius from Trench 10, Level 6 "backhoe pile") has been gnawed by a small rodent.

Extinct Large Mammals at Sunshine

Perhaps the most significant of the faunal remains from the Sunshine Locality are the 20 *Camelops hesternus* (yesterday's camel) specimens that have been recovered there. The first *Camelops* specimens to be identified from Sunshine were collected by the Desert Research Institute and the Nevada State Museum in 1990. These include three mandible specimens (two lefts and one fused right and left), a left upper third molar, a right lower first incisor, and two right lower second incisors. These elements were found in the alluvial gravels (Final Stratum E) of Backhoe Trench 17, between .15 and 2.00 m below the top of the marsh (see chapter 2).

In the 1995 Hamilton College excavations, seven additional *Camelops* specimens were recovered from the fluvial sediments in the Strat Trench 3 (ST3) area: a premolar, a right upper second molar, a left scapula, a proximal right radio-ulna, a proximal left radio-ulna, a left unciform, and a first phalanx (see Figures 3.31, 3.33). Several lithic artifacts were found in very close proximity to the scapula and the phalanx, including the basal portion of a stemmed point preform (see Figures 3.31–3.32).[4] The depositional context of these finds, however, precluded drawing a direct association between the artifacts and the bones because it is probable that all of these objects were redeposited by fluvial transport.

One of the primary goals of the 1996 season was to expand the ST3 excavation in order to recover more bones and artifacts, partly in hope of being able to draw a firmer association between humans and extinct fauna, an issue to which we return shortly. Six more specimens of *Camelops hesternus* were found in the 1996 excavation: a left upper third molar, two cheek tooth fragments, a molar enamel fragment identified as cf. *Camelops hesternus,* a distal left radio-ulna, and a proximal rib (see Figure 3.34). Also found during this season was the horse (*Equus* sp.) incisor.

Considered in total, the NSM–DRI and Hamilton College specimens represent the remains of at least two individual camels. The NSM–DRI assemblage contains two right lower second incisors, and two of the mandible specimens in this assemblage overlap substantially along the left diastemal crest. In addition, the Hamilton College and NSM–DRI assemblages each contain one left upper third molar.

Besides the specimens identified as *Camelops hesternus* or *Equus* sp., 22 specimens that are not identifiable to taxon, but which are from very large, camel- or horse-sized mammals, have also been recovered at Sunshine. The Hamilton College excavations recovered 16 such specimens from Final Stratum E: one left mandible fragment, two rib shaft fragments, one partial humerus head, one left tibia shaft fragment, and 11 specimens from unidentified elements. A portion of an alveolus or alveoli from a mandible or maxilla and two specimens from unidentified elements were also recovered by Hamilton College, but no provenience information is available for these specimens as they were found during the backhoe excavations. The Nevada State Museum and the Desert Research Institute recovered a portion of a right premaxilla, a right tibia midshaft fragment, and a left tibia distal shaft fragment from the alluvial gravels (Final Stratum E).

One of the *Camelops* specimens from Sunshine has been directly dated by AMS dating of bone collagen to 11,330 ± 60 radiocarbon years BP. Two additional dates of 11,340 ± 50 and 11,910 ± 50 rcy BP were obtained by the NSM on two different *Camelops* teeth recovered from the 1990 excavation of Backhoe Trench 17. The two younger of these dates are significant from a purely paleontological point of view as they make these specimens the youngest well-dated *Camelops* from the Great Basin (see dates in Grayson 1993:164). They are also two of the youngest dates on *Camelops* from anywhere in North America (R. Graham, personal communication 1998) and are among the youngest secure dates for any extinct Pleistocene taxon within the Great Basin (Grayson 1993:164). The only other Great Basin sites with well-dated extinct mammals younger than 12,000 rcy BP are both located in far southern Nevada: Gypsum Cave, with *Nothrotheriops shastensis* (Shasta ground sloth); and Tule Springs, with *Equus, Camelops,* and *Mammuthus columbi* (Columbian mammoth [Grayson 1993:164; see also Beck and Jones 1997]).

The dates are also significant as regards the issue of the possible association of these bones with human activity. All of the other dates from the fluvial sediments at Sunshine that were taken on charred organic material are between 200 and 1,500 radiocarbon years younger than the date on the *Camelops* specimen. This suggests that at least some of the camel bones may have been originally deposited hundreds of years prior to having been redeposited by fluvial transport.

However, it is almost certainly the case that the artifacts recovered in the terminal Pleistocene deposits were similarly redeposited by fluvial action. In addition to the stemmed point preform noted above that was found next to the bones of *Camelops,* one fluted point has been found buried in the fluvial deposits at Sunshine. If it can be assumed that fluted points in the Great Basin are contemporaneous with Clovis occupations in the southwestern United States and Great Plains—an assumption that may be incorrect (see Beck and Jones 1997; Beck et al. 2008; Bryan and Tuohy 1999; Grayson 1993)—then it is possible that this point was originally deposited as early as about 11,200 rcy BP before being redeposited to the location in which it was found. Because the two-sigma range on the *Camelops* AMS date (11,210 to 11,450 rcy BP) nearly overlaps 11,200, it is possible that the fluted point was originally deposited around the same time that some or all of the camel bones were. Figure 4.4, however, shows the one-sigma distribution of these dates after they have been calibrated, and there is no overlap between the three dates on the camel bone (Beta-105662) or teeth (UCR-3934, UCR-3933) and any of the other dates from the alluvial gravels. A two-sigma range for Beta-105662 may overlap with that of Beta-105658 and Beta-37515 (although the latter has a very large standard deviation). The possible overlap of the other two is intriguing but nothing more at this point.

Likewise, Beck and Jones (1997) have considered the dating of stemmed points in the Great Basin and have argued that, though the majority of these points fall between 10,000 and 7500 rcy BP, the early end of their temporal range may also be as old as 11,200 rcy BP; Smith Creek Cave, located only a few valleys to the east of Sunshine, has produced stemmed points that may date to as early as 11,140 rcy BP (Beck and Jones 1997; though see Bryan and Tuohy 1999). It is thus also within the realm of possibility that the buried stemmed point preform from Sunshine was originally deposited at about the same time that the Sunshine camels died. Clearly, the issue of the age of fluted points in the Great Basin is far from settled (Beck and Jones 1997; Beck et al. 2008; Bryan and Tuohy 1999; Grayson 1993), and it is by no means certain that the buried stemmed point preform from Sunshine is that old, but it is at least possible that people were present at the Sunshine Locality while camels still roamed the landscape.

Paleoenvironmental and Biogeographic Implications

In addition to the camel and horse specimens recovered at Sunshine, the remains of smaller mammals as well as those of fishes and birds were also found in the terminal Pleistocene strata here. Although samples are small, these specimens provide some information about environmental conditions at the time of their deposition, and this information is consistent with the geologic evidence.

Bird specimens recovered from the fluvial and cienega deposits are indicative of a wetland habitat. Taxa identified include two genera of ducks (*Anas* sp. and *Aythya* sp.), geese (*Branta* sp.), swans (*Cygnus* sp.), grebes (*Podiceps* sp.), and unidentified shorebirds (Scolopacidae). In addition to these waterbirds, the remains of sharp-shinned hawk (*Accipiter striatus*) and black-billed magpie (*Pica pica*) were also recovered from the lower strata; these birds are typical Great Basin desert species but are usually found in habitats more mesic than Long Valley is today.

A total of 25 fish specimens were also recovered from the fluvial deposits during the Hamilton College excavations at Sunshine. Unfortunately, because of the fragmentary nature of these specimens, none could be identified below the taxonomic level of family. The families represented include Cyprinidae (carps and minnows), Catostomidae (suckers), and Salmonidae (trouts, chars, whitefishes, and salmons). Two of the cyprinid specimens compare favorably in size to *Gila atraria* (Utah chub). Of course, the families present here include species that inhabit a wide range of aquatic habitat types, and even the Utah chub can be found living under a variety of conditions. As a result, beyond the indication that the area supported a permanent water source, no more detailed environmental inferences can be drawn from the Sunshine fishes.

Of the small mammal (i.e., leporid and rodent) remains recovered from the terminal Pleistocene strata at Sunshine, most of the taxa represented occur in the area today and, indeed, were also recovered in the upper strata here (Table 7.1). As most of the rodent taxa present are fossorial, it may simply be that many of these animals are relatively recent in age but burrowed their own way into the lower deposits, likely transporting additional bones and artifacts downward in the process. Alternatively, at least some of the small mammal specimens from the lower strata may truly date to the terminal Pleistocene. Supporting this possibility is the fact that few krotovinas were observed in the well-bedded fluvial deposits (see Figures 3.5, 3.18, 3.20, and 3.27). If this is the case, then it would indicate that the small mammal fauna of this area has changed relatively little since the terminal Pleistocene, at least on a presence/absence scale and at the genus or family taxonomic level to which the majority of the terminal Pleistocene specimens could be identified.

There are two possibly significant exceptions to this pattern, however: two rodent taxa were recovered in the fluvial strata but not in the overlying deposits, and these two taxa tend to inhabit areas that are more mesic than Sunshine is today (Tables 7.1–7.2). One of these taxa is the genus *Microtus* (meadow voles), 14 specimens of which have been identified at Sunshine. None of these specimens could be identified below the genus level, but meadow voles in general tend to prefer more mesic conditions than presently exist at Sunshine (Hall 1946). The only voles recovered from the upper eolian deposits are sagebrush voles (*Lemmiscus curtatus*), which were also recovered from the fluvial deposits at Sunshine and which are common in sagebrush (*Artemesia*)-covered areas such as are currently found in the area (Hall 1946).

The other exception is the single wood rat (*Neotoma*) specimen recovered at Sunshine. This specimen is a partial humerus that was identified as *Neotoma cinerea*, the bushy-tailed wood rat, based on its large size. This species favors cooler habitats and is usually found only at higher elevations within the Great Basin today, though a few individuals have been collected or sighted at elevations lower than that of the floor of Long Valley (Grayson et al. 1996; Hall 1946; see also Grayson and Madsen 2000). The specimen from Sunshine was found in the fluvial sands and, because wood rats do not burrow, was probably deposited by stream flow. However, this specimen does not exhibit any visible evidence of long-distance fluvial transport—indeed, it would have to have traveled many miles if it originated in any upland setting—thus, it likely provides a terminal Pleistocene low-elevation record for this species (see Grayson and Madsen 2000; Grayson et al. 1996).

Finally, the remains of three carnivore taxa have been identified from the fluvial strata at Sunshine: *Canis* sp., cf. *C. latrans* (coyote), *Vulpes vulpes* (red fox), and *Mustela vison* (American mink). Coyotes are common in Long Valley today, but the nearest records for red foxes and minks listed by Hall (1946; see also Hall 1981) are, respectively, from the Schell Creek Range to the southeast and Ruby Valley to the north. The fact that these two species appear to have occupied Long Valley in the past but have not been recorded in the area in historic times may simply be the result of insufficient sampling in museum collections (e.g., Grayson and Livingston 1993), or it may indicate that the ranges of these species have contracted since the terminal Pleistocene.

Conclusions

It is unfortunate that the vertebrate remains from the Sunshine Locality provide no direct evidence about the subsistence practices of Paleoarchaic people in this part of the Great Basin. However, the Sunshine faunal assemblage does provide a great deal of information that is important for understanding the environment in which the earliest residents of this region lived.

The radiocarbon dates on *Camelops* specimens from Sunshine may overlap with the earliest human occupations in this region, the age of which is still somewhat unclear (Beck and Jones 1997; Bryan and Tuohy 1999; Grayson 1993). If this is the case, it would mean that at least one type of highly profitable, and probably abundant, large-bodied vertebrate resource would have been available to early Paleoarchaic people in this area. If people made use of this resource, it is likely that their overall foraging returns would have been substantially higher than those obtained by later people following the extinction of this resource (e.g., Beck and Jones 1997). Until recently no firm association between humans and extinct megafauna had been found anywhere in the Great Basin, much less any direct evidence that people actually hunted or scavenged these animals (Beck and Jones 1997; Grayson 1993). However, in the re-excavation of the Paisley 5 Mile Point Cave site (35-LK-3400) in south-central Oregon, Dennis Jenkins (2007) and his colleagues have documented the contemporaneity of humans and Pleistocene megafauna. A camel bone from one of the four caves has been dated to 12,300 ± 40 rcy BP, and a horse bone yielded a date of 11,130 ± 40 rcy BP. Three human coprolites were also recovered and have been dated by two separate laboratories to 12,300 ± 40 rcy BP (Beta Analytic, Inc.) and 12,400 ± 60 rcy BP (Oxford AMS Radiocarbon Dating Laboratory [Gilbert et al. 2008; Jenkins 2007]). The details of these new finds have not yet been fully published, but they certainly confirm both the contemporaneity of humans and megafauna and quite likely that some extinct megafaunal species were human prey.

Even if the terminal Pleistocene residents of the Sunshine Locality did not make use of extinct large mammals, it is still likely that they had much more abundant and more profitable resources available to them than did people during later times. Both the faunal and the geologic data from Sunshine indicate a wetter environment at this time with a permanent source of surface water, though one that changed from an earlier braided stream to a later slower-moving marsh. Because the diversity of biotic communities is positively correlated with effective precipitation in desert environments like the Great Basin (e.g., Grayson 1998, 2000b), such a habitat would likely have supported resources that were both more abundant and higher in caloric returns than those that could have been sustained as conditions dried out in the early Holocene. In addition to the waterfowl and fishes that we know could be found at Sunshine during the terminal Pleistocene, this location probably supported abundant edible plant resources and attracted many terrestrial vertebrates as well. As these resources became more scarce or disappeared altogether with the onset of the Holocene, people would likely have begun to make greater use of a wider range of lower-return resources, and they probably obtained these resources from a wider variety of habitat types such as the uplands, which seem to have been used more frequently later in the Paleoarchaic period (Beck and Jones 1997; Grayson 1993).

Acknowledgments

Russell W. Graham and Donald K. Grayson identified some of the first *Camelops* specimens recovered in the Hamilton College excavations. Graham also assisted in identifying additional specimens and provided helpful information concerning dates on *Camelops*. Eugene Hattori of the Nevada State Museum provided the Nevada State Museum–Desert Research Institute Sunshine faunal assemblage for analysis and also assisted greatly in obtaining radiocarbon dates on the *Camelops* incisors from this assemblage. Diana Greenlee tested *Camelops* specimens for collagen content, and John Rozdilsky provided access to comparative specimens in the collections of the Burke Museum at the University of Washington. Charlotte Beck and Donald K. Grayson provided helpful comments on an earlier version of this chapter.

Notes

1. Faunal specimens from the 1997 Hamilton College excavations, which were limited to the upper deposits on the southwestern bank of the stream channel, have not been analyzed. However, observation of the bones that were recovered while in the field suggested that the taxa represented are essentially the same as those recovered from Strata A and B during the 1993 excavations.
2. Fifteen fish specimens were also recovered in the NSM–DRI assemblage, but these have not been identified.
3. There is also one rounded unidentified specimen in the Hamilton College assemblage for which no provenience information is available.
4. This specimen is a late-stage (Stage 3) biface in the stemmed point reduction sequence (see chs. 5–6). We refer to it in our subsequent discussions as a stemmed point preform.

8

Discussion and Conclusion

Charlotte Beck and George T. Jones

The Sunshine Locality represents a unique glimpse into the world of the terminal Pleistocene/early Holocene (TP/EH) peoples of the Great Basin. The sheer number and density of artifacts at the site (many times the number of artifacts that have been collected still remain), suggesting that the area was visited repeatedly over perhaps two millennia, are unprecedented in our experience. Shortly after 9000 rcy BP Sunshine Wash appears to have dried, and the locale grew less attractive to foraging populations, although it continued to be visited intermittently into the late Archaic. Studies at the Sunshine Locality since the early 1970s have focused principally on the Paleoarchaic lithic record that is in such great abundance. It was our hope in continuing these explorations to discover primary cultural deposits that would help to answer questions of long-standing interest. Although some of those hopes remain unfulfilled, the information gained from the Sunshine Locality has added significantly to our knowledge of this period. In this final chapter we focus on a number of issues that make the Sunshine Locality such an important site for Paleoarchaic archaeology.

The Sunshine Locality is one of a small number of TP/EH sites in the Great Basin from which large numbers of fluted points and crescents have been recovered. Further, it has an extensive stemmed point assemblage and a large number and variety of other tools. It is unique among these few sites to have yielded evidence of extinct mammals and artifacts in the same stratum, however uncertain that association might be. It is also distinctive in its paleoenvironmental record, including a relatively large Pleistocene fauna and a black mat. Finally, it is unique as an open site in its large number of radiocarbon dates, providing not only a good chronological sequence for the TP/EH but also a limiting date on a fluted point and two of the youngest dates in North America for *Camelops hesternus.* We organize our discussion around three general themes that encompass these aspects of the Sunshine Locality: paleoenvironment, Paleoarchaic technology, and Paleoarchaic land use.

Paleoenvironment

The environmental history of the Sunshine Locality has been developed from stratigraphic and sedimentologic studies of the Sunshine Wash deposits and from the faunal remains they contain. This summary reviews the results of those investigations and then draws comparisons with the environmental and climatic records of the region.

The Sunshine Locality, and more specifically, Sunshine Wash, contains a stratified sequence of lacustrine, alluvial, and eolian sediments that reach more than 5 m in thickness. From numerous stratigraphic profiles along a 1.5-km reach of the wash a consistent stratigraphic sequence is evident (Figure 3.49). A system of eight stratigraphic units was developed based on test excavations conducted in 1993 (Jones et al. 1996). This system was employed during subsequent excavations to maintain stratigraphic provenience (see chapter 3). Noting that some of the stratigraphic units recognized by Jones et al. were facies distinctions rather than discrete strata, Holmes (1998) and Huckleberry (Huckleberry et al. 2001) reduced the number of stratigraphic units and simplified the stratigraphic nomenclature. Figure 4.1 presents a schematic of this stratigraphic system, which is used in the following discussion.

In Holmes and Huckleberry's stratigraphic system the basal unit (Stratum F) is lacustrine silt and sand deposited in pluvial Lake Hubbs. Some beds within Stratum F contain oblate gravels, indicating their deposition in a nearshore setting. Stratum E is coarse alluvium that was deposited at the base of a channel (channels) incised into lake deposits. These high-energy braided stream deposits contain fluvially transported bones of extinct mammals, small mammals, birds, fish, and artifacts. Stratum D contains two facies. One, an alluvial sand containing cross-bedding and cut-and-fill structures (D), rests in the channel of Sunshine Wash. The second facies (D_{df}) is a distal fan deposit that is represented in the southeastern part of the Sunshine Locality. These deposits contain beds of fine sand and silt that represent a predominantly sheet-flow mode of deposition at the terminus of fans entering Sunshine Wash from the south. These beds, which are discontinuous along the southern margin of the wash, are incised by younger drainages and are strongly deflated.

In many locations within Sunshine Wash the upper part of Stratum D is a light gray marl, which is capped by Stratum C, a dark brown pedogenic unit. Stratum C contains faunal remains and a small number of artifacts and appears to represent either a shallow pond deposit or a wetland soil (or both). Stratum C reflects a period of reduced stream flow in Sunshine Wash but the persistence of an elevated water table. Strata B and A are, respectively, eolian and channel sheet-wash facies of a thick unit that caps the Sunshine sequence. These deposits reflect drier conditions, periods like today during which Sunshine Wash maintained ephemeral stream flow. Along with Stratum C, these units are strongly bioturbated. Stratum A contains variable concentrations of artifacts depending on its location in relation to high-density surface artifact deposits. As best we can tell, these artifacts are eroded from the banks along the wash and thus are in secondary context.

Mammal bones were recovered from every stratigraphic unit. Bird and fish bones, in contrast were largely confined to the alluvial sands and gravels of Stratum E. The mammalian faunas of Strata A and B are represented mainly by rodents and lagomorphs, which are common elements of the modern fauna. Indeed, many of the former are burrowing rodents, for example, ground squirrel and pocket gopher, and they may be much younger than their position in the stratigraphic column seems to indicate. One taxon of note in the Holocene fauna is pygmy rabbit (*Brachylagus idahoensis*), whose occurrence indicates the presence of denser shrub cover than occurs at the Sunshine Locality today.

The mammalian assemblage of Stratum C differs little from later ones with the exception of the occurrence of meadow voles, which prefer mesic settings. Stratum C also contains a small bird fauna, represented by diving ducks and sharp-shinned hawk, taxa that also indicate moister conditions. In view of the depositional and pedogenic processes that produced Stratum C, the appearance of these taxa is not at all surprising.

Certainly the most interesting faunal assemblage is contained in the fluvial deposits of Stratum E. Here, too, are meadow voles, plus a more diverse suite of avian taxa, including swan and geese, and several fish taxa. The presence of all of these taxa is consistent with the interpretation of Sunshine Wash as a vigorous permanent braided stream system during the terminal Pleistocene. Stratum E also contains two extinct mammals, yesterday's camel and horse. Neither occurrence is especially surprising. At Tule Springs, for example, fluvial deposits (Unit E_1) dating between 11,500 and 13,000 rcy BP contain these taxa (Haynes 1967; Mawby 1967). Terminal Pleistocene occurrences are represented in other paleontological contexts in Nevada and Utah as well (Grayson 1993). But none of these localities possesses geologic associations of extinct fauna and artifacts (Beck and Jones 1997).

Three radiocarbon dates on *Camelops* bone and teeth yielded ages of 11,910 ± 50, 11,340 ± 50 (not C^{13} corrected), and 11,330 ± 60 rcy BP (not C^{13} corrected). The latter two of these dates are among the youngest reported for camels, not only in the Great Basin but in all of North America. Alluvial charcoal from Stratum E has been dated between 10,930 ± 60 and 9860 ± 50 rcy BP. Even at three standard deviations there is no overlap in the dates on extinct fauna and charcoal, suggesting that the former were redeposited. (This is also true of the calibrated dates [Figure 4.4].)

Alluvium older than that containing the camel bone and artifacts, identified by mechanical trenching rather than hand-excavation, is preserved in the broader sections of Sunshine Wash. Inspections of long profiles containing the older alluvium revealed no artifacts. In contrast, artifacts were occasionally found in profiles representing Stratum E. On the face of it, these observations appear to suggest that the bones of extinct mammals and the artifacts recovered in Stratum E were derived from different stratigraphic units. Without identifying their sources, however, we cannot be certain that they were not originally contained within the same stratigraphic unit. Having a common source would imply an age of greater than 11,000 rcy BP for the cultural materials, which is not entirely inconsistent with the presence of fluted and stemmed projectile points at the locality. At present, however, our best conservative interpretation is that the artifacts postdate 10,930 rcy BP and the extinct fauna appear to date at least 400 radiocarbon years earlier.

Based on the sedimentary and faunal record we offer the following reconstruction of depositional events. Subsequent to its high stand, pluvial Lake Hubbs receded toward the center of Long Valley. Thereafter, streams flowing from the southeastern section of the valley coalesced east of Sunshine Well and incised a deep, wide channel. These events are undated in Long Valley, but recent studies in nearby valleys indicate that pluvial lakes were at high stands between 13,000 and 13,800 rcy BP (e.g., Garcia and Stokes 2006; Lilliquist 1994). Often one or more still stands date to ca. 13,500 and 12,400 rcy BP (Garcia and Stokes 2006), whereas the recession of Lake Franklin paused at ca. 13,300 and 12,700 rcy BP (Lilliquist 1994). The well-dated pluvial lake record of Lake Bonneville in northwestern Utah indicates that deep lake water may have persisted as late as 12,000 rcy BP, followed by a dramatic recession lasting about 500 years (Godsey et al. 2005). The lake reached its lowest late-glacial elevation several centuries before 11,000 rcy BP (Broughton et al. 2000; Oviatt et al. 2003) and then began a transgression phase. Surrounded by a small watershed and lower mountains, Lake Hubbs may have responded more rapidly to late-glacial climate changes, descending faster than Lake Bonneville. This suggestion remains conjectural because we only begin to pick up the chronology of events at the Sunshine Locality after 12,000 rcy BP during an episode of aggradation.

The stratigraphic and faunal records of the Sunshine Locality reveal a period of higher-than-modern effective moisture lasting at least 1,500 radiocarbon years, between about 11,300 and 9800 rcy BP. During this period, Sunshine Wash held a permanent stream that went through several episodes of downcutting and aggradation. These processes may correspond to a Younger Dryas–age transgression of Lake Hubbs, but there is no indication that lake waters ever expanded sufficiently to reach the Sunshine Locality. Elsewhere in the Great Basin various proxy records indicate greater effective moisture at this time. Lake transgressions (Briggs et al. 2005; Oviatt et al. 1992), the formation of organic layers (black mats [Quade et al. 1998]), and mammalian faunas (Grayson 2000a, 2000b) point to cooler and moister conditions during the Younger Dryas. The precise mechanisms for this increased moisture—for example, lower temperatures, intensified winter storms or summer monsoons—and the complex spatial and temporal patterns they induced are not well understood (Briggs et al. 2005; Oviatt et al. 2003).

Extinct mammals were components of the local fauna, at least during the early part of the period. Redeposition of bones by the Sunshine stream is apparent in the discrepancy between radiocarbon dates of charcoal in sediments encasing the bone and artifacts and of dates directly on bone and teeth. The stream grew less competent over the period, depositing finer alluvium, and finally became ephemeral. The end of this period is represented by marl deposits in the channel and the development of wetland soil across the floor of the wash. This soil reaches a thickness of nearly 1 m in some locations, probably as a result of the presence of local seeps and substantial contributions of eolian dust.

A shift to markedly dryer conditions, represented by the cessation of paludal deposition/wetland soil formation and the inception of eolian activity and channel margin erosion, occurred after 9800 rcy BP. This transition is coincident roughly with two wildfire events. These fires are represented by a charcoal couplet for which radiocarbon dates of 9800 and 8500 rcy BP (not C^{13} corrected) are available. These dates differ by about 1,300 radiocarbon years, and their difference is difficult to reconcile. The two lenses are separated by no more than 2 cm of sediment, which is hardly enough to suggest that these fires are of such different ages. The older of the two dates is an AMS assay on charcoal, whereas the younger date was derived by conventional dating methods on charcoal-rich sediment. Judging on the greater likelihood of contamination by soil humates, the younger date appears to be less secure.

The regional paleoenvironmental record does not help to resolve in favor of either date. The older date approximates a resumption of insolation-driven global warming at the end of the Younger Dryas. Thompson (1992) reports that Lake Franklin, in nearby Ruby Valley, became increasingly saline after 10,400 rcy BP. Madsen (2000) reports that after several centuries of increasing salinity Lake Bonneville dropped abruptly around 10,100 rcy BP. Black mats, like that represented by Stratum C, date to a period between 9500 and 10,500 rcy BP in southern Nevada (Quade et al. 1998). Oviatt et al. (2003) report organic mats in the Bonneville Basin dating between approximately 9400 and 9700 rcy BP. From these data, it appears that hydrologic systems in many parts of the Great Basin responded to climate change shortly after ca. 10,000 rcy BP. The end of the Younger Dryas is less evident in the regional biotic record (Rhode 2000), but this may reflect that these records are not well resolved at this time.

The biotic record does, however, record substantial drying in the millennium between 9000 and 8000 rcy BP. The Ruby Valley pollen record (Thompson 1992), for example, suggests a marked expansion of shadscale vegetation about 8750 rcy BP. Thompson (1992) attributes this to the retraction of shallow lakes and marshes and the consequent development of broad playa surfaces. Farther afield, at Homestead Cave in the northern Bonneville Basin, Grayson (2000a, 2000b) reports that the mammalian fauna reflect cool and moist conditions before 8300 rcy BP and much warmer and drier conditions after that time. At the Sunshine Locality, this period is marked by the accumulation of eolian sediments along the edges of the channel bottom.

In summary, the Sunshine Locality appears to have been a very inviting environment for humans between 11,300 and 9800 rcy BP, during which a permanent stream flowed in Sunshine Wash. Late in this period, as the stream became more ephemeral, marshes and meadows developed in the wash and perhaps along other drainages, providing a productive habitat, for both humans and other animals. Available fauna included numerous large and small mammals, such as camel, horse, artiodactyls, and lagomorphs, as well as fish and waterbirds, such as swans, geese, and diving ducks. Although we have no data on the plant species available at the site during this period, a number of edible species were undoubtedly available,

TABLE 8.1. Radiocarbon Dates Reported to Be Associated with Fluted Points in the Great Basin

SITE	UNCALIBRATED RADIOCARBON DATE	REFERENCE
Danger Cave, UT	10,080 ± 130 BP	Madsen and Rhode 1990
Sunshine Locality, NV	10,320 ± 50 BP	Huckleberry et al. 2001
Henwood Site, CA	8470 ± 370 BP	Douglas et al. 1988
Connley Cave No. 5, OR[a]	9540 ± 260 7 BP 7430 ± 140 BP	Beck et al. 2004

[a] It is debated whether this point is fluted (see Beck et al. 2004).

just as they were in similar environments elsewhere in the area, such as Ruby Valley to the north. It is unclear, however, whether early visitors to the site made use of floral resources because of the near absence of ground stone. Some time between 9800 and 8500 rcy BP the local climate dried considerably, making the site a much less attractive place to visit, and thus humans were present only intermittently after this time. Judging from the small number of Rosegate and Desert Series points in the assemblage, people visited the site very rarely in the last 1,500 to 2,000 years.

Paleoarchaic Technology

Analysis of the stone artifact assemblage from the Sunshine Locality has provided an opportunity to examine questions of long standing about Paleoarchaic technology. For instance, what is the relationship between Clovis and Great Basin Fluted points? What is the temporal and functional relation between fluted points and Great Basin Stemmed points? Aside from the differences in the point forms, are the tool kits different as well? Where do crescents, which are found nearly exclusively in the Great Basin, fit into the scheme? Here we address several of these issues using the Sunshine assemblage as a springboard for comparison.

Fluted Points in the Great Basin

The prevailing thought concerning Great Basin Fluted points is that they represent the earliest human occupation of this region as they do elsewhere in North America and are therefore representative of Clovis (Fagan 1988; Willig 1988). This inference has never been demonstrated, as we have argued previously (e.g., Beck and Jones 1997, 2007; Beck et al. 2004; Beck and Jones 2008). In fact, the few dates that are associated with Great Basin Fluted points are all younger than the dates for Clovis (Table 8.1). Most of these dates are believed to be in error (Beck and Jones 1997; Grayson 1993), but what if they are not? There are numerous fluted point types in other regions, including Barnes and Gainey in the northeast and Cumberland, Simpson, and Beaver Lake in the southeast, that postdate Clovis and are morphologically different from it. The best example, of course, is Folsom, which lasted on the Plains until 10,200 rcy BP (Haynes 1992; Taylor et al. 1996; Waters and Stafford 2007). There is no reason to assume that Great Basin Fluted points do not have a similar history; that is, even if Clovis *is* represented in the Great Basin, it could be followed by other, later fluted forms.

In chapter 6 we compared the Sunshine fluted points with those from a number of Clovis and Folsom contexts, finding that only two specimens exhibit a Clovis-like morphology. Further, the fluting technology of the fluted preform (Figures 6.8–6.9) is somewhat different from that of Clovis, more similar, in fact, to the fluting technology of Folsom but certainly not as complex. We concluded that the majority of the Sunshine points are not Clovis but more likely a later form, such as developed elsewhere across North America. The limiting date of 10,325 rcy BP suggests an occupation coeval with Folsom. Is this the case for other Great Basin Fluted points as well?

Recently we conducted a cladistic analysis comparing the morphological features of 343 Great Basin Fluted points (we expanded original data compiled by A. Taylor [2002, 2003]) with the Clovis data presented in Table 6.2, based on a similar set of criteria used in our analysis of the Sunshine fluted points in chapter 6 (Beck and Jones 2007). The results of this analysis reveal that some Great Basin Fluted points conform to Clovis point morphology and others do not, suggesting that a morphology indistinguishable from Clovis is represented among Great Basin Fluted points but that at least one other, non-Clovis, fluted form occurs as well. We have reason to believe, however, that the appearance of Clovis in this region was somewhat later than on the Plains.

Elsewhere (e.g., Beck and Jones 2007, 2008) we have made the argument that sites containing Clovis points appear to be oldest in the southern Plains and grow progressively younger to the north and west (but see Waters and Stafford 2007). If this pattern is accurate and represents the expansion of Clovis populations, their appearance in the Great Basin likely dates to the latter part of the accepted Clovis time period (i.e., 11,500–10,900 rcy BP). We have also argued that the presence or absence of Clovis blades, which Collins and Lohse (2004:176) suggest are almost as diagnostic as Clovis projectile points, might aid in establishing the relative timing of this entry. Clovis blades are quite prevalent in the southern Plains but decrease in number with distance from that area (Figure 8.1). Because the earliest Clovis sites are in the southern Plains, this pattern suggests that with time, use of blades

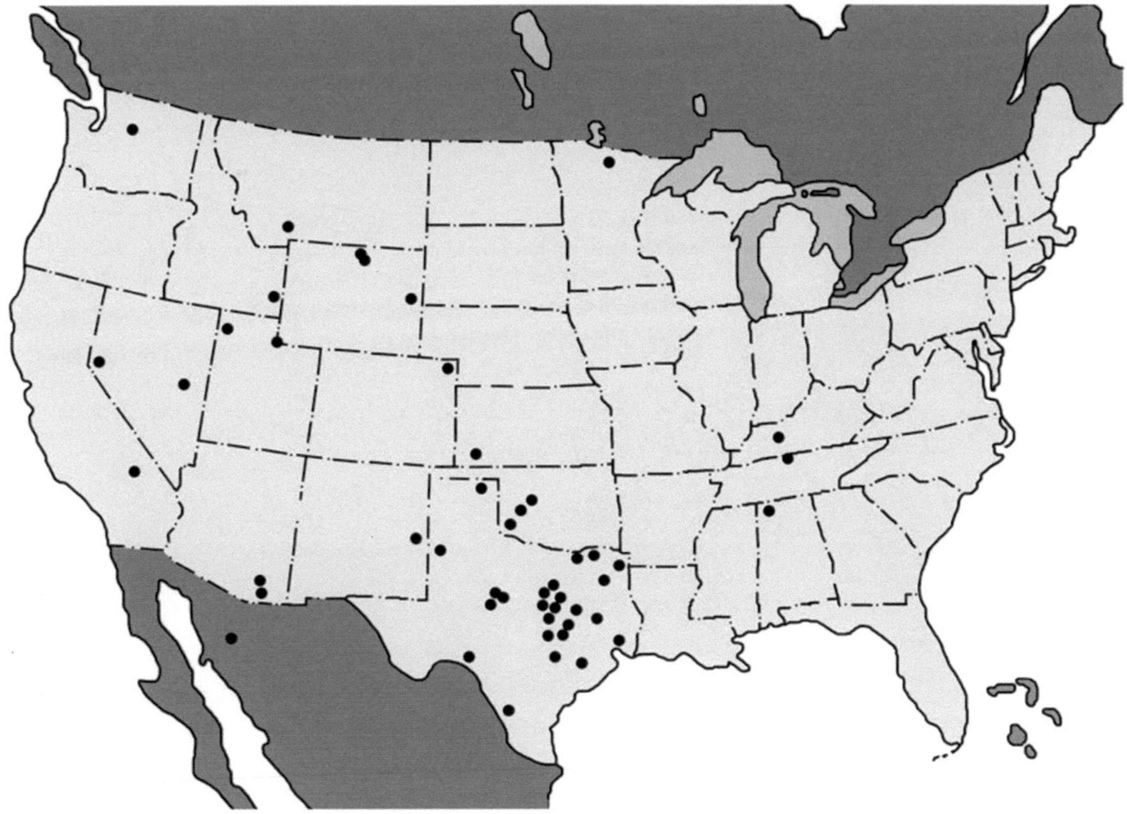

FIGURE 8.1. The distribution of Clovis blades and blade cores (from Collins 1999b; Dennis Stanford, personal communication 2005).

decreased. It would follow, then, that if Clovis people entered the Great Basin during the latter part of the Clovis time period, blades would be rare. This is indeed the case.

In the Great Basin, one Clovis blade was found in the Pine Grove Hills of western Nevada (David Rhode, personal communication 2002), at least three were collected at China Lake (Davis 1978a, 1978b), one was recovered from the alluvial gravels at the Sunshine Locality, and two possible blades were found in the Hutchinson–Noyes assemblage from the Sunshine Locality (see Figures 3.22A and 5.36). From the Columbia Plateau, five blades have been recovered from the East Wenatchee cache in Washington (Gramly 1993). In addition, two blade cores were reported by private collectors, one from southeastern Idaho and the other from northeastern Utah (Dennis Stanford, personal communication 2004). Although these cores are not associated with fluted points, Stanford confirms that they are quite similar to Clovis blade cores and suspects that they are Clovis.

The presence of blades in the Sunshine assemblage suggests that Clovis people may have passed through this area. This is supported by the fact that two of the Sunshine fluted points conform to Clovis morphology. However, only three blades have been recovered from this site; no blade cores have ever been collected or even noted. Because these cores are so distinctive, if Hutchinson or Noyes had found one, they certainly would have collected it. The earliest date from the alluvial gravels, 10,930 ± 60 rcy BP, adds support to a late arrival of Clovis to the area. Other dates from the Stratum E alluvium, however, range from 10,690 to 9860 rcy BP and more likely date the primary fluted point occupation. These dates, together with the paucity of Clovis blades and the morphological differences between Clovis and all but two of the Sunshine fluted points, suggest that Clovis is *not* represented at Sunshine in any significant way. Instead, these data suggest that the fluted point component represents a later form coeval with Folsom. The question remains, however, as to whether the fluted point occupation at Sunshine was coeval with at least some part of the stemmed point occupation.

Unfortunately, the Sunshine data do not help a great deal in answering this question. A fluted point and a stemmed point preform were both retrieved from the alluvial gravels (Stratum E), the latter in the same unit and

TABLE 8.2. Early Radiocarbon Dates Associated with Large Stemmed Points

REGION	SITE	DATE (RADIOCARBON YEARS BP)	POINT TYPE	REFERENCE
Columbia Plateau	Coopers Ferry, WA	11,320 ± 80 11,410 ± 130	Lind Coulee	Davis 2001
		10,740 ± 220	Windust	
	Marmes, WA	10,810 ± 275 10,750 ± 90	Windust	Rice 1972
	Sentinel Gap, WA	10,680 ± 190	Haskett	Galm et al. 2004
	Buhl, ID	10,675 ± 95	Lind Coulee?	Green et al. 1998
Great Basin	Connley Cave No. 4B, OR	11,200 ± 200 10,600 ± 190	Haskett	Bedwell 1973
	Smith Creek Cave, NV	11,140 ± 120 10,840 ± 250 10,740 ± 130 10,700 ± 180 10,660 ± 220 10,630 ± 190 10,570 ± 160	Lake Mohave?	Bryan 1979
	Wildcat Canyon, OR	10,600 ± 200	Parman Windust	Dumond and Minor 1983
	Handprint Cave, NV	10,740 ± 70	Lind Coulee?	Gruhn and Bryan 1988
	Sunshine Locality, NV	10,700 ± 180	Stem only	Huckleberry et al. 2001
Bonneville Estates	Rockshelter, NV	10,560 ± 50	Fragment	Goebel 2007; Graf 2007

15 cm above the camel bones recovered in 1995. This geologic association is suggestive of the contemporaneity of fluted and stemmed points, but only in the broadest sense.

We point out, however, that, except for the recent dates from the Paisley Caves in Oregon, which are not associated with any projectile points, all of the earliest radiocarbon dates in the Great Basin and Columbia Plateau are associated with stemmed points (Table 8.2); this suggests that the latter were coeval with, if not slightly earlier than, fluted points in those regions, an argument Alan Bryan (1980, 1991) has been making for years. After many years of searching for buried fluted point sites that date to, or in excess of, 11,000 rcy BP, Great Basin archaeologists still have not found them, and chances are, they never will.

In sum, the data from the Sunshine Locality and other sites in the Great Basin suggest that Clovis may be present in the region, but its occurrence dates to the latter part of the Clovis time period. Further, the temporal and morphological data suggest that Clovis was followed by a later fluted form, which is represented at the Sunshine Locality, although we do not know how long this form persisted. We do know that stemmed points persisted in the Great Basin until perhaps 7500 rcy BP (Beck and Jones 1997), and the large number of sites where these points occur without fluted points suggest that the latter did not persist as long. Finally, the data do not support a "Clovis-first" appearance in the Great Basin but, rather, are suggestive that stemmed point forms are at least as old, if not older, than Clovis in this region.

Stemmed Point Form and Function

A number of different types have been defined over the years that reflect modalities in stemmed point morphology. The general similarity of these types to one another has often been noted and led Tuohy and Layton (1977) to combine them into the Great Basin Stemmed Series. In fact, there has been some suggestion that these types represent nothing more than different "peaks" along a continuum of breakage and resharpening, beginning with the largest (Cougar Mountain) and ending with the smallest (Silver Lake [e.g., Amick 1996]). The Sunshine assemblage provides an excellent opportunity to examine this issue.

Even our preliminary studies of the morphology of Silver Lake points made it clear that these points are quite different from those of the other four types present in the Sunshine assemblage (e.g., Cougar Mountain, Ovate, Parman, and Lake Mohave). They have relatively short stems, which most often expand proximally from the neck and then contract, a shape that is almost impossible to have resulted from the resharpening of any of the other point forms given the average width and proximal shoulder angle of these stems. In addition, all of the other point forms have long, contracting stems that vary little from type to type except in length and cross-sectional shape. Thus, we concluded that the Silver Lake type *does* represent a different entity; that is, it is a valid type. The case for the other four types, however, is less conclusive.

On the one hand, an examination of size, raw material, and the degree of resharpening suggests that these four forms could indeed represent a continuum, resulting from breakage and resharpening, from the largest, Cougar Mountain, to the smallest, Lake Mohave. On the other hand, the location and mechanics of resharpening suggest otherwise. Certainly the resharpening of one form into another did occur, as evidenced by several Cougar Mountain stem fragments in the Sunshine assemblages reworked into Lake Mohave points. In other cases, however, it is clear that points of this type were not the result of resharpening but were the intended end product of the manufacturing process. This suggests that the more important issue is the intended function of a particular form.

Since the first discovery of stemmed points on the beaches of Pleistocene Lake Mohave, the general assumption has been that they served as projectile points. Some time after we started working in Butte Valley, however, we began to suspect that projectile use was not the sole reason for their manufacture; instead, we believed that these artifacts probably served a number of different functions (e.g., Beck and Jones 1993). Therefore, the initial question we addressed concerning their function was whether these different forms were used as part of a projectile system. Using the concept of performance characteristics (e.g., Schiffer and Skibo 1987), an object used exclusively as a projectile point should be designed for balance and stability, as evidenced by symmetry and weight distribution, as well as have the ability to penetrate the target, as evidenced by a sharp tip and edges as well as a relatively thin cross section (Christenson 1986; Flenniken and Wilke 1989; Frison 1973, 1976; Frison and Zeimens 1980; Van Buren 1974). In most cases, points of all five types are asymmetrical and excessively thick; they also are quite often worn, sometimes heavily so, suggesting some other use.

Focusing on the specific forms, the data indicate that Silver Lake and Lake Mohave points were not part of a projectile technology but that each form served a specific function or set of functions. We have already mentioned the morphological differences between Silver Lake points and those of the other four types. Almost all of the Silver Lake points in the Sunshine assemblage have been resharpened, and most are worn. Use-wear is almost always abrasion, although two specimens exhibit crushing and a third exhibits chipping along one edge of the blade. Small, abraded high points that remain along the edges of some resharpened blades suggest that these points were heavily abraded as well, before they were resharpened. Some specimens are so thoroughly resharpened that virtually nothing remains of the original edges, even on the stem. The abrasion present on these points is suggestive of intensive cutting or sawing motions, which could also result in the chipping and crushing mentioned above. These points occasionally may have been put to other uses as well. For instance, the tip of one specimen is resharpened into a narrow point that is abraded, suggesting possible use as a graver or drill. There is, however, nothing about these use-wear patterns that suggests Silver Lake points were used as projectile points.

The function(s) of Lake Mohave points appears to be related to the distinctive diamond shape of their blades. These blades are often beveled, which may have been a means of achieving this diamond shape. As in the case of Silver Lake points, Lake Mohave points often exhibit abrasion on the edge of the blades, again consistent with a cutting or sawing motion. In at least two cases, the edge is actually polished, indicating extensive sawing action of a medium like rawhide. Unlike Silver Lake points, however, a number of the Lake Mohave points exhibit arris abrasion or striations on one surface. This is especially true of those with chisel tips. The chisel tips also exhibit striations, which run perpendicular to the tip edge. Although some of these tips are quite thin, these use-wear patterns suggest that these particular points were, in fact, used as chisels.

The other three forms appear to have seen more general use, such as cutting, slicing, and sawing, suggesting use as knives. Haft abrasion on the surfaces of the stem and lower portion of the blade of some Cougar Mountain points, however, suggests that considerable pressure was exerted on the point while in the haft. Also, breakage patterns on points of this type indicate twisting motions that may have resulted from use as thrusting spears. All of these patterns argue against use as projectile points.

Interestingly, similar forms (e.g., Lind Coulee and Haskett) on the Columbia Plateau do fulfill the criteria for use as a projectile point. That is, they are symmetrical with sharp edges and point and are more finely made than the stemmed points in the Sunshine assemblage. The Lind Coulee type is also associated with the earliest radiocarbon dates in that region (11,410 ± 130 and 11,370 ± 40 rcy BP) from the Coopers Ferry site (Davis 2001; see Table 8.2). Although the dates associated with stemmed points in the Great Basin are younger, there are two instances of pre–11,000 rcy BP dates in this region at sites from which stemmed points were recovered (Table 8.2). There is a date of 11,200 ± 200 rcy BP associated with Haskett at Connley Cave No. 4 in central Oregon (Bedwell

1973). The other two dates from this stratum, however, are 10,600 ± 190 and 9760 ± 180 rcy BP, both from levels below that yielding the early date, which suggests that there was some degree of stratigraphic mixture.

The only other pre–11,000 rcy BP date possibly associated with a stemmed point in the Great Basin is from Smith Creek Cave. The Mount Moriah occupation is dated between 11,140 ± 120 and 9940 ± 160 rcy BP (Bryan 1979, 1988).[1] This occupation, however, consists of a number of dated hearths, which vary in age, the oldest of which has a single date of 11,140 ± 200 rcy BP. All of the other 11 dates are post–11,000 rcy BP. It is not clear with which hearth(s) the stemmed points are associated, but the likelihood is that they, too, are post–11,000 rcy BP in age, which would be consistent with all of the other dates associated with stemmed points in the Great Basin. If stemmed points actually represent the earliest human occupation of the Columbia Plateau, diffusing from there southward into the Great Basin and eastward onto the Plains, then it appears that, as this technology diffused into the Great Basin, it diversified in form *and* in function, no longer serving exclusively as a projectile.

In 1997 we argued that stemmed points and lanceolate points (fluted and unfluted) were not technological alternatives but, rather, forms that performed different functions within the same tool kit. The Paleoarchaic tool kit thus encompassed an evolving projectile technology—fluted to unfluted lanceolate, eventually replaced by the square-base form (i.e., Windust)—and a thrusting/processing technology—Cougar Mountain, Parman, and Lake Mohave (Beck and Jones 1997:204). We based this argument on the fact that the earliest dates in the Great Basin are associated with stemmed, not fluted, points, suggesting to us that stemmed points were at least coeval with fluted points in the Great Basin. However, at that time we had no technological data to support this argument. The results of our analysis of the Sunshine fluted, unfluted lanceolate, and stemmed points now provide some of those data.

First, the comparison of fluted and unfluted lanceolates suggests that they represent two distinct entities. Unfluted lanceolate points were not simply too thin to flute, as has been argued by Hofman (1992) for Midland points. Because fluted and unfluted points have never been found together in stratigraphic context, and because unfluted points are not associated with any radiocarbon dates, we have no way of knowing their temporal relation, but the fact that there are four times as many unfluted ($n = 72$) as fluted ($n = 17$) lanceolates in the Sunshine assemblage suggests that use of the former persisted much longer than that of the latter. This same logic should hold for Windust A, which in our scenario replaced unfluted lanceolate points as the projectile; that is, there should be an even greater number of Windust points, assuming population growth over time and continuing visitation at the site. There are, however, only 14 Windust A points in the Sunshine assemblage. The earliest date for this type in the Great Basin is 9920 ± 470 rcy BP from the Paulina Lake site in central Oregon (Connolly and Jenkins 1999). Intensive use of the Sunshine Locality ended between 9800 and 8500 rcy BP, which may account for the small number of Windust points there. Thus, in general, the Sunshine assemblage supports a succession of point forms, from fluted to unfluted lanceolate to square based.

The question remains, however, why the function of the stemmed point changed. We have an idea, although not much data to support it. This idea relates to the arrival of Clovis people on the Plateau at approximately 11,000 rcy BP, where they would have encountered people carrying a stemmed technology. These latter people, we argue, crossed the mountains onto the Plains carrying Lind Coulee and Haskett points. We might assume that as these people came into contact, they shared their technology with one another. As the combination of these technologies moved into the Great Basin, where the lithic terrain as well as the environment were very different from those in both the Columbia Plateau and the Plains, perhaps a combination of raw material availability, or limited knowledge of that availability, and changes in subsistence fostered a change in function of existing stemmed forms and the evolution of new ones. For example, Haskett is not well represented in the Great Basin. This type is present, for example, at Connley Caves in central Oregon but not in the Steens Mountain assemblage in southeastern Oregon (Beck 1984; Bedwell 1973; Jones 1984). There are five Haskett points in the surface assemblage collected from Dugway Proving Ground (Jones et al. 2002) in the western Bonneville Basin, but there are none in our assemblages from Butte, Long, and Jakes valleys to the west. This scarcity indicates that Haskett, as a projectile point, reached the Great Basin but did not persist.

The Cougar Mountain form is likely the Great Basin version of the Lind Coulee form (see discussion of typology in chapter 4). This type is much more prevalent in the northern half of the Great Basin (i.e., Oregon, northern Nevada, and northwestern Utah) than in the southern half, especially the Mojave Desert. And by the time it arrived at the Sunshine Locality, it no longer functioned as a projectile point.

Raw material becomes an important issue at this point in the discussion. In our original argument the projectile technology was always predominantly chert and the thrusting/processing technology was predominantly obsidian and fine-grained volcanics (FGV). If we look to

Clovis origins on the Plains, the primary high-quality raw material in that region is chert, which explains why all of the fluted points (both Clovis and Folsom) are manufactured from that material. In the southern Plains there are two extensive high-quality sources, Alibates and Edwards; these are quite distinctive and are recognized in most Clovis assemblages of the region, even in the far northern Plains. Obsidian is present in some areas of the Columbia Plateau, but although some fluted points in that region are made from this material, chert remains the toolstone of choice. In the Great Basin, however, more than half (56.9 percent) of the 343 points in the fluted point database are made from obsidian, and only 38.2 percent are made from chert. This change in raw material representation possibly reflects the different lithic terrain of the Great Basin, where, with the exception of the Tosawihi Quarries in northeastern Nevada, chert mostly occurs in small local outcrops. The material in these outcrops often comes in "small packages" and variable quality. Most of these occur on the slopes or at higher elevations, where fluted points are rarely found. In fact, there are several very distinctive, high-quality sources within about 25 mi of the Sunshine Locality that are not represented in the assemblage. They were, however, used by later Archaic populations in the region. One explanation for the neglect of these sources by the earliest populations in this region is that they had not yet been discovered.

Both the fluted and unfluted points from Sunshine, however, are predominantly chert, with only a few made from obsidian. Although this could be a sampling problem, it likely reflects the paucity of obsidian in this region. Three of the unfluted lanceolates are made from FGV, a material that fluted points are rarely made from. The use of FGV becomes even more pronounced among Windust points; only one is chert, seven are obsidian, and six are FGV. The use of this latter material is hard to explain other than the lack of obsidian sources or knowledge of good-quality chert.

Raw material use for stemmed points is similar to that for fluted points early on but, like that for fluted points, changed in the Great Basin. On the Columbia Plateau, Haskett and Lind Coulee points are most often made from chert, although they are sometimes made from obsidian. Cougar Mountain points, however, are much less often made from chert. They are made from obsidian where available but more often from FGV. We have argued elsewhere (Jones and Beck 1999) that this is related to access to raw material nodules large enough for the manufacture of these points. This does not preclude the selection of stone for functional reasons, of course, say, for hafted butchering tools, as well as for designs that extend the use-life of the tool. Once we see Cougar Mountain points in the Great Basin, we also begin to see other stemmed forms, and these are also manufactured predominantly from FGV. The evolution of these forms (and possibly the material from which they are made) likely had to do with subsistence diversification.

One of the important components of the TP/EH environment of the Great Basin was the abundant shallow-water resources, which appear to have been the focus of Paleoarchaic subsistence from the beginning. The Sunshine Locality provided such a setting, with a permanent stream when people first arrived and an extensive marsh by ca. 9800 rcy BP. The large numbers of artifacts over such a sizeable area are testimony to repeated visits to the site for more than 1,000 radiocarbon years. The earliest people in the area most likely focused more heavily on hunting and fishing than on plants, as evidenced by the almost total lack of ground stone at the site. Thus the uses to which stemmed points were put were likely related to the processing of meat and fish rather than plant foods, although the latter cannot be ruled out.

In summary then, we amend our 1997 scenario somewhat, based on the data from the Sunshine Locality. People colonizing the Columbia Plateau, likely via the Columbia River from the Pacific coast, carried a long, stemmed projectile in the form of Lind Coulee and possibly Haskett. People entering the Columbia Plateau from the Plains carried a fluted lanceolate projectile. Moving southward into the Great Basin, which had a different environment and lithic terrain, the stemmed point form and function began to evolve to fit the circumstances, and the fluted point became the projectile. At this point, then, there were two evolving technologies performing different functions within the same tool kit: an evolving projectile technology—fluted to unfluted lanceolate to square based—and a thrusting/processing technology—Cougar Mountain, Ovate, Parman, Lake Mohave, and Silver Lake.

Paleoarchaic Biface Technology

In all of the Paleoarchaic assemblages we have examined in eastern and central Nevada, biface reduction is a dominant theme. In fact, it is *the* dominant theme in all but the Sunshine assemblage (and perhaps the Limestone Peak Locality 1 assemblage from Jakes Valley). The assemblages from Butte Valley, for example, are composed almost completely of spent stemmed points, bifaces of all but the very earliest reduction stage, biface reduction flakes, and debitage. Besides stemmed points, there are few formal tools represented.

In the prevalence of bifaces, Paleoarchaic assemblages are similar to Paleoindian assemblages elsewhere in North America. This feature has led many archaeologists (e.g., Goodyear 1989; Kelly 1988; Kelly and Todd 1988) to suggest that Paleoindian lithic technology was organized around the use of bifacial cores because they were efficient material packages that were portable, supplied raw material for tools of different sizes and morphologies, and could be transformed ultimately into a critical tool form, a projectile point. Although Kelly (2001:72) notes that the efficiency of using bifaces as cores has not been systematically tested, archaeologists continue to be persuaded by the compelling logic of this argument. It is widely accepted that Clovis people, at least on the northern Plains and the Columbia Plateau, did practice such a strategy (e.g., Bradley 1982; Frison 1991; Hofman 1992; MacDonald 1985; Wilke et al. 1991; Woods and Titmus 1985; but see Collins 1999a, 1999b; LeTourneau 2000); this certainly was the case for Folsom (Collins 1999b). Clovis cache assemblages such as Anzick (Wilke et al. 1991), Simon (Woods and Titmus 1985), Fenn (Frison and Bradley 1999), and East Wenatchee (Gramly 1993; Mehringer and Foit 1990) contain a range of bifaces: relatively large bifacial flake cores, bifacial fluted point blanks, and fluted point preforms. Based on their analysis of the Anzick assemblage, Wilke et al. (1991) suggest that the bifacial flake core represents the primary reduction stage in Clovis technology and served as a source of flake blanks for tools such as scrapers and gravers.

We have suggested that highly mobile Paleoarchaic people also employed such a strategy (Beck and Jones 1997). More recently we have conducted analyses of biface assemblages from lithic quarry/workshop and occupation/task sites and now recognize that biface core technology is not a unitary phenomenon. There is good reason to believe that Paleoarchaic people employed a different core reduction strategy for lanceolate and stemmed forms (e.g., Fagan 1988; Pendleton 1979; Warren and Phagan 1988; but see Amick 2004). Pendleton (1979), for example, notes that there was a preference shown for the type of flake blank selected to manufacture the two forms. Beyond this, we have found that, in the case of stemmed points manufactured from FGV, flake blanks were reduced to a very considerable degree, either at the lithic source or at a nearby occupation site (Beck et al. 2002), and then transported with only final shaping and thinning to be completed. As such, these bifaces could not serve as effective sources of large flake blanks. Rather, little more than small flakes for expedient tools could be derived from these bifaces once they entered the traveling tool kit of Paleoarchaic foragers.

Biface reduction at Sunshine, however, appears to have been directed toward a wider range of end products. Fewer than half of all of the bifaces at Sunshine are production bifaces; the remainder are crescents, scrapers, drills, unique forms, or amorphous bifaces, all of which are made predominantly of chert. The presence of these tools (in both bifacial and unifacial form) is one of the aspects of the Sunshine assemblage that differs from most of the other Paleoarchaic assemblages we have examined. Certainly, the reduction of FGV toolstone at Sunshine was focused toward the manufacture of stemmed points as it was elsewhere. Also, a number of production bifaces are worn, indicating that they were used as tools themselves. But biface reduction of chert was focused toward a variety of end products.

This use of chert differs from that associated with the Clovis technology discussed above, where bifaces are often quite large and served initially as cores for flakes to be made into a variety of tools. Although the Clovis biface ultimately may have been reduced into a fluted point preform, it served as a toolstone source for all Clovis stone tools, such as scrapers, gravers, bifacial knives, drills, and ultimately, fluted points. This is not the case for bifaces in the stemmed point technology, evidenced by the raw material composition of other tools in the Sunshine assemblage. If FGV bifaces were transported for use as cores, other tools would also be made of this material, but they are not. They are most often made from chert (and sometimes obsidian where that material is plentiful): 94 percent of the tools from the Sunshine assemblage are made from chert; only 4 percent are made from FGV.

Of course raw material representation is, in part, a function of the mechanical requirements of the tools (Amick 1993; Beck and Jones 1990b). Thus, it could be that chert *was* carried in the form of bifacial cores. It is certainly true that the majority of chert flakes with platforms in the Sunshine assemblage are biface reduction flakes (see Table 5.20). We found this to be true in Paleoarchaic assemblages we have analyzed from Butte and Jakes valleys as well (e.g., Beck and Jones 1990a, 1990b). If chert was carried as bifacial cores, we would expect the majority of chert tools to have been made on biface reduction flakes. Very few of the unifacial tools from Sunshine retain their platforms, but about half of those are made on biface reduction flakes, whereas the remainder are made on flakes or chunks from general core reduction. Of the 22 cores represented in the Sunshine assemblage, 18 are chert (see Table 5.88); only 15, however, were subjected to special analysis. All are relatively small, and 13 of the 15 are amorphous cores. Two may be polyhedral (see Figure 5.35I, J), but none is bifacial. Thus, we cannot evaluate how chert was carried, but it is certainly the case that FGV, the predominant material used by the manufacturers of stemmed points, was carried as bifaces either for the purpose of general cutting functions or as late-stage preforms for stemmed points. Also, because of the numerous small chert sources located in the vicinity of Long Valley, as well as elsewhere in the region, it was probably not necessary to carry chert in the form of bifacial cores, but we are still left with the fact that a large number of chert flakes from Sunshine and other Paleoarchaic assemblages in the region are biface reduction flakes, a pattern that we still do not fully understand.

The Other Part of the Tool Kit

Since working at the Sunshine Locality, we have been struck by the remarkable similarity between the tools found there and those in Paleoindian assemblages in eastern North America and the Plains and that tool categories contained in Gramly's *Guide to the Palaeo-Indian Artifacts of North America* (1990) are applicable to the tools in the Sunshine assemblage. Similarities include general categories, such as several different kinds of scrapers, gravers, notches, drills, and chisels, but also more specific tool classes, such as spurred end scrapers and compass gravers. The morphological similarities of tool forms across such a large expanse of space suggests some similarity in subsistence strategy across much of North America, as argued by Kelly and Todd in 1988. It also suggests a relatively fast colonization of most parts of the continent, as Meltzer (2002) has argued.

There are, of course, several differences between Paleoarchaic tool kits and those of Paleoindians elsewhere, such as the rarity of burins and *pieces esquillees* in the former. There are two differences in particular, however, that we discuss here.

The first of these regards the high incidence of combination tools in the assemblage. About 25 percent of tool objects possess two or more functional units (e.g., employable units, or EUs). The most common combination tool is the scraper/graver, but others such as scraper/notches, chisel/scraper/gravers, and graver/notches are present as well. In seeking an explanation for this pattern we are drawn to cost-benefit arguments; that is, combination tools may represent a material-conservation strategy. With quite a large number of good-quality chert sources in the area (that are represented at the site) and along the route traveled by foragers on their way to Sunshine, we find this explanation unpersuasive. Still, to resupply from Sunshine required traveling about 10 km to chert and FGV sources represented in the assemblage.

Alternatively, the combination of two or more different types of EUs might also relate to the suite of activities in which the tool was used. For instance, as we discussed in chapter 5, end and side scrapers often occur in combination in the Sunshine assemblage. Frison believes that the side scrapers from the Horner I site in Wyoming were used in the butchering process but that this process included an "interplay of cutting and scraping actions" (1987:238). Thus for tasks that required different tools, perhaps used sequentially, EUs that are used at different stages in a process (i.e., the end scraper and the side scraper) might be present on the same tool. This would suggest that, in the case of scraper/gravers, these different EUs were used at different points in the same activity. Table 5.42 indicates that the majority (78.8 percent) of scraper/graver combinations occur on side scrapers or end/side scrapers, suggesting that the relation is between the side scraper and the graver.

Finally, the production of combination tools might be another means to anticipate future tasks while keeping the bulkiness of the transported tool kit to a minimum. We have little reason to doubt that the curation of unifacial chert tools was the equal of that of FGV stemmed bifaces.

The second difference between Paleoarchaic and other Paleoindian assemblages is the presence of crescents. Crescents continue to puzzle archaeologists studying this early record because questions regarding their temporal placement and function have never been satisfactorily answered. Arguments concerning temporal placement have centered on whether they are associated with fluted or stemmed points, but this argument is moot if fluted and stemmed points were coeval. Proposed functions for these tools range widely, from medical instruments to weapons used to stun birds and practically everything in between. The fact that crescents are rarely found outside the Great Basin, however, suggests that their appearance was directly related to the subsistence strategy that evolved in that region, and as we noted above, this strategy centered on shallow-water resources.

It is interesting, however, that crescents do not occur in all Paleoarchaic assemblages, even though the latter might have been deposited in areas associated with TP/EH lake or marsh environments. We have collected nearly 10,000 artifacts from Butte Valley, for instance, and have found only three crescents. Even the Dietz assemblage, which contains large numbers of both fluted and stemmed points, contains only a few of these artifacts. In fact, crescents are found in large numbers only in a few locations, including several sites in the Black Rock Desert (Clewlow 1968a, 1968b; Hester 1977), Coyote Flat (Butler 1970), and the Alvord Basin (Pettigrew 1984) in the northern Great Basin; on the beaches of Pleistocene Lake Tonopah in southern Nevada (Pendleton 1979); and in the southern Mojave Desert near Pleistocene Lake Mojave (Amsden 1937) and, of course, the Sunshine Locality. But they are notably rare in other areas, including the Nevada Test Site in southern Nevada (Amick 1993; Haynes 1996), Fort Irwin in the northern Mojave Desert (Basgall 1993a, 1993b; Basgall and Hall 1993; Hall 1993; Warren 1990), Paleoarchaic sites in eastern Nevada (with the exception of Sunshine), and the Bonneville Basin (Jones et al. 2002). Therefore, there must be something quite different about the activities performed at some sites and not at others that resulted in the deposition of large numbers of crescents.

Even when crescents are found only in small numbers they are rarely found as isolates. Nor, as we have learned from investigations of assemblages in the vicinity of Sunshine, do they occur where the dominant activity was the rejuvenation or replacement of stemmed points, such as at the sites in Butte Valley. Both of these contexts are suggestive of resource procurement rather than processing activities. Crescents, we believe, are more likely to have been part of a processing technology but not the processing activities of a group on the move. Instead, we believe that these processing activities are associated with longer residential stays at a particular location.

Our analysis results suggest that these artifacts were transversely hafted cutting implements (although use as handheld tools cannot be ruled out), in which the points constituted the tool segment. As to what was being cut, we can only speculate. As noted earlier, the almost complete lack of ground stone at the Sunshine Locality suggests that plant resources did not constitute a major portion of the diet, at least those that require grinding, such as seeds. But certainly plants were used quite early for the manufacture of such items as sandals, woven bags and mats, and basketry. The earliest date associated with woven artifacts is 11,250 ± 250 rcy BP from Fishbone Cave in the Winnemuca Lake Basin (Orr 1974). Whether or not these artifacts were truly being made at this early date, they were certainly being made shortly after 10,000 rcy BP, as the dates from a number of sites indicate (e.g., Danger Cave: Jennings 1957 [dates revised by Madsen and Rhode 1990]; Shiner: Hattori 1982; Spirit Cave: Tuohy and Dansie 1997). Thus, crescents could have been used to cut and process plants for this purpose.

On the other hand, these tools may have been used to process meat. Hattori et al. (1990) conducted protein residue analysis on 30 crescents and found proteins representative of the variety of animals, including fish, waterfowl, and rabbit. There are mixed opinions concerning the validity of results from protein analysis (e.g., Downs and Lowenstein 1995; Gurfinkel and Franklin 1988; Loy 1983; Smith and Wilson 1992), but the results of Hattori et al.'s analysis are consistent with a subsistence strategy focused on shallow-water resources.

The Sunshine assemblage contains a large number of crescents, indeed the largest number of these artifacts from a single site *anywhere* in the Great Basin, suggesting that their function was particularly relevant to Paleoarchaic activities at this site. It also suggests that the Sunshine Locality saw repeated visits over a longer period of time than most other Paleoarchaic sites in the Great Basin. Why this might be the case is the focus of our final section.

The Sunshine Locality and Paleoarchaic Land Use

Throughout the preceding chapters and in this final discussion we have remarked on the distinctive character of the Sunshine lithic assemblage. By comparison with other regional Paleoarchaic sites, Sunshine is large and contains a tool assemblage unprecedented in size and diversity. Although no doubt some of this tool diversity relates to assemblage size (the fact that it thus samples a wider suite of behaviors), we are struck that many kinds of tools have not before been seen in other regional samples. The size of the Sunshine assemblage surely relates to the length of use of this location, but we suspect that occupational intensity, another contribution, implies a distinctive piece of the land-use patterns of Paleoarchaic people in this region. Much longer residential stays, affording time for activities related not only to resource procurement but to food and material processing, are much in evidence here.

Recently, based on obsidian and FGV source attributions, we have hypothesized a set of five lithic conveyance zones in the Great Basin (Jones et al. 2003). The eastern conveyance zone, in which the Sunshine Locality is located, encompasses ca. 500 km from north to south. Its western edge is delimited by the fact that almost all of the obsidian within the zone comes from the north, south, or east; very little comes from the west. Only one obsidian source is local, and it is composed of small pebbles, none large enough to manufacture a Great Basin Stemmed Series projectile point, yet obsidian artifacts account for about 15 percent of the eastern Nevada assemblages. Aside from the local source, 19 other sources of known location have been identified in the eastern Nevada assemblages, all located at least 250 km from the study area.

Although the large majority of obsidian in the eastern Nevada assemblages is from within the conveyance zone, about 2 percent comes from areas outside the zone, such as eastern California, southern Nevada, and northwestern Nevada. All of these obsidians are represented in small numbers, most often a single artifact. Although a few of the obsidians occur in the larger Butte Valley and Jakes Valley assemblages, the majority occur in the Sunshine assemblage, which has the greatest source diversity of all of the eastern Nevada assemblages relative to the number of items sourced (Figure 8.2). It is difficult to argue that these items were obtained through direct access; it is much more likely that they were obtained through opportunistic reciprocal exchanges.

Speaking of colonizing populations, Meltzer suggests that dispersed groups would face trade-offs among a series of competing demands, including maximizing mobility, minimizing group size, and most importantly, maintaining contact "in order to sustain information flow, social relations, and most especially, demographic viability" (2002:36). Although we are not making the argument that the first visit to the Sunshine Locality was by a "colonizing population," given the earliest radiocarbon dates at the site that first visit must have been among the earliest incursions into the region, and the population is likely to have been highly mobile, as we have recently demonstrated (e.g., Jones et al. 2003). It is not impossible to imagine that the earliest records in the different conveyance zones might have been deposited by a few (or even a single) distinct groups of people, who would have been extremely vulnerable demographically. These groups must have come together periodically—if, as we believe, population density remained quite low throughout this period—as aggregation would have been a necessary factor to accomplish economic and social demands. Sunshine would have provided an ideal location for such aggregation, not only because of its lush habitat but also because it is located at the western edge of the most eastern zone, about midway between the northern and southern boundaries. The inclusion of groups from the adjacent zones to the west would account for the diversity of obsidian at Sunshine as well as the presence of obsidian from sources far to the west. In such a setting informal exchanges of material goods would likely have taken place. We note that 12 of the 17 artifacts made from extra-zone obsidian are projectile points and one is a biface, suggesting that exchanges were in the form of finished items.

With the drying of the area after ca. 9800 rcy BP, Sunshine became less attractive and was visited only intermittently after this time. The addition of obsidian sources from Utah to the eastern Nevada assemblages as well as a decrease in use of the far northern and southern sources suggest a change in mobility patterns about this time; people appear to have traveled less, perhaps remaining in patches longer, and with movement now in an east/northeast–west/southwest direction (Jones et al. 2003). Occupation of the Old River Bed area in the Bonneville Basin appears to have increased at this time as well (Jones et al. 2002). It may well be that movement between our eastern Nevada study area and the Old River Bed became the established strategy by the end of the early Holocene. But by about 8500 rcy BP, Sunshine no longer played an important part in human subsistence and mobility strategies.

Concluding Remarks

The Sunshine Locality is an exceptional site that has provided a wealth of information concerning terminal Pleistocene/early Holocene environment and Paleoarchaic technology. It is unique among other such sites in the number and diversity of tools, the large number of

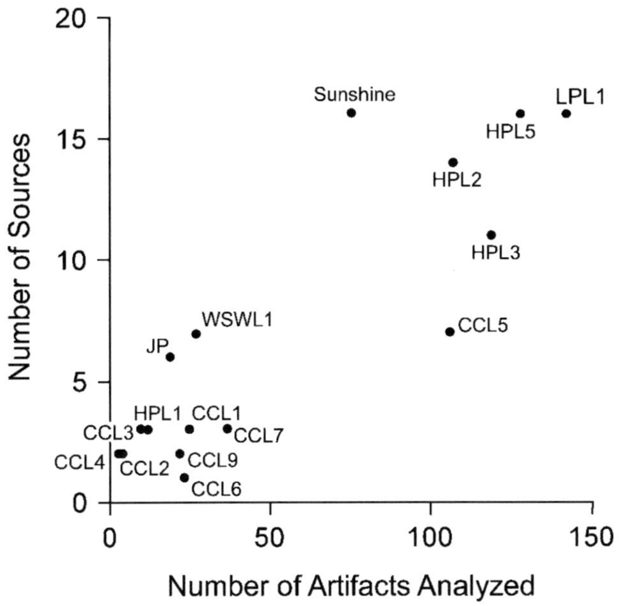

FIGURE 8.2. Scatterplot of the number of obsidian sources vs. the number of items analyzed in the eastern Nevada assemblages.

fluted points and stemmed points, the limiting date on a fluted point, the large collection of crescents, and the presence of extinct camels in the same strata with stone tools. We consider ourselves privileged to have become a part of its history. It is also fortunate that the private collectors at the site were Phil Hutchinson and Gary Noyes, who documented the provenience of many of the artifacts they collected, and that they donated their collection to the Nevada State Museum. Without this collection, we could not have completed many of the analyses we have presented in this monograph.

Note

1. Six other dates were reported by Bryan that we do not include in our discussion. The younger two, 9800 ± 190 and 9280 ± 160 rcy BP, were discounted by Bryan; the older four, ranging from 14,220 ± 650 to 11,680 ±160 rcy BP, have been challenged by Thompson (1985; see discussion in Beck and Jones 1997:192–193). Thus we chose in 1997 and here as well to use a conservative estimate of the age of the Mount Moriah occupation, beginning with the date of 11,140 ± 120 rcy BP.

Appendix

TABLE A.1. Identified Faunal Specimens Recovered in the 1993 Hamilton College Excavations at the Sunshine Locality

	STRATUM						
TAXON	A	B	C	D/E	F/G	N.A.[a]	TOTAL
Fishes							
Cypriniformes (Minnows and suckers)					3		3
Cyprinidae (Minnows)					11		11
Birds							
Anatidae (Waterfowl)					2		2
Branta sp. (Geese)					1		1
Anas sp. (Dabbling ducks)				3	1		4
Aythya sp. (Diving ducks)					3	1	4
Oreoscoptes montana (Sage thrasher)	1						1
Mammals							
Leporidae (Rabbits and hares)	30		8	2	14		54
Brachylagus idahoensis (Pygmy rabbit)	11				4		15
Sylvilagus sp. (Cottontails)	4		1		4		9
Lepus sp. (Jackrabbits)	6				4		10
Sciuridae (Squirrels)	211	29	11		6		257
Tamias sp. (Chipmunks)	1						1
Spermophilus sp. (Ground squirrels)	16		1				17
Spermophilus mollis (Piute ground squirrel)	107	19	14				140
Thomomys sp. (Pocket gophers)	134	20	25	1			180
Thomomys bottae (Botta's pocket gopher)	19	1	4				24
Dipodomys sp. (Kangaroo rats)	5				2		7
Dipodomys ordii (Ord's kangaroo rat)	3						3
Peromyscus sp. (Deer mice)	3		1				4
Neotoma cinerea (Bushy-tailed wood rat)				1			1
Arvicolinae (Voles)	18	2	1		9		30
Microtus sp. (Meadow voles)				1	4	1	6
Lemmiscus curtatus (Sagebrush vole)	6				2		8
Canidae (Dogs)					1		1
Vulpes vulpes (Red fox)					1		1
Artiodactyla (Even-toed ungulates)	1				4	2	7
Total number of identified specimens	576	71	66	8	76	4	801
Total unidentified	433	52	23	29	682	25	1,244

[a] Stratigraphic provenience is not available for these specimens.

Table A.2. Identified Faunal Specimens Recovered in the 1995 Hamilton College Excavations at the Sunshine Locality

Taxon	Excavation Unit: Stratum				Total
	LT: C	LT: F/G	ST3: F/G	N.A.[a]	
Birds					
Podiceps sp. (Grebes)			1		1
Anatidae (Waterfowl)	1		2		3
Cygnus sp. (Swans)			1		1
Branta sp. (Geese)			1		1
Anas sp. (Dabbling ducks)			2		2
Aythya sp. (Diving ducks)	2	1	3		6
Accipiter striatus (Sharp-shinned hawk)	1				1
Mammals					
Leporidae (Rabbits and hares)		2	5		7
Sylvilagus sp. (Cottontails)			1		1
Sciuridae (Squirrels)		1	1		2
Thomomys sp. (Pocket gophers)		1	1		2
Arvicolinae (Voles)	1	1			2
Microtus sp. (Meadow voles)	1	1			2
Canis latrans (Coyote)			1		1
Camelops hesternus (Yesterday's camel)			11	2	13
Total number of identified specimens	6	7	30	2	45
Total unidentified	128	30	124[b]	8[c]	290

Note: LT = Loader Trench; ST = Strat Trench.
[a] Stratigraphic provenience is not available for these specimens.
[b] Two of these are from very large, camel- or horse-sized mammals.
[c] Three of these are from camel- or horse-sized mammals.

Table A.3. Identified Faunal Specimens Recovered in the 1996 Hamilton College Excavations at the Sunshine Locality

Taxon	Stratum F/G
Fishes	
Cypriniformes (Minnows and suckers)	6
Cyprinidae (Minnows)	2
Catostomidae (Suckers)	2
Birds	
Podiceps sp. (Grebes)	1
Branta sp. (Geese)	1
Anas sp. (Dabbling ducks)	4
Aythya sp. (Diving ducks)	3
Scolopacidae (Shorebirds)	1
Passeriformes (Perching birds)	2
Pica pica (Black-billed magpie)	1

Taxon	Stratum F/G
Mammals	
Leporidae (Rabbits and hares)	5
Brachylagus idahoensis (Pygmy rabbit)	4
Sylvilagus sp. (Cottontails)	2
Lepus sp. (Jackrabbits)	2
Sciuridae (Squirrels)	1
Thomomys sp. (Pocket gophers)	2
Arvicolinae (Voles)	1
Microtus sp. (Meadow voles)	2
Mustela vison (American mink)	1
Equus sp. (Horses)	1
Artiodactyla (Even-toed ungulates)	1
Camelops hesternus (Yesterday's camel)	6
Total number of identified specimens	52
Total unidentified	253[a]

[a] Fourteen of these are from very large, camel- or horse-sized mammals.

References Cited

Ahler, S. A.
1989 Mass Analysis of Flaking Debris: Studying the Forest Rather Than the Tree. In *Alternative Approaches to Lithic Analysis,* edited by D. O. Henry and G. H. Odell, pp. 85–118. Archeological Papers of the American Anthropological Association No. 1.

Ahler, S. A., and P. R. Geib
2000 Why Flute? Folsom Point Design and Adaptation. *Journal of Archaeological Science* 27:799–820.

Aikens, C. M.
1970 *Hogup Cave.* University of Utah Anthropological Papers 93. Salt Lake City.

Alcock, L.
1987 *Economy, Society and Warfare Among the Britons and Saxons.* University of Wales Press, Cardiff.

Amick, D. S.
1993 Toolstone Use and Distribution Patterns Among Western Pluvial Lakes Tradition Points from Southern Nevada. *Current Research in the Pleistocene* 10:49–51.
1995a Raw Material Selection Patterns Among Paleoindian Tools from the Black Rock Desert, Nevada. Current Research in the Pleistocene 12:55–57.
1995b Patterns of Technological Variation Among Folsom and Midland Projectile Points in the American Southwest. *Plains Anthropologist*: 23–38.
1996 Early Technological Complexes in the Northern Great Basin. Paper presented at the 25th Biennial Great Basin Anthropological Conference, Kings Beach, Nevada, October 10–12.
1998 A Closer Look at Great Basin Crescents. Paper presented at the 26th Great Basin Anthropological Conference, Bend, Oregon, October 8–10.
1999 Using Lithic Artifacts to Explain Past Behavior. In *Models for the Millennium. Great Basin Anthropology Today,* edited by C. Beck, pp. 161–170. University of Utah Press, Salt Lake City.
2004 A Possible Ritual Cache of Great Basin Stemmed Bifaces from the Terminal Pleistocene–Early Holocene Occupation of NW Nevada, USA. *Lithic Technology* 29:119–145.

Amsden, C. A.
1935 The Pinto Basin Artifacts. In *The Pinto Basin Site,* by E. W. C. Campbell and W. H. Campbell, pp. 33–51. Southwest Museum Papers No. 9. Los Angeles.
1937 The Lake Mohave Artifacts. In *The Archeology of Pleistocene Lake Mohave,* by E. W. C. Campbell, W. H. Campbell, E. Antevs, C. A. Amsden, J. A. Barbieri, and F. D. Bode, pp. 51–98. Southwest Museum Paper No. 11. Los Angeles.

Anderson, D. G., L. D. O'Steen, and K. E. Sassaman
1996 Environmental and Chronological Considerations. In *The Paleoindian and Early Archaic Southeast,* edited by D. G. Anderson and K. E. Sassaman, pp. 3–15. University of Alabama Press, Tuscaloosa.

Andrefsky, B., Jr.
1998 *Lithics. Macroscopic Approaches to Analysis.* Cambridge University Press, Cambridge.

Antevs, E.
1948 Climatic Changes and Pre-White Man. *University of Utah Bulletin* 38(20):167–191.

Bamforth, D. B.
1991 Flintknapping Skill, Communal Hunting, and Paleoindian Projectile Point Typology. *Plains Anthropologist* 36: 309–322.

Barnosky, A. D., and D. L. Rasmussen
1988 Middle Pleistocene Arvicoline Rodents and Environmental Change at 2900-Meters Elevation, Porcupine Cave, South Park, Colorado. *Annals of Carnegie Museum* 57:267–292.

Barry, R. G.
1983 Late Pleistocene Climatology. In *Late Quaternary Environments of the United States,* Vol. 1, edited by S. C. Porter, pp. 390–403. University of Minnesota Press, Minneapolis.

Basgall, M. E.
1988 Archaeology of the Komodo Site, an Early Holocene Occupation in Central–Eastern California. In *Early Human Occupation in Far Western North America: The Clovis–Archaic Interface,* edited by J. A. Willig, C. M. Aikens, and J. L. Fagan, pp. 103–119. Nevada State Museum Anthropological Papers 21. Carson City.
1993a *The Archaeology of Nelson Basin and Adjacent Areas, Fort Irwin, San Bernadino County, California.* Report prepared for the U.S. Army Corps of Engineers, Los Angeles District, by Far Western Anthropological Research Group, Davis.
1993b Early Holocene Prehistory of the North-Central Mojave Desert. Unpublished Ph.D. dissertation, Department of Anthropology, University of California, Davis.

Basgall, M. E., and M. C. Hall
1991 Relationships Between Fluted and Stemmed Points in the Mojave Desert. *Current Research in the Pleistocene* 8:61–64.
1993 *Archaeology of the Awl Sites, CA-SBR-4562, Fort Irwin, San Bernardino County, California.* Report prepared for the U.S. Army Corps of Engineers, Los Angeles District, by Far Western Anthropological Research Group, Davis.

2000 Morphological and Temporal Variation in Bifurcate-Stemmed Dart Points of the Western Great Basin. *Journal of California and Great Basin Anthropology* 22:237–276.

Beck, C.

1984 *Steens Mountain Surface Archaeology: The Sites.* Ph.D. dissertation, University of Washington. University Microfilms, Ann Arbor.

1995 Functional Attributes and the Differential Persistence of Great Basin Dart Forms. *Journal of California and Great Basin Anthropology* 17:222–243.

1998 Projectile Point Types as Valid Chronological Units. In *Measuring Time, Space, and Material: Unit Issues in Archaeology,* edited by A. F. Ramenofsky and A. Steffen, pp. 21–40. University of Utah Press, Salt Lake City.

Beck, C., and G. T. Jones

1988 Western Pluvial Lakes Tradition Occupation in Butte Valley, Eastern Nevada. In *Early Human Occupation in Far Western North America: The Clovis–Archaic Interface,* edited by J. A. Willig, C. M. Aikens, and J. L. Fagan, pp. 273–301. Nevada State Museum Anthropological Papers 21. Carson City.

1990a Late Pleistocene/Early Holocene Occupations in Butte Valley, Eastern Nevada: Three Season's Work. *Journal of California and Great Basin Anthropology* 12:231–261.

1990b Toolstone Selection and Lithic Technology in Early Great Basin Prehistory. *Journal of Field Archaeology* 17:283–299.

1992 Paleoindian–Archaic Range Shifts in Eastern Nevada. *Current Research in the Pleistocene* 9:1–2.

1993 The Multi-Purpose Function of Great Basin Stemmed Series Points. *Current Research in the Pleistocene* 10:52–54.

1994 Dating Surface Assemblages Using Obsidian Hydration. In *Dating in Exposed and Surface Contexts,* edited by C. Beck, pp. 47–76. University of New Mexico Press, Albuquerque.

1997 The Terminal Pleistocene/Early Holocene Archaeology of the Great Basin. *Journal of World Prehistory* 11:161–236.

2007 Early Paleoarchaic Point Morphology and Chronology. In *Paleoindian or Paleoarchaic? New Insights of Late Pleistocene–Early Holocene Archaeology in the Great Basin,* edited by K. Graf and D. Schmitt, pp. 23–41. University of Utah Press, Salt Lake City.

Beck, C., G. T. Jones, D. L. Jenkins, C. E. Skinner, and J. J. Thatcher

2004 Fluted or Basally-Thinned? Re-Examination of a Lanceolate Point from the Connley Caves in the Fort Rock Basin. *University of Oregon Anthropological Papers* 62:281–294.

Beck, C., and G. T. Jones

2008 Is There Clovis in the Great Basin. *American Antiquity,* in review.

Beck, C., A. Taylor, G. T. Jones, C. Fadem, C. Cook, and S. Millward

2002 Rocks Are Heavy: Transport Costs and Paleoarchaic Quarry Behavior in the Great Basin. *Journal of Anthropological Archaeology* 21:481–507.

Bedwell, S. F.

1973 *Fort Rock Basin: Prehistory and Environment.* University of Oregon Books, Eugene.

Benson, L. V., D. R. Currey, R. I. Dorn, K. R. Lajoie, C. G. Oviatt, S. W. Robinson, G. I. Smith, and S. Stine

1990 Chronology of Expansion and Contraction of Four Great Basin Lake Systems During the Past 35,000 Years. *Palaeogeography, Palaeoclimatology, Palaeoecology* 78:241–286.

Bettinger, R. L., J. F. O'Connell, and D. H. Thomas

1991 Projectile Points as Time Markers in the Great Basin. *American Anthropologist* 93:166–172.

Bettinger, R. L., and R. E. Taylor

1974 Suggested Revisions in Archaeological Sequences of the Great Basin and Interior Southern California. *Nevada Archaeological Survey Research Paper* 5:1–26.

Beyries, S.

1988 Functional Variability of Lithic Sets in the Middle Paleo-Lithic. In *Upper Pleistocene Prehistory of Western Eurasia,* edited by H. Dibble and A. Montet-White, pp. 213–223. University Museum, University of Pennsylvania, Philadelphia.

Boldurian, A. T.

1990 *Lithic Technology at the Mitchell Locality of Blackwater Draw: A Stratified Folsom Site in Eastern New Mexico.* Plains Anthropologist, Memoir 24. Lincoln, Nebraska.

Boldurian, A. T., and J. L. Cotter

1999 *Clovis Revisited. New Perspectives on Paleoindian Adaptations from Blackwater Draw, New Mexico.* University Museum, University of Pennsylvania, Philadelphia.

Bonnichsen, R.

1977 *Models for Deriving Cultural Information from Stone Tools.* Archaeological Survey of Canada Paper No. 60. Mercury Series. National Museum of Man, Ottawa.

Bordes, F.

1968 *The Old Stone Age.* Translated by J. E. Anderson. World University Library, New York.

Bouyoucos, G.

1962 Hydrometer Method Improved for Making Particle Size Analysis of Soils. *Agronomy Journal* 54:464–465.

Bradley, B. A.e1982 Flaked Stone Technology and Typology. In *The Agate Basin Site: A Record of Paleoindian Occupation of the Northwestern High Plains,* edited by G. C. Frison and D. J. Stanford, pp. 181–208. Academic Press, New York.

1993 Paleoindian Flaked Stone Technology in the North American High Plains. In *From Kostenki to Clovis: Upper Paleolithic–Paleoindian Adaptations,* edited by O. Soffer and N. D. Praslov, pp. 251–262. Plenum Press, New York.

Bradley, B., and G. C. Frison

1987 Projectile Points and Specialized Bifaces from the Horner Site. In *The Horner Site. The Type Site of the Cody Cultural Complex,* edited by G. C. Frison and L. C. Todd, pp. 199–231. Academic Press, New York.

1996 Flaked-Stone and Worked-Bone Artifacts from the Mill Iron Site. In *The Mill Iron Site,* edited by G. C. Frison, pp. 43–70. University of New Mexico Press, Albuquerque.

Briggs, R. W., S. G. Wesnovsky, and K. D. Adams

2005 Late Pleistocene and Late Holocene Highstands in the Pyramid Lake Subbasin of Lake Lahonton, Nevada, USA. *Quaternary Research* 64:257–263.

Broilo, F. J.

1971 An Investigation of Surface Collected Clovis, Folsom, and Midland Projectile Points from Blackwater Draw and Adjacent Localities. Unpublished Master's thesis, Department of Anthropology, Eastern New Mexico University.

Brott, C. W.

1966 Artifacts of the San Dieguito Complex. In *Ancient Hunters of the Far West,* edited by M. Rogers Jr., pp. 141–193. Union-Tribune Publishing Co., San Diego.

Broughton, J. M., D. B. Madsen, and J. Quade

2000 The Homestead Cave Ichthyofauna and Implications for Terminal Pleistocene and Holocene Lake Level Fluctuation in the Bonneville Basin, Utah. *Quaternary Research* 53:392–401.

Bryan, A. L.

1979 Smith Creek Cave. In *The Archaeology of Smith Creek Canyon,* edited by D. R. Tuohy and D. L. Rendall, pp. 164–251. Nevada State Museum Anthropological Papers 17. Carson City.

1980 The Stemmed Point Tradition: An Early Technological Tradition in Western North America. In *Anthropological Papers in Memory of Earl H. Swanson, Jr.,* edited by L. B. Harten, C. N. Warren, and D. R. Tuohy, pp. 77–107. Idaho Museum of Natural History, Pocatello.

1988 The Relationship of the Stemmed Point and Fluted Point Traditions in the Great Basin. In *Early Human Occupation in Far Western North America: The Clovis–Archaic Interface,* edited by J. A. Willig, C. M. Aikens, and J. L. Fagan, pp. 53–74. Nevada State Museum Anthropological Papers 21. Carson City.

1991 The Fluted Point Tradition in the Americas—One of Several Adaptations to Late Pleistocene American Environments. In *Clovis: Origins and Adaptations,* edited by R. Bonnichsen and K. L. Turnmire, pp. 15–33. Center for the Study of the First Americans, Oregon State University, Corvallis.

Bryan, A. L., and D. R. Tuohy

1999 Prehistory of the Great Basin/Snake River Plain to About 8,500 Years Ago. In *Ice Age People of North America: Environments, Origins, and Adaptations,* edited by Robson Bonnichsen and Karen L. Turnmire, pp. 249–263. Oregon State University Press, Corvallis.

Bull, W. B.

1991 *Geomorphic Responses to Climatic Change.* Oxford University Press, New York.

Butler, B. R.

1961 *The Old Cordilleran Culture in the Pacific Northwest.* Occasional Papers of the Idaho State College Museum, No. 5. Pocatello.

1963 An Early Man Site at Big Camas Prairie, South-Central Idaho. *Tebiwa* 6:22–34.

1965 A Report on Investigation of an Early Man Site near Lake Channel, Southern Idaho. *Tebiwa* 8:1–20.

1970 A Surface Collection from Coyote Flat, Southeastern Oregon. *Tebiwa* 13:34–58.

Callahan, E.

1979 The Basics of Biface Knapping in the Eastern Fluted Point Tradition: A Manual for Flint Knappers and Lithic Analysts. *Archaeology of Eastern North America* 7:1–180.

Campbell, E. W. C.

1936 Archaeological Problems in the Southern California Deserts. *American Antiquity* 1:295–300.

Campbell, E. W. C., and W. H. Campbell

1940 A Folsom Complex in the Great Basin. *Masterkey* 14:7–11.

Campbell, E. W. C., W. H. Campbell, E. Antevs, C. A. Amsden, J. A. Barbieri, and F. D. Bode

1937 *The Archeology of Pleistocene Lake Mohave.* Southwest Museum Paper No. 11. Los Angeles.

Casjens, L. A.

1974 The Prehistoric Human Ecology of Southern Ruby Valley, Nevada. Unpublished Ph.D. dissertation, Department of Anthropology, Harvard University, Cambridge, Massachusetts.

Christenson, A.

1986 Projectile Point Size and Projectile Aerodynamics: An Exploratory Study. *Plains Anthropologist* 31:109–128.

Clark, J. D.

1958 Some Stone Age Woodworking Tools in Southern Africa. *South African Archaeological Bulletin* 13:144–152.

Clewlow, C. W., Jr.

1968a Surface Archaeology of the Black Rock Desert, Nevada. *University of California Archaeological Survey Reports* 73: 1–94.

1968b Projectile Points from Lovelock Cave, Nevada. *University of California Archaeological Survey Reports* 71:89–116. Berkeley.

COHMAP Members

1988 Climatic Changes of the Last 18,000 Years: Observations and Model Simulations. *Science* 241:1043–1052.

Collins, M. B.

1999a Clovis and Folsom Lithic Technology on and near the Southern Plains. In *Folsom Lithic Technology. Explorations in Structure and Variation,* edited by D. S. Amick, pp. 12–38. International Monographs in Prehistory, Archaeological Series 12. Ann Arbor.

1999b *Clovis Blade Technology.* University of Texas Press, Austin.

Collins, M. B., and J. C. Lohse

2004 The Nature of Clovis Blades and Blade Cores. In *Entering America. Northeast Asia and Beringia Before the Last Glacial Maximum,* edited by D. B. Madsen, pp. 159–183. University of Utah Press, Salt Lake City.

Connolly, T. J., and D. L. Jenkins

1999 The Paulina Lake Site (35DS34). In *Newberry Crater. A Ten-Thousand-Year Record of Human Occupation and Environmental Change in the Basin–Plateau Borderlands,* by T. J. Connolly, pp. 86–121. University of Utah Anthropological Papers No. 121. Salt Lake City.

Copeland, J. M., and R. E. Fike

1988 Fluted Projectile Points in Utah. *Utah Archaeology* 1:5–28.

Cowles, J.
1959 *Cougar Mountain Cave in South Central Oregon.* Private publication, Ranier, Oregon.
Cox, Steven L.
1986 A Re-Analysis of the Shoop Site. *Archaeology of Eastern North America* 14:101–170.
Crabtree, D. E.
1972 *An Introduction to Flintworking.* Idaho State University Museum Occasional Papers No. 28. Pocatello.
Craven, S. L.
2003 Lithic Variation in Hafted Bifaces at the Lind Coulee Site (45GR97), Washington. Unpublished Master's thesis, Department of Anthropology, Washington State University, Pullman.
Cressman, L. S., F. C. Baker, H. P. Harren, P. Conger, and R. F. Heizer
1942 *Archaeological Researches in the Northern Great Basin.* Carnegie Institution of Washington Publication No. 538. Washington, D.C.
Currey, D. R.
1990 Quaternary Paleolakes in the Evolution of Semidesert Basins, with Special Emphasis on Lake Bonneville and the Great Basin, U.S.A. *Palaeogeography, Palaeoclimatology, Palaeoecology* 76:189–214.
Dansie, A.
1990 Taphonomy and Taxonomy of Large and Small Fauna from the Sunshine Wells Locality. Paper presented at the 22nd Biennial Meeting of the Great Basin Anthropological Conference, Reno.
Daugherty, R. D.
1956 Archaeology of the Lind Coulee Site, Washington. *Proceedings of the American Philosophical Society* 100(3):223–278.
Davis, E. L.
1973 The Hord Site, a Paleoindian Camp. *Pacific Coast Archaeological Society Quarterly* 10:1–6.
1978a *The Ancient Californians: Rancholabrean Hunters of the Mojave Lakes Country.* Natural History Museum of Los Angeles County Science Series 29. Los Angeles.
1978b Associations of People and a Rancholabrean Fauna at China Lake, California. In *Early Man in America from a Circum-Pacific Perspective,* edited by A. L Bryan, pp. 183–217. Occasional Papers No. 1. Department of Anthropology, University of Alberta, Edmonton.
Davis, E. L., C. W. Brott, and D. L. Weide
1969 *The Western Lithic Co-Tradition.* San Diego Museum Papers No. 6. San Diego.
Davis, E. L., and R. Shutler Jr.
1969 Recent Discoveries of Fluted Points in California and Nevada. *Nevada State Museum Anthropological Papers* 14:154–179. Carson City.
Davis, L. G.
2001 The Coevolution of Early-Hunter-Gatherer Culture and Riparian Ecosystems in the Southern Columbia River Plateau. Unpublished Ph.D. dissertation, Department of Anthropology and Department of Earth and Atmospheric Sciences, University of Alberta, Edmonton.
Deller, D. B.
1980 Parkhill (Brophey) Site, AhHk-49: Analyses of Surface Materials. Unpublished Master's thesis, Wilfred Laurier University, Waterloo, Ontario.
Deller, D. B., and C. J. Ellis
1988 Early Palaeo-Indian Complexes in Southwestern Ontario. In *Late Pleistocene and Early Holocene Paleoecology and Archaeology of the Eastern Great Lakes Region,* edited by R. S. Laub, N. G. Miller, and D. W. Steadman, pp. 251–263. Bulletin of the Buffalo Society of Natural Sciences 33. Buffalo.
1992 *Thedford II: A Paleo-Indian Site in the Ausable River Watershed of Southwestern Ontario.* Memoir No. 24. Museum of Anthropology, University of Michigan, Ann Arbor.
Dorenbosch, S.
2000 Taphonomic Analysis of a *Camelops hesternus* Skeleton from the Sunshine Locality, Nevada. Unpublished Senior Honor's thesis, Hamilton College, Clinton, New York.
Douglas, C. L., D. L. Jenkins, and C. N. Warren
1988 Spatial and Temporal Variability in Faunal Remains from Four Lake Mojave–Pinto Period Sites in the Mojave Desert. In *Early Human Occupation in Far Western North America: The Clovis–Archaic Interface,* edited by J. A. Willig, C. M. Aikens, and J. L. Fagan, pp. 273–301. Nevada State Museum Anthropological Papers 21. Carson City.
Downs, E. F., and J. M. Lowenstein
1995 Identification of Archaeological Blood Proteins: A Cautionary Note. *Journal of Archaeological Science* 22:11–16.
Dumond, D. E., and R. Minor
1983 *Archaeology in the John Day Reservoir: The Wildcat Canyon Site 35-GM-9.* University of Oregon Anthropological Papers 30. Eugene.
Dunnell, R. C.
1970 *Systematics in Prehistory.* Free Press, New York.
Dunnell, R. C., and C. Beck
1979 *The Caples Site, 45-SA-5, Skamania County, Washington.* Reports in Archaeology No. 6. Department of Anthropology, University of Washington, Seattle.
Dunnell, R. C., and S. K. Campbell
1977 *Aboriginal Occupation of Hamilton Island, Washington.* Reports in Archaeology No. 4. Department of Anthropology, University of Washington, Seattle.
Ellis, C. J.
1984 Paleo-Indian Lithic Technological Structure and Organization in the Lower Great Lakes Area: A First Approximation. Unpublished Ph.D. dissertation, Simon Fraser University, Burnaby.
Ellis, C. J., and D. B. Deller
1988 Some Distinctive Paleo-Indian Tool Types from the Lower Great Lakes Region. *Midcontinental Journal of Archaeology* 13:111–158.
Fagan, J. L.
1988 Clovis and Western Pluvial Lakes Tradition Lithic Technologies at the Dietz Site in South-Central Oregon. In *Early Human Occupation in Far Western North America:*

The Clovis–Archaic Interface, edited by Judith A. Willig, C. Melvin Aikens, and John L. Fagan, pp. 389–416. Nevada State Museum Anthropological Papers 21. Carson City.

Figgins, J. D.

1927 The Antiquity of Man in America. *Natural History* 27:229–239.

Flenniken, J. J.

1985 Stone Tool Reduction Techniques as Cultural Markers. In *Stone Tool Analysis: Essays in Honor of Don E. Crabtree,* edited by M. G. Plew, J. C. Woods, and M. G. Pavesic, pp. 265–276. University of New Mexico Press, Albuquerque.

Flenniken, J. J., and A. W. Raymond

1986 Morphological Projectile Point Typology: Replication, Experimentation and Technological Analysis. *American Antiquity* 51:603–614.

Flenniken, J. J., and P. J. Wilke

1989 Typology, Technology, and Chronology of Great Basin Dart Points. *American Anthropologist* 91:149–158.

Frison, G. C.

1973 *The Wardell Buffalo Trap 48SU301: Communal Procurement in the Upper Green River Basin, Wyoming.* University of Michigan, Museum of Anthropology, Anthropological Papers No. 48. Ann Arbor.

1976 Cultural Activity Associated with Prehistoric Mammoth Butchering and Processing. *Science* 194:728–730.

1987 The Tool Assemblage, Unfinished Bifaces, and Stone Flaking Material Sources for the Horner Site. In *The Horner Site. The Type Site of the Cody Cultural Complex,* edited by G. C. Frison and L. C. Todd, pp. 233–278. Academic Press, New York.

1991 *Prehistoric Hunters of the High Plains.* 2nd ed. Academic Press, New York.

Frison, G. C., and B. Bradley

1999 *The Fenn Cache. Clovis Weapons and Tools.* One Horse Land and Cattle Company, Santa Fe.

Frison, G. C., and D. J. Stanford

1982 *The Agate Basin Site. A Record of the Paleoindian Occupation of the Northwestern High Plains.* Academic Press, New York.

Frison, G. C., and L. C. Todd (editors)

1987 *The Horner Site. The Type Site of the Cody Cultural Complex.* Academic Press, New York.

Frison, G. C., and George M. Zeimens

1980 Bone Projectile Points: An Addition to the Folsom Cultural Complex. *American Antiquity* 45:231–237.

Futato, E. M.

1996 A Synopsis of Paleoindian and Early Archaic Research in Alabama. In *The Paleoindian and Early Archaic Southeast,* edited by D. G. Anderson and K. E. Sassaman, pp. 298–314. University of Alabama Press, Tuscaloosa.

Gallagher, J. P.

1977 Contemporary Stone Tools in Ethiopia: Implications for Archaeology. *Journal of Field Archaeology* 4:407–414.

Galm, J. R., S. Gough, and F. L. Nials

2004 Climate Change and the Paleoindian–Archaic Transition in the Interior Pacific Northwest. Poster presented at the 69th Annual Meeting of the Society for American Archaeology, Montreal.

Gans, P. B., G. A. Mahood, and E. Schermer

1989 *Synextensional Magmatism in the Basin and Range Province: A Case Study from the Eastern Great Basin.* Geological Society of America Special Paper 233. Boulder.

Garcia, A. F., and M. Stokes

2006 Late Pleistocene Highstand and Recession of a Small, High Altitude Pluvial Lake, Jakes Valley, Central Great Basin, USA. *Quaternary Research* 65:179–186.

Gee, G. W., and J. W. Bauder

1986 Particle-Size Analysis. In *Methods of Soil Analysis, Pt. 1: Physical and Mineralogical Methods,* 2nd edition, edited by A. Klute, pp. 383–412. Soil Science Society of America, Madison.

Gifford, E. W., and W. E. Schenck

1926 Archaeology of the Southern San Joaquin Valley. *University of California Publications in American Archaeology and Ethnology* 25:1–122.

Gilbert, M. T. P., D. L. Jenkins, A. Götherstrom, N. Naveran, J. J. Sanchez, M. Hofreiter, P. F. Thomsen, J. Binladen, T. F. G. Higham, R. M. Yohe II, R. Parr, L. S. Cummings, and E. Willerslev

2008 DNA from Pre-Clovis Human Coprolites in Oregon, North America. *Science* 320(5877):786–789.

Gile, L. H., F. F. Peterson, and R. B. Grossman

1966 Morphological and Genetic Sequences of Carbonate Accumulation in Desert Soils. *Soil Science* 101(5):347–360.

Godsey, H. S., D. R. Currey, and M. A. Chan

2005 New Evidence of an Extended Occupation of the Provo Shoreline and Implications for Regional Climate Change, Pleistocene Lake Bonneville, Utah, USA. *Quaternary Research* 63:212–223.

Goebel, T.

2007 Pre-Archaic and Early Archaic Technological Activities at Bonneville Estates Rockshelter: A First Look at the Artifact Record. In *Paleoindian or Paleoarchaic? New Insights of Late Pleistocene–Early Holocene Archaeology in the Great Basin,* edited by K. Graf and D. Schmitt, pp. 156–184. University of Utah Press, Salt Lake City.

Goebel, T., R. Powers, and N. Bigelow

1991 The Nenana Complex of Alaska and Clovis Origins. In *Clovis Origins and Adaptations,* edited by R. Bonnichsen and K. L. Turnmire, pp. 49–79. Center for the Study of the First Americans, Oregon State University, Corvallis.

Goodyear, A. L.

1989 A Hypothesis for the Use of Cryptocrystalline Raw Materials Among Paleo-Indian Groups of North America. In *Eastern Paleoindian Lithic Resource Use,* edited by C. J. Ellis and J. C. Lathrop, pp. 1–9. Westview Press, Boulder.

Gould, R. A.

1970 Spears and Spear-Throwers of the Western Desert Aborigines of Australia. *American Museum Novitates* 2403:1–42.

Graf, K. E.

2001 Paleoindian Technological Provisioning in the Western Great Basin. Unpublished M.A. thesis, Department of Anthropology and Ethnic Studies, University of Nevada, Las Vegas.

2007 Stratigraphy and Chronology of the Pleistocene to Holocene Transition at Bonneville Estates Rockshelter, Eastern Great Basin. In *Paleoindian or Paleoarchaic? New Insights of Late Pleistocene–Early Holocene Archaeology in the Great Basin,* edited by K. Graf and D. Schmitt, pp. 82–104. University of Utah Press, Salt Lake City.

Gramly, R. M.

1982 *The Vail Site: A Palaeo-Indian Encampment in Maine.* Bulletin of the Buffalo Society of Natural Sciences, Vol. 30. Buffalo.

1990 *Guide to the Palaeo-Indian Artifacts of North America.* Persimmon Press, Buffalo.

1993 *The Richey Clovis Cache: Earliest Americans Along the Columbia River.* Persimmon Press Monographs in Archaeology, Buffalo.

Grayson, D. K.

1993 *The Desert's Past. A Natural Prehistory of the Great Basin.* Smithsonian Institution Press, Washington, D.C.

1998 Moisture History and Small Mammal Community Richness During the Latest Pleistocene and Holocene, Northern Bonneville Basin, Utah. *Quaternary Research* 49:330–334.

2000a The Homestead Cave Mammals. In *Late Quaternary Paleoecology in the Bonneville Basin,* edited by David B. Madsen, pp. 67–89. Utah Geological Survey Bulletin 130. Salt Lake City.

2000b Mammalian Changes to Middle Holocene Climatic Change in the Great Basin of the Western United States. *Journal of Biogeography* 27:181–192.

Grayson, D. K., and S. D. Livingston

1993 Missing Mammals on Great Basin Mountains: Holocene Extinctions and Inadequate Knowledge. *Conservation Biology* 7:527–532.

Grayson, D. K., S. D. Livingston, E. Rickart, and M. W. Shaver III

1996 Biogeographic Significance of Low-Elevation Records for *Neotoma cinerea* from the Northern Bonneville Basin, Utah. *Great Basin Naturalist* 56:191–196.

Grayson, D. K., and D. B. Madsen

2000 Biogeographic Implications of Recent Low-Elevation Recolonization by *Neotoma cinerea* in the Great Basin. *Journal of Mammalogy* 81:1100–1105.

Grayson, D. K., and D. J. Meltzer

2002 Clovis Hunting and Large Mammal Extinction. A Critical Review of the Evidence. *Journal of World Prehistory* 16:313–359.

Green, J. P.

1975 McKean and Little Lake Technology: A Problem in Projectile Point Typology in the Great Basin of North America. In *Lithic Technology: Making and Using Stone Tools,* edited by E. H. Swanson Jr., pp. 159–171. Mouton, The Hague.

Green, J. S., and J. T. Flinders

1980 *Brachylagus idahoensis. Mammalian Species* 125:1–4.

Green, T. J., B. Cochran, T. W. Fenton, J. C. Woods, G. L. Titmus, L. Tiezen, M. A. Davis, and S. J. Miller

1998 The Buhl Burial: A Paleoindian Woman from Southern Idaho. *American Antiquity* 63:437–456.

Grimes, J. R., and B. G. Grimes

1985 Flakeshavers: Morphometric, Functional and Life-Cycle Analyses of a Paleoindian Unifacial Tool Class. *Archaeology of Eastern North America* 13:35–57.

Gruhn, R., and A. L. Bryan

1988 The 1987 Archaeological Excavations at Handprint Cave, Nevada. *Nevada Archaeologist* 6(2).

Grunder, A. L.

1992 Two-Stage Contamination During Crustal Assimilation: Isotopic Evidence from Volcanic Rocks in Eastern Nevada. *Contributions to Mineralogy and Petrology* 112: 210–229.

Gurfinkel, D. M., and V. M. Franklin

1988 A Study of the Feasibility of Detecting Blood Residue on Artifacts. *Journal of Archaeological Science* 15:83–98.

Hall, E. R.

1946 *Mammals of Nevada.* University of Nevada Press, Reno.

1981 *Mammals of North America.* 2nd ed. Wiley, New York.

Hall, M. C.

1993 *Archaeology of Seven Prehistoric Sites in Tiefort Basin, Fort Irwin, San Bernardino County, California.* Report prepared for the U.S. Army Corps of Engineers, Los Angeles District, by Far Western Anthropological Research Group, Davis.

Harden, J. W., E. M. Taylor, L. D. McFadden, and M. C. Reheis

1991 Calcic, Gypsic, and Siliceous Soil Chronosequences in Arid and Semiarid Environments. In *Occurrence, Characteristics, and Genesis of Carbonate, Gypsum, and Silica Accumulations in Soils,* edited by W. D. Nettleton, pp. 1–16. SSSA Special Publication No. 26. Soil Science Society of America, Inc., Madison.

Harrington, M. R.

1948 *An Ancient Site at Borax Lake, California.* Southwest Museum Papers No. 16. Los Angeles.

1957 *A Pinto Site at Little Lake, California.* Southwest Museum Papers 17. Los Angeles.

Hattori, E. M.

1982 *The Archaeology of Falcon Hill, Winnemucca Lake, Washoe County, Nevada.* Nevada State Museum Anthropological Papers No. 18. Carson City.

Hattori, E. M., M. E. Newman, and D. R. Tuohy

1990 Blood Residue Analysis of Great Basin Crescents. Paper presented at the 22nd Biennial Great Basin Anthropological Conference, Reno.

Hayden, B.

1986 Use and Misuse: The Analysis of Endscrapers. *Lithic Technology* 15:65–70.

Hayden, B. (editor)

1979 *Lithic Use-Wear Analysis.* Academic Press, New York.

Haynes, C. V., Jr.

1967 Quaternary Geology of the Tule Springs Area, Clark

County, Nevada. In *Pleistocene Studies in Southern Nevada,* edited by M. Wormington and D. Ellis, pp. 15–104. Nevada State Museum Anthropological Papers No. 13. Carson City.

1991 Geoarchaeological and Paleohydrological Evidence for a Clovis-Age Drought in North America and Its Bearing on Extinction. *Quaternary Research* 35:438–450.

1992 Contributions of Radiocarbon Dating to the Geochronology of the Peopling of the New World. In *Radiocarbon After Four Decades,* edited by R. E. Taylor, A. Long, and R. S. Kra, pp. 355–374. Springer-Verlag, New York.

Haynes, G.

1996 Assemblage Richness and Composition at Paleoarchaic Sites near Yucca Mountain, Nevada. Unpublished Ph.D. dissertation, Department of Anthropology, University of Nevada, Reno.

Haynes, G.

2007 Paleoindian or Paleoarchaic? In *Paleoindian or Paleoarchaic? Great Basin Human Ecology at the Pleistocene–Holocene Transition,* edited by K. E. Graf and D. Schmitt, pp. 251–258. University of Utah Press, Salt Lake City.

Haynes, G., D. G. Anderson, C. R. Ferring, S. J. Fiedel, D. K. Grayson, C. V. Haynes Jr., V. T. Holliday, B. B. Huckell, M. Kornfeld, D. J. Meltzer, J. Morrow, T. Surovell, N. M. Waguespack, P. Wigand, and R. M. Yohe II

2007 Comment on Redefining the Age of Clovis: Implications for the Peopling of the Americas. *Science* 317:320b (online).

Hedges, R. E. M., and G. J. van Klinken

1992 A Review of Current Approaches in the Pretreatment of Bone for Radiocarbon Dating by AMS. *Radiocarbon* 34:279–291.

Heizer, R. F., M. A. Baumhoff, and C. W. Clewlow Jr.

1968 Archaeology of South Fork Shelter (NV-EL-11), Elko County, Nevada. *University of California Archaeological Survey Reports* 71:1–58. Berkeley.

Heizer, R. F., and C. W. Clewlow Jr.

1968 Projectile Points from Site NV-CH-15, Churchill County, Nevada. *University of California Archaeological Survey Reports* 71:59–88. Berkeley.

Heizer, R. F., and T. R. Hester

1978 Great Basin. In *Chronologies in New World Archaeology,* edited by R. E. Taylor and C. W. Meighan, pp. 147–199. Academic Press, New York.

Hester, J. J.

1972 *Blackwater Locality No. 1: A Stratified Early Man Site in Eastern New Mexico.* Fort Burgwin Research Center Publication No. 8. Rancho de Taos, New Mexico.

Hester, T. R.

1973 *Chronological Ordering of Great Basin Prehistory.* University of California Archaeological Research Facility Reports 17. Berkeley.

1977 Archaeological Materials from a Site in the Black Rock Desert of Northern Nevada. *University of California Archaeological Research Facility Contributions* 35:1–16. Berkeley.

Hicks, P.

1990 Lithics from Sunshine Wells Geological Test Trenches. Paper presented at the 22nd Biennial Meeting of the Great Basin Anthropological Conference, Reno.

Hofman, J. L.

1992 Recognition and Interpretation of Folsom Technological Variability on the Southern Plains. In *Ice Age Hunters of the Rockies,* edited by D. J. Stanford and J. S. Day, pp. 193–224. Denver Museum of Natural History, Denver; and University Press of Colorado, Niwot.

Hofman, J. L., D. S. Amick, and R. O. Rose

1990 Shifting Sands: A Folsom–Midland Assemblage from a Campsite in Western Texas. *Plains Anthropologist* 35:221–253.

Holmes, A. M.

1998 Geoarchaeology and Paleoenvironments of the Sunshine Locality, East-Central Nevada. Unpublished Master's thesis, Department of Anthropology, Washington State University, Pullman.

Hose, R. K., and M. C. Blake Jr.

1976 Part I, Geology. In *Geology and Mineral Resources of White Pine County, Nevada,* pp. 1–35. Nevada Bureau of Mines and Geology, Bulletin 85. Carson City.

Hostetler, S. W., and L. V. Benson

1990 Paleoclimatic Implications of the High Stand of Lake Lahontan Derived from Models of Evaporation and Lake Level. *Climate Dynamics* 4:207–217.

Hostetler, S. W., F. Giorgi, G. T. Bates, and P. J. Bartlein

1994 Lake–Atmosphere Feedbacks Associated with Paleolakes Bonneville and Lahontan. *Science* 263:665–668.

Howard, Calvin D.

1990 The Clovis Point: Characteristics and Type Description. *Plains Anthropologist* 35:255–262.

Howard, E. B.

1935 *Evidence of Early Man in North America.* Museum Journal 24(2–3). University of Pennsylvania Museum, Philadelphia.

1936 The Antiquity of Man in America. *Scientific Monthly* 43: 367–371.

Hubbs, C. L., and R. R. Miller

1948 The Zoological Evidence: Correlation Between Fish Distribution and Hydrographic History in the Desert Basins of Western United States. *Bulletin of the University of Utah* 38(20), *Biological Series* 10:17–166.

Huckleberry, G. A., C. Beck, G. T. Jones, and A. M. Holmes

1997 Further Excavations and Paleoenvironmental Data at the Sunshine Locality, Eastern Nevada. *Current Research in the Pleistocene* 14:162–163.

Huckleberry, G. A., C. Beck, G. T. Jones, A. M. Holmes, M. D. Cannon, S. D. Livingston, and J. M. Broughton

2001 Terminal Pleistocene/Early Holocene Environmental Change at the Sunshine Locality, North-Central Nevada, U.S.A. *Quaternary Research* 55:303–312.

Hughes, S. S.

1998 Getting to the Point: Evolutionary Change in Prehistoric Weaponry. *Journal of Archaeological Method and Theory* 5:345–408.

Hutchinson, P. W.
1979 Notes on the Prehistoric Dwellers at Lake Hubbs. Notes and Photographs of the Entire Collection Made at Lake Hubbs. Manuscript on file, Nevada State Museum, Carson City.
1988 The Prehistoric Dwellers at Lake Hubbs. In *Early Human Occupation in Far Western North America: The Clovis–Archaic Interface,* edited by J. A. Willig, C. M. Aikens, and J. L. Fagan, pp. 303–318. Nevada State Museum Anthropological Papers 21. Carson City.
1990 A Long-Term Study of Artifact Exposure at Early Human Sites. Paper presented at the 22nd Biennial Great Basin Anthropological Conference, Reno.
1993 The Prehistoric Dwellers at Lake Hubbs. Lithic Artifacts from Lake Terraces. Manuscript on file, Nevada State Museum, Carson City.

Ingbar, E. E., M. L. Larson, and B. A. Bradley
1989 A Non-Typological Approach to Debitage Analysis. In *Experiments in Lithic Technology,* edited by D. S. Amick and R. P. Mauldin, pp. 67–99. BAR International Series 528. Oxford.

Irwin, H. T., and H. M. Wormington
1970 Paleo-Indian Tool Types in the Great Plains. *American Antiquity* 35(1):24–34.

Jackson, M. L.
1975 *Soil Chemical Analysis—Advanced Course.* 2nd ed. Published by the author, Madison.

Janitsky, P.
1986 Organic Carbon. In *Field and Laboratory Procedures Used in a Soil Chronosequence Study,* edited by M. J. Singer and P. Janitsky, pp. 34–36. U.S. Geological Survey Office Bulletin 1648. U.S. Government Printing Office, Washington, D.C.

Jenkins, D. L.
2007 Distribution and Dating of Cultural and Paleontological Remains at the Paisley 5 Mile Point Caves (35LK3400) in the Northern Great Basin: An Early Assessment. In *Paleoindian or Paleoarchaic? New Insights of Late Pleistocene–Early Holocene Archaeology in the Great Basin,* edited by K. Graf and D. Schmitt, pp. 57–81. University of Utah Press, Salt Lake City.

Jennings, J. D.
1957 *Danger Cave.* University of Utah Anthropological Papers 27. Salt Lake City.

Johnson, J. K.
1981 *Yellow Creek Archaeological Project,* Vol. 2. Archaeological Papers of the Center for Archaeological Research, No. 2. Tennessee Valley Authority, Chattanooga.

Johnson, M. F.
1989 The Lithic Technology and Material Culture of the First Virginians: An Eastern Clovis Perspective. In *Paleoindian Research in Virginia: A Synthesis,* edited by J. N. Wittkofski and T. R. Reinhart, pp. 95–138. Special Publication No. 19. Archaeological Society of Virginia, Cortland.

Jones, G. T.
1984 *Prehistoric Land Use in the Steens Mountain Area, Southeastern Oregon.* Ph.D. dissertation, University of Washington. University Microfilms, Ann Arbor.

Jones, G. T., D. G. Bailey, and C. Beck
1997 Source Provenance of Andesite Artifacts Using Non-Destructive XRF Analysis. *Journal of Archaeological Science* 24:929–943.

Jones, G. T., and C. Beck
1990 An Obsidian Hydration Chronology of Late Pleistocene/Early Holocene Surface Assemblages from Butte Valley, Nevada. *Journal of California and Great Basin Anthropology* 12:84–100.
1992 Chronological Resolution in Distributional Archaeology. In *Place, Time, and Archaeological Landscapes,* edited by L. Wandsnider and J. Rossignol, pp. 167–192. Plenum Press, New York.
1999 Paleoarchaic Archaeology in the Great Basin. In *Models for the Millennium. Great Basin Anthropology Today,* edited by C. Beck, pp. 83–95. University of Utah Press, Salt Lake City.

Jones, G. T., C. Beck, and R. A. Kessler
2002 *Analysis of Artifacts from the Old River Bed Delta, Dugway Proving Ground, Utah.* Report prepared for and submitted to David B. Madsen in fulfillment of the contract agreement with the University and Community College System of Nevada, signed on June 6, 2002.

Jones, G. T., C. Beck, E. E. Jones, and R. E. Hughes
2003 Lithic Source Use and Paleoarchaic Foraging Territories in the Great Basin. *American Antiquity* 68(1):5–38.

Jones, G. T., C. Beck, F. L. Nials, J. J. Neudorfer, B. J. Brownholtz, and H. B. Gilbert
1996 Recent Archaeological and Geological Investigations at the Sunshine Locality, Long Valley, Nevada. *Journal of California and Great Basin Anthropology* 18:48–63.

Judge, W. J.
1973 *Paleoindian Occupation of the Central Rio Grande Valley in New Mexico.* University of New Mexico Press, Albuquerque.

Kelly, R. L.
1988 The Three Sides of a Biface. *American Antiquity* 53:717–734.
2001 *Prehistory of the Carson Desert and Stillwater Mountains. Environment, Mobility, and Subsistence in a Great Basin Wetland.* University of Utah Anthropological Papers No. 123. Salt Lake City.

Kelly, R. L, and L. C. Todd
1988 Coming into the Country: Early Paleoindian Mobility and Hunting. *American Antiquity* 53:231–244.

Knudson, R.
1973 Organizational Variability in Late Paleoindian Assemblages. Unpublished Ph.D. dissertation, Department of Anthropology, Washington State University, Pullman.
1979 Inference and Imposition in Lithic Analysis. In *Lithic Use-Wear Analysis,* edited by B. Hayden, pp. 269–281. Academic Press, New York.
1983 *Organizational Variability in Late Paleo-Indian Assemblages.* Washington State University, Laboratory of Anthropology, Reports of Investigations, No. 60. Pullman.

Krieger, A. D.
1947 Artifacts from the Plainview Bison Bed. In *Fossil Bison and Associated Artifacts from Plainview, Texas,* edited by E. H. Sellards, G. L. Evans, and G. E. Meade, pp. 927–954. Bulletin of the Geological Society of America 58. Boulder.

Kutzbach, J. E., and P. J. Guetter
1986 The Influence of Changing Orbital Parameters and Surface Boundary Conditions on Climatic Simulations for the Past 18,000 Years. *Journal of Atmospheric Science* 43:1726–1759.

Lahren, L.
1969 Wilsall Excavations: An Exercise in Frustration. *Proceedings of the Montana Academy of Science* 29:147–150.

Layton, T. N.
1970 High Rock Archaeology: An Interpretation of the Prehistory of the Northwestern Great Basin. Unpublished Ph.D. dissertation, Department of Anthropology, Harvard University, Cambridge, Massachusetts.
1972 Lithic Chronology in the Fort Rock Valley, Oregon. An Obsidian Hydration Study from Cougar Mountain Cave. *Tebiwa* 15:1–21.
1979 Archaeology and Paleo-Ecology of Pluvial Lake Parman, Northwestern Great Basin. *Journal of New World Archaeology* 3:41–56.

Ledbetter, R. J., D. G. Anderson, L. D. O'Steen, and D. T. Elliott
1996 Paleoindian and Early Archaic Research in Georgia. In *The Paleoindian and Early Archaic Southeast,* edited by D. G. Anderson and K. E. Sassaman, pp. 270–287. University of Alabama Press, Tuscaloosa.

LeTourneau, P. D.
2000 Folsom Toolstone Procurement in the Southwest and Southern Plains. Unpublished Ph.D. dissertation, University of New Mexico, Albuquerque.

Lilliquist, K. D.
1994 Late Quaternary Lake Franklin: Lacustrine Chronology, Coastal Geomorphology, and Hydrostatic Deflection in Ruby Valley and Northern Butte Valley, Nevada. Unpublished Ph.D. dissertation, University of Utah, Salt Lake City.

Loy, T. H.
1983 Prehistoric Blood Residues: Detection on Tool Surfaces and Identification of Species Origin. *Science* 200:1269–1271.

MacDonald, G. F.
1985 *Debert: A Palaeo-Indian Site in Central Nova Scotia.* Anthropology Papers No. 16. National Museum of Canada, Ottawa.

Machette, M. N.
1985 Calcic Soils of the Southwestern United States. In *Soils and Quaternary Geology of the Southwestern United States,* edited by D. L. Weide, pp. 1–22. Geological Society of America Special Paper 203. Boulder.

Madsen, D. B.
1999 Environmental Change During the Pleistocene–Holocene Transition and Its Possible Impact on Human Populations. In *Models for the Millennium. Great Basin Anthropology Today,* edited by C. Beck, pp. 75–82. University of Utah Press, Salt Lake City.
2000 *Late Quaternary Paleoecology in the Bonneville Basin.* Utah Geological Survey Bulletin 130. Salt Lake City.

Madsen, D. B., and D. R. Rhode
1990 Early Holocene Pinon (*Pinus monophylla*) in the Northeastern Great Basin. *Quaternary Research* 33:94–101.

Magne, M. P.
1985 *Lithics and Livelihood: Stone Tool Technologies of Central and Southern Interior B.C.* Archaeology Survey of Canada, Mercury Series No. 133. Ottawa.

Magne, M. P., and D. Pokotylo
1981 A Pilot Study in Bifacial Lithic Reduction Sequences. *Lithic Technology* 10:34–47.

Marshall, S. B.
1985 Paleoindian Artifact Form and Function at Shawnee Minisink. In *Shawnee Minisink: A Stratified Paleoindian–Archaic Site in the Upper Delaware Valley of Pennsylvania,* edited by C. McNett, pp. 165–209. Academic Press, New York.

Mason, R. J.
1962 The Paleo-Indian Tradition in Eastern North America. *Current Anthropology* 3:227–278.

Mawby, J. E.
1967 Fossil Vertebrates of the Tule Springs Site, Nevada. In *Pleistocene Studies in Southern Nevada,* edited by M. Wormington and D. Ellis, pp. 105–128. Nevada State Museum Anthropological Papers No. 13. Carson City.

McDevitt, K. B.
1994 Results of Replicative Hide-Working Experiments: The Roles of Raw Material, Hide Condition and Use Wear Patterns in the Determination of Rhyolite End Scraper Function. *Lithic Technology* 19:93–97.

Mehringer, P. J., Jr., and F. F. Foit Jr.
1990 Volcanic Ash Dating of the Clovis Cache at East Wenatchee, Washington. *National Geographic Research* 6:495–503.

Meltzer, D. J.
2002 What Do You Do When No One's Been There Before? Thoughts on the Exploration and Colonization of New Lands. In *The First Americans. The Pleistocene Colonization of the New World,* edited by N. G. Jablonski, pp. 27–58. Memoirs of the California Academy of Sciences No. 27. San Francisco.

Meltzer, D. J., and M. R. Bever
1995 Paleoindians of Texas: An Update on the Texas Clovis Fluted Point Survey. *Bulletin of the Texas Archaeological Society* 66:17–51.

Michie, J. L.
1990 Bioturbation and Gravity as a Potential Site Formation Process: The Open Area Site, 38GE261, Georgetown County, South Carolina. *South Carolina Antiquities* 22:27–46.

Mifflin, M. D., and M. M. Wheat
1979 *Pluvial Lakes and Estimated Pluvial Climates of Nevada.* Nevada Bureau of Mines and Geology Bulletin 94. Carson City.

Moeller, R. W.
1980 *6LF21: A Paleo-Indian Site in Western Connecticut.* American Indian Archaeological Institute, Occasional Paper No. 2.
Morris, E. A., and R. C. Blakeslee
1987 Comment on the Paleoindian Occurrence of Spurred Scrapers as Reported by Rogers. *American Antiquity* 52:830–831.
Morrow, J. E.
1997 End Scraper Morphology and Use-Life: An Approach for Studying Lithic Technology and Mobility. *Lithic Technology* 22:70–85.
Morrow, J. E., and T. A. Morrow
1999 Geographic Variation in Fluted Projectile Points: A Hemispheric Perspective. *American Antiquity* 64:215–231.
Musil, R. R.
1988 Functional Efficiency and Technological Change: A Hafting Tradition Model for Prehistoric North America. In *Early Human Occupation in Far Western North America: The Clovis–Archaic Interface,* edited by J. D. Willig, C. M. Aikens, and J. L. Fagan, pp. 373–387. Nevada State Museum Anthropological Papers 21. Carson City.
Nami, H.
1999 The Folsom Biface Reduction Sequence: Evidence from the Lindenmeier Collection. In *Folsom Lithic Technology. Explorations in Structure and Variation,* edited by D. S. Amick, pp. 82–97. International Monographs in Prehistory. Archaeological Series 12. University of Michigan, Ann Arbor.
Newcomer, M. C.
1971 Some Quantitative Experiments in Handaxe Manufacture. *World Archaeology* 3:85–94.
Nials, F.
1990 Stratigraphic Investigations at the Sunshine Well Locality, White Pine County, Nevada. Manuscript on file, Nevada State Museum, Carson City.
Nials, F., and J. O. Davis
1990 Late Quaternary Stratigraphy and Depositional Environments of the Sunshine Wells Locality. Paper presented at the 22nd Biennial Meeting of the Great Basin Anthropological Conference, Reno.
Nissen, K., and M. Dittemore
1974 Ethnographic Data and Wear Pattern Analysis: A Study of Socketed Eskimo Scrapers. *Tebiwa* 17:67–87.
Noyes, G. D., and P. W. Hutchinson
1972 The Prehistoric Dwellers at Lake Hubbs. Manuscript on file, Nevada State Museum, Carson City.
O'Brien, P. J.
1984 The Tim Adrian Site (14NT604): A Hell Gap Quarry Site in Norton County, Kansas. *Plains Anthropologist* 29:41–55.
O'Connell, J. F.
1975 *The Prehistory of Surprise Valley, Northeast California.* Ballena Press Anthropological Papers No. 4. Ramona, California.
O'Connell, J. F., and C. M. Inoway
1994 Surprise Valley Projectile Points and Their Chronological Implications. *Journal of California and Great Basin Anthropology* 16:162–198.
Odell, G. H.
1996 *Stone Tools and Mobility in the Illinois Valley. From Hunter-Gatherer Camps to Agricultural Villages.* International Monographs in Prehistory, Archaeological Series 10. University of Michigan, Ann Arbor.
Olsen, S. R., and L. E. Sommers
1982 Phosphorous. In *Methods of Soil Analysis Part 2: Chemical and Microbiological Properties,* edited by A. L. Page, pp. 403–430. Soil Science Society of America, Madison.
Orr, P. C.
1974 Notes on the Archaeology of the Winnemucca Lake Caves, 1952–1958. *Nevada State Museum Anthropological Papers* 16:47–59. Carson City.
Oviatt, C. G., D. R. Currey, and D. Sack
1992 Radiocarbon Chronology of Lake Bonneville, Eastern Great Basin, USA. *Palaeogeography, Palaeoclimatology, Palaeoecology* 99:225–241.
Oviatt, C. G., D. B. Madsen, and D. N. Schmitt
2003 Late Pleistocene and Early Holocene Rivers and Wetlands in the Bonneville Basin of Western North America. *Quaternary Research* 60:200–210.
Painter, F.
1985 Possible Evidence of Tattooing by Paleo-Indians of Eastern North America. In *The William Site, Dinwiddie County, Virginia,* edited by R. M. Peck, pp. 87–94. Privately published. Available from the Virginia Archaeological Society, Richmond.
Patterson, L. W.
1982 Replication and Classification of Large Size Lithic Debitage. *Lithic Technology* 11:50–58.
1990 Characteristics of Bifacial-Reduction Flake-Size Distribution. *American Antiquity* 53:550–558.
Pecora, A. M.
2001 Chipped Stone Tool Production Strategies and Lithic Debris Patterns in Lithic Debitage. In *Context, Form, Meaning,* edited by W. Andrefsky Jr., pp. 173–190. University of Utah Press, Salt Lake City.
Pendleton, L. S.
1979 Lithic Technology in Early Nevada Assemblages. Unpublished Master's thesis, Department of Anthropology, California State University, Long Beach.
Pettigrew, R. M.
1984 Prehistoric Human Land-Use Patterns in the Alvord Basin, Southeastern Oregon. *Journal of California and Great Basin Anthropology* 6:61–90.
Pinson, A. O.
1999 Foraging in Uncertain Times: The Effects of Risk on Foraging Behavior During the Pleistocene–Holocene Transition in the Oregon Great Basin. Unpublished Ph.D. dissertation, Department of Anthropology, University of New Mexico.
Pitblado, B. L.
1998 Peak to Peak in Paleoindian Time: Occupation of Southwest Colorado. *Plains Anthropologist* 43:333–348.
2003 *Late Paleoindian Occupation of the Southern Rocky Moun-*

tains. Early Holocene Projectile Points and Land Use in the High Country. University Press of Colorado, Boulder.

Prufer, O. H., and R. S. Baby

1963 *Paleo-Indians of Ohio.* Ohio Historical Society, Columbus.

Quade, J.

1986 Late Quaternary Environmental Changes in the Upper Las Vegas Valley, Nevada. *Quaternary Research* 26:340–357.

Quade, J., R. M. Forester, W. L. Pratt, and C. Carter

1998 Black Mats, Spring-Fed Streams, and Late-Glacial-Age Recharge in the Southern Great Basin. *Quaternary Research* 49:129–148.

Rhode, D.

2000 Holocene Vegetation History in the Bonneville Basin. In *Late Quaternary Paleoecology in the Bonneville Basin,* by David B. Madsen, pp. 149–163. Utah Geological Survey Bulletin 130. Salt Lake City.

Rice, D. G.

1972 *The Windust Phase in Lower Snake River Region Prehistory.* Washington State University, Laboratory of Anthropology, Report of Investigations No. 50. Pullman.

Riddell, F. A., and W. H. Olsen

1969 An Early Man Site in the San Joaquin Valley, California. *American Antiquity* 34:121–130.

Roberts, F. H. H.

1936 Additional Information on the Folsom Complex: Report on the Second Season's Investigation at the Lindenmeier Site in Northern Colorado. *Smithsonian Miscellaneous Collections* 95(10):1–38.

Rogers, M. J.

1939 *Early Lithic Industries of the Colorado River and Adjacent Desert Areas.* San Diego Museum of Man, San Diego.

Rogers, R. A.

1986 Spurred End Scrapers as Diagnostic Paleoindian Artifacts: A Distributional Analysis of Stream Terraces. *American Antiquity* 51:338–341.

Roosa, W. B.

1965 Some Great Lakes Fluted Point Types. *Michigan Archaeologist* 11:89–102.

1977a Fluted Points from the Parkhill Site. In *For the Director: Research Essays in Honor of James B. Griffin,* edited by C. Cleland, pp. 87–122. Anthropological Papers No. 61. Museum of Anthropology, University of Michigan, Ann Arbor.

1977b Great Lakes Paleo-Indian: The Parkhill Site, Ontario. In *Amerinds and Their Paleo Environments in Northeastern North America,* edited by W. S. Newman and B. Salwen. *Annals of the New York Academy of Sciences* 288:349–354. New York.

Ruedas, L. A.

1998 Systematics of *Sylvilagus* Gray, 1867 (Lagomorpha: Leporidae) from Southwestern North America. *Journal of Mammalogy* 79:1355–1378.

Ryser, F. A., Jr.

1985 *Birds of the Great Basin: A Natural History.* University of Nevada Press, Reno.

Schiffer, M. B., and J. M. Skibo

1987 Theory and Experiment in the Study of Technological Change. *Current Anthropology* 28:595–609.

Schroedl, A. R.

1991 Paleo-Indian Occupation in the Eastern Great Basin and Northern Colorado Plateau. *Utah Archaeology* 4:1–15.

Shott, M. J.

1994 On Size and Form in the Analysis of Flake Debris. *Journal of Archaeological Method and Theory* 1:69–110.

1995 How Much Is a Scraper? Curation, Use Rates, and the Formation of Scraper Assemblages. *Lithic Technology* 20:53–72.

1996 An Exegesis of the Curation Concept. *Journal of Anthropological Research* 52:259–280.

Sigler, W. F., and J. W. Sigler

1987 *Fishes of the Great Basin: A Natural History.* University of Nevada Press, Reno.

Simms, S. R.

1988 Conceptualizing the Paleoindian and Archaic in the Great Basin. In *Early Human Occupation in Far Western North America: The Clovis–Archaic Interface,* edited by J. A. Willig, C. M. Aikens, and J. L. Fagan, pp. 41–52. Nevada State Museum Anthropological Papers 21. Carson City.

Simms, S. R., and M. C. Isgreen

1984 *Archaeological Investigations in the Sevier and Escalante Deserts, Western Utah.* University of Utah Archaeological Center Reports on Excavations 83-12. Salt Lake City.

Smith, P. R., and M. T. Wilson

1992 Blood Residues on Ancient Tool Surfaces: A Cautionary Note. *Journal of Archaeological Science* 19:237–241.

Steward, J. H.

1938 *Basin–Plateau Aboriginal Sociopolitical Groups.* Bureau of American Ethnology Bulletin 120. Washington, D.C.

Storck, P. L.

1997 *The Fisher Site. Archaeological, Geological and Paleobotanical Studies at an Early Paleo-Indian Site in Southern Ontario, Canada.* Memoir No. 30. Museum of Anthropology, University of Michigan, Ann Arbor.

Stuiver, M, and P. J. Reimer

1993 Extended ^{14}C Database and Revised CALIB 3.0 ^{14}C Age Calibration Program. *Radiocarbon* 35:215–230.

Sullivan, A. P., III, and K. C. Rozen

1985 Debitage Analysis and Archaeological Interpretation. *American Antiquity* 50:755–779.

Tadlock, W. L.

1966 Certain Crescentic Stone Objects as a Time Marker in the Western United States. *American Antiquity* 31: 662–675.

Taylor, A.

2002 Results of a Great Basin Fluted Point Survey: Chronological and Functional Relationships Between Fluted and Stemmed Points. Unpublished Senior thesis, Department of Anthropology, Hamilton College, Clinton, New York.

2003 Results of a Great Basin Fluted-Point Survey. *Current Research in the Pleistocene* 20:77–79.

Taylor, R. E., C. V. Haynes Jr., and M. Stuiver
1996 Clovis and Folsom Age Estimates: Stratigraphic Context and Radiocarbon Calibration. *Antiquity* 70:515–525.
Teltser, P. A.
1991 Generalized Core Technology and Tool Use: A Mississippian Example. *Journal of Field Archaeology* 18:363–375.
Thaeler, C. S., Jr.
1980 Chromosome Numbers and Systematic Relations in the Genus *Thomomys* (Rodentia: Geomyidae). *Journal of Mammalogy* 61:414–422.
Thomas, D. H.
1970 Archaeology's Operational Imperative: Great Basin Projectile Points as a Test Case. *University of California Archaeological Survey Annual Report* 12:27–60.
1981 How to Classify the Projectile Points from Monitor Valley, Nevada. *Journal of California and Great Basin Anthropology* 3:7–43.
1983 The Archaeology of Monitor Valley, 2: Gatecliff Shelter. *Anthropological Papers of the American Museum of Natural History* 59:1–552.
1986 Points on Points: A Reply to Flenniken and Raymond. *American Antiquity* 51:619–627.
Thomas, D. H., and R. L. Bettinger
1976 Prehistoric Pinon Ecotone Settlements of the Upper Reese River Valley, Central Nevada. *American Museum of Natural History Anthropological Papers* 53:263–366.
Thompson, R.
1985 The Age and Environment of the Mount Moriah (Lake Mohave) Occupation at Smith Creek Cave, Nevada. In *Environments and Extinctions: Man in Late Glacial North America,* edited by J. I. Mead and D. J. Meltzer, pp. 111–119. Center for the Study of Early Man, University of Maine, Orono.
1992 Late Quaternary Environments in Ruby Valley, Nevada. *Quaternary Research* 37:1–15.
Titmus, G. L., and J. C. Woods
1986 An Experimental Study of Projectile Point Fracture Patterns. *Journal of California and Great Basin Anthropology* 8:37–49.
1991a Fluted Points from the Snake River Plain. In *Clovis: Origins and Adaptations,* edited by R. Bonnichsen and K. L. Turnmire, pp. 119–131. Center for the Study of the First Americans, Department of Anthropology, Oregon State University, Corvallis.
1991b A Closer Look at Margin "Grinding" on Folsom and Clovis Points. *Journal of California and Great Basin Anthropology* 13:194–203.
Tomenchuck, J.
1997 A Parametric Use-Wear Study of Artifacts from Areas C and C-East. In *The Fisher Site. Archaeological, Geological and Paleobotanical Studies at an Early Paleo-Indian Site in Southern Ontario, Canada,* by P. L. Storck, pp. 95–161. Memoir No. 30. Museum of Anthropology, University of Michigan, Ann Arbor.
Tomenchuck, J., and P. L. Storck
1997 Two Newly Recognized Paleoindian Tool Types: Single- and Double-Scribe Compass Gravers and Coring Gravers. *American Antiquity* 62:508–522.
Tompkins, C. N.
1993 Classifying Clovis Points: A Study in Metric Variability. Unpublished Master's thesis, Department of Anthropology, University of Arizona, Tucson.
Tuohy, D. R.
1969 Breakage, Burin Facets, and the Probable Linkage Among Lake Mohave, Silver Lake, and Other Varieties of Paleo-Indian Projectile Points in the Desert West. *Nevada State Museum Anthropological Papers* 14:132–152.
1974 A Comparative Study of Late Paleo-Indian Manifestations in the Western Great Basin. In *Collected Papers on Great Basin Archaeology,* edited by R. Elston, pp. 91–116. Nevada Archaeological Survey Research Paper No. 5. University of Nevada, Reno.
1985 Notes on the Great Basin Distribution of Clovis Fluted and Folsom Projectile Points. *Nevada Archaeologist* 5:15–18.
1986 Errata and Additional Notes on the Great Basin Distribution of Clovis Fluted and Folsom Projectile Points. *Nevada Archaeologist* 5:2–7.
1988 Paleoindian and Early Archaic Cultural Complexes from Three Central Nevada Locations. In *Early Human Occupation in Far Western North America: The Clovis–Archaic Interface,* edited by J. A. Willig, C. M. Aikens, and J. L. Fagan, pp. 217–230. Nevada State Museum Anthropological Papers 21. Carson City.
Tuohy, D. R., and A. J. Dansie
1997 New Information Regarding Early Holocene Manifestations in the Western Great Basin. *Nevada Historical Society Quarterly* 40:24–53.
Tuohy, D. R., A. J. Dansie, and W. L. Tadlock
1990 Overview 1990 and Prospects for Further Investigations. Paper presented at the 22nd Biennial Great Basin Anthropological Conference, Reno.
Tuohy, D. R., P. W. Hutchinson, and W. L. Tadlock
1990 Introduction to the Sunshine Locality. Paper presented at the 22nd Biennial Great Basin Anthropological Conference, Reno.
Tuohy, D. R., and T. N. Layton
1977 Towards the Establishment of a New Series of Great Basin Projectile Points. *Nevada Archaeological Survey Reporter* 10:1–5.
Van Buren, G. E.
1974 *Arrowheads and Projectile Points.* Arrowhead Publishing, Garden Grove.
Vaughn, S., and C. N. Warren
1987 Toward a Definition of Pinto Points. *Journal of California and Great Basin Anthropology* 9:199–213.
Walkley, A., and I. A. Black
1934 An Examination of the Degtjareff Method for Determining Soil Organic Matter and Proposed Modification of the Chromic Acid Titration Method. *Soil Science* 37:29–38.
Wallace, W. J., and F. A. Riddell
1988 Prehistoric Background of Tulare Lake, California. In *Early Human Occupation in Far Western North America: The Clovis–Archaic Interface,* edited by J. A. Willig, C. M. Aikens, and J. L. Fagan, pp. 87–119. Nevada State Museum Anthropological Papers 21. Carson City.

Wallman, S., and D. S. Amick
1991 Cody Complex Occupation in the Black Rock Desert, Nevada. *Current Research in the Pleistocene* 8:51–53.
Wardle, H. N.
1913 Stone Implements of Surgery from San Miguel Island, California. *American Anthropologist* 15:656–660.
Warren, C. N.
1967 The San Dieguito Complex: A Review and Hypothesis. *American Antiquity* 32:168–185.
1990 *Archaeological Investigations at Nelson Wash, Fort Irwin, California.* Report submitted to the National Park Service, Western Region, by Dames & Moore, San Diego.
Warren, C. N., and C. Phagan
1988 Fluted Points in the Mojave Desert: Their Technology and Cultural Context. In *Early Human Occupation in Far Western North America: The Clovis–Archaic Interface,* edited by J. A. Willig, C. M. Aikens, and J. L. Fagan, pp. 121–130. Nevada State Museum Anthropological Papers 21. Carson City.
Warren, C. N., and D. L. True
1961 The San Dieguito Complex and Its Place in California Prehistory. *University of California, Los Angeles, Archaeological Survey Annual Report* 1960–1961:246–338.
Waters, M. R., and T. W. Stafford Jr.
2007 Redefining the Age of Clovis: Implications for the Peopling of the Americas. *Science* 315:1122–1126.
Webb, S. David
1965 The Osteology of *Camelops. Bulletin of the Los Angeles County Museum: Science* 1.
Wheat, J. B.
1979 *The Jurgens Site.* Plains Anthropologist Memoir No. 15. Lincoln, Nebraska.
Whittaker, J. C.
1994 *Flintknapping. Making and Understanding Stone Tools.* University of Texas Press, Austin.
Wilke, P. J., J. J. Flenniken, and T. L. Ozbun
1991 Clovis Technology at the Anzick Site, Montana. *Journal of California and Great Basin Anthropology* 12:242–272.
Willig, J. A.
1988 Paleo-Archaic Adaptations and Lakeside Settlement Patterns in the Northern Alkali Basin, Oregon. In *Early Human Occupation in Far Western North America: The Clovis–Archaic Interface,* edited by J. A. Willig, C. M. Aikens, and J. L. Fagan, pp. 417–482. Nevada State Museum Anthropological Papers 21. Carson City.
1989 Paleo-Archaic Broad Spectrum Adaptations at the Pleistocene–Holocene Boundary in Far Western North America. Unpublished Ph.D. dissertation, Department of Anthropology, University of Oregon, Eugene.
1991 Clovis Technology and Adaptations in Far Western North America: Regional Patterns and Environmental Context. In *Clovis: Origins and Adaptations,* edited by R. Bonnichsen and K. Turnmire, pp. 98–108. Center for the Study of the First Americans, Corvallis.
Willig, J. A., and C. M. Aikens
1988 The Clovis–Archaic Interface in Far Western North America. In *Early Human Occupation in Far Western North America: The Clovis–Archaic Interface,* edited by J. A. Willig, C. M. Aikens, and J. L. Fagan, pp. 1–40. Nevada State Museum Anthropological Papers 21. Carson City.
Wilmsen, E. N.
1968 Lithic Analysis in Paleoanthropology. *Science* 161:982–987.
Wilson, Don E., and F. Russell Cole
2000 *Common Names of Mammals of the World.* Smithsonian Institution Press, Washington, D.C.
Wilson, Don E., and DeeAnn M. Reeder
1993 *Mammal Species of the World: A Taxonomic and Geographic Reference.* 2nd ed. Smithsonian Institution Press, Washington, D.C.
Woods, J. C., and G. L. Titmus
1985 A Review of the Simon Clovis Collection. *Idaho Archaeologist* 8:3–8.
Wormington, H. M.
1957 *Ancient Man in North America.* 4th ed. Denver Museum of Natural History Popular Series No. 4. Denver.
1979 *Ancient Man in North America.* Denver Museum of Natural History, Popular Series No. 4. Denver.
Wycoff, D. G.
1999 Southern Plains Folsom Lithic Technology: A View from the Edge. In *Folsom Lithic Technology. Explorations in Structure and Variation,* edited by D. S. Amick, pp. 39–64. International Monographs in Prehistory No. 12. University of Michigan, Ann Arbor.
York, Gigi
1995 Delineating Prehistoric Settlement Patterns, in Long Valley, Nevada. Unpublished Master's thesis, Department of Anthropology, Northern Arizona University.
York, Robert
1974 Test Excavations and Controlled Surface Collecting in Long Valley, Nevada. Manuscript on file, Nevada State Museum, Carson City.
1978 *Long Valley Archaeological Study 1978. Progress Report.* Cultural Resources Report, Bureau of Land Management, Nevada State Office, Reno.
1979 The Long Valley Archaeological Study: Fitting It All Together. Paper presented at the 44th Annual Meeting of the Society for American Archaeology, Vancouver.
Young, D. E., and R. Bonnichsen
1995 Cognition, Behavior, and Material Culture. In *Stone Tool Analysis: Essays in Honor of Don E. Crabtree,* edited by M. Plew, J. Woods, and M. Pavesic, pp. 91–133. University of New Mexico Press, Albuquerque.
Young, Michael A., and William D. McCoy
1984 Late Quaternary Histories of Long, Ruby, and Jakes Valleys, Nevada. *Abstracts of the Eighth Biennial Meeting of the American Quaternary Association*: 143.
Zeveloff, Samuel I., and Farrell R. Collett
1986 *Mammals of the Intermountain West.* University of Utah Press, Salt Lake City.

Index